Johannes Ungelenk
Literature and Weather

spectrum
Literaturwissenschaft/
spectrum Literature

―
Komparatistische Studien/Comparative Studies

Herausgegeben von/Edited by
Moritz Baßler, Werner Frick,
Monika Schmitz-Emans

Wissenschaftlicher Beirat/Editorial Board
Sam-Huan Ahn, Peter-André Alt, Aleida Assmann, Francis Claudon,
Marcus Deufert, Wolfgang Matzat, Fritz Paul, Terence James Reed,
Herta Schmid, Simone Winko, Bernhard Zimmermann,
Theodore Ziolkowski

Band 61

Johannes Ungelenk

Literature and Weather

Shakespeare – Goethe – Zola

DE GRUYTER

Also thesis at the Ludwig-Maximilians-Universität München, 2016.

ISBN 978-3-11-070913-1
e-ISBN (PDF) 978-3-11-056097-8
e-ISBN (EPUB) 978-3-11-055970-5
ISSN 1860-210X

Library of Congress Cataloging-in-Publication Data
A CIP catalog record for this book has been applied for at the Library of Congress.

Bibliographic information published by the Deutsche Nationalbibliothek
The Deutsche Nationalbibliothek lists this publication in the Deutsche Nationalbibliografie; detailed bibliographic data are available on the Internet at http://dnb.dnb.de.

© 2020 Walter de Gruyter GmbH, Berlin/Boston
This volume is text- and page-identical with the hardback published in 2018.
Typesetting: RoyalStandard, Hong Kong
Printing and binding: CPI books GmbH, Leck
♾ Printed on acid-free paper
Printed in Germany
www.degruyter.com

Acknowledgments

This book has been made possible by generous and faithful support of all kinds. I am grateful to Barbara Vinken, whose creative, carefree intellectuality has deeply shaped my love to literary studies. She not only supervised the project – she also defended it against critical voices of colleagues, while giving me free rein to pursue it wherever it would lead. I would not have dared to expose myself to the heavy weather of academia without the continuous intellectual as well as personal support of Tobias Döring. He is a witty Shakespearean (and more), he knows how to write thrilling texts – and the compassionate responsibility that he takes for his students as an academic teacher is exemplary. The study has profited immensely from his extensive reading of draft chapters during the process of writing. Annette Keck has – without knowing that she would later become part of the committee – contributed decisively to the study's focus when insisting on the weather's 'historical index' in the selection interview for the doctoral programme in which the project was to be realised. Her precise and challenging questions were not only instructive, they prooved also a source of intellectual pleasure.

I am grateful to Oliver Grill for the last four years of shared literary weather. I am indebted to his initiative that established a fruitful and very pleasant 'weathery' cooperation: a workshop and a seminar on the weather of literature promoted the topic to become a visible subject of study at the LMU's philologies. It tells a lot that our coffee meetings have outlived the discussion of our weather projects.

It was an honour to discuss the draft of the chapter on Shakespeare with Ewan Fernie. He encouraged me to work with an explicitly Foucauldian framing, which helped a lot to structure the book. I would like to thank Sandra Fluhrer for reading and giving feedback on the Shakespeare and Goethe sections, which did not only improve the text but made the best of strolls through the English Garden and along the Isar. Anna Leyrer has polished the introduction and the conclusion, intellectually as well as stylistically – I love to trust her sense of brevity, beauty and precision. I am hugely indebted to Kathleen Rabl who took the pains to approximate my non-native writing to the habits and taste of the English-speaking reader. I am well aware that the task was Herculean, no, impossible – and it is solely my German, baroque mind that is to blame for the hickups and stumbles that are left in the final version of the text.

This book would not exist without the financial support of several institutions. The doctoral study programme ProLit of the LMU Munich granted me a three months' scholarship at the beginning of the project. The Center for

Advanced Studies of the LMU Munich supported my work on Shakespeare and the weather as part of a research group directed by Tobias Döring. A dissertation scholarship of the Evangelisches Studienwerk Villigst enabled me to write this book without any financial worries or academic duties. I am grateful for these luxurious conditions and hope that I have made the most of them.

I think it an illusion that (academic) texts are produced by individuals – it is settings, assemblages, as Gilles Deleuze would call them, that kindle a desire to write and that guide the fingers on the keyboard without the typer even noticing it. I have been lucky to be part of several assemblages: the ProLit colloquium, with its wonderful but obviously challenging principle of group supervision and peer feed-back, Barbara Vinken's and Tobias Döring's colloquia or study days, to name the academic ones first. It is, however, the non-academic, perhaps even less 'professional' assemblages that I feel my work owes the most: the Arbeitsgemeinschaft 'Kritische Wissenschaft' of the Evangelisches Studienwerk, with all the lovely friends that I happened to find there over the years; the Mensa-Crew; my wonderful flatmates and not to forget my parents and family. The AG 'Kritische Wissenschaft' brought me into contact with what has intellectually fascinated and shaped me – and made me experience the pleasure of critical thinking that 'academia', with its careerism, its hierarchies, dependencies and its utter absence of (non-narcissistic) love could never have done. Two hours of lunch talk that oscillate between intense political discussions of world politics, mutual moaning and consolation, intellectual debates and a lot of hilarious comedy are the luxury I treat myself to every day. I am certain this book would look very different without the precious time with the Mensa-Crew – Dominik Aufleger, Jochen Gaab, Simon Gröger, Mara Matičević, Concetta Perdichizzi, Katharina Wagner, not to forget Steffi and Pocahontas...

Last but not least I am grateful to my parents, my grandparents, my uncle, who did all they could to guide me into life: it is not only their love, but also their struggling, their unfulfilled dreams, their suffering from tensions between sensitivity and ambition, between desires and the burdens of an unchosen everyday life that have made this book possible. It is the careful thirst for an open, unforeseeable future I owe to them – and I admire their courage to grant me the freedom to become what they could not know what it exactly is...

Table of contents

Acknowledgments —— v
List of Abbreviations —— ix
Introduction —— 1

I	***The Tempest*. Staging the Weather** —— 17	
1	Title —— 18	
2	Weather and theatre —— 21	
3	The tempest scene —— 25	
4	Miranda and Prospero – exposition —— 43	
5	God of power – temporal royalties —— 58	
6	The climate of th'isle —— 74	
7	Gonzalo's plantation and Prospero's masque —— 94	
8	Bringing the play to an end —— 127	
II	***Werther*. Reading the Weather** —— 147	
1	Werther and his environment —— 148	
2	The birth of a weathery medium – the ball-scene —— 159	
2.1	Breaking/Transgressing the circles —— 160	
2.2	Werther's "pretentious meteorology [*anmaßliche Wetterkunde*]" —— 171	
2.3	Love and weather – a parallel threat to order —— 181	
2.4	The waltz – flying like the weather —— 188	
2.5	Clever closures – restoration of order —— 210	
2.6	The epiphany of the weathery medium —— 216	
3	Well and hut – idyll and prison —— 233	
4	At the limits of human nature – the novel's storm and urge —— 266	
5	Werther's *passio* – and his Ossianic resurrection —— 290	
III	***Les Rougon-Macquart*. Describing the Weather – and a Changing Climate** —— 317	
1	From weather to climate —— 317	
2	Milieu —— 330	
3	Global warming – the old and the new Paris —— 361	
4	Meteorotopoi – the proliferation of the hothouse —— 389	
4.1	The bar – Paris inebriated —— 396	

4.2	The coal-pit – battle of weathers —— **404**
4.3	The department store – a weather machine —— **411**
4.4	The hothouse (effect) —— **425**
5	The weather of the masses —— **446**
6	Climate catastrophes, climate crises – the seasons and life —— **473**
7	Mastery – the end of modern aesthetics —— **531**

Conclusion —— **552**
Works Cited —— **566**
Index —— **585**

List of Abbreviations

A	L'Assommoir	FR	La Fortune des Rougon
Adl	'Adelung' (dictionary)	G	Germinal
Ar	L'Argent	H5	Henry V
AYL	As You Like It	JV	La Joie de vivre
BD	Au Bonheur des Dames	LLL	Love's Labour's Lost
BH	La Bête humaine	Lr.	King Lear
C	La Curée	Mac.	Macbeth
Cor.	Coriolanus	MM	Measure for Measure
D	La Débâcle	MND	A Midsummer Night's Dream
DP	Le Docteur Pascal	MV	The Merchant of Venice
DWB	Deutsches Wörterbuch	N	Nana
eA	L'Assommoir (English transl.)	OC	Œuvres complètes
eBH	La Bête Humaine (English transl.)	OED	Oxford English Dictionary
		PA	Une page d'amour
eBP	The Belly of Paris	PB	Pot-Bouille
eD	La Débâcle (English transl.)	PetRob	Le Petit Robert
eE	Earth	R	Le Rêve
eFR	The Fortune of the Rougons	RE	Le roman expérimental
eG	Germinal (English transl.)	RN	Les romanciers naturalistes
eK	The Kill	R2	Richard II
eLP	Ladies' Paradise	Rom.	Romeo and Juliet
eM	Money	Shr.	The Taming of the Shrew
eN	Nana (English transl.)	Son.	(Shakespeare's) Sonnets
ePL	Pot Luck	T	La Terre
eSAM	The Sin of Abbée Mouret	TN	Twelfth Night
eTR	Thérèse Raquin (English transl.)	TR	Thérèse Raquin
		Tr	Travail
FA	Frankfurter Ausgabe (Goethe)	VP	Le Ventre de Paris
FaM	La Faute de l'abbé Mouret	WA	Weimarer Ausgabe (Goethe)

Introduction

This project began with an observation: for a number of highly canonised texts, texts that influence the perception of western literature, the weather plays a surprisingly important role. Shakespeare, Goethe and Zola represent three different historical contexts and literary epochs, they are icons of three different national literatures and their works have been formative for different genres. However, despite the extensive spectrum that these names and their oeuvres evoke, their undoubted importance for literature and its development appears to be accompanied by an astonishingly consistent characteristic: a shared 'inclination' towards the weather.

In the literary texts I have in mind (Shakespeare's *Tempest*, Goethe's *Werther* and Zola's *Rougon-Macquart*) the weather is not only a favourite motif or theme and it is not merely in single, prominent scenes that it becomes evident. The 'inclination' towards the weather shapes the plays and novels as wholes, on their surface as motifs and imagery, but more importantly also in their deep structure and their self-conception as literary texts. Against the background of the huge historical, cultural and generic scope in which the observation of this 'inclination' was made, a suspicion arose: there appeared to be an affinity between 'the literary' and 'the weather'. It is this suspicion that the following chapters will explore and elaborate.

William Shakespeare's *King Lear* may serve as an initial example that introduces us to the core of the project and that explicates its concrete critical parameters. *King Lear* is extremely canonical, and it is famous for its 'storm scene', probably the most prominent of all 'weather scenes' in world literature. Viewed more closely, the storm not only rages in one, but several scenes – and is fundamental for the whole play, even beyond its acoustic representation on stage. The events that precede the storm can be summarised in a few sentences: King Lear has abdicated and divided his kingdom amongst two of his daughters, Goneril and Regan. His third daughter Cordelia, although apparently the one most loved by Lear, is disinherited and cast out, because she refused to take part in the rhetorical contest of expressing love to their father, which Lear had imposed on his daughters. Once the kingdom is distributed and the authority transferred to Goneril and Regan, they do not live up to their 'affectionate' words. On the contrary, Lear and his retinue are sent from one to the other and are treated by both without the respect that a former king and father deserves. In the end, Goneril and Regan threaten to close their doors on him, if he does not radically reduce his train that is accused of depravity. It is here that Lear speaks the following two verses that, in my opinion, are at the centre of the whole play:

> Lear: Rather I abjure all roofs and choose
> To wage against the enmity o'th'air (*Lr.* 2.2.397–398)

Lear's words weigh heavily and entail serious consequences. His fool had warned him only moments before that "Winter's not gone yet, if the wild geese fly that way." (*Lr.* 2.2.236–237) In fact, Lear takes the decision to "abjure all roofs" in the face of a brewing storm:

> Gloucester: Alack, the night comes on, and the high winds
> Do sorely ruffle; for many miles about
> There's scarce a bush. (*Lr.* 2.2.490–492)

Despite the impending heavy weather, Regan and her husband Cornwall carry out the threat and "oppose the bolt | Against [Lear's] coming in" (*Lr.* 2.2.365–366). Having already locked their own door, Regan and Cornwall command Gloucester, who expresses pity for the old king, to close his as well:

> Regan: [...] Shut up your doors.
> [...]
> Cornwall: Shut up your doors, my lord; 'tis a wild night.
> My Regan counsels well; come out o'the storm. (*Lr.* 2.2.494–499)

As a consequence, Lear finds himself on an open field, exposed to the storm and without shelter. The expectation of seeing him "wage against the enmity o'th'air" in an existential struggle of culture confronting nature is however belied. Lear does not fight the raging elements. On the contrary, he lays down his arms, surrenders to the weather and even appears to affirm and conjure up its violent forces:

> Lear: Rumble thy bellyful! Spit fire, spout rain!
> Nor rain, wind, thunder, fire are my daughters;
> I tax not you, you elements, with unkindness.
> I never gave you kingdom, called you children;
> You owe me no subscription. Why then, let fall
> Your horrible pleasure. Here I stand your slave,
> A poor, infirm, weak and despised old man. (*Lr.* 3.2.14–20)

Lear's famous address to the weather meticulously contrasts the "elements" to his daughters: *they*, "rain, wind, thunder, fire" are *not* his daughters, *they* do *not* "owe" Lear "subscription". Lear's decision to "abjure all roofs" and expose himself to "the enmity o'th'air" has created a completely new situation. The storm introduces a 'state of exception' that suspends the conventional structures of authority and social form: Lear's authority as a father and former king, as well as the conventionalities of adequate social behaviour ("unkindness"), of moral, judicial and economic obligations, cease to be of any import. Lear cannot be said to have been forced to "abjure all roofs" and to tragically end up exposed to heavy weather. He rather explicitly affirms the storm's 'state of exception', despite the fact that it suspends the very structure that his former reign and behaviour (cf. his rhetorical contest of praise, his expectancy of respect) had been based on. As the passage quoted effectively illustrates, Lear's formerly authoritative "I" is replaced by the elements' "You" and "Your" that take over the 'active' position at the beginning of the verses – Lear (the 'retired' king) subjects himself to the new authority that governs this state of exception, to the powers of the weather, and humbly retreats to the verse's 'passive' end position: as a "slave" and an "old man".

It is hard to understand Lear's decision or find rational grounds for it. By abjuring shelters and affirming the weather's authority, Lear apparently confutes all the rules of good judgment. It is no coincidence that the notorious list of instructions for practical life that his fool communicates to Lear at an early stage of the play culminates in the advice to "keep in-a-door":

Fool: Have more than thou showest,
Speak less than thou knowest,
Lend less than thou owest,
Ride more than thou goest,
Learn more than thou trowest,
Set less than thou throwest,
Leave thy drink and thy whore
And keep in-a-door,
And thou shalt have more
Than two tens to score. (*Lr.* 1.4.116–125)

Lear obviously defies the logic of life, of self-assertion and sound (or Machiavellian) gain in property and power. It is therefore only natural that when, instead of keeping "in-a-door", he opts to expose himself to the storm, only a few loyal souls follow him, as predicted by the fool:

Fool: That sir which serves and seeks for gain,
And follows but for form,
Will pack when it begins to rain,
And leave thee in the storm; (*Lr.* 2.2.267–270)

The two rhymes wittily confirm my argument of the weather's state of exception: the weather is somehow opposed to the rules and logic of 'conventional' life: "rain" answers "gain" and "storm" responds to "form". The weather does however not only erect a static opposition to the conventions of life and society; it critically questions their norms and habitual functioning. The weather's state of exception reveals the world's hypocrisy and the myopia of the principles (i.e. gain and form) that govern it. In a similar way the weather had once made Lear aware of his self-conceit with regard to apparently unlimited kingly authority, as he claims late in the play:

> Lear: When the rain came to wet me once and the wind to make me chatter; when the thunder would not peace at my bidding, there I found 'em, there I smelt 'em out. Go to, they are not men o'their words: they told me I was everything; 'tis a lie, I am not ague-proof. (*Lr.* 4.6.100–104)

By abjuring all roofs Lear thus retires a second time, this time in a radical way. He turns his back on the world and delivers himself to a different reign, to that of the weather. As we have just seen, the elemental state of exception is however not indifferent to the world of secular authority, of gain and form. When Lear declares himself a "slave" to the weathery powers, his position is thus not just the passive one of "A poor, infirm, weak and despised old man", who has retreated from the world and lost all hopes and visions. On the contrary, he has joined a 'critical' alliance:

> Kent: [...] Where's the King?
> Knight: Contending with the fretful elements;
> Bids the wind blow the earth into the sea,
> Or swell the curled water 'bove the main,
> That things might change, or cease; [...] (*Lr.* 3.1.1–7)

As the last verse demonstrates, the weather's state of exception 'affects' the world in a particular way: as a Hippocratic crisis. In ancient and early modern medicine, crisis was conceived of as the critical but necessary stage of an illness, as the 'decisive' moment (gr. κρίνω (*krínō*), 'to separate, part, select, choose'), when things either changed for the good, and the patient was heading towards the restoration of health, or to a fatal end.

Although the storm has divided the *dramatis personae*, has separated Lear's loyal followers (i.e. those that expose themselves to the heavy weather) from his Machiavellian opponents, who stay "in-a-doors", the weather's state of exception does not form an idyllic counter-world. Despite the fact that the characters grouped around Lear in the storm have not followed the old king for form or gain, the 'new', stormy setting is not characterised by authenticity or genuine humanness. On the contrary, the weathery 'community' of Lear and his caring 'company' is a community of histrionics, of outcasts and outsiders. The weather's state of exception creates a liminal space where the human being is not only exposed to the weather, but also to madness and the very limits of 'humanness': a space where it becomes impossible to distinguish between disguise and disorder, between mask and misery.

This is the "horrible pleasure" that the weather "let[s] fall" on Lear and his followers. The raging elements do not found a new, utopic community; as a crisis, they aim at an effect: "That things might change, or cease". As Lear's subjection to the weather has vividly demonstrated, this effect differs markedly from the effects brought about by the strategic, intentional behaviour of a rational human being. The effect of the weather's state of exception is ineluctably *mediated*. It is the effect of a medium that can be conjured up ("Rumble thy bellyful! Spit fire, spout rain!"), but that does not follow secular hierarchies, which ultimately resists human control.

The weather pervades Shakespeare's play. Lear's gesture of 'abjuring all roofs' and his conjuring up a 'weathery state of exception', which is connected to 'horrible pleasure' and to the critical attitude 'That things might change or cease', is, however, not only crucial for reading *King Lear*. I would like to suggest that it involves more: it involves literature in general. I do not mean to claim that Lear presents stable 'characteristics' of literature; it is rather dimensions or axes whose relation to each other can help to reconstruct the actualisation of 'the literary' in different contexts and under different epistemic and social conditions.

David Gwilym James's thesis that "*The Tempest* is a commentary on *King Lear*" (1967, 26) may lead us towards an understanding of how the literary medium reflects on its functioning in the practice of early modern theatre. In *King Lear*, the weather's state of exception not only 'carries away' the king's party, but very quickly also 'infects' the rest of the *dramatis personae*. The folio's famous stage direction, "Storm still" (*Lr.* SD, 3.1; 3.2; 3.4.3; 3.4.61; 3.4.98; 3.4.158), recurring six times, may be said to remain true for the whole play, even when the 'actual' storm has long ceased; the weather's state of exception and its "horrible pleasure" continue to the very end. "This cold night will turn us all to fools and madmen." (*Lr.* 3.4.77), the fool had predicted, and he again proves to be right. He even appears to speak truly on a dimension that surpasses the horizon and responsibility of a stage character, leaving the fictional world, and the internal communication system of drama: one may say that *King Lear* (the play!) 'enacts' the weather's state of exception, that *King Lear*, as a theatre performance, *is* this stormy state of exception. When the fool utters his prediction, turning to and focussing on the audience at the right moment, the "us all" that "This cold night will turn [...] to fools and madmen" then includes more than the play's *dramatis personae*. It is thus primarily the spectators who will experience the effect of the "cold night['s]" weathery medium; for them its "horrible pleasure" is produced. However, in *King Lear* these metatheatrical reflections remain in the shadow of the overwhelming tragic story that this play enacts. It is, as David Gwilym James claims, in Shakespeare's late *Tempest* that the weathery metatheatrical reflections, which were already present in *Lear*, literally move to centre-stage. My first chapter is therefore dedicated to a close reading of Shakespeare's *Tempest*. It will disclose a profound theory of early modern theatre that employs the dominant knowledge of the time to conceptualise the way the theatrical medium achieves effects on its audience that are analogous to the way the weather works on the human body.

"Rather I abjure all roofs" could also serve as the motto for the protagonist of Johann Wolfgang Goethe's epistolary novel *Die Leiden des jungen Werthers*, which appeared in 1774, more than one hundred and sixty years after *The Tempest* was first performed. Werther's name not only seems to exhibit his 'inclination' to the weather (in German: *Wetter*); like Lear, he "does not search for a roof that protects him from tempests", as Enzo Neppi notes (2010, 316; my transl.). He is, from the beginning to the end, drawn out of doors, always eager to experience overpowering nature:

> And – except when, from time to time, melancholy gets the better of me and Lotte allows me the miserable solace of weeping tears of anguish over her hand – then I must away, must go out [*Muß hinaus*]! and then I roam far and wide over the fields; then my joy lies in climbing a steep mountain [...]. (73; transl. altered; emph. J.U.)[1]

In contrast however to Lear, no 'weathery' community forms around Werther. He remains a solitary 'roamer', whose 'abjuring all roofs' is demonstrated to imply the abjuration of life itself. When Werther's decision to commit suicide is settled, he once more gives in to his characteristic urge to expose himself to the rough

---

[1] Here and in the following Stanley Corngold's translation is quoted. Since my argument refers to the German version of 1774 (footnotes provide the text of the *Frankfurter Ausgabe* edited by Waltraud Wiethölter), and Corngold's translation is based on the 1787 version, changes had to be made in a few passages to render the 1774 text. I have marked these changes with an explicit reference to the deviation between the versions. "Und wenn nicht manchmal die Wehmuth das Uebergewicht nimmt, und Lotte mir den elenden Trost erlaubt, auf ihrer Hand meine Beklemmung auszuweinen, so muß ich fort! Muß hinaus! Und schweife dann weit im Felde umher. Einen gähen Berg zu klettern, ist dann meine Freude [...]." (112)

elements. His nightly leaving of the town foreshadows his departure from life that will follow only twenty-four hours later:

> The watchmen, who knew him, let him go out [*hinaus*] without a word. A mix of rain and snow was whirling, and it was nearly eleven o'clock when he knocked at the gate again. His servant noticed, on Werther's return home, that his master's hat was missing. He did not venture to comment, helped him off with his clothes, which were soaked through. Only much later was the hat found on a crag that overlooks the valley from the slope of the hill [...]. (140; emph. J.U.)[2]

Werther would have fit well in Lear's 'weathery community': he is a 'liminal' figure, an outsider, associated with the notions of madness and excess; he embodies the limits of humanity. However, as his solitariness and, above all, the apparently necessary connection between abjuring the roofs and abjuring life indicate, Werther's enlightened world does not leave room for the formation of the weather's state of exception. It is here that the epistemic differences between the early 17th and the late 18th century become evident. In the second chapter of my study I attempt to show how literature solves the exemplary problem of Werther's 'unliveable' inclination to the weather and finds a way to establish a weathery state of exception and a critical weathery community in the 'weather-free' surrounding of enlightened society. In other words, the 'old' affinity of the literary and the weather is still prevalent, the transformed epistemic environment demands however a re-invention of the 'literary' as a 'weathery medium', of its role and functioning. The fact that the "horrible pleasure" of Werther's tragic story has affected generations of readers appears to testify to the success of literature's creating a space for a collective experience of the 'impossible', 'placeless' 'weathery state of exception'.

At first glance, Émile Zola's cycle of novels called *Les Rougon-Macquart*, which was published between 1871 and 1893, might appear to be much closer to Goethe's novel than *Werther* could be claimed to be to Shakespearean theatre. A closer look at the parameters with which our reading of *King Lear* has equipped us reveals a deep rupture. "Rather I abjure all roofs" could here no longer serve as the motto of a solitary doomed outsider, it rather appears to be the motto of the world of the Second Empire itself that Zola's cycle depicts. It can no longer be understood as the label for an impossible, an unliveable experience, but

---

[2] "Die Wächter die ihn schon gewohnt waren, ließen ihn stillschweigend hinaus, es stübte zwischen Regen und Schnee, und erst gegen eilfe klopfte er wieder. Sein Diener bemerkte, als Werther nach Hause kam, daß seinem Herrn der Huth fehlte. Er getraute sich nichts zu sagen, entkleidete ihn, alles war naß. Man hat nachher den Huth auf einem Felsen, der an dem Abhange des Hügels in's Thal sieht gefunden [...]." (246)

reflects a key characteristic of 'modern' urban life: the whole city of Paris seems to have 'abjured all roofs', all the cycle's protagonists, despite their huge differences in social status, form one gigantic weathery collective. Whenever some of them look down on the city's rooftops, they do not see the culture's shielding itself against nature's raging elements; what they encounter is 'the elements' themselves: a "sea of houses with blue roofs, like surging billows [*flots*] that filled the horizon" (*eK*, 67), a "living, seething ocean" (*eK*, 67);[3] "grand Paris which rolled out in front of [them] the turbulent sea of its roofs" (*PA*, II 822; my transl.),[4] "the ocean, with all the infinity and mystery of its waves" (*PA*, II 850; my transl.),[5] "the vast sea of roofs" (*PA*, II 1070; my transl.).[6] In fact, Zola's description of the Second Empire is the description of weather processes and their very own logic. My third chapter reveals this constellation to be another expression of the affinity of literature and weather. It is dedicated to reconstructing the universal pervasion of the weather in Zola's narrated world, which indicates a decisive social and epistemic shift that separates it from the enlightened weather-free world depicted in Goethe's *Werther*. How does the role and function of literature change when the 'weathery state of exception' that had been the paradigm and the differentiating characteristic of the literary medium has become the paradigm of a society, of modernity and progress? What about literature's "horrible pleasure" and its critical attitude "That things might change or cease"? These are the questions that my reading of Zola raises against the background of the two contrasting constellations of literature's affinity to the weather.

The relation of literature and weather is obviously a broad subject. The particular approach that I pursue with this study cannot and does not aspire to cover all the various associations one might have when considering the two topics. It is a contribution to a field of study that the humanities discovered for themselves quite some time ago. In the wake of the growing attention that the

---

[3] Here and in the following translations of the *Oxford World Classics* series have been used, if available. Footnotes provide the French original of the *Pléiade* edition. I have introduced title abbreviations (an initial 'e' marks English translations) so that the quotes can easily be referred to single novels. A list at the back gives an overview of the abbreviations used. "Ce jour-là, ils dînèrent au sommet des buttes, dans un restaurant dont les fenêtres s'ouvraient sur Paris, sur cet océan de maisons aux toits bleuâtres, pareils à des flots pressés emplissant l'immense horizon. [...] Et ses regards, amoureusement, redescendaient toujours sur cette mer vivante et pullulante, d'où sortait la voix profonde des foules." (*C*, I 387–388)

[4] Here and in the following, the translations of *Une page d'amour* are my own, based on C. C. Starkweather's translation published by the Société des beaux arts (1905). "[...] grand Paris qui déroulait devant elle la mer houleuse de ses toitures [...]." (*PA*, II 822)

[5] "C'était la pleine mer, avec l'infini et l'inconnu de ses vagues [...]." (*PA*, II 850)

[6] "[...] la mer immense des toitures [...]." (*PA*, II 1070)

theme of climate change has attracted in the media and the public perception especially in the last decades, the former rather esoteric niche is beginning to develop into a fashionable and highly productive field of knowledge.

Literary studies had been concerned with the weather long before criticism divested it of its questionable reputation as an unappealing and banal subject of enquiry. As, for instance, George E. Williams's (1951) and E. Catherine Dunn's (1952) early topical articles on the storm in *King Lear* may indicate, the reason for this is simple: there are literary texts in which the weather plays a crucial role, so that one cannot read them without making sense of its function. The critical choice of the weather as a subject of literary study was thus not primarily motivated by an interest in it or meteorology, but emerged from the literary texts themselves, as a problem with which their readers were confronted. This tradition of 'internally-motivated', 'non-institutionalised' 'weathery' readings still exists today, as Andreas Höfele's article (2006) on *The Tempest* exemplarily indicates.

The range of literary texts that have motivated this kind of 'conventional', old-school criticism of the literary weather overlaps strikingly with the small corpus of texts on which my study is based: my project takes a similar point of departure. I do not select and approach the literary texts with a certain interest in 'their weather'; the weather and its importance for 'the literary' is not brought to the texts, it is not a question for which the texts are supposed to provide answers. Above all, it is a question that the texts themselves raise. The observation precedes the systematisation. What differentiates my study from sporadic and singular 'weathery' readings is that I attempt to bundle these observations within a wider perspective. I assume that there is some sort of structural correlation of weather and literature that must naturally remain concealed in articles concentrating on single texts.

Friedrich Christian Delius is considered one of the pioneers for the literary studies' interest in the weather: his *Der Held und sein Wetter* [The Hero and His Weather] (1971) was the first book-length work that included 'the weather' in its title. As the book's subtitle, *Ein Kunstmittel und sein ideologischer Gebrauch im Roman des bürgerlichen Realismus* [An Artistic Device and Its Ideological Employment in the Novel of Bourgeois Realism] indicates, the weather remains, as in Delius's famous phrase, a "relatively banal subject" (1971, 8) that is not of any interest in itself, but in its authorial employment as an artistc device. The very rigid frame of one literary epoch and one genre eliminates the epistemic and historical dimension that is inherent in the weather and its knowledge and replaces it by presupposing an ideological frame that it brings to the texts from the extra-fictional world. It is this framing that reduces the weather to an apparently transparent motif, to the *Kunstmittel*, that serves as the analytical instrument for Delius's comparative study.

My approach attempts the opposite: I would like to create an awareness for the fact that prominent literary texts present the weather as a challengingly complex subject; a subject complex enough to reflect on the medium of literature, its functioning and its social and epistemological embeddedness. In fact, there might be hardly anything less specific to the 'literary weather' than its authorial employment as an artistic device. Not without reason is Eberhard Lämmert, Delius's supervisor, reported to have called it "a means for creating atmosphere for bad authors [*Stimmungsmacher für schlechte Autoren*]" (Delius and Vogel 2008, 78). The weather is perhaps the one paradoxical exception from the author's absolute rule over her fictional universe: it appears to be inherently connected to a notion of uncontrollability, so that one can only have it at one's full disposal at the cost of aesthetic devaluation. The question of weather, mastery and its aesthetic and ideological implications is important and we will come back to it with regard to Zola.

More than ten years after Delius's work, Arden Reed published the second book-length study with the weather in its title: *Romantic Weather. The Climates of Coleridge and Baudelaire* (1983). It operates on a much more advanced theoretical level. In the introduction Arden Reed sketches an archaeology of the weather, which points out its epistemological, cultural and literary transformations throughout the centuries. In this part, his study resembles the project I am pursuing. Unfortunately, these interesting reflections are marginalised: the conventional layout of Reed's book, which focuses on one literary epoch and uses the weather as a means of comparing two authors is similar in effect to the one that Delius's study exhibits: despite Reed's interesting readings and his high degree of theoretical reflection, the weather is reduced to a mere motif that is used to make poetological observations. The substantial parts of his book do not therefore provide evidence for the archaeology sketched in the book's introduction, and the two thus remain largely unconnected.

In the late 1990s, the rising public perception of climate change made itself felt: the humanities systematically conquered the field, beginning with histories of the interaction between climate and culture (Fleming 1998, Stehr and Storch 1999, Stevens 1999, Acot 2003, Strauss and Orlove 2003, Le Roy Ladurie 2004–2009, Boia 2005, Linden 2006, Behringer 2007), which was followed, somewhat later, by research in the history of meteorology and its cultural implications (Janković 2000, Riskin 2002, Taub 2003, Anderson 2005, Fine 2007, Golinski 2007, Fleming 2010, Janković 2010). Within a decade dozens of studies were published, of which Emmanuel Le Roy Ladurie's three-volume *Histoire humaine et comparée du climat* (2004–2009) is certainly the most monumental. This historical project enjoyed an immediate echo in literary studies: under the supervision of Ladurie Anouchka Vasak has written a dense monograph that bears the title *Météorologies. Discours sur le ciel et le climat, des lumières au romantisme* (2007). Her study does not subject itself to any exterior principle of organisation and can therefore assemble a huge amount of material from various areas (literature, natural history, theory) and develop highly interesting insights. Vasak's method of distilling her observations exclusively from her readings, her interest in the constitution of the modern subject and her historical perspective that reveals epistemic and cultural transformations have inspired my project. Vasak's approach nevertheless involves a problem: the title's reference to a 'discourse of the sky and the climate' evokes associations of a structured field, with its own rules and regulations, of a 'discourse' in the narrow Foucauldian sense. This is however not the case – there is no Foucauldian discourse 'of the weather'. As a consequence, Vasak confronts a vast and very heterogeneous group of texts and observations that is not coordinated and arranged by intrinsic rules and regulations, and she does not develop an overarching question that would put these diverse texts into perspective or organise the selection of material. Furthermore, although her study fills more than five hundred pages, the sheer mass of texts and the wide scope of her project do not provide for detailed close readings of literary texts. In fact, the 'literary' does not appear to be of specific interest for her. She does not develop an approach to literary texts; they form part of her corpus, and are read, with philological care, but not differently than texts of natural history or philosophy.

Although Anouchka Vasak's project enjoys a special status in the academic field of literary studies and its 'schools', institutions and research networks, the role that literary texts play in her study represents a strong general tendency: over the last decades, literary studies have tended to shift their focus and broaden their area of competence. This 'cultural turn' implies that scholars are not primarily interested in the literary text itself, but in 'broader' questions of 'culture'. One might say that 'good', engaged literary criticism has always pursued this project. However, especially the nascent fields, like the one of literature and weather, are dominated by a 'monoculture' of a certain critical attitude towards literary texts: elaborate, non-literary frameworks and questions induced by these frameworks are applied to the literary texts, which are not supposed to raise questions but are approached in this way to generate or legitimise answers. Large areas of the critical production influenced by 'Ecocriticism' and 'Science Studies' operate in this way. In the best cases, these frameworks facilitate interesting readings; in the worst, the literary texts degenerate to a mere reservoir of material that is somehow representative of 'culture' and 'society' or serves as evidence for 'general' arguments that derive from the non-literary framework and precede the selection and the reading of the literary texts.

Projects like Michael Gamper's 'literary meteorology' (2014), which is supported by a framework of Science Studies, face these 'dangers': although the thesis of a genuinely 'literary' knowledge of the weather draws attention to the literary text and its peculiarities, it is nevertheless the framework that guides the approach to the text and presupposes the literary text's relation to its non-literary surroundings. As we will see, the role of the literary text as a knowledge producer in the epistemic assemblage is a special case with a clear historical index, a fact that might be neglected by merely positing this function. The dominant background of Science Studies with its historical matrix of discoveries and developments threatens to replace careful readings of the literary texts and their own, often much more complex, conceptual framing of the literary weather. The interest in literature's contribution to the production of (meteorological) knowledge is always in danger of regressing to the study of the weather as a motif, which only the non-literary background brought to the text helps to structure and make meaningful.

In 2009 the historian Dipesh Chakrabarty published his article "The Climate of History. Four Theses" in *Critical Inquiry* and thereby contributed significantly to the establishment of the notion of 'the anthropocene' in the humanities. Literary studies quickly adopted Chakrabarty's ideas; an extremely productive field of knowledge has formed around this notion of 'the anthropocene', which is a multifaceted concept that can be strategically employed for very different aims. It has been used to argue for a broadening of the 'jurisdiction' of literary scholars, who now feel qualified and entitled to lecture on climate and climate history. It has, however, also been regarded as an important conceptual background that questions, challenges and shifts criticism's view of its 'traditional' subject 'literature', and thereby inspired new, creative interpretations of widely-read, 'old' texts. In this respect Chakrabarty's contribution mirrors those of his 'predecessors', the critical thinkers Michel Serres and Bruno Latour. Both have provided essential conceptual work for the exploration of a realm of knowledge that abrogates the difference of subject and object, of nature and culture. With his *Feux et signaux de brume. Zola* (1975) Michel Serres has himself furnished evidence that an interest in science and conceptual, epistemic backgrounds and a very detailed, philologically challenging close reading of literary texts can be mutually inspiring and strengthening, without the one providing the rigid and structuring background for the other. This is also the path I would like to pursue.

The layout of my study owes much to the work of Michel Foucault (cf. 1966, 1969). I attempt to do an archaeology; the archaeology of the relation, or the affinity, between literature and the weather. This has several 'methodological' implications.

(1) An archaeology does not begin with definitions; I therefore will not and cannot abstractly explicate *a priori* what I understand as 'weather' and clearly demarcate it from the notion of 'climate'. It is exactly the particular and historically variable filling of this general and vague term, its role, pervasion and

proliferation in the world, that I would like to explore as the project of this book. Although 'represented' by the 'same' or at least similar phenomena of wind, rain, etc., the early modern 'weather' of Shakespeare's time plays a very different role in the contemporary understanding of the world than the weather in Goethe's enlightened society or in Zola's France of the Second Empire. As a consequence, it is therefore important to follow up the proliferations of the weather, the 'official' meteorological knowledge of the time, as well as its infiltration in neighbouring epistemic fields and in the contemporary use of language. This always implies moving on the very boundary of 'literal' and 'figural' weather and examining both sides and what is undecidable in-between. As we will see, the transformation of 'literal' weather to 'figural' weather is one of the dominant shifts that can be observed. An archaeology thus encounters and dissects various concrete 'actualisations' of notions like the weather (the same holds true, as we will presently see, for literature and its genres) but refrains from declaring one of them to be definitive and ahistorical. One of these 'actualisations', located in the 19th century, registers the entry of a new understanding of 'climate' that decisively supplements the role of the 'weather' in the world. Our reading of Zola will give an account of this development.

(2) An archaeology reveals, above all, historical, cultural and epistemic ruptures. It is therefore essential to broaden the perspective and deliberately avoid the academic conventions of focusing on one literary epoch, on established transitional periods like the 'long XYth century', or on one literary genre. In order to circumvent the dipartite pattern 'from the unfamiliar to the familiar', or 'from the unenlightened to the enlightened', the layout of my study is inspired by Michel Foucault's *Les mots et les choses* and examines three constellations that are separated by two ruptures. The particularities and characteristics of each actualisation of the affinity between literature and weather only acquire a form against the contrasting background of the two other actualisations. The ambitious adventure of broadening the perspective does therefore not aim at 'covering' a more extensive period of time, but, on the contrary, at sharpening the view of the particular by discovering its historical index and its epistemic specificities. It goes without saying that the discovery of ruptures and contrasts relies on a certain consistency and continuity of themes and structures that are shifted, displaced and reordered. There is no *a priori*, methodological 'proof' that a particular 'archaeology' will excavate relevant results apart from its very performance itself. I hope that this book will, in the end, have testified to the existence of an affinity of literature and weather.

(3) An archaeology does not fabricate a new master narrative. It consciously remains a sketch with a limited representative force. The genealogical story of 'abjuring all roofs' inspired by *King Lear*, a story of the negotiations of the 'weathery medium' of literature that my introduction relates does not merely

summarise the 'results' of my study. It unfolds the frame of my archaeological examination. It is in the nature of this sort of critical research, which relies completely on readings of texts and defies prefigured conceptual frameworks, that the structuring parameters are themselves part of the results. However, the genealogical story itself should not be overestimated in its status as a constative speech act: a genealogy does not merely, and perhaps not primarily, analyse the status quo and the developments of a certain phenomenon (here the relation between literature and the weather) in and in-between different historical settings in a positivistic fashion; a genealogy has to be understood by what it does: it is always a more or less provocative (cf. the subtitle *Eine Streitschrift* [A Polemic] of Friedrich Nietzsche's *Zur Genealogie der Moral* (1988a)), or at least unsettling strategic intervention that denaturalises the phenomena on which it focuses. It shows that things have become the way they are, that they were different in the past and therefore will be potentially different in the future. The 'actual' 'results' of my study are to be found where the frame has to prove itself in practice: in the course of the chapters when it crystallises from the literary texts and is at the same time challenged by their complexity.

In one aspect my approach differs decisively from Michel Foucault's archaeological or genealogical writings: instead of assembling a huge amount of texts in order to derive their shared historical *a priori*, I have decided to work with single, paradigmatic 'examples'. The three sections of my study all take one literary text or cycle of texts as their point of departure and attempt to carefully develop a historical, cultural and epistemic constellation from it. The literary texts I have selected are typical examples of texts in which the weather plays a crucial role: *The Tempest*, by William Shakespeare, *Die Leiden des jungen Werthers*, by Johann Wolfgang Goethe and Émile Zola's *Les Rougon-Macquart*. As stated above, the observation of the weather's importance preceded the methodological reflections. The three texts' historical distance, their being situated in nascent cultural formations and their formative influence on Western literature predetermine them to become the pillars of an archaeological approach.

Working with examples must raise questions: What are these texts exemplary for, what do they represent? A genre, a literary epoch, a century? I would suggest to bracket, or at least to postpone these questions. My study aims at exploring and reconstructing three concrete constellations or assemblages in which the literary texts are embedded, of which they give an account and with which they interact. These constellations or assemblages and their characteristic 'manner of interaction' transcend the literary texts. They are not part of their fictional universes, but the factual conditions that make the texts possible. They can therefore, with some caution, be called exemplary. It is however impossible to determine in an abstract way the historical, generic or geographic reach of these constellations. In the best case the constellations explored in this study are exemplary for the discovery of other constellations that might work differently. Nevertheless, the formative influence of the selected, canonical texts to some extent ensures that the constellations examined here can claim a certain relevance.

The decision to work with exemplary texts in great detail derives essentially from the type of texts on which this study is based. As Michel Foucault has emphasised, literature has a complicated relation to the epistemic systems of its time (cf. 2001 [1965], 1966, 58–59); literary texts do not form part of the dominant discourses of knowledge production and therefore do not have to comply with these discourses' rules and norms. They are however not indifferent to them either. Each literary text or at least each genre negotiates its epistemic and social environment and positions itself in the assemblage of conditions responsible for its existence. The (self)understanding of 'the literary' and the 'function' of literature (entertainment, education, critique, production of alternative knowledges, …) are products of these negotiations. They are historically as variable as the role of the weather. It is the literary realm itself that creates room for these reflections and negotiations: literary texts are thus not only 'symptoms' for a certain cultural, social or epistemic 'situation'. On the contrary, their very special and variable position towards discourses of knowledge production and their rules and norms might even render them rather unreliable symptoms. Literary texts, some extensively, some rather implicitly, reflect and produce their relation to their non-fictional 'outside'; they are sensitive to the language-use of their time, they analyse and take strategic positions related to the epistemic, cultural and social developments of their environment. It is therefore important to take the literary texts' characteristic complexity seriously. This is what I attempt to do with my study. It consists of three detailed close readings that aim at recognising the texts' complexity by patiently reconstructing their subtle and intricate reflections and negotiations.

It may be against the current trend of literary studies to spend so much time 'on the surface' of only three 'texts': it appears to be much more promising to process huge amounts of texts with a specific theoretical framework in order to gather 'literary' arguments for cultural phenomena that satisfy a certain 'broader' popular or public interest. However, if literary studies are not to disavow or compromise their subject, which is the literary text, it is crucial to practice and cultivate the art of reading, to dwell on its textual surface of significants and participate in the processes of signification and creation of meaning. This is not to be misunderstood as silencing the social, political or cultural conditions and implications of these texts. On the contrary, as New Historicism has taught us, close readings are to be connected with close readings of co-texts (philosophical, poetological, 'scientific',...) and it is the textual surface itself that guides us to important and relevant material. In my study, these 'additional' texts are not of a framing or contextualising character; I incorporate them into my reading whenever they shed light on the literary text and contribute to unfolding the constellation that I am about to reconstruct. As a result, a variety of material finds its way into the book: medieval and early modern encyclopaedias, poetological writings of the authors treated, excerpts from other literary texts of the time, dictionary entries, philosophical texts by historical philosophers like Herder, Kant, Hegel, as well as by philosophers and thinkers of the 20th century, like Freud, Kristeva, Deleuze, Foucault and Serres, woodcuts and edgings,...

Each of the following three chapters relates one particular, exemplary story of literature's 'abjuring all roofs'. I have consciously refrained from embedding the readings in a framing master-narrative: they stand for themselves, they are conceptualised as autonomous texts that have their own consistency as extensive close readings of a literary classic. Contrastive connections are inserted in the course of the readings only when the observations made them appear helpful and adequate. The idea is to reduce the synthesising forces of a rigid systematic approach in order to allow the emergence of the particular consistency of the phenomena that I am pursuing. I have also decided not to tell the (biographical) story of the obvious continuities of influence and poetological inspiration that links the three authors. The readings themselves give testimony of the fact that these very different texts stand in dialogue with each other. The institutionalisation of national philologies may have foreclosed the 'European' character of the dense intertextual net of literature; in spite of crossing the realms of three 'national literatures', reading Shakespeare, Goethe and Zola is in no need of justification; it rather suggests itself.

Nevertheless, it is of highest priority to respect and emphasise the distance that separates the three examined constellations. It is this distance, the existence of distinct 'archaeological levels', that makes the genealogical perspective possible. The archaeology that this study pursues is not a linear, continuous narrative to be found in the studied objects; it emerges in retrospect from the 'triad' of readings that are assembled in this book.

This is the moment when the methodological roof of introductions and the illusion of mastery that lives under it has to be abjured. All that remains is to ask you, dear reader, for patience and generosity, and invite you to expose yourself together with me to the fascinating, sometimes sunny, mostly heavy, literary weather gathered in this book.

I *The Tempest*. Staging the Weather

Shakespeare's *Tempest* has generated a remarkable spectrum of criticism. In several waves that tell much about the theoretical and academic fashions of literary criticism, biographical, allegorical, Christian and humanist readings have been challenged and supplemented by cultural materialist, metatheatrical and postcolonial approaches. The enormous range and amount of such various and often conflicting critical endeavours is perhaps the key feature of *The Tempest*'s text and performance history. Hundreds of different stagings and elaborate close readings have testified to the fact that it is not merely an openness, a symbolical indeterminateness that makes this play particularly suitable for all sorts of appropriations and speculations, but a dense and intricate complexity that provides stunning textual evidence for an extensive range of fruitful interpretations. As a contribution to this spectrum of interpretations I venture to add another, perhaps quite exotic, reading. My aim is however not merely to find a niche that has not yet been sufficiently explored or to follow a thread to the margins of the text, but to give an account of the interplay of some of *The Tempest*'s most central concerns.

When considering the leading question of the study that this chapter is a part of it comes as no surprise that this endeavour involves early modern ideas of 'the weather'. With the following detailed analysis of *The Tempest* I would like to propose that the traces of temperance, climatic and humoral disturbances and infections prominent in the play provide us with an elaborate reflection on early modern theatre. This reflection situates the relatively new cultural institution, 'public theatre', in a faltering cosmological system of the world and examines effectiveness and role of the theatre in this system in terms borrowed from contemporary natural philosophy. By doing so, this investigation will attempt to give complex answers to some controversial questions in Shakespeare studies of the last decades: the political stance, the subversiveness of Shakespearean theatre, its role in negotiating orders of the world, the pragmatic frame that brings together stage and audience, to name only a few.

It is the beauty of *The Tempest* that it stages these abstract questions in a most concrete and spectacular way. Meaning created on the level of plot and characters is wittily made to comment on the medium and pragmatics of theatre in a vivid and at the same time dizzying fashion. The task for this chapter must thus be to follow the Christian, colonial, utopian and political threads without selecting one of them as the definite, transparent background for an explanatory reading, and to read them as dimensions of the question of the cultural site theatre. This means foregrounding the metatheatrical reading of the play only insofar as theatre is regarded as a space of controversial political, cultural and philosophical negotiations instead of a self-absorbed aesthetic enclave.

1 Title

The first hint that puts us on the track of the weather's role in Shakespeare's *Tempest* is undoubtedly its title. It appears to be striking for several reasons. First of all it is "remarkable, since the storm takes place only in the first scene, though its consequences are immense" (Walter 1983, 2). As D. S. McGovern notes, there have even been suggestions "that a more appropriate title for *The Tempest* would be *The Island* because the self-contained strangeness of Prospero's isle pervades the play, whereas the storm is limited to its opening scene" (1983, 201).[7] Is 'the storm' however really limited to the first scene? The title that Shakespeare gave his play questions this all-too 'literal', denotative reading of *"Tempest"*. Shakespeare's title calls on us to follow up more wide-ranging implications; it forces us to relate the play's first scene to the play as a whole and to find arguments for the claim that in attending *The Tempest* we experience "a play that is throughout its length a storm" (Brook 1957). We cannot dismiss this claim as a mere allusion to the title that serves as a hardly present, rather academic, paratext to the experience of what is taking place in-between the stage and audience during a performance. Prospero himself is alluding to the title's metatheatrical dimension when towards the end of the play he tells Alonso that "In this last tempest" "I | Have lost my daughter" (5.1.147–148; 5.1.153).[8] His witty histrionic gesture is a textbook case of dramatic irony: the audience shares Prospero's awareness that Alonso is fooled by his wrong 'literal' reading of "this last tempest", believing it to refer to the first scene's tempest in which he was shipwrecked with his party and lost his son. Prospero is not lying: in a sense he has lost his daughter (to Ferdinand) as Alonso has lost his son (to Miranda). The tempest of the first scene has been part of Prospero's stagecraft that initiated, but not accomplished, this double loss. However, Prospero's speaking of "this last tempest" is not merely a feeble, misleading fibbing; it is what could be called a dramatic metalepsis.[9] The phrase alludes to the title of

---

[7] The title of William Davenant's John Dryden's adaptation of *The Tempest*, called *The Tempest, or The Enchanted Island* (first performed 1667) very much illustrates this claim.

[8] All the Shakespeare quotes refer to editions of the Arden Shakespeare. Here and in the following *The Tempest* is quoted from Virginia Mason Vaughan's and Alden T. Vaughan's edition only referring to act, scene and line, other Shakespeare texts are marked by the conventional abbreviations (see the List of Abbreviations).

[9] Cf. Gérard Genette's notion of "métalepse narrative" (1972).

the play of which he is, at the moment of speaking this phrase, the protagonist. The deictic demonstrative "this" makes the paradoxical crossing of pragmatic boundaries, of internal and external communicative system, from the level of characters to the level of stage and audience, possible. The play *The Tempest* as a whole tells the story of Miranda's betrothal to Ferdinand that re-establishes Prospero's role in the dynasties of Milan and Naples. The dramatic irony produced by this brief comment thus re-enacts the important relation between the tempest of the first scene and the play as a whole that its title already makes us think about.

The title is unusual as well, in a way that might help us explicate the system of intricate threads that establishes the relation between the title, the tempest scene and the play set on the island. As James Walter notes, "*The Tempest* is unusual among Shakespeare's plays in that its title calls first attention, not to a great personage or to some human mood or effect, but to a natural phenomenon" (1983, 62). The influential tradition of romantically reading *The Tempest* as a metaphor of the retiring "poet-magician, poet creator" (Kott 1965, 178) and decades of refuting and deconstructing this view in postcolonial and other terms, have contributed much to the negligence of paying attention to the play's actual title. It is not "*Prospero*", not centring on a great personage, but "*The Tempest*". It indeed calls attention to a natural phenomenon, however, to be more precise, not in a general manner. The title's definite article designates a singular event of such a natural phenomenon. It is responsible for the double entendre that equates a specific theatre event and the event of a natural weather phenomenon ('Have you heard of *The Tempest*/the tempest at Whitehall?').

And there is more that this title has to tell. Peter Hulme (1981) has made us aware of the fact that by calling the play "*The Tempest*" Shakespeare took a decision: there was another word available that he could have resorted to for signifying the central weather event: the noun *hurricane* or *hurricano*, which had only recently entered the English language as a result of the colonial encounters in the Americas. According to Hulme, the use of this term would have strengthened the Caribbean dimension of the play that is particularly present in the name *Caliban*, an anagram of a similarly recent linguistic colonial import, *can(n)ibal*. Instead, Shakespeare "prefers the Mediterranean *tempest*" (1981, 59). Peter Hulme can demonstrate that by opting for *tempest* like his "narrative sources" for the shipwreck, William Strachey and Sylvester Jourdain (who reported on a shipwreck that had taken place near the Bermudas), Shakespeare actualises the familiar ideological framework of Christian providence and redemption (1981, 59). As we will see, this framework will in fact be of particular importance for the play as a whole.

The Caribbean *hurricane* was however not the only alternative available to Shakespeare; D. S. McGovern refers us to a term still more familiar than the 'Mediterranean' *tempest*, to an older, Anglo-Saxon alternative:

> For the title of the play Shakespeare could have chosen instead the more common word *storm*, which descends from Old English. He may have preferred *tempest* because it is a word of a more literary register and for that reason would draw more conscious attention to itself. It is also possible that the word was felt to have a greater figurative capacity to express specifically inward turmoil in addition to its literal meaning. (1983, 201)

Whether of a more literary register or not, the word *tempest* certainly does draw attention to itself. I agree with John Gillies that "Shakespeare cannot have been unaware of the pun on the Latin word for weather (*tempestas*) that lurks in the very title of his play" (1986, 686–687).[10] This pun brings the title into contact with a field of atmospheric, physiological, affective, emotional and, as we will see later, also of political 'communication'. Contemporary natural philosophy (as well as medicine) was rooted in this field, which had also left its traces in language and common sense during its long history from antiquity through the Middle Ages. To our modern understanding, however, this extensive, proliferating system of communication and correspondences must remain alien and hardly traceable. My translation into the terms of 'atmosphere', 'physiology', 'affects' and 'emotions' indicates how much our modern understanding has lost the decisive link that made phenomena and notions communicate for a long time. Luckily enough the memory of language provides us with cues, and the title "*The Tempest*" buys into this linguistic (and conceptual) reservoir: tempest, (dis)temperature, temperament, (dis)temper, tempering, temperance. The "figurative capacity", its potential of 'metaphorising' "inner turmoil" that D. S. McGovern ascribed to the word *tempest* might turn out to be less figurative than it appears to our modern way of thinking. By translating "inner turmoil" into "distemper" (we will later come to the famous "Never till this day | Saw I him touched with anger so distempered!" (4.1.144–145)), we see that *tempest* (*tempestas*) and *distemper* (i.e. "inner turmoil) are not merely figuratively linked. Renaissance knowledge centred on a notion of temperance, on establishing a balance between conflicting, instable, transforming and fluid pairs of antagonists. These antagonists might also be on a different scale, microcosmic humours and macrocosmic elements, that are not only linked analogically but also communicate

---

10 Lat. "Tempestas, atis, f.g. *Time, a seasonable time and faire weather, a faire or good season: a tempest or storme, a boysterous or troublous weather, be it winde, haile, or raine: commonlie it signifieth a tempest or storme of rain & haile together. also great trouble, busines or ruffling in a common weale, a storme or trouble of adversitie, daunger or perill, a commotion.*" (Thomas 1587, Tempestas, atis).

effects, that interact in a complex, bi-directional and causally hardly conceivable fashion.

When claiming that 'the weather' plays a decisive role in *The Tempest*, that *The Tempest* is in fact in a certain way a play about 'the weather', I am using the term *weather* as an umbrella term for this huge field of distemperature and temperance, reaching from atmospheric phenomena to the tempers of the human body and the body politic. The weather, understood in these terms, accounts for the endless, ever-imperfect processes of ordering and dis-ordering, for the fundamental imperfection and disorder at the heart of every (at least non-divine) order. As a consequence, *The Tempest* is, as its title promises, a play about the "duress of tempestuous inner and outer weather" (Peterson 1973, 220). It is a play about temperance, that is not only "the central virtue of all comedies", as Northrop Frye writes (1965, 153), but also inseparable from tempestuous weather, its dialectical counterpart, so to speak. As Ernest B. Gilman claims with regard to *The Tempest*, "the cure for distemper lies not in withdrawing from time's sometimes violent jars but in tempering oneself to them" (1980, 223).

2 Weather and theatre

Is it bold to claim that *The Tempest* is a play about the weather, when it is so obviously a play about theatre? Despite the extensive theoretical and thematic scope of criticism that *The Tempest* has engendered, it does not seem too controversial to emphasise the metatheatrical dimension that pervades the play. Katherine Steel Brokaw calls it a "meta-theatrical reverie" (2008, 37), Karol Berger reads it as Shakespeare's

> most consistently metatheatrical play, the play that destroys the illusion of immediacy and, regardless of its subject, offers constant interpretation of the medium in which this subject is meditated upon – an interpretation, I might add, which is far from enthusiasm and full of distrust. (1977, 235)

In the course of this chapter, we will come across dozens of instances, some more prominent, some less, that underline Karol Berger's claim of the play's "constant interpretation of the medium". However, notwithstanding the play's title, the astonishing fact that most of these instances of metatheatrical situations and reflections, including all the prominent ones, are conceptualised with the help of notions of the weather has gone unnoticed in decades of criticism. To put it in an extemporary and surely reductionist way: the theatrical medium is an 'airy' one, one in which air moves and thickens, clouds form and dissolve, in which gusts of wind circulate from stage to audience and from audience to stage, generating effects on the audience's and the players' tempers, on their "inner weather". In using these terms to sketch what I would claim is a specifically early modern vision of theatre, the problem that arises and that is likely to be responsible for the lack of critical attention to the weather in metatheatrical readings, can hardly be missed: to our modern eyes and ears the relation between the medium theatre and the natural phenomenon weather seems to be merely metaphorical. However, it is the question of this 'metaphor's' arbitrariness that distinguishes our modern reading of it from its early modern function. Michel Foucault has taught us in *The Order of Things* that "[i]n its raw, historical sixteenth-century being, language is not an arbitrary system" (Foucault 1970, 35).[11] Resemblance and analogy are not categories of abstract and retrospective ordering (undertaken by (metaphorical) language); in the early modern age, resemblance and analogy *are* still the organising principles of the world, they form the basis of what is regarded as true knowledge. The 'metaphor' of theatre as weather is thus motivated by an underlying system of correspondences and analogies that retains a close connection to the sixteenth-century knowledge of the world. It is built on the very premises of contemporary (natural) philosophy and medicine. In other words, it is backed by what we would today call 'science', by a 'state of the art' truth. I am well aware that drawing this conclusion is not an uncontroversial point to make. Shakespeare's use of language is the least related to the "raw, historical sixteenth-century being" of language as could be imaginable, the playful and witty exhibition of the arbitrariness of language in fact being one of his indisputable skills. However, this is not the point. What I am suggesting is a system of knowledge behind the weather-theatre 'metaphor', supporting this metaphor, making it possible. As has been shown in great detail by Simeon K. Heninger (1960) and as will be evident in the following sections, Shakespeare makes extensive use of contemporary natural-philosophical and medical conceptions of weather and its humoral effects. As a consequence, he writes his metaphor into the system of knowledge that Foucault attempts to make us more familiar with in the first part of his famous book. The wide-reaching analogical conceptions alluded to in many of Shakespeare's plays, and especially in *The Tempest*, formed a central part of the medieval and early modern worldview. They were thus shared by his audience, they were built on ground so common that there was no need to explicate them in greater detail. Unfortunately, having been born four centuries later than Shakespeare and his audience and living in a world that is ordered and presented to us in a completely different manner, we do not share the ground on which Shakespeare established his metatheatrical reflections. Moreover, we do not share the historical *a priori*, to use another Foucauldian term (cf. 1969, 174), that made the early modern theatre experience as such possible. Although a lot

---

11 "Dans son être brut et historique du XVIe siècle, le langage n'est pas un système arbitraire [...]." (Foucault 1966, 49)

of work has already been done in this direction, the task of excavating this historical *a priori* is still great and risky. Following up the 'metaphor' of theatre and weather, taking the motivation of the analogy behind this link seriously, may help us to reconstruct parts of the common ground lost to us.

In order to understand the critical strategy of my argument, it might be useful to dedicate a few words to the early modern epistemological background and the important and perhaps unexpected role it plays for my intervention in the debate of reading *The Tempest* and Shakespeare in general. At first glance, the project of explicating one analogy, the one of theatre and weather, and assembling evidence for it must look imbalanced and uncritical. One might be inclined to know more about the resistances to this analogy and also be referred to the instances where the play exhibits its limitations and contradictions. However, the epistemic framework behind the modern readers' expectations (i.e. for example, the expectations of a process of verification that would have to include observations for and against the proposed thesis) is not compatible to the early modern epistemological background and thus to the epistemic efficacy of 'an analogy' as such. An analogy, like the one between weather and theatre, does not function the way an argument or a proposition works in a modern *system* of knowledge. As a result of a completely different epistemological framing, which is devoid of stable limits and stable references, it can neither be verified nor contradicted. As Michel Foucault has pointed out in *The Order of Things*, it is a long and potentially unending process for "even the slightest of analogies" to be "justified and finally take on the appearance of certainty":

> First and foremost, the plethoric yet absolutely poverty-stricken character of this knowledge. Plethoric because it is limitless. Resemblance never remains stable within itself; it can be fixed only if it refers back to another similitude, which then, in turn, refers to others; each resemblance, therefore, has value only from the accumulation of all the others, and the whole world must be explored if even the slightest of analogies is to be justified and finally take on the appearance of certainty. It is therefore a knowledge that can, and must, proceed by the infinite accumulation of confirmations all dependent on one another. And for this reason, from its very foundations, this knowledge will be a thing of sand. The only possible form of link between the elements of this knowledge is addition. Hence those immense columns of compilation, hence their monotony. (Foucault 1970, 31)[12]

---

12 "Et d'abord le caractère à la fois pléthorique et absolument pauvre de ce savoir. Pléthorique puisqu'il est illimité. La ressemblance ne reste jamais stable en elle-même ; elle n'est fixée que si elle renvoie à une autre similitude, qui en appelle à son tour de nouvelles ; de sorte que chaque ressemblance ne vaut que par l'accumulation de toutes les autres, et que le monde entier doit être parcouru pour que la plus mince des analogies soit justifiée, et apparaisse enfin comme certaine. C'est donc un savoir qui pourra, qui devra procéder par entassement infini de confirmations s'appelant les unes les autres. Et par là, dès ses fondations, ce savoir sera sablonneux. La seule forme de liaison possible entre les éléments du savoir, c'est l'addition. De là ces immenses colonnes, de là leur monotonie." (Foucault 1966, 45)

This "monotony" and the principle of "addition" will therefore also shape the presentation of my reconstruction of the analogy of theatre and weather. Nevertheless, despite the plethora of hints and evidences that Shakespeare's *Tempest* will help us accumulate, the analogy will remain of frail epistemological force, it will remain "a thing of sand". There is therefore 'no need to deconstruct this analogy'. On the contrary, excavating this frail piece of early modern knowledge and asserting it against the hegemony of modern, systemic thinking that has become naturalised appear to me in itself to be a critical strategy. To be sure, the analogy of theatre and weather that my chapter focuses on is only one analogy, and only one approach among many. It cannot and does not intend to claim any privilege for understanding the play, as it does not intend to foreclose alternative approaches by turning the play merely into a 'metatheatrical monument', which it clearly is not. In other words, my reading aspires to work as a "critique" (cf. Barker and Hulme 2002, 198) rather than as a taming confirmation of the play's reception in conventional criticism. The monotony of compiling evidence for the analogy of theatre and weather is a calculated strategic necessity for this endeavour.

The way taken is a winding path, picking up the allusions, hints and direct references scattered all over the play, and trying to understand, on the one hand, their systematic coherence and, on the other, the connections this conceptual web offers to the manifold themes that Shakespeare's play negotiates. Wherever a fruitful resonance can be produced, I will bring in early modern philosophical, medical and popular co-texts which may help us increase our footing. Nevertheless, the search for the lost 'historical literality' behind what appears to us as arbitrary instances of figural speech will remain a very thin line to balance. As an incentive to follow me along this path I have nothing but a double promise to offer: reading *The Tempest* with an eye on the role of the weather and its relation to the theatrical medium will deepen an understanding of this play, as regards certain passages as well as the relationship of particular themes. Moreover, we will discover in Shakespeare's *Tempest* a pragmatic theory of theatre, or rather, we will read Shakespeare's play as a staging of such a media-theoretical reflection. That is to say that the play's title, "*The Tempest*", not only describes what the audience *sees*, what takes place in one scene that has to be read as a symbolically charged synecdoche (*pars pro toto*) of the whole play. Rather, it signifies what the audience *experiences*, or is to experience, in the two or three hours' time at the Blackfriars, the Globe or at Whitehall. That is what I would like to argue in the following sections, starting with a reading of the play's prominent opening, the tempest scene.

3 The tempest scene

The first scene of Shakespeare's *The Tempest* undoubtedly enjoys a special and unusual status: it is at the same time structurally and topographically separated from the rest of the play, but is the main reference point for the play's title. At first glance, it does not really serve any obvious expositionary function. It seems instead to translate the highly common picture of a shipwreck, known from emblem books and recognisable as an "intertextual topos that pointed almost inevitably to the world of fiction" (Mowat 2000, 30),[13] into an unprecedented stage spectacle. The scene's isolated position at the beginning of the play and the fact that the viewer is not provided with any context or semantic framework that the scene's impressions could be related to strengthens the impact of the rather unspecific allegorical force that the well-known image of the shipwreck brings to the London stage: we see the "ship of state" (Pieters 2000, 142), "a traditional metaphor for society" (Wright 1977, 248), "and when it founders the cries are of the severing of social bonds" (Fowler 2000, 37). The prominence of allegorical approaches to the scene is hardly astonishing, since Shakespeare's tempest scene is related to one of the forefathers of allegorical reading. For his theory of allegory Quintilian had chosen Horace's famous ode 1.14, "O navis" and, as Elizabeth Fowler notes, the same allegorical hinge organises the two literary ships' contact with heavy weather: the Latin verb *gubernare* links the meaning of steering a ship with statecraft, with governing (cf. 2000, 38). Despite the generality of this allegorical picture, the art of steering a ship as a metaphor for 'the political' appears promisingly pertinent for *The Tempest* as a whole: Steering a ship always means combining the notions of fighting against the weather's turmoil and of being completely dependent on the weather's forces in order to progress. It is not really apt to say that a sailing ship *confronts* the weathery elements – its relation to the weather is a very different one from the relation of a modern ship driven by steam, diesel or nuclear energy. It literally cannot withdraw from the elements: it has to temper itself to them.

These very general remarks lead straight to the difficult but also teasing question of the first scene's relation to the rest of the play, to what is going to follow. In the discussion of the play's title it became clear that this question is markedly central. However, when thinking about the links and correspondences that hold together the first scene and the rest of the play set on the island, we should always keep in mind the viewers' experiencing the spectacle: the structure of *The Tempest* (a play, I assume they are watching for the first time

---

13 For this claim Hans Blumenberg's famous *Shipwreck with Spectator* (1997) provides an abundance of material.

and did not know before) forces them to take the first scene, as it is – as a self-sufficient little theatre play. All links and correspondences with the less condensed, less allegorical and symbolical plot on the island will have to be recognised only in retrospect. In contrast to modern academic writing on Shakespeare's *Tempest*, which is essentially an exercise in re-reading, thinking, and, again, re-reading, the audience in the early modern playhouse does not have the opportunity to skim back a few pages and compare two passages at remote ends of the play. As a consequence, the effect of the correspondences between the first scene and the play as a whole has to function on a much less conscious level. That does not mean that the links were merely rough, feeble or vague, but that, not unlike connections produced by what Sigmund Freud calls dream-work, the links are less systematic, too heterogeneous and many-faceted to establish a clear-cut passage from the first scene to the rest of the play. It might thus be too optimistic to label the tempest scene's ship a "microcosm of the whole play" (Wells 1994, 350), if only because there is no time for the audience to reflect on the net of analogical relations that this label presupposes. However, Stanley Wells surely has a point with regard to the astonishing richness of connections that the first scene produces. Instead of using the concept of microcosm I would suggest following Douglas L. Peterson and characterising the status of the first scene as an "emblem"[14] of the play:

> As the play progresses we realize that in addition to initiating the action of the play the scene has also functioned as a dramatic version of the "tempest-tossed bark" emblem – as a "speaking picture" announcing the thematic significance of the action it initiates (1973, 219).

Without the audience noticing in the moment they see it, "Shakespeare raises in the first scene fundamental issues of temperament, authority, and political power that haunt the play" (De Gooyer 2001, 515); "he reveals the climate, themes, and thrust of the whole play at its onset" (Hall 1999, 42). As a dramatic emblem, the first scene's relations to the 'text' of the following scenes set on the island are complex and not easily traced in few general words. However, Shakespeare has provided us with an unusually finely drawn emblem, etching

---

[14] An exemplary emblem in Helkiah Crooke's famous medical treatise *Mikrokosmographia* resembles the emblematic first scene of Shakespeare's *Tempest* in theme and allegorical horizon: "The world is a Sea, the accidents and divers occurentes in it are waves, wherein this small Bark is tossed and beaten up and downe, and there is betwixt us and our dissolution, not an inch boord, but a tender skinne, which the slenderest violence even the cold aire is able to slice through. How then, may some say, commeth it to passe, that so weake a vessell should live in so tempestuous a Sea, should ride out so many stormes and dangers?" (Crooke 1615, 60)

rather than woodcut, that gives us plenty of occasions through which to explore these relations. An important condition for this endeavour is that we listen carefully to the text. It is not without cause that Guy Back feels urged to remind the directors of this world that the "point of the scene would be in what was said rather than in stage effects" (1971, 78). Shifting the attention away from the stage's "effort to simulate a storm's 'hurly-burly'" (1971, 78) to what the characters on stage have to say facing this dreadful weather might paradoxically lead us much closer to an assessment of "stage realism" (Holland 1995, 223), involving stage-weather, than speaking about wind-machines, squibs and rolling canon balls along wooden trays. The first scene's tempest is more than a "central symbol named in the play's title" (Mebane 1988, 33); it is emblematic, because of "the storm that is associated with tragic experience" (Mebane 1988, 33); this 'little' first scene already touches on the issues and their metatheatrical implications that are elemental to *The Tempest* as a whole. Let us begin to work out the questions that the first scene raises, and hope that this will, perhaps in a more literal way than intended by Grace Hall, reveal something about the "climate [...] of the whole play" (1999, 42).

The Tempest begins with an appellation:

Master:	Boatswain!
Boatswain:	Here Master. What cheer?
Master:	Good, speak to th' mariners. Fall to't yarely or we run ourselves aground, Bestir, bestir! (1.1.1–4)

This appellation constitutes the first of the hierarchical relationships of master and servant, an emblematic pairing on which the much-discussed relationships of Prospero and Ariel and Prospero and Caliban will be moulded. Hardly anyone in the audience would have noticed the theatrical trick disclosed by this short exchange of words: as a result of the appellation, the audience knows in seconds what characters the two actors onstage are impersonating; the character of the boatswain is 'produced', is instantiated by one, by the very first word. The power of speaking this word also introduces the second character onstage, as the boatswain's reply acknowledges the master as master. In the context of drama, this Althusserian appellation, famous from his "Ideology and Ideological State Apparatus" (1971), takes on a metatheatrical significance: it is as if the theatre director casts his roles and 'transforms' an actor into a character. This is, I would suggest, exactly what the audience experiences in these first words. Having been acknowledged/recognised as the master, the master hands the power of speech down the ladder of hierarchies to the boatswain, thereby (constitutively) introducing a third now recognisable party to the stage: "speak to the mariners".

Prospero's sending Ariel on theatrical duty will later recall this imperative. The master has hardly finished his sentence and left the stage when, as if by magic, the mariners enter. Within few sentences the beginning of the first scene erects a hierarchical power structure that works mainly in a theatrical mode: by the evocative and conjuring power of words.

In this way the short passage already indicates the two main themes of the famous tempest scene: it is all about hierarchy and about the power of words. To be more precise, it is about a particular state of exception that affects these two themes in a specific way.

Alonso, King of Naples, who is one of the passengers on board the ship experiences this state of exception when he comes on deck and attempts to speak with the Boatswain:

> *Alonso:* Good boatswain, have care. Where's the master? Play the men!
> *Boatswain:* I pray now keep below! (1.1.9–11)

Although he is of the highest 'worldly' rank on board, and although the ship might very probably even be part of his royal possessions, the Boatswain does not answer the king's question. In contrast to the authority that the master exerted over the Boatswain in the play's first exchange of words, the king's imperative ("Play the men!") does not meet with a loyal response; on the contrary, the Boatswain brusquely answers with another imperative, commanding the king (!) to leave the deck. This strange suspension of 'worldly' hierarchy does not concern the king alone. His whole entourage has come on stage without being directly addressed (and thereby introduced to the audience) by the master or his deputy, the boatswain. In stark contrast to the ship's hierarchy of master, boatswain and mariners that had been established instantly by the power of appellations, the worldly hierarchy of the king, duke and courtiers lacks a spoken embodiment in this scene. Although the viewers become aware that the group of people must be of high rank ("remember whom thou hast aboard" (1.1.19)), even a court party, the audience's theatrical experience of the scene confirms the boatswain's stance in the dispute over the hierarchies on board. He does not address his interlocutors by their rank, as would be appropriate (different from Alonso, who addresses him as "Good boatswain"). He even mocks their high positions in the worldly hierarchy of authority: "What cares these roarers for the name of king?" (1.1.16–17); and to Gonzalo, "You are a councillor; if you can command these elements to silence and work the peace of the present, we will not hand a rope more. Use your authority!" (1.1.20–23).

As the boatswain's cynical comments indicate, it is the heavy weather that accounts for the suspension of the worldly hierarchy: the "roarers" (i.e. the high waves) do not care for the "name of king", "the elements" do not obey the "councillor's" commands. The social assemblage on board appears to have merely adopted the weather's 'state of exception', its suspension of worldly authority. In fact, the manoeuvres that the boatswain commands the mariners to enact confirm this strategy of adapting to the weather rather than countering it: in order to prevent the ship from "run[ning] *aground*" (1.1.4; emph. J.U.), the mariners are called to "*fall* to it yarely" (1.1.3; emph. J.U.) and "[t]ake in the *top*sail" (1.1.5–8; emph. J.U.):

> Boatswain: Down with the topmast! Yare! Lower, lower! Bring her to try with main course. (*A cry within.*) A plague upon this howling. They are louder than the weather or our office. (1.1.33–36)

The heavy weather forces the crew to sacrifice the ship's top structures. They *temper* the ship to the tempest by removing its vertical extension to a large proportion. Paradoxically, 'obeying' the weather's movement of pushing downwards, following it to a certain degree ("Fall to it", "Down with the topmast!", "lower, lower!") seems to be the appropriate and only possible means of preventing an absolute, fatal sinking ("we run ourselves aground"): this perhaps counter-intuitive measure accords well with Renaissance ideas of medicine and curing 'distempers', and may give us a first idea of how the notion of 'tempering' functions, one that has become so alien to us.

The act of ridding the ship of its upper rigging is certain to be allegorically charged with political meanings. It is no coincidence that the famous revolutionary battle cry, "Down with the king" uncannily reverberates in one of the boatswain's commands ("Down with the topmast!"). In *The Tempest*, the (allegorical?) image of a vessel bereft of its top structures occurs twice: in the tempest scene it is, as we have seen, a reigning king, Alonso and the reigning duke of Milan, Antonio who lose their authority; remarkably, also Prospero's fall, or rather the usurpation of his power in Milan involves the same image (cf. Back 1971, 81, Neill 1983, 46, Fowler 2000, 39):

> Prospero: In few, they hurried us aboard a bark,
> Bore us some leagues to sea, where they prepared
> A rotten carcass of a butt, not rigged,
> Nor tackle, sail, nor mast – the very rats
> Instinctively have quit it. There they hoist us
> To cry to th' sea that roared to us, to sigh
> To th' winds, whose pity, sighing back again,
> Did us but loving wrong. (1.2.144–150)

Both times the 'topless' ship is associated with a political state of exception that suspends worldly hierarchies. The 'old' hierarchies are not simply replaced by new, or different ones. Both vessels, the one transporting Alonso and his courtly party as well as the bark carrying Prospero and his daughter, are kept in a state of suspension that makes itself felt by the uncanny absence of the governing authority. Prospero and Miranda could not address their complaints to the usurpers responsible for their suffering, and the same appears to be true on board of the kingly ship: "Where is the master?" (1.1.11), Alonso and Antonio repeatedly ask during the storm; and, although the audience has seen the ship's master leave the stage moments ago, the two most highly ranked passengers of the ship are not given the favour of his presence. The master's absence throughout the scene (and the whole play) is indeed remarkable.

Instead of facing the 'new' (revolutionary or usurped) hierarchy, all that the vessels' crews encounter is – weather. The "roar[ing]" "sea" and the "sighing" "winds" in the case of Prospero and Miranda, and the emblematic storm with its *"tempestuous noise of thunder and lightning"* (SD 1.1) for the court party surrounding Alonso. This violent presence of the weather does however not satisfy the search for the 'master of it all'. For the early modern mariners, as well as for the early modern theatre audience, the weather is not just a manifestation of atmospheric contingency, but a medium of divine intervention that has to be deciphered:

> In the first scene, the storm winds of the play's title clearly arouse divine associations in the minds of the mariners, who are awed and terrified into unaccustomed prayer [...]. The sailors' credulity is understandable; frequently in biblical apocalyptic, from Job to Isaiah to Ezekiel to Daniel to Revelation, wind is a sign of divine presence [...] (Job 38:1; Is. 29:6, 66:15; Ez. 1:4–5; Da. 7:2, 40:6; Rev. 7:1). (Hodgkins 2010, 159)

In other words, with the heavy weather dominating the scene, the court party's search for "the master" gains another, a theological dimension that supplements the literal reference to the person in charge on board: another absent 'master' appears to be directing the ship's course, a master whose province and jurisdiction is not limited to the ship, but who also 'commands' over the globe and its weather. It is therefore not astonishing that the presence of the weather even increases the desire for someone on stage who could give interpreting testimony of this weather and of its spectacles, who could perhaps even claim authority over it! Heather Campbell observes that the scene indeed articulates this desideratum in Christian terms:

> The Boatswain's challenge to Gonzalo ["You are a councillor; if you can command these elements to silence and work the peace of the present, we will not hand a rope more. Use your authority!" (1.1.20–23)] clearly evokes the episode in the Gospels in which Christ stills the storm (Matthew 8.23–27; Mark 4.35–41; Luke 8.22–25) [...]: "What manner of man is this, that even the winds and the sea obey him!" (Matthew 8.27) (Campbell 1993, 81).

Andreas Höfele supports Christopher Hodgkins's description of wind as "a sign of divine presence" by referring to the cultural phenomenon of the "*Wetterpredigt* (weather sermon)", a popular form of preaching ruefulness by interpreting weather phenomena, especially thunderstorms, as signs of divine wrath (2006, 25). The impression of a divine presence evoked by the scene's noises and weather is strengthened by the spoken words in the scene that are interspersed with carefully placed allusions and intertextual links. John D. Rea has convincingly argued for an intertextual link between the scene and Erasmus's "Naufragium" (1919), where a shipwreck is chosen as a scenario to test belief and differentiate it from (Catholic, worldly, egoist) superstition.

Although neither Jesus Christ nor a theologically schooled person prove to be on board to silence or at least to interpret the storm, the appropriate Christian reaction to the heavy weather appears to have a representative amongst the crew: the boatswain. Strikingly, he twice answers the question after the master with the order to retreat to under deck ("I pray now keep below!" (1.1.11); "Keep your cabins!" (1.1.14)). A little later he explains that when he sends them "To cabin!" (1.1.17), it is "to make [themselves] ready [...] for the mischance of the hour" (1.1.24–25). As preached in the weather sermons, he thus instructs them to answer the weather's significant expression of God's deprivation of *caritas* (we could say, being led by a wrong, but helpful 'folk' etymology) with the 'appropriate' Christian response: by withdrawing from the turmoil of the outer world, and probing one's conscience in order to repent. The noun *cabin*, besides its obvious denotation of a "room or compartment in a vessel for sleeping or eating in" (*OED*, cabin, *n.* 5. a.), also carries exactly these Christian connotations of retreating from the world for contemplation and repentance: "A cell: e.g. of an anchorite or hermit, in a convent or prison" (*OED*, cabin, *n.* †3. a.).

However, the court party follows the Boatswain's command only temporarily: after a few seconds they re-appear on stage and will not be told off again. Shakespeare clearly actualises the Christian horizon of interpreting the tempest and its theological hierarchy only to suspend it: the state of exception on board follows a different logic, a logic that suspends the worldly as well as the theological hierarchies. More than that, the 'state of exception' that Shakespeare emblematically sketches with the help of the 'image' of the ship encountering heavy weather *is defined by its characteristic suspension of all sorts of hierarchies* that structure the 'ordinary' world of the early modern audience. The state of exception on board the vessels is essentially *theatrical*.

Against this background, the boatswain's sending the noblemen to their cabins translates into the theatrical language of sending them offstage. Their intimate, personal inner transformation from sinner to repentant in their private cabin is not suited to the medium theatre. The transformations that theatre is concerned with take place onstage. Onstage, "the master", representing absolute authority, control and the 'true' meaning (the significate!), is not to be found. There seems to be, above all, one 'thing': 'only' weather.

However, as the boatswain demonstrates to the court party, this does not have to mean there is 'nothing' to be found, out there, in the middle of the raging weather. By wittily answering Antonio's question, "Where is the master, boatswain?", with a glib "Do you not hear him?", he displaces the question, probably intending to be brought to speak to the master, and refers the impatient courtiers to *a medium*. The master's apparent absence is thus translated into a somewhat remote, inapproachable presence. What do the noblemen hear that would make the seemingly absent master present? The boatswain's briefing of the mariners, before the entrance of the court party, has given the audience the hint that this has to be the master's whistle:

> Boatswain: Heigh, my hearts; cheerly, cheerly, my hearts! Yare! Yare! Take in the topsail. Tend to the master's whistle! [*to the storm*] Blow till thou burst thy wind, if room enough. (1.1.5–8)

Despite this clear hint, a close reading of the boatswain's chain of commands upsets the straightforward reference to the master's whistle. Modern editors have in unison felt the need to insert the extrapolated stage direction "[*to the storm*]" that separates the master's whistle from the Boatswain's addressing the tempest. The stage direction is indeed motivated by the text and represents the dramatic necessity of marking the address to the wind as spoken to a new addressee. However, this pragmatic break should not foreclose the semantic current that flows across the break: "Blow till thou burst thy wind", spoken to the weather, uncannily resonates with the master's whistle of the preceding command. The syntactical realisation of the phrase does not even allow the actor to speak his address to the weather as contrastive to the master's blowing the whistle ("Tend to the master's whistle! And thou, tempestuous wind, *thou* blow till thou burst thy wind"). The audience cannot avoid hearing the ambivalent, double reference to the whistling sound's source, which can be both: either the ship's master, or the raging weather. The intricate semantic current of blowing a whistle thus exemplifies a phenomenon that is of great importance for the first scene and for the play as a whole. The noun *whistle* denotes a sound that can be produced both by human beings and by the weather: "Any similar sound [to the act of whistling], as of wind blowing through trees or rigging [...]" (*OED*, whistle, *n.* 3. d.).

The boatswain's question, "Can you not hear him?" directs the court party as well as the theatre audience to the ambivalence, to the unknown source of the sound and thus links it to a question that is central to *The Tempest*: "the question of authority" (Hall 1999, 42). When taking in the topsail, to whose whistling do the mariners, ultimately, "tend"? The winds', or the master's – or are the two even 'collaborating', in a way? Whose whistling does the Boatswain mean, when he rhetorically asks the courtiers: "Do you not hear him?" as an answer to their "Where is the master [...]?"? This time, the Arden[3] editors have not equipped us with an added stage direction asking for an offstage whistle to be blown – and how should the audience tell that this whistling sound is to be heard as the ship master's and not the wind's whistling in the rigging? What the court party and the audience are sure to hear is "*A tempestuous noise of thunder and lightning*" (SD 1.1).

In other words, the suspension of hierarchies on board the vessels (Alonso's ship and Prospero's bark) is linked to the increased importance of a certain, intense and ambivalent, but highly significant manner of 'acoustic expression'. As the 'episode' of the 'master's whistle' so vividly indicates, a medium of 'meaningful' sounds supplements the absence of the usual, of the familiar hierarchy. The 'state of exception' on board the vessels, which I have suggested to be emblematically *theatrical*, is characterised by these two inseparable traits: by a suspension of hierarchies that is supplemented by the intense presence of a medium of 'meaningful sounds'. Strikingly, as we have seen, both traits are connected to the dominant role of the heavy weather. It is the tempest's irresistible power that questions and suspends the worldly authority; it is its manifold array of sounds that foregrounds the supplementary role of the medium, its making present what is absent (i.e. the master).

Prospero's and Miranda's miserable time aboard the unrigged bark reveals interesting things about the weathery medium of sounds that is constitutive for the state of exception:

> Prospero: In few, they hurried us aboard a bark,
> Bore us some leagues to sea, where they prepared
> A rotten carcass of a butt, not rigged,
> Nor tackle, sail, nor mast – the very rats
> Instinctively have quit it. There they hoist us
> To cry to th' sea that roared to us, to sigh
> To th' winds, whose pity, sighing back again,
> Did us but loving wrong. (1.2.144–150)

All that Prospero and his little daughter can do on board the rigless bark exposed to the elements is use their voices and 'vent' their emotions. There is no one they could communicate their sorrows to, except for the sea and the wind. However, quite surprisingly, the sea does a quite similar thing – it roars, they cry, which are both ways of using 'one's' voice with some passion. More than that, the passage's parallel construction intensifies this impression, in that the winds seem to echo Prospero's and Miranda's sighs by "sighing back", which, as an assonance, even echoes their initial cries. The relentless sea and winds seem to be 'moved' by Prospero's and Miranda's 'venting' their 'emotions', the sea and the winds seem to be susceptible to feeling pity and love. Certainly, this anthropomorphic image could be qualified as a mere projection: Prospero could be said to displace the humanity that his human surroundings have not shown him to the elements, to his new, and in a way, much more 'loyal' (since at least indifferent and not malignant) surroundings. However, as we will see, *The Tempest* is strikingly preoccupied and fascinated with the notion of 'roaring' and its powerful effects, not only on humans, but also on animals, and, quite similar to the 'image' we are analysing, on Ariel, who is "but air" (5.1.21). As a consequence I would suggest taking the claim of a 'weathery communication', as absurd as it might appear, seriously for a moment, and focus on its material foundations. In my paraphrase of the passage I have attempted to use expressions that, as signifiers, bear testimony to a 'literal' (or rather 'material', 'factual') foundation of the apparently figural, anthropomorphic image: *to vent, emotion, to move*. Viewing the passage's linguistic material more closely, we recognise that a related thing is happening there: like the noun *whistle*, the verbs *to roar* and *to sigh* oscillate between 'expressive' sounds that are produced by human beings and typical sounds produced by the weather (cf. *OED*, sigh, *v.1*. c.; roar, *v.* 2. b.). Shakespeare thus does not invent a daring metaphor, he merely uses and foregrounds an existing semantic link of his time. In today's vocabulary we would perhaps say that it is the bodily, the physical rather than the intellectual dimension of communicating that he emphasises.

With regard to the 'episode' of the ambiguous sound of the whistle, the scene of Miranda's and Prospero's sighing to the sea that sighs back in response adds another 'turn of the screw': the intricate structure of parallelisms and assonances as well as the use of signifiers that testify to the shared material foundation of human sounds and sounds of the weather place them on one and the same plane. Human 'utterances' and the weathery movement of the elements (air/wind and water/sea) do not only coexist, they even communicate. An analogy of dramatic speech and the weather begins to form and articulate the specificity of the 'weathery medium' that is characteristic for the theatrical 'state of exception'. The weather thus serves as the paradigm for the very materiality and the way this medium works and brings about effects.

Strikingly, the exchange of roars and sighs, of noisy air apparently has the power to evoke pity. It is, at the latest, when this key term of Aristotle's theory of tragedy is mentioned that we hear the metatheatrical innuendoes of this episode narrated by Prospero. Is not the "rotten carcass of a butt, not rigged, | Nor tackle, sail, nor mast" where the only thing to do is cry and sigh and evoke pity a fitting metaphor for the early modern platform-stage? "[P]layhouses are like ships in many ways", Douglas Bruster writes, "[b]oth are wooden structures", and both are windy places, as according to "a common trope" the theatre is filled with "windy shouts of acclaim" (2001, 260). In this light, "To cry to th' sea that roared to us, to sigh | To th' winds, whose pity, sighing back again, | Did us but loving wrong" (1.2.148–150) reads like a theory of the medium of theatre, in a condensed form. It centres on the notion that dramatic communication, traversing the seam between stage and audience, works as a voiced motion of air, as weather, a motion travelling in two directions, tempering the offstage sea and the staged 'inner weather'. The episode thus turns out to translate the epilogue's famous metatheatrical formulas, often read as mere conventional words more or less outside the play, into a narrated dramatic image at its very heart.

The situation of the court party on board the ship mirrors Prospero's and Miranda's case on the bark. However, against the background of what we have just discussed, one of the most famous sentences of the first scene gains new meaning. The boatswain's "What cares these roarers for the name of king? To cabin! Silence! Trouble us not." (1.1.16–18) appears to comment on the "sea that roared to [Prospero and Miranda]" and that "Did [them] but loving wrong". Why does the fate of Prospero and Miranda arouse the roaring sea's "pity", while the "roarers" (i.e. the violent waves) do not seem to care for Alonso? As Stanley Wells (1994, 351) notes, it is important to pay attention to the exact formulation: the roarers are not said not to care for the king (i.e. for Alonso), but for the "*name* of king". The waves' lack of care does not express utter indifference, it merely expresses indifference to names and ranks. In other words, as already stated above, the boatswain's rhetorical question, first of all, actualises the weathery suspension of hierarchies. The fact that the noun *roarer* can also denote a "noisy, riotous reveller" (*OED*, roarer, *n*. 1. b.) emphasises the explicitly political, rebellious dimension in the waves' violence. However, the (political) suspension of hierarchies alone cannot account for the 'difference in pity' between Alonso and Prospero and Miranda. It is not ranks or hierarchy (no matter, as we will see, whether usurped or rightful) that raises pity – but its weathery supplement. In contrast to Alonso and Antonio, whose questions after the master indicate that they are still 'acting' in the worldly mode of hierarchy and ranks, Prospero and Miranda have adapted to the dominance of the weathery medium that characterises the *theatrical* state of exception: they join the weather, they "sigh" and "cry", in a way they themselves become "roarers" ("A person who or thing which roars" (*OED*, roarer, *n.1*. 1. a.). It is through this medium that they 'manage' to bring about pity.

Nevertheless, the court party does not obey the boatswain's commands. They only unwillingly and for a short time retreat "[t]o cabin" as they were told, and, as a consequence, the boatswain's demand, "Trouble us not!" goes unheard. Even during their short absence from the stage they already begin to "[t]rouble the boatswain: "A plague upon this howling" the Boatswain shouts, "They are louder than the weather or our office" (1.1.35–36). As already indicated by the boatswain's associating his passengers' noises with the noises of the weather, the court party has joined the 'weathery medium'. Their "howling" is similar to Prospero's and Miranda's answering the sea's roars with their sighs and cries. It is another instance of Shakespeare's using an ambivalent notion of sound that can both be ascribed to living beings as to the weather (cf. *OED*, howling, *n.* 1. a.) and prepares the court party's re-appearance on stage: the stage is the paradigmatic space for the weather and the medium of significative effective/affective sounds that it epitomises. In other words, by disobeying the boatswain the court party accepts and makes itself part of the *theatrical* state of exception that the tempest scene stages. It is therefore not astonishing that, like Prospero and Miranda, the court party finally arouse pity in their exemplary audience, as we will see in the next section.

With regard to the logics of this scene, we have to conclude that the theatre's relation to the weather is one of exposing oneself to it, rather than retreating from it. Theatre is played 'on deck' (not in the cabins), and it is a matter of joining the weather, of 'assisting to it'. The boatswain appears to be the character who can best testify to this tempestuous (stage-)weather. He is professionally exposed to it – and he tempers himself to it:

Gonzalo: Nay, good, be patient.
Boatswain: When the sea is! (1.1.15–16)

The tempestuous sea is not the only 'weather' to which the boatswain finds himself exposed. The court party's "mar[ring] [the mariners'] labour" (1.1.13) on deck is with much subtlety and care also figured as another 'weather'. Not only are they, as we have seen, howling "louder than the weather" (1.1.35–36) when offstage, also onstage they "do assist the storm" (1.1.14). What is it, precisely, they do that assists the storm? They do what the theatre audience expects and wants them to do: they talk. The boatswain's response to the noblemen's 'venting' forth all sorts of questions, commands, curses, anecdotes and observations shows that their talking has an effect on him similar to the storm his ship is facing: "Silence! Trouble us not." (1.1.18) Again, we have to listen carefully and consult the *OED* in order to 'hear' the analogy the verb *to trouble* expresses.

Its familiar meaning in the given context is derived from the verb's astonishingly 'weathery' standard meaning:

> *trans.* To disturb, agitate, ruffle (water, air, etc.); *esp.* to stir up (water) so as to make it thick or muddy; to make (wine) thick by stirring up the lees[15]; to make turbid, dim, or cloudy. (*OED*, trouble, v. I. 1. a.)

The boatswain is troubled by the noblemen's talk as sea, air and ship are by the weather. As has been repeatedly emphasised, this connection is not merely a metaphorical one, but gives testimony to the fundamental analogy at the heart of the early modern humoral theory of passions. The boatswain thus finds himself in-between two analogous, *and* communicating, interdependent storms. Ironically, by shouting to the noblemen "Silence! Trouble us not" (1.1.18), he attempts with regard to the one storm what he mocks the court party for in the face of the other: "if you can command these elements to silence and work the peace of the present we will not hand a rope more" (1.1.21–23). He does not prove to be able to command the noblemen to silence any more than they can command the elements. The scene reflects this impotence of the characters on stage as a question of authority: both boatswain and noblemen lack the power to "Use [their] authority" (1.1.23). Some higher authority seems to be controlling and watching over the scene. Some higher authority seems to test, re-negotiate and challenge the worldly order represented by the titles and names of rank. This higher authority that makes itself felt through the forces of weather seems to be responsible for the fact that the "state totters from the very first scene" (Porter 1993, 34), that "the world of Renaissance space is broken apart" (Kirkpatrick 2000, 91). It introduces a "moment of crisis" (Ryan 2003, 41) that shapes the tempest scene. The weather's enormous power of penetrating and infecting, of troubling not only the microcosmic bodies on board but also the body politic with its "roarers" and "mutinous winds" (5.1.42) furnishes the absent, the supposed master presiding over it with unequalled authority.

All in all, the scene has confronted the audience with a situation of crisis in which an existing order is suspended and re-negotiations are beginning

---

15 The 'wine-image' is very common for describing the humours and their different nature: "And as there are foure elements of which our bodies are compounded, so there are foure sorts of humors answerable to their natures, being al mingled together with the blood: as we may see by experience in blood let out of ones body. For uppermost wee see as it were a litle skimme like to the stoure or working of new wine, or of other wine when it is powred foorth. Next, we may see as it were small streams of water mingled with the blood. And in the bottome is seene a blacker and thicker humour, like to the lees of wine in a wine vessell." (La Primaudaye 1594, 358–359) See also Batman (1582, 28ᵛ).

to take place. All the 'trouble', the suspension of hierarchies as well as the renegotiations, are related to the weather and make use of the huge net of its analogical effects (on the individual mind, the body politic, the rigging of the ship). Furthermore, the scene's violent weather invokes a Christian framework that introduces the notion of a higher authority at play in and responsible for this scene. However, this Christian framework, present to all early modern spectators, turns out to be only an auxiliary structure: unlike a weather sermon in church, the ambivalence of the scene's 'mastery' is not resolved by an interpretation that finally lifts the veil and makes present God's motivations by the true speech of the preacher. Ultimately, the scene's suspension of hierarchies also captures the theological hierarchy of the Christian framework. Instead of taking the Lutheran way, instead of going to the cloister's cabin (cf. Höfele 2006, 25) the court party, and with it the play as a whole, opt for the stage, for the theatrical; they opt for joining and exposing themselves to the weather. The 'state of exception' that has been asserted to be characteristically theatrical affirms the very mediality of the medium that Shakespeare conceptualises as analogous to the weather. Instead of asking for the significates 'behind' this weathery medium ("Where's the master?" What are his intentions? What is it that he wants to say to us with this weather? What does this weather stand for?) this *theatrical* mode asks its participants (including actors *and* audience) to *join* this weather, to expose and temper themselves to it. It is, as we have seen, in this way that tragedy works and that pity is produced.

Nevertheless, it is interesting, especially from a cultural-historical point of view, that Shakespeare uses the auxiliary construction of Christian divine authority to reflect on theatre. An observation that Michael Witmore makes in his book on the early modern dealing with 'the accident' seems to be of interest for our purposes:

> In addition to serving as a lightning rod for debates about God's providence, for example, we find the accident at the center of Shakespeare's highly reflexive theatrical practice, engaging basic questions about the nature of theatrical artifice and the relationship between the playwright's ordered world and that of a providential God. (2001, 4)

I would like to suggest that the first scene (and *The Tempest* as a whole) can indeed be understood as a reflection on the question about "the relationship between the playwright's ordered world and that of a providential God". However, I think we should be very careful not to read this "ordered world" too harmoniously and optimistically. Shakespeare's *Tempest* does not celebrate the omnipotence of a master ruling over his world, ordered according to his will. The "usual sentimental reading of *The Tempest*" (Berger 1969, 265) overlooks the simple fact that *The Tempest*'s world "is neither ideal nor idyllic" (Bulger

1994, 39), not at the beginning, and not at the end. The same holds true, naturally, for the world presided over by God's providence. What the play's reflection on the relation between the playwright's ordered world and the world of a providential god focuses on is the uneasy, complex and mediated relation that the master figures entertain to their respective worlds. And it is here that the weather comes into play: the masters are not present. We should not be deluded by Prospero's entering the stage and claiming responsibility for the storm in the first scene. As we will see in the next section, this responsibility is always belated, *après-coup*, literally after the *coup de théâtre* – and after the scene's prominent *coups de vent*. The masters, as masters, are absent and remain so. When masters are present on stage, they prove to be not the masters of the present situations, not in direct control but separated from their world by time, and by an airy medium (Ariel). Neither the heavenly, nor the theatrical master is moving his subjects (his characters, so to speak) on strings, like puppets. It is not the vanity of the scripted role that Shakespeare aims at when reverting to the prominent image of *theatrum mundi*. He is fascinated by the process of mediation, by the way divine providence, the caring and the wrathful master, 'speaks' to the world – and the way his audience 'listens'.

'Speaking' and 'listening' are mere metaphors: it is through the weather that this communication is mediated and effected. As a consequence, 'listening' is not a straightforward action: it means being tempered by the weather and tempering oneself to it, which, surely, involves interpretation, though it is not reducible to this alone. In his appropriation of the *theatrum mundi* image, Shakespeare thus appears to emphasise a fundamental doubleness or split that is constitutive of every theatrical situation: the split between stage and audience, players and watchers. It is the effect being produced through and across this split between stage and audience that defines the surplus of theatre, that differentiates the theatrical situation from most other pragmatic situations. In this view, theatre is no mere representation in relation to other original, authentic, real-life situations. It is not a representation of an order, produced and controlled by its master, the playwright, somehow competing with the more authentic order created by divine authority. Theatre is performance (also in its non-theatrical sense) – it is an event which happens to a very particular, a pre-defined 'little' world. As the metatheatrical image of the ship amidst the raging waves transports very well, the wooden, hyper-weathery space of the theatre is limited and well marked-off from the rest of the world. In this artificial world, the hierarchies of the 'real' world are suspended for a limited amount of time, and the weathery medium of noises and dramatic speech is made to take on an exceptionally dominant role. Despite the setting's 'artificiality' and limitedness, the crisis that the theatrical event 'performs' should not be underestimated as merely metaphorical: Like the tempest of the play's first scene, theatre as weather is a 'bodily' endeavour. The analogy of the theatrical and weather that Shakespeare posits is based on a material foundation: as we will see in the following sections, theatre affects and 'infects' the individual body as well as the collective body assembled in its little world. It may question and upset naturalised hierarchies and orders, not in a direct way of intervention, but mediated through the complex processes of tempering. Undoubtedly, tragic experience, if 'successful', is, as we will see, (also and mainly) a bodily experience, a cathartic purging of superfluous humours.

In addition to the (bodily) dimension of 'curing affection', Shakespeare's early modern theatre may share another, a rather 'aesthetical' trait with the divine intervention of heavy weathers. Ultimately, God's weathery interventions, as the weather sermons preach, have one specific goal: not only to lead humankind towards the true way of life and worldly organisation, but to make them admire the aspect of His greatness, delivered to mankind through his mysterious spectacles. It is beyond debate that Shakespeare's plays are also shaped by this dimension of bravura, by a witty will to admiration.

The analogy of theatre and a weathery 'state of exception' that the first scene of Shakespeare's *Tempest* introduces (and that is explicated throughout the play) may thus help us find the balance between, 'the political' and 'the aesthetic', as well as the practical-economical dimension of Shakespeare's stagecraft. Following up this analogy provides a nuanced way of reflecting on the early modern theatre's potential for political 'intervention' in considered, careful terms and at the same time giving an account of its self-promoting and self-reflecting aspects as an economic, mass-oriented as well as aesthetical practice for the people and the court. Both of these dimensions are examined with regard to the question of how theatre bridges the gap between stage and audience – that is why we could well call this process a reflection on the medium, the weathery medium of theatre.

At first glance, the play's opening tempest-scene appears to be rather an impressive instance of stage spectacle than an elaborate commentary on the theatre medium. It is, however, precisely the connection of spectacle and metatheatrical importance that provides the key for understanding the scene's central role for the play and lays the decisive foundation for the metatheatrical analogy that pervades *The Tempest* as a whole. Despite its condensation into less than seventy lines of text, even the audience's most easily distracted viewer can hardly miss the crucial Christian framework and the question of the weather's role as mediating higher authority. This is not the result of a didactic, mediating approach but of an unprecedented, highly unconventional and highly spectacular *coup de théâtre* that opens the play. Peter Holland (1995, 223) demonstrates the unconventionality of Shakespeare's staging a shipwreck in tempestuous weather with reference to two plays by Thomas Heywood: "Our Stage so lamely can expresse a Sea | That we are forst by Chorus to discourse | What should have been in action [...]", the chorus in *The Fair Maid of the West* (1964, 319) complains; in his earlier *The Four Prentices of London* (1592) a "Presenter" is used to help the audience "Imagine now yee see the aire made thicke | With stormy tempests, that disturbe the Maine" (Heywood 1964, 175). Both voice the "conventional acknowledgement that showing sea-storms was beyond the stage's capabilities" (Holland 1995, 222). With *The Tempest*'s first scene, Shakespeare dares to break with convention and stage a spectacle that pushes the stage's – and also the audience's limits. According to Andrew Gurr, "Shakespeare may have designed his opening scene mischievously, with the intention of giving the Blackfriars audience a deliberate shock" (2010, 17). *The Tempest*, arguably written for the Blackfriars' stage, does not at all comply with the toned-down, less noisy and more subtle style that the indoor audience was used to and expected. At least its first scene does not follow the conventions; it, however, differs markedly in this respect from the rest of the play. "There is one thing that exists outside the Unities, and that is the storm of act I, scene I" writes Raphael Lyne, noting that "this separate scene" "occupies a less substantial space" but "itself observes dramatic Unity" (2004, 132).

The shocking, daring first scene is situated uneasily next to the much more framed and controlled rest of the play. Its own "dramatic Unity" and its different setting almost make it appear a play of its own, a sort of theatrical warm-up before the main act of the evening. So much so that Jan Kott's observation "[o]n the surface, the first prologue [...] seems unnecessary" (1965, 180) does not at all seem far-fetched. Not surprisingly, however, it does not take Jan Kott long to follow this superficial impression with an analysis that is very interesting for our purposes: "But this dramatic prologue has one other purpose. It is a direct exposition of one of the great Shakespearian theses, a violent confrontation of nature with the social order." (1965, 180) It is probably the same argument that I am pursuing by looking at Shakespeare and the weather. In contrast to Jan Kott I would suggest putting less trust in the 'nature'/'social order'-dichotomy; 'the weather' may provide a term that allows us to modify his argument in a way that avoids this rather misleading binary. Its "dramatic prologue", as Jan Kott calls it, does indeed work as a kind of exposition. However, it is crucial to emphasise its dramatic nature: Prospero's narrative exposition that follows the scene could not differ from it in a more contrasting fashion. The first scene stages its message, and that is to say more than that it merely translates the "violent confrontation of nature with social order" into dramatic language, into spectacle. The first scene not only depicts the confrontation, it performs this violent confrontation, so that it actually takes place between the stage and the audience. "Nature", to retain Jan Kott's terminology a bit longer, not only confronts the social order represented on stage – it also, and perhaps foremost, confronts the 'social order' attending the spectacle, it confronts the audience. That is why the scene's spectacle, the "shock" it makes the audience feel, is so important. This shock is at the same time 'weathery' as it is 'theatrical'. Here we see why I hesitate to use the notion of "nature" for the power challenging and unsettling, or at least making itself felt on the "social order": the problematic term "nature" neglects the central analogy of divine and of theatrical authority watching over and intervening through the forces of weather. It is in this first scene that the audience experiences this particular 'theatrical weather' in the most immediate and intense fashion.

Paradoxically enough, the scene that is so often read as a sort of prologue lacks the mediating, guiding and reflecting dramatic instance that characterises all the following scenes. With regard to the pragmatic dimension of the theatrical situation, the tempest scene provides absolutely no "transition", no "way into the world of the play" (McNamara 1987, 186). Despite its evocation of a ship sailing to the island where the rest of the play is set, the theatrical experience of the scene is an abrupt beginning *in medias res*. It is, *pragmatically*, the most conventional, non-reflexive, non-metatheatrically broken scene of the whole play. Here the unparalleled, difficult tension of the scene emerges: How are we to understand the scene that presents itself purely as a spectacle on stage (no play-within-play situation, no mediating agent on stage) as the symbolically highly charged emblem for the whole, for the pragmatically much more complicated play that is to follow? On the one hand, the first scene does not explain anything, in the least the new pragmatic situation in which the audience finds itself involved when the play begins. It is rather involving us in something that the play will then explain. It provides the audience with violent theatrical experience, making it feel the "howling" and "roaring", exposing it in the most immediate way to the theatrical weather, a theatrical experience that the metatheatrical ponderings of the rest of the play appear to presuppose and require in order to unfold. On the other hand, it is already, although in a less explicit way, occupied with the medium theatre. We have mentioned the master's initial theatrical appellation, transforming actor into character. His being sent offstage and the absence it creates are meaningful, because he could well have been the mediating agent of a prologue, the agent we miss, whose absence we feel. David Norbrook agrees that the "master's whistle" (he does not notice the weathery undertones of "whistle" that we have elucidated) is "a figure for the playwright's authority" (1992, 46). When the master has left the stage, the weathery turmoil on deck takes on innuendoes of dramaturgical turmoil on stage; the clashing nautical and state hierarchies also stage a conflict about authority over the stage. Alonso's question about the master is directly followed by an ambiguous command that receives an equally ambiguous answer:

> *Alonso:* Good boatswain, have care. Where's the master? Play the men!
> *Boatswain:* I pray now keep below! (1.1.9–10)

Both, Alonso's "Play the men!" as well as the boatswain's "keep below!" can be understood as a theatre director's commands, the first similar to the master's initial appellation, the second as ordering the figures offstage. In the vicinity of the question "Where's the master?", this dramaturgical struggle further deepens the scene's central impression of the absence of a controlling, omnipotent and transparent instance of authority. All we apprehend of this authority on stage is its effective force, the weather. This constellation of the absence of the controlling, transparent authority and the being exposed to powerful but ambiguous (weathery) forces is a very apt description of the theatrical situation as such. It is important to appreciate the first scene's constellation of the absence of the master and the difficult, but effective presence of a 'medium'. It is this constellation that makes the title-giving scene emblematic for the rest of the play and prevents the most dangerous misreading *The Tempest*'s metatheatrical layout has to offer: the acceptance of Prospero's presence on stage as the transparent presence of higher (theatrical) authority which Alonso exemplarily longed for in the first scene. This would not only transform the play into a highly questionable fantasy of total power, but also lead the play's metatheatrical reflections *ad absurdum*: theatre with its own, absolutely transparent truth present on stage denies its constitutive split between audience and actors and its own existence as a *medium*. Reading the play with a focus on the weather avoids falling into this interpretative trap by directing attention to the theatrical mediality. It is this medial link between weather and theatre that will continue to be followed up in the next chapters.

4 Miranda and Prospero – exposition

The first words spoken in the second scene are no less theatrically transformative than the master's appellation that opened the tempest scene. This time, however, it is not an actor that is transformed into a character, but a whole scene is retrospectively transformed into a play-within-a-play:

> Miranda: If by your art, my dearest father, you have
> Put the wild waters in this roar, allay them.
> The sky, it seems, would pour down stinking pitch
> But that the sea, mounting to th' welkin's cheek,
> Dashes the fire out. (1.2.1–5)

The transformation brought about by the master's appellation had been a conversion from 'real' to 'theatrical' ('what you see on stage is not a man walking on stage, but an actor playing the boatswain for you') on a first level; the transformation taking place in the play's second scene seems to repeat the first transformation on a second level ('what you see on deck of the ship is not a boatswain, but a spectacle for an audience'). It transforms 'theatrical reality' into 'theatrical theatricality' and creates a new "theatrical reality" that now serves as the reference point of the whole theatrical spectacle: the Chinese-boxes-structure of pragmatic levels that is so characteristic for *The Tempest* is set in place. However, the second 'transformation' is merely a retrospective one. As such, it does not have the same effect on the viewers as the first one had. This time the transformation is not the initial constitutive condition for the audience's viewing of the scene, for anyone's taking part in the theatrical spectacle. The second, retrospective transformation cannot undo the audience's theatrical impression of the first scene. Its effect is rather on the scenes to follow than on the one the audience witnessed some minutes before. It instantiates a new, a more complex pragmatic situation that differs markedly from the pragmatics of the tempest scene:

> It is only after the physical and material tempest has been depicted [or rather performed! J.U.] that the morality will be performed. All that happens on the island will be a play within a play, a performance produced by Prospero. (Kott 1965, 180)

So when we emphasise that "[s]tructurally, *The Tempest* is a play within a play" (Nevo 1999, 80), that a "theater-within-the-theater is the basic formal device of *The Tempest*" (Berger 1977, 234), we should hasten to add that this holds true for all of the play except its first scene, the scene to which the play owes its name. Only by stressing the pragmatic difference between the first scene and the rest of the play, can one become aware of the effect that this transformation at the beginning of the play's second scene produces: the two different pragmatic systems put the audience in two different pragmatic positions. The position the viewers occupied in the first scene is now, after the transformation, occupied by the figures on stage, by Miranda, Prospero, Ariel – so that the audience can, from its new position one pragmatic level up, watch on stage embodiments of its old position. In other words, from the beginning of the second scene, the audience finds itself, as audience, on stage. The metatheatrical reflection of the piece is exposed in this scene as a reflection on the theatrical experience that all the viewers share: their having experienced the tempest scene.

The pragmatic transformation is brought about by a lengthy sequence of narratives, two of which are a retelling of the tempest that the audience has seen performed only minutes before. The narrators of these two retrospective renderings of the tempest held key positions in its theatrical set-up: Miranda as spectator and Ariel as actor. In their narrations of the storm both reflect on the effect the weathery spectacle had on its audience. Critics have in Miranda often found "the ideal spectator of tragedy and catharsis" (Garber 2004, 857):

> *Miranda:* [...] O, I have suffered
> With those that I saw suffer – a brave vessel
> (Who had no doubt some noble creature in her)
> Dashed all to pieces. O, the cry did knock
> Against my very heart! Poor souls, they perished.
> Had I been any god of power, I would
> Have sunk the sea within the earth or ere
> It should the good ship so have swallowed and
> The fraughting souls within her.
>
> *Prospero:*   Be collected;
> No more amazement. Tell your piteous heart
> There's no harm done.
>
> *Miranda:*   O woe the day.
>
> *Prospero:*   No harm! (1.2.5–15)

And indeed, her suffering "with those [she] saw suffer" has more specific implications than displaying some universal trait of intelligent life, it is not merely a case of "neural mirroring" (Wehrs 2011, 547). Prospero's calming response hints at the Aristotelian undertones that characterise the dialogue as one about the tragic effect of theatre on the audience. Amazement and pity are two key concepts that Aristotle uses to describe the effect of tragedy in the famous ninth chapter of his *Poetics*:

> But again, Tragedy is an imitation not only of a complete action, but of events inspiring fear or pity. Such an effect is best produced when the events come on us by surprise; and the effect is heightened when, at the same time, they follow as cause and effect. The tragic wonder [τὸ θαυμαστὸν] will there be greater than if they happened of themselves or by accident; for even coincidences are most striking [θαυμασιώτατα] when they have an air of design. (1452a; transl. S. H. Butcher)

Miranda is thus, according to Aristotle's theory, "articulating the ideal audience response of terror and pity" (Höfele 2006, 29). She is amazed and moved by the spectacle and thereby 'performs' (acts out and exhibits for the audience) the "catharsis-effects" that theatre, in this case the storm scene, aims at producing (cf. Trüstedt 2011, 92). However, the fact that Prospero quite desperately tries to cure her of these 'theatrical' effects (and we will come back to why cure here is a particularly apt term) seems to indicate that Miranda was probably not the 'intended' audience for the spectacle. Her very name punningly tells us that her 'intended' place is on the other side of the spectacle's seam: not to be amazed, not the 'one who wonders', but 'one to be wondered at'; not an audience but a spectacle herself. Katrin Trüstedt has dissected the wittily punning connection of Prospero's "art" (1.2.1) and his telling Miranda about her being "ignorant of what thou art" (1.2.18), a connection that uncovers Miranda's identity as being part of Prospero's cunning artful spectacle and political plans (2011, 91). The framework of intentions is his; Miranda's being moved by the spectacle does not fit the framework, does not serve any obvious function in Prospero's plan. It seems rather to be prompted by a master, still absent, despite Prospero's presence on stage, prompted with an "air of design", as Aristotle would say, for us, for the 'real' audience, mirroring and reflecting our tragic experience of the first scene. Prospero's harsh, imperative attempts at undoing the spectacle's effects on Miranda refute any claim that Miranda's watching the shipwreck could have been part of Prospero's plans. It does not seem as if he intends to turn her pity into love for Ferdinand, or any similar thing:

> *Prospero:* Be collected;
> No more amazement. Tell your piteous heart
> There's no harm done.
> *Miranda:* O woe the day.
> *Prospero:* No harm! (1.2.13–15)

Prospero's urging Miranda to have her "thoughts, feelings, or mental faculties at command or in order: composed, self-possessed" (*OED*, collected, *adj.*) is typical for the mastery that he claims for and over himself. However, he will later be brought to feel that this intellectual mastery over the (bodily) passions is an illusion. His reading of Aristotle's concept of catharsis seems to deny what his attempt at mastering, the necessity of mastering, nevertheless acknowledges: pity and amazement are no purely intellectual but also 'somatic', humoral events. His "Tell your piteous heart" underlines the paradoxical endeavour of discursively 'convincing' a bodily process. The futility of Prospero's position is further exposed by the fact that his argument – that "There's no harm done" – is merely a description of the theatrical situation as such; it is precisely this 'magic' of theatre that, according to Aristotle, brings about terror and pity despite our knowledge that, in actuality, there is really no harm done! Miranda's heart is not moved by the propositional force of true arguments, but by other, more 'weathery', and more theatrical forces of language: "O, the cry did knock | Against my very heart!" (1.2.8–9). We have already come across this weather dimension of "roaring", "sighing", "whistling" when comparing the first scene to Prospero's story of his floating on the "carcass of a butt", which he narrates later in this second scene. Miranda now feels the pity that for some reason the first scene's weather and waves lacked. In fact her reaction as a viewer, knowing no harm is done, not being in any danger herself, is indistinguishable from Prospero's reaction to his misery as the actual victim; Miranda's suffering with those she saw suffer produces the same cleansing humoral reaction, she weeps:

Prospero:	When I have decked the sea with drops full salt, Under my burden groaned, [...] (1.2.155–156)
Prospero:	[to Miranda] Wipe thou thine eyes, have comfort; (1.2.25)

However, Miranda's tears, perhaps too hastily wiped away, have not really cured her of her pity yet. Interestingly, she asks about the "design" behind the storm, a promising attempt to rid herself of the amazement, heightened, according to Aristotle, by the impression of "an air of design":

Miranda:	[...] And now I pray you, sir, For still 'tis beating in my mind, your reason For raising this sea-storm? (1.2.175–177)

It is however not the notion that knowledge of the design, that the presence of the intention behind the spectacle destroys its theatricality, its theatrical force, but the formulation "still 'tis beating in my mind" that I would like to point to. The *OED* tells us that the adjective *beating* can bear a distinctly weathery meaning: "Of wind, rain, etc.: That strikes violently, or batters; driving" (*OED*, beating, *adj.* 2.). The "sea-storm" still "beating" in Miranda's mind has a double reference: either it is 'literally' the 'memorised' storm that still "beat[s]" in her mind, or the effect of the spectacle, her suffering with those she saw suffer, that "beats". The first 'literal' beating provides the basis for the second, seemingly 'more figural' beating: the 'weathery' effect of the spectacle, its beating in Miranda's mind, is motivated by the spectacle's being indeed one of heavy weather.

Significantly, we encounter two 'beating minds' later in *The Tempest* that are both reactions to theatrical spectacles, although these are not motivated by depicted storms: Prospero's "beating mind" (4.1.163) following the spectacle of the masque that Karen Flagstad (1986, 223) and John Gillies (1986, 698) have brought into connection with Miranda's "beating in my mind" (1.2.176) and Prospero's telling Alonso not to "infest your mind with beating on | The strangeness of this business" (5.1.246–47), a comment on the whole spectacle played to the king's party on the island. The sequence of usages of the term *beating* tells us a lot about the emblematic function the tempest scene and its reflection in the second scene fulfil. The first scene's spectacle, the tempest, is not just any spectacle. By depicting a storm, it depicts how a theatrical spectacle 'works' on its audience: like weather. It represents Shakespeare's attempt to reflect on the medium of theatre by positing that it functions analogously to the weather. In this way, it can literally speak about the spectacle's content, the tempest, and thereby always also speak, in a double way, about the medium theatre, about *The Tempest*. Once this analogy is established (as by Miranda's "beating" in her mind caused by the sea-storm being a phenomenon of weather *and* theatrical spectacle) the 'weathery' terms are applied to the theatrical spectacle without having to be motivated by the spectacle's weathery 'content' anymore. It is now only the spectacle's analogical 'weathery' nature and functioning that account for the weather's presence in the metatheatrical reflections.

John Gillies's reading of Alonso's 'beating mind' at the end of the play is a prime example of an interpretation which is sensitive to the importance of the weather established in the play's first scene, although he does not notice the metatheatrical dimension of the weather and the question of temperance:

> In Prospero's advice to the newly healthy Alonso, "Do not infest your mind with beating on | The strangeness of this business" (5.1.246–47), the fen imagery of disease is linked to the "beating" of "sea-sorrow," thereby combining in one image the two most important symbolic loci of intemperance in the play – fens and sea. (Gillies 1986, 684)

Ariel's rendering of the storm scene from the perspective of the actor could have helped John Gillies to link the field of weather and temperance that he has so brilliantly followed up in his essay to the play's reflection on the pragmatics of theatre:

> *Prospero:*   Hast thou, spirit,
> Performed to point the tempest that I bade thee?
> *Ariel:*   To every article.
> I boarded the King's ship: now on the beak,
> Now in the waist, the deck, in every cabin
> I flamed amazement. Sometime I'd divide
> And burn in many places – on the topmast,
> The yards and bowsprit would I flame distinctly,
> Then meet and join. Jove's lightning, the precursors
> O' th' dreadful thunderclaps, more momentary

	And sight-outrunning were not; the fire and cracks
	Of sulphurous roaring, the most mighty Neptune
	Seem to besiege and make his bold waves tremble,
	Yea, his dread trident shake.
Prospero:	My brave spirit,
	Who was so firm, so constant, that this coil
	Would not infect his reason?
Ariel:	Not a soul
	But felt a fever of the mad and played
	Some tricks of desperation. [...] (1.2.193–210)

This dialogue between Prospero and Ariel is one of the play's most important metatheatrical passages, because it is here that the link between Prospero's "art" and "theatre" is made explicit for the first time. In his behaving "like the director of a play who has missed the premiere of his show and inquires whether his instructions were followed to the letter" (Popelard 2009, 25), Prospero openly confirms what we have inferred from the first scene: his way of acting on the world is crucially a mediated one. A remarkable gap yawns between the articles of the playwright's script and the performance acted out in his absence. The need for mediation has the effect that, although the intervention seems to be a powerful one, and the questions about its success verge on being rhetorical, the intervention is not fully under control. I therefore agree with Katherine Steele Brokaw that "Ariel is a crucial meta-theatrical site" (2008, 37), and that this metatheatrical site calls attention to the actor's pragmatic position in the constellation of theatre. However, I am not exactly sure whether *The Tempest* gives us suitable material for claiming that this site "calls attention to itself as the creation of a skilled actor, inviting audiences and critics to reflect on its constructedness and reauthorization" (2008, 37), and I do not think that Ariel is really "representing an actor's imagination" (2008, 37). Rather, I would suggest that it is Ariel's name that provides us with the key to the implications of this "crucial meta-theatrical site" and thereby follow up a path that Katherine Steele Brokaw has discovered but not exploited fully for her argument.

The First Folio's list of roles tells us that Ariel is "an airy spirit", and this is also what we hear, when we hear his name: air. Prospero repeatedly addresses him as spirit in the dialogue we are currently discussing ("Hast thou, spirit", "My brave spirit") and thereby lends weight to the second part of the Folio's role description: Ariel is a spirit. This term opens a wide and complex, but interesting semantic field, as the *OED* tells us:

> The earlier English uses of the word are mainly derived from passages in the Vulgate, in which *spiritus* is employed to render Greek πνεῦμα *pneuma n.* and Hebrew rūaḥ. The translation of these words by *spirit* (or one of its variant forms) is common to all versions of the Bible from Wyclif onwards. (*OED*, spirit, *n.* Etymology)

Thanks to its consistent use in Bible translations for rendering, via the Latin *spiritus*, the Greek πνεῦμα, the English *spirit* has inherited the crucial double meaning that characterises the Greek πνεῦμα, denoting both wind and breath (cf. Brokaw 2008, 27). What we find in these etymological searches is that one word, spirit, contains in its etymological history the central analogy that I have suggested as the basis for *The Tempest*'s metatheatrical reflections. Ariel, the spirit, the actor, is a "crucial meta-theatrical site", because his "act of breathing; (a) breath" (*OED*, spirit, *n.* IV. 15. †b.) as an actor is an analogy to "A movement of the air; a wind; a breath (of wind or air)" (*OED*, spirit, *n.* IV. 15. a.).

We will see that *The Tempest* plays with these weathery innuendoes of *breathe* (as it played with the weathery innuendoes of *roar, sigh, whistle*): *to breathe* in the meaning of "To give forth audible breath or sound; to speak, sing, etc." (*OED*, breathe, *v.* 7.), as in "they [...] scarce think | [...] their words | Are natural breath" (5.1.155–157); and *to breathe* in the meaning of "Of wind, air, etc.: To blow softly" (*OED*, breathe, *v.* 8.), as in the famous "The air breathes upon us here most sweetly" (2.1.49). Significantly, in *The Tempest*, the breathing of air and the speaking of words cannot really be distinguished:

> Alonso: Methought the billows spoke and told me of it;
> The winds did sing it to me, and the thunder,
> That deep and dreadful organ-pipe, pronounced
> The name of Prosper. [...] (3.3.96–99)

What this analogy, inscribed into Ariel's being "an airy spirit", provides us with is a model of the ('physiological', humoral) effect of theatre – and of dramatic speech. This effect is produced despite, or rather *through* the actor's problematic embodiment of a theatrical character, which is a reflection of the pragmatic seam that characterises the relation between character, actor and audience. The character presented by the actor is of a different 'substance' than the audience's material bodies (we will come across many occasions in the following sections where the play reflects on this crucial pragmatic difference). And again we find this theatrical problem reflected in a semantic dimension of the term *spirit*: Ariel is an "Incorporeal or immaterial being, as opposed to *body* or *matter*; being or intelligence conceived as distinct from, or independent of, anything physical or material" (*OED*, spirit, *n.* I. 1. d.). In the language of the play this translates into his being "but air" (5.1.21), not a body tempered by the four elements, "perfectly mixed" that "will not easely be changed and resolved from that forme which [it is] in" (Fulke 1563, 1ᵛ), but of the order of an element not tempered in a body so that it can easily transform and change into other elements. We see quite easily how this semantic dimension of *spirit* ties in well with Ariel's metatheatrically representing an actor's (weathery) changeableness.

However, Ariel's 'being' a "spirit" involves other implications as well. In relation to the magus Prospero and with regard to his 'job' of haunting Prospero's enemies, he is obviously also

> A supernatural, incorporeal, rational being or personality, usually regarded as imperceptible at ordinary times to the human senses, but capable of becoming visible at pleasure, and freq. conceived as troublesome, terrifying, or hostile to mankind. (*OED*, spirit, *n*. I. 3. a.)

At times Shakespeare seems to lose control of his witty juggling with the different facets of Ariel's being a 'spirit'. For example, in a much-discussed scene, Ariel's histrionic qualities obviously conflict with his supernatural capabilities when Prospero commands him to dress up as a nymph *and* to be invisible (why then dress up?):

> *Prospero:* Go make thyself like a nymph o'th' sea:
> Be subject to no sight but thine and mine, invisible
> To every eyeball else. Go take this shape
> And hither come in't. Go! Hence with diligence. (1.2.302–305)

A last less obvious and quite complicated semantic dimension of *spirit* has to be added to the picture. This dimension will enable us to understand the important analogical mechanism on which all these 'spirits' are founded and which operates with the breath/wind, microcosm/macrocosm analogy. The *OED* describes this sort of 'humoral' spirit as "One or other of certain subtle highly-refined substances or fluids (distinguished as *natural*, *animal*, and *vital*) formerly supposed to permeate the blood and chief organs of the body" (*OED*, spirit, *n*. IV. 16. a.). Put by Helkiah Crooke, physician to James I, the definition of this spirit reads quite similar:

> A subtle and thinne body alwayes moovable, engendred of blood and vapour, and the vehicle or carriage of the Faculties of the soule. [...] It followeth in the definition, that they are engendred of blood and a thin vapour; so that they have a double manner, an exhalation of the bloode and aire; and therefore it is, that all our spirits are cherished, preserved and nourished by aire and blood. (1615, 174)

In Crooke's definition the role of *pneuma* for this "subtle and thinne body" becomes apparent. However, his definition tells us more about the *pneuma* involved than that air plays a role in the spirit's engendering. The words he uses for giving an account of this engendering are the *termini technici* for describing the engendering of meteorological phenomena. Following Aristotle's *Meteorology*, early modern theories of the meteors were built on two basic processes: dry exhalations and moist exhalations (vapours). "The mater whereof the moste part of *Meteores* dooth consiste, is either water or earth, for out of the water, proceade vapors, and out of the earth come exhalations" (Fulke 1563, 2ʳ). So, for example, "The wind is an exhalation hote and dry" (Hill 1574, 34ʳ), and "many kynde of moist *Meteors* are generated, as sometime cloudes and rayne, sometime snowe and hayle" when "vapors are drawen up from the waters and watry places, by the heate of the sunne" (Fulke 1563, 2ᵛ). The exhalations of blood and air that Crooke sees at play in the generation of spirits are interesting: in the worldview of micro- and macrocosm (that is to say of the four humors and the four elements) blood and air form an analogical pair. The microcosmic humour blood corresponds to macrocosmic elemental air: "the proper nature of blood is to bee hote and moist: wherein it answereth to the nature of the aire" (La Primaudaye 1594, 359). As a consequence of being engendered of both an element and of its corresponding humour, the "spirits" can act as a hinge in-between microcosm and macrocosm, they are of a "middle Nature" in a wider sense than Helkiah Crooke's explanation intends:

> As in the Heavens the Angels are the Messengers of God, carrying down his commandements unto men whome also they guard and defend; so in this *Microcosme* the dull Flesh being of too slow a kind to ensue the noble motions of the Soule, which with his counterpoise it oftner doth oppresse, our wise Creator ordained spirites of a middle Nature betweene the Soule and the Body, which like quicke Postes, Like Pursevants or Heralds might travel betweene them, and communicate their commission to the particular partes which they receive either at the first hand from the Soule it selve in the Brayne, or have it sealed in the Heart or the Liver, as in her subordinate offices.
>
> These Spirits *Galen* calleth ἐνορμῶντα Impetuous bodies, because their motion is sudden & momentanie like the lightning, which in the twinkling of an eye shooteth through the whole cope of Heaven; yea so much more subtle are they then the Lightning, as that the one is visible the other invisible: or they are like the winde which whiskes about in every corner and turns the heavy saile of a Wind-mill, yet can we not see that which transports it. (Crooke 1615, 824)

On the one side of the analogy, we find communication across the hierarchy of divine power and men, mediated by a Messenger – a constellation strongly resonating with the relation of Prospero, Ariel and their audiences, a relation that, as we have seen, *The Tempest* explicitly reflects in exactly these religious terms. On the other side of the analogy, in a process of the "*Microcosme*", the hierarchy of Soule and Body is to be crossed, the third term this time being the spirits called "Impetuous Bodies". What makes these two analogical sequences communicate and thus produces effects across the microcosm-macrocosm seam is the weather. Gail Kern Paster emphasises that Helkiah Crooke "uses meteorology to explain the invisible, instantaneous action of spirits" (2004, 40). More precisely, it is the mediating nature of the spirits, their role as "Messengers", "Postes", "Pursevants" or "Heralds" travelling "between" and "communicat[ing] their commission" that is explained with the help of meteorological phenomena like "Lightning" and "Wind". As their "double manner" as "exhalation[s] of the bloode and aire" (1615, 174) already indicated, the spirits do not only function *like* supernatural or weathery spirits, they are also susceptible to them: they are "affected [...] by (among other things) angels and evil spirits and ghosts, alcoholic spirits and music, climate and airs and waters" (Sutton 2007, 19).

> "The Aire works on all men," says Burton, "when the humours by the Aire bee stirred, he goes in with them, exagitates our spirits, and vexeth our Soules: as the sea waves, so are the spirits and humours in our bodies, tossed with tempestuous windes and stormes" (1:237). (Paster 2004, 41)

This is the way that Ariel as a "meta-theatrical site" produces an effect on the audience: as an *airy spirit* he moves the audience's *spirits*. He acts "as minister[ ] of the sovereign will, as physical extension[ ] of the immaterial soul" (Roach 1985, 40), however not "by divine right" (Roach 1985, 40), but by the convention of theatre. Shakespeare's *Tempest* thus provides us with an extensive metatheatrical reflection on what Joseph R. Roach in his book on theories of acting delineates as an early modern way of theatrical communication, which is based on an

> explanation of communication founded on the ancient concept of pneuma. It was widely believed that the spirits, agitated by the passions of the imaginer, generate a wave of physical force, rolling through the aether, powerful enough to influence the spirits of others at a distance. (1985, 45)

In the passage where Ariel informs Prospero about his having performed the tempest, the analogy that makes the spirit Ariel produce an effect on the spirit of his audience is clearly marked: Ariel "burn[s] in many places", "flame[s] distinctly" "on the topmast, | The yards and bowsprit" – and he "flame[s] amazement":

> Ariel: To every article.
> I boarded the King's ship: now on the beak,
> Now in the waist, the deck, in every cabin
> I flamed amazement. Sometime I'd divide
> And burn in many places – on the topmast,
> The yards and bowsprit would I flame distinctly,
> Then meet and join. Jove's lightning, the precursors
> O' th' dreadful thunderclaps, more momentary
> And sight-outrunning were not; the fire and cracks
> Of sulphurous roaring, the most mighty Neptune
> Seem to besiege and make his bold waves tremble,
> Yea, his dread trident shake. (1.2.195–206)

In this scene Ariel resembles a sort of 'exteriorised' microcosmic spirit, an "Impetuous Bodie": the tempestuous fiery spectacle he delivers, emphasised by his narration's strong semantic topology of fire ("flame", "burn", "flame" "lightning", "fire", "sulphurous"), makes him appear to match in substance these animal spirits of the microcosm: "In substance animal spirits resemble wind and fire, more subtle than matter, more material than soul." (Roach 1985, 40) As in Helkiah Crooke's definition, the microcosmic spirit "is sudden & momentanie like the lightning, which in the twinkling of an eye shooteth through the whole cope of Heaven" (1615, 824), Ariel's flaming is so swift that even "Jove's lightning" was not "more momentary | And sight-outrunning". This quickness is perhaps the key feature that characterises Ariel as a spirit:

Ariel:	Presently?
Prospero:	Ay, with a twink.
Ariel:	Before you can say 'come' and 'go',
	And breathe twice and cry 'so, so',
	Each one tripping on his toe,
	Will be here with mop and mow.
	Do you love me, master? No?
Prospero:	Dearly, my delicate Ariel. (4.1.42–48)

Ariel earns the epithet "delicate" (also: "Delicate Ariel" (1.2.442)) for this quickness, and, vice versa, his quickness results from his being delicate. Ariel's 'substance' 'is' a subtle spirit: "And, for thou wast a spirit too delicate | To act her earthy and abhorr'd commands" (1.2.272–273). "Ariel, all air and fire – elements of sublimation in alchemy [...] is etherealised, spirirtualised" (Nevo 1999, 83–84). According to Bartholomaeus, it is also this 'unearthy' substance, that could account for his strong thirst for freedom that, in the end, distinguishes him from the earthy Caliban: "For though the world seeme father and forth bringer and feeder of bodies, yet it is prison of spirites, and most cruell exiling of soules" (1582, 119ᵛ).

The strategic "commission" with which Prospero entrusts his "Messenger" Ariel is therefore not by chance quite a 'weathery one': The fact that Ariel is to perform a specific and well-known meteorological phenomenon exhibits his similarity to the microcosmic spirit. The piece of weather, so to speak, that he brings to the audience has been chosen with some care: as a fiery meteorological phenomenon it matches Ariel's subtleness and emphasises the analogy of spirit-actor and the audience's animal spirits. So much so that Ariel's narration can play with the double import of his 'flaming':

> Ariel: [...] now on the beak,
> Now in the waist, the deck, in every cabin
> I flamed amazement. [...] (1.2.196–198)

Ariel flames 'outwardly', on the ship, as a meteorological phenomenon, and he flames 'inwardly', in the viewers' minds, he stirs their spirits and humours and evokes amazement. Shakespeare's audience was certainly familiar with one of the most talked of and most miraculous meteorological phenomena at sea, "the bright and shynyng exhalations that appear in tempestes, *whiche the Mariners call* Santelmo, or Corpus sancti" (Cortés 1630, 51^v), and which were discussed under the name of *Helena* and *Castor* and *Pollux* in the early modern natural philosophy's treatises on weather:

> It is also very often seen in the night, of them that sayle in the Sea, & sometime will cleave to the mast of the shyp, or other highe partes, somtyme slyde around about the shyppe, and either rest in one part till it go out, or els be quenched in the water. This impression [...] if it be but one, is named *Helena*, if it be two, it is called *Castor* and *Pollux*. (Fulke 1563, 11^v)

If we listen carefully, we can hear in Ariel's words a gentle reverberation of the typical tone that characterises the descriptions of this phenomenon we find in natural philosophers' and encyclopaedic texts. His use of the term "Sometime" ("Sometime I'd divide | And burn in many places") is a good example for this, echoing the conventionally ubiquitous use of this term in early modern natural philosophy. Ariel's narration even reflects the distinction of the two phenomena called "*Castor* and *Pollux*" and "*Helena*" that also appeared in William Fulke's treatise on early modern meteorology: Ariel relates that he first burned "distinctly" in two places before burning only in one ("Then meet and join"). By making Ariel realise both these nautical meteorological phenomena, Shakespeare avoids these phenomena's clear-cut and much-discussed prognostic forces that his audience is very likely to be familiar with: Castor and Pollux signify a happy, Helena a terrible outcome.

My interest is not in speculating about whether Shakespeare may have had one of the many, and often astonishingly similar (plagiarised!) treatises at hand when he wrote the scene. However, it is important to note that he chooses a meteorological phenomenon whose strong effect on the viewers was well known, a meteorological phenomenon that conjures up religious awe:

> among certayne simple and ignoraunt people, it is accounted for a miracle, that in certayne tempestes on the sea, the Mariners see certayne shyning & bright fyres, which with great superstition they kneele downe unto, and pray unto, affirming that it is Santelmo that appeareth unto them (Cortés 1630, 52^r).

In a surrounding only quite recently permeated by "the Protestant insistence that the age of miracles had ceased" (Witmore 2001, 22), the metatheatrical reflections of Shakespeare's *Tempest* reveal that the mechanism of miracle and religious awe can now be effectively used for theatrical purposes: not only for producing awe, but also for "flaming" Aristotelian "amazement" (1.2.198) instead. Or, to put it the other way round, the spectacles of theatre work the way that religious miracles did – and therefore satisfy a 'spiritual', emotional, passionate demand that the new religious dogma fails to address.

However, we should hasten to add that Prospero's heritage is more ambiguous than was perhaps suggested by talking about awe and miracles. The powers of weather have always also been (ab)used by darker forces: "In dede the devil hath used these lightes (although they be naturally caused) as strong delusions to captive the myndes of men" (Fulke 1563, 12ʳ). In fact, Prospero's theatrical use of St. Elmo's fire very much resembles the devil's manipulative "strong delusions to captive the myndes of men". Allegedly, Ferdinand was even brought to cry: "'Hell is empty, | And all the devils are here'" (1.2.214–215):

> *Prospero:* My brave spirit,
> Who was so firm, so constant, that this coil
> Would not infect his reason?
> *Ariel:* Not a soul
> But felt a fever of the mad and played
> Some tricks of desperation. [...] (1.2.206–210)

What appears in these few lines is a description of how (Ariel's) theatrical spectacle works on his audience. The uncommon term *coil* is an ingenious choice of word to express and pool the spectacle's doubleness of voice and weather that we already saw at work in terms like *roar, sigh, whistle, breathe*: "Noisy disturbance, 'row'; 'tumult, turmoil, bustle, stir, hurry, confusion' (Johnson)" (*OED*, coil, *n.2*. 1.). The spirit's coil works on the souls of the viewers; a striking similarity of position underlines the analogical relation that the dialogue explicates: "spirit" and "soul" occupy the end position of a line that in both cases serves as a kind of pick-up phrase for the ensuing, also strikingly similarly-phrased lines. The semantic proximity of spirit and soul cannot go unnoticed; what mediates these two notions, occupying the end position of the line in-between spirit and soul is the theatrical "coil". Thus the semantic play at the end position of lines wittily performs the mediating role this "coil" plays, bringing the spirit-actor Ariel in communication with the viewers' souls.

The passage offers a consistent explanation of how this communication works: as an "infection", causing "fever", nobody being so "firm" in the sense of "Healthy, robust" (*OED*, firm, *adj.* 4.) to withstand this infection. To early-modern ears, this explanation ties in well with the weathery undertone of "coil" and the fiery and tempestuous nature of Ariel's theatrical spectacle: "infection" was seen as the way that unwholesome weather could act upon the human body, or as the *OED* puts it: "Originally: contaminated condition or unhealthy quality (of air, water, etc.)" (*OED*, infection, n. 2. I.). Fortunately, *The Tempest* gives us the opportunity to get an idea of this concept of infection in Caliban's cursing of Prospero:

> Caliban: As wicked dew as e'er my morther brushed
>   With raven's feather from unwholesome fen
>   Drop on you both. A southwest blow on ye
>   And blister you all o'er. (1.2.322–325)
>
> Caliban: All the infections that the sun sucks up
>   From bogs, fens, flats, on Prosper fall, and make him
>   By inchmeal a disease! (2.2.1–3)

John Gillies has persuasively read this "'fen' imagery as a ubiquitous mirror of intemperance" (1986, 684) and contrasted it with the play's prominent instances of temperance. I completely agree with him that the play's "idiom of disease and distemper" (1986, 684) together with its depictions of temporal harmony constitute a "structural axis of the motif of temperance" (1986, 686) that is crucial for the play as a whole. However, I do not think that following up the "dialectic of temperance and intemperance" (1986, 683) merely on the level of plot, as a feature of the fictional world, allows us to make this observation as productively as it can and should be made. As we have seen with regard to Miranda's as well as to Ariel's recapitulations of the tempest scene, the play as a whole strongly reflects on the pragmatics of the theatrical situation, with the central question of how a theatrical effect is produced. These first reflections, from both the audience's as well as the actor's point of view, have already provided us with dozens of hints that are leading us towards a reading that takes into account this "structural axis" of temperance *and* the play's characteristic metatheatrical play-within-the-play structure. The second scene's retrospective narratives, unmasking the first scene's tempest as a weathery theatre spectacle, have reflected on the audience's Aristotelian reaction, on pity as well as amazement. The fact that the spectacle performed by Ariel and witnessed by Miranda had chanced to be a tempest, a phenomenon of weather, emerges as a metatheatrical trick: it implies that speaking about the effect of the first scene does always mean speaking about a phenomenon of weather and about a theatrical spectacle at the same time. As a consequence, the elaborate pattern that contemporary natural philosophy has developed for the weather's effect on the microcosmic body, its being conceived of as a medium between some higher, absent authority and the lower world, can be appropriated for speaking about theatre and its effects. The "dialectic of temperance and intemperance" that John Gillies diagnoses in *The Tempest* thus gains a new, metatheatrical dimension: it begins to introduce an early modern way of conceptualising the functioning of the medium theatre, a medium that Shakespeare reflects upon as an analogue of the weather. If we are to believe contemporary accounts, Miranda and the court party were not the only early modern viewers of theatrical spectacles who felt a "beating mind", flaming "amazement" or a "fever", being infected by theatrical "coils": Anthony Munday reports about theatre-goers who "have received at those spectacles such filthie infections, as have [...] turned their bodies into sicknes" (Munday 1580, 54).

5 God of power – temporal royalties

Miranda's and Ariel's narratives are not the second scene's only ones: there is a third, lengthy one presented to us by Prospero. At first glance this narrative does not as much reflect on the first scene's performance as the other two did, but seems to provide the audience with an account of the events that preceded the action which it witnesses on stage, in the conventional manner of a narrative exposition. However, as Miranda and Ariel held important pragmatic positions in the first scene's theatrical constellation as viewer and actor, Prospero occupies a third, perhaps the most important, theatrical position. It is this position in the theatrical constellation, I would like to claim, that his narrative implicitly portrays in interaction with the other two.

The tempest scene had closed with Gonzalo's remark that "The wills above be done, but I would fain die a dry death" (1.1.66–67). This remark summarises what I have called the first scene's characteristic 'Christian framework': the complicated, weathery intervention in the lower world of an absent, but powerful authority situated in a transcendent "above". The very first sentence of the second scene, spoken by Miranda, associates Prospero and his "art" with this authorial, 'godly' position and power:

> *Miranda:* If by your art, my dearest father, you have
> Put the wild waters in this roar, allay them. (1.2.1–2)

Her description of the storm emphasises that the power over the wild water's roar, over weather and elements is a power over hierarchies that finds expression in a vertical topology of rising and sinking:

> *Miranda:* The sky, it seems, would pour down stinking pitch
> But that the sea, mounting to th' welkin's cheek,
> Dashes the fire out. [...] (1.2.3–5)

Miranda depicts the storm as an extreme elemental struggle, upsetting the hierarchical order of the four elements, which are 'normally' located in layers, one above the other, according to their lightness and their qualities:

> The highest is the sp[h]ere of the fire, which toucheth the hollowness of the Moones heaven, the next is the ayre, whiche is in the hallowness of the fyer, the ayre within his hollowness, comprehendeth the water and the earth, whiche bothe make but one *spheare* or *Globe*, or as the commen sort may understand it one Bal. So eche element is within another as the skales of a perle, are on above another, or (to use a grosse similitude) as the pieles of an onion, ar one within another [...]. (Fulke 1563, 5ʳ)

The topological order (fire above air above water above earth) follows the logic of a chain that links each element, characterised as a combination of two qualities, by correspondence to both adjoining elements in one quality respectively:

> Water, as arm'd with moisture and with cold,
> The cold-dry Earth with her one hand doth hold;
> With th'other th'Aire: The Aire, as moist and warme,
> Holds Fire with one; Water with th'other arme:
> As Country Maydens in the Month of *May*
> Merrily sporting on a Holy-day,
> And lustie dauncing of a lively Round. (Sylvester 1605, 42)

As a result, "the sea, mounting to th' welkin's cheek" threatening to "dash the fire out" is the heftiest of elemental conflicts, because the tempest's turmoil that Miranda is talking of upsets the elemental hierarchy in a way that two elements of contrary nature (here water and fire) that are usually separated by a third (air) come to clash and fight:

> Those, whose effects doo wholy contradict,
> Longer and stronger strive in their Conflict.
> The hot-dry Fire, to cold-moist Water turnes-not;
> The cold-dry Earth to hot-moist Aire, returnes-not,
> Returnes not eas'ly: for (still opposite)
> With tooth and nailes as deadly Foes they fight.
> But Aire turne Water, Earth may Fierize,
> Because in one part they doo simbolize:
> And so in combat they have lesse to doo,
> For't's *easier farre, to conquer one then two.* (Sylvester 1605, 40)

Interestingly, not only the powerful intervention causing the storm works by unsettling the 'natural' hierarchy and topological order of elements, but also Miranda's suggestion of allaying it (sinking the sea within the earth!):

> Miranda: Had I been any god of power, I would
> Have sunk the sea within the earth or ere
> It should the good ship so have swallowed and
> The fraughting souls within her. (1.2.10–13)

As a consequence, the allaying of the storm is not put into effect by a more or less automatic, evident return to the 'natural' order of the elements, but marks the necessity of another authorial intervention. As small a hint as this might be, it is significant, nonetheless: *The Tempest* is not concerned with an assessment of orders, it is not discerning 'unnatural' ones from the 'natural', it does not stage the passage "from the chaos and terror of the storm [...] to the order and delight of the marriage" (Belton 1985, 127).

Undoubtedly, on the surface, *The Tempest* mimics the common plot of "[g]rowing chaos followed by a reordering of elements", "a process inherent in any storm as well as being basic to the structure of any play" (Harris 2001, 562). Its "dissolving [order] into chaos" (Wright 1977, 248) in the tempest scene is therefore as conventional as the subsequent "countertheme of new order out of chaos" (Wright 1977, 248), instantiated by Prospero's "foundation of his new order" (Hillman 1985, 152) that answers "the passing away of the old" (Oseman 2003, 78). As Claudia W. Harris rightly remarks, "this chaotic process is especially apparent in *The Tempest*" (Harris 2001, 562) – it is especially apparent, because the play's metatheatrical Chinese-boxes-structure of pragmatic levels puts this "process" on display. It does, however not do so to celebrate its outcome, the romance's "true ordering of the good and real" (Wehrs 2011, 522), but to reflect on this process itself. As Rose Abdelnour Zimbardo puts it, "the theme of *The Tempest* is not regeneration through suffering, but the eternal conflict between order and chaos" (1963, 50). To be more precise, I would say that the theme of *The Tempest* is theatrical intervention in this eternal conflict between order and chaos, an intervention that always crosses the pragmatic levels of stage and audience: *The Tempest* does not *represent* the production of a superior fictional order, it stages, it *performs* theatre's own (dis)tempering force.

It was Miranda's depiction of the storm and her suggestion of allaying it, both formulated as authorial interventions upsetting the 'natural' order of elements, that led to the claim that it is the interventions and not the natural order that *The Tempest* focuses on. This observation could also support Heather Campbell's important assertion that "Most particularly, Prospero never figures as the divine delegate, restoring order out of chaos" (Campbell 1993, 86). Miranda, were she "any god of power" would not have restored the topological hierarchy of the elements, would not have re-separated water and fire by air, she "would | Have sunk the sea within the earth", she would have answered with another upsetting intervention.

The terminology of Prospero's answer very much underlines that he does indeed occupy the position of a "god of power":

> *Prospero:* The direful spectacle of the wreck which touched
> The very virtue of compassion in thee,
> I have with such provision in mine art
> So safely ordered, that there is no soul –
> No, not so much perdition as an hair,
> Betid to any creature in the vessel
> Which thou heard'st cry, which thou saw'st sink. (1.2.27–32)

The terms "virtue of compassion", "provision", "soul" and "perdition" clearly introduce a Christian register. Especially Prospero's "provision in mine art" establishes what Michael Witmore calls "the relationship between the playwright's ordered world and that of a providential God" (2001, 4): "The action of God in providing for his creatures; the divine control and ordering of events; divine providence" (*OED*, provision, *n.* 3. †b.). There is another instance of the analogy of Prospero's role in the theatrical constellation and the role of a providential god, very similar to the term "provision":

> *Prospero:* [...] and by my prescience
> I find my zenith doth depend upon
> A most auspicious star, whose influence
> If now I court not, but omit, my fortunes
> Will ever after droop. [...] (1.2.180–184)

Prescience, "Knowledge of events before they happen; foreknowledge" (*OED*, prescience, *n.* 1.), is like *provision* a capacity or potentially caring action that is moulded on the notion of divine providence, "an attribute of God" (*OED*, prescience, *n.* 1. a.), that can, however, also be attributed to human beings. The scene's obvious preoccupation with the analogy of Prospero's role and that of a providential god is perfected by the presence of divine providence 'itself' in Prospero's narrative:

> *Miranda:* How came we ashore?
> *Prospero:* By providence divine. (1.2.159)

This unique intervention of providence in a world that seems to be nearly utterly under the control of Prospero's "provision" is indeed striking and has evoked controversial interpretations of the relationship between Prospero's provision and this "providence divine". Is Prospero's art "a means through which God's will is accomplished" (Mebane 1979, 176), does he "obtain genuine power by aligning [himself] with the order of Providence" (Mebane 1979, 179)? Is he a "providential instrument" (Ide 1991, 104)? Or merely a "showman displaying to best advantage the craft of Providence" (Slover 1978, 185)? Or, rather, is Prospero "emphatically not Providence" (Campbell 1993, 87)? To my mind all these interpretations are too much focussed on the fictional world of one pragmatic level only, speculating about whether Prospero's rising back to worldly power accords with a divinely sanctioned order or not. I do not think that the relation of Providence and Prospero's provision is a question of plot and assessment of orders. I would rather suggest reminding ourselves of the fact that Prospero's provision was presented to us as "provision in mine art": Prospero's provision is a director's provision for his play, this play being a pragmatic level of which Prospero himself does not form a part, from which he is absent. On this level over which Prospero exercises his "provision", people are "cast ashore" (2.2.121) exactly as Prospero and Miranda "came ashore". This holds true not only for Stephano and Trinculo, but also for the king's party:

> Antonio: We all were sea-swallowed, though some cast again,
> And by that destiny to perform an act
> Whereof what's past is prologue, what to come
> In yours and my discharge! (2.1.251–254)

The strong semantic isotopy of theatre ("perform", "act", "prologue") that follows the party's weathery arrival on the island punningly activates the theatrical meaning of the verb *to cast*. In a movement already very familiar to us, a phenomenon of weather "The simple action: To throw" (*OED*, cast, *v.* I.) as "Said of the sea, waves, wind, or the like: esp. in *cast ashore*" (*OED*, cast, *v.* I. 3.) is brought into connection with the practice of theatre: "To put 'into shape' or into order; to dispose, arrange" (*OED*, cast, *v.* VIII.), "To allot (the parts of a play) *to* the actors; to appoint (actors) *for* the parts" (OED, cast, *v.* VIII. 48. a.). In short: Prospero's 'provisionary' theatrical intervention is figured as a 'providential' intervention of the weather. Actually, his authority of "playwright and book-holder" (Holland 1995, 214) consists to an important part of the "dramatist's ability to determine who is present on stage" (Lyne 2004, 134) – who is cast ashore, so to speak. In the play, Ariel actualises Prospero's weathery power of 'casting':

> Ariel: [...] as thou bad'st me,
> In troops I have dispersed them 'bout the isle. (1.2.219–220)

Thus it is Prospero who decides over Antonio and Sebastian's "destiny", who decides over the "act[s]" they "perform", who has cast them ashore and cast their parts. Prospero is the master over confinements and entrances of all the figures of the play, a fact that is communicated to the audience in detail and with a long breath. Caliban is "[d]eservedly confined into this rock" (1.2.362) from where he can be ordered at will, as the second scene shows. Sycorax "did confine" (1.2.274) Ariel "Into a cloven pine" (1.2.277) and only Prospero's "art" can make "gape | The pine and let [him] out" (1.2.291–293) – threatening him to "peg" him in the "knotty entrails" of an oak (1.2.294–295), if he does rebel. Ferdinand finds himself, similar to Caliban, imprisoned by Prospero, although comforted by Miranda's presence:

> *Ferdinand:* Might I but through my prison once a day
> Behold this maid. All corners else o'th' earth
> Let liberty make use of; space enough
> Have I in such a prison. (1.2.491–494)

The spirits of act four are by Prospero's "art" "from their confines called to enact | [His] present fancies" (4.1.120–122). Prospero's summoning the king's party on stage at the beginning of act five works in a very similar way:

> *Ariel:* Confined together
> In the same fashion as you gave in charge,
> Just as you left them; all prisoners, sir,
> In the line-grove which weather-fends your cell.
> They cannot budge till your release. (5.1.7–11)

However, for his own and Miranda's coming ashore, for their being 'cast' ashore, Prospero's dramaturgical "provision" cannot claim responsibility. The casting of this part takes place on a higher pragmatic level, it is watched over by an authority that is absent from Prospero's fictional world, an authority now called "providence divine". The analogy of Prospero's "provision" to this authority's "providence" is thus an analogy that links two pragmatic levels in a hierarchical relationship, two boxes of the play's pragmatic Chinese-boxes-structure. Regarded from this metatheatrical perspective, Prospero's falling back to "providence divine" to give an account of an absent authority corresponds to Gonzalo's trusting the "wills above" in the first scene: this time not only crossing the boundary of a play-within-the-play but pointing beyond drama's internal communication system. The play's metatheatrical resolution of Gonzalo's trust in the "wills above", presenting a "poet and stage-manager figure[ ]" (Garber 1974, 188) to the audience thus teaches us to read the Christian framework as being analogically appropriated by a reflection on the pragmatic constellation of theatre. Consequently, I would argue that what we are to expect from Prospero's appeal to "providence divine" is less an assessment of his plans and plotting in terms of divine order or will, but a contribution to the play's metatheatrical reflections. In other words, I do not think that Prospero is referring to a divine authority inside the fictional world – but quite literally to a 'Will above' – to a poet and stage-manager of the external communication system.

It is the Epilogue, at the latest, that confirms this crossing of pragmatic levels, this dramatic metalepsis: Prospero, as we have shown above, the master over the characters' confinements (i.e. their exits and entrances), reveals his own confinement, his presence on stage, being a matter of the outer communicative system, here of the viewers themselves: "I must be here confined by you" (Epilogue. 4). This metalepsis, crossing the play's internal and external communicative system is indeed a major contribution to the play's metatheatrical setup: it mirrors the crossing of pragmatic levels of the play-within-play situation and refers it to the play's own boundary of internal and external communication systems, a boundary that cannot be controlled from within the play, by Prospero. This is the decisive step of making the piece speak about theatre – and not about the absolute power of its stage-managing protagonist. It is important to mark the instances where the play alludes to what transcends it, to the pragmatic levels that cannot be present on stage, because this complicated 'absent presence' of the play's "providence divine", of the authority and w/Will above it, accounts for its mediality, for its being a piece of theatre. With Prospero's presence on stage the play offers us the tempting opportunity to solve this tension of an absent-presence or present-absence and (mis)take Prospero's will and his intentions as responsible for all there is and happens on stage. This transparency, although showing us a man of the theatre and his spectacles, his "present fancies" (4.1.122), does not at all talk about theatre, but, when read naively as has been too often done, presents a totalitarian vision of power. We should thus not only pay attention to "the limitations of art in [Prospero's] endeavour" (Zimbardo 1963, 50) but listen carefully to the play's allusions to the pragmatic boundaries of its Chinese-boxes-structure that account for these limitations. Only then *The Tempest* does reveal much about the medium theatre in the early modern age. The hierarchies of pragmatic levels always constitute 'transcendent aboves', authorities of a higher level, presently-absent to the lower level. It is in-between the above transcendence and the audience below that theatre takes place. Like the weather, as the medium of divine providence, theatre can cross this gap (without transcending it!) and produce effects.

With these precautions in mind we can now turn to Prospero's role in the theatrical constellation and to what his narration tells us about it. First of all, George Slover quite rightly reminds us of the fact that Prospero is also an actor (1978, 186); however, this is not the specific position we are interested in at the moment. What differentiates him from Ariel, expressed by their characteristic master-slave relationship, is his role as "manager of shows" (Miko 1982, 8): no matter whether we regard him as "director" (Popelard 2009, 25), "playwright" (Slover 1978, 186), "scenarist-lyricist" (Slover 1978, 186) or "controlling figure[ ]" (Homan 1973, 74), Prospero holds a position in the theatrical constellation that is one level above the respective level of the play. This is best demonstrated by Ariel's first words to Prospero, who has summoned the spirit on stage, thus effecting his theatrical entrance:

> *Prospero:* [to Ariel] Come away, servant, come; I am ready now.
> Approach, my Ariel. Come.
> Enter Ariel
> *Ariel:* All hail, great master; grave sir, hail! […] (1.2.187–189)

Ariel's addressing Prospero as "great master" answers the most pertinent question of the tempest scene: "Where's the master?" (1.1.9) – *le-voilà*, here he is! It was his will, that was done in the tempest scene, and that has not betrayed Gonzalo's trust, saving the whole party without any harm done. With regard to this weathery spectacle Prospero is indeed the "god of power" (1.2.10) that Miranda aspires to be in order to allay the storm and rescue ship and crew. However, this position is not a result of Prospero's superhuman, magical forces inherent in his person. As we have learned, he cannot give an account of his being 'cast' into the godlike role, although he tries his very best in providing us with the circumstances of 'his casting' in his expositional narrative. What Prospero's narrative *does* is transform him from "master of a full poor cell" (1.2.20) to a "great master" (1.2.189) of godlike status before the exemplary eyes of his daughter that represent the audience's 'eyes' on the stage. What it *speaks of* is how he went from being a "prince of power" (1.2.54) in Milan to becoming a "god of power" (1.2.10) on the island. Both these movements, one beginning years ago in Milan, the other taking Prospero's present existence on the island as its starting point, converge in his new authorial (threatrical!) position, as a "god of power" once the court party has arrived near the island. Interestingly, both starting points, the "poor man" Prospero's "library" (1.2.97) in Milan and Prospero's "full poor cell" (1.2.20) on the island, denote some kind of spiritual retreat from the world, not only for their common 'poorness'. *Cell* similar to the first scene's *cabin* bears traces of Prospero's housing on the island resembling a spiritual retreat (cf. *OED*, cell, *n.1*. 1. a. and 4. a.). Prospero's library in Milan is the place where he dedicated himself to "secret studies" and retreated from government and worldly affairs:

Prospero:	[the liberal arts] being all my study,
	The government I cast upon my brother
	And to my state grew stranger, being transported
	And rapt in secret studies. [...] (1.2.75–77)
Prospero:	[...] Me, poor man, my library
	Was dukedom large enough. Of temporal royalties
	[Antonio] thinks me now incapable; [...] (1.2.109–111)

Again the conscious use of end position marks the semantic centre of Prospero's narrative: his seclusion in the library is contrasted with Antonio's "temporal royalties". It is this being set in opposition with "temporal royalties" that adds a strong sense of the 'spiritual' to Prospero's retreat in his library (cf. *OED*, temporal, *adj.1.* 2.). Interestingly, Prospero's 'spiritual' retreat into his library is made possible by a last worldly and theatrical or stage-managing act: Prospero "cast" "The government" "upon [his] brother" (1.2.76). It is no coincidence that we here again find the term *cast*, with all its theatrical and weathery innuendoes. In fact, it is here, in its first use, that we are made aware of its theatrical connotations by the scene's taking up the theatrical thread some lines later:

Prospero:	Being once perfected how to grant suits,
	How to deny them, who t'advance and who
	To trash for overtopping, new created
	The creatures that were mine, I say, or changed 'em,
	Or else new formed 'em; having both the key
	Of officer and office, set all hearts i'th' state
	To what tune pleased his ear, that now he was
	The ivy which had hid my princely trunk
	And sucked my verdure out on't. [...] (1.2.79–87)
Prospero:	[...] He being thus lorded,
	Not only with what my revenue yielded
	But what my power might else exact, like one
	Who, having into truth by telling of it,
	Made such a sinner of his memory
	To credit his own lie, he did believe
	He was indeed the duke, out o'th' substitution
	And executing th'outward face of royalty
	With all prerogative. Hence his ambition growing –
	[...]
	To have no screen between this part he played
	And him he played it for, he needs will be
	Absolute Milan. Me, poor man, my library
	Was dukedom large enough. Of temporal royalties
	He thinks me now incapable; [...] (1.2.97–111)

Antonio's "executing th'outward face of royalty", having been 'cast' into this role by Prospero, strikingly resembles Prospero's later theatrical magic on the island: "trash[ing] for overtopping" (we remember the tempest scene's *top*sail that had to be taken down), "new created | The creatures", "new formed 'em" "or changed 'em" could be descriptions of what Prospero tries to do with Antonio or Alonso on the island, the island "full of noises" (3.2.135), orchestrated by Prospero, whose project is, indeed, also to "set all hearts i'th' state | To what tune please[s] his ear". In Milan, Prospero did not occupy himself with this theatrical "outward face of royalty" and instead devoted his attention to the affaires inside his library.

As it turns out, this is Prospero's tragic "error" (Lindenbaum 1984, 167): the usurpation of his dukedom takes place in this outer realm – and it seems to be a very theatrical affair. According to Prospero's words, the usurpation is brought about as a collapse of theatre's pragmatic levels: Antonio "credit[ed] his own lie", "did believe | He was indeed the duke", thereby dissolving the distinction of actor and character; moreover, "To have no screen between this part he played | And him he played it for" collapses the distinction of part and playwright/stage-manager, or audience, of the internal and external communication systems. The result of the collapsing of theatre's pragmatic levels into one of worldly power is Antonio's becoming "Absolute Milan". The authority he gains by collapsing the theatrical layers is "Absolute" – as can only be rightfully said of God's omnipotence. It does therefore not come as a surprise that this hubris will be punished in the course of the play. Especially, since this question of absolute, despotic, rule happened to be an enormously important political topic of the time when the play was first performed, as Donna Hamilton shows by pointing to the "centrality of the debates on the royal prerogative" (1990, xi) during James's I reign. So why, could be asked with Andreas Höfele (2006), does the play's poetic justice not punish Prospero's theatrical, godlike manipulations as hubris?

What distinguishes Prospero from Antonio is that he respects theatre's pragmatic levels and restrictions. He is aware of the "screen between this part he played | And him he played it for" as both his references to "providence divine" and to the audience's power in the Epilogue indicate. Prospero's understanding of "temporal royalties" differs fundamentally from Antonio's: for Antonio, "temporal royalties" signifies a ruler's claim to the worldly power over this material world, in contrast to God's divine claim to power over an ensuing, transcendent spiritual realm, whereas for Prospero's understanding, another dimension of the term *temporal* might be decisive: *temporal* understood as "Lasting or existing only for a time; passing, temporary" (*OED*, temporal, *adj.1.* 1.).

Obviously, this 'temporality'/'temporariness' distinguishes Prospero's understanding of "temporal royalties" from Antonio's equating these royalties with absolute worldly power. Prospero's authority and power is limited, it is subject to an external restraint and it is not completely 'worldly': it is bound to and restricted by the theatrical constellation.

This limitation suggest a reply to the uneasy observation that, as Ole Martin Skilleås puts it, "[i]t seems that [Prospero's] powers do not go beyond the vicinity of the island" (1991, 123). Generations of critics have attested to the fact that there is no reason to be found on the level of plot and fictional world that could account for this strange range of Prospero's powers. This logical problem of the play's fictional world does indeed appear to be its very omphalos: it testifies to *The Tempest*'s fundamental, ineluctable metatheatrical nature. The play, I would propose, is not about Prospero, it is about theatre: it is about an institution, a heterotopos in Foucauldian words (cf. Foucault 2001), that for a limited amount of time brings together a variety of very different people in a certain limited space; an institution that suspends, to a certain degree, social hierarchies and, temporarily, hands the authority to a group of people of marginal status in worldly terms. This is *The Tempest*'s core, around which the story of Prospero's usurpation and the dynastic marriage of Miranda and Ferdinand is arranged. That is not to say that the political machinations and negotiations are mere padding to the play's metatheatrical centre. On the contrary, they clearly mark the political import of Prospero's theatrical spectacle and its transformative effects. However, by limiting Prospero's power to the theatrical constellation, by not allowing him to exercise his magical powers outside 'the theatre' of the island, by not allowing him to use it as a direct political means in Milan, the specifically theatrical way of dealing with politics and power, the political dimension of the *medium* theatre, can be observed.

It is possible to assume that Prospero's quest (and at the same time the theme of *The Tempest*) is to make known to the world a form of "temporal royalties" (i.e. the relatively new cultural practice of theatre) of which Antonio "thinks [him] now incapable" (1.2.110–111). These temporal royalties are temporary, and no form of worldly power: before his "temporal royalties" on the island start, he has been a "prince of power" (1.2.54), and as his changing clothes, adding "hat and rapier" as to "present" himself "As [he] was sometime Milan" (cf. Antonio's being "absolute Milan" (1.2.109)!) (5.1.84–86), indicates, he returns to the "prince of power" in the end, which coincides with his abjuring his art.

On the island, he is not "prince of power", but "god of power" (1.2.10), not only in command of his few subjects, but also of the weather. If we thus watch and listen closely, we can see and hear Prospero rise and sink as we heard of

Antonio's illegitimate rise to power and with Miranda saw him "sink" (1.2.32) – with the difference that Prospero decides to abjure his magic and leave the island, whereas Antonio had no "mind to sink" (1.1.38). However, Prospero's rise is not a rise back to political power, it is a rise to his theatrical power. The craving to rise is first expressed when Prospero finds himself at the lowest, usurped and exposed to the elements, when he

> Prospero: Under my burden groaned, which raised in me
> An undergoing stomach to bear up
> Against what should ensue. (1.2.155–158)

However, Prospero's rise does not start, as one might expect, with his being cast ashore, with his taking mastery over the isle, his subjecting Ariel and Caliban and his building a little state of which he holds the reign. It is thus not the "colonialist aspects of location" (Albanese 1996, 69) that is responsible for Prospero's ascent to power. Prospero's "Now I arise" (1.2.169) does not easily refer to a narrated point of time inside his story, not only because his command to Miranda to "Sit still and hear the last of our sea-sorrow" directly follows and makes it rather appear, as the Ard[3] editors gloss, "an implied SD, indicating that Prospero gets up from a sitting position". The deictic "now" reoccurs some lines later, this time accompanied by an explanation of its reference:

> Prospero: By accident most strange, bountiful fortune
> (Now, my dear lady) hath mine enemies
> Brought to this shore; and by my prescience
> I find my zenith doth depend upon
> A most auspicious star, whose influence
> If now I court not, but omit, my fortunes
> Will ever after droop. [...] (1.2.178–184)

What makes Prospero "arise" is the arrival of his "enemies" – and that is to say the arrival of his audience, of the subjects of his theatrical transformations. Prospero's rise is inherently a theatrical one. The play's characteristic, "abundant 'now'" (Hall 1999, 45), spread all over *The Tempest*, (there being "no text in the canonical history of playwriting where the word 'now' occurs as often as in *The Tempest*" (Pieters 2000, 150)) is indeed the most obvious sign of the play's characteristic metatheatrical configuration. The characters' and the audience's sharing the same theatrical "now" has important things to tell about weather and theatre.

Not only that Prospero's rise begins "Now", when the audience arrives, but also that it reaches its peak, its "zenith", when Prospero comes to embody the theatrical/dramaturgical "wills above", observing Ariel clad as a harpy present his performance to Prospero's enemies: "*Solemn and strange music, and* Prospero *on the top (invisible)*" (SD 3.3). It is here that Prospero occupies the position of a "god of power" (1.2.10), the absent presence/present absence of a higher authority according to whose will and provision the performance is acted out. I do not think it fruitful at all to compare Prospero's "quasi-divine powers" (Homan 1973, 71) to 'real', genuinely divine powers. Classifying "Prospero's power [...] as (at best) worldly, harshly repressive and narcissistic, rather than absolute by divine decree" (Campbell 1993, 89) completely misses the play's metatheatrical frame and the analogical function that divine power plays for that frame. As we have shown above, it is the limitation to theatre that distinguishes Prospero's "temporal" royalties from Antonio's absolute worldly royalties. This is the only reason why Prospero's rise is not a case of hubris, not a "blasphemous temptation (worthy of Antichrist) to [...] play[ ] a 'god of power'" (Hodgkins 2010, 156). Indeed, measured in terms of either spiritual or worldly ends, Prospero's "victory is essentially an empty one" (Campbell 1993, 89): he achieves only a "severely limited – because wholly temporal – version of immortality" (Campbell 1993, 89)) and, back in Milan, Prospero will again be "subject at any moment to disturbance by the ill will of Antonio and Sebastian or the inexperience of Ferdinand and Miranda" (Magnusson 1986, 59). However, Prospero's descent in the end, from "god of power" back to "prince of power", indicated, as Andreas Höfele has shown (2006, 35), by Prospero's burying his broken staff "certain fathoms in the earth" and drowning his book "deeper than did ever plummet sound" (5.1.55–57) cannot be read as the protagonist's failure, punished by the play's system of poetic justice. The play does not stage Prospero's abjuration of magic as a result of his failure, or his triumph; apart from the dynastic marriage the play seems even to end in striking indifference to who has achieved what and to how the future in Milan will look like. Instead, the play's final moments are governed by the spectacle of Prospero's abjuration of magic that is not really motivated by anything, that seems to follow a higher necessity. It is just the other side of the play's metatheatrical omphalos: as *temporal* royalties, Prospero's theatrical reign as a god of power has also come to an end! The performance is over, the constellation's very own power structure dissolves, and the world will again begin to follow a worldly order, not governed by theatrical "gods of power" but by "princes".

The play is very thorough, almost concerned, to emphasise its "eliminating the convention that stage time is not the same as real time" (Sokol 2003, 127). Again and again we encounter the mentioning of "three hours": first, as a likely allusion to Prospero's dramaturgical office as a "book-holder" (Holland 1995, 214), when Miranda tells Ferdinand that he, for the moment, does not have to fear her father, because Prospero "Is hard at study; [...] | He's safe for these three hours" (3.1.20–21). The hints crowded in act five to prepare for Prospero's abjuration (i.e. for the end of the play) are much more explicit: Alonso talks of being wrecked "three hours since" (5.1.136) as does the Boatswain some lines later, speaking of "three glasses" (5.1.223). The same "three hours" occur in Alonso's astonished comment to Ferdinand's obviously quite recent "acquaintance" (5.1.186) with Miranda. I think it quite obvious that the three hours are to be read as a metatheatrical reference to the duration of the play itself. It is interesting and significant that Shakespeare does not resort to the famous "two hours" that was more conventional for talking about the length of an early modern play, as the Prologue of *Romeo and Juliet* prominently does by referring to "the two hours' traffic of our stage" (*Rom.*, Prologue, 12). *The Tempest*'s "three hours" do not simply establish a comical because uncannily self-referential and metaleptical link to the 'typical' length of an Elizabethan or Jacobean play. It denotes the amount of time that the staging of *The Tempest* actually took.[16] Why does it, and I agree with T. R. Langley that it does, "come[ ] as something of a shock to be reminded that the playing time [...] and the fictional time correspond so straitly [sic!]" (1991, 132)? It is surely not an abstract correspondence in duration that "partly dissolves the distance between the play's fantastic action and the 'real lives' of its first spectators" (Sokol 2003, 127). The temporal structure of *The Tempest* is so unsettling, because it dares a very fundamental dramatic metalepsis; *The Tempest*'s fictional time does not only correspond to the audience's real time in duration, it is indistinguishable from it:

> *Prospero:* Now does my project gather to a head.
> My charms crack not; my spirits obey; and time
> Goes upright with his carriage. How's the day?
> *Ariel:* On the sixth hour; at which time, my lord,
> You said our work should cease. (5.1.1–5)

Prospero could have asked any member of the audience for the time – he would have received the same answer. It is hardly possible to mark in a more outright fashion the astonishing game that Shakespeare is here playing with what T. G. Bishop has described as theatre's characteristic relation between 'the now' of the "remote moment of the story being told" and 'the now' of the performance (Bishop 1996, 1). It is the 'real' time of performance, being limited to three hours, that sets the 'fictional' time for Prospero's project: it has to "gather to a head",

---

16 As Tiffany Stern has shown, the reference to two hours is more conventional than the reference to three hours, which, however, was also in use for denoting the length of plays. Plays, especially in the later Elizabethan and in the Jacobean age, tended to be longer than two hours, so that the reference to two hours is rather conventional than 'adequate' (2015).

because the theatre is running out of light (either natural, or candles) and its audience is getting hungry. And when Prospero tells Miranda that "The hour's now come; | The very minute bids thee ope thine ear" (1.2.36–37), the "kairos" (Sokol 2003) (the propitiousness of the moment) is a very theatrical "kairos", alluding to the need to provide the audience with expositional knowledge. This is even more explicit in the "kairos" summoned up by "the accident most strange" of "A most auspicious star, whose influence" Prospero has "now" to court, a moment that we have already identified with the arrival of his fictional *and* real audience.

The Tempest provides us with an abundance of undisputable hints that make us aware of the uncanny metatheatrical identification of the story's and the performance's 'now':

> The characters of the play go through the tempest, and through a trial. The spectators witness the tempest with them, at exactly the same time. The characters go to supper; at the same time the actors and the spectators will go to supper. The tempest is over, the magic is over, and so is the performance. Life begins again, in the same way as before the tempest, before the performance, for characters and audience alike. Has nothing changed? (Kott 1965, 176)

Jan Kott, to my mind, poses *The Tempest*'s central question: "Has nothing changed?" Viewed from "th'outward face" of Antonio's absolute "royalty" (1.2.104), we would have to answer: No. As the first scene's tempest had caused "not so much perdition as an hair" (1.2.30), leaving Gonzalo's "doublet as fresh as the first day [he] wore it" (2.1.103–104), the audience leaves the three hours of theatre probably also looking much the same as before. However, what about Prospero's "temporal royalties"? As Jan Kott's commentary on the simultaneity of the story's and the performance's time suggests, the audience, has also "gone through" the tempest/*The Tempest*; the viewers have, "for the length of the performance", also "submit[ted] to being bound" (Ward 1987, 99) to Prospero's temporal royalties. By coming to the theatre they have made a decision similar to the court party on the first scene's ship: instead of retreating to the lonely inwardness of cabins or cells in order to take a pause from worldly orders, they have chosen to expose themselves to the publicity of a London theatre. Prospero, being transformed from "master of a full poor cell" (1.2.19–20) to the "potent master" (4.1.34), whose "so potent art" (5.1.50) makes him even control the weather and thus assume the position of a "god of power", has made a similar decision for publicity. It is the meeting of these three decisions, bringing together characters, audience and stage-managing playwright that accounts for the "kairos" that *is The Tempest*. "The hour's now come" (1.2.36) when these three parties are summoned to one place, at the same time and thus constitute a theatrical constellation.

The "kairos" of the theatrical constellation provides for the fact that "something" changes: as D. S. McGovern and Douglas Peterson have observed, *The Tempest*'s metatheatrical configuration stages a "crisis" (Peterson 1973, 220, McGovern 1983, 207), whose old, medical meaning gives an account of how the "change" is brought about:

> *Pathol.* The point in the progress of a disease when an important development or change takes place which is decisive of recovery or death; the turning-point of a disease for better or worse; also applied to any marked or sudden variation occurring in the progress of a disease and to the phenomena accompanying it. (*OED*, crisis, *n.* 1.)

So what about this theatrical crisis, brought about in the "kairos" of the theatrical constellation, as a result of our subjection to Prospero's (dis)tempering temporal royalties? "Has nothing changed?"

Prospero's "temporal royalties" are weathery: the three hours' "time" ("Weather; (in *pl.*) meteorological conditions" (*OED*, time, *n.* I. †20.)) that he presides over as a "god of power" work on the viewers' bodies as a *Tempest* was thought to affect bodies exposed to it according to the medical knowledge of the time: Miranda feels flaming amazement, and pity beating in her mind. Ariel diagnoses a fever whose infection no one of the court party could withstand. Prospero, as we will see, cannot help being "touched with anger so distempered" (4.1.145). As even Ariel, who is "but air" has "a touch of feeling | Of [the court party's] afflictions" (5.1.20–21), it is not beside the point to assume that the audience is expected to share some of these 'inner', humoral movements.

However, what about Antonio's famously not saying a word after he has been restored, not one word of repentance, not one word signalling a 'moral change'? His future political submissiveness? Would not that be the true "sea-change" (1.2.401) theatre is to bring about, bettering its audience in three hours, intervening in recent political affairs, exercising some kind of direct, calculated impact on its viewers? Like Ferdinand, Antonio and the others, the audience has seen "something rich and strange" (1.2.402) in these three hours, and has, like Ferdinand and Antonio, believed in these strange things. However, the tempest has neither drowned and transformed Alonso into the pure, innocent, ideal but lifeless beauty of "coral" and "pearls" (1.2.399–400), nor supposedly changed Antonio and the audience, into ideal (but lifeless?) personifications of stainless moral beauty. The play's milieu has not been the bottom of the sea – but the weathery region of an island. The weather's transformative power does not engender ideals – its power is a power of (dis)temperance, not transforming the outward shell, but the inner weather of the humours and spirits. The analogy of weather and theatre that *The Tempest* stages may thus warn us to project the all-too modern expectation of a Schillerian educational moral and political theatre – and make us more susceptive to the early modern climate of the isle.

6 The climate of th'isle

In our explorations of this isle, "full of noises, | Sounds and sweet airs" (3.2.135–136), we are not alone. However, it is not Caliban that accompanies us, leading us around the isle as a sort of 'tourist guide', as he will later do for his companions Stephano and Trinculo. Thus there is, at this moment in time, no one to tell us: "Be not afeard"; only the expectations we brought to the theatre may give us some hope that this isle's "noises, | Sounds and sweet airs [will] give delight and hurt not" (3.2.135–136). We, as the audience, are exploring the island together with the party cast there after the shipwreck, whose arrival mirrors our coming to the theatre. However, we do share more than merely the newness to a location: "The 'actuality' of the island is always at a dream-like remove from the characters' perception of it" (Magnusson 1986, 59), "*The Tempest* itself is, in a sense, a vision for the audience as well as for some of the characters in the play" (Semon 1974, 100). Put in other words: the future "victims [of Prospero's manipulations] are also, of course, an audience" (Miko 1982, 9). According to Alvin B. Kernan this is a typical technique deployed by Shakespeare:

> He did not harangue and instruct his audience directly like Ben Jonson, but he did often put an audience on stage in ways which suggest his conception of the relationship of playwright, play, actors, and audience. (1982, 141)

As Miranda's narration retrospectively established her as a figure of the audience in the second scene, reflecting on the first scene's tempest, our viewing position is again, and now permanently doubled on stage. However, this time we are simultaneously confronted with the spectacle and the audience of this spectacle that share the same acting space. And, oddly enough, the stage audience experience the theatre situation more intensely and more consciously than the 'real' audience itself. "In no other play of Shakespeare's [...] is the gap between the knowledge and expectations of the audience and the characters as great as it is here" (McNamara 1987, 183); Prospero's letting us in on his plans and their theatrical execution early in the play has changed our perspective on the staged events. We are no longer witnessing the stage spectacle as a stage spectacle that we have chosen to expose ourselves to when going to the theatre, co-suffering with the characters on stage, as we have done during the tempest scene. The metatheatrical setting of the events on the island with representatives of the audience, actor and stage-managing playwright on stage shifts our attention from the spectacle itself to the 'seam' in-between spectacle and audience, spectacle and stage-manager, actor and character that are now present on stage. Our exploration of this wondrous island differs thus markedly from that of our company on stage: whereas their impressions are intensely theatrical impressions evoked by the spectacles that Ariel and Prospero perform for them, we are watching them being exposed to these spectacles, we focus on *how* these spectacles work on the (stage!) audience.

The climate of th'isle that we are exploring is the way that theatre, as a medium, crosses the pragmatic seam of audience and stage, of internal and external communication system. These crossings – and I think this is the central metatheatrical thesis of *The Tempest* – are indeed a question of climate: theatrical spectacle and weather work the same way. They act as mediums or milieus that exercise a power of (dis)tempering.

The first of the shipwrecked party to arrive on the island is Ferdinand. Significantly, he seems to be a bit early: in contrast to all the other victims of the shipwreck, his being cast on shore/stage does not take place as a scene of the second act, but is crammed into the second scene of act one, a scene that would even without Ferdinand's entrance have already been by far the longest of the play. Obviously, his early arrival associates him with Prospero and Miranda and prepares his serving as a dynastic link between the two fractions later on. However, Ferdinand's arrival forming part of the highly functional second scene of the first act means more. It serves as a dramatic transition into the new metatheatrical situation that will shape the play from the second act onwards. It puts into practice what Miranda, as viewer, and Prospero, as stage-managing playwright, have with their narratives established. In contrast to Ferdinand, the audience can see that it is Ariel who performs the piece of music that Ferdinand hears, it is thus introduced to the dramatic convention so important for the rest of the play. The audience always sees and knows what the characters on stage do not see and know; the way that Prospero's theatrical manipulations work is metatheatrically exhibited all the time:

> *Ferdinand:* Where should this music be? I'th' air, or th'earth?
> It sounds no more, and sure it waits upon
> Some god o'th' island. Sitting on a bank,
> Weeping again the King my father's wreck,
> This music crept by me upon the waters,
> Allaying both their fury and my passion
> With its sweet air. [...] (1.2.388–394)

By ambiguously alluding to two characteristics that we have already come across Ferdinand's initial questions aim right at the heart of the vision of theatre that *The Tempest* advocates. Firstly, the location of "this music" is a question of vertical topology, of hierarchy. The question "I'th' air, or th'earth?" represents the distinction of earthly, terrestrial/heavenly, divine, as Ferdinand's own answer to his question a few lines later shows:

> Ferdinand: This is no mortal business nor no sound
> That the earth owes. I hear it now above me. (1.2.407–408)

The music's not being of the earth indicates the island's otherworldliness, its being governed by "Some god o'th' island". The fact that Ferdinand hears the music from "above" alludes to the "wills above" of the tempest scene that we have already identified as figuring for the higher pragmatic level of dramaturgy and playwriting. Although the semantic isotopy that establishes the opposition of terrestrial/divine is strong ("earth", "god o'th' island", "no mortal business", "earth", "above"), it is not as stable and closed as it might seem: whereas its earthly pole is established with insistence, the divine pole is rather extrapolated from the negation of the terrestrial. The only positive term we encounter is doubly qualified, "*sure* [...] *some* god o'th' island" and thus marked as an extrapolation. Furthermore, and here we come to the second characteristic of theatre that Ferdinand is unknowingly hinting at, the topological binary of earth and heaven is unsettled by another topological hierarchy that does not directly involve transcendent divinity: that of the elements. The insistence of "air" in the passage distorts the neat earth/heaven distinction: "I'th' air, or th'earth?" can be read quite literally, as the passage seems to do itself: "This music crept by me upon the waters",[17] alludes to the topological order of the three elements, earth, water and air, and emphasises the air's moving "close to the ground [in this case the water surface], as a short-legged reptile, an insect, a quadruped moving stealthily, a human being on hands and feet, or in a crouching posture" (*OED*, creep, *v.* 1. a.). The fact that the air (always playing with its associations with the name *Ariel*, who might perhaps literally creep by the sitting Ferdinand) seems to move rather horizontally should warn us of too hastily identifying the music capable of allaying the storm with the heavenly music of the spheres. Ferdinand's wondering about the origin of the music does not merely reveal the "Renaissance veneration of music as pleasurable experience in itself and as an expression of order and harmony [...] too widely documented to need detailing here" (McNamara 1987, 187). The ambiguity of "I'th' air, or th'earth?",

---

[17] This passage also seems to allude to one of the first sentences of the Bible, "the Spirit of God moved upon the waters" (Gen. 1.2; Whittingham 1560, 1ʳ), establishing an intertextual link between "air" and holy "spirit" that could be of interest for my reading of *The Tempest*.

referring both to a transcendent and an elemental origin expresses in this first magic performance on the island what Joseph Ortiz interprets as a common trait of all the "magical episodes":

> On the one hand, the magical episodes allow the audience to see firsthand the harmonizing, civilizing effects of music that are usually described in speculative texts. [...] On the other hand, by calling attention to Prospero's agency in engineering these scenes, Shakespeare suggests that music, because it can work unseen, is a useful tool for making magical phenomena seem credible. (2011, 169)

It is important to stress the ambiguity of music, because in *The Tempest*, "music is not simply, as so many have said, harmonious, the 'very symbol of order' [Zimbardo 1963, 50]" (Fox-Good 1996, 248). "The Tempest radically deconstructs this kind of musical symbolism" (Fox-Good 1996, 247), a symbolism that opposes earthly chaos and heavenly, musical order: the island is "full of noises, | Sounds and sweet airs" (3.2.135–136) that come from somewhere "above", supposedly controlled by some kind of authority, "some god o'th' island". However, we should take the ambiguity of "noises, | Sounds and sweet airs" seriously: as Joseph Ortiz writes, it is "ambiguity and illegibility that is the condition of music as constitutive of Prospero's – and the dramatist's power" (2011, 171). Ferdinand's question "I'th' air, or th'earth?" expresses exactly this "ambiguity and illegibility": the answer to this question, despite his extrapolating a "god of power" is suspended, remains 'in the air', so to speak. The island's 'god' remains absent, what allays "the waters[']" "fury" and Ferdinand's "passion" is an intermediary between earth and heavens, music's "sweet air".

Jacquelyn Fox-Good (1996, 248) and Robert Lanier Reid (2007, 502) have noted the central pun linking the *air* as "Melody" (*OED*, air, *n.1*. II.) to "Atmospheric air" (*OED*, air, *n.1*. I.). The play will come back to this pun, supporting its musical side, as we have seen, when Caliban famously characterises the isle as "full of noises, | Sounds and sweet airs" (3.2.135–136), and its weathery part in Adrian's assessment of the island's climate: "The air breathes upon us here most sweetly" (2.1.49) or Prospero's talking of "sweet aspersion" (4.1.18), aspersion in the sense of a weathery "shower or spray" (*OED*, aspersion, *n.* 2.). The pun on *air* connects (musical) performance and a phenomenon of weather – and states that the two have the same effect:

> Ferdinand: [...]
> This music crept by me upon the waters,
> Allaying both their fury and my passion
> With its sweet air. [...] (1.2.388–394)

What Ariel's musical performance does is temper the outward weather, the fury of the sea and Ferdinand's inner humoral weather, his passion. Thus the music's "sweet air" functions as the counterpart of or antidote to the first scene's whistling winds and roaring waves. The first scene's noisy performance of tempestuous winds had a distempering, the second scene's sweet air of music a tempering effect. In this early stage of the play, when nothing has yet changed between the tempest and the allaying of its winds we can quite clearly see that *The Tempest* is not using the weather as the *expression* of a larger "conflict between order and chaos" (Zimbardo 1963, 50) but as a means of achieving a strategic (dis)tempering effect – a theatrical means of achieving a theatrical effect, an effect of (dis)temperance. In other words, the weather does not *represent* (a disordered state of the world), but 'performs', it does something to the 'viewers' exposed to it. This manipulative theatrical effect works perfectly on Ferdinand, almost too perfectly: his being easily tempered by the music's sweet air and his readily believing in "no mortal business" of the "god o'th' island" portray him as an exemplary theatregoer. In our discussion of his reaction to the masque staged by Prospero we will later see that his theatrical enthusiasm verges on naivety, he (too easily) forgets about the limits of theatre and the worldly world outside. In this scene, however, Ferdinand's reaction to the storm and to Ariel's musical performance quite exactly mirrors Miranda's reaction to the first scene's spectacle. Ferdinand is moved to tears and he links the events to the authority of some "god o'th' island", as Miranda has done. This is the first step of passing the role of spectator, of audience, that Miranda has 'abstractly' and retrospectively explained to us, on to other characters; characters that are on stage simultaneously with the spectacle they are witnessing and that is strategically performed for them.

Miranda's encounter with Ferdinand also plays with casting characters in the role of theatrical spectators. In the beginning, it is Miranda's turn to view a scene, later Ferdinand will wonder at her:

Prospero [to Miranda]:
>The fringed curtains of thine eye advance,
>And say what thou seest yond.

Miranda: What is't, a spirit?
>Lord, how it looks about. Believe me, sir,
>It carries a brave form. But 'tis a spirit.

Prospero: No, wench, it eats and sleeps and hath such senses
>As we have – such. [...] (1.2.409–414)

I agree with Harry Berger Jr. that the "fringed curtains" of Miranda's eyes suggest "that Miranda's eyes open on Prospero's play world" (Berger 1969, 282 note 26). There is no doubt that Prospero's directing Miranda's attention to the spectacle of Ferdinand's entrance is a theatrical event; it is closely related to Prospero's drawing the curtain when he "*discovers Ferdinand and Miranda, playing at chess*" (SD 5.1.171) to the court party towards the end of the play. Miranda's reaction to the spectacle reveals its metatheatrical nature: her insisting on the impression that what she encounters is "a spirit" refers to the pragmatic seam that is characteristic for theatre in general, and present on stage in so many of *The Tempest*'s scenes. Miranda asks whether Ferdinand is merely a theatrical character, an apparition, a spirit, like Ariel "but air" (5.1.21) – or indeed a 'real' human being. Prospero's answer, that "it [!] eats and sleeps and hath such senses | As we have" must for the audience sound rather funny: in our world, actors are not spirits, they do eat and sleep; nevertheless, this does not prevent them from acting like "spirits" on stage, carrying "brave forms" that are not 'theirs', and 'infecting' their audience, moving their spirits and humours. We know that this is exactly what they do at the time that Prospero is speaking those words. Not only for the audience, who is watching human actors on the stage of the Globe, at Blackfriars or Whitehall, but also for Miranda and Ferdinand:

> Prospero: *[aside]*   It goes on, I see,
> As my soul prompts it. [...] (1.2.420–421)

The complex constellation that makes of the encounter of the two a spectacle for each of them, mutually occupying the position of the audience for the spectacle of the other's surprising entrance brings about the effect that Prospero has prompted: their love. Miranda somehow notices this theatrical manipulation: her 'suspicions' that Ferdinand was no 'real' human being may be wrong in the fictional world that they both inhabit. However, she is aware of the fact that some spirit, controlled by a higher authority, is exercising an influence on her. In other words, she is aware of the theatrical situation that she is taking part in.

Miranda is not the only character on the island to 'mistake' human beings for spirits. In fact, only Ferdinand once gets it right when he allows himself to "be bold | To think" the actors of Prospero's masque "spirits" (4.1.119–120). However, he is lucky, the case obvious, and the list of mistaken identities much longer: at the entrance of Trinculo, Caliban thinks "Here comes a spirit of [Prospero's], and to torment me | For bringing wood in slowly" (2.2.15–16); Prospero is himself aware that the court party cannot be sure of beholding "a living prince", "The wronged Duke of Milan, Prospero!" when they finally encounter him in person, and offers them, "For more assurance", an embrace. Even that does not seem to be too effective in the island's theatrical climate:

> *Alonso:* Whe'er thou be'st he or no,
> Or some enchanted trifle to abuse me
> (As late I have been), I not know. Thy pulse
> Beats as of flesh and blood; and since I saw thee,
> Th'affliction of my mind amends, with which
> I fear a madness held me. (5.1.111–116)

Ironically, Caliban's and Alonso's mistaking human beings of the fictional world for mere spirits of the island, repeating Miranda's reaction on the entrance of Ferdinand, speaks metatheatrical truth of the theatrical situation of which they form a part as characters of the play *The Tempest*. The climate of the island seems to make characters aware of their being characters of a piece of theatre, aware of their spirits being controlled by a higher authority. It seems to bring them to the 'metaleptic limit' of desperately wanting to jump out of their fictional world.

Miranda's encounter with Ferdinand is the model for what all the characters will experience on the island, an experience that Gonzalo describes as a time "When no man was his own" (5.1.213). In the present scene, the transitional scene leading to the events on the island, Miranda feels, without fully realising it, that she is played upon, that on the island, one is somehow under a spell – more and at the same time less than simply oneself. This holds true for both pragmatic positions of theatre that are negotiated in this scene: the character, embodied by an actor, on stage, is a mere spirit, "but air", it [!] is to a large degree controlled by script and dramaturgical command; however, the actor, is also, for the time of the play, not himself, but something other, representing a character that somehow adds to his human body. Similar things could be said of the audience: they are under the play's weathery spell, submit to it for the time of the play, but they also, as we will see, participate with their imagination in the engendering of the theatrical climate that gives shape to the airy apparitions of these three hours.

Both sides of the characteristic theatrical climate of spiritual control are exhibited by crucial experiences of the court party on the island. For example when Ariel "*playing solemn music*" (SD 2.1.185), unseen and unheard by the characters on stage, all of a sudden, lulls everyone to sleep in the midst of their explorations of the island, except for Sebastian and Antonio. These two wonder about the strange coincidence, sense some sort of higher power, and yet act the way that they were prompted to act by Prospero who snares them into temptation:

Sebastian:	What a strange drowsiness possesses them!
Antonio:	It is the quality o'th' climate.
Sebastian:	Why Doth it not then our eyelids sink? I find not Myself disposed to sleep.
Antonio:	Nor I. My spirits are nimble. They fell together all, as by consent; They dropped, as by a thunderstroke. What might, Worthy Sebastian, O, what might – ? No more; And yet, methinks I see it in thy face What thou shouldst be. Th'occasion speaks thee, and My strong imagination sees a crown Dropping upon thy head. (2.1.199–209)

Although Antonio does not know that it was not the wind's sweet air, but Ariel's sweet musical air that accounts for the "strange drowsiness" of the rest, he is not mistaken blaming "the quality o'th' climate". On the contrary, it is indeed the island's theatrical climate that works on the "spirits" of the characters on stage; their falling "together", their dropping "as by thunderstroke" follows indeed from a certain "consent": however, not in the sense of a "Voluntary agreement to or acquiescence in what another proposes or desires" (*OED*, consent, *n*. 1. a.), but understood as one and the same sympathetic reaction to an affection of the spirits coming, "dropping" from somewhere above: "*Physiol.* and *Pathol.* A relation of sympathy between one organ or part of the body and another, whereby when the one is affected the other is affected correspondingly" (*OED*, consent, *n*. †5). As we have been repeatedly made aware, a "god o'th' island" reigns over these affections, deciding whose spirits are "nimble" and whose heavy, as he reigns over weather, and decides over dropping thunderstrokes. What Antonio is not aware of is that this "god o'th' island" is not only dropping thunderstrokes and drowsy human beings, but also the "crown" that his "imagination sees [...] | Dropping upon" Sebastian's head. This is strikingly similar to the "riches" that Caliban sees in his dreams, when the "clouds [...] open", "Ready to drop upon [him]" (3.2.141–142). The position of this god in the vertical hierarchy, his power over the weathery phenomenon 'dropping from the sky', makes him, in the theatrical setting of this island, also a god over the fortunes of the characters; their plotting, Antonio's as well as Caliban's, is prompted as futile from the very start. More than that, the temptation of their plotting, however, forms itself part of Prospero's theatrical plan: it is Ariel lulling all but the two future usurpers that provides them with the tempting occasion to plot and execute this usurpation: Antonio's "strong imagination" is thus also a product of Ariel's and Prospero's theatrical manipulations.

As another, very similar scene indicates, the spiritual control that characterises the theatrical climate of the island is not only exercised on the characters as actors, acting according to what a higher authority prompts them to act, but also on the audience of these spectacles. Again it is a "weariness" that manipulates the characters on stage, this time transforming them to an audience for a spectacle:

> Alonso: Old lord, I cannot blame thee,
> Who am myself attached with weariness
> To th' dulling of my spirits. Sit down, and rest. (3.3.4–6)

Unlike the effect of weariness in the related scene of act two, this time, "th' dulling of [...] spirits" does not put Alonso and his companions to sleep, it rather transports them into a sort of intermediary state between waking and sleeping. It is no coincidence that this scene follows Caliban's famous speech on sleep and dreaming ("Be not afeard. The isle is full of noises"; "when I waked | I cried to dream again" (3.2.135–143)): Shakespeare's play consciously approximates the experiences of dream and of viewing a theatrical spectacle, it emphasises the similarity of the effect that these two phenomena have on the imagination and 'spirits' of the person experiencing them. Sitting down, 'taking a rest' from the toils of exploring the island does not recreate the court party in the usual sense: it prepares them for the breath-taking and ('spiritually') highly disturbing experience of the theatre spectacle they are about to view. What is to follow is the banquet scene that culminates in Ariel's harpy speech. The character-spectators' drowsiness, their reduced, resting outward and their intensified, 'humoral' 'inner' activity is similar to dreaming. Shakespeare uses this analogy to illustrate the weathery spell to which theatre viewers submit themselves for the time of the play.

Their reactions to this spectacle are well known to us from the scene that has led us to this passage: Alonso's question "What were these?" (3.3.20) and Gonzalo's answer, mistaking the spirits for "people of the island" (3.3.30), mirror Miranda's taking Ferdinand for a spirit. The symptoms of the theatrical climate of the island seem to be always and reliably the same: amazement and the readiness to believe in a higher authority responsible for the island's miracles. "O wonder!" (5.1.181), Miranda exclaims, "A most high miracle!" (5.1.177), Sebastian stammers, after Prospero had discovered the new-formed couple to Alonso's court party towards the end of the play, confirming Gonzalo's dictum that "All torment, trouble, wonder and amazement | inhabits here [on the island/the theatre]" (5.1.104–105). Again, this late and final encounter that re-unites all the fractions is clearly moulded on the transitional encounter between Ferdinand and Miranda, an encounter that had transformed Miranda from the 'false' position of spectator to the 'correct' one of spectacle, now to be wondered at:

> Ferdinand: [...] (O, you wonder!)
> [...]
> Miranda: No wonder, sir (1.2.427–428).

Amidst all this wonder, everybody seems to agree that divinity is apparently somehow present: seeing Miranda, Ferdinand identifies "Most sure the goddess | On whom these airs attend!" (1.2.418–420). Mirroring this attribution, Miranda does not follow her father's suggestion "thou mightst call him | A goodly person" (1.2.416–417), but decides that "I might call him | A thing divine, for nothing natural | I ever saw so noble" (1.2.418–420). Alonso will in the final scene react in a similar fashion when encountering Miranda:

> Alonso: Is she the goddess that hath severed us
> And brought us thus together? (5.1.187–188)

'Mistaking' humans for either spirits or goddesses and gods while being rapt in a state of enthusiastic wonder can thus be counted among the main influences that the island's climate exercises on its visitors. What looks like an ontological instability at first sight, or rather, an instability of perception, easily remediable by getting the categories right again, turns out to be a question of 'spiritual' control: Caliban, Alonso, Ferdinand and Miranda, are all not wrong in suspecting a higher authority, a "god o'th' island" is in control of the island's 'spirits', as they are not wrong in suspecting the 'shapes' that they are encountering are not humans, with body and will, but mere 'spirits' in the service of some larger project, stirred by some higher authority. As we have seen, the word *spirits* not only denotes Prospero's army of helping hands, Ariel and "the rabble" (4.1.37), over whom Prospero commands directly, "To th' syllable" (1.2.501), but also the visitor's "spirits", their vital principle, their passions, their inclinations and their tempers. Speaking about the metatheatrical *climate* of the island is thus not just some metaphoric expression, but analogically characterises Prospero's power as the "god o'th' island", who exercises an influence on the 'spirits', as the climate does "affect human, animal, or plant life":

> The characteristic weather conditions of a country or region; the prevalent pattern of weather in a region throughout the year, in respect of variation of temperature, humidity, precipitation, wind, etc., esp. as these affect human, animal, or plant life. (*OED*, climate, *n.1.* 2. a.)

The intricate analogy of Prospero's theatrical and weathery power covers both sides of the pragmatic seam simultaneously staged by *The Tempest*: (1) Prospero commands directly over the spirits as actors. As the early modern theory of acting would have it, the art of acting consisted in literally embodying the passions that were prompted by the book, a reason why the profession of acting was regarded as unhealthy (cf. Roach 1985, 49). (2) Via these embodied passions Prospero engenders a climate that 'infects' and thereby controls the audience's spirits, causing "torment, trouble, wonder", "amazement" (5.1.104) and even "madness" (5.1.116). As we have seen with Ferdinand and Miranda and as we will see with Sebastian and Antonio, most of the figures on stage will come to feel Prospero's theatrical power from both sides, once as audience, once as actors, because they fill both roles, being spectators of Prospero's spectacles and performing a part in Prospero's – and Shakespeare's play.

The court party's first impressions of the island have been received as the most problematic and superfluous passage of the whole piece, and are rarely played in modern productions. However, for those who are interested in the connection of weather and theatre the scene's punning on mere trivia holds in store the key terms on which the analogy of theatre and weather hinges. It is no coincidence that the court party's first impression of the island now literalises what had already been alluded to in the "sweet air" welcoming Ferdinand on the island, an impression of its climate:

> Adrian: Though this island seem to be desert –
> [...]
> Uninhabitable and almost inaccessible –
> [...]
> It must needs be of subtle, tender and delicate temperance. (2.1.37–45)

Antonio's and Sebastian's rather feeble punning on Adrian's meteorological observations may not be too funny – however, it repeats and sharpens the important key terms so that they cannot easily be missed by the audience:

> Antonio: Temperance was a delicate wench.
> Sebastian: Ay, and a subtle, as he most learnedly delivered. (2.1.46–48)

The *OED* lists Adrian's usage of *temperance* as an example for the word's obsolete and rather rare meaning "Moderate temperature; freedom from the extremes of heat and cold; mildness of weather or climate; temperateness" (*OED*, temperance, *n.* II. †4.). However, the attributes "subtle, tender and delicate" are unusual to express "temperance" signifying a temperate climate. Only *delicate*, in its denoting "Delightful, charming, pleasant, nice" (*OED*, delicate, *adj.* I. 1.) "Said of the air, climate, or natural features" (*OED*, delicate, *adj.* I. 1. †c.) fits *temperance* in the sense of a temperate climatic state. The adjectives *subtle* and *tender* are however synonyms of other meanings of *delicate* – and thus indicate another reading of *temperance* that supplements the superficial one of the isle's temperateness. The *OED* tells us that *tender* in its basic meaning denotes being "Soft or delicate in texture or consistence; yielding easily to force or pressure; fragile; easily broken, divided, compressed, or injured" (*OED*, tender, *adj.* I. 1. a.) which can be said "Of animals or plants: Delicate, easily injured by severe weather or unfavourable conditions; not hardy; needing protection" (*OED*, tender, *adj.* II. b.). The adjective *subtle* bears a meaning that can function as a complement to the tenderness of being "easily injured by severe weather or unfavourable conditions": "Esp. of a gas or liquid: thin (in consistency); not dense; not viscous; clear. Also: penetrating or pervasive by reason of lack of density" (*OED*, subtle, *adj.* II. 11.). In our analysis of Ariel's epithet "delicate" we have seen that his substance as "a spirit too delicate" (1.2.272) is the substance of a *subtle* spirit, quick and effective because of its subtleness/delicateness:

> One or other of certain subtle highly-refined substances or fluids (distinguished as *natural*, *animal*, and *vital*) formerly supposed to permeate the blood and chief organs of the body. (*OED*, spirit, *n.* IV. 16. a.)

Thus what the series of attributes "subtle, tender and delicate" conjures up are a process's two possible complementary conditions: one expressing the high susceptibility to "weather or unfavourable conditions", the other the characteristic quality of easily "penetrating or [being] pervasive by reason of lack of density". This process is called temperance:

> The action or fact of tempering; mingling or combining in due proportion, adjusting, moderating, modification, toning down, bringing into a temperate or moderate state (*OED*, temperance, *n.* II. †3. a.)

When Adrian says of the island that "It must needs be of subtle, tender and delicate temperance" he not only refers to the completely irrelevant and superfluous information of the island's mean temperature, winds and rainfall, he, unknowingly, characterises it as an exemplary, a special place of temperance. As the active ending *-ance* shows, *temperance* in its original meaning signifies an action, or a process, not a state – only its derived meanings later began metonymically to signify the process's result. The island's "mildness of weather or climate" that we and the punning court party hear when Adrian speaks of "delicate temperance" reminds us of the fact that the weather is the paradigm for these processes of tempering; we may also hear the play's title "*The Tempest*" resonate in this "delicate temperance", as we may hear the notion of 'temperament' or 'tempers'. Adrian's babbling, constantly interrupted by Antonio and Sebastian who are obviously getting annoyed by Adrian's talkative mood, seems to present us with a knot of the play's threads, a knot that we were looking for.

Following Antonio and Sebastian, as so many critics as well as theatre directors have done, and omitting this passage from their readings and productions thus gives away the key for a metatheatrical reading of the play. Adrian's "delicate temperance" is at the same time a characteristic of the fictional world's island and a very interesting conceptualisation of early modern theatre. As we have seen, "delicate" points to a specific 'readiness' for temperance on both sides of theatre's pragmatic seam: in the theatrical constellation, the audience is not "firm [and] constant" (1.2.208) but "Tender or feeble in constitution; very susceptible to injury; liable to sickness or disease; weakly, not strong or robust" (*OED*, delicate, *adj.* II. 8. b.) – the actor, "delicate Ariel" (4.1.49), being of the subtle substance of "a spirit [so] delicate" (1.2.272), "penetrating or [being] pervasive by reason of lack of density" (*OED*, subtle, *adj.* II. 11.) can easily "infect" (1.2.208) this audience with "a fever" (1.2.209). From above, the stage-managing playwright watches and prompts these processes. The authority of "god o'th' island" provides him with the power of "temporal royalties", the power to initiate (not necessarily to accomplish!) the weathery temperance that takes place in-between actors and audience, that crosses the pragmatic seam. We will see that whenever we hear of the "subtleties o'th' isle" (5.1.124) or its "quality o'th' climate" (2.1.200) in the course of *The Tempest*, the elaborate analogy of theatre and weather is referred to: not as a mere metaphor, but, as the humoral innuendoes of "subtleties" and "quality" ("In early use: † = humour *n.* 2b" (*OED*, quality, *n.* II. 7. a.)) indicate, with the tempering efficacy of theatre as weather in mind.

A few lines later, Adrian continues his observations about the island's climate:

Adrian: The air breathes upon us here most sweetly.
Sebastian: As if it had lungs, and rotten ones.
Antonio: Or as 'twere perfumed by a fen. (2.1.49–51)

As we have already noted above, this line of Adrian's echoes the "sweet airs" that had welcomed Ferdinand to the island, and establishes the analogy of (musical) performance and the phenomena of weather by indicating the pun on the polysemous *air*. It is no coincidence that all the explicit keys to the analogy of weather and theatre are put into Adrian's mouth: his is neutral voice, in fact, he is not established as a discernible character at all. In quoting what he has to say about the island's weather we have quoted more than half his lines. Apart from the island's climate, he utters some words in the court party's discussion about Claribel in Tunis, and here Adrian adds the correct and learned information to the discussion's comparison of Claribel with Dido that the latter "was of

Carthage, not of Tunis" (2.1.83). If this tells us anything about Adrian, then that he is not as naïve as Gonzalo and not as cynical as Antonio and Sebastian. If it was not for this neutrality, for his not being established as a dramatic character at all, the part of Adrian would be highly superfluous. However, the message to be conveyed seems to have been too important and fragile to tinge it with a character's humoral status.

Sebastian's and Antonio's replies to Adrian's praising the island's "air" that "breathes upon" them "most sweetly" underlines the metatheatrical reading that we have suggested of the island's clime: as John Gillies has noted, their contradicting Adrian's "sweet air", rather smelling the stink of "a fen", is a "theatrical joke at the expense of the audience who 'breathe' upon the stage castaways with their collectively 'rotten lungs'" (1986, 682). This "theatrical joke" quite wittily inverts the double entendre of *pneuma* (linking wind and human breath) that we have identified as an important pillar of the play's analogy of theatre and weather. Whereas the tempest scene and the passages following it had, as we have shown, used the notion of *pneuma* to establish an analogy of theatrical spectacle and dramatic speech in order to give an account of the 'stage side' of theatre's pragmatic seam, the notion of 'windy breath' is here employed for the 'audience side'.

Obviously, the audience participates in the island's climate as well. Especially the groundlings in their "fen", known according to "a common trope" (Bruster 2001, 260) for 'airing their lungs' with "windy shouts", surely not only "of acclaim" (Bruster 2001, 260) seem to be hinted at with this theatrical joke. The fact that this breath, crossing the pragmatic seam from audience to stage, smells "as 'twere perfumed by a fen" links this joke to an important topos of the play: as John Gillies has noted, the "'fen' imagery [is] a ubiquitous mirror of intemperance", one of the "two most important symbolic loci of intemperance in the play" (Gillies 1986, 684), the other being the sea. The audience's participation in the climate of the island is in this instance clearly marked as an action of distemperance. The epilogue will indicate the opposite pole of the viewers' contribution to the theatrical climate, by telling them that "Gentle breath of yours my sails | Must fill" (Epilogue, 11), asking for temperance. Like the windy breath of spectacle, exposing both its distempering, tempestuous (the tempest scene), as well as its tempering, harmonious side (Ariel's music, the marriage masque), the audience's breath is presented in its complete range from the distemperance of fens (disturbance of the play) to the temperance of winds driving the theatrical sailing ship (shouts of acclaim, applause for the actors).

However, the audience's "intensive cooperation" (Bruster 2001, 260) in the island's climate is not limited to the "windy shouts" to which Sebastian's and Antonio's theatrical joke, or the epilogue's address to the audience refer. The whole passage, starting with the unsettling contradictoriness that haunts Adrian's initial statement, is concerned with the audience's cooperation in a theatrical event; the metatheatrical joke we have just analysed merely sets us on the right track to relate this question of cooperation to the metatheatrical question of the island's climate. Let us again have a look at Adrian's first, repeatedly interrupted, sentence: "Though this island seem to be desert – | [...] | Uninhabitable and almost inaccessible – | [...] | Yet – | [...] | It must needs be of subtle, tender and delicate temperance." (2.1.37–45) How does he come to the conclusion that the island "must needs be of subtle, tender and delicate temperance"?

The fact that "Adrian, Gonzalo, Sebastian, and Antonio cannot agree about the nature of the island" (Sousa 2001, 450) seems to provide us with the possibility of finding the reason for Adrian's conclusion in the fictional world of the island, an island that may not prove to be as "desert" and "Uninhabitable" as it seemed to Adrian at first glance:

Gonzalo:	Here is everything advantageous to life.
Antonio:	True, save means to live.
Sebastian:	Of that there's none, or little.
Gonzalo:	How lush and lusty the grass looks! How green!
Antonio:	The ground indeed is tawny.
Sebastian:	With an eye of green in't. (2.1.52–57)

However, taking sides with Gonzalo and reading the island's climate as tropical, green and "advantageous to life" in its abundance, as Wolfgang Clemen has done (cf. Flagstad 1986, Fitz 1975) is neither a less, nor more convincing argument than L. T. Fitz's reading the island as "bare" and covered by "nothing but uncultivated grass" (1975, 43). A strange, fundamental contradictoriness seems to characterise this island:

> This alien habitat seems to have few trees and yet yields thousands of logs; it has a scarcity of food and fresh water, and yet it sustains human life. It seems to be a wasteland, and yet has great natural resources (Sousa 2001, 451).

Karen Flagstad has found a source for this "question insistently raised (but left open) by the play": she identified the play's unsolvable question of whether the island "is a green world or a wasteland" as reflecting "a fundamental contradiction inherent in the collective text of contemporary travel accounts" (1986, 221). Her reading of one of the play's important topoi thus very much resembles John Gillies's reading of the topos of temperance: he too identifies this topos as an important one in contemporary colonial accounts, in his case specifically of "the discursive portrait of Virginia" (1986, 683). I think it important to keep this connection to colonial writing in mind, and will come back to it in due course. However, it is not enough simply to mark this connection in order to account for these central topoi or loci in *The Tempest*. No matter how familiar these early overseas colonial and travel accounts were to the audience of London's theatres at the beginning of the 17th century, merely reflecting this "external context" (Gillies 1986, 700) is too weak a link as to explain the specific theatrical experience that Shakespeare creates from these two topoi in the play. Unlike John Gillies I do not maintain that the topos of temperance (and this holds true for the contradictoriness of the island's climate as well) is "external rather than internal to the play's essential nature" (Gillies 1986, 700). On the contrary, these two topoi negotiate the very nature of *The Tempest* as a stage play. Both, Karen Flagstad as well as John Gillies miss the metatheatrical significance of the topoi they so thoroughly analysed by linking them to colonial discourse.

The court party's apparently so superfluous and irrelevant discussion about the climate of the island links these two topoi and relates them to a significant contribution of the audience to this climate. Gonzalo's and Antonio's disagreement about whether the island's ground is "green", covered by "lush and lusty [...] grass" or "tawny" is not merely a disagreement about the qualities of the fictional world, but about the dramatic constitution of this fictional world. It addresses a problem of crossing the pragmatic seam that is characteristic of early modern theatre: the stage on which the actors playing Gonzalo and Antonio are standing is wooden, and as such "tawny", "brown with a preponderance of yellow or orange" (*OED*, tawny, *adj.*). This stage is now supposed to be representing the island on which the castaways have been washed ashore: in early modern theatre that did not make use of scenery, this representation was mainly the task of the audience's "imaginary forces" (*H5*, Prologue, 18), guided by some hints of the play's text, as in Sir Philip Sidney's lively description in his *An Apologie for Poetry*:

> Now ye shal have three Ladies, walke to gather flowers, & then wee must beleeve the stage to be a Garden. By & by, we heare newes of shipwracke in the same place, and then wee are to blame, if we accept it not for a Rock.
>
> Upon the backe of that, comes out a hidious Monster, with fire and smoke, and then the miserable beholders, are bounde to take it for a Cave. While in the mean-time, two Armies flye in, represented with foure swords and bucklers, & then what harde heart wil not receive it for a pitched fielde? (1595, [no pagination])

In the scene we are reading, Shakespeare plays with Antonio's and Gonzalo's being audience and stage characters at the same time. As an audience that arrives on the scene of Prospero's spectacles, their "filling the gaps" (Dessen 1980, 6) of this yet uncharacterised fictional island with their imagination brings forth very different results. Whereas Gonzalo's rich imagination lets him revel in the lushness of a tropical paradise, Antonio seems to reject any use of his imagination, seeing the stage as what it is – a tawny, wooden structure, without "any means to live". The result for us, the audience, is highly paradoxical: Gonzalo and Antonio, as stage characters, are to provide the audience with hints that guide how it imagines the island. However, as a result of their quarrelling over the island's climate, which they (as a stage audience), had to imagine as well, these hints are so contradictory that it is no longer possible for the 'real' audience to imagine the scenery. In the end, this dysfunction, this breaking down of our imaginary contribution to the theatrical constitution of this scene, is evidence of the spectators' conventional and active involvement in this crucial process.

The scene provides the key to a kind of running gag that keeps surfacing throughout the play. Its first instance, although quite obscure, may be Gonzalo's pleading for solid ground at the end of the tempest scene, when the shipwreck has become inevitable: "Now would I give a thousand furlongs of sea for an acre of barren ground – long heath, brown furze, anything. [...]" (1.1.65–67). Gabriel Egan points to the homophony of what the folio text prints as "firrs" that could both signify the "furze" that the Ard³ editors very convincingly emend, and the brown firs, referring to the very "shaped boards" of the stage on which the actor playing Gonzalo is standing:

> If Gonzalo is referring to the playhouse fabric just as the scene closes then his wish acquires the ironic overtone of wanting to be anywhere but the dramatic location (aboard ship), including being where he actually is, standing on the stage. This would give the opening scene of *The Tempest* the same quality as the analogous Dover Cliff scene (Egan 2006, 153–154).

The pun referring both to a possible ground covering in the fictional world and the brown ground of the wooden stage is very similar to Gonzalo's and Antonio's discussion about the island's ground covering, tawny or green, two scenes later, almost too similar to be pure coincidence.

Gabriel Egan has, like George Slover (1978, 194), found another instance that metatheatrically makes fun of the stage's double nature as a location of the fictional world and a concrete location in London: Trinculo's "Were I in England now (as once I was) and had but this fish painted, not a holiday fool there but would give a piece of silver." (2.2.27–29). In a sense, he was in England "now", and a lot of fools, all the London playgoers, had given at least a piece of silver, the entrance fee for the pits, or more, for the galleries, to see "this fish".

The masque play-within-the-play provides us with another version of what we have called the running gag of the interplay between stage and audience in the constitution of the fictional world. Kevin R. McNamara addresses an important point when he emphasises the fact that unlike the court masques written by Ben Jonson or others and furnished with sumptuous scenery as of Inigo Jones, the scenery of Prospero's masque has to be "conveyed by word-painting" (1987, 186). Against the background of Gonzalo's arguing with Antonio about the green- or 'tawnyness' of the island's ground, the masque's insistence on the 'word-paint' of its scene as taking place on green grass is striking: "Here on this grass-plot, in this very place" (4.1.73), "hither, to this short-grassed green" (4.1.83), "on this green land" (4.1.130). This time the hints guiding the audience's "imaginary forces" are strong and unambiguous. No wonder that they prove successful: not only the stage spectator Ferdinand's reaction, claiming to see "paradise" (4.1.124), but also John Gillies's conjecture that "possibly a green carpet" (1986, 691) served as a prop and reference for the ubiquitous demonstratives "this" testifies to the efficacy of these hints. I do not assume there was such a carpet – and if there were one, the groundlings from their low standpoint could not have been able to see it anyway. There is no need for that carpet, because for the groundlings as for John Gillies, the textual hints suffice to imagine the grassy scenery (or even a green carpet). It is this "cooperation" that "[b]oth Prospero's show and Shakespeare's [play] demand […] to sustain 'our spell'" (Slover 1978, 192); more than that, it is this cooperation that the play exhibits. When Prospero's "charms are all o'erthown" (Epilogue, 1), and that is, as we have learned, also a result of our not sustaining this "spell" any longer with our "imaginary forces", the island becomes "bare" (Epilogue, 8), indistinguishable from the bare stage (cf. McNamara 1987, 187).

With this background we are now capable of understanding what Adrian actually says when he babbles about the island's "delicate temperance": There is no contradiction between the island's "seem[ing] to be desert" and its "subtle, tender and delicate temperance". On the contrary, its delicate temperance follows from the island's being desert – from its being a bare, early modern platform stage. All that is conjured up on this stage, the island's lushness, Prospero's spectacles, Trinculo's clownery, the masque's scenery, is of a different, a rather 'insubstantial', "subtle" substance: it is the product of a cooperation between the actor-spirits on stage, typified by the "airy spirit" Ariel, and the audience's spirits of imagination. This "airy charm" (5.1.54) of an early modern stage play, of an "insubstantial pageant" (4.1.155) that "melt[s] into air, into thin air" (4.1.150) after three hours thus "must needs be of subtle, tender and delicate temperance": the "action or fact of tempering; mingling or combining in due proportion, adjusting, moderating, modification, toning down, bringing into a temperate or moderate state" (*OED*, temperance, *n.* II. †3. a.) the subtle substances of these spirits, crossing theatre's pragmatic seam of audience and stage, is what the play metatheatrically negotiates under the heading of 'the climate of the island'.

We learn another important thing from the court party's discussion about the island's climate: the island's "delicate temperance" is not an affair of only two, abstract, uniform 'spirits', one of the spectacle's actors, one of the audience's imagination, but a process dependent on individual humours. A rather mysterious comment made by Sebastian to Antonio's and Gonzalo's disagreement about the isle's climate and ground covering has been cause for conjecture: his "With an eye of green in't." (2.1.57) that answers Antonio's claim that "The ground is tawny" (2.1.56). What does Sebastian's comment mean? As the Ard³ editors gloss, the *OED* "credits the first application of 'eye' as 'Slight shade, tinge' to this line" (cf. *OED*, eye, *n.1*, †II. 9. a.). Does Sebastian offer a sort of compromise between Gonzalo's viewing the island as lush and green and Antonio's emphasising its tawny barrenness? This slight concession, mainly confirming Antonio's observation, but admitting to Gonzalo's claim also a very limited amount of truth, would mirror Sebastian's first contribution to this discussion, "Of that there's none, or little". However, the formulation "an eye of green" is too unfamiliar as to merely express a "Slight shade, tinge" of green discernible in the more or less tawny ground. I would suggest that "an eye of green" refers to the viewer whose eye perceives this "tinge", "expressing the disposition or feeling of the person looking" (*OED*, eye, *n.1*, 5. c.). Thus Sebastian does not so much refer to the ground itself, but to the viewers perceiving it, so that the "eye of green in't" is Gonzalo's, so to speak, only "an eye", since the others' eyes, Antonio's and probably also Sebastian's, see only the barren, wooden, tawny stage. Their cynical, unfeeling, humoral state thus contributes in a very different way to the island's "delicate temperance", producing a very different climate of the isle than Gonzalo's sympathetic humour. Shakespeare can express this dependence of the island's temperance, and that is to say, of the theatrical effect, on the humoral status of every single viewer only by passing the talk about the island's climate on from Adrian to Gonzalo. Adrian's neutrality, his not being portrayed as a character with a certain humoral disposition makes him the perfect choice to convey the important key information, the abstract facts to the audience, to provide it with the frame that is needed to understand the characters' debates. Gonzalo's, Antonio's and Sebastian's different 'inner weather' is however much better suited to further characterise the island's "delicate temperance":

Gonzalo:	[...] You rub the sore
	When you should bring the plaster.
Sebastian:	Very well.
Antonio:	And most chirurgeonly!
Gonzalo:	It is foul weather in us all, good sir,
	When you are cloudy.
Sebastian:	Foul Weather?
Antonio:	Very foul. (2.1.139–143)

As will turn out only slightly later, Alonso's inner cloudiness, his foul 'inner weather' is not shared by all the members of the court party. His misery rather gives Antonio "[t]h'occasion" (2.1.207) to "teach" Sebastian's "standing water", "how to flow" (2.1.221–222), making an end of Sebastian's "hereditary sloth" that "instruct[ed] him "To ebb" (2.1.222–223) in terms of dynastic claims. Without ever learning about their attempt at usurpation, Gonzalo very early senses Sebastian's and Antonio's deviating 'inner weather' – his trying to cover the fact that Antonio and Sebastian prefer "rub[bing] the sore" instead of "bring [ing] the plaster" with the avowal of sympathy with Alonso's "foul weather" spoken in the name of everyone is helpless, at best. However, Gonzalo's avowal and the medical vocabulary in which he puts his observation of Sebastian's unsympathetic behaviour is an occasion the play uses to spell out a connection that we have taken for granted in our previous discussions of the play: the connection of humoral status and weather. Similar to Adrian's exposing the key terms of "delicate temperance", the key terms of an inner, humoral "foul weather" are repeated by Sebastian and Antonio, so that they cannot be missed by the audience. The semantic isotopy of medicine/health ("sore", "plaster", "chirurgeonly") makes us also susceptible to the 'medical' meaning of this "foul weather", *foul* connoting "Of a disease or a person affected with disease" (*OED*, foul, *adj*. I. 1. b.) or "Charged with defiling or noxious matter" (*OED*, foul, *adj*. II. 4. a.) thus also transporting the infecting nature of "Unfavourable; wet and stormy" (*OED*, foul, *adj*. III. 15.) weather. Sebastian's reaction to Gonzalo's avowal, his "Foul weather?" seems to question, undermine, and reject it; Antonio's "Very foul" rather cynically confirms and probably displaces the meaning of *foul* towards a more aggressive tone that foreshadows his revolutionary plans.

The differences in 'inner weather' that this scene indicates contributes productively to establishing the climate of the play in two ways: (1) On the level of plot and characters it provides a situation of crisis, analogous to the tempestuous outer weather and creates the very theatrical possibility of using this crisis to 'plot' one's own future, "to perform an act | Whereof what's past is prologue, what to come | In yours and my discharge!" (2.1.252–254), as Antonio puts it. This level is reminiscent of the famous and weathery "fair is foul and foul is fair | Hover through the fog and filthy air" (*Mac.*, 1.1.10–11) from *Macbeth*. (2) On the level of stage and audience, the one concerned with crossings of the theatre's pragmatic seam, we have learned that the island's climate, its green lushness or barrenness is dependent on the viewer's individual inner weather. The "delicate temperance" of the island's climate that Adrian evokes is thus created as an interaction of the spectacle's outer and the viewers' inner weather.

7 Gonzalo's plantation and Prospero's masque

The newly arrived characters' lengthy discussions about the climate of the island are interrupted by a strange and very prominent interlude: Gonzalo's utopic vision of an ideal commonwealth. It is no coincidence that our analysis has evaded, 'circumvented' this interlude; we have found rich material for our interest in the weather in the direct vicinity of it, but Gonzalo's vision itself is conspicuously free from any weather at all, at least at first glance. Moreover, with regard to the abundance of weather-related material in *The Tempest*, there is no need to read the weather into one of the few passages where it obviously does not surface. However, I agree with Dean Ebner that Gonzalo's utopia "is central to an understanding of the play" (1965, 164), in so far as "Gonzalo's commonwealth has the dramatic function of raising questions about Prospero's" (Seiden 1970, 16). It is these vital connections to *The Tempest*'s web, especially to Prospero's "present fancies" (4.1.122) of the betrothal masque, that establish Gonzalo's 'unweathery' utopia as an important reference point for *The Tempest*'s reflections on theatre and weather. Despite the complete thematic absence of weather in the vision itself, this reference to the play's theme of climate and tempering does not come as an intellectual sophistry perceivable only to the expert who re-reads the play for the fifth time in her ivory tower: the framing of the utopic vision, its position as an abrupt interlude motivated by the characters' lively discussions on the island's climate clearly marks its relation to the theme of weather:

> *Gonzalo:* It is foul weather in us all, good sir,
> When you are cloudy.
>
> *Sebastian:* Foul weather?
>
> *Antonio:* Very foul.
>
> *Gonzalo:* Had I plantation of this isle, my lord –
>
> *Antonio:* He'd sow't with nettle-seed.
>
> *Sebastian:* Or docks, or mallows. (2.1.142–145)

Gonzalo's talking of his utopic commonwealth as a "plantation" continues the argument on the island's barrenness or fertility, an argument, as we have seen, that was deeply steeped in metatheatrical discussions. Antonio and Sebastian naturally insist on their opinion of the island's barrenness by hinting at the 'agricultural' meaning of *plantation*, signifying "The action of planting seeds or plants in the ground" (*OED*, plantation, *n.* 2. a.) and suggesting sowing seeds of plants characteristic for waste, uncultivated ground. However, similar to their sarcastic comments before, Antonio's and Sebastian's playing with words is more than mere feeble punning: their comments further a semantic level that was already prominent in Gonzalo's choice of the word "plantation", a semantic dimension that due to Antonio's and Sebastian's remarks cannot now be missed by the spectator. *Plantation* in the sense of "The settling of people, usually in a conquered or dominated country; *esp.* the planting or establishing of a colony" is not only a synonym for "colonization" (*OED*, plantation, *n.* 2. b.), it also parallels and thereby 'translates' the etymology of *colony* into English: "Middle English *colonie*, < (partly through Old French *colonie*) Latin colōnia, < colōnus tiller, farmer, cultivator, planter, settler in a new country" (*OED*, colony, *n.* Etymology) (cf. Strier 1999, 18). This agricultural etymology of *plantation/colony* is important, because it reveals the central paradox that haunts Gonzalo's utopic commonwealth: his "plantation" is a place characteristically devoid of planting:

> Gonzalo: Letters should not be known; riches, poverty
> And use of service, none; contract, succession,
> Bourn, bound of land, tilth, vineyard – none;
> No use of metal, corn, or wine or oil; (2.1.151–154)

Despite its being positioned in the midst of a seemingly random enumeration, the absence of "tilth" in Gonzalo's "plantation" is not just any article among others. As has been extensively noted in criticism, Shakespeare takes most of the articles of Gonzalo's list verbatim from John Florio's translation of Michel de Montaigne's essay "Of the Caniballes". There we find a similar list that is presented as an answer to Plato's political utopia developed in *The Republic*:

> It is a nation, would I answer *Plato*, that hath no kinde of traffike, no knowledge of Letters, no intelligence of numbers, no name of magistrate, nor of politike superiorities; no use of service, of riches, or of poverty; no contracts, no successions, no dividences, no occupation but idle, no respect of kinred, but common, no apparrell but naturall, no manuring of lands, no use of wine, corne, or mettle. (Montaigne 1603, 102)

In Montaigne's text, the notion of tilling features as well, but in a more prominent place than as part of a list. It serves as a sort of allegorical motto for the whole political utopia that he finds realised in a far-off country:

in divers fruites of those countries that were never tilled, we shall finde, that in respect of ours they are most excellent, and as delicate unto our taste; there is no reason, arte should gaine the point of honour of our great and puissant mother Nature. (Montaigne 1603, 102)

Gonzalo echoes this motto in his summing up of the core of his imaginary commonwealth, where he relates the fact that the violence of political "arte" is absent from his "plantation" to a particular state of nature:

> Gonzalo: All things in common nature should produce
> Without sweat or endeavour; treason, felony,
> Sword, pike, knife, gun, or need of any engine
> Would I not have; but nature should bring forth
> Of its own kind all foison, all abundance,
> To feed my innocent people. (2.1.160–165)

"[P]uissant mother Nature['s]" abundance remarkably frames the problems of political violence that she effectively prevents: the universal harmony of Gonzalo's commonwealth relies on nothing but a primordial naturalness of abundance. As the Ard[3] editors gloss, Gonzalo gives us a broad hint of a first well-known example for such "innocent people" living in perfect harmony from nature's foison "Without sweat or endeavour":

> 17 Also to Adám he said, Because thou hast obeied the voice of thy wife, and hast eaten of the tre (whereof I commanded thee, saying, Thou shalt not eat of it) cursed *is* the earth for thy sake: in sorowe shalt thou eat of it all the dayes of thy life.
>
> 18 Thornes also, and thystles shal it bring forthe to thee, and thou shalt eat the herbe of the field.
>
> 19 In the sweat of thy face shalt thou eat bread, til thou returne to the earth: for out of it wast thou taken, because thou are dust, and to dust shalt thou returne. (Gen. 3.17–19; Whittingham 1560, 2ᵛ)

Once the "sweat and endeavour" mark Gonzalo's commonwealth as a prelapsarian world, we begin retrospectively to realise that already his talking of a "plantation" carries biblical undertones: "8 And the Lord God planted a garden Eastwarde in Eden, and there he put the man whome he had made" (Gen. 2.8; Whittingham 1560, 1ᵛ). The reasons John Calvin identifies in his commentary on Genesis for the choice of the signifier *garden* provide the apparent link that connects Montaigne's text "Of the Caniballes", Gonzalo's utopian commonwealth and the Bible's prelapsarian world:

> God therefore had planted Paradise, which he had garnished alone with muche pleasantnesse, with plentie of all fruites, and with all maner of the best giftes. For this cause it is called A garden, both because of the pleasantnes of the situation, and also because of the beautie of the forme and fashion. (Calvin 1578, 58–59)

We have already cited above the "divers fruites of those countries that were never tilled" that are "as delicate unto our taste" (Montaigne 1603, 102) as our own agricultural products and that allegorically characterise Montaigne's land of the cannibals. This is a land of "naturall ubertie and fruitefulnesse", that is, in its "plenteous aboundance" (Montaigne 1603, 104), doubtlessly moulded on the biblical garden Eden. From *The Tempest*'s discussions we have learned that nature's "all foison, all abundance" (2.1.164) is a question of the "quality o'th' climate" (2.1.200), of the island's "air breath[ing] [...] most sweetly" (2.1.49), of its "delicate temperance" (2.1.44–45). The same holds true for Montaignes cannibals: "they live in a country of so exceeding pleasant and temperate situation, that as my testimonies have tolde me, it is very rare to see a sicke body amongst them" (Montaigne 1603, 102). Again, one influential model behind this "temperate situation" is the Bible. A passage in the account of the creation has provoked interpretations of the prelapsarian perfect temperance, that is to say of an absence of weather that seems to be alluded to in Montaigne's and Gonzalo's text:

> 5 [...] the Lord God had not caused it to raine upon the earth, nether *was there* a man to til the grounde,
>
> 6 But a myst went up from the earth, and watred all the earth. (Gen. 2.5–6; Whittingham 1560, 1ᵛ)

A gloss in the margins of the Geneva Bible specifies the significance of this absence of raine by characterising drought and rain as means of godly interference applied not as part of nature's perfect order, but "according to [God's] pleasure: "God onely openeth the heavens and shutteth them, he sendeth drought and raine according to his good pleasure." (Whittingham 1560, 1ᵛ) At this prelapsarian point there is no need for wrathful godly interference, since, as another gloss puts it, despite God's now having "finished his creacion, [...] his providence stil watcheth over his creatures and governeth them". Gonzalo's claim that he "would with such perfection govern, sir, | T'excel the Golden Age" (2.1.168–169) adopts this exact notion of prelapsarian perfect governance. The abundance of fruit, the absence of human tilling and the fact that his people are "innocent" (2.1.165) clearly and unmistakably indicate that Gonzalo's commonwealth is an emulation of the biblical prelapsarian world. Shakespeare borrows this constellation from Montaigne's famous essay: here, as well, the state of the land and people is characterised by the important keyword "perfection" (Montaigne 1603, 102). Montaigne further explicates this state of perfection by adding that "lawes of nature do yet commaund them" (Montaigne 1603, 102). The same holds true in Gonzalo's commonwealth: in a world where nature produces "All things [...] | Without sweat or endeavour", "bring[ing] forth | Of its own kind all foison, all abundance", political violence, "treason, felony, | Sword, pike, knife, gun, or need of any engine" (2.1.160–165), are simply not needed. From John Calvin's commentary we learn that, again, this thought derives from the Bible: "Adam being as yet perfect and uncorrupt, had no neede of the lawe" (Calvin 1578, 70).

The state of perfection is a state of perfect temperature. Since there is not yet any intemperance in the world, the notion of temperance cannot really be applied to this prelapsarian setting – perfect *temperature* is not a balancing dynamic temperance, it is a perfect, timeless state:

> And therefore GOD had so tempered them [the humours of man's body] in the first creation of man as was requisite, so that hee woulde have preserved him in a perpetuall life, if by true obedience hee had always beene knit and united unto God his Creatour. But since man fell at variance with God through sinne, all this goodly concorde, which God had placed not onely in mans bodie, but also betweene the rest of his creatures, hath been troubled and turned into discord by meanes of sinne. So that all this goodly temperature and harmonie of the humours in which mans bodie was created was dissolved and broken asunder, and that in such sort that it was never since sounde and perfect in any man, of how good constitution soever hee hath been. (La Primaudaye 1594, 367)

According to John Calvin it is Adam's decisive act of "filthie intemperancie" (Calvin 1578, 61) that disrupts the perfect prelapsarian temperature and creates the rupture between the perfect harmony of the heavenly regions whose "moving [...] is first and everlasting" (Bartholomaeus 1582, 141^v) and "The region Elementall, which is continually subiect to alterations" (Cortés 1630) and "subiect to corruption" (La Primaudaye 1601, 177). As a consequence, the "varietie of tymes in sundry climates" and the "varietie of divers complexions, fourmes, and dispositions of all creatures under the face of heaven" (Cortés 1630, preface) are generated: "the whole order of nature was turned upside downe through mans default" (Calvin 1578, 115). Adam's act of "filthie intemperancie" thus introduces intemperance into the world – and, importantly, this intemperance finds its most immediate and intense expression in the phenomena of weather:

> The intemperature of the aire, yce, thunders, unseasonable raines, drouthe, hailes, and what soever is extraordinarie in the world, are the fruites of sinne. (Calvin 1578, 114)

As Andreas Höfele has shown in his article "Raising Tempests: Religion, Science, and the Magic of Theatre" (Höfele 2006), the theological role of weather as a manifestation of man's fall and god's intervention in a postlapsarian world was ubiquitous in the dogma preached at the time. However, it is mainly the glosses of the Geneva Bible that contain this interpretation; the text itself, except for the passage in the account of the creation we have cited above, does not really prominently elaborate on the link of the fall and the introduction of (heavy) weather. That is why Gonzalo, despite the unmistakable allusions presented above, does not explicitly refer to the Bible's garden of Eden, but to another well-known rendering of perhaps the same, or at least a closely related, myth: "I would with such perfection govern, sir, | T'excel the Golden Age" (2.1.168–169). In Ovid's version of the golden age myth that Shakespeare was definitely familiar with it is the weather that marks the difference between "the golden age, which of it selfe maintainde, | The truth and right of every thing unforct and unconstrainde" (Ovid 1567, 2^r) and the ensuing silver age:

> There was no feare of punishment, there was no threatning lawe
> In brazen tables nayled up, to keepe the folke in awe.
> There was no man would crouch or creepe to Judge with cap in hand,
> They lived safe without a Judge, in everie Realme and lande.
> [...]
> The fertile earth as yet was free, untoucht of spade or plough,
> And yet it yeelded of it selfe of every things inough.
> And men themselves contented well with plaine and simple foode,
> That on the earth of natures gift without their travell stoode,
> [...]
> The Springtime lasted all the yeare, and Zephyr with his milde
> And gentle blast did cherish things that grew of owne accorde,
> The ground untilde, all kinde of fruits did plenteously avorde.
> [...]
> The rule and charge of all the worlde was under Jove unjust,
> And that the silver age came in, more somewhat base than golde,
> More precious yet than freckled brasse, immediatly the olde
> And aunciant Spring did Jove abridge, and made therof anon,
> Foure seasons: Winter, Sommer, Spring, and Autumne of and on.
> Then first of all began the ayre with fervent heate to swelt.
> Then *Isycles* hung roping downe: then for the colde was felt
> Men gan to shroud themselves in house. their houses were the thickes,
> And bushie queaches, hollow caves, or hardels made of stickes.
> The first of all were furowes drawne, and corne was cast in ground.
> The simple Oxe with sorie sighes, to heavie yoke was bound. (Ovid 1567, 2^r–2^v)

In Ovid's text we find all the important components that we already identified as connecting Gonzalo's speech to contemporary Bible-commentary: (1) absence of law, (2) absence of tilling and labour, (3) natural abundance of fruit. The golden age myth might not give as thorough an account of the fact of Gonzalo's people's being "innocent" (2.1.165) as the one in the Bible. However, its linking the end of the golden age with the introduction of the "Foure seasons" and their particular phenomena of weather provides us with the decisive key for understanding the relation of Gonzalo's utopian commonwealth to *The Tempest* as a whole: the *absence* of seasons (lat. *tempestates*), the perfect, stable temperature that characterises the golden, paradisiacal age of Gonzalo's commonwealth, defines it as a sort of counterpart to the theatrical world tellingly subsumed under the play's title *"The Tempest"*.

Josuah Sylvester's widely circulated translation of Guillaume de Salluste Du Bartas's didactic poem *La Sepmaine ou Création du monde* (1578) helps to understand this crucial relation. Du Bartas's poem mixes notions of the Bible and of ancient (Greek or Latin) mythology in exactly the way we have done in our analysis of Gonzalo's utopian commonwealth, giving us an idea of the syncretistic understanding of the world common in early modern times. The first passage I would like to quote describes the golden, paradisiacal state that might have inspired Gonzalo for his vision of an ideal commonwealth:

> If there I say the Sunne (the Seasons stinter)
> Made no hot Sommer, nor no hoarie Winter,
> But lovely VER kept still in lively lustre
> The fragrant Valleys smiling Meades and Pasture:
> That boistrous *Adams* body did not shrinke
> For Northren winds, nor for the Southern winke:
> But *Zephyr* did sweet muskie sighes afford,
> Which breathing through the Garden of the Lord,
> Gave bodies vigour, verdure to the field,
> That verdure flowers, those flowers sweet savor yield:
> That day did gladly send his sister night,
> For halfe her moisture, halfe his shining Light:
> That never frost, nor snow, nor slipp'rie ice
> The fields enag'd: nor any stormy stower
> Dismounted Mountaines, nor no violent shower
> Poverisht the Land, which frankly did produce
> All fruitfull vapours for delight and use:
> I thinke I lie not, rather I confesse
> My stammering Muses poore unlearnednes.
> If in two words thou wilt her praise comprise,
> Say 'twas the type of th'upper Paradice; (Sylvester 1605, 276)

As already indicated in this account of perfect temperature that mainly works by negating any weathery disruption, Du Bartas sets the state of perfect temperature off from the ensuing corrupted ages that are defined by their intemperance of weather:

> Heav'n, that still smiling on his Paramoure
> Still in her lap did *Mel* and *Manna* poure,
> Now with his haile, his raine, his frost and heate,
> Doth partch, and pinch, and over-whelme, and beate,
> And hores her head with Snowes, and (ielous) dashes
> Against her browes his fierie lightning flashes. (Sylvester 1605, 330)

Remarkably, *The Tempest* alludes to both these notions of perfect, provident temperature and of punishing distemperance. It is in the mode of dream, which is not reconcilable with reality, that the notion of provident perfection is actualised:

> Caliban: [...] in dreaming,
> The clouds, methought, would open and show riches
> Ready to drop upon me, that when I waked
> I cried to dream again. (3.2.139–143)

Like the "smiling" "Heav'n" of Du Bartas's paradisiacal world that "*poure[s]*" "Mel and Manna", Caliban dreams of a sunny sky, revealing "riches | Ready to *drop*". Not coincidentally, both imply a higher, transcendent authority that governs benevolently over the earthly regions. However, Caliban is well aware that the godly intervention he is dreaming of is a nostalgic longing irreconcilable with postlapsarian reality. More than that, the very notion of a godly intervention modelled on the concept of rain (cf. "poure" and "drop"), of a *weathery* intervention, is not compatible with the state of paradisiacal perfect temperature: God's nourishing his people with Manna is not an episode of Adam and Eve in the fruitful garden of Eden, but of the murmuring, highly malcontent people's march through seemingly endless deserts (cf. Exodus 16.1–36). Caliban is one of the few characters who knows that a rather wrathful authority is watching over him, an authority whose punishment is very consistently characterised by the verb *to pinch*:

> Prospero: [...] thou shalt be *pinched*
> As thick as honeycomb, each *pinch* more stinging
> Than bees that made 'em. (1.2.329–313; emph. J.U.)
>
> Caliban: [...] His spirits hear me,
> And yet I needs must curse. But they'll nor *pinch*,
> Fright me with urchin-shows, pitch me i'th' mire,
> Nor lead me, like a firebrand in the dark,
> Out of my way unless he bid 'em. (2.2.3–7; emph. J.U.)
>
> Caliban: [...] If he awake,
> From toe to crown he'll fill our skins with *pinches*,
> Make us strange stuff. (4.1.233–235; emph. J.U.)
>
> Prospero: Go, charge my goblins that they grind their joints
> With dry convulsions, shorten up their sinews
> With aged cramps, and more *pinch*-spotted make them
> Than pard or cat o'mountain. (4.1.258–261; emph. J.U.)
>
> Prospero: Thou art *pinched* for't now, Sebastian! – Flesh and blood,
> You, brother mine, that entertained ambition,
> Expelled remorse and nature, whom Sebastian
> (Whose inward *pinches* therefore are most strong)
> Would here have killed your king (5.1.74–78; emph. J.U.)
>
> Caliban: I shall be *pinched* to death (5.1.276; emph. J.U.)

It does not seem to be a coincidence that this verb carries innuendoes of political violence and torture, notions, as Richard Strier (1999) and Curt Breight (1990) have shown, that are inseparable from Prospero's political 'handling' of treason. At the same time *to pinch* is one of the verbs that Sylvester chooses in his translation of Du Bartas to render God's wrathful weathery interventions in the postlapsarian world:

> Now with his haile, his raine, his frost and heate,
> Doth partch, and *pinch*, and over-whelme, and beate,
> And hores her head with Snowes, and (ielous) dashes
> Against her browes his fierie lightning flashes. (Sylvester 1605, 330; emph. J.U.)

In his famous "Ye elves"-speech Prospero himself stylises his powerful and violent interventions in very similar terms – in terms of weather:

> *Prospero:* [...] I have bedimmed
> The noontide sun, called forth the mutinous winds,
> And 'twixt the green sea and the azured vault
> Set roaring war; to the dread-rattling thunder
> Have I given fire and rifted Jove's stout oak
> With his own bolt: the strong-based promontory
> Have I made shake, and by the spurs plucked up
> The pine and cedar; graves at my command
> Have waked their sleepers, ope'd and let 'em forth
> By my so potent art. (5.1.41–50)

It is not difficult to find in this speech allusions to what the audience has seen on stage or at least heard talked about in the previous two and a half hours: not only the tempest scene's "mutinous winds", the "roaring war" "'twixt the green sea and the azured vault" that Miranda had experienced as a "roar" of the "wild waters" "mounting to th' welkin's cheek" of the sky (1.2.2–5), but also Ariel's being imprisoned in the "rift" of "a cloven pine" (1.2.277) of which only Prospero's "art" (1.2.291) could free him, as well as Prospero's threatening Ariel to "rend an oak" and "peg [him] in his knotty entrails" (1.2.294–295). Prospero's interventions are paradigmatically the interventions of an age that is defined by the introduction of weathery seasons, of *tempestates*, and are therefore diametrically opposed to Gonzalo's paradisiacal golden age utopia that envisions a prelapsarian, weather-free world of perfect temperature.

Astonishingly enough, Du Bartas chooses for his narration of the transition from Paradise to our postlapsarian world a vignette that must appear very familiar to viewers of *The Tempest*: "The tumbling Sea, the Ayre with tempests driven" (Sylvester 1605, 332) provide the scenery for a shipwreck:

> But mortall *Adam*, Monarch heere beneath,
> Erring, draws all into the pathes of death;
> And on rough Seas, as a blind Pylot rash,
> Against the rock of Heav'ns just wrath doth dash
> The Worlds great Vessel, sailing yerst at ease,
> With gentle gales, good guide, on quiet Seas. (Sylvester 1605, 331)

Put next to this last verse of Du Bartas's, Prospero's "promis[ing] [the court party] calm seas, auspicious gales" (5.1.315) may take on a religious, Christian tinge; however, whether or not we read the end of the play as "a vision of apocalyptic judgment" (Ide 1991, 116), Prospero's promise aims beyond the play's world. The paradisiacal, perfectly tempered "calm seas, auspicious gales" must remain outside the boundaries of this rather weathery play; his promise provocatively contrasts with the play titled "*The Tempest*".

It is this contrast, this total, utter 'misplacement' that accounts for the comic effect of Gonzalo's utopian vision. What is talked about and made fun of here is however not one single character's exuberant naivety, but a collective fantasy, popularised in the early modern age by prominent personages: as Karen Flagstad notes, both Vespucci and Columbus thought they were "destined to rediscover Eden" (1986, 219), and we know by Sir Thomas More's "own account [that] Vespucci's report provided a direct inspiration for *Utopia* (1516)" (Flagstad 1986, 219). A possible pun discovered by John X. Evans supports the thesis that Shakespeare alludes to and positions himself critically in these debates of colonising America and the political role of utopianism. The lines in question are Alonso's enervated response to Gonzalo's utopian vision:

> *Alonso:*   Prithee, no more.
>   Thou dost talk nothing to me. (2.1.171–172)

Here is what John X. Evans makes of these lines:

> Realizing that the word *Utopia* means "nowhere" (literally, "not a place"), quick and well-educated playgoers in Shakespeare's audience might well have detected a play on words and reconstructed the lines something like this: "Prithee no Thomas MORE. Thou dost talk UTOPIA to me." (Evans 1981, 81)

Although philologically not completely convincing (after all, there is, and remains a difference between "nowhere" and "nothing") the play's overall explicit, critical position towards utopianism fits the punning allusion "no MORE" too neatly to dismiss it as unintended and purely coincidental. Paying closer attention to the contradictions for which Antonio and Sebastian criticise Gonzalo's vision, we would have to say that it is not logically flawed in a way that would make the reality of his vision inconceivable: planting a perfectly tempered garden where there is no law, "No sovereignty" but a king, a "governour", was widely believed as having already been done once and famously documented – in the Bible: God himself had this "plantation", in Gonzalo's words, and it was Him who made Adam "governour and overseer of the garden", "governour" in a world without laws, without political violence. The unsolvable contradictions are obviously contradictions haunting the colonial idea of r*ediscovering* Eden: as Ovid's and Montaigne's accounts state in astonishing accordance, the idea of colonial expansion is characteristically alien to 'the colony's' respective golden age people:

> They contend not for the gaining of new landes; for to this day they yet enjoy that naturall ubertie and fruitefulnesse, which without labouring-toyle, doth in such plenteous aboundance furnish them with all necessary things, that they neede not enlarge their limites. (Montaigne 1603, 104)

> The loftie Pynetree was not hewen from mountaines where it stood,
> In seeking straunge and foren lands, to rove upon the flood.
> Men knew none other countries yet, than where themselves did keepe:
> There was no towne enclosed yet, with walles and diches deepe. (Ovid 1567, 2ᵛ)

In Ovid's account, the shipman, "hoyst[ing] his sailes to wind" is used as the paradigm that serves as a recognizable visual image of all the corruptions, such as political violence and "bound" (2.1.153) of tilled, agricultural land and therefore characterises the most base, the iron age:

> For when that of this wicked Age once opened was the veyne
> Therein all mischief rashed forth. then Fayth and Truth were faine
> And honest shame to hide their heades: for whom stept stoutly in,
> Craft, Treason, Violence, Envie, Pride and wicked Lust to win.
> The shipman hoyst his sailes to wind, whose names he did not knowe:
> And shippes that erst in toppes of hilles and mountaines had ygrowe,
> Did leape and daunce on uncouth waves: and men began to bound,
> With dowles and diches drawen in length the free and fertile ground,
> Which was as common as the Ayre and light of Sunne before. (Ovid 1567, 3ʳ)

The more we follow the traces that are alluded to in Shakespeare's text, traces that give us an idea of the shared background against which the early modern theatre audience viewed *The Tempest*, the more we begin to understand the import of the play's initial storm- and shipwreck-vignette and the wide-ranging implications of its title. In the context of a play as metatheatrical as *The Tempest*, Gonzalo's vision of a weather-free, perfectly tempered "plantation" is more than a critique of the absurd, naïve and contradictory colonial dreams of rediscovering Eden. The reason why Gonzalo's utopia is incompatible with the circumstances of the island, why its seemingly not relating at all to the world he and the others are inhabiting cannot be found simply in his misapprehension of the place he has landed on: on the contrary, as we have tried to show with regard to Columbus, Vespucci and Thomas More, Gonzalo gives voice to a longing widely shared in the early modern world. The cultural diagnosis of the status quo behind this longing provides the common basis for all the texts we have read so far: for Ovid and Calvin, for Montaigne – and for Shakespeare! They all agree, I would suggest, that somehow 'the world is out of joint', that its having lost its perfect temperature (especially expressed by increasing political violence and social disorder) is becoming a problem that has to be urgently confronted.

However, the island on which Gonzalo finds himself stranded is neither the fictional exotic island of a travel account, nor the perfectly tempered world of an epic myth's nostalgic report. The island Gonzalo has landed on is the stage of a theatre. Obviously, this theatrical isle's temperance contrasts with the mythical perfect temperature that Gonzalo dreams of. Nevertheless, this contrast is not inherent in the medium theatre, per se. Gonzalo's utopic vision could well be read as a programmatic theatrical statement: "Had I plantation of this isle, my lord – | [...] And were the king on't, what would I do?" (2.1.144–146) – 'were I in charge of this theatre, writing plays and directing the performances, what would these theatrical displays be like?' They would probably confront their audience with a similar situation to the one that Montaigne's eyewitness experienced when encountering the 'noble' Brazilian indigenous people. We would see a fictional play-world constituting itself as at least closer to perfect temperature as the world outside the theatre walls; the theatre would then be a heterotopic place where a fictional utopia can be attended, at least for a certain amount of time. It could be a place, again analogous to Montaigne's ideas, where we learn about our own corruptions, our own savageness in contrast to the nobleness of the characters – and perhaps leave this heterotopos as morally bettered people. Put in these slightly ironic words, the programmatic theatrical statement (rather Schillerian than early modern!) I imputed to Gonzalo may appear rather ridiculous. However, we have to take this vision of theatre seriously, especially since there is a strong tradition of reading *The Tempest* in exactly this way. David G. Brailow, for example, diagnoses in Prospero a "desire to withdraw from reality, to create a golden world of his own fancy" which finds its most explicit expression in his trying "to create perfect love" (1981, 290). Thomas Bulger follows this interpretation: for him, Ferdinand's and Miranda's love is, "on an individual level", a sort of realisable utopia (1994, 41), and that is why he can rejoice in the fact that "in the final balance, a kind of utopia has been achieved" (1994, 44). Bulger's longing for a utopic, perfect temperature also tinges his reading of the rest of the play: despite the recurring rebellions on the island and Prospero's staged violence against the unruly, Bulger finds that "Under his governance, the island society is free from (or limits) the problems that plague all political states" (1994, 39).

Thomas Bulger is only one, random example of this quite influential tradition – a tradition that cannot be separated from reading *The Tempest* as a 'romance'. This genre label carries the expectations of the "true ordering of the good and real" (Wehrs 2011, 522) and of "effecting changes from discord to harmony" (Mebane 1988, 33) to a theatrical text, and thereby creates mirages of perfect temperature:

> Purity and isolation so great lie beyond any pastoral dream; this is Eden, an unfallen world where the air is full of music, the virgin sand bears no footprint as the spirits dance over it (Bradbrook 2001, 191).

The ambassador, representing this way of reading *The Tempest* in the play's own fictional world is not Prospero – it is Gonzalo. As we have seen above, Prospero's role is intrinsically linked with his acting as the wrathful, punishing, 'postlapsarian' "god o'th' island", as a "god of power" whose interventions usually take the shape of more or less violent weather affecting his victims' tempers. It is this 'Gonzalonian' reading of *The Tempest* as constituting a fictional world of perfect temperature on stage that Alonso's "Prithee, no more!" (2.1.171) explicitly dismisses. The "desire to withdraw from reality" that David G. Brailow, as quoted above, claims for Prospero is in fact Gonzalo's, it is a desire for utopia. In a way, this desire is anti-theatrical: reading *The Tempest* in a Gonzalonian fashion means reading it as a 'romance' – that is to say reading it as if it were a piece of poetry that narrates mythical events of a distant pastoral past or of an ideal pastoral world. In fact, theatre staging the utopian fantasy of a perfectly tempered world would not only "excel the Golden Age" in "perfection" of fictional government (2.1.168–169), as Gonzalo boasts of his (theatre) project, it would rather "exceede all the pictures wherewith licentious Poesie hath prowdly imbellished the golden age" (Montaigne 1603, 102); however, not as Montaigne envisioned by finding this utopia in some Brazilian village, but by acting these pictures out on a London stage.

I have called these staged poetical images anti-theatrical, because despite the possibility of their being staged, their understanding of a representation of perfect temperature does not differ substantially from genuinely poetical forms of *representing* a weather-free world: in Gonzalo's plantation, perfect temperature is a trait of the fictional world, it remains diegetic, it is narratable. Its relation to the non-fictional world outside is one of withdrawal, one of retreat, replacing the weathery factual reality with fictional perfect temperature. In contrast to Gonzalo's plantation, "On Prospero's island, Shakespeare's history of the world is played out, in an abbreviated form. It consists of a struggle for power, murder, revolt and violence" (Kott 1965, 188), Jan Kott rightly observes. It is highly significant, emblematic even, that, as already mentioned above, the characters that function as the stage-audience do not follow the boatswain's command to "Keep [their] cabins" (1.1.14), to "give thanks [they] have lived so long and make [themselves] ready in [their] cabin for the mischance of the hour" (1.1.24–25). They do not withdraw, pray for and dream of Paradise's perfect temperature (dreams shaped by all those "pictures wherewith licentious Poesie hath prowdly imbellished the golden age", and by the huge number of travel accounts leaving the printer's press every day). "Gonzalo's 'commonwealth'[, a] [...] utopian pastoral world where man coexists in perfect harmony with nature and his own kind" (Brailow 1981, 298) is a sort of withdrawal from the realities of the outer world into the pastoral landscapes of the imagination's interior.

It is no coincidence that Gonzalo, facing the first scene's disastrous storm that threatens to wreck their ship would "give a thousand furlongs of sea for an acre of barren ground" (1.1.65–66); this barren, but solid, untossed, weather-free acre offers enough of a platform for his imagination to stage a world of perfect temperature, a world where, as he says, "everything is advantageous to life" (2.1.52), where "the grass looks" "lush and lusty" (2.1.55). However, the theatre audience of Shakespeare's *The Tempest* notices from the start that the stage spectacle it experiences differs fundamentally from what Gonzalo envisions; in coming to the theatre, the viewers have, like the court party of the first scene, decided to expose themselves to heavy weather – no big surprise, going to see *The Tempest*. Are they affected, moved, disturbed in their tempers, as the play's stage audience is? This is one of the main questions that this play raises.

In short: instead of serving as a sterile space for projecting unrealisable utopian fantasies, as an as-blank-as-possible screen in a space as totally screened from the postlapsarian, weathery, imperfect world as possible (in what could be called a 'representational-imaginary mode'), *The Tempest* metatheatrically develops a notion of theatre as a hyper-weathery space: a space of delicate temperance, where the circulation of air and spirits is intensified, where microcosm and macrocosm communicate in an even higher degree than usual; a space where temperance is literally *performed* between the stimuli-generating stage and the audience that believingly assists in giving these stimuli a space of resonance (a 'pragmatic-performative mode').

At first glance, the betrothal masque that Prospero stages seems to resemble Gonzalo's utopian vision: according to critics, it "pictures a fertile paradise reminiscent in some ways of Gonzalo's ideal commonwealth" (Ebner 1965, 170), it performs "a brief withdrawal into the golden age, Gonzalo's dream as magical theater" (Berger 1969, 272), it creates "a golden world, sealed off from all perturbation and flaw" (Gilman 1980, 219), and draws the picture "of a life of pastoral bliss in a timeless Edenic setting" (Lindenbaum 1984, 168). However, apart from the "abundance similar to that Gonzalo earlier assumed" (Lindenbaum 1984, 163), Prospero's masque world differs markedly from Gonzalo's Edenic vision: the masque's very first line, spoken by Iris and addressing Ceres, the goddess of agriculture and fertility, unmistakably differentiates this world from Gonzalo's golden age utopia: "Ceres, most bounteous lady, thy rich leas | Of wheat, rye, barley, vetches, oats and peas" (4.1.60–61), her "bosky acres" (4.1.81) in general, are not compatible at all with Gonzalo's commonwealth that characteristically makes "No use of metal, corn, or wine or oil" (2.1.154) and knows no "tilth" (2.1.153). It is no coincidence that the masque mentions a "pole-clipped vineyard" (4.1.68) that, again, contrasts to Gonzalo's vision that explicitly excludes the "vineyard" (2.1.153) from its world. Significantly enough, the masque tells us that not even the favourite places of the gods are perfectly tempered and paradisiacal in any way: Ceres "air[s]" herself at the "sea-marge, sterile and rocky-hard" (4.1.69).[18] In short, the world of Prospero's masque is not at all Edenic, not at all a world of the golden age's perfect temperature. It is not a setting of "No occupation, all men idle, all" (2.1.155), not, as Melissa E. Sanchez notes, "the typical Jacobean masque setting of a locus amoenus", but "a foisoning plantation that requires apparently endless labor to keep it from rot and excess" (Sanchez 2008, 76). No matter whether the "pion[ing] and twill[ing]" (4.1.64), the "betrim[ming]" (4.1.65) and "clipp[ing]" (4.1.68) is done by 'nature', "spongy April" (4.1.65) or human labourers like the "weary" "sunburned sicklemen" (4.1.134), it does not comply with the paradisiacal *state* of perfect temperature, but indicates a *process* of temperance. The fact that the central theme of Prospero's masque is harvest (and not merely natural abundance of fruits) is founded on this processuality, this temporality of temperance: the life that Prospero's masque depicts is precisely *not* "a life of pastoral bliss in a timeless Edenic setting" (Lindenbaum 1984, 168). As John Demaray rightly describes it,

> All action occurs [...] in a moving masque-like iconographic cosmos composed of the elements of earth, air, fire and water and subject to the movements of the seasons, storms, tides and heavens. (1998, 13)

---

[18] The desertedness of Ceres's earthly residuum probably has to do with the myth of the rape of Proserpine, her daughter: according to Ovid's report in the fifth book of his *Metamorphosis*, Pluto had abducted her into the underworld, and Ceres searching her daughter in vain on earth caused a terrible draught on Sicily when she learned about her rape and abduction (cf. Ovid 1567, 62–65).

The very fact and necessity of composition, of balanced interplay between the gods and their elemental realms marks this world's contrast with the perfect temperature of Eden. If anything, the iconography of Prospero's masque could be said to strive for a "postdiluvian regeneration", as Ruth Nevo has decided to call it:

> Juno, goddess of the rain-bestowing sky, Ceres of the receiving earth, and Iris, the rainbow messenger who joins above and below with promise of a postdiluvian regeneration, a return of the natural cycle of seedtime and harvest (Nevo 1999, 89–90).

However, it is not the "promise of a postdiluvian regeneration" that appears important in these words. (Donald R. Wehrs has a point claiming that "To pray for fertility is to accept mortality" (2011, 564), and we will see in a minute that the deceitful security that this promise might produce is easily misunderstood.) What is of fundamental import in Ruth Nevo's analysis of the masque's iconography is the intermediary role of Iris, "who joins above and below". Iris is between the worlds, a messenger travelling between the heavens and earth – and as a messenger, bridging the gap, she also affirms this very gap, the split between the worlds. The prelapsarian immediacy of heavens and earth, of god and creation, has already been ruptured. As a postlapsarian medium, Iris is "a mythological personification of temperate weather" (Gillies 1986, 686). She "combines the elements of air and water in her rainbow, [...] [s]he is weather in bono where the storm is weather in malo" (Gillies 1986, 686). I agree with John Gillies that the tempest scene and the masque scene correspond in their central 'weatheriness' and that they thereby provide the play with its organising principle and structure.

However, focussing too much on the juxtaposition of storm and shipwreck as initial "intemperance" and Iris and the masque as final "temperance" (Gillies 1986, 687) runs the risk of hypostasising these two poles of the process of (dis)tempering as two substantial, independent states. As tempting as the romance structure of telling a story leading from a disordered to an ordered state of things might be, strengthening this juxtaposition neglects the important difference that separates Prospero's masque from Gonzalo's commonwealth and the important similarity that makes the theatrical events of the first scene's tempest and the late masque correspond. This difference consists of the absence of weather in Gonzalo's imaginary world of perfect temperature and the tempering effect of weathery (theatrical) intervention in the tempest and masque scene. It is important not to forget that Prospero's conjuring up the masque does not merely represent the 'oh so ordered' state of the fictional world near the end of the performance, just as little as the initial storm *represented* disorder. Prospero stages the masque as a strategic (dis)tempering intervention, the same way that he staged the storm – not as beautiful or ugly representations of the respective status quo, but as aiming for a certain effect, for a certain pragmatic force that spectacle is meant to produce.

The betrothal masque is not merely "a celebration of the betrothal of Ferdinand and Miranda" (Gillies 1986, 686) that represents and revels in the harmony of tempers that their love has achieved. On the contrary, from the very start *The Tempest* displays the worryingly distempering effect of love, as for example in Prospero's aside commenting on Ferdinand: "Poor worm, thou art infected!" (3.1.31). The masque is preceded by Prospero's attempting to curb the temperamental side effects of this love-relationship that he "infected" the pair with for dynastic reasons and that now could endanger the honour of his daughter. He does not even shy away from threatening Ferdinand with a curse of distemperance on the lovers' union in the case of premarital sex:

> *Prospero:* [...] But
> If thou dost break her virgin-knot before
> All sanctimonious ceremonies may
> With full and holy rite be ministered,
> No sweet aspersion shall the heavens let fall
> To make this contract grow; but barren hate,
> Sour-eyed disdain and discord shall bestrew
> The union of your bed with weeds so loathly
> That you shall hate it both. (4.1.14–22)

It is not difficult to see in this curse the counterpart to the marriage masque; whereas the masque sketches the promise of fertile temperance, Prospero here voices a threat of barren intemperance. Despite their apparent juxtaposition, both, promise and threat, are different strategies aimed at the same goal, and, more importantly in the same weathery fashion: to temper Ferdinand's passion in order to protect Miranda's honour. However, Prospero does not seem to trust too much in Ferdinand's answer:

> *Ferdinand:* [...] the murkiest den,
> The most opportune place, the strong'st suggestion
> Our worser genius can, shall never melt
> Mine honour into lust to take away
> The edge of that day's celebration (4.1.25–29).

At least, only a few lines before the beginning of the masque, Prospero sees himself forced to renew his warnings, using explicitly temperamental vocabulary, an isotopy that Ferdinand continues in his answer:

Prospero [to Ferdinand]:
>Look thou to be true. Do not give dalliance
>Too much the rein. The strongest oaths are straw
>To th' fire i'th' blood. Be more abstemious
>Or else good night your vow!

Ferdinand: I warrant you, sir,
>The white cold virgin snow upon my heart
>Abates the ardour of my liver. (4.1.51–56)

The masque that sets in at exactly this point mirrors the isotopy of problematic (humoral) heat ("melt", "lust", "straw", "fire", "blood", "ardour of my liver") and the necessity of tempering it with some source of coldness. However, this theme will only start after a caesura, in the masque's second part, so to speak. Interestingly enough, the bipartite structure of the masque has been widely overlooked. The fact that (as Prospero even makes the audience aware), "Juno and Ceres whisper seriously" (4.1.125) in the interval between the parts clearly marks that some sort of problem has arisen; it is in the stage audience's (i.e. Ferdinand's) response to the masque's first part that this problem seems to have surfaced.

Before turning to this problem (and in order to understand it) we have to take a closer look at the masque's initial section. Ferdinand has good reasons for describing it as "a most majestic vision, and | Harmonious charmingly" (4.1.117–118). It does indeed possess or is "characterized by majesty; [it is] of imposing dignity or grandeur; stately" (*OED*, majestic, *adj.*) since it shows us goddesses conversing in a highly stylised manner. The picture of the interplay of their respective elements or realms that these goddesses draw is rightfully called "harmonious": the world of their dialogue is "Marked by harmony, agreement, or concord; [...] having the parts or elements in accord so as to form a consistent or agreeable whole" (*OED*, harmonious, *adj.*). Although the weather is obviously an important, if not the most important, component of this so harmonious setting, this world's delightful temperance and its fertility and abundance seem to approximate the Edenic, weather-free, perfect temperature of Gonzalo's utopia: "Harmonious charmingly", as Ferdinand very rightly calls it, "highly pleasing or delightful to the mind or senses" (*OED*, charming, *adj.* 2. a.). However, almost too delightful to be true, the majesty and harmony of this so well tempered masque world already indicates its magic origin: it is harmonious "Using charms; exercising magic power" (*OED*, charming, *adj.* 1.). The illusory nature of this well-tempered vision even forms a central part of its fictional world; a quarter of the first part's lines are dedicated to assuring and discussing Venus's and Cupid's absence from the scene:

> Ceres: Tell me heavenly bow,
> If Venus or her son as thou dost know,
> Do now attend the queen? Since they did plot
> The means that dusky Dis my daughter got,
> Her and her blind boy's scandaled company
> I have forsworn. (4.1.86–91)

In other words, the masque's world can only be harmonious if Venus and Cupid remain absent. As the viewers familiar with Roman and Greek mythology would immediately notice, the importance of their absence has wider implications for this harmony than a mere personal conflict among gods and goddesses. The story that Ceres alludes to, known as 'The rape of Proserpine', relates the origin of winter and the seasons: Cupid, encouraged by his mother Venus, has shot one of his arrows at Pluto, "dusky Dis", who, as a result, falls in love with Ceres's daughter Proserpine. He rapes her and abducts her into his kingdom, the underworld. Ceres complains about this incident to Jove, Proserpine's father (and Pluto's brother), and is granted the right to divorce her daughter from Pluto, and bring her back from the underworld, under one condition: "But yet conditionly that she have tasted there no foode: | For so the destnies have decreed" (Ovid 1567, 65r). Unfortunately, Proserpine had violated this condition:

> In Plutos Ortyard rechlessely from place to place to stray,
> She gathering from a bowing tree a ripe Pownegarnet, tooke
> Seven kernels out and sucked them. (Ovid 1567, 65r)

In the end, Jove ordains a compromise between his brother Pluto and Ceres, the mother of his daughter:

> But meane betweene his brother and his heavie sister goth
> God Jove, and parteth equally the yeare betweene them both.
> And now the Goddesse Proserpine indifferently doth reigne
> Above and underneath the Earth, and so doth she remaine
> One halfe yeare with hir mother and the resdue with hir Feere
> Immediatly she altred is as well in outwarde cheere
> As inwarde minde. for where hir looke might late before appeere
> Sad even to Dis, hir countnance now is full of mirth and grace
> Even like as Phebus having put the watrie cloudes to chace,
> Doth shew himselfe a Conqueror with bright and shining face. (Ovid 1567, 65v)

In short, Jove's compromise gives an account of the change of seasons, and especially of the barren and uncomfortable winter period. As a consequence, only Venus's and Cupid's absence and the repression of the fact that 'Proserpine's Rape' (as John Gillies notes, in many ways "equivalent to the Christian idea of the fall" (1986, 697)) has already happened, can produce the blessings of the masque that culminate in the two verses spoken by Ceres:

> Spring come to you at the farthest,
> In the very end of harvest. (4.1.114–115)

These words sit very uneasily in Ceres's mouth, who is so intimately connected with Proserpine's, her daughter's, abduction and the introduction of seasons. The situation does not change when we regard the blessings from a Christian viewpoint and interpret rainbow-Iris as the symbol for the postdiluvian promise. As Kevin R. McNamara has shown (1987, 192), this promise outrightly contradicts Ceres's blessing; more than that, her blessing may even sound blasphemous against the Lord's promise to Noah:

> 22 Hereafter sede time & harvest, & colde & heate, & sommer and winter, & daie & night shal not cease, so long as the earth remaineth. (Gen 8.22; Whittingham 1560, 4ᵛ)

If it was indeed "Prospero's attempt to elide winter with the fullness of harvest flowing directly into spring" (McNamara 1987, 192), then Kevin McNamara is right to claim that he "is belated and misguided" (1987, 192). However, the masque's complex and paradoxical staging of its own foundational repression, its lengthy reasoning on Venus's and Cupid's absence, shields it from criticism like McNamara's. By focussing on what has to be excluded in order to achieve a harmoniously tempered world, the masque indicates that temperance cannot be separated from its dialectical double, distemperance. The masque explicitly demonstrates that conjuring up this charmingly harmonious world implies spiriting away the distempering forces of Venus and Cupid.

Iris, however, not only relates the happy coincidence of Venus's and Cupid's absence, her account ends with Cupid's abjuring his amorous activities:

> *Iris:*   Of her society
> Be not afraid. I met her deity
> Cutting the clouds towards Paphos, and her son
> Dove-drawn with her. Here thought they to have done
> Some wanton charm upon this man and maid,
> Whose vows are that no bed-right shall be paid
> Till Hymen's torch be lighted, but in vain.
> Mars's hot minion is returned again;
> Her waspish-headed son has broke his arrows,
> Swears he will shoot no more, but play with sparrows
> And be a boy right out. (4.1.91–101)

The picture of Cupid breaking his arrows and playing with sparrows is of such a parodying and satirical tinge that it does not, at least to my understanding, comply with the "majestic" register of the masque's celebratory blessings. And, what is more, Cupid's "wanton charm" and the fact that he "broke his arrows" reflect and foreshadow in an uncanny way Prospero's magic (theatrical) interferences and his abjuration:

> *Prospero:* [...] But this rough magic
> I here abjure; and when I have required
> Some heavenly music (which now I do)
> To work mine end upon their senses that
> This airy charm is for, I'll break my staff,
> Bury it certain fathoms in the earth,
> And deeper than did ever plummet sound
> I'll drown my book. (5.1.50–57)

In this light, read together with Prospero's "airy charm", the choice of words in "wanton charm" that Venus and Cupid "thought [...] to have done" on Ferdinand and Miranda takes on some interesting meaning. Without doubt the charm that Cupid and Venus are famous for is characterised by the adjective *wanton* in its meaning "Lascivious, unchaste, lewd. †Also, in milder sense, given to amorous dalliance" (*OED*, wanton, *adj.* 2.). Cupid's concluding decision to "be a boy right out" activates a second, the basic, meaning of *wanton*, signifying "Of persons: Undisciplined, ungoverned; not amenable to control, unmanageable, rebellious. Of children: Naughty, unruly" (*OED*, wanton, *adj.* †1. a.). Shakespeare's perhaps most famous usage of *wanton* bears exactly this meaning:

> *Gloucester:* As flies to wanton boys are we to the gods,
> They kill us for their sport. (*Lr.* 4.1.38–39)

And yet, I would suggest it is no coincidence that it was an encounter "I'the last night's storm" (*Lr.* 4.1.34) that inspired this 'aphorism'. The adjective *wanton* is in Shakespeare's works (and this is what makes "wanton charm" so closely related to "airy charm") exceptionally frequently used with reference or in connection to phenomena of weather or season, especially to warm, moving air:

> So are those crisped, snaky golden locks
> Which makes such *wanton* gambols with the wind, (*MV*, 3.2.92–93; emph. J.U.)

> When we have laughed to see the sails conceive
> And grow big-bellied with the *wanton* wind (*MND*, 2.1.129–129; emph. J.U.)

> How long a time lies in one little word!
> Four lagging winters and four *wanton* springs
> End in a word; such is the breath of kings. (*R2*, 1.3.213–215; emph. J.U.)

> A lover may bestride the gossamers
> That idles in the *wanton* summer air,
> And yet not fall, so light is vanity. (*Rom.*, 2.6.18–20)
>
> The canker blooms [...]
> Hang on such thorns, and play as *wantonly*,
> When summer's breath their masked buds discloses (*Son.*, 54.5–8; emph. J.U.)
>
> Adonis painted by a running brook
> And Cytherea all in sedges hid,
> Which seem to move and *wanton* with her breath
> Even as the waving sedges play with wind. (*Shr.*, Introduction 2.48–51; emph. J.U.)
>
> [...] the *wanton* spoil
> Of Phoebus' burning kisses (*Cor.*, 2.1.211–212; emph. J.U.)

The semantic core or the decisive knot in the semantic web that holds these usages of *wanton* together seem to me to be indeed Cupid and his "wanton charm". He combines the main meanings of *wanton* in an emblematic way: he is pictured as a boy and thus can embody the notion of undisciplined, rebellious, unruly child (*OED*, wanton, *adj.* †1. a.); furthermore, as the god of love, infecting his peers and the human lot with his arrows, he is the one responsible for the lascivious, the unchaste, the lewd, for being given to amorous dalliance (*OED*, wanton, *adj.* 2.). Unfortunately, the *OED* cannot really help us understand the connection to the weather that is so prominent in the passages cited above. However, Shakespeare's *Love's Labour's Lost* can:

> Berowne: For your fair sakes have we neglected time,
> Played foul play with our oaths. Your beauty, ladies,
> Hath much deformed us, fashioning our humours
> Even to the opposed end of our intents;
> [...]
> As love is full of unbefitting strains,
> All wanton as a child, skipping and vain (*LLL*, 5.2.749–755).

It is the "fashioning [of] humours | Even to the opposed end of our intents" that links the weather and Cupid's charm. His "wanton charm" thus works the same way as Prospero's "airy charm": like the weather it (dis)tempers the humoural 'inner weather', causing "*wanton* stings and motions of the sense" (*MM*, 1.4.58; emph. J.U.) – only "a man whose blood | Is very snow-broth" (*MM*, 1.4.56–57) will not be affected by this. It achieves an effect by delicately and subtly penetrating the human microcosm and "fashioning [its] humours":

Dumaine:	Love, whose month is ever May,
	Spied a blossom passing fair
	Playing in the *wanton* air.
	Through the velvet leaves the wind,
	All unseen, can passage find;
	That the lover, sick to death,
	Wished himself the heaven's breath.
	"Air," quoth he, "thy cheeks may blow;
	Air, would I might triumph so!" (*LLL*, 4.3.99–107; emph. J.U.)

Cupid's "wanton charms" and Prospero's "airy charms" correspond: Prospero's abjuration and his breaking his staff does not only mirror Cupid's breaking his arrows and abjuring his charming activities; Prospero has also exercised Cupid's "wanton charm" on Ferdinand and Miranda, he has "infected" (3.1.31) Ferdinand with love for Miranda. Moreover, also Prospero's other weathery charms work in the same humoral way: the first scene's "mutinous winds" (5.1.42) and "roarers" (1.1.17) semantically buy into the isotopy of the wanton child; the airy charms of music with their allaying, tempering effect function as 'antidotes', with regard to the intended effect they are thus comparable to the aim of the masque scene.

In focussing on the weathery innuendoes of Cupid's and Prospero's charms, we should not overlook their theatrical quality: a charm, "The chanting or recitation of a verse supposed to possess magic power or occult influence" (*OED*, charm *n.1*. 1. a.) may be regarded as very aptly describing the theatrical situation with its centrality of the spoken, or formerly, in ancient Greece, sung verses (cf. Döring 2013); especially since the notion of charm puts the emphasis on the pragmatic force of these words on the audience, on the effect that these words have on the audiences' tempers. It is time we direct our attention to the fact that Berowne's comment on love's force as "fashioning our humours" in *Love's Labour's Lost* is part of a metatheatrical reflection, as the beginning of the passage quoted above indicates: "For your fair sakes have we neglected time, | Played foul play with our oaths". The same holds true for Ferdinand's remark that "This is a most majestic vision and | Harmonious charmingly" that directly leads into his discussing with Prospero about the actors' being spirits.

However, what does this correspondence of Cupid's wanton charms with Prospero's theatrical, weathery, airy charms mean for the masque scene and *The Tempest* as a whole? As analysed above, the masque exposes that the absence of Cupid and Venus, the absence of their "wanton charm" is the very condition of possibility for its own harmonious world. With regard to the fact that Shakespeare's play explicitly categorises the masque as one of Prospero's charms, with spirits as actors, conjured up for the betrothed couple, the fictional world's abjecting its theatrical origin is highly significant: the masque as a play-within-the-play evokes a world that defines itself as neatly as possible as an anti-world of the (theatre) world it features in. It is a charm depicting and celebrating a world without charms. If *The Tempest* is a play that stages a fictional world that is itself a world full of theatre, then the masque world radically breaks with this self-reflecting *mise-en-abîme* structure. What it does, is the very opposite: it is a theatrical spectacle that depicts a world devoid of theatre.

In order not to rush this thesis, we should perhaps take the first step first and say that it is depicting or, envisioning rather, a world devoid of intemperance, and that is to say: a world without winter:

> Spring come to you at the farthest,
> In the very end of harvest. (4.1.114–115)

This blessing has proved very tempting for critics: it seemed appropriate as a motto for the play as a whole, especially since the play's first recorded performance took place on Hallowmas: "Read as a play for Hallowmas, *The Tempest* becomes a conjuration against winter" (Bender 2001, 208). However, the play's resistance to this reading is immense. Especially its title serves as a strong argument against this motto: as John Gillies writes, "winds and tempest [...] for mythographers such as Cesare Ripa were identified with winter" (1986, 697); John B. Bender agrees that "tempests are [...] simply symbols for winter" (2001, 208). Interestingly enough, as L. T. Fitz has noted, Prospero measures time in winters (1975, 44). Moreover, to me the mysterious labour of carrying logs speaks against reading the play as "a conjuration against winter". I do not see Prospero brewing magic potions, to me he is not a magician of the druidical, but of the (prompt)bookish type. I would therefore suggest reading the obviously quite urgent necessity to carry logs, like the initial tempest, as a symbol for winter, exactly in the way it is used in the concluding song of *Love's Labour's Lost*:

> When icicles hang by the wall
> And Dick the shepherd blows his nail
> And Tom bears logs into the hall (*LLL*, 5.2.900–902).

Speculative as it might be, I would also count Bent Holm's and Clifford Davidson's anagrammatically connecting Prospero's name to the name of Proserpine ("proserp- [...] combined with a ferd-inand, suggests the name of Proserpina" (Holm 1999, 6); "proserpo" (Davidson 1976, 15)) amongst the arguments for the fact that "the play taken as a whole presents the winter omitted from the masque" (Bender 2001, 210): comparable to the year that Jove "parteth" as a compromise between his brother Pluto and his daughter's mother Ceres, Shakespeare's *Tempest* is divided into parts that envision perfect temperature (Gonzalo's utopia) or pure temperance (excluding distemperance) (the masque) and parts showing and performing the processes of temperance and distemperance (the rest). However, in *The Tempest*, this division is by no means equal, and it does not function as a compromise. This has to do fundamentally with the fact that the weathery world of winter, the world where distemperance and temperance interact and bring forth tempering effects, happens to be the world of charms: of Prospero's "airy charms" as well as of Cupid's "wanton charms". Obviously, the 'coexistence' of weather and charms, as already stated so often, is no coincidence, but a result of the charms' pragmatic force that functions in the (dis)tempering way of weather. As a metatheatrical play, reflecting on its own theatricality, *The Tempest* undertakes to explore this, *its*, theatrical world – that is to say the world of charms and (dis)temperance. The two other, 'alternate' worlds that *The Tempest* sketches, Gonzalo's commonwealth of perfect temperature and the masque's pure temperance are worlds that are projected by the theatre world as opposing models in order to contrast them with the theatrical.

This can also be read as a reflection on the relation of contemporary cultural practices: it appears that in *The Tempest*'s metatheatrical ponderings, public theatre also attempts to set itself off from rivalling literary/poetic or cultural forms. With regard to Gonzalo's Edenic pastoral world we might – and this is mere speculation –, claiming support in Montaigne's criticism of "licentious Poesie" (1603, 102), suspect an allusion to the pastoral romance world of the epic – however, the feeblest and coarsest of allusions, if an allusion at all. The situation is different concerning the court masque: here *The Tempest* clearly and explicitly takes a stance. Nevertheless, critics cannot agree on this position: on the basis of my reading of the masque, I come to the conclusion that interpretations like David Bevington's, stating that "The masque in *The Tempest* is a demonstration of, and a tribute to, dramatic art and poetry of the imagination" (Bevington 1998, 237) have missed the point. Paying close attention to the contrasting conditions of masque and play world in terms of temperance/ distemperance, it does not seem adequate to say that "the extremes may be tempered nowhere but on the magic island and in the masque where love is guided by gods" (Berger 1969, 272). On the contrary, the play clearly marks the absence of winter and charms from the masque world and thereby explicitly distinguishes it from the play world, a weathery ('winter') world that is, as a "magic island", a world of charms! Therefore *The Tempest* cannot "operate[ ] more obviously as masque than as drama" (Grant 1976, 1) – what it does is explicate the important differences between these two. There is no evidence at all that the masque's goddesses "express the power of art to inform, to move, to persuade" (Bevington 1998, 236), on the contrary, the most adequate word to describe the masque is the adjective "ineffective" (Holland 1995, 222):

> To this point [Prospero] has been performing for both onstage and theater audiences with his work presented as reality and as having an effect upon it. When he presents his idea of order toward which the whole play is supposed to be moving, he offers a "second world" that does not cross but remains wholly other. (McNamara 1987, 190)

This failure of "not cross[ing]" (a brilliant way of putting it) does not result from the players' flawed execution. Nothing has gone wrong with the masque, on the contrary: this failure, this inefficacy proves that the masque, at least in its first part, has worked perfectly well and performed what it had hoped and said to perform: as Karen Flagstad describes it, "The masque is [...] a 're-vision' in which the loss of perpetual spring [...] is effectively reversed" (1986, 209). It has, if Karen Flagstad is right, succeeded in conjuring up a weather-free world – and that is to say a world without the (dis)tempering forces that could cross the pragmatic boundaries and move/temper its audience. The masque is a charm without any magic powers; the emptiest of charms, a charm without effect, merely spiriting away its own being a charm, and celebrating its own perfect impotency. I agree with Irwin Smith that "Whatever else the masque may be, it is not an exhibition of Prospero's art" (1970, 214), not so much because "[n]othing turns out as he planned it" (1970, 214), but rather because the masque, in contrast to all other spectacular instances of Prospero's magic spectacles, does not really achieve a theatrical effect on his audience. Its spectacle is so ineffective that it would never feature in the 'Ye elves'-speech's famous list of his magical doings and accomplishments.

The audience reaction to the masque seems to be rather an accident and a problem instead of an integral part of a theatre performance, nothing "planned", for sure:

> *Ferdinand:* Let me live here ever!
> So rare a wondered father and a wise
> Makes this place paradise. (4.1.122–124)

There is no question that Ferdinand's "edenic quivering [is] exposed as a naïve and infatuated audience response to the masque" (Gilman 1980, 221), not only because Prospero tells him to "Hush and be mute, | Or else our spell is marred" (4.1.126–127), but also because Ferdinand's response provokes "Juno['s] and Ceres['s] whisper[ing] seriously" (4.1.125). Ferdinand's mistake seems to be that he is taken in by the masque's fiction, that he "is willingly captured by the masque's easy promise" (McNamara 1987, 195). He does not respect its "illusoriness" (Knowles 1999, 114), but wants to cross from the play world into the masque world. By marking Ferdinand's response as "naïve and infatuated" the play further strengthens the difference that separates the play world from the masque world and that makes crossing impossible and even unthinkable. As James Knowles notes, the categorical difference between the illusory fictional world and the real world that stages this masque has to be read as a commentary on the contemporary cultural practice of the court masque:

> This illusoriness contrasts markedly with the Stuart masque, where performers crossed between the illusionistic space of the scene into the dancing space, and where fictions became actual individuals. (Knowles 1999, 114)

Significantly, Prospero's reflective comment on the masque undermines the Jacobean court masque's cosmological aspirations: his masque does not aim at "present[ing] a grand and permanent vision of order" (McNamara 1987, 188). It does not aspire to be "a revelation of the generative principle of the universe" (Davidson 1976, 12), or to "disclose[ ] the fruitful unity of the natural world [...], human society [...], and the divine" (Bulger 1994, 42). What Prospero envisions with his masque does not celebrate or testify to an existing cosmological unity of the ideal and the real. All that the spirits do in performing the masque is "to enact | [Prospero's] *present fancies*" (4.1.121–122):

> In early use synonymous with imagination *n.* (see fantasy *n.* 4); the process, and the faculty, of forming mental representations of things not present to the senses; chiefly applied to the so-called creative or productive imagination, which frames images of objects, events, or conditions that have not occurred in actual experience. (*OED*, fancy, *n.* 4. a.)

Furthermore, as the attribute *present* tells us, the masque as an enactment of Prospero's fancies bears a temporal index; it negotiates a present thought that moves or troubles Prospero and visualises this inner process in the form of a masque. The world devoid of charms, devoid of winter's weathery distemperances, is, I would claim, the product of one quite clearly identifiable 'fancie': Prospero foreshadows his abjuration, he imagines a world without charms and weathery interventions; or, to be more precise, he produces a wishful fantasy of a world where weathery and magic intervention is not necessary, because any notion of distemperance is excluded from this world. The 'dreamer' Prospero's role, whose wish finds expression in this 'fancie', is displaced on the absent but paradoxically present Cupid: his breaking his arrows, swearing to give up exercising his wanton charms are the decisive hints this fancie provides to identify Prospero and reconstruct at least parts of the latent 'dream' content.

However, all of a sudden, Ferdinand interrupts the masque with his enthusiastic comments and wakes the fantasising Prospero. At this moment, stimulated by Ferdinand's misreading and at the same time revealing Prospero's fantasy as a mere vision/illusion of Paradise, the discrepancy between the masque's wish and the reality of its occasion and circumstances makes itself felt. We remember that the masque was preceded by the worries about Ferdinand's ardent love and lust that Prospero apprehended as a threat to Miranda's premarital virginity and honour. Up to now, in this first part, the masque has not at all served as an answer to this problem. On the contrary, it has, as a betrothal masque, presented the viewers with a world devoid of love, devoid of lust, devoid of problematic temperance! Prospero's ambiguous "There's something else to do" (4.1.126) on the one hand points to the first part's inability to do something about this problem of temperance, of achieving an effect on the audience instead of revelling in fantasies. On the other hand, it refers to the fact that the key part of the masque as a court masque is still missing. Both these aspects combine quite fortunately, since the missing element, the "cosmic dance" (Davidson 1976, 16) is exactly the element that "serves to erase barriers between the mythological fiction and the present reality of courtly celebration" (Bevington 1998, 235): "every masque moved toward the moment when masque and spectator merged, joining in the great central dance, affirming thereby the identity of fictive and real" (Orgel 1971, 369). However, in Prospero's masque, he and the rest of the viewers remain "sealed off from the masque by a fictional barrier that is like a one-way mirror" (Bevington 1998, 235).

The masque's second part does indeed reflect the problem of love's and lust's excessive heat that requires some kind of temperance, and displays this temperance as a rustic dance:

> *Iris:* [...]
> Come, temperate nymphs, and help to celebrate
> A contract of true love. Be not too late.
> *Enter certain Nymphs.*
>
> You sunburned sicklemen, of August weary,
> Come hither from the furrow and be merry;
> Make holiday! Your rye-straw hats put on,
> And these fresh nymphs encounter every one
> In country footing. (4.1.132–138)

We can quite easily refer the sicklemen's "rye-straw hats" back to Prospero's image of "The strongest oaths [that] are straw | To th' fire i'th' blood" (4.1.52–53), the "temperate" or "fresh nymphs" mirror the "white cold virgin snow" (4.1.55), i.e. Miranda, cooling, as Ferdinand claims, his heart and liver. Obviously, and this is only a winking note in passing, the masque world's absence of winter could not really match Ferdinand's wintery snow – giving another argument for the presence of winter on the island, at least in its metaphorical realms. However, more importantly, the whole second, very short part of the masque seems strangely half-hearted. It comes across as an improvised annex to the first part without any obvious connection to it. It appears to be an absent-minded attempt at mending the initial inattention to the masque's occasion and its tempering task. Despite the fact that the masque's obligatory dance seems to take place in this second part, the one we see does not comply at all with the court masque's conventions of the concluding "cosmic dance". Its cast of nymphs and "sunburned sicklemen" is too base of rank as to make an identification of the aristocratic world of the (stage) audience and the world of the masque possible. This dance "in country footing" cannot be understood as the climax of the masque; there is an unresolvable tension between the low cast of the second and the stylised conversation in the first of the goddesses in the "majestic vision". Neither should this dance be interpreted as an antimasque either, as David Bevington (1998, 235) and others have proposed. This section of the quite recently introduced dipartite structure of the Stuart court masque would have to depict an instance of distemperance or disorder, mostly effected by lower rank characters, that is then defeated by the victory of the masque's restitution of true order. However, the rustic dance we see does not introduce disorder or chaos, on the contrary, it displays the temperance that Prospero is envisioning for Ferdinand and Miranda. To my understanding, Prospero's masque distorts the highly conventionalised court masque in a too extreme way as to be claimed merely "seemingly unfinished" (Bevington 1998, 235). It rather acts out the illusoriness and the impossibility of identifying the fictional world of the masque and the real world of the court.

Prospero's masque thus dismisses the simplistic, idealising cosmological worldview on which both the notion of absolutism's divine right and the cultural practice of the court masque are based. His masque exposes that in the postlapsarian world inhabited by him and his contemporaries the barrier between spectacle and audience cannot be crossed in the simple way practiced in the court masque, that is by postulating cosmological harmony. If the Elizabethan theatre is "a Theatrum Mundi after an earthquake" (Kott 1965, 180) as Jan Kott so famously described, then we have discovered one of the decisive rifts this earthquake has caused. Ferdinand is right "[t]o think these [actors] spirits" (4.1.120) – they are not courtiers, "royalty itself" (Bradbrook 2001, 198) is not participating, as it often did in the Stuart court masque, so that the categorical, in some sense even the ontological difference between the fictional and the real world is marked from the very start.

With regard to this characteristic trait of Prospero's masque that is revealed to the audience in the break between the two parts, the fact that the masque ends "without the participation on the dance floor of the marrying couple" (Bevington 1998, 235) cannot come too much as a surprise. Nevertheless, the effect of the masque's abrupt ending is immense: As Kevin R. McNamara states, the "masque's dissolution must have been as jarring to the Whitehall audience as it was to the onstage viewers" (1987, 195). By quoting the cultural practice of the court masque Shakespeare's *Tempest* evokes the expectation of a stable cosmological order towards which the fictional world is moving and which serves as a point of reference for both the fictional and the real world. With the masque's distortion and its abrupt ending, this expectation is frustrated: this is why Kevin R. McNamara can, quite rightly, I think, claim that "the 'tragic' moment is the play's rejection of the masque's simple answers" (1987, 198). The fact that the simple answer of a concluding picture of ideal order is made to fail has wide-reaching implications: not only for the courtly worldview that can no longer imagine itself as cosmological and continue repressing the realities of a postlapsarian world.

Most importantly, the failure of the masque's simple answers has implications for the *relation* between the real and the fictional. The practice of theatrical spectacles can no longer rely on telling the story of an anamnesis of the true order that is attained as in a romance, the true order that would automatically connect it with the real world. Since the cosmological, common ground automatically linking reality and fiction has been exposed as an illusion, fiction and reality cannot transparently communicate on the level of diegesis any longer. The order represented in the fictional world has ceased to have an inherent relation to the ideal order organising the world – stepping over from one world into the other, as the masque would have it, has become impossible. The unity of fiction and reality via cosmological harmony has, once and for all, experienced Jan Kott's 'earthquake', making the crossing of the rift between fiction and reality an interesting problem. As a result, instead of focussing on the representation of truth, theatre finds itself confronted with a question of pragmatics: A question, as I am attempting to demonstrate, for which Shakespeare's early modern public theatre has found a weathery solution.

How complex this relation between fiction and reality can be surfaces in the moment of the masque's abrupt end:

> *Prospero* [aside]:
>> I had forgot that foul conspiracy
>> Of the beast Caliban and his confederates
>> Against my life. The minute of their plot
>> Is almost come. [*to the Spirits*] Well done. Avoid, no more!
>> (4.1.139–142)

At first glance it seems uncontroversial to say that at this very moment "the masque vision is punctured by a reality clearly outside its bounds and imaginings" (Knowles 1999, 113). However, is what punctures Prospero's masque really an "intrusion of extra-theatrical reality" (Egan 1972, 179)? Prospero's comment spoken aside sounds rather like one of the narrator's famous comments in Laurence Stern's *Tristram Shandy*, when he has, over one of the many digressions, again forgotten about a character and his or her strand of narrative so that the character has to 'wait' upon the narrator in a perhaps very uncomfortable and odd situation (the last one described by the narrator, the one where the narrator left the character and set off for the digression).[19] This "foul conspiracy" that breaks into the well-tempered world of the masque and puts an end to it is not reality's foul weather, it is the theatrical foul weather of one of *The Tempest*'s subplots (cf. Barker and Hulme 2002). This is what Prospero's "The minute of their plot | Is almost come" implies: the noun *plot* plays not only with its literary undertones (cf. *OED*, plot, *n.* 6.); most importantly, the fact that Prospero knows "the minute of their plot" reveals that it is actually him, the playwright/stage-manager, who has plotted and timed their rebellion and its defeat. Similar to Prospero's metaleptically alluding to the play's three hours of performance, his referring to "the minute" of Caliban's rebellion that "is almost come" locates this event on a time scale that is not part of the diegetic, fictional world, but of the play's (i.e. *The Tempest*'s) time frame and composition.

In conclusion, with the words "Avoid, no more" (clearly echoing Alonso's "Prithee, no more" (2.1.171) that had put an end to Gonzalo's weather-free utopia) Prospero returns to the theatrical, the weathery world of *The Tempest*. As Ernest B. Gilman writes, the "masque vanishes with a tempest" (1980, 216), a tempest that brings forth "the play's most memorable yet perplexing moment" (Greenblatt 1988, 144). Prospero himself is moved by this theatrical weather, these now very human "mutinous waves" – "the princely artist puts himself through the paralyzing uneasiness with which he has afflicted others" (Greenblatt 1988, 144):

Ferdinand [to Miranda]:
    This is strange. Your father's in some passion
    That works him strongly.
Miranda: Never till this day
    Saw I him touched with anger so distempered!
    (4.1.143–145)

---

19 Cf. the odd situation of Caliban's party being left "I'th' filthy-mantled pool beyond [Prospero's] cell" (4.1.182) and the court party's being "Confined together | [...] | In the line grove which weather-fends [Prospero's] cell (5.1.7–10).

Prospero: [...] Sir, I am vexed;
Bear with my weakness; my old brain is troubled.
Be not disturbed with my infirmity.
If you be pleased, retire into my cell
And there repose. A turn or two I'll walk
To still my beating mind. (4.1.158–163)

The play here does not economise on the instances expressing Prospero's humoral movement, the distemper of his 'inner weather'. This is not only to emphasise the intensity of his passion, but to intricately mark, word by word, the fact that what he is going through is indeed the very same "with which he has afflicted others": the "passion | That works him strongly" will be mirrored by Prospero's "charm [that] so strongly works 'em" (5.1.17). The verb *to work* is repeatedly used to express the achievement of an effect on the humours: in "My high charms work, | And these, mine enemies, are all knit up | In their distractions" (3.3.88–90) or in "Like poison given to work a great time after" (3.3.106). Prospero's "passion" alludes to Ferdinand's "fury and my passion" (1.2.388–394) that is allayed by Ariel's music. Prospero is "touched" as the "direful spectacle of the wreck [...] touched | The very virtue of compassion in [Miranda]" (1.2.27–28). His being "distempered" resonates with the masque's "temperate nymphs" (4.1.132) and the island's "subtle, tender and delicate temperance" (2.1.44–45). In Prospero's "vexed" condition the "vexations" (4.1.5) that Prospero has put Ferdinand through as "trials of [his] love" (4.1.6) are unexpectedly reflected. The fact that Prospero's "old brain is troubled" refers to what we have called the "'weathery' standard meaning" of the verb *to trouble* when analysing the boatswain's "Silence! Trouble us not" (1.1.18) or the island's characteristic that "All torment, trouble, wonder and amazement | inhabits [t]here" (5.1.104–105). As already discussed above, Prospero's "beating mind" after the masque again links his reaction to Miranda's response to the spectacle of the initial tempest that was "still [...] beating in [her] mind" (1.2.176) after the performance had ended.

There are therefore good reasons for claiming that, in this very moment, *The Tempest* culminates: the island's theatricality, its charm, its delicate and (dis)tempering air is demonstrated as also affecting the "god o'th' island", Prospero himself. In retrospect, Prospero's comment that "There's something else to do" (4.1.126), uttered in the break in-between the masque, may 'actually' have referred to countering Caliban's rebellion. The masque's second part seems to have only repressed and deferred this thought that than suddenly re-emerges with the well-known consequences. However, there is no reason why Prospero's forgetting about handling the rebellion should have had such an intense distempering effect on him, should have refocused his theatrical charms onto himself. As we learn only shortly after, dealing with the rebellion is not at all a difficult or urgent problem: Ariel has safely "left [Caliban and his partners in crime] | I'th' filthy-mantled pool beyond [Prospero's] cell" (4.1.181–182), awaiting Prospero's punishment of their offences. What Prospero has to experience when noticing that he "had forgot that foul conspiracy" is that the ominous "There's something else to do" (4.1.126) cannot be ultimately satisfied. There is no last thing that has to be done before perfect, endless and final harmony is reached: not the temperance of Ferdinand's and Miranda's love, nor the defeat of Caliban's uproar. That is why this culmination breaks into Prospero's "present fancies" of the masque and destroys them: his vision of a well-tempered, harmonious world achieved by his art and outliving his abjuration – and that is also to say a theatrically bettered world that can now dispense with theatre – is, painfully, experienced as an illusion. Prospero is made to feel that he, despite his role as "god o'th' island", does not occupy a position outside this weathery world of temperance and distemperance. He may, with his "art" well interfere and, as we would perhaps say today, effect some humoral and weathery displacements. However, there is neither an absolute ideal state, that could be achieved, or towards which the whole system could be made to move, nor is there the outside position of an absolute 'will' exercising absolute control.

It nevertheless appears wrong to read this experience as conveying the message of the failure of Prospero's theatrical project and, consequently, of the cultural form of theatre as a whole. On the contrary, it demonstrates a conceptualisation of theatre that is embedded in a complex net of forces that 'work' its power on the individuals' but also the institutions' tempered bodies. Theatre does not hold a privileged position in this net: it is not an observation point providing a clearer vision of the truth of the real or the truth of the ideal, it is not exceptionally talented, so to speak, in representing either the status quo or the ideal model that should serve as orientation. As a consequence, what breaks into Prospero's fantasy of a well-tempered world without charms and theatre is not only the foul weather of a rebellion, it is also the foul weather of lovely disturbances – lovely distemperances not only of love, but also of theatre. However, the frustration of Prospero's vision introduces one practical problem to his theatre project, a frustration, I would suggest, that makes itself felt among the audience of his play: taking the illusoriness of an absolutely harmonious, well-tempered world seriously, accepting the insatiability of the "There's something else to do", renders the ending of a theatre performance, "the necessity of bringing their 'play' to an end" (Tonning 2004, 378) problematic. The critics' boundless debate about Antonio's silence at the end of *The Tempest* and the unanswered questions of Ariel's and especially Caliban's future, or rather, of all the characters' futures, attests to this observation. Theatre working its effect on the audience as weather in the radically relative processes of temperance and distemperance, in weathery processes without an ideal, normal state, thus turns out to be an intervention of the 'interminable' kind.[20]

(The theatre companies of early modern theatre might, however, even have economically exploited this problem: as the epilogue of *Twelfth Night* famously tells us, its theatrical rain was "rain it raineth every day" (*TN*, 5.1.385) . . .)

8 Bringing the play to an end

From the moment of the masque's interruption, *The Tempest* is preoccupied with one central question: what does it mean to bring the play to an end, and how can this end be properly brought about? Gonzalo formulates this question as a 'beseeching' motto:

> *Gonzalo:* All torment, trouble, wonder and amazement
> Inhabits here. Some heavenly power guide us
> Out of this fearful country. (5.1.104–106)

Gonzalo's appealing to "Some heavenly power" indicates that the question of the play's end is a question of its specific pragmatic structure and relations. To be guided "Out of this fearful country" involves crossing the boundaries of theatre's fictional world and re-entering the 'real' world that has hosted and produced theatre's "fearful country". The masque as the play's "one scene where theatrical illusion and the play's supposed reality are kept rigidly separate" (Magnusson 1986, 63) provides ideal conditions for reflecting on these negotiations of pragmatic boundaries at the end of a theatre performance. Commenting on the abrupt end of the masque, Prospero's famous 'Our revels' monologue attempts the first sketch of an answer to this particular problem:

> *Prospero:* [. . .]
> Our revels now are ended. These our actors,
> As I foretold you, were all spirits and
> Are melted into air, into thin air;
> And – like the baseless fabric of this vision –
> The cloud-capped towers, the gorgeous palaces,
> The solemn temples, the great globe itself,
> Yea, all which it inherit, shall dissolve;
> And like this insubstantial pageant faded,
> Leave not a rack behind. We are such stuff
> As dreams are made on, and our little life
> Is rounded with a sleep. (4.1.148–158)

---

20 This term is inspired by Sigmund Freud's famous text "Terminable and Interminable Analysis" (1964).

Prospero's monologue is divided into three distinct movements of dissolution, three crossings that are brought into relation with each other. Its first crossing exhibits the pragmatic problem of theatre that he is faced with: "An occasion or period of exuberant merrymaking or noisy festivity", in this case "an organized item of entertainment; a dance, a masque, a play" (*OED*, revel, *n.1*. 1.) has come to an end. Its "melt[ing] into air, thin air" reverses the movement that Thomas Heywood describes when conjuring up the theatrical scenery of a storm in his play *The Four Prentices of London*:

> Imagine now yee see the aire made thicke
> With stormy tempests, that disturbe the Maine (Heywood 1964, 175).

The second movement of dissolution concerns the "great globe itself", "towers", "palaces" and "temples", examples underlining the worldliness of the finite macrocosm that is central here. Significantly, places like "palaces" and "temples" are paradigmatic locations for "revels", so that the second movement seems to involve in its dissolution the very level that had staged the conjuration and the dissolution of the theatrical spectacle; the very level of 'real' life onto which we had to cross when the fictional world of the masque ceased to exist. The third movement of dissolution addresses a very general, or rather universal, "We", and "our little life": in contrast to the second movement's macrocosm ("the great globe") it is here the human microcosm, "our little life", that is in the focus of this last movement of dissolution. Prospero's monologue links these three movements of dissolution in the way of analogy: in an astonishing regularity, his monologue is structured by the recurrence of the analogic formula "And [–] like ..." that begins every fourth line and marks the division of the 'Our revels' speech in three parts. The basis of this analogical system that spans the whole elemental realm of macrocosm and microcosm is strikingly provided by theatre. The actors' "melt[ing] into air, into thin air" after the "revels [...] are ended" serves as the model that is 'imitated' by macro- as well as microcosm. Both analogical formulas paraphrase the 'theatrical dissolution': "And – like the baseless fabric of this vision – [...] shall dissolve" actualises the isotopies of 'dissolution' ("melted", "dissolve", later "faded") and of insubstantiality ("spirits", "air", "baseless", later "insubstantial"). The noun *fabric*, in its basic meaning, signifying "A product of skilled workmanship" (*OED*, fabric, *n*. I.), may refer to the analogy of the macrocosm's being created by a god as demiurge, and the playwright's or stage-manager's fabrication of the theatre piece, *ex nihilo*. I would, despite the Ard[3] editors' as well as the folio edition's punctuation, which seems to indicate another reading, suggest that the second analogical formula belongs and refers to the movement of dissolution that concerns the microcosm and is introduced by the famous "We are such stuff | As dreams are made on":

not the least because "And like this insubstantial pageant faded" quite ingeniously plays with the polysemy of *pageant* that links this formula to the concept of microcosm. The noun *pageant* on the surface clearly refers to the realm of theatre: it denotes "A play in a medieval mystery cycle; an act or scene in such a play. Later also: a play on a religious theme" (*OED*, pageant, *n*. 1. a.) and, metonymically also "A stage or platform on which scenes were acted or tableaux represented" (*OED*, pageant, *n*. 2. a.). However, very early a figurative meaning came into use that applies this theatrical meaning to the concerns of the human microcosm: "*fig*. A part played by someone in a situation; the role which a person takes in life, in society, etc. Esp. in *to play one's pageant* : to act one's part" (*OED*, pageant, *n*. 1. †b.). I would argue that the difficult "We are such stuff | As dreams are made on, and our little life | Is rounded with a sleep" echoes and transposes the analogy of microcosm and theatre that was alluded to by the polysemy of *pageant*. Using a strategy similar to the epilogue of *A Midsummer Night's Dream*, the vision of a theatre spectacle is reflected upon as an analogue to a dream:

> Robin: If we shadows have offended,
> Think but this, and all is mended:
> That you have but slumbered here,
> While these visions did appear; (*MND*, Epilogue, 1–4)

It is no coincidence that this analogy of dream and theatre surfaces when the question of a transformation of pragmatic boundaries, of finding a way out of the theatrical spectacle arises. Caliban's famous monologue on dreaming is a prime example of the fact that reflecting upon dreaming does inseparably and inevitably involve questions of waking, and of the relations between dreamworld and real world:

> Caliban: [...] in dreaming,
> The clouds, methought, would open and show riches
> Ready to drop upon me, that when I waked
> I cried to dream again. (3.2.139–143)

As already shown above, the court party's (theatrical) experiences on the island are repeatedly characterised as dream-like: so when the Boatswain in the end gives an account of his and the master's being brought from their ship to the final assembly of Prospero and the rest, "On a trice, so please you, | Even in a dream, were we divided from them | And were brought moping hither" (5.1.238–240), or, when Ferdinand reports that "My spirits, as in a dream, are all bound up" (1.2.487). This latter quotation may help us understand the dark "We are such stuff | As dreams are made on": The "stuff", the "substance or 'material' (whether corporeal or incorporeal) of which a thing [in this case "we", the human microcosm] is formed or consists" (*OED*, stuff, *n.1.* 3.) seamlessly incorporates itself into the isotopy of 'insubstantial material' constituted by "baseless fabric", "insubstantial pageant", and, most importantly, by "rack" and "spirits". The link between the human microcosm (the "We") and dreams is, again one of analogy. As Karol Berger rightly notes, it is important to pay attention to the little particle *as*: "The stuff that dreams are made on is, technically, spirit", furthermore, "Men are not spirits, but *like* spirits they melt into nothingness when they die" (Berger 1977, 233; emph. J.U.). However, paying attention to one she overlooks another particle that Kevin R. McNamara has, for good reasons, insisted on (1987, 194): we can learn from Ferdinand's telling us that his "spirits, as in a dream, are all bound up" (1.2.487) that the spirits that dreams are made *of* are not materially independent of the human microcosm; on the contrary, the human microcosm can be said to be "stuff" that dreams are made *on*, providing the material basis for these dreams. Shakespeare's uncanny formulation "We are such stuff | As dreams are made on" thus functions as a complex hinge: on the one hand it establishes the analogical relation of dream and microcosmic reality as Karol Berger emphasises; on the other hand it refers to the hierarchical relation of one serving as the material basis for the other, the human microcosm as the material basis *on* which dreams are made.

This latter hierarchical, material relation of dream and microcosm mirrors the material relation of theatrical revels and the macrocosm's temples and palaces we have analysed above. However, in both instances, no matter whether microcosm or macrocosm is taken as the material basis of theatre or (theatrical) dream, the very materiality, the durability of this material basis is counteracted by the analogy: the materiality of the basis is characterised as being as insubstantial, as temporal and dissolving as the materiality of theatre or dream that is 'emanating' from this basis. In other words, the theatrical analogy dissolves the pattern of material basis/insubstantial emanation by complicating it in an inescapable circle.

Again rather wittily, Shakespeare depicts this circle in the phrase he attaches to the "We are such stuff | as dreams are made on", which is followed by: "and our little life | Is rounded with a sleep". Many critics have agreed that in this context "sleep" activates its figurative meaning of "The repose of death" (*OED*, sleep, *n.* 4. *fig.* a.), so that the whole sentence could be paraphrased as: 'we, who produce dreams, are made of a similar, insubstantial material, proved by the fact that we have to die in the end'. However, the noun *sleep* uncannily interferes with the notion of dreaming, so that paradoxically the dissolution of the material basis for dreams, the death of the microcosm, seems to produce another undeniable basis for dreams – sleep. A paradoxical circle is established, a circle to which the word *rounded* seems to allude. And indeed, what Prospero's monologue prompts us to think about here is a circle – or rather, *circulation*.

Prospero's monologue, I would suggest, develops the notion that theatre, macro- and microcosm are all situated in and share and also constitute the elemental realm, the realm that is characterised by fundamental instability, by the circulation of the elements or humours.

The corresponding elemental nature of micro- and macrocosm that Prospero's 'Our revels' speech is built upon formed the very basis of the early modern worldview, and was certainly more than familiar to the audience:

> For in Man's self is Fire, Aire, Earth, and Sea,
> Man's (in a word) the World's Epitome,
> Or little Map, which heere my Muse dothe trie
> By the grand Patterne to exemplifie. (Sylvester 1605, 205)

However, the decisive facet of this early modern worldview that Prospero is hinting at with his speech lies beyond this analogy, it is shared by both micro- and macrocosm, because it follows from their elemental nature:

> True it is, as we have else-where touched, that no body is so framed, or hath such an harmony and equality throughout, but that there is some disagreement & inequality. (La Primaudaye 1594, 380)

We have seen that this facet was a focus of *The Tempest* long before Prospero's famous monologue: Gonzalo's utopia as well as Prospero's masque were attempts to transcend or repress this postlapsarian "disagreement & inequality" that fundamentally distinguishes the elemental world's imperfect, temporal and dissolving circulation from the divine world's or heavens' perfect and timeless circular movements. Prospero now affirms this postlapsarian "disagreement & inequality" in his 'Our revels' speech – not only as a comment on the world's present status quo, but as a statement about theatre and its relation to the world. This statement is not merely another version of the all-too common theatrum mundi metaphor, it does not simply rephrase the familiar "All the world's a stage, | And all the men and women merely players" (AYL, 2.7.140–141) (cf. Lipmann 1976, 233). It is imprecise to say that this speech "coalesce[s]" "the metaphors of the world as theater and life as dream" (Lipmann 1976, 243), or that it

> collapses the levels of representation with which *The Tempest* has juggled: the globe that is the world, the Globe that was the theatre, fantasy, reality, dream, all are one, a little life islanded in an ocean of non-existence (Nevo 1999, 91).

These general theses overlook the specificity of the vocabulary Prospero uses. His monologue prominently resorts to *termini technici* of elemental circulation and transformation: "melt", "dissolve" and "faded" signify processes of elemental transformation and circulation also in a literal, not only in a metaphorical way. As will be seen, by using these *termini* Prospero quotes 'physiological' descriptions and explanations of natural phenomena that were state of the art knowledge of natural philosophy. He also names the phenomena that these *termini* were used for: weather and humours! The central information for identifying this reference is surely the actors' being "spirits" that "melted into air, into thin air": here, both the notions of vital spirits and of macrocosmic, meteorological phenomena are hinted at. Vital spirits were thought to evaporate from the humour of blood, in a way analogous to the engendering of the macrocosmic phenomenon of wind:

> [God] hath appointed the blood to water all the body, and to give life and nourishment unto it, out of which also the vital spirits arise, as smal & mild windes proceed out of rivers and fountaines (La Primaudaye 1594, 368).

This corresponding system of outer and inner (humoral) weather constitutes the paradigmatic axis of the elemental world's imperfect nature, of its instability, its temporalness, its transformations and dissolutions. The individual experience of one's changing humoral condition, not only in terms of sickness, but also of the fluctuation of one's tempers may help us to develop, literally, a feeling of the imperfect, transitory nature of the elemental world. In the same way phenomena of weather are the exemplary illustrations of the elemental world's imperfect, instable, temporal nature. As in Pierre de la Primaudaye's explanation of spirits, the weather thus serves as an important analogical paradigm in the way natural philosophy explains the functioning of the elemental world.

This is also what happens in Prospero's speaking of "melt[ing] into air, into thin air" as well as in "Leave not a rack behind". *Rack* is here used in its meaning "A bank of cloud, fog, or mist; a wisp of cloud or vapour" (*OED*, rack, *n.2*, 2. b.), and even to modern readers unfamiliar with the notion of elements transforming into each other, the notion of melting into thin air without leaving a rack behind can claim intelligibility and a certain illustrative force. However, as James Walter notes, with a love for detail and completeness, the noun *rack* "binds together" a rich bundle of meanings and allusions that supplement this dominant 'meteorological' meaning: "senses of storm, wreckage, instrument of torture, mental or physical torment, dregs of wine, exorbitant rent, wisp of cloud, frame for holding cases of type, as well as theatrical scaffold" (1983, 70). Especially the last meaning listed by James Walter, "theatrical scaffold", must catch our eye, since it resonates with one of the central patterns of Prospero's monologue: similar to "the baseless fabric of this vision" and "this insubstantial pageant" the polysemy of "rack", signifying both "wisp of cloud or vapour" and "theatrical scaffold", identifies the temporality, the insubstantiality shared by weather phenomena and the notion of theatre. Remarkably, Prospero does not characterise theatre by connecting it to familiar notions of macrocosmic weather and microcosmic humours; what he actually does is using theatre, supported by allusions to weather and humours, as another exemplary, visualising instance of the elemental world's temporality and imperfection.

Nevertheless, Prospero's monologue is first and foremost about theatre; however, his rhetorical strategy of reading theatre as one exemplary instance of the postlapsarian, imperfect world, a world that is always in the process of (dis)temperance, fulfils a crucial function. As noted above, the question Prospero addresses with this monologue aims at determining the pragmatic boundaries of theatre and negotiates the dissolution of the theatre situation: What is at stake here is the relation of theatre and real world. If theatre is, as Prospero seems to insist, an exemplary instance of the instable, imperfect elemental world, then theatre cannot define itself as 'other' to that world: it can neither be regarded as an utopic space where ideals are developed and 'fostered', nor can it claim a superior position for reflecting on quanderies of the real world. As a consequence, crossing the pragmatic boundaries from theatre situation to 'real life' does not involve a radical change of 'medium': *The Tempest* takes place in a weathery 'real' world, so to speak. Theatre is conceptualised as one particular weather phenomenon that works on the same 'physiological' or rather humoral basis and is of a similar 'temporal' nature as all the other weather events that the human microcosm encounters in the elemental world. *The Tempest* is thus literally "air made thick", as Thomas Heywood said, which then, after three hours, "melt[s] into air, thin air" again. When the audience has finally found its way "Out of this fearful [theatre] country", temperance may not be as delicate as it has been during the last three hours in the hyper-weathery space of the theatre, but the 'real' world is still weathery, still imperfect, as we are taught not least by the fact that we all have to die, that we will dissolve, melt, fade away.

It does not take long for this dialogue's quite abstract ponderings to become connected to the concrete action of the play. The theme of 'bringing the play to an end' is now explicitly voiced:

Prospero: Let them be hunted soundly. At this hour
Lies at my mercy all mine enemies.
Shortly shall all my labours end, and thou
Shalt have the air at freedom. (4.1.262–265)

The ambiguous deixis of "At this hour", referring both to the fictional world's as well as the real world's time, exactly designates (in a metaleptical way) the crossing of pragmatic boundaries that is to be achieved shortly, when Prospero's "labours end". Interestingly, the end of these "labours" goes hand in hand with Ariel's having "the air at freedom", which again supports my thesis that *The*

Tempest conceptualises Prospero's theatrical labours as a weathery manipulation of air. The quoted passage of the fourth act is followed by an astonishing twin passage at the start of the fifth act:

> Prospero: Now does my project gather to a head.
> My charms crack not; my spirits obey, and time
> Goes upright with his carriage. How's the day?
>
> Ariel: On the sixth hour, at which time, my lord,
> You said our work should cease.
>
> Prospero: I did say so,
> When first I raised the tempest. (5.1.1–6)

As noted above, we encounter here the same metalepsis, conflating fictional and factual time. Against this background of metatheatrical innuendos and of playing with the internal and the external communication systems, Shakespeare's employing the words "labour" and "work" may allude to the serious business side of this entertaining "project", to the hard conditions of the players' profession, to the fact that the players had to earn their bread and butter with this their job. Peggy Muñoz Simond's interpretation of the passage presents a different approach; in its first lines she has discovered the main evidence for her famous reading of *The Tempest* as a play about alchemy (cf. Simonds 1997): "project", "charms" that "crack not", obeying "spirits" do indeed allude strongly to alchemistic practices. However, alchemy and theatre do here have more than a metaphoric connection. Both are, literally and 'physically', manipulations of the world's temperance, of the imperfect circulation of the elements in the nether world. As we have seen, the "Something projected or thrown out; [the] projection, [the] emanation (of some being or thing)" (*OED*, project, *n.* †3.) must not be the philosopher's stone producing gold or something metaphorically resembling this process; it can well, and literally, refer to the theatrical tempest, to the play called *The Tempest*, that Prospero has conjured up, has made emanate. The metaleptic comments on the performance's time and Prospero's own mentioning of the tempest he raised (i.e. *The Tempest*) are strong indications for reading this whole passage metatheatrically. The formulations "Now" Prospero's project "gather[s] to a head" and "At this hour | Lies at [his] mercy all [his] enemies" mark a crucial point in time for this tempering (theatre) "project" that in previous sections I attempted to capture with the Hippocratic notion of 'crisis'.[21]

And indeed, Prospero, in his god-like position of deciding over the destiny of those he has troubled these last three hours with the tempestuous distemperance of his art will now effect an important, tempering change:

---

[21] Cf. 6 and 68.

Prospero:	[...] Go, release them, Ariel.
	My charms I'll break; their senses I'll restore;
	And they shall be themselves. (5.1.30–32)

These words announce the end of Prospero's theatrical project, and the transformative crossing of pragmatic boundaries that his audience will have to go through. Furthermore, these words also announce that *The Tempest* undertakes the paradoxical attempt at staging the transformation taking place at the end of a play: the dissolution of the fictional world, the breaking of the distempering theatrical charm, and the "restor[ation]", the re-tempering of the audience's senses.

The Tempest depicts this transformation as a sort of magical ceremony. Prospero has traced a magic circle, Ariel leads the "spell-stopped" stage-audience, the court party, into this circle, and Prospero speaks to them in an uncanny, half-descriptive, half-enchanting way:

Prospero:	A solemn air and the best comforter
	To an unsettled fancy, cure thy brains
	(Now useless) boiled within thy skull. There stand,
	For you are spell-stopped. – (5.1.58–61)

The impression that Prospero's project culminates in a Hippocratic crisis is confirmed by the medical vocabulary that characterises and organises his speech: "A solemn air" is the "best comforter", that is to say "A thing that produces physical comfort" (*OED*, comforter, *n.* 5.) – either, as in the play's second scene, a "thing" like sleep, that "seldom visits sorrow; when it doth, | It is a comforter" (1.2.195–196) or a thing like "An invigorating agent; a cordial (*OED*, comforter, *n.* †4.) – to "cure" the stage audience. We also are given the diagnosis of the actual ailment from which Alonso and his fellows are suffering: their "brains" are "boiled within [their] skull" leading to the brain's being "useless", out of function, since the faculty of "fancy" is decisively affected. This faculty is said to be "unsettled" in the specifically pathological meaning of having lost its (healthy) balance (cf. *OED*, unsettled, *adj.* 1. a.; 2. b.; and 5. a.). These "brains | [...] boiled within th[e] skull" might look to us like a strong metaphorical, perhaps even poetical description; however, the notion of heat troubling the brain reflects state of the art medical knowledge:

So, too-much Heat, doth bring a burning Fever,
Which spurres our Pulse, and furres our Pallat ever;
And on the tables of our troubled braine,
Fantastikely with various pensill vaine
Doth counterfaite as many Formes, or mo,
Then ever Nature Arte, or Chaunce could show (Sylvester 1605, 36)

Too much heat seriously troubles the brain because this organ was thought to be cold, and therefore functioned decisively in maintaining the body's healthy temperance:

> For like as in man's *Little World*, the Braine
> Doth th'highest place of all the Frame retaine,
> And tempers with it's moist-full coldnes so,
> Th'excessive heate of th'other parts below (Sylvester 1605, 71).

In fact, the moist and cold brain tempers the body's inner, humoral weather analogous to the clouds of the outer weather:

> And first we must know, that besides the distribution of all the humours together with the blood into all parts of the bodie by the veines, and that for the causes before learned, there is yet another meane whereby these humors, especially the flegmatike humour, which is of the nature of the water, ascend up unto the braine, by reason of vapours arising upward out of the stomacke, like to the vapour of a potte seething on the fire with liquor in it, and like to vapours that ascend up from the earth into the ayre, of which raine is engendred. Now when these vapours are come up to the braine, they returne to their naturall place, and into the nature of those humours of which they were bred, as the vapours that are held in the aire turne againe into the same nature of water of which they came. Therefore as the waters are contained within the cloudes in the region of the aire allotted unto them, so is it with our braine which is of a colde nature, and of a spongie substance fitte for that purpose. So that we always carie within it as it were cloudes full of water, and of other humours that distil and runne downe continually by the members and passages, which God hath appointed to that ende, as wee have alreadie hearde. (La Primaudaye 1594, 364)

Thus what Prospero has manipulated with his weathery theatrical interventions in the course of the last three hours is, very 'physically', his victims' inner humoral weather: their "fever of the mad" (1.2.209) is a disturbance of their humours' temperance, a lack of coldness in the brain that interrupts the tempering circulation of humours.

Manipulating interventions from without like Prospero's were not uncommon to the medical theories of the time. They formed part of the theories of the humoral and elemental circulation, as the "evill spirits" in Pierre de la Primaudaye's encyclopaedic *French Academie*:

> evill spirites might trouble the imagination, fantasie, and mindes of men. We may say as much of the humours of the body, whose motions and nature they knowe very well. (1594, 381)

Despite his not being overtly "evill", the "airy spirit" Ariel's role and powers in these theatrical manipulations seem to be accounted for by this capacity of intervening in the microcosmic humoral temperance that natural philosophy attributed to "evill spirits". Prospero's role is different; as we have already observed above, he rather holds the position of a "god of power" (1.2.10):

> And on the other side, although we had no examples of floods and inundations of waters, of earthquakes and such other judgementes of God whereby he punisheth men, nevertheles these water-floods which we alwaies carie about us, ought to admonish and induce us to feare him, to call upon him by prayer, and day and night, yea hourely, to recommend our life unto him, seeing he can take it from us by stopping our breath, yea by a very small matter: or at least deprive us of all motion and sense, as though our bodies had neither soule nor life in them, but were like to poore dead carkases. For the doing hereof hee needeth not to thunder or light from heaven against us, but onely to cause a small showre of water to powre downe from our head, which is the highest, the goodliest and most noble part of the bodie, and as it were the heaven of the litle world: or if it please him to cause a fewe droppes onely to distill downe upon the sinewes and joyntes, it will torment men more grievously then if they were in some continuall torture [...] (La Primaudaye 1594, 365).

Prospero indeed "punisheth men": he not only "too austerely punished [Ferdinand]" (4.1.1), he also punishes the other "men of sin" (3.3.53) in order to reach their being "penitent" (5.1.28). Moreover, he "deprives [his enemies] of all motion and sense": twice people drawing swords at him or Ariel are *"charmed from moving"* (SD, 1.2.467), Ferdinand in act one and the court party in act three, scene three. Act five emphasises Prospero's power of controlling his victims' motions and senses: when Ariel tells him that "They cannot budge till your release" (5.1.11) and when the court party stand on stage "spell-stopped" (5.1.61), explicitly deprived of their senses. Similar to the punishing god that Pierre de la Primaudaye describes, Prospero "torment[s] men" by interfering in their microcosmic processes of temperance: it is not without reason that Gonzalo very explicitly characterises the (theatrical) island as a fearful place where "All torment, trouble, wonder and amazement | Inhabits" (5.1.104–105). Caliban, who knows this island best lives in permanent fear of these torments: "Here comes a spirit of his, and to torment me | For bringing wood in slowly" (2.2.15–16); "Do not torment me! O!" (2.2.55); "The spirit torments me! O!" (2.2.63). The end of act four even stages the reason for his fears: Prospero here brutally tortures Caliban and his confederates, aiming at the "sinews and joyntes" that Pierre de la Primaudaye also listed as possible points of attack:

> *Prospero:* Go, charge my goblins that they grind their joints
> With dry convulsions, shorten up their sinews
> With aged cramps, and more pinch-spotted make them
> Than pard or cat o'mountain. (4.1.258–261)

When Prospero puts his plans of "restor[ing]" "their senses" (5.1.31) into practice, he has to re-establish the circulation and temperance of his (former) enemies' inner weather. This is exactly what happens when the end of the play is approaching:

> *Prospero:*　[...] [*aside*] The charm dissolves apace,
> And as the morning steals upon the night,
> Melting the darkness, so their rising senses
> Begin to chase the ignorant fumes that mantle
> Their clearer reason. (5.1.64–68)

This passage continues the precise description of the characters' changing humoral weather that Prospero's diagnosis of their "boiled" brains and "unsettled fancy" had started. Especially the keyword, "ignorant fumes", that is analogically connected with the daily meteorological phenomenon of the sun's "melting the darkness"[22] is a case in point. As we have seen above, "vapours arising upward out of the stomacke", "ascend[ing] up unto the braine" are like "vapours that ascend up from the earth into the ayre, of which raine is engendred" (La Primaudaye 1594, 364); "ignorant fumes" not "melting" into rain as a result of excessive heat in the brain thus create a serious problem:

> And sometime that malitious smoke smiteth to the rootes of the sinews of feelyng, and passeth into the innermost partes of the sinewes in his sharpnesse and force, and letteth the spirite of feelyng that is therein and grieveth him: and so it distempereth the substance and the use of reason, and taketh away the kindlye moving of the tongue, that telleth what reason meaneth, and maketh the tongue stammer and fayle, as it is seene in dronken men. Also oftentimes, it letteth and destroyeth altogether kindly moving: as appeareth in them that shake and quake, and have the palsie. And no wonder: For the powers that should rule in the sinews and all the members and lymmes be overset, as overflowed with a vapor infecting kindly juyce in the bodye, but that sharpe smoake having masterie, and coveting to subdue that kindly vertue, purposeth and striveth to beare downward the member or lymme. (Bartholomaeus 1582, 28^v–29^r)

However, now, Prospero's magic procedure works as a cure; it makes the court party's "rising senses" "chase" and ultimately "dissolve[ ]" these distempering "ignorant fumes" – as the rising sun dissolves the morning fog. It is no coincidence that we encounter here again the isotopy of 'dissolution' that so strongly characterised Prospero's 'Our revels' monologue. Whereas in the monologue the

---

[22] As Otto Gilbert notes in his monumental *Die meteorologischen Theorien des Griechischen Altertums* the 'older' Greek natural philosophers believed that the night's – and winter's – darkness was a phenomenon of the maximal condensation of air (cf. 1907, 18, 112, 448, 490, 682). What we encounter here with Shakespeare's "melting the darkness" is thus a sort of atavism of the early modern meteorological theory's foundation in ancient thought.

isotopy of 'dissolution' referred to the fading theatre performance, here the transformative dissolution has two points of reference that are both set in analogical relation to the meteorological phenomenon of the morning sun's "melting the darkness": (1) "The charm dissolves apace"; (2) "the ignorant fumes that mantle | Their clearer reason [dissolve]". "The charm", singular with definite article, I would claim, represents, as a metaleptic cypher, the theatre piece *The Tempest*, similar to what we have said about "airy charm" (5.1.54) and "wanton charm" (4.1.95) above. The "ignorant fumes" that are melting designate the audience's 'physiological' reaction to this theatrical charm, and to its dissolution, respectively. Thus what cures the audience's unsettled humoral weather is a change of the outer weather (the end of *The Tempest*, the (stage) audience's being led out of this fearful, theatrical country, with its troubling delicate temperance). Prospero's aside that we are discussing here thus establishes a link between the audience's "unsettled fancy" (5.1.69) and Prospero's "present fancies" (4.1.122). The opposition of "unsettled fancy" and "clearer reason" that is exhibited by this passage is not by chance 'weathery': *unsettled* can mean "Not peaceful, tranquil", "Changeable, variable" "Of weather" (*OED*, unsettled, *adj.* 1. a. + b.), *clear* "Free from cloud, mists, and haze" (*OED*, clear, *adj.* 2. c.). It was Prospero's "present fancies", very rightfully titled "*The Tempest*", that unsettled his (stage) audience's and his own humoral, inner weather. The boatswain's initial appeal "to work the peace of the present" (1.1.22) is not and cannot be followed until the end of Shakespeare's play: *The Tempest* as such is this troubling disturbance. Ariel-harpy's words to the court party can therefore stand as a motto for the three hours of performance:

> Ariel: The powers delaying, not forgetting, have
> Incensed the seas and shores – yea all the creatures –
> Against your peace. (3.3.73–75)

As we have seen, Prospero himself is not exempt from this humoral heavy weather: his distemper after the masque's abrupt ending makes Ferdinand and Miranda univocally "wish[ing] [him] peace" (4.1.163) as well. Moreover, Prospero's asides commenting on what is happening in the transformation that takes place on stage uncannily unsettles the actual addressees of his words and disenchantments:

> Prospero: [...] [*aside*] Their understanding
> Begins to swell, and the approaching tide
> Will shortly fill the reasonable shore
> That now lies foul and muddy. Not one of them
> That yet looks on me or would know me. (5.1.79–83)

We could here again follow up the echoes of contemporary natural philosophy emerging from this passage: metaphorising "their understanding" as an "approaching tide" mirrors the early modern conviction that "according as [the moon] encreaseth or decreaseth, so doe the humours in all creatures augment and diminish", and similarly, "so doth the weather change in disposition, turning sometimes into raine, sometimes being faire, and sometimes tempestuous" (La Primaudaye 1601, 160). However, the last sentence of this passage appears to be more important than emphasising another time that bringing the tempestuous theatre piece to an end means effecting a change of weather. The sentence reads: "Not one of them | That yet looks on me or would know me". It uncannily refers to the strange communication situation that characterises the scene. The decisive question seems to be: To whom is Prospero actually speaking? According to Harry Berger Jr., Prospero's speech

> is, in effect, a soliloquy. It is as if he hesitates to put on the real scene without one more dress rehearsal; or as if he is primarily aiming the words at himself, reminding himself of the part he has decided to play, and of the parts he has written for them, as penitents. (1969, 276)

In my opinion, it is much too late in the play for a "dress rehearsal". The actors as well as the audience are rather on their own way out of the theatre. I therefore agree with Günther Walch that "[t]he dramatist seems concerned about reactions by the audience off stage rather than on stage" (1996, 229). Prospero's talking *of* the stage audience that neither "looks on [him] or would know [him]" is addressed at the 'real' audience, represented by this stage audience: the 'real' audience that does 'look on him' and has come to know him in the last almost three hours! The transformation that is described and effected in this scene not only involves leading the characters off stage, leading them out of this fearful country, transforming them from characters to actors-off-duty: it also, and perhaps primarily, involves the 'real' viewers, it leads them from the theatre situation back to their real life, it 'dissolves' the pragmatic system of theatre, it 'melts' the "ignorant fumes" that their over-active imagination, their fancies, have produced in their assisting the performance they have been a part of.

Shakespeare marks the success of Prospero's transforming the stage audience back to real life by one decisive characteristic, a characteristic familiar to theatre goers: a change of *belief*. This is the central theme dominating the play's last minutes after Prospero has brought the court party back to their senses. Suddenly, a fundamental uncertainty haunts the perception of Alonso and his confederates:

> Alonso: Whe'er thou be'st he or no,
> Or some enchanted trifle to abuse me
> (As late I have been), I not know. [...]
> [...]
> Th'affliction of my mind amends, with which
> I fear a madness held me. This must crave –
> An if this be at all – a most strange story. (5.1.111–117)

Only few lines later Gonzalo echoes Alonso's impression and thus emphasises that this uncertainty of perception is not an individual psychological disturbance but results from the transformation 'in pragmatics' that they have all gone through:

> Gonzalo: Whether this be
>   Or be not, I'll not swear.
> Prospero: You do yet taste
>   Some subtleties o'th' isle that will not let you
>   Believe things certain. (5.1.122–125)

It would be a serious misunderstanding to read Prospero's explanation of this uncertainty as attributing it simply to the island – things are more complicated than that. Surely, when the victims of the shipwreck first arrive on the island, what they encounter is strange, hard to believe and somehow unreal: Sebastian wonders at the "strange drowsiness" that suddenly "possesses" Alonso and Gonzalo, an event that Antonio, as we have seen, significantly attributes to "the quality o'th' climate" (2.1.199–200); Trinculo wonders at the "strange fish" Caliban (2.2.27); the court party wonder at "*several strange shapes, bringing in a banquet*" (SD, 3.3.17) that seconds later "vanish[ ] strangely" (3.3.40). However, despite all this initial strangeness, all the characters believe in this strange new world, as Ferdinand believes in Ariel's famous song that gives an account of the transformation the characters and their world go through when they enter the (theatre) island:

> Ariel [Sings]:   Full fathom five thy father lies,
>   Of his bones are coral made;
>   Those are pearls that were his eyes,
>   Nothing of him that doth fade
>   But doth suffer a sea-change
>   Into something rich and strange. (1.2.397–402)

By entering the new pragmatic context of the theatre island, the characters are affected and transformed by this "sea-change". The transformation to which Prospero subjects them when preparing them for leaving the island inversely corresponds to the initial "sea-change". In-between these two transformations everyone is wholly committed to the island's world, so that the "subtleties o'th' isle" are not questioned or doubted at all. Nobody notices that "no man [is] his own" (5.1.213), or that Ariel has "made [them] mad; | And even with such-like valour, men hang and drown | Their proper selves" (3.3.58–60). On the contrary, Ferdinand is not alone in attesting to a heightened belief in the (strange!) circumstances when he tells Prospero that he "do[es] believe [that Miranda will outstrip all praise] | Against an oracle" (4.1.11–12). Sebastian and Antonio have already confessed their wondrous belief in an earlier scene:

> *Sebastian:*   A living drollery! Now will I believe
> That there are unicorns; that in Arabia
> There is one tree, the phoenix' throne, one phoenix
> At this hour reigning there.
> *Antonio:*   I'll believe both;
> And what does else want credit, come to me
> And I'll be sworn 'tis true. [...] (3.3.21–26)

After the transformation, Gonzalo forthrightly contradicts this statement: "Whether this be | Or be not, I'll not swear". It is primarily in retrospect that the events of the last hours appear "not natural [...]; they strengthen | From strange to stranger" (5.1.227–228). Only when "all of [them]" have re-found "their proper selves" (3.3.60) do they realise what "strange a maze" (5.1.242) they have trod, what "strange [a] thing" (5.1.290) they have looked on. In short, the strangeness, the uncertainty of perception, the doubtful status of reality are an effect of the co-presence or overlap of two pragmatic levels, the fading theatrical and the rising 'real' world.

Significantly, this rising 'real' world does not immediately re-establish stable truth and certainty; on the contrary, it not only casts doubt on the 'theatrical' past events, but also on the perception of the new 'real' reality. "[T]his last tempest", despite its being 'theatrical', has unsettled the 'real' perception of 'reality':

> *Prospero:*   In this last tempest. – I perceive these lords
> At this encounter do so much admire
> That they devour their reason and scarce think
> Their eyes do offices of truth, their words
> Are natural breath. – But howsoe'er you have
> Been jostled from your senses, know for certain
> That I am Prospero [...]. (5.1.153–159)

Undoubtedly, this passage speaks of the effects of theatre, the disturbances that a theatrical tempest brings about. It also discusses the most basic of theatrical conventions: the belief that our "eyes do offices of truth", although we know that what we see is fiction, and the belief that the words we hear, despite their being dramatic speech, "are natural breath". It is surely no coincidence that "In this last tempest. –" and "Are natural breath. –" are constructed as parallel isocola: the linking of this last theatrical tempest with natural breath actualises the intricate net of the Greek *pneuma*, bringing together the notion of macrocosmic wind and microcosmic breath and thereby providing, as I have attempted to show, the 'physiological' essence of Shakespeare's understanding of theatre.

It does not take long for Prospero to lead all the characters out of the fearful country – all, except one: himself. Despite his abjuration, despite his changing clothes, he seems to remain unchanged, he seems to occupy the very same powerful position of a "god o'th' island" (1.2.390), commanding Ariel, as ever:

> *Prospero:* I'll deliver all,
> And promise you calm seas, auspicious gales
> And sail so expeditious that shall catch
> Your royal fleet far off. [*aside to Ariel*] My Ariel, chick,
> That is thy charge. Then to the elements
> Be free, and fare thou well! (5.1.314–319)

Sam Mendes's 1993 scandalous RSC production of *The Tempest* (cf. Vaughan and Vaughan 2011, 116–117) directed the scholars' attention to the question of whether Prospero proves capable of keeping his promise, and that is to say whether Ariel follows Prospero's last command, or not. Sam Mendes has famously argued for the latter, making Ariel spit at Prospero as an answer to his "fare thou well". This reading seems to be supported in the "Epilogue | spoken by Prospero" that follows almost directly the passage quoted above:

> Now my charms are all o'erthrown,
> And what strength I have's mine own,
> Which is most faint. Now, 'tis true
> I must be here confined by you,
> Or sent to Naples. Let me not,
> Since I have my dukedom got
> And pardoned the deceiver, dwell
> In this bare island by your spell;
> But release me from my bands
> With the help of your good hands.
> Gentle breath of yours my sails
> Must fill, or else my project fails,
> Which was to please. Now I want
> Spirits to enforce, art to enchant;

And my ending is despair,
Unless I be relieved by prayer,
Which pierces so that it assaults
Mercy itself, and frees all faults.
As you from crimes would pardoned be,
Let your indulgence set me free. (Epilogue, 1–20)

Once *The Tempest* has 'really' ended, Prospero finally himself undergoes the transformation that he announced, and delayed over and over again. But has *The Tempest* 'really' ended, when Prospero speaks this epilogue? As Kevin McNamara notes, "Prospero does not, like Rosalind, step out of character to deliver the epilogue; he speaks as a character to an audience" (1987, 199) – which can be understood as a strong hint that *The Tempest*'s epilogue somehow appears to be "more than" the "conventional appeal for applause" (Berger 1977, 236). Shakespeare uses the epilogue's liminal status in-between the pragmatic levels to perform what the whole play, especially its last scenes, had been reflecting on and speaking about: the theatrical relation between stage and audience. The epilogue repeatedly points to its special pragmatic 'location' in-between: the temporal deixis "now" ("Now my charms", "Now, 'tis true", "Now I want") as well as the local deixis "here" and "on this bare island" mark this reference to the epilogue's particular pragmatic situation. Prospero's epilogue stages an intricate dialogue, or rather an interplay between an "I" of the stage and a "you" of the audience: "my charms" transform into "your spell", "own" rhymes on "o'erthrown", and is followed by a "you" that rhymes on "true". In these few lines Prospero performs in words the transformation he, as a stage character goes through at the end of a theatre performance: "I must be here confined by you", he says, starting the sentence with the once so powerful "I" and ending it with the "you", with an address to the audience. With the "you", the audience, now takes over the very position that the "I", Prospero, had occupied for the last three hours. Therein consists the epilogue's magic: it at once completely transforms, it inverts the constellation that *The Tempest* had erected – and at the same time it reads like a perfect summary of the play that the audience has seen.

As David Porter contends, the epilogue "seems to resonate with a number of passages earlier in the play where Prospero appears strangely anxious about the reception of stories of his own" (1993, 33). It continues the series that stretches back at least to his famous 'Our revels' speech (cf. McNamara 1987, 199), however, this time not addressing a fictional, representative double of the real audience on stage (the court party), not speaking of a fictional double of the 'real' performance on stage (the masque), but referring to the very relation between stage and audience, to the limits of the play called *The Tempest*. "The epilogue is not an end to illusion but an extension of it" Sherron Knopp writes (2004, 349), and I think, in a certain sense, she is right: the epilogue draws the audience into the constellation of the fictional world, because Prospero in the epilogue "places himself in the same relation to the audience as previously Ariel, the Italians, and also Caliban, had stood to him" (Berger 1969, 278). The evidence for this claim is abundant: as we have seen, Prospero had governed as the master of confinements, he has decided over the entries and the exits, he has in this way very much directed the play called *The Tempest*. He has emblematically "free[d]" Ariel from the "torment" of the pine tree (1.2.251), he has not only called spirits "from their confines" on stage to "enact" (4.1.120) the masque, he has also asked Ariel to "release" (5.1.30) the court party from their being "Confined together | [...] | In the line grove which weather-fends [his] cell (5.1.7–10)" to be brought before the audience's eyes. "Now", everything has changed. "Now", it is Prospero who "must be here confined by" the viewers, or "released" by them, "from [his] bands". The epilogue is an elaborate explication, or rather, a humble and desperate celebration of this contrast and of the inversion of roles that accompanies the transformation of the pragmatic situation.

Moments before Prospero had promised to "set [Ariel] free" (1.2.443), "[n]ow" that *The Tempest* has 'ended', his last three words, from beyond the performance, so to speak, beg for his own liberation: "set me free." "Now", with this aspiration, Prospero has become indistinguishable from his arch-enemy Caliban, whose longing for freedom demanded Prospero's most violent governance: "Freedom, high-day; high-day freedom; freedom high-day, freedom" (2.2.181–182). As a result of the crisis called *The Tempest* that is now overcome – 'weathered', so to speak – the audience holds now the position in relation to Prospero that Prospero once held in relation to the other characters. Surely this is "an extension" of the play's "illusion" (Knopp 2004, 349); however, as I would argue, not in the sense that the audience is "invited to enter the play-world" (Egan 1972, 173). This play-world, as marked by Prospero's words, has ceased to exist: his "charms are all o'erthrown" "this bare island" is "now" rather "an apron in the theater [...] than an island in the sea" (Berger 1969, 277). And yet it continues to live on, not because we uphold the illusion, but because, as Stephen Lipman writes, "Shakespeare establishes continuity between the world of his drama and the real world of the audience" (1976, 244). The epilogue does not speak from the play-world to the 'real' world, and it does not talk about the play-world: it speaks from the in-between and focuses on this in-between.

Shakespeare uses the conventional communication from the audience to the stage at the end of a play – that is to say the convention of applause and shouts of acclaim – to once again strengthen the metatheatrical, metapragmatic theory of theatre that he has staged with *The Tempest*. What gets passed on in the epilogue from Prospero's "I" to the audience's "you" is the capacity to communicate across what I have called the 'theatrical seam' via the medium of 'weather'. Prospero's "charm", his "art to enchant" and to "enforce spirits" is continued in the audience's "spell". With their "good hands" and their "gentle breath" the spectators are said to be capable of producing the "calm seas, auspicious gales" that Prospero promised the court party, and that Ariel apparently, despite being charged, did not "deliver" (5.1.314–315). Peter Holland rightly notes that the epilogue, "conjur[ing] up its own particular noise, a storm of clapping" and, we could add, of "windy shouts of acclaim" (Bruster 2001, 260), can be read as a "transformed echo of the play's opening storm-scene" (Holland 1995, 225). The initial tempest led the audience and its representatives on stage, the court party, onto the theatre island – the "auspicious gales" of the viewers applause and shouts of acclaim finally lead everyone "Out of this fearful country" again. The audience's applause therefore not only, once and for all, melts *The Tempest* "into air, into thin air", so that the character of Prospero "[l]eave[s] not a rack behind"; the applause not only "constitutes at once an affirmation of his worthiness to return to Naples and a proclamation of his fictionality; [and] thus simultaneously vindicates and ends Prospero's existence" (Tonning 2004, 379); with the epilogue's few lines Prospero turns a mere convention into a statement of complicity. Harry Berger Jr. has good cause to wonder whether Prospero "is entirely sincere in claiming that his project was to please" (1969, 278): I think that he charges the conventional applause with performative force. In a clever way, this applause now figures as the audience's signature under Shakespeare's pragmatic theory of theatrical communication working like weather. The spectators, however, are not entirely free in their decision to countersign this theory: like Ariel, their collaboration is a condition for being able to leave the theatre's fearful country: "My [audience], | That is [your] charge" the epilogue tells them. "Then to the elements | Be free, and fare thou well!"

II *Werther*. Reading the Weather

It was more than 150 years later that a young German, the son of a rich citizen of Frankfurt, published a little book that brought him immediate fame. *Die Leiden des jungen Werthers* (1774) by Johann Wolfgang Goethe was a European bestseller. Within a few years it ran through several editions and was very quickly translated into a range of languages. It not only promoted the twenty-four year old to a leading figure in the European literary scene, above all, *Werther* was an unprecedented popular success with a far-reaching cultural impact that became known as the famous '*Werther*-fever'. None of Goethe's many and prominent works that were to follow in more than fifty years of intensive literary production would match the popular resonance of *Werther*. When his 'mature' work remained somewhat in the shadow of the early novel and its success, Goethe soon developed a rather ambiguous relationship to *Werther*, a relationship that might be reflected in the book's reputation today. It enjoys the existence of a typical 'classic' that is read in schools; everyone has heard about it, but it is not the best of memories or thrilling reading experiences that are associated with it. Nevertheless, in literary criticism *Werther* has always had its place: the number of publications on Goethe's first novel is immense. However, it is rather the obvious cultural importance and its formative (intertextual) influence on European literature that accounts for the scholars' interest than an aesthetic evaluation that differs from Goethe's view of his work. Academically, *Werther* and Goethe's *Sturm und Drang* writing are overshadowed by the monument of Weimar Classicism.

As I would like to demonstrate with my reading, *Werther* and its context of origin deserve more and closer critical attention. The *Sturm und Drang* period is particularly formative with regard to epistemic, social and aesthetic developments that inform our understanding of 'modernity': an analysis of Goethe's early novel thus promises to explore *in statu nascendi* what has become the latent and implicit foundation of a worldview that still decisively influences the way we perceive ourselves and our surroundings today.

Despite the distance of 150 years and completely different linguistic, cultural and epistemic circumstances, Shakespeare plays a decisive role in the intellectual climate of the second half of the 18th century. The enthusiasm for the 'rediscovered' Shakespeare that Goethe shared with Herder and the circle formed in Straßburg is well documented. Without doubt, the admiration, the intense study and the profound knowledge of 'the Bard' has left its traces, especially on Goethe's early work. Dedicating a chapter to Goethe's *Werther* after having closely read Shakespeare's *Tempest* is thus not an unreasonable endeavour. However, since it is not my intention to write a history of influence, these few remarks on the intellectual connection that bridges the rupture between Goethe's and Shakespeare's very different worlds must suffice. The fact that it is the epistolary and autobiographically inspired novel *Werther* and not Goethe's slightly earlier (and in some aspects overtly 'Shakespearean') drama *Götz von Berlichingen* (1773) that made it a European bestseller, emphasises the complexity of Shakespeare's 'influences' on the 18th century literary production. Due to the distance and diversity in genre, *Werther* is not an adequate object for a comparative reading and thus stresses the important epistemic, cultural and social differences that separate Goethe's late 18th from Shakespeare's early 17th century.

In the following sections I will therefore not analyse the novel against the background of early modern Shakespearean theatre, but read it 'separately' and attempt to reconstruct its specific embeddedness in the epistemic, social, aesthetic and cultural surroundings of its time. Herder's and Goethe's enthusiasm for Shakespeare and their characteristic 18th century reception of 'the Bard' form a part of this constellation and will be examined as one of its dimensions in the course of my reading of *Werther*.

It is the weather that appears to be a particularly pertinent focus of study and that captures both the continuities as well as the rupture between the early modern and the *Sturm und Drang* circumstances of literary production. I therefore think it feasible to suggest that the importance of the weather in *Werther* is unconceivable without its Shakespearean prefiguration; however, the weather fulfils a different role in the enlightened world and thus demands a critical approach that will make it productive for literature in a different way. This is what a close reading of the novel will have to demonstrate.

1 Werther and his environment

Werther's first of his famous descriptions of landscape, presented to us in his second letter, dated May 10th, exhibits a curious characteristic of the whole text that has not received adequate critical attention:

> When the vapor of this lovely valley rises *around me* and the midday sun rests on the impenetrable dark of my woods and only a few stray gleams steal into the inner sanctuary [...] My friend! when the light fades *around my eyes* and the world *around me* and the heavens rest in my soul like the shape of a beloved – then I often yearn and think: Oh could you express that [...] – but I am dying of this, I succumb to the force of the splendour of these displays. (23–24; emph. J.U.)[23]

---

[23] "Wenn das liebe Thal *um mich* dampft, und die hohe Sonne an der Oberfläche der undurchdringlichen Finsterniß meines Waldes ruht, und nur einzelne Strahlen sich in das innere Heiligthum stehlen [...]. Mein Freund, wenn's denn *um meine Augen* dämmert, und die Welt *um mich her*

Joachim von der Thüsen is one of the few readers of Werther who have noted that the adverb *rings umher* ['around'] occurs strikingly often (1994, 466) in Goethe's text. In the German original, various phrases that the English translation usually renders as "around" do indeed feature prominently: "rings umher" can be found six times, "rings" in combination with particles other than "umher" eleven times, the phrase "um mich" [around me] even twenty-one times – and there are various other formulations of the same circular constellation to be found in the novel, as we will see in the following.

The passage quoted above gives us some decisive hints concerning the structure of this constellation. First of all, the "around" has a clear centre: it is consistently accompanied by a pronoun of the first person. The constellation thus reflects *Werther*'s innovative form as an epistolary novel that is exclusively centred on only one writer of letters and depicts the singular perspective of only one correspondent. An answer to Lorna Martens's questions of why "the epistolary novel *Werther* provide[d] the impetus for the first modern diary novels" and why it exercised "such a lasting influence on the genre as a whole" (1985, 90) may thus be found in Werther's letters themselves. Not only because they are, according to Gerhard Kurz, rather diary entries than letters (1982, 101), but rather because his letters furnish us with a thorough meditation on a subjective centre and the relation to its surrounding – or, more precisely, on subjectivity. Examining this specific constellation may thus add flesh to the bones of a critical commonplace regarding the novel, the commonplace so memorably described by David Wellbery when he says that "*Werther* is the first European novel in which subjectivity per se – the per se of subjectivity – attains aesthetic concretization" (1994, 181).

But there is more to the passage quoted above and its exposition of the circular constellation whose meaning we are pursuing. Apart from the repeated connection of the "around" with a pronoun of the first person, striking references to the constitution of 'interior' spaces are encountered: we read of an "inner sanctuary" into which "only a few stray gleams steal", and later of the protagonist's "soul" where his impressions finally "rest" when they have "fade[d]" in the outside world. Topographically speaking, these two spaces that are curiously denoted as 'interiors' define the opposing ends of a concentric constellation: at the centre, there is the focalising subject, and, at its very heart, in a literal sense, the interior of its soul. Limiting its vision, at the far end of the vista, so-to-speak, there is the "surface" [*Oberfläche*, missing in the English translation] of "the

---

und Himmel ganz in meiner Seele ruht, wie die Gestalt einer Geliebten; dann sehne ich mich oft und denke: ach könntest du das wieder ausdrücken [...] – Aber ich gehe darüber zu Grunde, ich erliege unter der Gewalt der Herrlichkeit dieser Erscheinungen." (14; emph. J.U.)

impenetrable dark of my woods". All that Werther perceives and delights in takes place "before [his] eyes" (23), in-between these two surfaces, one separating the outer world from Werther's inner soul, one limiting the "lovely valley" lighted up by the midday sun, and thereby also limiting his vista and vision. However, and this is the point one cannot avoid stumbling over when reading the passage quoted above, the outer limit of his vista and of the place he is enjoying is not only a limiting "surface", it constitutes an interior space: "the inner sanctuary". The fact that the outer limitation of the in-between, "my woods", is constructed with the same possessive pronoun as "my soul", as the inner limitation, emphasises that these two constructions of interior spaces are related to each other in a Chinese-box-structure: viewed as limitations, they are concentric circles, drawn around the first person pronoun.

The seemingly enthusiastic passage thus describes a very precise constellation: the topography of the place constitutes an interior space that sur*rounds* the subject, which, in turn, is constituted as another interior space. The passage shows that it is the negotiations, or rather the penetrations, taking place at the topological limitations, that are of interest for the novel. The outer limitation works like a shielding filter, protecting the "inner sanctuary": the force of the "midday sun", contrasting sharply to the "dark of my woods", cannot penetrate "into the inner sanctuary" except for "only a few stray gleams" that manage to "steal into it". This seclusiveness emphasises, or rather creates, the sanctity of the place and is responsible for an ambiguous aura of dark awe and homely bliss.

Without doubt, the letter of May 10th celebrates enthusiastically the "wonderful gaiety", the "eternal bliss" (23) that Werther experiences. However, what is taking place at the two concentric limitations at second glance betrays a certain threat to this gaiety: although both the outer sun and Werther's inner impressions of the scene seem to "rest" peacefully, one on the outer limitation, the "impenetrable dark of my woods", the other inside of the inner limitation of "my soul", the ending of the passage clearly articulates the danger of the limitations' fatal collapse: "but I am dying of this, I succumb to the force [*Gewalt*, i.e. violence] of the splendour of these displays". What looks very much like a typical formulation of the topical problem of artistic expression, turns out in hindsight to have been a foreshadowing of Werther's death.

Apparently, forces are working on the limitations, and the bliss of the idyllic place is not as stable and guaranteed by the "All-loving" "Allmighty" (23) as Werther seems to imagine. In this scene, it is the 'inner interior' space (i.e. Werther's subjective boundaries) that are in danger of being burst open. As will be evident later, the outer limitation, shielding the *locus amoenus*, the bliss of the idyllic place in-between, is as much in danger of succumbing to violence from without as the inner limitation. It is no coincidence that the German formulation of "zu Grunde gehen" that is here translated as "I am dying of this" reoccurs in Werther's conjuration of the "torrent of the genius", whose "rushing in on a spring tide" does not only "shatter your amazed soul", but also makes sure that "the sedate gentlemen['s]" "little summer houses, their tulip beds and cabbage patches would be ruined [*zu Grunde gehen*]" (30–31). As both Robert H. Brown and Karl Nikolaus Renner note, the famous inundation scene described in Werther's letter of December 8th "realize[s]" (Brown 1991, 104) what he had pondered on a metaphorical level (Renner 1985, 13) with regard to the "torrent of the genius". However, it is not only the flooding of Werther's "dear valley" (122) that literally realises a 'zu Grunde gehen', Werther himself is also on the brink of literally 'going to ground':

> Oh, with my arms wide open I stood facing the abyss [*Abgrund*] and breathed down! down! and was lost in the bliss of hurling my torrents, my suffering raging down! roaring away like the waves! (123)[24]

Werther's "dying of this", his succumbing "to the force [*Gewalt*, i.e. violence] of the splendour of these displays", that closes the passage we have been analysing thus foreshadows the violent forces that the novel shows working on the defining constituents of the concentric constellation. This is important to note, because the fact that these dark threats are already latently present within the bliss of this early letter indicate that they are not something that happens to the constellation, owing to unfortunate circumstances, or to Werther's increasing psychic disorder. Rather, these threats are inherent in the constitution of this constellation; they are inseparable from it, a necessary by-product or result of its make up, as will be shown in the following sections. Werther's first of his famous landscape descriptions thus indicates that the quiet idyll is situated in a concentric constellation that is constructed around a focal point; it is located in a specific in-between space that is limited by two boundaries: one outer limitation, shielding the idyll from exterior forces, here the midday sun, and one inner limitation, separating the subject's interior from the outer world that it perceives "around [his] eyes", here "my soul".

Werther's second letter is not the only occasion when the 'concentric constellation' surfaces. The constellation proves rather to be a set structure to which the novel keeps returning, from the first to the last letters. The novel prominently actualises this constellation in different topographical ensembles that strikingly

---

[24] "Ach! Mit offenen Armen stand ich gegen den Abgrund, und athmete hinab! hinab, und verlohr mich in der Wonne, all meine Quaalen all mein Leiden da hinab zu stürmen, dahin zu brausen wie die Wellen." (194)

resemble each other, all sharing the elements that we have worked out with regard to the passage quoted above.

A good example for this is a famous section that is centred around a well:

> I do not know whether deceitful spirits *hover around* this region or whether it is the warm, divine fantasy *in my heart* that makes everything *around me* appear like paradise. Just outside the town there is a well [...]. The low wall above, which forms the *surrounding enclosure*, the tall trees *that cover the place all around*, the coolness of the place; all this has something so attractive [*anzügliches*], so awesome [*schauerliches*] about it. [...] When I sit there, the patriarchal idea comes to life so vividly *around me*; they are there, all our forebears, meeting others and courting at the well, while benevolent spirits *hover around* the wells and springs. (24; transl. altered; emph. J.U.)[25]

The topographical setting of the well exhibits a familiar pattern: the "low wall above, which forms a surrounding enclosure" constitutes a first, inner circle, the "tall trees that cover the place all around" a second, concentric outer circle around the well as its focal point. Again, the notion of seclusiveness is emphasised: "enclosure" designates the inner interior space, the "tall trees" are there to "cover the place all around", which, very similar to the "dark woods" of the passage analysed above, is responsible for the wholesome "coolness of the place". Yet whether this place is really as idyllic as it seems (and as some critics have read it)[26] remains far from clear. Similar to the "inner sanctuary" that oscillated between gloomy awe, and homely bliss, the place is carefully characterised as ambiguous: it has something "schauerliches" (that is 'awe-some' or rather nightmarish) and "anzügliches", which means it exercises an attraction that may well imply danger.[27] The interesting framing of the scene stresses this ambiguity. The "deceitful spirits" that "hover around" the place at the beginning of the scene and of which Werther is not quite sure whether it is they who are responsible for his paradisiac impressions, or not, turn into "benevolent spirits", still "hover[ing] around the wells and springs" at the end of the scene.

---

[25] "Ich weiß nicht, ob so täuschende Geister *um* diese Gegend schweben, oder ob die warme himmlische Phantasie *in meinem Herzen* ist, die mir alles *rings umher* so paradisisch macht. Da ist gleich vor dem Orte ein Brunn' [...]. Das Mäuergen, das oben *umher* die *Einfassung* macht, die hohen Bäume, die den Platz *rings umher bedecken*, die Kühle des Orts, das hat alles so was anzügliches, was schauerliches. [...] Wenn ich da sizze, so lebt die patriarchalische Idee so lebhaft *um mich*, wie sie alle die Altväter am Brunnen Bekanntschaft machen und freyen, und wie *um* die Brunnen und Quellen wohlthätige Geister schweben." (16; emph. J.U.)
[26] Cf. Hohendahl (1972), Pabst (2010) and Powers (1999).
[27] Cf. the entry of Grimm's *Deutsches Wörterbuch* for *anzüglich* that lists the very sentence from Werther that we are analysing and adds the Latin words "ad se rapiens, periculosus, malignus, acerbus" as qualifiers to the German word in question (*DWB*, anzüglich, *adj.*).

Importantly, an allegorical dimension is woven into the scene's framing: the well is introduced as an allegory of the human heart. Quite playfully, the well takes over the central position in the concentric constellation that the heart had occupied before its introduction: the first "around" is related to the "me", then Werther begins to talk about the well, which all of a sudden, and without mediation, continues the concentric topology, in the position of the focal point. Curiously enough, this shifts again and thereby closes the frame: the phrase "When I sit there" reintroduces Werther, "around" whom the "patriarchal idea comes to life", however not without referring back, once again, to the "spirits", still "hovering around the wells". It is not without reason that the novel so carefully builds up this allegory. When the constellation has ceased to work properly, the allegory will be taken up again, and will thereby provide us with another decisive key for the understanding of the (problematic) functioning of the concentric constellation. We will dedicate a detailed analysis to this allegory of the well in a later section, however, at this point it was its characteristic, concentric topology that had to be stressed.

It is hardly surprising that Werther's "spot" of his choice in Wahlheim once more confirms the topological setting that has become familiar to us:

> About an hour's ride from town there is a village called Wahlheim.* [...] At the inn a good woman, pleasant and sprightly despite her age, sells wine, beer, and coffee; and what tops everything are two linden trees whose widespread limbs *cover* the little square in front of the church, which is *surrounded* by peasant cottages, barns, and homesteads. I have rarely found a spot so cozy, so homey [...]. (29; emph. J.U.)[28]

The fact that Werther even has, as he puts it, "my little table brought out from the inn, and my chair" (29) emphasises that he positions himself in the centre of this place, by the linden trees. Werther describes this procedure as "setting up a little hut at some cozy spot" (29), so that we, here again, encounter the double, concentric structure: Werther erects a "little hut" that in turn is "cover[ed]" by trees and "surrounded by peasant cottages, barns, and homesteads". No wonder that the atmosphere emanating from this place is similar to the ambiguity that characterised the other examples of the concentric constellation. "So vertraulich, so heimlich", as the German original has it, cannot but remind us of a notion that Sigmund Freud will make famous more than 150

---

28 "Ohngefähr eine Stunde von der Stadt liegt ein Ort, den sie Wahlheim* nennen. [...] Eine gute Wirthin, die gefällig und munter in ihrem Alter ist, schenkt Wein, Bier, Caffee, und was über alles geht, sind zwey Linden, die mit ihren ausgebreiteten Aesten den kleinen Plaz vor der Kirche *bedecken*, der *ringsum* mit Bauerhäusern, Scheuern und Höfen eingeschlossen ist. So vertraulich, so heimlich hab ich nicht leicht ein Pläzchen gefunden [...]." (26; emph. J.U.)

years after Goethe wrote his novel: the notion of the uncanny (cf. 1970 [1919]). The English translation "so cozy, so homey" suppresses the connotation of the 'occult' that both, "vertraulich" [also: confidential, esoteric] and "heimlich" [also: covert, clandestine] transport.[29] This trace of the ambiguous, uncanny atmosphere, one of the key elements of the concentric constellation (and that is to say, of the constellation of modern subjectivity), the use of the very same linguistic material with which the Viennese founder of psychoanalysis will play in a similar way, seems undeniably to point towards Freud. Against the background of what Susanne Lüdemann has demonstrated in her book on literature and psychoanalysis (1994), the constitutive connection between the literature of Goethe's time and the fundamental concepts of psychoanalysis is not revolutionary: her claim that the model of subjectivity that psychoanalysis conceptualises emerged in the late 18th century, and, to a considerable extent, in and through the novel, is confirmed by our findings in *Werther*. We can, at this stage, only take the constellation's dipartite structure of interiority and the resulting uncanny atmosphere of this interiority as first, weak indicators. However, this idea will be followed up and what still has to be discussed is perhaps the strongest argument for a proximity of what Goethe's novel relates and the field of psychoanalysis: the insight "that we are not masters of ourselves and least of all able to dictate our feelings" (49).[30] As will be seen, Werther is not master of his hut – not only because heavy weather keeps storming on it from the outside, but also and mainly because equally heavy weather urges from the inside and threatens to burst the hut open. The forces of the storming, urging, uncontrollable 'inner interior' are, that is one of the main claims of this chapter, rightfully also called 'weather', because they maintain an intrinsic relation to the 'outer' weathery forces, as will be shown in the following sections.

In the analyses of the topographic ensembles we have so far neglected one obvious trait: the concentric constellation is characterised as a 'lonely' place, as

---

29 The entry "heimlich" in Grimm's *Deutsches Wörterbuch* quotes this very passage from Goethe's *Werther* as an example for the word's denoting the "homey and domestic, from where the notion of the cosy and familiar emanate [aus der bedeutung des heimatlichen und häuslichen fliesz die vorstellung des traulichen und vertrauten]" (*DWB*, heimlich, *adj. adv.*, 3.; my transl.). However, it also lists the semantic dimension that will become so important for Freud: "the meaning of the hidden, dangerous [...] develops further, so that *heimlich* takes on the sense that *unheimlich* [...] used to carry. [die bedeutung des versteckten, gefährlichen [...] entwickelt sich noch weiter, so dasz heimlich den sinn empfängt, den sonst unheimlich [...] hat.]" (*DWB*, heimlich, *adj. adv.* 9.; my transl.)
30 "[...] daß man nicht Herr über sich selbst sey, und am wenigsten über seine Empfindungen gebieten könne" (66).

the place of one, solitary subject. "I am alone and glad to be alive" (23),[31] these are the words with which Werther introduces his landscape description of May 10th that was analysed above as the first sketch of the concentric constellation. The same notion of loneliness characterises the setting of the well: when Werther returns to it some months after the famous scene we have read, it reminds him of "the time when my heart was so alone" (51).[32] And "when one fine afternoon [Werther] chance[s] upon the spot under the linden trees", in Wahlheim, he finds "the place lonely" (29; transl. altered).[33] The last example of a topographic ensemble is also described as containing an inner, "enclosed spot around which hover all the thrills of solitude", a solitude that is explicitly connected with the notion of the uncanny:

> First, you have the distant prospect between the chestnut trees – Ah, I remember, I have already written you, I think, a lot about it, how high walls of beeches finally *enclose* you, and how an abutting grove makes the avenue ever darker, until finally everything ends in an *enclosed spot around* which hover all the thrills of solitude. I still feel the sense of hominess/uncanniness [*wie heimlich mir's ward*] experienced when I entered for the first time one day at high noon; I dimly felt what a stage that could become for bliss and for pain. (74; transl. altered; emph. J.U.)[34]

It might almost be tiring to discover again the topological structure of the concentric constellation, with its two enclosing circles, here the "high walls of beeches" as an outer limitation and the "enclosed spot" as an 'inner interior' – especially since even the wording remains similar to the description of Werther's other familiar spots. The "tall trees that cover[ed] the place all around" the well have simply been turned into a "high wall of beeches"; this time it is not "deceitful" or "benevolent spirits", but a "thrill of solitude" that "hover[s]" "around" the central spot. We also find the notion of darkness, first conveyed to us in the formulation of "my dark woods", here produced by an "abutting grove". And, as already mentioned, the concentric constellation produces a

---

31 "Ich bin so allein und freue mich meines Lebens [...]." (14)
32 "[...] die Zeit, da mein Herz so allein war [...]." (70)
33 "Das erstemal als ich durch einen Zufall an einem schönen Nachmittage unter die Linden kam, fand ich das Plätzchen so einsam." (26)
34 "Erst hast du zwischen den Castanienbäumen die weite Aussicht – Ach ich erinnere mich, ich habe dir, denk ich, schon viel geschrieben davon, wie hohe Buchenwände einen endlich einschliessen und durch ein daran stoßendes Bosquet die Allee immer düstrer wird, bis zuletzt alles sich in ein geschlossenes Plätzgen endigt, das alle Schauer der Einsamkeit umschweben. Ich fühl es noch wie heimlich mir's ward, als ich zum erstenmal an einem hohen Mittage hinein trat, ich ahndete ganz leise, was das noch für ein Schauplaz werden sollte von Seligkeit und Schmerz." (116)

constitutive ambiguity: it is a place "for bliss and pain", of which the feeling of the uncanny/homey proves an apt foreboding.

The reason why we have worked our way through all these examples in great detail is simple: this constellation, its problems and merits, its "bliss and pain", is what the whole novel is about. The few traits of this constellation, its double structure of interiority, its being threatened externally as well as internally by astonishingly similar forces, and the uncanniness that issues from it constitute the backbone of the present reading of the novel. This approach follows Werther's claim that the topography of his familiar places sets the "stage" for all the "bliss and pain" of his sufferings.

However, there is one important qualification: pragmatically speaking, especially with regard to what we have said about Shakespeare and early modern theatre, this "Schauplatz", this setting is not a stage. It suffices to remember the boatswain's sending the court party "To cabin!" (1.1.17) in the first scene of Shakespeare's *Tempest*, to realise the fundamental difference in the two text's meta-topographical – and that is also to say meta-medial – awareness: as we saw in the first chapter, the court party refuses to go to the cabins and opts for the public, for exposing themselves to the stormy weather on board. They thereby choose the open space of the theatrical. The metatheatrical reflections of *The Tempest* make it quite clear that 'the cabin' itself cannot be staged. Appearing on stage always means abandoning the cabin, entering an open space, either being let loose from confinements by the directing stage-master Prospero, like Ariel, Caliban, the rebelling party or the sailors, or deliberately preferring the stage over the cabin, like the court party. Goethe's *Werther*, on the contrary, is a novel about the cabin; the cabin not as a place of religious retreat, not as a place where one belongs to God – but as the place where one belongs only to oneself, as the single, proper room of one's own.

Unfortunately, all the English translations have covered the traces that the novel leaves, disclosing itself explicitly as a novel about 'the cabinet': the very first letter introduces the "ruined little cabinet [*Cabinetgen*]" (23; transl. altered) in the garden that Werther immediately declares his "favorite spot" (23). The necessity of Werther's death is given topological expression when Lotte, in their last encounter, retreats into her "little room [*Cabinet*[ ]]" (140), her cabinet, and does not answer Werther's pleading for a farewell. This takes on symbolical meaning against the background of the scene that finishes off the novel's first part and that we have just examined as the last example of the concentric constellation. The "enclosed spot around which hover all the thrills of solitude" turns out to be "the dark little garden house [*düstern Cabinette*]". Werther remembers well the moment "when [he] entered for the first time one day at high noon"; now it is "Lotte[, who] enter[s]", with her husband – and Werther.

Their relation to this shared interior may be read as an allegory for the novel's main question, which is a question of the cabinet:

> Lotte entered and sat down, Albert beside her, and I as well; but my restlessness did not let me sit for long; I stood, went over to her, paced back and forth, sat down again: I was in an anxious state. (74–75)[35]

Whereas Lotte and Albert calmly accept the domesticity of the cabinet, Werther's "restlessness" drives him beyond that construction of interiority. As Joachim von der Thüsen puts it, his "need for movement, in contrast [to Lotte], does generally not stop at those boundaries of the domestic and the uncontained [*ungeborgenen*] life" (1994, 477; my transl.). The necessity of Werther's restlessness and the irresistible attraction of the cabinet's shelter account for the fact that the story of the cabinet is ultimately tragic: a story of "bliss and pain". The cabinet is thus not a topographical metaphor of what the individual, as an individual, structurally is, must be, and has ever been, for all time. The novel unmistakably reveals this setting as a place of contestation. Goethe's *Werther* is dedicated to the resistances that a well-defined, life-centring and, for the late 18th century, 'unavoidable' constellation faces.

With regard to Shakespeare's theatre and its contrasting choice against the cabin we have seen that this constellation is not universal – it has a rather recent historical pedigree, more or less in the making when *Werther* was being written, as will soon become clear. If we are to call this constellation by 'its name', this would sound very familiar to us all: modern subjectivity. This prominent tag has been avoided as far as possible and 'the concentric constellation' or 'the cabinet' preferred, because it is the characteristics of this constellation, its detailed construction and functioning that is the object of analysis. The rather abstract term of the 'concentric constellation' seems to be more promising for analysing phenomena of culture and society than merely accepting the phenomenon that has attracted attention under so overused a label as 'modern subjectivity', which has long lost its accuracy and appeal. The idea is to follow closely the conceptual material and the narrative elaboration that Goethe's *Werther* offers to its readers, which may provide us with new insights into the historical constellation that emerged around the time when the novel was written, and which is itself thoroughly reflected in it. This may shed some light on the circumstances of the modern subject's birth, the process of constitution of a constellation that has grown so natural to us and our understanding of

---

[35] "Lotte trat hinein und sezte sich, Albert neben sie, ich auch, doch, meine Unruhe lies mich nicht lange sizzen, ich stand auf, trat vor sie, gieng auf und ab, sezte mich wieder, es war ein ängstlicher Zustand." (116)

the world that we intuitively would not suspect it to be only one, historically specific way of making sense of that world – amongst many others, like the Shakespearean one, which we have long forgotten.

What can be learned from the novel is that the cabinet is more than merely a symbol for the abstract notion of interiority that is specific for what we conceive of as 'the subject'. It is embedded, as the inner interior, in the concentric constellation. Consequently, identifying the subject with the notion of a simple interiority can hardly be adequate. What 'the subject' finds beyond this "sanctuary", or "enclosed spot", the vista it perceives is not its other, but, as Werther tells us again and again, another, larger interior space, the limited space of what is "around" him. His surroundings form an inseparable part of the constellation, a defining element of the concentricity that the novel indicates is so characteristic. The concept of modern subjectivity thus consists of these two interplaying, concentric components: the subject's inner interiority and his environment.

It is no coincidence that the notion of environ-ment (*Um-welt*) resonates so intensely with the striking accumulation of formulations involving 'the around' which were encountered in this reading of *Werther*. Furthermore, we should not be too astonished by the fact that despite the many variants of 'the around' that the novel employs to express the notion of circular arrangement (*um herum, rings umher, um mich*), the simple term *Umwelt* (environment) that so pertinently captures this constellation does not occur once. The reason for this is as simple as it is hard for us to imagine, who are so used to the naturalised notion of *Umwelt*: it was not at Goethe's disposal, because it had not yet been coined! Despite its sixty-eight thousand pages, Johann Heinrich Zedler's *Grosses vollständiges Universal-Lexicon aller Wissenschafften und Künste* (1732–1754) does not list an entry for the term *Umwelt*. According to Jacob and Wilhelm Grimm's *Deutsches Wörterbuch* (1838–1971) the term *Umwelt* has only been in circulation "since the beginning of the nineteenth century" (*DWB*, umwelt, *n.*), its first occurrence is recorded for the year 1800, in an ode by Baggesen. Goethe features prominently among Grimm's examples of the early users of the term, however, more than thirty years after he, in his *Werther*, so concisely developed the concept that this term designates. In *Werther*, then, with the 'concentric constellation', the birth of a concept can be observed, before it has been widely recognisable under its proper name, and, more importantly, before it has been naturalised as the uncontested way that we, still today, perceive ourselves and the world around us.

The role of the weather in this dipartite constellation of subject and environment is shown as ambiguous in *Werther*: on the one hand, the weather is situated beyond the outer limitation, excluded or at least shielded, filtered away, from the idyllic setting of well, valley and cabinet; on the other hand,

Werther can sometimes quite calmly observe it "beating against the windowpane" (84). However, despite examples like the "snow and hailstones" (84) that Werther watches while he is writing Lotte (I think it is important that his writing a love-letter supplements the containment of the weather in this scene) the weather has not yet been domesticated into the controllable environment. The novel rather represents the weather as a dangerous force, somehow shut out or away, certainly not featuring in the 'abstract conception' of modern subjectivity. As much as it seems to storm from somewhere beyond, the novel in its explorations of the concentric constellation stresses the supplementary character of these weathery forces. Especially the fact that 'the storm' is always uncannily lashing against the limitations from the outer outside *and*, at the same time, from the inner inside, undermines the assumption that the weather is the subject's unknown and hostile other. The scene in which Werther, having "taken refuge from a heavy storm" (84), writes a love-letter to Lotte proves a good case in point: Werther's urge to write is directly triggered by the storm outside; the novel unmistakably states that only when "snow and hailstones [are] beating against the windowpane", had the "moment" come "in which [Werther's] heart urged [him] to write to [Lotte]" (84). This act of writing challenges as much, from within, the narrow limitations of "this solitude, [...] this confinement" provided by "this lowly peasant tavern", as the weather "beating against the windowpane" from without. It is this uncanny connection or correlation between (outer) storm and (inner) urge – a connection so happily depicted in the expression *Sturm und Drang* ('Storm and Urge')[36] – that is the underlying subject of this chapter. Thus far our readings of passages from *Werther* have fuelled the intuition that Goethe's novel explores the weathery underside of modern subjectivity. Perhaps more than that: with regard to the role that the medium of writing (and reading, as will be seen) plays in these explorations we could even suppose that the novel, as a novel, is *dedicated* to this weathery underside. For this approach a thorough analysis of the famous ball-scene promises further insight.

2 The birth of a weathery medium – the ball-scene

Werther's letter of June 16th is doubtless the most famous of the collection. It narrates the story of a moment that is widely conceived of as the decisive moment for romantic love relationships in general: Werther's "mak[ing the]

---

[36] Instead of resorting to the conventional 'Storm and Stress' I prefer to translate 'Sturm und Drang' as 'Storm and Urge', because *stress* does not convey as precisely as *urge* the fact that the German *Drang* does not refer to objective, 'outer' but to subjective, 'inner' processes, to processes taking place 'inside' the human being.

acquaintance" of Lotte, "who has won [his] heart" (34) – that is to say their (?) falling in love. However, besides the thrill of the situation and the obvious implications that this diegetic step has for the rest of Werther's story (the tragic turn that will issue from this fatal encounter), there is still something special about this letter, something that accounts for the letter's importance. Despite Werther's warning his addressee Wilhelm that "To narrate to [him] in an orderly fashion [...] will be a hard task" (34; transl. altered)[37] and that he is "full of joy and hence not a good chronicler" (34),[38] his letter turns out to be the most comprehensive and also the most 'chronicling' piece of narrative that we get from him. It not only assembles most of the key motives of the novel, it also sets them into relation with one another by embedding them into a story. This is in stark contrast to the dominating texture of *Werther* to which this special epistolary novel owes some of its fame: being fragmented into short, almost lyrical impressions of very different tone and motif. In the letter of June 16th what the novel presents as a whole takes place or happens in miniature: assembling the different motifs and impressions, inducing resonances and thus constituting a mosaic-like picture out of them. A thorough analysis of this scene thus promises to introduce us to 'the gist' of the novel – the weathery proceedings of and around the concentric constellation and the role of literature in this context.

2.1 Breaking/Transgressing the circles

The letter of June 16th starts with one of the novel's surprisingly rare reflections on the writing situation, with Werther's pondering on the alternatives of experience and writing, which could be of extreme interest with regard to the pragmatics of the epistolary novel:

> No, not some other time, I want to tell you right now. If I don't, I never will. For, just between us, since I started to write, I have three times been on the point of putting down my pen, saddling my horse, and riding out [*hinaus*] to see her. And yet I swore this morning not to ride out [*hinaus*], and yet every minute I go to the window to see how high the sun still is. –
>
> I could not resist, I had to go out to her [*zu ihr hinaus*]. Here I am again, Wilhelm, I'll have my evening bread and butter and write to you. How my soul delights to see her amid [*im Kreise*] those dear, lively children, her eight brothers and sisters. (35; transl. altered)[39]

---

37 "Dir in der Ordnung zu erzählen, wie's zugegangen ist [...] wird schwer halten [...]." (36)
38 "[...] ich bin vergnügt und kein guter Historienschreiber [...]." (36)
39 "Nein, nicht ein andermal, jetzt gleich will ich dir's erzählen. Thu ich's jetzt nicht, geschäh's niemals. Denn, unter uns, seit ich angefangen habe zu schreiben, war ich schon dreymal im

One could argue that the scene exhibits and interrupts the epistolary novel's illusion that experience is transported transparently through writing, and that writing does not stand in the way of experiencing, but is somehow taking place effortlessly, automatically. However, the novel does not develop this pragmatic argument, it does not come back to this question – that is why I would suggest that this is not what the scene at hand is ultimately about. Instead, the writing scene at the beginning of the letter introduces us to a central topic of the novel: the urge to go out, something is irresistibly drawing Werther *hinaus*. The scene stages this urge with unmistakable emphasis: *hinaus* features three times in only two sentences, culminating in the "I had to go out to her" that stresses the urge's victory over Werther's intentions to stay in and write to Wilhelm. The novel repeatedly readopts the catch-phrase that is highlighted in this writing scene. For example, in a letter two and a half months later, also triggered by Lotte; this time it is the interior space shared with Lotte, that Werther feels moved to leave:

> And – except when, from time to time, melancholy gets the better of me and Lotte allows me the miserable solace of weeping tears of anguish over her hand – then I must away, *must go out* [*Muß hinaus*]! and then I roam far and wide over the fields; then my joy lies in climbing a steep mountain [...]. (73; transl. altered; emph. J.U.)⁴⁰

A scene shortly before Werther's death also echoes this urge to go out and connects it with the quite desperate joy of climbing steep mountains:

> The watchmen, who knew him, let him *go out* [*hinaus*] without a word. A mix of rain and snow was whirling, and it was nearly eleven o'clock when he knocked at the gate again. His servant noticed, on Werther's return home, that his master's hat was missing. He did not venture to comment, helped him off with his clothes, which were soaked through. Only much later was the hat found on a crag that overlooks the valley from the slope of the hill [...]. (140; emph. J.U.)⁴¹

Begriffe die Feder niederzulegen, mein Pferd satteln zu lassen und hinaus zu reiten, und doch schwur ich mir heut früh nicht hinaus zu reiten – und gehe doch alle Augenblicke ans Fenster zu sehen, wie hoch die Sonne noch steht. Ich hab's nicht überwinden können, ich mußte zu ihr hinaus. Da bin ich wieder, Wilhelm, und will mein Butterbrod zu Nacht essen und dir schreiben. Welche eine Wonne das für meine Seele ist, sie in dem Kreise der lieben muntern Kinder ihrer acht Geschwister zu sehen! –" (36–38)

40 "Und wenn nicht manchmal die Wehmuth das Uebergewicht nimmt, und Lotte mir den elenden Trost erlaubt, auf ihrer Hand meine Beklemmung auszuweinen, so muß ich fort! Muß hinaus! Und schweife dann weit im Felde umher. Einen gähen Berg zu klettern, ist dann meine Freude [...]." (112)

41 "Die Wächter die ihn schon gewohnt waren, ließen ihn stillschweigend hinaus, es stübte zwischen Regen und Schnee, und erst gegen eilfe klopfte er wieder. Sein Diener bemerkte, als

In this episode narrated by the editor the 'outside' to which Werther obviously feels so attracted is quite skilfully characterised as a 'weathery' space. In order to unravel the role that the weather plays in this passage, we have to take a look at the scene's topography. What we perceive must look familiar to us: Werther crosses two boundaries, the outer one is the town gate, controlled by the watchmen, the other, inner one, is his home, where his servant is in charge. Of his wandering and experiences outside the town gates no description is given – what is narrated is just his crossing the boundary to get outside, and, after quite some time obviously, it has become late, his return into the town. In contrast to the richness of detail with which Werther's two crossings of the outer town boundary are related, the lack of the story of his wanderings outside the town limitations deserves to be called a narratological ellipsis. However, the editor does not narrate just nothing in-between the crossings. There is one, as I would suggest, weighty and meaningful half sentence inserted, standing in for the absent story, eight words dedicated to the weather: "A mix of rain and snow was whirling". As astonishing as it might already be to read of the weather instead of the hero's experiences and adventures, what becomes evident when viewing the passage more closely is that this weather description makes, as a weather description, very little sense. At least when we assume, and I think this is plausible, that the weather beyond the town gates does not differ significantly from the weather inside the town. Surely a "mix of rain and snow" must still have been "whirling" on Werther's way from the gate to his home. However, this is obviously not what the novel intends. By positioning these eight words of 'weather description' right within the narratological gap of Werther's experiences outside, substituting them for a story, the novel skilfully characterises the topographical and topological relations that it is so constantly working with. The outer outside, the realm beyond the outer limitation (here the town gate) is a space of rough, uncontrollable weather. That is why a reference to this weather can perfectly well substitute for the story of Werther's actions and experiences: what he is essentially doing by leaving the town in the late evening and night is exposing himself to the weather. In contrast to Shakespeare, where we have identified this condition as the standard of the pragmatic situation of early modern theatre, what Werther is doing in this situation (and whenever he yields to the urge of having to go out [*hinaus*]) is highly exceptional, crazy, irrational. His servant's reaction on Werther's return emphasises this exceptionality: "He did not venture to comment", as if what Werther had been doing the last hours

---

Werther nach Hause kam, daß seinem Herrn der Huth fehlte. Er getraute sich nichts zu sagen, entkleidete ihn, alles war naß. Man hat nachher den Huth auf einem Felsen, der an dem Abhange des Hügels in's Thal sieht gefunden [...]." (246)

was beyond discussion – and narration. However, what does reveal something about Werther's nightly journey beyond the town gates is the state of his clothes: his "hat was missing", his clothes "were soaked through". Both of these details bespeak how successful and intense Werther's exposing himself to the weather, or rather his merging with the weather, had been: clothes and especially the hat are, it would seem, the last layer, protecting Werther from the fierce forces of nature. The missing hat and soaked clothes do not fulfil this function any longer. More than that, the missing, perhaps abandoned hat, and the fact that Werther does not even seem bothered by its being missing, underline the impression that what his servant, and probably most of the readers, interpret as a miserable state, may for Werther be merely the remnants of an ecstatic natural experience. In any case, what can be said with certainty is that this experience seems to have been beyond social acceptance and is thus transformed to the sign of some sort of mental derangement.

An earlier scene had set the course for this reading of Werther's longing for the weathery outside: "Last night I had to go outside" (122; transl. altered),[42] Werther writes using the usual catch-phrase, when "all brooks were swollen and [his] dear valley flooded from Wahlheim down" (122). He "had heard already in the evening that the river had overflowed its banks" (122; transl. altered); why, then, is it so late as "[l]ast *night*", "[i]n the night, after eleven o'clock" that he "ran outside" (122)? Obviously it is not curiosity that drives Werther "outside", but some "unfamiliar inner frenzy [*Toben*]":

> I am in the state that must have been experienced by those unfortunate creatures who were thought to be ridden by an evil demon. At times it takes hold of me; it is not terror, not lust – it's an unfamiliar inner frenzy that threatens to rip my breast apart, that constricts my throat! Woe! Woe! and then I roam through the frightful night scenes of this hostile season. (122)[43]

Significantly enough, this passage directly precedes the mentioning of the flooding so that it becomes quite obvious that Werther rather uses this natural event to create a "frightful night scene[ ]" (the reason why he waits until after nightfall to go outside) where he can roam to give way to what he calls his "inner frenzy". Unfortunately the English translation "frenzy" for the German

---

[42] "Gestern Nacht mußt ich hinaus. Ich hatte noch Abends gehört, der Fluß sey übergetreten [...]." (194)

[43] "[...] ich bin in einem Zustande, in dem jene Unglükklichen müssen gewesen seyn, von denen man glaubte, sie würden von einem bösen Geiste umher getrieben. Manchmal ergreift mich's, es ist nicht Angst, nicht Begier! es ist ein inneres unbekanntes Toben, das meine Brust zu zerreissen droht, das mir die Gurgel zupreßt! Wehe! Wehe! Und dann schweif ich umher in den furchtbaren nächtlichen Scenen dieser menschenfeindlichen Jahrszeit." (194)

Toben misses an important semantic dimension, the crucial dimension for our interest: the verb *toben* is most commonly used in connection with a storm, or heavy weather, as in *Draußen tobte ein Sturm* [A storm was raging outside] – or, of the passions, as in *Er tobte vor Wut* [He was raging with anger]. It is, as we learn from Johann Christoph Adelung's *Grammatisch-kritisches Wörterbuch der hochdeutschen Mundart* (1811) another example of the group of verbs that featured so prominently in Shakespeare's *Tempest*, expressing the production of sound, applicable both to human action and to the weather, like *to howl, to whistle, to beat* and others. The entry "Toben" summarises this semantic dimension as the verb's first meaning: "To cause a high degree of vehement noise" (*Adl*, toben, *v.* 1.; my transl.).[44] The examples for this meaning list "an angry man", shouting vehemently or stamping his foot, as well as the winds, the sea, the must in the barrel, the passions, the waves: they all do what the German verb *toben* in its first meaning signifies. By translating *Toben* with *frenzy*, Stanley Corngold opted for the semantic dimension that Adelung categorises under 2): "Anciently used in the narrower sense for insane, being bereft of one's understanding, raving, because this is often linked to the actual *Toben*" (*Adl.* toben, *v.* 2.; my transl.).[45] Corngold's choice is thus no mistake, it however covers up that Werther's "inner" urge and the outside to which this need is driving him are of an uncannily equal *weathery* nature. As we have seen in the first chapter, the insight that the human passions and the weather are analogues would have counted merely as a commonplace in Shakespeare's time, when the analogy of microcosm and macrocosm constituted the system of the world. As Adelung's entry shows, the epistemological reference system has changed: his distinction between an "actual Toben" and its metaphorical and metonymical derivatives refers to the fact that the 'physiological' explanation of frenzy as a bad weather of the humours does not seem to be intelligible any more. The 18th century's system of the world, and, as a consequence, also the understanding of the human being and his body differs strikingly from its early modern predecessor; the weathery notions that for Shakespeare still represented the way the world was constituted and operated have been degraded to the realm of metaphor. Against this background it becomes understandable that the weathery "inner"

---

[44] "Einen hohen Grad des ungestümen Lärmens verursachen. Ein Zorniger tobet, wenn er ungestüm schreyet, mit den Füßen stampft u. s. f. Warum toben die Heiden? Die Tiefen toben, Ps. 77, 17. Die Winde toben, Sir. 39, 34. Und wenn er noch so tobte. Das tobende Meer. Der Most tobt in den Fässern. Die tobende Leidenschaft. Wenn über seinem Haupt der Wellen Donner tobt, Kleist." (*Adl*, toben, *v.* 1.)

[45] "Ehedem wurde es in engerer Bedeutung häufig für unsinnig, des Verstandes beraubt seyn, rasen, gebraucht, weil dieses oft mit einem eigentlichen Toben verbunden ist." (*Adl*, toben, *v.* 2.)

Toben seems so "unfamiliar" to Werther. However, this lack of familiarity does not render the weathery nature of his "inner" *Toben* that urges him to go out and expose himself to the weather any less noteworthy. On the contrary, the novel seems to re-discover something, something weathery, that has vanished from the vista of 'scientific', authoritative knowledge. If this proves true, then the uncanny interest in the unfamiliar that turns out to be a suppressed familiar (not on a personal level and not according to social, or parental norms in a stricter sense, but according to a new regime of knowledge) emphasises again the proximity of psychoanalysis and Goethe's novel.

Returning to the scene that introduced *hinaus*, the urge to go out, we have learned from this longish detour that when Werther "must go out to [Lotte]" instead of writing to Wilhelm, this is not a singular event triggered by his fresh love. It is one instance in this motif's chain of recurring instances, and this motif pervades the whole novel. This is certainly not the first notice taken of this motif, but it still seems to be quite difficult to grasp. Peter Pütz's interpretation that Werther is permanently escaping (1983, 56) is not convincing: it does not account for Werther's urge to go out and see Lotte. Even for the late instances where his leaving the town in the middle of the night might indeed look like an escape, the central element of Werther's inner drive to do so and the uncanny similarity of his inner storm and the outer weather remain unexplained. Erdmann Waniek's observation of a theme of "Vergehen" [decay/going away/ vanishing] (1982, 57) seems to come closer to what we have thus far found out about *hinaus*. As will become clear in the analysis of the dance scene, the novel not only bemoans the tragic aspect of decay and departing – it also joyfully affirms the "Vergehen". This is an important observation, because Werther's need to go out cannot simply be treated as a pathological symptom. Its connection with his suicidal last days should not cover up the rich spectrum of shades in which the novel presents this motif to us. Especially the early forms of this urge deserve critical attention: not only Werther's falling in love with Lotte, but earlier still, the longing to go out in his youth: "At that time, in blissful ignorance, I longed to set out [*sehnt ich mich* [...] *hinaus*] into the unknown world" (93).[46] This childhood longing, Werther's urge to see Lotte and his "inner frenzy [*Toben*]" are all instances of the same structural 'movement' – a movement that is best captured by conceptualising it with the concentric constellation. Werther's letter of June 16th gives us a first opportunity to do so – and we will repeatedly come back to this in later sections.

---

[46] "Damals sehnt ich mich in glüklicher Ungewissheit hinaus in die unbekannte Welt [...]." (150)

It is no coincidence that Werther's breaking the first circle (that is leaving his home and penfriend to see Lotte) promptly conjures up the next circle, the iconic one of Lotte, surrounded by her siblings:

> I could not resist, I had to go out to her [*zu ihr hinaus*]. Here I am again, Wilhelm, I'll have my evening bread and butter and write to you. How my soul delights to see her amid [*im Kreise*] those dear, lively children, her eight brothers and sisters. (35; transl. altered)[47]

Werther here prepares us for one of the most prominent tableaus of European literature. Furthermore, he introduces a miniature of the scene that increases our awareness of the importance of the masterpiece to come. However, the little miniature already transports the characteristic trait of this tableau: the constellation in a circle around Lotte. All the tableau does is stage the "most charming spectacle" of this circular constellation:

> I walked across the yard to the handsome house, and when I had gone up the front steps and entered the doorway, I caught sight of the most charming spectacle that I have ever witnessed. In the vestibule six children from eleven to two years old *crowded around a girl* with a lovely figure, of medium height, wearing a simple white dress with pink ribbons on her sleeves and at her breast. She was holding a loaf of black bread and cutting off a slice for each of *the little ones surrounding her*, in proportion to their age and appetite, giving it to each one with such kindness, each shouting out so unaffectedly their: Thank you! after having reached up for so long with their little hands even before the slice had been cut, and now, delighted with supper, either dashing off or, if they were of a quieter nature, walking calmly toward the *courtyard gate* to see the strange persons and the *carriage in which their Lotte was to drive off*. (36; emph. J.U.)[48]

What we encounter in the tableau is the concentric constellation. However, in this particularly idyllic instance it is not Werther, who is in the centre, but

---

47 "Ich hab's nicht überwinden können, ich mußte zu ihr hinaus. Da bin ich wieder, Wilhelm, und will mein Butterbrod zu Nacht essen und dir schreiben. Welche eine Wonne das für meine Seele ist, sie in dem Kreise der lieben muntern Kinder ihrer acht Geschwister zu sehen! –" (38)
48 "Ich gieng durch den Hof nach dem wohlgebauten Hause, und da ich die vorliegenden Treppen hinaufgestiegen war und in die Thüre trat, fiel mir das reizendste Schauspiel in die Augen, das ich jemals gesehen habe. In dem Vorsaale wimmelten sechs Kinder, von eilf zu zwey Jahren, *um* ein Mädchen von schöner mittlerer Taille, die ein simples weisses Kleid mit blaßrothen Schleifen am Arm und Brust anhatte. Sie hielt ein schwarzes Brod und schnitt ihren Kleinen *rings herum* jedem sein Stük nach Proportion ihres Alters und Appetites ab, gabs jedem mit solcher Freundlichkeit, und jedes rufte so ungekünstelt sein: Danke! indem es mit den kleinen Händchen lang in die Höhe gereicht hatte, eh es noch abgeschnitten war, und nun mit seinem Abendbrode vergnügt entweder wegsprang, oder nach seinem stillern Charakter gelassen davon nach dem *Hofthore* zugieng, um die Fremden und die *Kutsche* zu sehen, darinnen ihre Lotte *wegfahren sollte*." (40; emph. J.U.)

Lotte. The entire scene "is crowded around her", the children are "surrounding her" exactly paralleling the way the world was grouped in circles around Werther in the examples of the constellation discussed above. Interestingly enough Werther will soon enter Lotte's circle, he will even share the centre with her. This is aptly expressed by the fact that despite Lotte's claim that her siblings "have their bread sliced by no one else but [her]" (36),[49] only two months later, Werther is allowed to take over even this central task: "I sliced their bread for supper, which they now accept almost as gladly from me as from Lotte" (68).[50] Up to now, having described this process, it must look as if Werther is simply changing circles, leaving his old, solitary circle, entering a new, better one, because it is shared and crowded with Lotte and her little siblings. However, although Werther experiences this scene as an initiation, the tableau's end indicates that it in fact depicts something very different: Lotte's leaving her family circle. The "courtyard gate" is one marker (we will presently encounter another) of this concentric constellation's outer, limiting circle, the inner circle having been constituted by the children crowding around their sister. Beyond that outer limitation there are "strange persons", and the most worrying sight is the "carriage in which their Lotte was to drive off". Lotte is not only, like Werther, a centre around which a circular constellation has been constituted, around which her little world groups itself, she obviously also shares his urge or longing to go out.

Astonishingly enough, the scene's character as a farewell scene, and more importantly, the parallel of Werther's and Lotte's leaving their circles, has not received adequate critical attention. This is all the more striking, because the scene extensively stages Lotte's departing and thereby also discloses the double concentric topology of the scene's setting. Lotte takes leave twice: first from her little ones that remain in the inner circle, now under the tutelage of their oldest sister Sophie, then from "the two oldest boys" who are allowed to leave the inner circle with the departing Lotte:

> The two oldest boys had climbed up on the coach, and at my request she allowed them to ride with us to the edge of the woods as long as they promised not to tease one another and to hold on tight. (37)[51]

---

49 "[...] sie wollen von niemanden Brod geschnitten haben als von mir [...]." (40)
50 "Ich schnitt ihnen das Abendbrod, das sie nun fast so gerne von mir als von Lotten annehmen [...]." (102)
51 "Die zwey ältesten der Knaben waren hinten auf die Kutsche geklettert, und auf mein Vorbitten erlaubte sie ihnen, bis vor den Wald mit zu fahren, wenn sie versprächen, sich nicht zu necken, und sich recht fest zu halten." (42)

Again it is trees, here "the edge of the woods", that define the outer limitation of the concentric constellation. Here Lotte says farewell to her two oldest brothers, here she "had the coachman stop and her brothers dismount; *once again*, they were eager to kiss her hand" (37; emph. J.U.).[52] And as if this "once again" did not suffice to indicate that it is a second farewell, emphasising the double concentric structure of the constellation, Lotte explicitly reminds us of the first farewell by having her brothers "send her love to the little ones *once again*" (37; transl. altered; emph. J.U.).[53]

The novel celebrates Lotte's leaving her circles and thereby exposes similarities to Werther that are important to recognise: Lotte might certainly be said to be a 'stronger' character than Werther, because she is of a more 'balanced sentimentality' (Sauder 2010, 36), less erratic, less rash. This is displayed most obviously in their different ways of 'going out', one urged spontaneously, the other rather in control, quietly. However, structurally and topologically her leaving her children and home, crossing the outer limitation of a constellation usually centred around her, mirrors in detail Werther's situation and longings to go out, to break out of the habitual circles. Lilian R. Furst's labelling her a "communal ideal" (1990, 151) holds true with regard to Lotte's care for her siblings inside the homely constellation; her leaving them behind, under the tutelage of a twelve-year-old, to go to a ball (in the absence of her quasi-fiancé, as will turn out) does however not quite fit the ideal picture. We might feel compelled to question the impression of so many readers of *Werther*, here exemplarily put by Erdmann Waniek, that Lotte finds herself in "accordance with herself and her world" (1982, 73; my transl.). A thorough reading of the famous scene where Lotte feeds her siblings – and leaves them – can result in nothing but a refutation of Heinz Schlaffer's claim that Lotte, "like Don Quijote's Dulcinea", is but a "hollow mould" of a beloved figure, "ready even before [Werther] sees her for the first time" (1978, 216; my transl.). On the contrary, Lotte, despite their difference in temperament, uncannily resembles Werther. Their 'spiritual kinship' [*Seelenverwandtschaft*] (Kittler 1994, 150) is not limited to a particular attitude towards reading; it is founded on a structural similarity of their being-in-the-world. As will be evident at a later point, it is this particular being-in-the-world that conditions and necessitates their common attitude towards literature and reading. Literature serves an important function in the particular constitution as modern subjects that Werther and Lotte share.

It is of crucial importance to note this similarity of Werther and Lotte, in order to avoid falling prey to the novel's main trap: The problem that the

---

[52] "[…] als Lotte den Kutscher halten, und ihre beiden Brüder herabsteigen lies, die *noch einmal* ihre Hand zu küssen begehrten […]." (42; emph. J.U.)
[53] "Sie ließ die Kleinen *noch einmal* grüßen, und wir fuhren weiter." (42; emph. J.U.)

novel scrutinises is not Werther's idiosyncratic problem, the novel is neither a pathography of the eccentric, nor of the frustrated, unproductive writer. The problem cannot be put to rest with Werther's death, it does not die out with him, because it is of a general nature. It is indeed about the eccentric, about the ec-centric, about a concentric constellation and the longing, the thrill, the urge to go out, *hinaus*, to leave the homely circle's limitations: an urge engendered in the very 'inner interior' of the centre. Lotte is the best example for the fact that this ec-centric urge can perfectly well go unnoticed, that it may be regarded as a highly superfluous, needless eccentricity, troublesome and therefore to be abandoned: "it cannot, it cannot go on this way" (126).[54] However, despite her own efforts to master and suppress this urge we have already seen that it is present in her as well. The novel's staging of the farewell scene will not remain the only indicator for this; as we will see, Lotte surprisingly takes the initiative in almost all of the key scenes of the novel. These observations are very important for a reading of the novel, because they show that Werther's eccentricity is not a pathological aberration, but a necessary, inherent, albeit hardly recognisable, trait of the concentric constellation – that is, of modern subjectivity. It is its underside, or, rather its 'weather side', to borrow a term from Oliver Grill.[55]

As soon as the coach starts rolling and the conversation begins, the journey towards ecstasy, towards a weathery breaking of circles is on the way. Tellingly, it is a list of Lotte's favourite books, foreshadowing their deep literary affinity, that produces the first noted effects on Werther:

> I found so strong a personality expressed in everything she said, with every word I saw new charms, *new rays of intelligence bursting from her features*, which gradually appeared to blossom with delight because she sensed that I understood her. (38; transl. altered; emph. J.U.)[56]

The violence expressed by the weather metaphor of the "rays of intelligence bursting from her features" [*Strahlen des Geistes* [...] *hervorbrechen*] is in stark contrast with the calm and caring Lotte encountered in the domestic tableau scene. This "bursting" [*hervorbrechen*] may well be read as a breaking free of the concentric constellation's limitations, a movement that issues from within, that is amplified by the effect it has on Werther. Lotte's "blossom[ing] with

---

54 "[...] es kann nicht, es kann nicht so bleiben!" (218)
55 Cf. Oliver Grill, *Die Wetterseiten der Literatur*, forthcoming.
56 "Ich fand so viel Charakter in allem was sie sagte, ich sah mit jedem Wort neue Reize, *neue Strahlen des Geistes aus ihren Gesichtszügen hervorbrechen*, die sich nach und nach vergnügt zu entfalten schienen, weil sie an mir fühlte, daß ich sie verstund." (44; emph. J.U.)

delight" is the result of her recognising that he "understood her". Consequently, they mutually build up an ecstatic tremulous excitement, and Werther is pushed beyond himself by Lotte's radiance and words:

> I made an effort to conceal my emotions at these words. Of course I did not get very far; for when I heard her speak in passing with such perceptiveness about *The Vicar of Wakefield* and about* –, I was beside myself [*kam ich eben außer mich*] (38).[57]

These last words expressing Werther's ecstasy deserve that we listen carefully to them: "I was beside myself", that is how Stanley Corngold translates Goethe's "kam ich eben außer mich"; more literally, this little phrase would have to be rendered as "I came outside myself" – and it is now that we realise that this wording very precisely characterises the topological nature of the sort of overwhelming, positive emotion it signifies. Here the explicit legitimation becomes evident for using the notions of 'eccentricity' and 'ecstasy' that we have without great ado been operating with to characterise Werther's and Lotte's urge to go out, to the *hinaus*. Both these notions very accurately capture the thrill that is produced by a topological movement: *ecstasy*, Greek "< ἐκ out + ἱστάναι to place", "to put out of place"; *eccentric*, Greek "< ἐκ out of + κέντρον centre", "eccentric as opposed to concentric" (*OED*, ecstasy, n.; eccentric, adj.).

What we thus learn during the conversation taking place in the carriage on the way to the ball is crucial for our understanding of the concentric constellation: the pleasure principle governs over the urge to go out, pleasure that is created by a centrifugal movement of de-limitation, of leaving, of losing oneself:

> How I feasted on her black eyes during this conversation! How my entire soul was drawn to her animated lips and her fresh, glowing cheeks! How completely *immersed* [*versunken*] I was in the splendid sense of her conversation, so that at times I did not even hear the words with which she expressed herself! – You have some idea of this because you know me. In a word, when we came to a halt at the ballroom house, I got out of the carriage as if in a dream, and I was so *lost in my dreams in the twilit world around me* [*so in Träumen rings in der dämmernden Welt verlohren*] that I hardly registered the music pealing down to us from the brightly lit hall. (39; transl. altered; emph. J.U.)[58]

---

[57] "Ich bemühte mich, meine Bewegungen über diese Worte zu verbergen. Das gieng freylich nicht weit, denn da ich sie mit solcher Wahrheit im Vorbeygehn vom Landpriester von Wakefield vom* – reden hörte, kam ich eben ausser mich [...]." (44)

[58] "Wie ich mich unter dem Gespräche in den schwarzen Augen weidete, wie die lebendigen Lippen und die frischen muntern Wangen meine ganze Seele anzogen, wie ich in den herrlichen Sinn ihrer Rede ganz *versunken*, oft gar die Worte nicht hörte, mit denen sie sich ausdrukte! Davon hast du eine Vorstellung, weil du mich kennst. Kurz, ich stieg aus dem Wagen wie ein Träumender, als wir vor dem Lusthause still hielten, und war so *in Träumen rings in der dämmernden Welt verlohren*, daß ich auf die Musik kaum achtete, die uns von dem erleuchteten Saale herunter entgegen schallte." (44–46; emph. J.U.)

The German words expressing Werther's being "immersed" and "lost", *versunken* and *verloren*, exhibit, more strongly than their English pendants, a structural similarity, a similarity of movement. Grimm's *Deutsches Wörterbuch* teaches us that the particle *ver-* that these two German verbal adjectives share goes back to "the original Indo-Germanic meaning of the particles 'away, off [*fort, hinweg, ab*]'" (*DWB*, ver, vorsilbe, III.; my transl.).[59] *Versunken* and *verloren* thus form part of the theme of "Vergehen" (decay/going away/vanishing) that, as already mentioned above, Erdmann Waniek (1982, 57) claims as crucial for the *Werther*. It is, however, important to note that this theme is founded on and embedded in a topological structure and movement: *ver-gehen*, as being *ver-sunken* and *ver-loren* can only be understood in relation to the concentric constellation. They indicate the pleasure that is set free when the rigidity of the constellation is burst open, when the circles are transgressed and broken. As the passage quoted above indicates, Werther's being "lost" is not simply a relieving escape from some repressing state, it is an active movement 'out' of the centre, and a merging with the "twilit world" that is usually only perceived as a surrounding vista. This ecstatic eccentricity is emphasised by the fact that Werther's sensual perception, here of the "music pealing down to us from the brightly lit hall", is decisively weakened: he has left his central observation point; in these moments, perception and the rationality of consciousness is not the way he is relating to the world. He "got out of the carriage as if in a dream" – and this 'dream' will find its continuation in the actual ball-scene that is to follow. What the letter of June 16th has thus far narrated has merely foreshadowed what is to come. However, the journey to the ball has introduced the topology of ecstasy, of joy and pleasure, the thrill of eccentricity, and therefore perfectly well prepared us for an analysis of the letter's continuation.

2.2 Werther's "pretentious meteorology [*anmaßliche Wetterkunde*]"

Before coming to our reading of the letter's core, the ball-scene and its weathery negotiations, it is necessary to pause and reflect on some seemingly insignificant marginalia that this letter also includes:

> The sun was still a quarter of an hour from setting behind the hills when we arrived at the courtyard gate. The air was sultry, and the women expressed their concern about a thunderstorm that seemed to be gathering at the horizon in grayish-white, damp [*dumpfig*]

---

59 "die ursprüngliche indogermanische bedeutung der partikel ‚fort, hinweg, ab' (s. sp. 51) hat sich auch als germanische grundbedeutung erhalten, doch hat sie in der zusammensetzung manigfache nebenbedeutungen angenommen." (*DWB*, ver, *vorsilbe*, III.)

little clouds. *I duped their fears with pretentious meteorology [anmaßliche Wetterkunde]*, although I too was beginning to suspect that our party would suffer a blow. (36; transl. altered; emph. J.U.)[60]

I would suggest briefly disregarding the striking topological similarity of weather and the situation that is narrated (we will come back to this in the next section) and direct attention to Werther's playful reference to meteorology. This is the only passage, in a novel that is considered to be centred on the weather, where contemporary meteorological discourse is explicitly referred to. The note is marginal, at best, and neither informative, nor too affirmative, to say the least. However, the novel's relation to the official, authorised knowledge of meteorology could not be expressed more tellingly: Werther's "pretentious meteorology" stands as a representation of the novel's relation to contemporary, official 'scientific' knowledge in general. Werther's bluff does not so much consist in pretending to have knowledge that he has not, and therefore failing to forecast the weather adequately. Werther rather appropriates the authority of expertise in order to willingly and strategically deceive, "dupe[ ]" his companions. He, as well as his female company, is capable of reading the weather correctly; however, his 'scientific' male authority (pure pretence!) rules over common sense.

It is not that the novel does not accept the official knowledge of the weather produced and distributed by contemporary meteorology, a discipline that was developing as a 'science' during the 18th century. On the contrary, Werther's "pretentious meteorology" presupposes a general readability of the weather. In this scene, everyone knows about the thunderstorm: his female companions sense it, Werther "suspect[s]" it, and his readers, too, are well aware that Werther's meteorology will, sooner or later, indeed turn out to be only pretentious. An entry in Goethe's famous "Ephemerides" (autumn 1770 – August 1771) proves that he had by that time acquainted himself with the status quo of meteorological research: "Hartmann Verwandtschaft der Elecktr. Materie mit den schröcklichen Lufft Erscheinungen. Hannov. 1759." (FA 28, 236). Johann Friedrich Hartmann's book (1759) compiles recent findings, mostly of nascent experimental physics, and derives explanations for almost all of the weather

---

[60] "Die Sonne war noch eine Viertelstunde vom Gebürge, als wir vor dem Hofthore anfuhren, es war sehr schwühle, und die Frauenzimmer äusserten ihre Besorgniß wegen eines Gewitters, das sich in weisgrauen dumpfigen Wölkchen rings am Horizonte zusammen zu ziehen schien. Ich täuschte ihre Furcht mit *anmaßlicher Wetterkunde*, ob mir gleich selbst zu ahnden anfieng, unsere Lustbarkeit werde einen Stoß leiden." (38; emph. J.U.)

phenomena. His explanations break with the traditional, cosmological framework dominant from antiquity through the Middle Ages, and, as we have seen, still prevailed in thinking about the weather in Shakespeare's time. Goethe's own later meteorology, dating from 1815, refers back to the ancient models rather than resemble contemporary theories like Hartmann's, but that is just a remark in passing. In any case, Johann Friedrich Hartmann's book teaches the basics that suffice to see through Werther's pretentious meteorology. His chapter "Why summer lightning shows itself only on a clear sky" (Hartmann 1759, 225; my transl.)[61] reads like an antidote to Werther's meteorological fabrications. In the light of the "grayish-white, damp [*dumpfigen*] little clouds" "gathering at the horizon" (36) Werther's explaining the "flashing on the horizon" as "only summer lightning" (41)[62] is very easily exposed as mere pretence. They might not yet be "black", as Hartmann's "clouds which cover the sky when it thunders or wants to thunder" (1759, 171; my transl.),[63] however, their quality as "damp", *dumpfig*, is unmistakably characteristic for thunderstorms; Hartmann uses the related *terminus technicus* "dämpfigte Materie", "damp matter" (1759, 247; my transl.). Despite all these clear signs, the novel stages Werther's bluff as successful: "Other people that did not pay so close attention had taken it for summer lightning" (1759, 235; my transl.), Johann Friedrich Hartmann writes, as if commenting on this scene, acknowledging and at the same time chiding some people's lack of scientific knowledge.

Despite all of these resonances, the novel does not take sides with meteorological knowledge. On the contrary, it adopts a fundamentally a-meteorological perspective: Werther's "pretentious meteorology" is the precondition for all that is to follow. His wilfully wrong weather forecast provokes the ball-scene with its weathery hurly-burly, that is to say Werther's meeting Lotte, his falling in love with her. As we will see in the next section, these scenes are not at all independent of the violent weather. On the contrary, had Werther and his companions listened to the orthodoxy of meteorology, had they read the weather correctly and re-acted accordingly, they would have stayed at home, within the safe shelter of their houses, inside their domestic circles, and nothing would have happened worthy to write a novel about. Werther's letters consciously part with the contemporary official knowledge of the weather. They do not, as

---

[61] "Warum sich das Wetterleuchten nur bei klaren Himmel zeiget [...]." (Hartmann 1759, 225)
[62] "[...] die Blizze, die wir schon lange am Horizonte leuchten gesehn, und die ich immer für Wetterkühlen ausgegeben hatte [...]." (50)
[63] "schwarze Wolken welche den Himmel bedecken, wenn es donnert oder donnern wil" (Hartmann 1759, 171).

Shakespeare's theatre had done, employ the authoritative knowledge of the weather for their own ends, they do not search for support for their literary efficacy by looking for a symbiosis of literary practice and contemporary, authoritative knowledge of the world.

If an outspoken testimony is to be found for an aversion rather than an attraction to meteorology and (literary) writing at the time, then it is Johann Gottfried Herder's polemics against a French letter writer, taken from his *Journal meiner Reise im Jahr 1769*:

> writing letters like water; they were watery letters, indeed, that contained nothing but meteorological registers about the rain etc. [...] in short, notwithstanding all his good manners, the most worn out, sleepy human soul that had yawning enough to put to sleep and make yawn ten others around him. (1997, 106; my transl.)[64]

Herder's reference to the "meteorological registers" is not a random metaphorical remark but criticises a recent, proliferating scientific method: as Vladimir Janković (2000) and Jan Golinski (2007) have shown in their studies on 18th century meteorology, meteorological observations undertaken by laymen, often as a sort of hobby, in private forms of weather diaries, or exchanged via letters, formed the backbone of this developing science. They became more and more standardised in order to be collected in huge central databases organised by scientific societies.

Curiously enough, about forty-five years after the publication of *Werther* it is the old Johann Wolfgang von Goethe, privy councillor in Weimar, who initiates and lives through the success story of the meteorological register in Germany that Janković and Golinski reconstruct for Britain. His enthusiasm for the observations of the weather, also strengthened by Luke Howard's cloud classification, is highly visible in Goethe's letters especially of the years 1819 to 1823. There can be no doubt that Herder would have found a great number of "watery letters" among Goethe's, especially longish diary letters to his son August or to the Grand Duke Carl August from his stays at Carlsbad or Marienbad, consisting in substantial parts of weather records. Having, for instance, communicated the barometer levels at the hour of his departure from Jena, Goethe writes to the Grand Duke:

---

64 "Briefe schreiben wie Wasser; es waren aber auch gewässerte Briefe, die nichts enthielten als Meteorologische Verzeichnisse über Regen usw. [...] kurz, bei allen guten Seite<n> die abgebrauchteste, entschlafenste Menschliche Seele, die Gähnendes gnug hatte, um zehn Andre um sich einzuschläfern und gähnend zu machen [...]." (Herder 1997, 106)

[Carlsbad, May 7th 1820]

[...]

Since I, rising daily before sunrise, always happened to reside towards morning, thereafter travelling the whole day under the open sky, and could watch the course of the weather in its development, in sequence, I have, since such an opportunity may return rarely, noted down everything, carefully from hour to hour. (WA 33, 19; my transl.)[65]

For a time span of about three years, Goethe's professional correspondence with the Grand Duke is dominated by their shared enthusiasm for meteorology. Only three months after the letter from Carlsbad Goethe acknowledges "great difficulties" with his meteorological enterprise:

These accounts have great difficulties. The most important one consists in the fact that although all characters of clouds persist throughout the year and in all regions of the earth, they do, however, change expression and meaning according to season, climatic and altitudinal conditions. (WA 33, 154–155; my transl.)[66]

There is only one solution for tackling this problem: collecting more data, which will need more "good attenders and witty observers" that are "distributed over Germany" (WA 33, 157; my transl.).[67] In the course of a few years, a meteorological network develops that not only includes several observation points on the Grand Duke's territory, like Weimar, Jena and Schöndorf, but also registers data from "Halle" (WA 34, 55), "Carlsruh" (WA 34, 164), "Tepl" (WA 35, 246), "Wien" (WA 35, 297), "Breslau" (WA 35, 297), Pilsen (cf. WA 37, 141), the Rhön (WA 38, 167), "London" (WA 36, 291), "Boston" (WA 36, 291) and even "Brasilien" (WA 36, 292). In order to "bring the whole together, to put it on record and enliven it forever with means at hand" (WA 33, 202; my transl.) ("a precarious task" (WA 33, 202; my transl.)[68], as Goethe warns right at the beginning of the

---

65 "Da ich nun, täglich vor Sonnenaufgang aufstehend, zufällig immer gegen Morgen wohnte, sodann den ganzen Tag, unter freyem Himmel dahinfahrend, den Witterungsgang in seinem Verlauf, der Reihe nach, betrachten konnte, so habe ich, weil ein solcher Fall wohl selten wiederkehren möchte, alles sorgfältig von Stunde zu Stunde niedergeschrieben." (WA 33, 19)
66 "Diese Darstellungen haben große Schwierigkeiten. Die wichtigste liegt darin, daß die sämmtlichen Wolkencharaktere zwar durch's Jahr und durch sämmtliche Weltgegenden durchgehen, daß sie aber nach Jahreszeiten, klimatischen und Höhe-Verhältnissen Ausdruck und Bedeutung verändern." (WA 33, 154–155)
67 "Man sieht, was für gute Aufmerker und geistreiche Beschauer in Deutschland vertheilt sind." (WA 33, 157)
68 "[...] das Ganze zusammenzubringen, festzuhalten und durch baare Mittel für immer zu beleben scheint freylich eine bedenkliche Aufgabe [...]." (WA 33, 202).

project) the standardisation of data gains high priority. First, a "windscale" [*Windscala*] (WA 34, 55; my transl.), modelled on the one the Mannheimer Meteorologische Gesellschaft had developed, was sent round in order to make possible "comparison" [*Vergleichung*] (WA 34, 55; my transl.).[69] Later, Goethe reports to Carl August that "blank copies of the meteorological registers to be filled in have been communicated" (WA 35, 223; my transl.)[70] in order to achieve "conformity with the other institutes" (WA 34, 174; my transl.).[71] A "carefully elaborated and approved instruction for those persons, who are assigned with the task of weather observation in the Grand Duchy of Weimar" (WA 35, 162; my transl.)[72] attempted to make sure of the quality of the data and was supported by a supervision journey undertaken by Heinrich Ludwig Friedrich Schrön, assistant at the observatory in Jena, who reports that "the observers have been instructed and encouraged anew" (WA 38, 167; my transl.).[73]

The immediate aims of the project were formulated at an early stage of Goethe's correspondence with the Grand Duke: a "graphical presentation of the baro- and thermometer levels etc." which Goethe had seen undertaken by "*Winkler* in Halle" and found "astonishing" (WA 33, 290; my transl.)[74] as well as the publication of the meteorological data "in a public paper or booklet" (WA 34, 222; my transl.).[75] It does not take long until both these goals are attained: in the year 1821, a "weather book" [*Witterungsbuch*] is started in the "local library" (WA 34, 120; my transl.)[76] and Goethe's suggestion is followed to extract a monthly register from it, a register that Goethe will keep sending over

---

[69] Cf. a letter to Herbig, containing a windscale and explanations, where Goethe writes that "If Schöndorf followed registering the weather according to it, then a comparison would be possible." [Wenn darnach auch in Schöndorf aufgezeichnet würde, so könnte eine Vergleichung stattfinden] (WA 34, 55; my transl.)
[70] "[...] Exemplare der meteorologischen Tabellen zum Ausfüllen mitgetheilt worden [...]." (WA 35, 223)
[71] "[...] Conformität mit den übrigen Anstalten [...]." (WA 34, 174)
[72] "[...] die sorgfältig ausgearbeitete und geprüfte Instruction für diejenigen Personen, welchen in dem Großherzogtum Weimar die Wetterbeobachtung aufgetragen ist [...]." (WA 35, 162)
[73] "[...] die Beobachter auf's neue belehrt und ermuntert worden sind. Eine erweiterte Instruction hat jeder erhalten [...]." (WA 38, 167)
[74] "Sodann überreicht *Winkler* zu Halle ein schönes Exemplar seiner Tafeln, zugleich eine graphische Darstellung der Baro- und Thermometerstände etc., welche in Verwunderung setzen muß [...]." (WA 33, 290)
[75] "[...] daß Serenissimus gerne sehen würden, wenn von denen in Höchst Ihro Landen angeordneten Wetterbeobachtungen in einem öffentlichen Blatt oder Hefte regelmäßige Nachricht gegeben würde [...]." (WA 34, 222)
[76] "Das auf hiesiger Bibliothek zu diesem Jahr neu angefangene Witterungsbuch [...]." (WA 34, 120)

to the Grand Duke as the "local monthly weather register" (WA 34, 273; my transl.).[77] As far as the graphical presentation is concerned, Johann Friedrich Posselt, director of the observatory in Jena and scientific head of the meteorological enterprise, proved some talent, he "provided a barometrical inter line [*Zwischenlinie*] for Weimar" (WA 34, 120; my transl.)[78] and, to Goethe's and the Grand Duke's satisfaction, presented the data he was given in lines and coloured charts:

> Highly interesting for us, how Posselt has drawn the Schöndorfer line with red colour beneath the black line, indicating the barometric level of Halle; the accordance is striking.
>
> With the thermometrical lines a double indication has been undertaken as well, these however have to intersect more. (WA 33, 290; my transl.)[79]

However, the ultimate aim Goethe pursued with his meteorological project was more ambitious, and it is again Johann Friedrich Posselt, to whom he describes his meteorological vision:

> The constant – same course of the barometer changes in very distant places will, in my opinion, soon be regarded as the foundation of the whole meteorology; therefore, no efforts are to be spared in order to enlighten [*aufklären*] oneself about it and also about the disparities and deviances. (WA 36, 291; my transl.)[80]

Unfortunately, the addressee of the letter died quite unexpectedly only four days after this letter had been sent – and with him the Grand Duke's and also Goethe's visionary enthusiasm for meteorology. The letter Goethe sent to Carl August informing him about Johann Friedrich Posselt's death still contained an immediate plea for a successor, a "strenuous open-minded meteorologist" (WA 36, 315; my transl.);[81] in the course of the next year, however, what had been Goethe's vision of modern meteorology gave way to deep disappointment:

---

77 "[...] hiesige monatliche Witterungstabelle [...]." (WA 34, 273)
78 "[...] dieser [Posselt] besorgte denn auch für Weimar eine barometrische Zwischenlinie [...]." (WA 34, 120)
79 "Höchst interessant ist für uns dabey, wie Posselt unter die schwarze Linie, welche den Barometerstand von Halle andeutet, den Schöndorfer mit rother Farbe untergezeichnet hat; die Übereinstimmung ist auffallend.
Mit den thermometrischen Linien ist ein doppeltes Bezeichnen gleichfalls geschehen, doch diese müssen sich mehr durchschneiden." (WA 33, 290)
80 "Der regelmäßig – gleiche Gang der Barometer-Veränderungen an weit entfernten Orten wird nach meiner Überzeugung bald als das Fundament der ganzen Meteorologie angesehen werden; es ist daher keine Bemühung zu scheuen, um sich darüber wie über Ungleichheiten und Abweichungen derselben aufzuklären." (WA 36, 291)
81 "[...] tüchtigen vorurtheilsfreyen Meteorologen zu wünschen hätten [...]." (WA 36, 315)

> As far as meteorology is concerned I am of the same opinion that it cannot be understood completely, one may especially abandon all hopes that even the weather closest at hand could be forecast or something rational predicated about the past. (WA 38, 207; my transl.)[82]

Goethe thus conceded that it was not possible to "enlighten [*aufklären*] oneself" about the weather – meteorology could never "provide complete enlightenment" [*zu völliger Aufklärung dienen*] (WA 38, 208). Meteorology as a science had failed. Goethe's choice of words, however, alludes to a greater epistemological question: the fact that he repeatedly resorts to the notion of 'enlightenment' [*Aufklärung*] integrates his meteorological interest into the epochal epistemological movement. As Michel Serres has famously asserted, the 18th century's epistemology (and that is to say the spirit of the Enlightenment) "can be defined as the erasure of 'meteors'" (1977a, 229; my transl.).[83] *Meteor*, from Greek μετέωρος meaning 'raised from off the ground', 'hovering', comes to figuratively signify the 'oscillating', the 'uncertain', the 'unpredictable'. Meteorology can thus be understood as the navel of enlightened science, as a project that paradigmatically subjects the unpredictable to the dominance of the logos, that aims at getting control of the uncontrollable. It is thus, as Arden Reed rightly claims, "an oxymoronic science":

> As its name implies, meteoro*logy* is rooted in the field of logic, and is governed by the supreme authority of the *logos*. It aims, by the exercise of rational powers, to determine the regularity or order behind phenomena, which it will express in laws that govern the data it investigates. (1983, 13)

It is exactly this enterprise that Goethe bemoans as failed – "the regularity or order behind phenomena", "the laws that govern the data" could not be derived, that is why "all hopes" had to be abandoned, neither "forecast" nor "something rational predicated about the past" prove to be possible. However, this failure is not just any failure that could be supplemented by successes "in other places" as Goethe comforts himself in the closing of his letter to Carl August. If Michel Serres is right, then the whole project of Enlightenment [*Aufklärung*] suffers a heavy blow with the defeat of 18th century meteorology.

The reservoir of language provides us with one indicator that this might indeed be the case: the German word for Enlightenment, *Aufklärung*, is a weather

---

[82] "Was die Witterungslehre betrifft so bin ich gleicher Überzeugung daß sie nicht auszulernen sey, besonders möchte man alle Hoffnung aufgeben, selbst das nächstbevorstehende Wetter voraus zu verkünden, oder auch von dem vergangenen etwas Rationelles zu prädiciren." (WA 38, 207)

[83] "L'âge classique peut être ainsi aisément défini, dans son épistémologie et son histoire : l'effacement des Météores [...]." (Serres 1977a, 229)

metaphor. *Aufklärung* literally means 'clearing of the sky'; the metaphorical use of *Aufklärung* for the epistemological revolution starting to take place in the 18th century thus demands an equiprimordial counter-force: a force of 'clouding', so to speak. The naturalisation of the metaphor *Aufklärung*, its association with the immediate and transparent light of the dominant ratio, has led to the oblivion of its weathery character. It is only at its navel (i.e. with regard to meteorology) that the *Aufklärung* gets reminded of its own lack of inherent foundation, of its own situation in a field of conflicting forces. *Aufklärung* signifies *one* process, one weather phenomenon, that cannot be separated from others with which it interacts and from which its own individuation – no clearing without the formation of clouds – is dependent.

Against the background of what we have learned from Michel Foucault about the modern practices of discipline (cf. 1975), it is not astonishing that, when 'enlightened meteorology' is disillusioned, Goethe reinterprets the net of institutions, once established for scientific purposes, as institutions of schooling:

> However, there are beautiful aspects to be found, and to me, as already said earlier, the institutes want to stay interesting in that they are schools where for all purposes exact attention and registration is demanded. (WA 38, 207; my transl.)[84]

There is some irony in the fact that these institutes, where the limits of the enlightenment and its methods of observing and systematic registering (with a theory of thermodynamics missing) were experienced most intensely, were simply turned into schools of these very methods: they effectively collected huge masses of data to no avail – and nevertheless, or rather exactly for this reason, used for promoting and spreading this practice of collecting data.

> In that at so many points in Your Highness' country attention is attracted to general natural phenomena, sharp observation advised, tabular noticing made obligatory [*zur Pflicht machen*], the individual will certainly not miss to spread the like in his circle [...]. When I put myself to think that such a point is planted on the highest summit of the Rhön, I like to imagine what a solitary schoolmaster will gradually effect from there, and my imagination puts a special trust into this mission. (WA 38, 168; my transl.)[85]

---

84 "Indessen gibt es doch mitunter schöne Ansichten, und mir wollen die Anstalten, wie schon früher gesagt, dadurch interessant bleiben, daß sie eine Schule sind zu allen Zwecken genaues Aufmerken und Aufzeichnen erfordert wird [...]." (WA 38, 207)
85 "Indem an so vielen Puncten Ew. Königlichen Hoheit Lande die Aufmerksamkeit auf allgemeine Naturphänomene erregt, scharfe Beobachtung empfohlen, tabellarisches Bemerken zur Pflicht gemacht wird, so verfehlt der Einzelne gewiß nicht auch in seinem Kreise dergleichen zu verbreiten [...]. Wenn ich nun denke, daß ein solcher Punkt auf den höchsten Röhngipfel verpflanzt ist, so stelle ich mir gerne vor was ein einsamer Schulmeister von da aus mit der Zeit wirken werde, und meine Einbildungskraft setzt auf diese Mission ein besonderes Vertrauen." (WA 38, 168)

Privy Councillor Goethe's reaction to the failure of the scientific project of meteorology is paradigmatic: there was no 'scientific' alternative available to the doctrines of enlightenment ('science' being itself a child of the Enlightenment), no alternative to its methods and procedures. When these methods proved inadequate, the reaction could not be to question them, but, on the contrary, to turn them back on themselves, to erect schooling grounds serving as a disciplinary machinery for their spreading and embodiment – and that is to say to increase and stabilise its social monopoly.

When Goethe wrote *Werther* almost forty years earlier, he could not have known about the failure of meteorology. However, the novel voices a deep distrust of 'school knowledge', a distrust, as we will see, that is more than just youthful rebellion against the epistemological establishment:

> When Ulysses speaks of the immeasurable sea and the infinite earth, is it not more true, more human, more heartfelt than when now every schoolboy thinks himself marvelously sage, when he can parrot that it is round. (94; transl. altered)[86]

It is no coincidence that Homer's Odyssey comes to feature as the paradigm for another, alternative knowledge of the world. Goethe here refers to an important contemporary debate that had been initiated in England twenty years before, and had reached Germany in the late sixties and early seventies: the idea of the genius. Both Edward Young's *Conjectures On Original Composition* (1759) and Robert Wood's *An Essay on the Original Genius of Homer* (1769) (the latter reviewed in the *Frankfurter Gelehrte Anzeigen* of the year 1772) base their idea of the genius and his special relation to the world on the great ancestor Homer. This relation to the world is not simply an aesthetic one and thus merely the source of a new theory of art. Achim Aurnhammer's discovery of allusions to Robert Wood's text on the genius in the context of his essay on Werther as a painter could evoke these suggestions (cf. 1995, 94). The idea of the genius forms indeed a central part of what is called the 'Sturm und Drang' [Storm and Urge]; however, the passage quoted above makes very clear that what is at stake is more than a poetics or a theory of painting: it is about knowledge, about truth, about an access to the world. The "immeasurable sea and the infinite earth" is what resists the arduous collection of data, the discovery of the underlying laws that Goethe will supervise forty years later. The adjectives "immeasurable" and "infinite" immediately call attention to the fact that measuring, counting and registering are not adequate means of accounting for this dimension of reality,

---

[86] "Wenn Ulyß von dem ungemessenen Meere, und von der unendlichen Erde spricht, ist das nicht wahrer, menschlicher, inniger, als wenn jezzo jeder Schulknabe sich wunder weise dünkt, wenn er nachsagen kann, daß sie rund sey." (152)

that there are surely no laws to be discovered behind these phenomena in order to subjugate them to human control.

Nevertheless, despite being 'not merely aesthetic', the access to this alternative knowledge, this knowledge barred by the enlightened access to the world, is inherently literary, as the reference to Homer and the practice of what is known as 'Sturm und Drang' indicate. It is probably not too bold to claim that literature in its modern form, as an autonomous social, cultural and also epistemological practice, is born in the wake of this desideratum. The weather thus can be said to form the navel of the 18th century's knowledge of the world: it exposes the *Aufklärung*'s [Enlightenment's] inherent limits, unmasks the illusion of its epistemological monopoly and serves as the *Sturm und Drang*'s [Storm and Urge's] paradigmatic object.

Werther's "pretentious meteorology" condenses these complex epistemological negotiations into a catch phrase, a catch phrase explained to us by the little narrative that the letter of June 16th provides us with. If it represents the novel's relation to contemporary, official 'scientific' knowledge, as suggested above, then because it sarcastically turns the official meteorology's persuasive power against itself in order to make a different 'meteorology' possible: a literary meteorology, a meteorology of the *Sturm und Drang* instead of a meteorology of the *Aufklärung*, a meteorology that is not seeking for control over all that is foreign to the human being's ratio, but a meteorology that attempts to explore the reality of what is and will remain 'other' to the logos. This meteorology is thus rather a supplement to the enlightened knowledge than a concurring alternative. It does not question authoritative knowledge, it does not question that the earth is round – it just questions the monopoly, the exclusivity of rational truth. Although the weather, as I tried to show, serves as the paradigm, the field of this 'meteorology' of the *Sturm und Drang* is not limited to this 'object'. As the twofold name already indicates, there is a second paradigmatic object (and others, of course) under scrutiny; an 'object', that the letter of June 16th exposes as deeply related to the weather: love.

2.3 Love and weather – a parallel threat to order

The narrative of Werther's letter written on June 16th is constructed according to a fundamental parallel: a parallel of weather and love. These two 'phenomena' are not too easily brought into a harmonious relation, because we are used to attributing them to very different regions of being: the weather belongs to the realm of nature, love to the realm of society. The weather takes place 'outside', love concerns our 'inner inside', and so on. Constructing a parallel as this letter does, a parallel bridging the gap that our epistemological intuition regards as fundamental for our understanding of the world, looks very suspicious and demands an explanation.

The easiest way to account for the uncanny parallel would be to delegate the responsibility for it to the author of the fictional text in which it occurs: this is how Friedrich Christian Delius treats the weather in his study of realist fiction titled *Der Held und sein Wetter* [The hero and his weather] (1971). Heroes and weather cannot be said to form a parallel in a strong sense; they rather assume a dissymmetrical relation, one being the 'actual object' that is to be described and characterised, the other the means the author uses to do so. To be sure, it is the 'hero' and his social surroundings that are under scrutiny, the weather is regarded as "a comparatively banal object" (1971, 8; my transl.) that serves merely as a "Kunstmittel", as Delius claims in the book's subtitle, a machinery, a 'means of art'. "Each author builds his own sky" (1971, 77; my transl.), Delius writes, the weather is at his or her disposal like the lighting that the theatre director employs in order to support the characterisation of his hero.

Regardless of the adequacy of Delius's interpretations for the realist novels that form his corpus, it certainly appears that Goethe's *Werther* withstands his method of reading. However, the weather can neither be called a "banal object" in *Werther*, nor is it possible to determine whether the weather is used to characterise love, or love to cope with the weather. Furthermore, it seems to me that exactly what Delius takes for granted – the epistemological setting, the clear-cut distinction of the realm of love and the realm of weather – is what is at stake in Goethe's novel. It is this distinction of realms that makes Delius's basic distinction between the 'proper, actual object' and the 'means of characterisation' possible. Instead of using one (controllable) 'banality' to characterise an 'actual object' (and running the risk of thereby reducing it to just another banality) Goethe's *Werther* relies on a rather different strategy: the novel parallels two 'phenomena' that *both* elude 'orderly', rational description and control. The only viable way to characterise these phenomena consists in observing this parallel and shedding some light on the two phenomena by letting the one mirror the other. The novel does not try to merge love and weather into something 'banal' in order to subjugate them to the understandable, the rational, to the dominant epistemology. On the contrary, by bringing into focus what resists our enlightened understanding of the world, *Werther* reveals how the reigning rational order copes with these resistances. As will become evident, the main strategy of enlightened society consists in a double displacement: ex-pulsion into the 'outer outside' on the one hand, internalisation into the 'inner inside' on the other. In other words, the novel stages the birth of the epistemological setting that Delius, like most modern day readers, takes for granted. It demonstrates that the enlightened world has to tame the forces that are alien to its dominant epistemology and to the contemporary social system that has crystallised this epistemology into a social reality. It is thus important to take the parallel of weather and love seriously, in order to avoid projecting onto the scene what it actually questions.

In Goethe's *Werther* the parallel is introduced with a sense of danger that emanates from love as well as from the weather – and Werther's indifference to it:

> Be careful, her cousin added, that you don't fall in love! – Why is that? I said. – She is already engaged, she replied, to a very good man, who is away on a trip. He has gone to put his affairs in order, because his father has died, and he means to apply for a good position. – The information left me quite indifferent. (35–36)[87]

Not coincidentally this passage is directly followed by the corresponding weather passage already familiar to us:

> The sun was still a quarter of an hour from setting behind the hills when we arrived at the courtyard gate. The air was sultry, and the women expressed their concern about a thunderstorm that seemed to be gathering at the horizon [*rings am Horizont zusammen zu ziehen schien*] in grayish-white, sullen little clouds. I duped their fears with a pretense at meteorological expertise, although I too was beginning to suspect that our party would suffer a blow. (36)[88]

Both weather and love send forerunners signalling "that our party would suffer a blow". Both are introduced as threats that are somehow readable. However, it is the weather that makes itself heard more successfully: its signal cannot merely be answered with (pretended) indifference. Werther is forced to "dupe" his companions and thereby betrays, at least to the readers, his obvious partiality: far from being indifferent, he is expecting something special to happen at the ball. Even before having seen Lotte, he thus confirms the cousin's reading of an impending danger emanating from an impossible love affair to come. Goethe's ingenious construction, paralleling the threats of love and weather, makes the one characterise and emphasise the other: Werther's suspicion "that

---

[87] "Nehmen sie sich in Acht, versetzte die Baase, daß Sie sich nicht verlieben! Wieso? sagt' ich: Sie ist schon vergeben, antwortete jene, an einen sehr braven Mann, der weggereist ist, seine Sachen in Ordnung zu bringen nach seines Vaters Tod, und sich um eine ansehnliche Versorgung zu bewerben. Die Nachricht war mir ziemlich gleichgültig." (38)

[88] "Die Sonne war noch eine Viertelstunde vom Gebürge, als wir vor dem Hofthore anfuhren, es war sehr schwühle, und die Frauenzimmer äusserten ihre Besorgniß wegen eines Gewitters, das sich in weisgrauen dumpfigen Wölkchen rings am Horizonte zusammen zu ziehen schien. Ich täuschte ihre Furcht mit anmaßlicher Wetterkunde, ob mir gleich selbst zu ahnden anfieng, unsere Lustbarkeit werde einen Stoß leiden." (38)

our party would suffer a blow", despite being related to the impending thunderstorm also actualises the cousin's warnings. Stanley Corngold's choice of "blow" for Goethe's German "Stoß" is a happy one: it accurately transports the weather dimension of this word. In Grimm's *Deutsches Wörterbuch*, this semantic dimension is paraphrased as "in extended use (of blow-like movements): [...] of the wind [...] especially as forebodes of thunderstorms" (*DWB*, stosz, n. 4.; 4. e.; my transl.).[89] In the course of the ball-scene Goethe also links the notion of "blow" to the notion of love, using a rather marginal episode to metonymically foreshadow Werther's jealous relation to Albert: when "a neighbor" eats part of the lemons that Werther had set aside for Lotte, "with each little segment [...] a pang [*Stich*] went through [his] heart" (40).[90] *Stich* is a synonym for *Stoß*, which, according to the *Deutsches Wörterbuch* can also be dealt "with a sharp weapon intending to penetrate a body and to wound it" (*DWB*, stosz, n. 1. b.; my transl.).[91] Werther's formulation "that our party would suffer a blow" thus, in its very choice of words, aptly alludes to both, parallel, impending dangers, *Windstoß* and *Stoß ins Herz*, to weather and love.

Furthermore, the description of the approaching storm contains the sketch of a topology that must look familiar to us: the thunderstorm "gathers" in a centripetal movement that is more explicit in the German version, where the little word "rings" [encircling] emphasises the notion of circularity. What the weather description depicts is indeed a very specific meteorological process, a process that in 'early meteorology', from antiquity throughout the Middle Ages, and right up to the Renaissance, was conceptualised as 'concentration'. The process of 'concentration' forms an important part in accounting for the violent forces set free in the thunderstorm itself: these forces gather by concentrating, by condensing matter until at some point the cloud bursts and the heat and the difference of pressure produced by the violent rupture serve as explanations for thunder and lightning. As is inscribed in the word itself, *concentration* implies a topological dimension that also informs the direction of the "blow" [Stoß] to follow: the forces gathering towards a centre in a centripetal movement prepare and forebode the violent bursting, that takes a centrifugal direction. It is not only the topology of the concentric constellation and its inherent urge to go, to break out, that is encountered here; this weather description also provides a

---

[89] "[...] in erweitertem gebrauch (von stoszartigen bewegungen): [...] e) des windes (s. unten windstosz) [...] *besonders als vorboten des gewitters* [...]." (*DWB*, stosz, n. 4.; 4. e.)
[90] "[...] nur daß mir mit jedem Schnittgen das ihre Nachbarinn aus der Tasse nahm, ein Stich durch's Herz gieng [...]." (48)
[91] "[...] mit einer spitzen waffe und in der absicht, in den körper einzudringen und ihn zu verwunden [...]." (*DWB*, stosz, n. 1. b.)

structural representation of what Rolf Christian Zimmermann has identified as the central trait of young Goethe's view of the world (1968): the dialectics of centrifugal and centripetal pulses. Instead of reading *Werther* as illustrating "the degeneration of one pulse of life, the concentrating pulse" [*Verkümmerung eines Lebenspulses, nämlich des konzentrativen*] (1968, II, 190; my transl.) as Zimmermann does, I would like to assert that this dialectics resists degeneration or sublation: what Goethe's novel exposes is the insistency of the dialectics, the fact that the concentric constellation as a social mechanism of inherently centripetal, concentrating character produces exactly the opposing centrifugal movement it seems to be holding off. This is what the topological structure of the impending thunderstorm demonstrates: the process of concentration warns Werther and his companions of the following centrifugal violent blow. I am not convinced that Goethe's novel illustrates a shortcoming, a degeneration of or deviation from something regarded as a reachable ideal: the readers do not find a representation of this ideal in the novel's narrated world that would make this evaluation possible. The novel merely observes and describes the functioning of contemporary reality and the way it deals with the uncontrollable complexity that challenges the 18th century's epistemic and social system.

Werther's coming "out of [him]self" in the discussion about literature with Lotte in the coach that we discussed in the previous section can be read as a first centrifugal "blow" that the weather's centripetal movement of concentration has prepared. The parallel of weather and love becomes however even more explicit in the ball scene's most prominent moment of transgression that takes place in Werther's dance with Lotte:

> As we danced through the line and I, God knows with how much bliss, hung on her arm and eyes, which were full of the most genuine expression of the frankest, purest pleasure, we encountered a woman whom I had noticed earlier for the gentle expression on her aging face. Smiling, she looks at Lotte, lifts a minatory finger and, as we fly past, twice utters the name Albert very meaningfully. (40–41)[92]

We will return to this scene in the next section, especially to the cultural and media-theoretical implications of the dance. Before going into the details it is however important to situate it in the overarching parallel of weather and love

---

92 "Wie wir die Reihe so durchtanzten, und ich, weis Gott mit wie viel Wonne, an ihrem Arme und Auge hieng, das voll vom wahrsten Ausdrukke des offensten reinsten Vergnügens war, kommen wir an eine Frau, die mir wegen ihrer liebenswürdigen Mine auf einem nicht mehr ganz jungen Gesichte merkwürdig gewesen war. Sie sieht Lotten lächelnd an, hebt einen drohenden Finger auf, und nennt den Nahmen Albert, zweymal im Vorbeyfliegen mit viel Bedeutung." (48)

that are being examined here. The dance-scene neatly connects with the scenes preceding it. As with the dark clouds or Werther's losing himself in the coach, the impending danger of transgression can be anticipated: This time it is not the cousin, but an uncanny, strange [*merkwürdig*] woman characterised by the weird opposition of chiding and being gentle, who smilingly lifts "a minatory finger". As we learn, her observation may even be called 'meteorological'. The transgression she is reacting to is sketched in only a few words: "as we fly past" [*im Vorbeyfliegen*]. However, these words allude to the central and important characterisation of Lotte's and Werther's dance: "to fly around with her like the weather" (40; transl. altered).[93] This mediated reference to the weather is an important one: in it the parallel threats of weather and love meet. With the weather's entering the interior space of the ballroom, a stage of threat seems to have been reached that requires an intervention. The dance's weather has to be eliminated, banned, to restore order. It is the 'weird' lady's task to do so. Smiling, but purposeful, she mentions the decisive term: a name suffices, "Albert", "twice utter[ed] [...] very meaningfully". A chain of actions and reactions is set into motion that indeed fulfils the purpose intended. Lotte is brought to speak the quasi-magic formula, "Albert is a fine man to whom I am as good as engaged" (41),[94] which all of a sudden 'cures' Werther of his illusion of indifference, and thereby brings the conflict into the open:

> Enough, I became confused, lost count, and came in between the wrong couple, so that everything went awry, and it took all of Lotte's presence of mind and tugging and pulling quickly to restore order.
>
> The dance was not yet over when the lightning that we had long seen flashing on the horizon and that I had always pretended as only summer lightning began to grow far more pronounced and thunder drowned out the music. Three ladies broke out of the line, followed by their partners; the confusion became general, and the music stopped. (41)[95]

What had been constructed as parallel threats is here realised as a parallel transgression: "It is an act of transgression that takes place", Gerhard Neumann writes, an act "constructed in parallel to the frightening experience of the

---

[93] "[...] mit ihr herum zu fliegen wie Wetter [...]." (48)
[94] "Albert ist ein braver Mensch, dem ich so gut als verlobt bin!" (50)
[95] "Genug, ich verwirrte mich, vergaß mich, und kam zwischen das unrechte Paar hinein, daß alles drunter und drüber gieng, und Lottens ganze Gegenwart und Zerren und Ziehen nöthig war, um's schnell wieder in Ordnung zu bringen.
  Der Tanz war noch nicht am Ende, als die Blizze, die wir schon lange am Horizonte leuchten gesehn, und die ich immer für Wetterkühlen ausgegeben hatte, viel stärker zu werden anfiengen, und der Donner die Musik überstimmte. Drey Frauenzimmer liefen aus der Reihe, denen ihre Herren folgten, die Unordnung ward allgemein, und die Musik hörte auf." (50)

thunderstorm in nature" (2000, 529; my transl.). Werther's dancing with Lotte "like the weather" (or rather Werther's awareness that this 'weather' is socially out of place) had caused him to end up in such a state that the whole party is set in "confusion" when suddenly the weather enters the ballroom. Topologically speaking, this parallel is not established by analogy, it is rather metonymically linked, and only differs in scale: in both cases the weather is present in the same interior, strictly ordered and controlled place where it is not supposed to be. It breaks into this place from two different 'fronts': on the one hand, from Werther's and Lotte's 'meeting souls', from their 'inner interiors' (we have already come across this bursting movement when Werther noticed the "rays of intelligence bursting from her features" [*Strahlen des Geistes* [...] *hervorbrechen*] when Lotte was talking about literature in the coach); on the other hand, from the 'outer outside', as 'real' violent weather.

These two 'weathers' are different in scale as far as their impact on the party is concerned: whereas Werther's confusion creates only a temporary loss of order that "Lotte's presence of mind and tugging and pulling [can] quickly" restore, as a result of the intruding weather "the confusion became general", and even brings the whole party to a halt, indicated by the fact that "the music stopped". Interestingly, as will be seen in the section on the restoration of order, Lotte will again play a decisive role in remedying the party's general turmoil by initiating a game.

The parallel of weather and love, with its readable threats and simultaneous transgressions that ultimately actualise the presaged event of the party's "suffer [ing] a blow" is constructed too neatly, carefully and comprehensively as to be simply dismissible as mere artifice, employed to heighten the scene's impact. It establishes a proximity between these two notions that must appear striking and irritating against the background of modern epistemology. In our reading of Shakespeare's *Tempest* we have seen that our way of making sense of the world, our strict separation of distinct realms of being (outside/inside, the spheres of weather and the spheres of love) cannot claim a-historicity. As we have seen, the early-modern knowledge of the world to which Shakespeare's play testifies did indeed conceptualise the processes of weather and the processes of the human passions as inherently similar. Atavisms of this similarity can still be found in the sediments of our language, as in the love 'metaphors' of 'storm' or 'raging'. The parallel of love and weather that structures the central scene of Goethe's *Werther* definitely relates to these older conceptualisations of the world. However, this parallel cannot merely be understood as an atavism, as recurring to an older layer of knowledge. In contrast to Shakespeare, where language was wittily used to exhibit the analogies according to which the world was said to work, Goethe does not spell out the similarity responsible for the parallel of weather and love. All that remains in *Werther* is the parallel as such, hollowed out, so to speak, a pure form that must appear striking and highly questionable. Goethe's correlation of weather and love is, in itself, not a positive epistemological statement. The role it plays defines itself only through the topology in which it is situated: the dominant ordering of the world into a concentric constellation grouped around the rational subject. It is no coincidence that the parallel of love and weather challenges this dominant model (and all its social implications) in a way that reflects its double structure: as a force attacking both the defining boundaries, its external limits from the outer outside, and the internal limits from the inner interior. This weathery questioning does not aim at destroying the constellation of modern subjectivity, it is not a revolutionary attack. As its uncanny structural correspondence with the concentric constellation indicates, this (double) weathery threat is constitutive for the constellation. It forces this order to re-establish itself, and thereby demonstrates that the concentric constellation's architecture is constructed as a mechanism of defence. It indicates that there are forces beyond the orderly, rational edifice, that have to be expulsed into the 'outer outside' and internalised into the 'inner inside'; forces that are real, without having a place in the enlightened system of the world; forces that have to be disavowed, situated beyond the field of knowledge, truth, or sense in order to create the stability of the enlightened world. From within the concentric constellation these forces can, at best, be observed as 'the other' in relation to knowledge, as contingent or insane.

2.4 The waltz – flying like the weather

Critics agree that the dancing narrated in Werther's letter of June 16th is of greatest significance not only for the development of the novel, but also for the relation of literary writing and dance as cultural and social practices in general. Lotte's waltz with Werther may not be the "first couple dance in German literary history", as Lars Friedrich claims (2010, 263; my transl.), we should not forget its important predecessor, the "sittenlosen, frechen Wirbeltanz der Deutschen" in Sophie La Roche's *Geschichte des Fräulein von Sternheim* (2011, 194). However, it is, according to Gabriele Brandstetter, only "since Goethe's *Werther*-novel" that the dance has achieved "fundamental significance as a poetic argument" (1997, 1011; my transl.). Although the dance scene, especially the waltz, has been readily appropriated for all sorts of broader arguments, most prominently in the wake of Niklas Luhmann's theory of love as a generalised medium of communication (cf. Luhmann 2012), it does not function as straightforwardly as it might seem. Gabriele Brandstetter's observation that the dance in *Werther* "is paradigmatically staged as an exploratory pattern [*Erkundungsmuster*] of cultural formation" (1997, 1011; my transl.) thus not only puts the situation we find in *Werther* in carefully chosen words, it also demands an adequately careful close reading of this complex setting. As her formulation "exploratory pattern" clarifies, the waltz does not just represent a particular social situation that could simply be decoded and discovered 'behind' the dance. It rather probes this formation, explores its limits and structure and points out the problems that a new social coding will then have to elucidate.

The central waltz is prepared for in two steps, first a conversation about "the joy of dancing" (39) and then Werther's watching Lotte dance:

> You should see her dance! You see, she is so absorbed in it with her whole heart and whole soul [*mit ganzem Herzen und mit ganzer Seele dabey*], her whole body one harmony, so carefree [*sorglos*], so natural [*unbefangen*], as if this were all, as if she thought or felt nothing else; and in such moments everything else surely does vanish [*schwindet*] from her mind. (39; transl. altered)[96]

Werther's impressions confirm Lotte's "joy of dancing" that she was talking about in the carriage. "If this passion is a fault", Lotte had said, "I gladly confess to you that I know nothing better than dancing" (39). It should be added that the dance Werther sees her participate in is a minuet, the traditional social dance that the majority of critics in their interpretation of the dance scene contrast with the later waltz as a pair dance, the former standing for the old, feudal and cosmological order, the latter for the 'modern, differentiated social system'. This is important to note since Werther's description of Lotte's dancing a minuet does not differ significantly from his later description of their dancing the waltz. On the contrary, it is strikingly similar, his observations prepare for the subsequent scene, neatly paving the way from their leaving their homely circles towards the waltz and the window scene.

Lotte's dancing does indeed appear as a passion in Werther's description. Its insistent wording makes very clear that dancing is an act of de-limitation: the passage is dominated by notions of wholeness ("whole heart", "whole soul", "whole body") and totality ("as if this were all", "everything else surely does vanish"). We should not too quickly let these notions lead us to read the scene as a coming to itself of the authentic, full subject. The scene rather relates the collapse, the dissolution of the constellation that the novel has hitherto erected as the structure of modern subjectivity: the environment vanishes,

---

[96] "Tanzen muß man sie sehen. Siehst du, sie ist so mit ganzem Herzen und ganzer Seele dabey, ihr ganzer Körper, eine Harmonie, so sorglos, so unbefangen, als wenn das eigentlich alles wäre, als wenn sie sonst nichts dächte, nichts empfände, und in dem Augenblikke gewiß schwindet alles andere vor ihr." (46)

instead of a body defined by its (two) limitations a new 'whole' and infinite body emerges. David Wellbery has called the event that occurs in the waltz scene a "specific morphism of the phantasmagoric body" (1994, 183). It is however significant that the waltz as "site and occasion" (1994, 183) of this morphism, as David Wellbery claims, does not seem to be necessary for this event to happen. It is rather the passage quoted above, narrating Lotte's dancing the minuet (and not the waltz!), that unfolds the important observation that "the surrounding field of objects that would relativize the body – the field, let us say, of corporeal alterity – disappears" (1994, 183). What remains is a limitless body defined by its own wholeness.

The passage that relates Lotte's minuet dancing voices precise suggestions that distinguish the dance-body from the subjects defined by the concentric constellation. Unfortunately these hints are embedded in the semantic spectrum of two little German words, so that they must be lost in the English translation: the words "unbefangen" [natural, impartial, literally: 'non-captured'] and "sorglos" [carefree, careless]. In their dominant meaning, actualised in this passage, both words express a notion of freedom: not captured, not held back by constraints of any sorts, free of duty and sorrows. In this sense these adjectives can well be understood as signifying Lotte's real, authentic character, as a positive, life-affirming human being. However, in the context of the novel, both of these words transcend Lotte's character and refer to two topoi that run through the novel as its essential thread. "[U]nbefangen" clearly relates to the omnipresent topology of the human being as defined by its limitations. As discussed above, it is a key trait of the human being, not only of Werther, to "set[ ] up a little hut at some cozy spot, and settl[e] in there with all its limitation [mit aller Einschränkung zu herbergen]" (29; transl. altered).[97] The iconic tableau of Lotte giving her little siblings their dinner (consisting of bread only) is nothing but a visualisation of this limitation of a "cozy spot". However, the early letter of Mai 22nd already teaches us that this "Einschränkung" [limitation] is, as we will analyse in detail in a later section, also a prison: "When I observe the narrow limits [Einschränkung] in which man's powers of action and investigation are imprisoned" (27–28; transl. altered),[98] Werther writes, resorting again to the notion of "Einschränkung". The definition that Johann Christoph Adelung's dictionary gives of "unbefangen" marks the relation this adjective assumes to

---

[97] "[…] an einem vertraulichen Orte ein Hüttchen aufzuschlagen, und da mit aller Einschränkung zu herbergen […]." (26)
[98] "Wenn ich die Einschränkung so ansehe, in welche die thätigen und forschenden Kräfte des Menschen eingesperrt sind […]." (22)

the dominant notion of "Einschränkung": "in no disadvantageous way limited [*eingeschränkt*]" (*Adl.*, unbefangen, *adj. adv.*; my transl.).[99] The contrast between Lotte as the icon of the "cozy spot's" limitation and Lotte as the impassioned, "unbefangen[e]" dancer that the letter of June 16th presents emphasises the impression that she, like Werther, has a longing drawing her out of, urging her beyond the concentric constellation. Her "joy of dancing" turns out to be of the same eccentric, ecstatic quality as the feelings that drive Werther out of doors.

The second hint, given by the little word "sorglos" [carefree, careless] confirms this reading. Again this word refers to the idyllic scene of Lotte caring heartily for her siblings. As a later passage describes, since her mother's death, her whole existence has become centred on this caring role:

> how she, in her concern [*in Sorge für*] for the household and in her seriousness, had become a true mother, how not a moment of her time passes without active love, without work, and yet despite this, her good cheer, her blitheness have never left her. (61)[100]

It is Albert who gives this information to Werther in a long and important conversation. What the piece of information mirrors is indeed Albert's world, a world of work and concern and care. This is how the reader, and Werther, first heard of him:

> a very good man, who is away on a trip. He has gone to put his affairs in order, because his father has died, and he means to apply for a good position/provision/supply [*um eine ansehnliche Versorgung*]. – The information left me quite indifferent. (36)[101]

Albert is concerned, we could say, about everyone's *Versorgung*, he may even be considered as a personification of this term. However, the reader as well as Werther know that the characterisation he gives of his fiancée is not quite right: there are moments "of her time" that pass "without work", that pass without her fulfilling the caring role of the mother. The little word "sorglos" [carefree, careless] unmistakably marks that the ball, for which she leaves the circle of her siblings, is such an occasion. The "joy of dancing" that Lotte confesses to be her passion is inherently linked to the absence of care, to Lotte's

---

[99] "[...] auf keine nachtheilige Art eingeschränkt." (*Adl.* unbefangen, *adj. adv.*)
[100] "[...] wie sie in Sorge für ihre Wirthschaft und im Ernste eine wahre Mutter geworden, wie kein Augenblick ihrer Zeit ohne thätige Liebe, ohne Arbeit verstrichen, und wie dennoch all ihre Munterkeit, all ihr Leichtsinn sie nicht verlassen habe [...]." (90)
[101] "Sie ist schon vergeben, antwortete jene, an einen sehr braven Mann, der weggereist ist, seine Sachen in Ordnung zu bringen nach seines Vaters Tod, und sich um eine ansehnliche Versorgung zu bewerben. Die Nachricht war mir ziemlich gleichgültig." (38)

breaking free from the circles of her motherly duties. Nevertheless, the fact that her dancing is so "unbefangen" and "sorglos" does not simply mean that she is enjoying a licensed moment, set free from her duties for some hours. As Grimm's *Deutsches Wörterbuch* tells us, the adjective "sorglos" includes quite an ambivalent range of meanings: "free of sorrow, sorrows, not worrying about, lacking care, carefulness" (*DWB*, sorglos, *adj.*; my transl.).[102] Lotte's "sorglos" dance therefore does not merely signify that she is "free of agonising thoughts", or "not having knowledge of a present danger" and is thus "calm, harmlessly blithe, easy-going" (*DWB*, sorglos, *adj.* 1. a.; 1. b.; 1. c.; my transl.),[103] she may also be made responsible for lacking in care or concern for impending danger. As we have seen, the ball-scene is, even before it starts, characterised by a parallel threat of love and weather, a threat that draws attention to itself. Lotte is not among the "women [who] expressed their concern [*Besorgniß*] about a thunderstorm that seemed to be gathering at the horizon" (36). While the storm is brewing, she, "so carefree, so natural", is enjoying her dance. Her lack of concern may at least be said to be complicit with Werther's duping of the others' fears. This becomes even more obvious with regard to the danger of love: the information of Albert's existence as Lotte's as-good-as fiancé, and his being absent for the purpose of caring for their common future [*Versorgung*] "left [Werther] quite indifferent"; Lotte, does not seem to care about the danger of falling in love either. On the contrary, it is she who arranges their dancing the waltz, which is, as the novel explicitly tells us, against social custom. There is no need to suspect that Lotte "is a habitual breaker of hearts", as Benjamin Bennett (1980, 66) suggests. The question raised by this scene and by the novel in general is not the question of 'guilt' (cf. Dumiche 1995, Saine 1981), Lotte is not cheating on Albert – Werther does not replace Albert in any way. If Lotte "acts in a way that merits Albert's (and Kestner's) dissatisfaction" (Saine 1981, 57), then it is because Werther can share a joy with Lotte that is and will remain completely alien to Albert and his enlightened, ordered, 'concerned' world.

Viewed more closely, it does not even seem adequate to say that Lotte and Werther are indifferent to, uncaring about, the threats of the impending dangers. They are rather conjuring up these dangers, because joy and danger do not seem to be distinguishable. Their joy is what threatens the order, the neatly

---

[102] "[…] frei von sorge, sorgen, sich keine sorgen machend, der sorge, sorgfalt ermangelnd […]." (*DWB*, sorglos, *adj.* 1.)

[103] "a) ohne furcht, besorgnis vor einer bestimmten gefahr […] b) keine kenntnis von vorhandener gefahr habend […] c) allgemeiner sich keine quälenden oder ernsteren gedanken machend, ruhig, harmlos heiter, unbekümmert […]." (*DWB*, sorglos, *adj.* 1. a.; 1. b.; 1. c.;)

regulated world of ball and life. More than that, what they enjoy is the threat and danger, their joy is anarchic, the joy of de-limitation. Lucia Ruprecht's observation that what Lotte and Werther are acting out in their dance is an "(im)possibility" (2011, 55; my transl.) has a point; however, this (im)possibility is not "phantasmatic", as she claims, but perfectly real and impossible, at the same time. It is impossible from the perspective of the current social and epistemological order – that is why it can only be real as an anarchic threat, as a disrupting event that has to be silenced, overcome and forgotten as soon as possible to restore the order. The confusion that Werther's and Lotte's joy, their passion, provokes has to be read as a symptom of the reality of these 'impossible' forces. They are as real as the weather's forces disrupting the ball.

Here I think we are touching on the very core of the novel and its poetological self-reflections: there are forces, real but impossible, not accounted for, somehow beyond the epistemological reach of the established discursive regime that are waiting for 'their place', for a medium to host them, to give an account of them and to lend them 'possibility'. The weather's forces are the most intuitive and indisputable proof of the existence of this kind of real impossibility. They indicate the blind spot of the hegemonic enlightened regime that promotes a worldview based on the notion of the reign of ratio and of all-encompassing human control. The parallel of love and weather that Goethe constructs in Werther's letter of June 16th thus claims that the reality we intuitively accept for the weather's forces is also to be accepted for the phenomena of love and passion, another area not to be brought under the governance of human rationality.

Coming back at this point to Gabriele Brandstetter's dictum that Goethe's novel stages dance as "an exploratory pattern [*Erkundungsmuster*] of cultural formation" we are now in a position to see the whole range of interesting implications that this formulation entails: Lotte's "so carefree, so natural" dance has already given Werther a taste of the transgressive potential, of the underlying anarchic forces that are in the air from the beginning of the scene. It had already carried the "destructive overtones" (Brown 1991, 98) that the description of Lotte's waltz with him, though not different in quality, then explicitly characterises as 'weathery':

> So it began! and for a while we were delighted with the various ways our arms intertwined. How charming she was, how nimbly [*Mit welchem Reize, mit welcher Flüchtigkeit*] she moved! And now, as we began the waltz and, like the heavenly spheres, circled around one another, there was, of course, a good deal of confusion at first, because few were adept. We were clever and let them exhaust [*austoben*] themselves, and once the clumsiest ones had left the floor, we moved in [*fielen wir ein*] and, together with one other couple, Audran and his partner, carried on valiantly. Never have I danced so effortlessly. I was no

longer a mere mortal. To hold the loveliest creature in my arms and to fly around with her like the weather [*herum zu fliegen wie Wetter*], so that everything else around me vanished, and – Wilhelm, to be honest, I nevertheless vowed to myself that a girl whom I loved, to whom I was attached, should never waltz with anyone but me, even if it were to cost me my life. You understand what I mean! (40; transl. altered)[104]

It is not only the one, central simile, "to fly with her like the weather", that likens the dance to the weather. Regarded more closely, the weather pervades the whole passage. Again it is rather small words, easily lost in translation, that establish this analogy. The characterisation of Lotte's movement, rendered in English as "charming" and "nimbl[e]", in the German original resorts to notions that transport the idea of an event rather than of stable qualities. "Reize" signifies 'charms' as well as 'stimuli', as in the phrase "I saw new charms, *new rays of intelligence bursting from her features*" (an observation, as already analysed above, that Werther makes in the carriage while Lotte talks about literature). "Flüchtigkeit" is indeed to be read as meaning "nimble" or 'quickly', it however also carries the sense of 'fleeting', 'vanishing' that will become important towards the end of the passage, as we will presently see. The words that describe Lotte's and Werther's waiting for the confusion on the dance floor to stop are 'weathery' as well: as already discussed, the verb *toben* forming the root of "austoben" used in the passage, is very common for signifying the 'raging' of a storm.[105] It is no coincidence that the notion of confusion is early in this scene connected to the notion of the weather. Having waited for the confusion on the dance floor to cease, as if waiting under some shelter for the heavy rain to stop, Werther and Lotte "move[ ] in", at least in the German original, like another front of bad weather: "fielen wir ein", literally 'we fell in', 'we invaded', a phrase often used for (destructive) natural events, "*incidere, mainly of natural events*", as Grimm's *Deutsches Wörterbuch* tells us (*DWB*, einfallen, v. 3.; my transl.).[106]

---

[104] "Nun giengs, und wir ergözten uns eine Weile an mannchfaltigen Schlingungen der Arme. Mit welchem Reize, mit welcher Flüchtigkeit bewegte sie sich! Und da wir nun gar an's Walzen kamen, und wie die Sphären um einander herumrollten, giengs freylich anfangs, weil's die wenigsten können, ein bisgen bunt durch einander. Wir waren klug und liessen sie austoben, und wie die ungeschiktesten den Plan geräumt hatten, fielen wir ein, und hielten mit noch einem Paare, mit Audran und seiner Tänzerinn, wakker aus. Nie ist mir's so leicht vom Flekke gegangen. Ich war kein Mensch mehr. Das liebenswürdigste Geschöpf in den Armen zu haben, und mit ihr herum zu fliegen wie Wetter, daß alles rings umher vergieng und – Wilhelm, um ehrlich zu seyn, daß ich aber doch den Schwur, daß ein Mädchen, das ich liebte, auf das ich Ansprüche hätte, mir nie mit einem andern walzen sollte, als mit mir, und wenn ich drüber zu Grunde gehen müßte, du verstehst mich." (48)
[105] Cf. 149.
[106] "[...] *incidere, meist von naturerscheinungen* [...]." (*DWB*, einfallen, v. 3.)

Despite the explicit hint of the simile "to fly around with her like the weather" only a few critics reading this dance scene (one of the most prominent scenes of the novel) have noticed the important part that the weather plays. As some exemplary interpretations show, the observation of the weather's role in this scene makes a crucial difference for the way it is read. Gerhard Neumann belongs to those who have given attention to the weather, which has led him to see the waltz as "replacing the old code of a domestication of the bodily dynamic with a new of chaotic de-limitation" (2000, 527; my transl.). The "kinetic flush/ecstasy [*Rausch*]" of an "anarchic dynamic of flying, hovering, rotating, tumbling and unifying" is interpreted by Gerhard Neumann as a "threshold experience" (2000, 529; my transl.) that cannot be understood without "the thunderstorm, the 'chaos' of the natural" that enters the scene "as a question for the social fate, so-to-speak, breaking out of nature's numinous" (2000, 527; my transl.). He interprets the dynamic "of the whirl, of the tumbling" as "beyond the system's capacities of integration [*systematisch nicht mehr integrierbar*[ ]]", as a "'thermodynamic' movement" (2000, 527; my transl.). Gerhard Neumann's resorting to thermodynamics may however not have been the happiest of choices for bringing the knowledge of the weather and Werther's novel together: not only since the notion of a "thermodynamic movement" does not seem to be helpful for reconstructing the scene (thermodynamics is about the transformation of energies, thus different forms, not just kinetic energy, would be needed for an analogy); more importantly, the theory of thermodynamics is blatantly anachronistic. It is exactly the piece of theory missing in contemporary science that would generations later allow scientists to make sense of the data that Goethe and his contemporaries were so eagerly collecting without being able, as we have seen, to prognosticate or explain anything from them. However, Neumann's anachronism may also be read as a useful indicator of the dance's excessive quality: it is indeed a weathery moment that cannot be integrated into the epistemic and social system of the time. By resorting to a *terminus technicus* not available to Goethe and his contemporaries, Gerhard Neumann is able to capture what is "unheard of/the unprecedented in Goethe's novel [*das Unerhörte des Goetheschen Romans*]" (2000, 529; my transl.): an "aporetic moment, in which dance becomes the pattern of social order and at the same time its anarchic subversion" (2000, 529; my transl.). What makes this moment aporetic, what accounts for this aporia, is the fact that Neumann reads the novel as affirming both sides of the contradiction, order and subversion. Identifying the centre of the novel as an aporia, that is to say, granting the forces of subversion, the forces not domesticated by the reigning order (the ecstatic, the excessive) their own, positive existence seems to be inseparable from paying attention to the role of the weather.

Lucia Ruprecht's reading proves a case in point: she, like Neumann, characterises the waltz as "ecstatic [*rauschhaft*]" (Ruprecht 2011, 45; my transl.). In the course of her argument, however, she feels motivated to add that the dance is "conceptualised so excessive that it brings to life a pathologic dynamic which predetermines the further tragic course of events" (Ruprecht 2011, 45; my transl.). Her reading is exemplary: she does not take any interest in the weather, and very quickly qualifies excess and ecstasy as an idiosyncratic pathology. Without being fully aware of it, readings like hers take the stance of the ordered, enlightened, regulated world that the novel portrays to be Albert's world. Werther is 'othered', excess and ecstasy are identified as the corrupting flaws leading to the final fall – sad, but 'healthy' from the perspective of social order. No aporia remains, we are told a story of disturbances and aberrations that are overcome in the end. I think it questionable whether a story like the one reconstructed by Lucia Ruprecht can finally be called 'tragic' in a fuller sense of the word: it is rather moralistic than tragic, since it lacks the important element of fate, of transcending personal agency.

In contrast, Gerhard Neumann's reading sees the "question for the social fate" raised. It is his sensitivity to the weather's impact on the scene that enables him to give an account of the intuition that Werther's story is not simply pathologic, but tragic. If we were to speak of pathology, the dominant parallel of weather and dance would unmistakably indicate that this pathology could not be located on the level of the individual, but had to be thought of as effective on a 'higher' level – the heavy weather disrupts the ball as such, independent from Werther's and Lotte's waltz. This would then perhaps lead towards conclusions like: 'something's 'ill' in the state of 18th century society'. However, this does not seem to be adequate either, since our modern ears (in contrast to early-modern Shakespearean) are used to understanding a (temporal) aberration from the 'healthy', the 'right', 'correct' state when hearing the word 'pathologic'. In the face of the complex aporia that forms the core of Goethe's novel and the impossibility of determining any healthy state, this does not seem to make much sense. Furthermore, speaking of "pathologic dynamics" always denies these forces their own, positive existence and assumes a position in control of deciding between health and aberration.

David Wellbery, however, perhaps most explicitly claims a mode of existence for the forces at work in Lotte's and Werther's waltz, and it does not seem astonishing that his reading, like Gerhard Neumann's, is based on the role of the weather:

> The feature of this historical mutation that interests me here is that the waltz, as it enters the fiction, becomes the site and occasion of a specific morphism of the phantasmagoric body. Waltzing with Charlotte, Werther experiences a transformation of his own corporeality: the heaviness of the body falls away ("light"); the dancing couple attains equivalence to a meteorological or cosmic movement, flying "like the wind" ("wie Wetter"); finally, the surrounding field of objects that would relativize the body – the field, let us say, of corporeal alterity – disappears. (1994, 183)

David Wellbery thus interprets Werther's and Lotte's waltz as a "transcendence of human corporeal limitation" (1994, 184), as a positive, a productive movement that produces a new "transfinite body" (1994, 184). The "specific morphism" that Wellbery describes seems to be fuelled by a strong source of energy about whose relation to the weather Enzo Neppi has very aptly observed: "there is in [Werther] also a desire of metamorphosis, the urge [*l'envie*] of escaping the limits of his corporeal existence, of merging with the elements, of becoming wind or thunderstorm" (2010, 335; my transl.). In these few words many of the observations of our close reading undertaken so far culminate: Enzo Neppi condenses Werther's and Lotte's urge of going out, of leaving their circles and the important role the weather plays for this desire of transcending one's limitations in one handy, but ultimately puzzling formula. Puzzling, because the desire of becoming wind must, at least at first, appear unfamiliar, perhaps even incomprehensible. The reason for this lack of familiarity may be found in the fact that the conceptualisation of the body that this desire of becoming wind attempts to escape has grown even more naturalised, more monolithic and unquestioned for us than it was for Werther and his contemporaries.

The conceptualisation of the body that I am speaking of has become known under the term *homo clausus*. The implications of this concept of the body are not only of a 'physiological' nature, they are not limited to the way our 'biological' bodies are thought of, either as open, communicating vessels exchanging all kinds of material and standing in a certain (dis)balance with the rest of the world (the ancient model, still predominant in Shakespeare's time), or as closed, self-regulated organisms for which intrusion from the outside, or leaking from the inside is the main source of illness (the modern successor). The concept of *homo clausus* is at the heart of a new episteme, one may perhaps even say that the emergence of this conceptualisation has had a great share in revolutionising the epistemic field, with all its manifold social and political effects. Albrecht Koschorke's book *Körperströme und Schriftverkehr. Mediologie des 18. Jahrhunderts* [Streams of the Body and the Correspondence of Letters. Mediology of the 18th Century] (2003) explores a huge range of facets that the emergence of this new conceptualisation of the body brings forth in the world of the 18th century. From Koschorke's study we learn that the process of "The body's closure" (the title of one section) had not happened once and for all, but was still on-going in the course of the 18th century, and was still virulently contested when Goethe was writing his novel. Thus "the limits of [ones] corporeal existence" were still quite fresh, still felt as uncomfortable and contestable, not yet grown quite natural and inescapable.

Despite the odd fact that Goethe's *Werther* does not play a central role in Koschorke's book (on the contrary, we will see that in his reading, as a solitary exception among hundreds of examples, it even resists his argument in one point) Goethe's *Werther* may, with good reasons, even be called a predecessor of Koschorke's study: it in fact explores the contemporary negotiations and transformations taking place with the establishment of the concept of the *homo clausus*. In Koschorke's study as well as in Goethe's novel these transforming processes culminate in the emergence of new media for hosting the forces of 'the streams' that have lost their place in the processes of a new episteme constituting itself. The only manifest difference between Koschorke's study and Goethe's novel concerns the role of the weather: the weather is not included in Koschorke's focus, whereas the weather is a dominant theme in *Werther*, being very much at the centre of what the novel is about. This difference is striking, since Albrecht Koschorke does not seem to realise that his object of study forces him again and again to resort to notions of the weather: even the 'streams' of his title, referring to the medieval and early modern concept of a world governed by analogies, may be said to be imbued with weather, to be part of the dynamic processes of 'natural' correspondence, circulation and transformation of fluids for which the weather served as the paradigm – 'streams' is, in the broadest sense, a weather metaphor.

A greater sensitivity for the weather would have helped Albrecht Koschorke to connect Goethe's novel to his theory of the 18th century emergence of media: it would have helped to understand the dance scene's role in the wider context of the novel. The waltz marks, as we have seen, indeed one peak of delimitation that is characterised as a meteorological event: as 'flying like the weather'. However, this explicit reference to the weather is not singular and does not introduce something new and unheard of. On the contrary, as shown above, the subversive potential of the weather and its connection to the theme of delimitation are well established by the time of the waltz. Viewed more closely, even the wording of the actual delimitation looks astonishingly familiar. The waltz scene uses the following words: "To hold the loveliest creature in my arms and to fly around with her like the weather, so that everything else around me vanished [*daß alles rings umher vergieng*]". Two earlier passages are worth being brought to mind: Firstly, Werther watching Lotte dance: "You should see her dance! [...] [I]n such moments everything else surely does vanish [*schwindet*] from her mind"

(39; transl. altered). Secondly, even earlier, Werther's ecstasy when listening to Lotte on the way to the ball:

> How my entire soul was drawn to her animated lips and her fresh, glowing cheeks! How completely *immersed* [*versunken*] I was in the splendid sense of her conversation [...]! – [...] I was so *lost in my dreams in the twilit world around me* [*so in Träumen rings in der dämmernden Welt verlohren*] that I hardly registered the music pealing down to us from the brightly lit hall. (39; transl. altered; emph. J.U.)

"[E]verything else around me vanished [*alles rings umher vergieng*]", "everything else surely does vanish [*gewiß schwindet alles andere*]" – there can be no doubt that Werther's impression of seeing Lotte dance, his speculating about what is going on in her mind, in other words, his projecting his own ecstasy while watching her is indistinguishable from the ecstasy he experiences while waltzing with her. This is an astonishing observation, because it undermines all interpretations that regard the waltz as the decisive step for the ecstasy described in the novel, an ecstasy that would be that of the loving union of a pair. Albrecht Koschorke's reading of the waltz is paradigmatic in this respect:

> a circling, that with the vanishing [*schwindender*] control of the senses makes the external world as a whole sink away [*versinken läßt*] and thereby corresponds to the demand for exclusivity produced by the new rituals of pair formation as well as to the attacks of fainting that were expected in this context especially from women [...]. (Koschorke 2003, 201; my transl.)

Despite the plausibility that Koschorke's reading can claim for itself, despite the fact that Goethe indeed, as we will see, plays with the pseudo-etymology of *Schwindel* [dizziness] and *schwinden* [to vanish], neither the waltz's circling nor its ritualistic character of pair formation can be made responsible for the ecstasy it effects. The desire to find in this scene a paradigmatic visualisation of Luhmann's theory of love as a generalised medium for the two lovers' intimate communication has led Albrecht Koschorke astray, away from a close reading of the text that is telling a more complex story. As his wording betrays, Albrecht Koschorke has all three formulations of ecstasy in mind, the formulations that we above demonstrated to be strikingly similar: Koschorke's words, "vanishing control" [*mit* schwindender *Kontrolle*], refer to Werther's observation of seeing Lotte dance ("everything else surely does vanish from her mind" [*gewiß* schwindet *ihr alles andere*]); Koschorke's phrase, "makes the external world as a whole sink away" [*die Außenwelt als ganze* versinken läßt], takes up the wording of Werther's sensation when listening to Lotte in the carriage ("How completely *immersed* I was in the splendid sense of her conversation" [*wie ich in den herrlichen Sinn ihrer Rede ganz* versunken]). Albrecht Koschorke is surely right in reading these three formulations together as expressions of the same ecstatic movement. However, the novel's assigning this ecstasy to three distinct situations, only one of them being the waltz, resists Koschorke's reading the waltz as being responsible for the ecstatic state.

As a consequence, the relation between ecstasy and pair formation that the novel presents us with is more complicated. First of all, the moment of ecstasy cannot be conceptualised as an effect of pair formation and the "demand of exclusivity". Reading the three similar formulations of ecstasy together, it is far from clear what exactly 'sinks', 'vanishes' and 'is immersed' or 'lost', and what remains present and in touch. In each case it is the concentric constellation from where the movement starts, with just one single person – and not a pair – at its centre: Werther is "immersed" [versunken] "in the splendid sense of [Lotte's] conversation"; it is from Lotte's mind that "everything else surely does vanish", including the watching bystander Werther! Importantly, Werther's being "so lost in [his] dreams in the twilit world around [him]" indicates a different direction of vanishing: here it is not the surrounding, but the centre that collapses, this time Werther is lost. Thus the novel neither puts a pair at the centre of the ecstatic moment, nor is this ecstasy characterised as a movement of concentration, constituting a new unity. It does therefore appear worthwhile to have a look at the personal pronouns marking the centre of reference in the waltz scene:

> So it began! and for a while *we* were delighted with the various ways our arms intertwined. How charming *she* was, how nimbly *she* moved! And now, as *we* began the waltz and, like the heavenly spheres, circled around one another, there was, of course, a good deal of confusion at first, because few were adept. *We* were clever and let them exhaust themselves, and once the clumsiest ones had left the floor, *we* moved in and, together with one other couple, Audran and his partner, carried on valiantly. Never have *I* danced so effortlessly. *I* was no longer a mere mortal. To hold the loveliest creature in *my* arms and to fly with her like the wind, so that everything else around *me* vanished, and – Wilhelm, to be honest, *I* nevertheless vowed to myself that a girl whom *I* loved, to whom *I* was attached, should never waltz with anyone but me, even if it were to cost *me my* life. You understand what *I* mean. (40; transl. altered; emph. J.U.)[107]

---

107 "Nun giengs, und wir ergözten uns eine Weile an mannchfaltigen Schlingungen der Arme. Mit welchem Reize, mit welcher Flüchtigkeit bewegte sie sich! Und da wir nun gar an's Walzen kamen, und wie die Sphären um einander herumrollten, giengs freylich anfangs, weil's die wenigsten können, ein bisgen bunt durch einander. Wir waren klug und liessen sie austoben, und wie die ungeschiktesten den Plan geräumt hatten, fielen wir ein, und hielten mit noch einem Paare, mit Audran und seiner Tänzerinn, wakker aus. Nie ist mir's so leicht vom Flekke gegangen. Ich war kein Mensch mehr. Das liebenswürdigste Geschöpf in den Armen zu haben, und mit ihr herum zu fliegen wie Wetter, daß alles rings umher vergieng und – Wilhelm, um ehrlich zu seyn, daß ich aber doch den Schwur, daß ein Mädchen, das ich liebte, auf das ich Ansprüche hätte, mir nie mit einem andern walzen sollte, als mit mir, und wenn ich drüber zu Grunde gehen müßte, du verstehst mich." (48)

The beginning of the scene seems to play into Albrecht Koschorke's hands, the first person plural pronoun we is dominant, only shortly interrupted by an observation of Lotte's nimble movement, which resembles Werther's earlier observations of seeing her dance a minuet. However, when the scene gets closer to its ecstatic peak, the pronoun suddenly changes to the first person singular *I*. The passage repeatedly postpones the waltz's actual beginning: the intertwining arms indicate that the waltz to come is preceded by an Allemande; when the circling of the waltz starts, we are told that Werther and Lotte cleverly take their time before moving in. It is as late as here that their actual, intense waltzing begins – and it is here that the personal pronoun changes to the singular: "Never have *I* danced so effortlessly. *I* was no longer a mere mortal." The English translation even puts the ecstatic formula in a way that centres on a dominant first person pronoun: "To hold the loveliest creature in *my* arms and to fly with her like the wind *[herum zu fliegen wie Wetter]*, so that everything else around *me* vanished". In the German original this formula is more neutral, using an infinitive construction that evades any pronouns; however, the clause's implicit subject is indeed Werther as an individual *[mit ihr herumzufliegen]*. The novel thus gives no evidence that the ecstasy has to be read as the ecstasy of a pair. On the contrary, the description of the ecstasy rather moves away from the dancing couple, towards the experiencing individual.

The waltz scene in *Werther* has an important predecessor in one of Goethe's letters. This passage from a letter that Goethe wrote to his friend Salzmann at Sessenheim on the 29th of May 1771 is not only interesting for thematic reasons, it also has clearly served as a reservoir for important formulations that, three years later, found their way into the novel:

> I have danced together with the Oldest on Whit Monday, from two o'clock after lunch until 12 in the night, continuously, except for some intermezzos of food and drink. Mister Magistrate of Reschwog had given us his hall, we had found some honest musicians it went like weather *[da giengs wie Wetter]*. I forgot about the fever, and it has been better since then.
>
> You should at least have seen it. The whole *me* immersed in the dancing *[Das ganze mich in das Tanzen versuncken]*.
>
> And yet if I could say: I am happy, then everything would be better than all that.
>
> Who is allowed to say I am the most unfortunate says Edgar. That is his comfort dear man.
>
> My head is like a weather vane, when a thunderstorm is brewing and the gusts of wind changing. (FA 28, 229; my transl.)[108]

---

[108] "Getanzt hab ich und die Älteste Pfingstmontags, von zwey Uhr Nachtisch biss 12 Uhr in der Nacht, an einem fort, ausser einigen Intermezzos von Essen und Trincken. Der Herr Amtschulz von Reschwog hatte seinen Saal hergegeben, wir hatten brave Schnurranten erwischt da giengs wie Wetter. Ich vergass des Fiebers, und seit der Zeit ists auch besser.

In an odd fashion, almost as if distorted and displaced by Freud's dreamwork, we find in this letter many of the motives that the novel's letter of June 16th will then unfold and elaborate on: most prominently, for sure, the simile "like weather"[109] characterising the experience of dancing; but also small, rather stylistic idiosyncrasies recognisable only in the German original, like the "da giengs" that will resurface in *Werther* as introducing the dance passage ("Nun giengs"). The letter also includes in its brief description the dimension of watching the dance, that is to say the point of view of the observing bystander: "You should at least have seen it". This is interesting, because in *Werther*, Goethe will split the scene in two, so that his watching Lotte dance introduces the dimension of the watching bystander, while his waltzing with Lotte renders his subjective impression as the dancer. The similarity in formulation clearly indicates the intertextual relation between the letter and the dance scene in the novel: "You

---

Sie hätten's wenigstens nur sehen sollen. Das ganze *mich* in das Tanzen versuncken.

Und doch wenn ich sagen könnte: ich binn glücklich, so wär das besser als das alles.

Wer darf sagen ich binn der unglückseeligste sagt Edgar. Das ist auch sein Trost lieber Mann. Der Kopf steht mir wie eine Wetterfahne, wenn ein Gewitter heraufzieht und die Windstösse veränderlich sind." (FA 28, 229)

109 David Wellbery (cf. footnote 1994, 183) has discovered another similar link of weather and the waltz in a poem by Goethe called "An Christel", written before 1774, which assembles all the major motives that will feature in the novel's dance scene. These are the last three stanzas of the German version:

"Und wenn ich sie dann fassen darf
Im lüftgen deutschen Tanz
Das geht herum, das geht so scharf
Da fühl ich mich so ganz.
Und wenn's ihr tummlich wird und warm
Da wieg ich sie sogleich
An meiner Brust in meinem Arm
Ist mir ein Königreich.

Und wenn sie liebend nach mir blickt
Und alles rund vergißt
Und dann an meine Brust gedrückt
Und weidlich eins geküßt
Das läuft mir durch das Rückenmark
Bis in die große Zeh
Ich bin so schwach ich bin so stark,
Mir ist so wohl, so weh!

Da mögt ich mehr und immermehr,
Der Tag wird mir nicht lang,
Wenn ich die Nacht auch bei ihr wär
Dafür wär mir nicht bang
Ich denk ich halte sie einmal
Und büße meine Lust,
Und endigt sich nicht meine Qual,
Sterb ich an ihrer Brust." (FA 1, 222)

should at least have seen it [*Sie hätten's wenigstens nur sehen sollen*]" the letter says, which is echoed by the novel's "You should see her dance! [*Tanzen muß man sie sehen*]". In the letter, it is not clear whether the ecstatic formula "The whole *me* immersed in the dancing" refers to the external or the experiencing point of view, it oscillates between the two. However, what the letter makes more than clear is the subject of this being "immersed" [*versuncken*] in the dancing, which is even typographically emphasised. It thus unmistakably marks the point of reference of the dancing's ecstasy and excess: the "*me*" – not a word of 'we'! The ecstatic dancing experience is not about pair formation, not about exclusivity, not about a new intimate system of references. This is not to say that the experience is not inherently one of love, one brought about by another person. The point of reference, however, the place where ecstasy and excess unleash their forces and thus need to be coped with is the individual. Instead of building up a new system of reference, as Koschorke believes, along with Luhmann, Goethe here rather describes the excessive demands that are directed at the one system already available, at the individual. The way the letter continues, having narrated the dance's ecstasy is telling: "And yet, if *I* could say: *I* am happy". We see the individual, bemoaning its unfortunate self, finding itself at the centre of whirling weathery forces: "My head is like a weather vane, when a thunderstorm is brewing and the gusts of wind changing".

The persistent reference to the weather, not just as a simile characterising the dance but as expressive of a bigger problem troubling the individual, further adds to the evidence that the letter to Salzmann tells the 'primal scene' of dance and ecstasy, which the novel then expands and works with. The novel, however, opts for two decisive additions to the motives already present in the letter: characterising the dance as a waltz and bringing up the theme of the pair's exclusivity towards the end of the passage. It is these additions on which Albrecht Koschorke's reading focuses and it is important to understand these two related aspects as additions in the context of the constellation set up around the ecstasy overpowering the individual.

The waltz can be understood as a variation of the image of the weather vane that features so prominently in the letter but does not appear in the novel. Another letter to Salzmann, hardly two weeks later, takes up the image of the weather vane and illustrates its semantic core:

> It is raining outside and inside, and the nasty winds of the evening rustle in the vine leaves outside the window, and my anima vagula is like the little weather vane over there on the spire; turn, turn [*dreh dich, dreh dich*], that is how it goes all the day [...]. (FA 28, 230; my transl.)[110]

---

[110] "Es regnet draussen und drinne, und die garstigen Winde von Abend rascheln in den Rebblättern vorm Fenster, und meine animula vagula ist wie's Wetter Hähngen drüben auf dem Kirchturm; dreh dich, dreh dich, das geht den ganzen Tag [...]." (FA 28, 230)

Albrecht Koschorke rightly claims that the waltz's "circling" accompanies the "vanishing control of the senses"; characterising the dance as a waltz thus adds the information that it takes over the turning, the spinning of the weather vane caused by changing gusts of wind. Substituting the image of the weather vane with the waltz not only means shifting images for something that is hard to grasp and cannot be addressed 'literally'. As Lucia Ruprecht writes, the dance has "a substitution function comparable to the sentimental culture of writing [*eine der empfindsamen Schriftkultur vergleichbare Substitutionsfunktion*]" (2011, 45; my transl.). Since it is far from clear what the 'authentic', 'immediate', 'original' object (?) / feeling (?) / longing (?) / action (?) is that is said to be substituted by the dance or by writing, I would prefer to refer to the dance as a medium, a medium that opens a cultural space for these weathery forces, where these forces find expression and a cultural signification and are at the same time domesticated "by regulation and elaboration" (Ruprecht 2011, 59; my transl.). This new medium is thus characterised by the paradoxical fact that eccentricity is an essential part of its defining architecture: the centrifugal forces, accounting for the "vanishing control of the senses" are what the waltz, as waltz, is all about. As Gerhard Neumann puts it, the waltz is a "pattern of social order and at the same time its anarchic subversion" (2000, 529; my transl.). The dance however ultimately frames this subversion, tames it, gives it an appropriate, liveable, socially acceptable cultural form: it 'de-paradoxalises' its defining paradox, as Niklas Luhmann would say, so that, in this sense, the waltz is indeed a paradigmatic example for the generalised communicative medium of 'love as passion'.

The price for this 'liveability' of passion (that is to say of eccentricity), the side-effect of this medium produced by its specific codification, is as well-known to us as it is disturbing and fatal for Werther: exclusivity. The novel very early, before the waltz has been arranged and got under way acknowledges the waltze's constitutive exclusivity: "It's the custom here, she continued, that every couple that belongs together remain together for the German dance" (40).[111] It is no coincidence that the theme of exclusivity surfaces at the peak of the waltz's ecstasy:

> To hold the loveliest creature in my arms and to fly with her like the wind [*herum zu fliegen wie Wetter*], so that everything else around me vanished, and – Wilhelm, to be honest, I nevertheless vowed to myself that a girl whom I loved, to whom I was attached, should never waltz with anyone but me, even if it were to cost me my life. You understand what I mean. (40; transl. altered; emph. J.U.)[112]

---

[111] "Es ist hier so Mode, fuhr sie fort, daß jedes paar, das zusammen gehört, beym Deutschen zusammen bleibt [...]." (46)

[112] "Das liebenswürdigste Geschöpf in den Armen zu haben, und mit ihr herum zu fliegen wie Wetter, daß alles rings umher vergieng und – Wilhelm, um ehrlich zu seyn, that ich aber doch

Lucia Ruprecht has directed attention to the "abruptly emerging dash" (2011, 54; my transl.) that interrupts the description of the waltz and switches over to the theme of exclusivity. However, the dash not only signifies the "loss of visual perceptions" and the point "where description breaks off" (2011, 54; my transl.) as Ruprecht writes, but also expresses a contrastive passage, a passage to 'the other side of the medal'. In the German original the two small words "aber doch" [but yet] ("Wilhelm, um ehrlich zu seyn, that ich aber doch den Schwur") indicate a contrast, a defensive, admitting gesture. It is revealing that Stanley Corngold's English translation, deservedly famous for its unreached precision, in this case just eliminates the rather unsettling contrast by leaving the two small words untranslated: in doing so it follows the dominant reading promoted by Koschorke and others that attempt to link the ecstasy of the dance with pair-formation and exclusivity, declaring the latter the condition of the former. The two words that I tried to translate as "nevertheless" contradict this reading, so much so that they have to be left out, ignored, in order to uphold this interpretation. The exclusivity of pair formation does not bring about the ecstatic moment, nor does it seamlessly follow from it: exclusivity is the side effect of the particular medium in which this moment of ecstasy finds its socially acceptable realisation – it follows from the waltz as a cultural practice ("every couple that belongs together remain together for the German dance"). The ominous dash thus indicates a contrast that very much qualifies the aptness of the waltz medium with regard to the weathery, ecstatic forces on the verge of making a cultural appearance. Whereas the part of the description preceding the dash formulates the resonance of weathery forces and waltz, the part following the dash reveals this medium's incompatibility to Werther's problem. The dash also introduces a change in tone and perlocutionary mode. The second last word before the dash, "vanished [*vergieng*]", sums up the semantic field that the passage presents as bringing dance and weather into resonance: a de-reification, one could say, "the heaviness of the body falls away", David Wellbery writes, "the dancing couple attains equivalence to a meteorological or cosmic movement, flying 'like the wind' [*wie Wetter*]" (1994, 183). Fleetingness and movement are the passage's dominant semes linking weather and dance: "How charming she was, how nimbly she moved! [*Mit welchem Reize, mit welcher Flüchtigkeit bewegte sie sich*]". From this affirmation of fleetingness Werther's vow that follows the dash could not differ more: the perlocutionary mode of the vow already affirms and relies on stability, it denies the forces of time and change

---

den Schwur, daß ein Mädchen, das ich liebte, auf das ich Ansprüche hätte, mir nie mit einem andern walzen sollte, als mit mir, und wenn ich drüber zu Grunde gehen müßte, du verstehst mich." (48)

which is emphasised by the assertive "never" of Werther's "a girl whom I loved [...] should never waltz with anyone but me". Werther imposes a rigid rule on Lotte and himself that does not seem to be compatible at all with the "flying like the weather", with the anarchic fleetingness of the dancing experience – and, most importantly, with his own former indifference to the information that this girl "is already engaged" (35). In short, Werther's vow does not belong to the same world of weathery forces, the world where his urge to go out, his eccentricity and search for the ecstatic are engendered. The medium of the waltz has connected these forces to the codification of Albert's world. It is here that the unbridgeable conflict arises and that the impossibility of the weathery forces' realisation in this medium of waltz and 'love as passion' makes itself felt: the problem is not, as Lucia Ruprecht claims, that the substitution is enacted "in such a full-bodied fashion that the substitution itself turns into satisfaction [*dass die Substitution selbst zur Erfüllung gerät*]" (2011, 59; my transl.), but that the medium of the waltz, of 'love as passion', with its codification of exclusivity is not capable of capturing the weathery forces that resist being brought under the law of exclusivity. As Werther's and Lotte's ecstatic moments preceding the famous waltz show (moments overtly indifferent to the marital or even a relationship status of the beloved other), these weathery forces are also of a promiscuous nature, not to be tamed by pair formation. In the narrated world of *Werther*, it is Albert who occupies the place of exclusivity, and it is well known that he is not the novel's icon for passion. When Friedrich Nicolai's *Die Freuden des jungen Werthers* (1775) tells the story of Albert's ceding Lotte to Werther, its mocking sarcasm is derived from the obvious incompatibility of Albert's and Werther's longings and positions – Albert's position does not offer a solution to Werther's problem.

In the face of the codification of exclusivity that the medium of the waltz and 'love as passion' pre-supposes, Werther's fate is sealed: "even if it were to cost me my life". Reading this as an ultimate failure, however, is a misunderstanding and underestimation of the project the novel pursues. Werther's losing – or sacrificing? – his life does not merely communicate the general impossibility of integrating the weathery forces into the enlightened system of life and culture. It is, as we will see, the price he pays for his transformation into another medium, into a book's title protagonist. The fact that he, by fulfilling his vow and giving his life, keeps faith with the weathery forces surfaces in the novel's very choice of words, unfortunately, again, only in the German original: "und wenn ich drüber zu Grunde gehen müßte", a formulation which obviously cannot be transferred into English, signifying something like 'even if I were to perish, to be ruined [in the sense of to die] as a consequence of this'. The German phrase *zu Grunde gehen* (literally: 'going to the ground') is important and revealing for two reasons.

Firstly, as shown above, it is a recurring formulation that the novel employs for expressing the violent effect of the weather.[113] Secondly, Werther's vow of "zu Grunde gehen" resonates strikingly with the weathery description of his ecstatic moment in the waltz preceding the dash, for which the German verb *vergehen* is used. The notion of dissolving, expressed by these two formulations in a very similar way as a movement out of existence, as going somewhere where(by) one loses one's defining unity, gives this whole passage a remarkable turn: it reintroduces the weather's fleetingness into the stability of Werther's vow. In fact, it discloses fleetingness as a defining condition of vows and stability: the law is re-embedded in the inescapable logic of life (life that carries this fleetingness, the '*Entstehen* und *zu-Grunde-Gehen*' [coming into existence and perishing] in itself).

The notion of death and the important role it plays for the novel will be analysed in greater detail at a later point. It is, however, crucial when thinking about the role of the dance and the medium of the waltz and 'love as passion' to see the inherent connection between these two forms of transgressing human limitations, between these two forms of ecstasy, erotic *jouissance* [little deaths, so to speak] and 'deadly' death – Eros and Thanatos. What I have called weathery forces is not limited to promiscuous longings, but also, as will be seen in a later section, consists in an ontological dimension of constitutive fleetingness of the life and world. Werther's threat, his radical 'solution' to the problem of leaving this life if the exclusivity following from the codification of the medium at hand (dance, 'love as passion') does not prove to be liveable for him, is thus more than a capitulation or confession of failure. His suicide is a meaningful and provocative performative act, confronting the system with the forces it denies, urging a reaction. Despite the manifold cultural mechanisms of mourning and moral codification, Thanatos cannot be coped with routinely and silently, especially not when it surfaces in the radical form of a longing to die that finally manifests itself in being acted out. The existence of the novel is a case in point: Karl Wilhelm Jerusalem's suicide had a violent effect on Goethe and his contemporaries and in its role can hardly be overestimated for the project of writing *Werther*. Moreover, the assertion of the impossibility of routinely coping with Thanatos also holds true for the overwhelming reaction to Goethe's novel itself: the majority of contemporary responses to it are induced by the appalling suicide, a suicide somehow overburdening moral categories.

The equation that Lucia Ruprecht observes between "delirium [*Taumel*] of dance" and "delirium [*Taumel*] of death" (2011, 52; my transl.) is thus not so

---

113 Cf. 138.

much expressive of Werther's pathological constitution and fate as it is indicative of the inadequateness of the medium of the waltz to domesticate and contain the weathery forces of both Eros and Thanatos. Once the waltz has disclosed the codification of exclusivity that governs the system of 'love as passion', it has fulfilled its function as "an exploratory pattern [*Erkundungsmuster*] of cultural formation" (Brandstetter 1997, 1011; my transl.). Robert H. Brown is surely right in noticing that "[w]hile waltzing with Lotte like a storm, the corporative context of the ball vanishes" (1991, 98); however, it is not correct that "the sequence of dances [in Werther] stages in miniature the chronology of social styles of dance" (Ruprecht 2011, 45; my transl.). The novel in fact frames the waltz, as the most recent style of dancing, with a preceding minuet and Allemande and a "country dance [*Englischen*]" that succeeds it. This is done in order to work out the contrast effected by the waltz and the notion of exclusivity it discovers: whereas Werther can watch Lotte dance a minuet without even saying a word about her dancing partner or taking notice of the information that she is already promised to another man, it is during the "third country dance", not during the waltz, that Werther and Lotte are reminded of the decisive information that reveals the impossibility of their forming an exclusive pair: "As we danced through the line and I, God knows with how much bliss, hung on her arm and eyes" a woman emerges, "lifts a minatory finger and, as we fly past, twice utters the name of Albert very meaningfully" (40–41).[114] Without doubt the two words, "fly past", remind us of the waltz's ecstatic "flying like weather"; nevertheless, the scene also extensively emphasises that the style of dancing is now again a social dance, not a pair dance: not only when the strange, threatening woman emerges, but also when Lotte feels urged to confess her being promised to Albert:

> Who is Albert? I said to Lotte, if I may ask. – She was about to answer when we had to separate in order to move into the great figure eight, and it seemed to me that I saw signs of pensiveness on her forehead as we crossed in front of one another. – Why should I hide it from you, she said as she gave me her hand for the promenade, Albert is a fine man to whom I am as good as engaged. (41)[115]

---

[114] "Wie wir die Reihe so durchtanzten, und ich, weis Gott mit wie viel Wonne, an ihrem Arme und Auge hieng, das voll vom wahrsten Ausdrukke des offensten reinsten Vergnügen war kommen wir an eine Frau [...]. Sie sieht Lotten lächelnd an, hebt einen drohenden Finger auf, und nennt den Nahmen Albert zweymal im Vorbeyfliegen mit viel Bedeutung." (48)

[115] "Wer ist Albert, sagte ich zu Lotten, wenns nicht Vermessenheit ist zu fragen. Sie war im Begriffe zu antworten, als wir uns scheiden mußten die grosse Achte zu machen, und mich dünkte einiges Nachdenken auf ihrer Stirne zu sehen, als wir so vor einander vorbeykreuzten. Was soll ich's ihnen läugnen, sagte sie, indem sie mir die Hand zu Promenade bot. Albert ist ein braver Mensch, dem ich so gut als verlobt bin!" (49–50)

Very wittily Goethe here makes extensive allegorical use of the dance: its figures of separation and re-joining illustrate the strange oscillation between close proximity and distance that takes place in Lotte when the conflict of pair-formation and exclusivity, the 'rivalry' between Albert and Werther emerges. I do not see the novel playing off one style of dance against another, promoting the more modern waltz as standing for a functionally differentiated social system against the older social dances representing the old, feudal, cosmological order, as so many readers like Brown, Ruprecht and Koschorke have done. The moment of ecstasy that the waltz was more apt to bring about has already surfaced in the minuet and is now explicitly transferred to the "country dance", as Lotte and Werther are still referred to as "fly[ing]". Since the dimension of (an imposed) order is more prominent in the "country dance", the novel uses this style of dancing to illustrate the disturbance of order when Werther realises that the 'weathery' forces of love brewing in him cannot be realised in the form of pair-formation and 'love as passion':

> Enough, I became confused, lost count, and came in between the wrong couple, so that everything went awry, and it took all of Lotte's presence of mind and tugging and pulling quickly to restore order. (41)[116]

Remi Hess is surely right in observing that "[t]he intellectuals, having the writers of the German *Sturm und Drang* in their mind, will make use of [the waltz] in order to demarcate themselves from the values of the Enlightenment" (1998, 157; my transl.). In *Werther*'s famous dance scene, however, the dance ultimately fails as a medium for including and domesticating weathery forces, no matter whether as a waltz or as the older social 'country' form. The waltz is indeed in its form excessive, is ecstatic, it is 'weathery' – but, nevertheless, it is not weathery enough. Its codification of exclusivity proves unaccomplishable for Werther. His falling out of the country dance's order gives a visual representation of the fact that there is no social place available for him (and the weathery forces), and of the fact that his search for another medium capable of capturing the weathery energy has to continue. Before we turn to this medium that emerges at the end of the scene, we should have a closer look at the restorative reactions that the weathery disturbances provoke – not only in the figure of the skilful dancer Lotte, who pulls Werther back into the correct spot, but also with regard to the whole ball interrupted by the intrusion of the thunderstorm.

---

116 "Genug ich verwirrte mich, vergaß mich, und kam zwischen das unrechte Paar hinein, daß alles drunter und drüber gieng, und Lottens ganze Gegenwart und Zerren und Ziehen nöthig war, um's schnell wieder in Ordnung zu bringen." (50)

2.5 Clever closures – restoration of order

The latent sense of danger that accompanies and characterises the scene, and actualised by repeated warnings, signals that the situation of the ball is exceptional. Some devices of protection, granting the overall safety, seem to be suspended for the ball's occasion of enjoying oneself:

> It is natural, when a misfortune or something terrible takes us by surprise while we are enjoying ourselves, that the impression it makes on us is stronger than usual, partly because of the contrast, which we feel so vividly, partly, and even more, because our senses are open to perception and therefore take in an impression all the more readily. (41)[117]

The formulation of "our senses" being "open" [*weil unsere Sinnen einmahl der Fühlbarkeit geöffnet sind*] stresses the topological dimension of this exceptional situation. *Homo clausus* opening his closure, the concentric constellation's opening its limiting circles, not only makes excess and ecstasy possible, it also increases the risk of being shaken by the intruding weather. This is exactly what happens when the thunderstorm interrupts the party, which can best be observed by paying attention to the reactions this interruption provokes:

> I must attribute to these causes the amazing grimaces that I saw on some of the ladies' faces. The smartest one sat in a corner, her back to the window, and covered her ears. Another knelt in front of her and hid her face in this lady's lap. A third pressed herself between them and embraced her sisters amid a thousand tears. Some wanted to go home; others, who knew even less what they were doing, lacked the presence of mind to control the impertinences of our young gourmands who seemed to be very busy snatching from the lips of those harassed beauties all the anxious prayers intended for heaven. (41–42)[118]

The passage's satirical tone and its obvious gendering of the reactions to the thunderstorm challenge a straightforward reading of the symptoms. In my

---

[117] "Es ist natürlich, wenn uns ein Unglük oder etwas schrökliches im Vergnügen überrascht, daß es stärkere Eindrükke auf uns macht, als sonst, theils wegen dem Gegensazze, der sich so lebhaft empfinden läßt, theils und noch mehr, weil unsere Sinnen einmahl der Fühlbarkeit geöffnet sind und desto schneller einen Eindruk annehmen." (50)

[118] "Diesen Ursachen muß ich die wunderbaren Grimassen zuschreiben, in die ich mehrere Frauenzimmer ausbrechen sah. Die Klügste sezte sich in eine Ekke, mit dem Rükken gegen das Fenster, und hielt die Ohren zu, eine andere kniete sich vor ihr nieder und verbarg den Kopf in der ersten Schoos, eine dritte schob sich zwischen beyde hinein, und umfaßte ihre Schwesterchen mit tausend Thränen. Einige wollten nach Hause, andere, die noch weniger wußten was sie thaten, hatten nicht so viel Besinnungskraft, den Kekheiten unserer jungen Schlukkers zu steuern, die sehr beschäftigt zu seyn schienen, alle die ängstlichen Gebete, die dem Himmel bestimmt waren, von den Lippen der schönen Bedrängten wegzufangen." (51)

opinion Robert H. Brown underestimates these two factors, claiming that "[i]n an age still attuned to the traditional premise that nature reflects God's will, the storm's disruption of the dance likely signals divine disapprobation of events" (1991, 100). Werther's narration is tinged in a way that transports a certain evaluation of the ladies' reactions to the weather event: he interprets their facial expression as "grimaces", he seems to be in a position to discern the "smartest" of them. Furthermore, his phrase, "who knew even less what they are doing" emphasises the general impression that their reaction is judged by Werther as not being adequate, let alone self-evident. The stark contrast to the male responses to the weather event confirms this impression: "Some of our gentlemen had gone downstairs to smoke their pipes in peace" (41–42), Werther tells us, positing male peace against the ladies' struggle with their agitation, which, in contrast, must appear as 'hysterical', *avant la lettre*. Werther's narration of the events in a way resembles the smoking gentlemen's, or even the impertinent "young gourmands[']", making use of the ladies' being overcome by their excited state. Like them, he seems to be profiting from a superior, more controlled standpoint that grants the gentlemen a calm smoke and provides Werther with some ladies' intimate secrets not intended for his ears as well as with material for a mocking story of great detail.

However, and this is crucial, the novel does not merely make fun of the ladies' ridiculous superstitious reaction. On the contrary, it adopts the stereotypical topos of women's lacking rational self-control, of their being closer to nature and their senses therefore being automatically more "open to perception",[119] in order to exhibit what had been taking place in the moments of ecstasy and to visualise the topology of measures that have to be taken to restore the order. The ladies' reaction to the intruding thunderstorm is thus not ridiculous, it is emblematic, revealing the modern subject's defining structure shared by man *and* woman – with the only difference that this structure has gained such stability in the majority of male representatives that it does not seem to be troubled by this weathery intrusion (implying that the susceptibility to ecstasy is decreased, producing 'dry' male characters like Albert).

The ladies' reaction to the intruding weather once again refers us to the concentric constellation's double structure of limitations/boundaries: it is all

---

119 A topos, for example also featuring in Friedrich Schiller's poem "Würde der Frauen" (1795/1800), according to Sebastian Donat "perhaps one of [...] Friedrich Schiller's worst poems" (2003, 252; my transl.), notorious already among his contemporaries as shallow and clichéd:
"[...]
Aber wie, leise vom Zephyr erschüttert
Schnell die äolische Harfe erzittert,
Also die fühlende Seele der Frau.
[...]" (Schiller 1992, 186).

about undoing, re-closing the openness, about shutting the gates and restoring the defining limitations/boundaries. The reaction of "the smartest one [*Die Klügste*]" shows that there are two 'rows' of boundaries, edifices and orifices, to be closed: turning "her back to the window, [she] covered her ears". Around her as the centre of 'security-to-be-gained', ladies group without really knowing how to help themselves, the one "hid[ing] her face in this lady's lap" at least arrives at closing her senses very effectively (although thereby completely abandoning her environment, only relying on one single, sealed limitation), another merely trusting herself to the security of the others by "press[ing] herself between them". Some, however, fail completely in their attempts to restore their order: those, "who knew even less what they were doing", are the ones that decided to pray. Instead of closing their battered barriers they open their lips, giving those "snatching from the lips [...] all the anxious prayers intended for heaven" access to their intimate inner interiority, which would have been hermetically sealed from them under normal circumstances.

There is, however, another smart lady taking measures for restoring the order: "the landlady", who comes up with "the clever idea of showing [the party] to a room with shutters and curtains" (42).[120] She finally takes care of restoring the outer limitation in its concrete, tangible manifestation. "[S]hutters and curtains" will shut out the weather and its forces which had entered through the windows and therefore create a room independent from the heavy weather outside, a room completely under human control, a clean human environment, without weathery disturbances.

Once the problem of the outer limitation is solved, a third clever woman steps in to put back in order the inner limitations as well:

> No sooner had we arrived [in the room with shutters and curtains] than Lotte busied herself arranging a circle of chairs, requesting the company to take seats, and proposing the rules of a game. (42)[121]

The circle of chairs that Lotte arranges for her game very well visualises the topography of the order that her game re-establishes in a quasi-ritualistic way. The game is one that punishes the breach of order, which is a breaking out of the circle:

---

[120] "[...] und die übrige Gesellschaft schlug es nicht aus, als die Wirthinn auf den klugen Einfall kam, uns ein Zimmer anzuweisen, das Läden und Vorhänge hätte." (52)
[121] "Kaum waren wir da angelangt, als Lotte beschäftigt war, einen Kreis von Stühlen zu stellen, die Gesellschaft zu sezzen, und den Vortrag zu einem Spiele zu thun." (52)

I saw several young men pursing their lips and stretching their limbs in the hope of a juicy forfeit. – We're going to play at counting, she said. Now pay attention! I am going to go around the circle from right to left, and you must count, also going around, each with the number of your turn, and that has to go like wildfire, and whoever hesitates or makes a mistake gets a slap in the face, and so on up to one thousand. – It was fun to watch. She went around the circle with an outstretched arm. One, the first began; his neighbor, two; the next one, three; and so on. Then she began to move more and more quickly [*geschwinder zu gehen, immer geschwinder*]. Then someone made a mistake: smack! A slap, and amid the laughter the next one too: smack! And faster and faster [*Und immer geschwinder*]. I myself was hit twice, and it was with intense pleasure that I believed I noticed that these slaps were harder than the ones she handed out to the others. General laughter and commotion broke up the game before the company had counted to one thousand. Those who were most intimate drew each other aside, the thunderstorm had passed, and I followed Lotte back to the dance floor. On the way she said: The slaps made them forget the storm and everything else [*Wetter und alles*]! (42)[122]

Lotte's game maximises the velocity of movement that can be kept within the circle, resisting the centrifugal forces drawing or rather pushing towards the outside. The passage's insistent reference to the structure of the circle actualises the circular concentric constellation. Lotte's moving "more and more quickly", "faster and faster" alludes to the ecstasy of the dance described only a few lines above. The German word, denoting this increasing velocity, repeated three times, carries this connection in itself: "geschwinder zu gehen, immer geschwinder", "Und immer geschwinder". As Albrecht Koschorke implies in his analysis of the waltz (2003, 201), Goethe here plays with the pseudo-etymologic connection between *geschwind* [fast, quickly], *schwinden* [to vanish] and *Schwindel* [dizziness]. This semantic field being important for the theme of ecstasy resurfaces on several occasions throughout the novel: when "everything else surely does vanish [*schwindet*] from [Lotte's] mind" (39) while dancing; when "all [Werther's]

---

[122] "Ich sah manchen, der in Hoffnung auf ein saftiges Pfand sein Mäulchen spizte, und seine Glieder rekte. Wir spielen Zählens, sagte sie, nun gebt Acht! Ich gehe im Kreise herum von der Rechten zur Linken, und so zählt ihr auch rings herum jeder die Zahl die an ihn kommt, und das muß gehen wie ein Lauffeuer, und wer stokt, oder sich irrt, kriegt eine Ohrfeige, und so bis tausend. Nun war das lustig anzusehen. Sie gieng mit ausgestricktem Arme im Kreise herum, Eins! fieng der erste an, der Nachbar zwey! drey! der folgende und so fort; dann fieng sie an geschwinder zu gehen, immer geschwinder. Da versahs einer, Patsch! eine Ohrfeige, und über das Gelächter der folgende auch Patsch! Und immer geschwinder. Ich selbst kriegte zwey Maulschellen und glaubte mit innigem Vergnügen zu bemerken, daß sie stärker seyen, als sie den übrigen zuzumessen pflegte. Ein allgemeines Gelächter und Geschwärme machte dem Spiel ein Ende, ehe noch das Tausend ausgezählt war. Die Vertrautesten zogen einandery beyseite, das Gewitter war vorüber, und ich folgte Lotten in den Saal. Unterwegs sagte sie: über die Ohrfeigen haben sie Wetter und alles vergessen!" (52)

senses grow dizzy [*mir wird's so schwindlich vor allen Sinnen*]" (55) as a consequence of his and Lotte's finger or feet touching by chance; when Werther thinks about the transitoriness of man, that "he must be extinguished, must vanish [*verlöschen, verschwinden muß*], and so soon" (106). Lotte's moving "immer geschwinder" [more and more quickly] in her game resembles the waltz's delimiting circular movement. And, indeed, this movement is also, etymologically, one "like weather": *geschwind* derives from *schwind*, adj. adv., which, as Grimm's *Deutsches Wörterbuch* tells us, denotes "boisterous, violent, impetuous", "of natural events, weather" and "of sentiments" (*DWB*, schwind, *adj. adv.* 1.; 1. a.; 1. d.; my transl.).[123] The similarity of movement makes Lotte's game the perfect antidote to the waltz: instead of the waltz's aiming for the centrifugal forces, for ecstasy and excess, the game strengthens the centripetal forces of holding together, of staying centred and punishes break-outs. It is similar to an astronaut training procedure, exposing the participants to forces in order to increase their resistance to them. Robert H. Brown rightly observes that "Lotte's game approximates her parental role in the circle of her siblings" (1991, 100) – not only because she is the one standing in the centre, explaining the rules, caring for the party, but also, and mainly, because the game affirms the structure of the concentric constellation. In the scene of dances it is Lotte's game that functions as the purest ritual, as the "emblem of the institution of social order [*Sinnbild sozialer Ordnungsstiftung*]" (Neumann 2000, 529; my transl.).

The clever landlady had taken care of the outer limitation, coping with the forces threatening from without, Lotte's game now tackles the forces urging against the inner limitation from within. The topology of the game, with its circle of chairs and its punishing of centrifugal break-outs gives clear evidence for this, emphasising that the forces it tames are forces that are directed outwards, attacking the limitation from within. There are, however, other, perhaps more direct signs of what is taking place and what is at stake in Lotte's game. Abstractly speaking, the game is about coping with and redirecting 'libidinous energy'. "I saw several young men pursing their lips and stretching their limbs in the hope of a juicy forfeit", Werther tells us, and he himself participates in this exercise of intrapersonal, emotional tidying: "I myself was hit twice, and it was with intense pleasure that I believed I noticed that these slaps were harder than the ones she handed out to the others." In the transgressive moments of ecstasy, the urging forces had sought their way out by breaking through the inner limitation/boundary (no matter whether Lotte was talking about literature,

---

123 "1) ungestüm, gewaltig, heftig. a) von naturerscheinungen, wetter u. ähnl. [...] d) von empfindungen [...]." (*DWB*, schwind, *adj. adv.* 1.; 1. a.; 1. d.)

Lotte was dancing, or in Werther's waltz) and had thereby disturbed the established order. In contrast, the forces activated in Lotte's game are effectively redirected so that they stay within and do not cause any 'outer' trouble: they are (re-)interiorised. Werther reads the intensity of Lotte's slaps as a token of love; however, the difference to their waltzing, another token of love, consists in the fact that this love does not unfold its anarchic, weathery power; it does not shatter the secure structures ordering human life, but is tamely interiorised, imperceptible from without, except for some signs requiring subjective interpretation. Apparently, Werther is not the only one enjoying Lotte's slaps. This does not undermine his reading of the situation, it rather emphasises that Lotte's game is of a general nature. It does not only 'cure' or rather tame Werther's anarchic love, but makes use of and exhibits the functioning of a mechanism (a technique of self-discipline) on which the contemporary social order is founded: the mechanism of internalisation (cf. Foucault 1975).

As Lotte puts it with great generality: "The slaps made them forget the storm and everything else [*Wetter und alles*]!" Lotte's formulation expresses very well how this disciplinary measure works: it is not violent punishment that makes Werther and his peers shy away from breaking the circle and from living out the ecstasy of the weathery forces urging in their interior, but a process of forgetting. I would suggest reading this forgetting in a Freudian way: the forgetting of "weather and all" is obviously no conscious act, rather a form of unconscious repression that is facilitated by Lotte's 'joyous' disciplinary measure. Lotte's game thus demonstrates the neat correspondence of mechanisms of social ordering and mechanisms of intrapsychic ordering: it is impossible to say which one serves as the model that the other copies; they rather seem to be co-original, coping with the same problem. They are part of the same larger mechanism that acts on different levels. This mechanism polices the order of a certain status quo and guards the absolute control over it by shielding, draining off, discharging and re-directing threatening weathery energy (at its two 'weather fronts': the outer and the inner one).

The 'imprecise', 'cloudy' reference of "weather and all" refers to the shock of the interrupted party, to the intruding thunderstorm as well as to Werther's and Lotte's promiscuous love. For this label, the weather functions as a synecdoche, being the signified part, standing as a *pars pro toto* for the "all". Lotte's label thus works the same way as my speaking of 'weathery forces': it speaks of a complex of forces, threatening the current order of things; forces of which the weather's are the most concrete, most intuitive and objective representatives, therefore very handily 'representing' the rest.

The complex of "weather and all" does not refer to one singular event, one specific, singular crisis taking place at the ball that has been overcome with Lotte's game, at the latest. This complex is rather, as I am trying to demonstrate, one of the major themes of the whole novel. Werther's letter of June 16th not only narrates a weathery, ecstatic crisis, it also gives a detailed account of the protective structures and mechanisms that the threatened order has developed to cope with these weathery forces. The singular situation of Lotte, Werther, their falling in love and the intruding thunderstorm is thus used to exhibit in an emblematic way these protective structures and mechanisms. We learn from the clever closures undertaken in this scene that it is the defining structures of what we have called 'the concentric constellation', the tightening of the outer and the inner limitation/boundary, that are responsible for warding off the threatening weathery energy. In other words, the protective mechanisms against the weather and the mechanisms responsible for the constitution of the current order are the same. The weathery threat is not external to the enlightened way of ordering the world; the weather is not just any threat troubling the order from without. It is, on the contrary, constitutive for the concentric constellation with its two defining limitations/boundaries. The restoration of the order undertaken by the clever landlady and by Lotte thus re-enacts the constitution, 'the birth' of the current order, of the concentric constellation, of the enlightened world centred around the rational human being. The realm of human control, of objective, rational order is created in-between two limitations/boundaries, by driving the weathery forces beyond these limitations/boundaries: the 'outer' weather is shut out, its influence erased by withdrawing to "a room with shutters and curtains"; the inner weather of love, passion and also, as we will see later, of madness and irrationality is driven out of the public, tidy realm, beyond the inner limitation; it is 'neutralised' by internalisation. The restoration of order depicted in the letter of June 16th reveals the enlightened, clear, weather-free space in-between, the space of human mastery, to be a product of these two processes of "forget[ting] the weather and all", of repressing the weather.

2.6 The epiphany of the weathery medium

For many critics reading the letter of June 16th the true, ultimate restoration of order is not achieved by Lotte's game but moments later, when Lotte and Werther walk "over to the window", watch the thunderstorm move away and Lotte voices her famous: "Klopstock". Gerhard Neumann, for example, is one of those who see in this invocation of poetry the actual "antidote" (2000, 528; my transl.) to the waltz:

The novel soon – in the legendary window-scene between Werther and Lotte – adds an established pattern to the untamed and uncomprehended [*Diesem Ungezähmten wie Unverstandenen*] that overpowers the dancers; an established pattern of the institution of order and of the reconciliation of the chaotic, that is poetry in the form of a text by Klopstock. It is poetry that imposes the pattern of order of a reconciled nature and a reconciled deity on the threatening thunderstorm, it is poetry that leads the natural and the religious code to fuse in the literary code. (2000, 527; my transl.)

Gerhard Neumann's reading hinges on the intertextual link that Goethe indicates, in the first version of the novel, with one word only – the name of the poet, "Klopstock!", the "best-known tribute to Klopstock within German literature" (Lee 1990, 1). Even without the second version's hint to "the splendid ode that was in [Lotte's] thoughts" and that Werther "immediately recall[s]" (43) when hearing her invoke the poet's name, it does not seem too difficult to reconstruct why it is exactly this ode, Klopstock's "Frühlingsfeyer" that comes to Lotte's mind in this very situation and can be "immediately recalled" by Werther: it simply resonates with their experience of a brewing, threatening and eventually fading thunderstorm. Is it, however, adequate to infer from Lotte's and Werther's thinking of the same poem at the same time that they silently accept this poem's specific interpretation of the world and its theological framing?

Both Clayton Koelb and Gerhard Neumann answer this question in the positive. For them, Klopstock's "Frühlingsfeyer" offers a reading of the events (thunderstorm, their falling in love) that Werther and Lotte share by associating the poem: "love as religion; the restoration of the pietist patterns of edification as a formula for life [*pietistische Erbauungsmuster als Lebensformel*]" (Neumann 2000, 529; my transl.); the thunderstorm as "not only a particular meteorological event" but as "a mythic re-enactment of a universal rite of revivification, the 'Rites of Spring [Frühlingsfeier]' celebrated in Klopstock's poem" (Koelb 2008, 56). The theological frame accounting for the harmony and ultimate restoration of order that both Neumann and Koelb claim for this scene is an import from Klopstock's ode. Despite its not being present in the text of Goethe's novel, Neumann and Koelb feel entitled to read the explicit intertextual link to Klopstock's "Frühlingsfeyer" as representing and affirming this theological framework. However, Goethe's difficult relation to questions of theological orthodoxy and, more importantly, the novel's rather heterodox approach to theological 'material' cast severe doubts on this reading. All the more so, since the passage itself raises a theological issue, the deification/idolisation of the poet, that does not comply easily with the supposed theological framework:

> We walked over to the window. Thunder rumbled in the distance, a splendid rain was falling on the land, and the most refreshing scent rose up to us in the fullness of a rush of warm air. She stood leaning on her elbows, her gaze penetrating the scene; she looked up at the sky and at me, I could see tears in her eyes, she put her hand on mine and said, Klopstock! –
>
> I sank in the flood of feelings that she poured over me with this byword. I could not bear it, I bowed over her hand and kissed it as I wept the most blissful tears. And I looked again into her eyes – Noble poet! If you had but seen yourself idolized in this glance [*hättest du deine Vergötterung in diesem Blikke gesehn*] – and now I never want to hear your name, so often blasphemed, ever mentioned again! (43)[124]

It is not God's name, so often blasphemed by the infidels, that is now praised for his providence and the harmony he sends to earth, as would be expected by Werther's taking over the theological attitude of Klopstock's ode. It is the "noble poet" that is "idolized" (or rather deified, since the German *vergöttern* does not have the notion of false idolatry in its immediate semantic proximity), "idolized in [Lotte's] glance". The hint that it is her "glance" that idolizes the poet, not her invocation, is important: it has been widely overlooked that the whole scene is organised around a complex game of glances and looks. These glances and looks make the scene the famous window-scene it is – not only linking the inside and the outside, but also acknowledging a third, *mediating* agent, responsible for the scene's intense character.

The opening of the passage relates a change of settings that triggers the scene: the couple's walking over to the window revokes the party's moving to "a room with shutters and curtains". The crisis is apparently overcome; the protective measure of hermetically sealing oneself off from the outside not being necessary any more, careful contact to the outside has ceased to be dangerous. Not too surprisingly, the mentioning of the window is immediately followed by a glance outside. The focaliser of this glance is not clearly indicated; the description of what there is to see outside is framed by the "we" that walked over to the window and to whom the "refreshing scent rose up". This is important, because the next sentence, focalised by Werther, retrospectively offers us one possible

---

124 "Wir traten an's Fenster. Es donnerte abseitwärts, und der herrliche Regen säuselte auf das Land, und der erquikkendste Wohlgeruch stieg in aller Fülle einer warmen Luft zu uns auf. Sie stand auf ihrem Ellenbogen gestüzt und ihr Blik durchdrang die Gegend, sie sah gen Himmel und auf mich, ich sah ihr Auge thränenvoll, sie legte ihre Hand auf die meinige und sagte – Klopstock!

Ich versank in dem Strome von Empfindungen, den sie in dieser Loosung über mich ausgoß. Ich ertrugs nicht, neigte mich auf ihre Hand und küßte sie unter den wonnevollsten Thränen. Und sah nach ihrem Auge wieder – Edler! hättest du deine Vergötterung in diesem Blikke gesehn, und möchte ich nun deinen so oft entweihten Nahmen nie wieder nennen hören!" (52–54)

focaliser of the latter sentence's glance: Werther watches Lotte viewing the scene. The formulation "her gaze penetrating the scene [*die Gegend*]" clearly indicates that this look through the window transgresses a limitation/boundary: her glance penetrates the boundary of inside/outside, more than that, it also merges with, permeates [*durchdringen*] the scene. The best evidence for this is provided by a topical correspondence that connects Lotte to the landscape she is watching: the "tears in her eyes" correspond to the "splendid rain" outside and thereby actualise the old, classical topos of corresponding macrocosmic and microcosmic weather. A significant parallelism that gets lost in Stanley Corngold's translation indicates that Werther's glance at Lotte (noticing the tears in her eye) in turn corresponds to Lotte's two glances, to her glance outside and to her glance at Werther: "ihr Blick durchdrang die Gegend, *sie sah* gen Himmel und auf mich, *ich sah* ihr Auge thränenvoll" [her gaze penetrating the scene; *she looked* [*sah*] up at the sky and at me, *I saw* [*sah*] tears in her eye]. Whereas Lotte's glances bridge the outside and the inside, looking at the sky *and* at Werther, Werther has only eyes for Lotte. His attention stays inside the room, whereas Lotte makes this scene a window-scene: she is the centre of perception, she stands at the threshold, linking via her glances the outside and the inside. From the perspective of gender something seems to be at odds with Lotte's occupying this position. As her "penetrating gaze" already indicated quite explicitly, this position in the contact-zone to the outside seems to be an overtly masculine one. Holding this position, as Meredith Lee emphasises, "Lotte is one set apart. She, after all, initiates the moment" (1990, 5), "[i]t is Lotte, after all, who voices the name 'Klopstock', and it is Lotte, who will in the end encourage Werther to read from his translation of Ossian'", Peter Pütz adds (1983, 64; my transl.). Nevertheless, Goethe's novel does not stage a subversion of gender roles; Lotte's feminine occupation of a masculine role is a well-calculated, necessary step in a very conventional, phallogocentric project. She is the (female) agent granting the apotheosis of the male poet – or (male) poetry as such. She contributes the universality, the proximity to nature and sentiment that only a female agent can do. Clayton Koelb is right that "[i]t becomes impossible to tell where 'Klopstock' leaves off and 'Lotte' begins" (2008, 58): "Klopstock" takes over the liminal, mediating position that Lotte holds in this scene. He emerges as a sublation of the threshold between outside and inside: "she looked up at the sky and at me, I could see tears in her eyes, she put her hand on mine and said, Klopstock! –". "Klopstock" steps in-between "the sky", the place of the weather, and Werther, sublating the two directions of Lotte's glances and establishing a connection between the weather outside and Werther inside. Werther's reaction to this connection is telling of its success: Werther's "blissful tears" mirror Lotte's eyes full of tears, Werther's 'mediated' reaction not only resembles Lotte's 'immediate' 'correspondence', it is even much more intense:

> I sank [*versank*] in the flood of feelings [*Strom von Empfindungen*] that she poured over me with this byword. I could not bear it, I bowed over her hand and kissed it as I wept the most blissful [*wonnevollsten*] tears. (43)[125]

It is important to note that the tone changes as soon as the famous "byword" "Klopstock!" is voiced, a rupture marked by the dash following the invocation. Whereas the description of the landscape, or rather the weather outside, is solemn and contained (as symbolised by Lotte's tears, not rolling but staying contained in her eye) Werther's reaction is excessive: the tears he weeps are sure to be shed, the whole two sentences being pervaded by notions of pouring and (over)flowing. The contrast to the preceding description of the harmonious weather outside is most effectively illustrated by the weather imagery expressing Werther's being moved. His sinking "in the flood of feelings" does not correspond to the "splendid rain" "falling on the land" or to the "refreshing scent" rising up to Lotte and Werther "in the fullness of a rush of warm air". This scene is not one of containment in a re-erected religious framework, it is not merely "antidote" to (Neumann 2000, 528; my transl.) or "domestication of the waltz-scene" (2000, 529; my transl.), but stages another, perhaps the central ecstatic moment of the letter. This ecstatic moment unmistakably reveals itself with the very words following the ominous dash:

> Klopstock! – I sank [*versank*] in the flood [*Strom*] [...].

The German verb *versinken* continues the series of ecstatic moments marked by verbs of a similar semantic field, denoting a losing or disintegration of oneself, all sharing the prefix or particle *ver-*: "versunken [immersed]" and "verlohren [lost]" (Werther, caused by Lotte's conversation on literature) (44–46); "daß alles rings umher vergieng [so that everything else around me vanished]" in the waltz scene; and also later, again referring to the German verb *verlieren*, in the scene when an inundation has flooded Werther's beloved valley:

> Oh with my arms wide open I stood facing the abyss and breathed down! down! and was lost [*ver-lohr mich*] in the bliss [*Wonne*] of hurling my torments, my suffering raging down [*hinab zu stürmen*]! roaring away like the waves! (123)[126]

---

[125] "Ich versank in dem Strome von Empfindungen, den sie in dieser Loosung über mich ausgoß. Ich ertrugs nicht, neigte mich auf ihre Hand und küßte sie unter den wonnevollsten Thränen." (54)

[126] "Ach! Mit offenen Armen stand ich gegen den Abgrund, und athmete hinab! hinab, und verlohr mich in der Wonne, all meine Quaalen all mein Leiden da hinab zu stürmen, dahin zu brausen wie die Wellen." (194)

I quoted this much later passage at length, because we here encounter the corresponding outer weather to Werther's inner weather of the situation. The elements linking these two passages are not only the flood, but also the notion of disintegration, of merging with the elements that is inseparable from the bliss [*Wonne*] it sets free. The connection between these two passages reveals that Werther's reaction to the "byword" is not the "peak of [his] illusions" as Heinz Schlaffer claims (1978, 218; my transl.). The ecstasy of love and the ecstasy of suicide rather turn out to be indistinguishable; the distinction between sentimental illusion and enlightened truth that guides Schlaffer's reading is alien to Goethe's novel. The "bliss" [*Wonne*], no matter whether of Werther's "most blissful tears [*wonnevollsten Thränen*]" or of "hurling [his] torments, [his] suffering raging down" is ecstatic: it is, as the later passage explicitly tells us, "the bliss of [...] roaring away like the waves [*Wonne*, [...] *dahin zu brausen wie die Wellen*]". As already quoted above, Werther seems indeed to be driven by "a desire of metamorphosis, the urge [*l'envie*] of escaping the limits of his corporeal existence, of merging with the elements, of becoming wind or thunderstorm" (Neppi 2010, 335; my transl.). This holds true for both passages, for Werther's sinking in the flood of his sentiments as well as for the real inundation, flooding his beloved valley of which he desires to become a part. For an apt understanding of the famous window-scene, of Lotte's "Klopstock" and Werther's reaction to it and the general role this scene plays for the whole novel, it is vital to notice and take seriously the scene's weather: not only the harmonious weather outside, observed through the window, but also the stormy, heavy weather of Werther's ecstatic reaction triggered by the word "Klopstock!".

Werther's "flood of feelings [*Strome der Empfindungen*] that [Lotte] poured over him with this byword" and his "most blissful tears" may be accused of being the most conventional, formulaic and unoriginal of all sentimental clichés. However, I do not think that readings focusing on the emptiness of these formulas, imputing to the novel a need to reveal this emptiness and reflect on it, reach to the core of what this novel is about. In her commentary in the *Frankfurter Ausgabe* Waltraud Wiethölter quite affirmatively summarises these readings in the following way:

> Werther, as they say, were to be understood as a character, contrary to what its mawkish enthusiasts have read into it, that reveals bit by bit the precious achievements of the aforementioned culture of sentimentality in its symbolic [*zeichenhaft*] emptiness, meaning: as an effect of an albeit impressive, but anthropologically insubstantial ritual of communication [*anthropologisch substanzlosen Kommunikationsrituals*]. (FA 8, 944; my transl.).

There can be little doubt that the novel and "Werther's world is nothing but an accumulation of collectanea and optical reminiscences" (FA 8, 947; my transl.), and we will presently follow precisely this track for the passage we are reading. However, the fact that the thesis of the novel's exposing sentimental emptiness has to accuse the vast majority of Goethe's contemporary (as well as later critical) readers of having fundamentally misunderstood the novel – and label the singular success of the novel an unprecedented history of bad reading, could serve as a warning: apparently, interpreting the novel's dealing with sentimental formulae as disclosing their emptiness does not give sufficient account of the novel's unbelievable potential for identification. The fact that this strategic, critical move does not seem to have been noticed by the majority of contemporary readers, probably much more familiar with the 'discourse' of sentimentality and its formulae than the scholars of the 20th and 21st centuries, speaks against this being the gist of the novel, all the more so since this move is so simplistic: there are many more, and many more interesting things one can do with conventional formulae than believe in their potential authenticity (the critics whose readings Waltraud Wiethölter summarised seem to believe in 'anthropologically *substantial* rituals of communication'), and show that some of them turn out to be merely 'conventional', that is to say, empty, illusive and false.

Goethe, I would suggest, is obviously well aware of the fact that he quotes a conventional, clichéd formula with Werther's sinking in the flood of feelings. However, instead of merely exhibiting the emptiness of this formula, the novel performs something much more intricate: it listens to its very words, takes them more seriously than a conventional formula is usually taken – and discovers its weathery character. The phrase "flood of feelings [*Strome von Empfindungen*]" is no coincidence: not in the environment of Lotte's (contrasting) description of the weather outside; not as the final turn of a scene dominated by the weather's forces; not as one of the key-scenes of a novel that is as a whole deeply steeped in weather. Another much-discussed key-scene to which we will return in a later section uses the same conventional formula to unfold a poetological reflection, making extensive use of its weathery denotations:

> Oh, my friends! Why does the torrent of genius [*Strom des Genies*] gush out so rarely, so rarely come rushing in on a spring tide to shatter your amazed soul? – Dear friends, these sedate gentlemen dwell on both banks of the stream, where their little summer houses, their tulip beds and cabbage patches would be ruined [*zu Grunde gehen*], and who therefore have the sense in good time to use dams and flood channels to ward off the impending threat of danger. (30–31)[127]

---

[127] "O meine Freunde! warum der Strom des Genies so selten ausbricht, so selten in hohen Fluthen hereinbraust, und eure staunende Seele erschüttert. Lieben Freunde, da wohnen die gelaßnen Kerls auf beyden Seiten des Ufers, denen ihre Gartenhäuschen, Tulpenbeete, und Krautfelder zu Grunde gehen würden, und die daher in Zeiten mit dämmen und ableiten der künftig drohenden Gefahr abzuwehren wissen." (28)

Consequently, when only a few letters later Werther sinks in the flood [*Strome*] of feelings, the weathery character of this flood has already been explicated by the novel, it is present and actualised.

Furthermore, the weathery connotations of the German substantive *Strom* are also used in an intertextual way: *Strom*, its plural form *Ströme* and the related verb *strömen* form the backbone of Klopstock's ode "Die Frühlingsfeyer" so famously invoked by Lotte. The ode's extensive use of this word and its derivatives (featured six times in the poem, in prominent positions and function) exhibit its semantic potential for signifying all sorts of meteorological phenomena, hinging on the weather's central characteristic of a 'flowing movement': "die Ströme des Lichts rauschten [the streams of light rushed]" (Klopstock 1771, 24), "Wolken strömen herauf [the clouds are streaming up]" (Klopstock 1771, 26), "wie hebt sich der Strom [how the stream rises]" (Klopstock 1771, 26), "der Strom fliehet [the stream flees]" (Klopstock 1771, 26), "die Gewitterwinde [...] | Wie sie rauschen! Wie sie die Wälder durchrauschen! [the winds of the thunderstorm | How they rush! How they rush through the forests!]"[128] (Klopstock 1771, 28). This weathery character of the substantive *Strom*, "the elementary natural force of the stream [*Strom*], oppressing/distressing [*bedrückende*] man, terrifying him, often destroying his work, this natural force which he faces powerlessly" (*DWB*, strom, n. 2. b. α.; my transl.)[129] forms the centre of Klopstock's "Frühlingsfeyer". The poem also speaks of tears that are shed – and that are linked to the weather's streams. Although not directly associated with the word *Strom*, these tears form part of the semantic field of flowing and streaming, as the verb introducing the notion of tears indicates: "Ergeuß von neuem, du mein Auge, | Freudenthränen! [Pour out anew, you, my eye, | Tears of joy!]" (Klopstock 1771, 25) Echoes of the German verb *ergießen* [to pour out] that Klopstock here uses can also be found in Goethe's *Werther*, having been transformed to the closely related verb *ausgießen* [to pour out] and are now explicitly joined to the notion of the stream [*Strome*]:

---

128 In the 1759 and the 1771 version that Goethe knew, the word *Strom* and its derivatives do not feature in this passage. It is, in these two versions, dominated by another weathery verb, *rauschen*, that is as prominent in the poem as *Strom/strömen*. The fact that Klopstock for the later version of 1798 replaces the second mentioning of *rauschen* in this passage with the verb *strömen* underlines the central role of these two, apparently, interchangeable verbs, signifying the weather's forces. In the 1798 version the passage reads: "die Gewitterwinde [...] | Wie sie rauschen! wie sie mit lauter Woge den Wald durchströmen! [the winds of the thunderstorm [...] | How they rush! how they stream through the forest with a loud surge!]" (Klopstock 2010, 179)

129 "[...] die den menschen bedrückende, elementare naturkraft des stroms, die ihm furcht einflöszt, die sein werk oft zerstört, der er machtlos gegenübersteht." (*DWB*, strom, n. 2. b. α.)

> I sank in the flood of feelings that she poured over me [*über mich ausgoß*] with this byword. I could not bear it, I bowed over her hand and kissed it as I wept the most blissful [*wonnevollsten*] tears. (43)[130]

This brief example of close intertextual links between Klopstock's ode and Goethe's *Werther* raises suspicions that the intricate play of allusions and borrowed formulations might not be limited to these two sentences. "Lotte's [and Werther's!] reaction to the thunderstorm" is likely not to be as "affected" as Benjamin Bennett claims (1980, 64), since "Lotte" (or rather the novel) "manage[s]" more than merely "to pronounce the poet's not very euphonious surname" (1980, 65). Nevertheless, Friedrich Kittler is not wrong when he writes that "what is spoken aloud between [Lotte and Werther] is only the author's name" (1994, 150; my transl.). However, the "text of the 'Frühlingsfeyer'" does *not* merely "remain remembered in the literal sense: sunk in two reader-inwardnesses that have translated it into inner feelings" (1994, 150; my transl.). A closer look at the text of the window-scene reveals that Klopstock's poem is present from the very beginning of the passage right to its end.

It is as if Klopstock was standing behind the writing Goethe, whispering catchwords in his ear around which the latter developed the text we now read as the 'authentic' description of a scene. More or less all the keywords responsible for the scene's very own, solemn tone are material borrowed from Klopstock's ode. The signifier *herrlich* of the novel's "herrliche Regen [splendid rain]" appears twice in the poem as "Immer herrlicher offenbarest du dich [Ever more glorious you reveal yourself]" and "Angebetet, gepriesen | Sey dein herrlicher Name! [Worshiped, praised | Be your glorious name!]" (Klopstock 1771, 27) The phrase's verb, "der herrliche Regen *säuselte* auf das Land [the splendid rain was falling/ whispering/murmuring on the land]", is also taken from Klopstock's "Die Frühlingsfeyer", from its important last group of verses:

> See, now Jehova does not come in the weather any more,
> In quiet, gentle murmur/whisper [*Säuseln*]
> Comes Jehova,
> And below him bends the bow of peace! (Klopstock 1771, 28; my transl.)[131]

The "*erquikkendste* Wohlgeruch [the most refreshing scent]" that is invoked by the novel following the mentioning of the splendid rain is again informed by

---

[130] "Ich versank in dem Strome von Empfindungen, den sie in dieser Loosung über mich ausgoß. Ich ertrugs nicht, neigte mich auf ihre Hand und küßte sie unter den wonnevollsten Thränen." (54)

[131] "Siehe, nun kommt Jehova nicht mehr im Wetter, | In stillem, sanftem Säuseln | Kommt Jehova, | Und unter ihm neigt sich der Bogen des Friedens!" (Klopstock 1771, 28)

the poem, where we read the line: "Nun ist, wie dürstete sie! die Erd' *erquickt* [Now is, how she thirsted! the earth refreshed]" (Klopstock 1771, 28). The "Fülle einer warmen Luft [The fullness of a rush of warm air]" that completes the novel's description of the scene/weather outside the window finds a counterpart in the poem as well: Goethe's "Fülle [fullness]" echoes Klopstock's "Seegensfüll' [fullness of blessing]" (Klopstock 1771, 28), the praising of the rush of "warme[ ] Luft" [warm air] refers to the poem's question "Euch, wunderbare Lüfte, | Sandte der Herr? [You, wonderful airs/breezes, | Has sent the Lord?]" (Klopstock 1771, 26) In fact, there is hardly one word of the novel's glance through the window that is not informed by Klopstock's "Die Frühlingsfeyer". Goethe's novel not only relates a similar weathery situation – it borrows many of Klopstock's central signifiers. "[T]he passing of the thunderstorm through the natural landscape is [indeed] experienced initially by Lotte through the medium of Klopstock's ode" as Meredith Lee writes (1990, 5), so that "[i]t becomes impossible to tell where 'Klopstock' leaves off and 'Lotte' begins" (Koelb 2008, 58).

However, is it really Lotte who experiences the passing thunderstorm? As already noted above, the focalisation of the scene's and the weather's description is not marked in an unambiguous way: the glance through the window is motivated by a sentence that has Lotte and Werther as subjects, represented collectively by the first person pronoun in the plural, "we": "We walked over to the window", a collective that is again referred to in the description "the most refreshing scent [that] rose up to *us*". The intuition that agency and perception are based on the individual rather than on a collective (an intuition to which most of the narratological instruments remain faithful) seems to be so strong, and collective focalisation so complex a problem, that most readers readily accept the retrospective explication of glances: the "we" is dissolved, Lotte declared to be the focaliser of the glance outside, while Werther fills the role of an observer of the second degree, watching Lotte look through the window. However, what if Clayton Koelb's observation, already quoted above, that "Lotte shows that she reads the world the way Werther does, through the lens of poetry" (2008, 56), is correct in a very literal, narratological way? What if Clayton Koelb gives us a very interesting answer to our question of the passage's focalisation?

The glance through the window is indeed focalised "through the lens of poetry". Our detailed comparative analysis of the linguistic material shared by the passage and Klopstock's poem confirms this thesis. Even the novel itself seems to give us a hint about how to sublate the complex game of glances, how to solve the window-scene's riddle:

> And I looked again into her eyes [*Und sah nach ihrem Auge wieder*] – Noble poet! [– Edler!] If you had but seen yourself idolized in this glance [*hättest du deine Vergötterung in diesem Blikke gesehn*] – and now I never want to hear your name, so often blasphemed, ever mentioned again!

As the beginning of the passage indicates, it is a re-enactment, a second glance, it repeats a scene that has taken place only seconds earlier: "she looked up [*sie sah*] at the sky and at me, I could see [*ich sah*] tears in her eyes, she put her hand on mine and said, – Klopstock!". Whereas Werther's glance of the earlier scene is indeed of a second degree, holding a certain distance, watching Lotte's emotions and hearing her invocation of the poet, his second, re-enacted glance triggers a different movement, leads him somewhere else: he now himself invokes the poet, a parallel emphasised in the German original by mirroring the punctuation of Lotte's invocation, '[dash] object of invocation [exclamation mark]': "– Klopstock!"; "– Edler!". The half-sentence that follows this surprising invocation explains the decisive step that has led to it: "If you had but seen yourself idolized in this glance" [*hättest du deine Vergötterung in diesem Blikke gesehn*]. On the surface it is an old topos that brings about the idolisation: "beautifully and often our language employs *Blick* [glance] for the light and ray of the eye, that is itself the seeing, shining [...]. The eye glances, flashes/ fulgurates and shines [*das auge blickt, blitzt und leuchtet*]" (*DWB*, blick, *n*. 3.; my transl.).[132] Etymologically, this flashing/fulgurating/shining *Blick* is a weathery phenomenon, it once signified 'lightning':

> the OHG [Old High German] meaning, fulgor, fulgur, fulmen, fast shooting ray of light, initially hints at the natural phenomenon and is very frequent also in MHG [Middle High German], more rare in NHG [New High German]. We do not use the simple *Blick* for fulgur any longer, but the closely related *Blitz* instead. (*DWB*, blick, *n*. 1.; my transl.)[133]

Against the background of the German noun *Blick* and its semantic implications, the idolising effect of Lotte's glance begins to look familiar to us: we are reminded of the ecstatic moment in the coach, discussed above, the moment when speaking about literature "with every word [Werther] saw new charms, *new rays of intelligence bursting* from [Lotte's] features" (38; transl. altered;

---

[132] "[...] schön und oft verwendet unsere sprache blick vom licht und strahl des auges, das ja selbst das sehende, leuchtende ist [...] das auge blickt, blitzt und leuchtet [...]." (*DWB*, blick, *n*. 3.).

[133] "[...] die ahd. bedeutung fulgor, fulgur, fulmen, schnell schiesszender lichtstrahl geht zunächst auf die naturerscheinung und ist auch mhd. sehr häufig, nhd. seltner. wir gebrauchen für fulgur nicht mehr das einfache blick, sondern das nahverwandte blitz [...]." (*DWB*, blick, *n*. 1.) Only a few lines later, Goethe is quoted for making use of this old meaning of *Blick*.

emph. J.U.).¹³⁴ Lotte's ecstatic glance thus sets free shining light that contributes to Klopstock's epiphany, to his deification, which seems to have captivated Werther as well. The English word that Stanley Corngold chooses for translating the German *Blick*, glance, is capable of transporting this explication: *glance* not only signifies a "brief or hurried look" (*OED*, glance *n*.1 4.), but, being related to the German *Glanz*, also "[a] sudden movement producing a flash or gleam of light; also, the flash or gleam itself" (*OED*, glance *n*.1 3.). However, this reading of Lotte's ecstasy that somehow infects Werther, does not really solve the riddle of the glances; Werther stays a distanced observer of the second degree, watching Lotte who is doing all the work of looking outside and evoking Klopstock.

There is, I would claim, another reading encoded in this passage, a reading that solves the riddle and explains why this passage, despite its surface, does not narrate the deification of a poet, but "the auratization [*Auratisierung*] of a text" (Neumann 2000, 528; my transl.). This reading is possible only with regard to the German original, because it relies on a meaning of the German noun *Blick* that is not transported by the English *glance*: "*Blick* can express, like *Anblick* and similar others, intransitively the looking [*das Blickende*], shining [*Scheinende*], as well as transitively the looked at [*Angeblickte, Erblickte*]" (*DWB*, blick, n. 8.; my transl.),¹³⁵ the *Deutsche Wörterbuch* entry of *Blick* notes, directly referring to the use of this meaning in Goethe's works. This second option introduces considerable changes with regard to our sentence:

> Noble poet! If you had but seen yourself idolized in this glance [*hättest du deine Vergötterung in diesem Blikke gesehn*] –

If glance refers to what Lotte had supposedly seen with "this glance", it suddenly becomes possible to re-enact this idolisation – and this is, I think, what is going on in the scene. Or rather, this is what we, as readers, are called to do. As Klopstock (a potential reader of the novel) is supposed not to have noticed his idolisation, so are the rest of the novel's readers assumed to have read the description of the look out of the window without reading it as a homage to the poet. The game of glances is here brought to a new level, a level that sublates the hierarchy of looks that the novel's protagonists have exchanged and now includes the readers and the novel's own act of enunciation. "If you had but seen" may thus be read as a calling to re-read the passage and read it as what

---

134 "Ich fand so viel Charakter in allem was sie sagte, ich sah mit jedem Wort neue Reize, *neue Strahlen des Geistes aus ihren Gesichtszügen hervorbrechen*, die sich nach und nach vergnügt zu entfalten schienen, weil sie an mir fühlte, daß ich sie verstund." (44; emph. J.U.)
135 "[...] blick kann, wie anblick und alle ähnlichen, sowol intransitiv das blickende, scheinende, als transitiv das angeblickte, erblickte ausdrücken [...]." (*DWB*, blick, *n*. 8.)

it really is: not as Lotte's look through the window, describing the weather outside but as the epiphany of literature as a medium.

As we have shown above with our re-reading of the scene with Klopstock's poem in mind, what we get is not a vista focalised by Lotte – but by Klopstock's poem. That is why Werther can join Lotte, share 'her' idolising *Blick*. They have discovered a 'collective', a 'shared focalisation',[136] that is to say, a (literary) medium!

It is no coincidence that Klopstock's "Frühlingsfeyer" has triggered this epiphany, as it is no coincidence that this epiphany is taking place at a window, on the threshold between outside and inside. The weather, the obvious common ground that Klopstock's poem and the ballroom-scene of Goethe's novel share, constitutes the basis for this meta-poetic move. "Die Frühlingsfeyer" narrates the weather's role as the medium for God's provident reconciliation of heaven and earth:

> Alas, now rushes, now rushes
> Heaven, and earth of the gracious rain. (Klopstock 1771, 28; my transl.)[137]

In Goethe's novel, the "splendid rain" that Werther watches at the window "does not lead him to the divine-natural [*göttlich-natürliche*] source of experience that the text merely communicated [*vermittelte*]", as Stephan Pabst (2009, 139; my transl.) writes. Goethe's *Werther* does not pass on the ideological-theological statement of Klopstock's poem. In this scene Goethe's novel is less concerned with the communication of concepts and worldviews than with its own meta-poetical performance: it is less saying or stating but doing something. The connection that is established in *Werther* is not of "heaven, and earth", but of Lotte and Werther. It is, however, again the weather, that plays a decisive part in making this connection possible:

> she looked up at the sky and at me, I could see tears in her eyes, she put her hand on mine and said, Klopstock! –

Obviously, Klopstock's poem does not talk about a loving couple, it talks about the "sky" and about "tears". It sublates what Lotte and what Werther see, fuses their views into one. The novel performs this fusion most artistically and wittily by focalising the look through the window through Klopstock's poem.

---

136 Unintendedly, this narratological reflection uncannily approximates Niklas Luhmann's theory of love as a generalised medium of communication (cf. Luhmann 2012).
137 "Ach! schon rauscht, schon rauscht |Himmel, und Erde vom gnädigen Regen!" (Klopstock 1771, 28)

Lotte's "Klopstock!" therefore does not so much invoke an individual poet or poem, but the literary medium as such. The famous window-scene of Goethe's novel is all about mediality – a theme that is already inherent in its topographical setting, which by itself raises the question of bridging the inside and the outside, of finding a medium that makes communication across the threshold possible. The setting also emphasises that the question of mediality cannot be separated from the question of the weather. The window in its functions of warding off the weathery forces and at the same time allowing for some sort of contact to this weathery outside equals the demands that are made of the (literary) medium in the context of the whole letter. It is therefore no coincidence that the epiphany of the literary medium takes place in the setting of a window scene. Klopstock's "Frühlingsfeyer" as a text about the weather not only resonates with Lotte's and Werther's experiences at the window, the epiphany of the literary text as a medium provides the lovers with a solution to their problems experienced during the ballroom scene: they find 'a reality', a place for their love.

The literary medium that emerges in the window scene continues and sublates the ballroom-scene's conflict with the weathery forces. We have analysed the ecstasy and the pleasure of the weathery forces' breaking the boundaries of the concentric constellation, threatening the established order in an anarchic way. We have also seen that this contemporary, enlightened order, producing a space of human mastery and control, is constituted by shutting out and containing these weathery forces, so that any threat of weather is countered by even more effective mechanisms to restore that order and seal off the human space even more hermetically than before. Consequently, there is no socially acceptable place for weathery forces, not for the outer weather's resisting man's technical control over the world, not for the inner weather of passion, irrationality and ecstasy. With the invocation of "Klopstock!" a 'piece of social reality' emerges that 'traverses' the concentric constellation's limitations/boundaries – without breaking it apart, without disturbing its workings in an anarchic way, that is to say without provoking immediate restorative reactions. Literature as a medium gives the weathery forces a social place, assigns a well-defined, autonomous position to them within the established and accepted order of the world. The discursive system of literature is itself this very place. To be sure, the emergence of this weathery medium has to be called a "domestication" (Neumann 2000, 529; my transl.): the weathery forces are now housed within the well-defined boundaries of what is called 'literature'. However, as the window scene so vividly and concretely demonstrates, this medium of literature has the power and capacity of supplementing the enlightened order of the world, of which it itself forms part. It is not merely a collection of empty fantasies, its presence as a medium within the enlightened world makes a difference: 'things' become possible, can be said, shared, felt, realised within the boundaries, within the system of limitations that were not possible, not realisable without this medium.

When Lotte invokes "Klopstock!" at the window, it is not only the correspondence of the harmonious weather, of the "splendid rain" outside and the ode's concluding "gracious rain" that she brings to her and Werther's mind, that she makes present through the literary medium. The reference to the "Frühlingsfeyer" also transports the poem's heavy weather, its so vivid description of the thunderstorm rushing and flooding through the world. As we have seen, Werther's ecstatic reaction, his sinking "in the flood of feelings [*Strom von Empfindungen*]", his weeping "the most blissful [*wonnevollsten*] tears" (43) does not correspond to the harmonious weather outside: it breaks the letter's logic of correspondence or parallel of outer weather and inner weather, the correspondence of weathery events and love. The literary medium Lotte introduces with her invocation has effected an unlinking of (contingent) weather events and her love with Werther. It has, however, not unlinked the correspondence of love and weather in general: it is now the poem's weather that Werther's (and Lotte's) inner weather is answering. In other words: Lotte and Werther are in contact with the weather, without breaking their circles, without causing a conflict and without anyone at the ball or even most of the critical readers of the scene sensing a transgression. Through the weathery medium of literature their love has found a place.

This place is real and objective; it is not a fantasy, not a subjective projection. The weather is here not repressed into an interiority where it cannot be shared, cannot have any effect on public life. Werther's and Lotte's "reader-inwardnesses [*Leser-Innerlichkeiten*]" (Kittler 1994, 150; my transl.) differ markedly from Werther's internalisation of love we observed in the context of Lotte's game: his sensing Lotte's love in the intensity of the slaps he receives from her hand remains indeed a subjective impression, probably one which other participants in the game, without any objective reason, may have as well. What Friedrich Kittler calls "reader-inwardnesses" transcends the limits of subjective interiority. The medium literature, the text in its objectivity, traverses the intimate, the private, the lonely inner interior so that these interiors and their weathery forces can interact, can be shared, can form something new. The novel underlines this objectivity of the medium by performing what is taking place on the diegetic level: by narrating the window-scene through the lens of Klopstock's text, and thus choosing a mode of focalisation that transcends the perception and consciousness of the characters, and calling attention to the mediality of literature that is capable of constituting a collective for which the intimate, the private, plays a foundational role.

This new collective that is produced by the medium of the literary text is not a reality of the second degree, not merely a simulacrum. Olaf Reinhardt's interpretation of the window scene is symptomatic of the logocentric prejudice that text as reality must be secondary to 'real' reality: "where the exclamation of the poet's name seems to express the encounter [*Zusammentreffen*] of two sentimental souls", he writes, "it, in reality, rather replaces their get-together [*Zusammenkunft*]" (2003, 57; my transl.). Erdmann Waniek's warning that "there is the danger, that a voluntary and perhaps hasty-unnecessary [*voreilig-unnötige*] escape to reading-experiences blocks the own experiencing" (1982, 72; my transl.) takes a similar track. I think it important to notice that literature emerging as an autonomous medium is actually a specific piece of reality with specific capacities. It is surely (as is probably most of what we call 'culture') a product of sublimation, perhaps, at that time, "the most modern, sentimental, anti-rationalist" "medium of a sublimate" (Gille 1998, 15; my transl.). However, 'text' does not simply replace 'body', the reality of Lotte's and Werther's shared "Klopstock!" does not replace their waltz. It is simply a different piece of reality – as (Luhmann's system of) love is a piece of reality different from sex, both bringing forward their own, specific modes and contents of experiencing. Without doubt, there is a close connection between both (as there is a close connection between waltz and Klopstock). However, the question of whether one is a danger for the other, whether one is the 'actual', real thing, the other merely an illusion, cannot be answered in a simple, obvious way. What can be said is that literature proves to be a much better medium for the weathery forces than the waltz. The emergence of literature is thus no substitution, but a supplementation. Through it, an encounter of Werther and Lotte proves to be possible without causing chaos and provoking restorative forces. As the story that the novel tells demonstrates, and as already the ending of the waltz scene indicated, Lotte's and Werther's love remains reliant on the literary medium. It cannot exist without it. Nevertheless, by suggesting that this love ultimately finds its realisation in the novel called *Werther*, I do not want to say that this love is merely fictive, Werther's illusion, not based on (diegetic) factual truth. It is 'real', 'true', (diegetic) factual love that can, however, only exist in and through the literary medium.

If "Werther pleads for the autonomy of love", his tragic story does not relate the reaching of its ends in the full sense, because this love remains dependent on another autonomous medium: as Hans-Edwin Friedrich observes, "*The Sufferings of Young Werther* [plead] for the autonomy of the novel as a form of art" (2000, 215; my transl.). Goethe's Werther is thus not a novel on the art of love, it is not about how to love in a liveable way – it is a novel on the role of the novel, a novel about the necessity of the autonomy of the novel. It is a novel that presents the novel to create a much-needed place for the weathery forces, of love, passion, but also of irrationality, of suicide, of death, in the enlightened order of the world where these phenomena and forces only feature as antagonists to be expelled and repressed.[138]

The literary medium does not drive out the weather by taming it, once and for all. It does not erect walls against the weather, does not enclose it to be handled safely for the future. The window scene re-enacts the complete ballroom-scene, with all its weather and its ecstasy in words taken from Klopstock. It does, however, not mirror Klopstock's story line, leading towards benevolent, divine harmony: as is hardly ever noticed, the window scene in *Werther* does not end with Klopstock's "bow of peace" – it does not articulate the promise of no future flooding. On the contrary, the "splendid rain" outside is followed by Werther's ecstatic flood of feelings and tears; the heavy, uncontrollable weather lives on. Werther's words even explicitly testify to the loss of control on which the scene ends, and thereby emphasise their ecstatic nature: "I could not bear it, I bowed over her hand [*neigte mich auf ihre Hand*] and kissed it as I wept the most blissful tears" (43).[139] This is not merely a conventional, sentimental gesture. The novel's very words indicate that the kiss is a transgression, a loss of control. Werther not only proves to be incapable of following Lotte and containing his tears; in this scene he cannot contain himself. We all know that this will not remain the only occasion where Werther loses self-control: the window-scene's kiss uncannily prefigures the transgression of its "parallel-scene [*Parallelszene*]" (Reinhardt 2003, 57; my transl.) late in the novel, when it is again a literary text, *Ossian*, that nourishes the protagonist's love and passion and triggers a promiscuous kiss. The fact that Goethe chooses to end the window-scene and the famous letter of June 16th with Werther's "bow[ing] [*neigte*] over" Lotte's hand, not with Klopstock's "bow of peace" is significant: strikingly using the same verb (*neigen*), replacing the symbol of peace with what is to

---

138 In her *La révolution du langage poétique* Julia Kristeva appears to develop a similar thought when she links 'the literary' or 'the poetical' with constitutive but usually inaccessible "residues" or uncontainable 'forces':

> "C'est ainsi que nous pouvons penser d'ailleurs toutes les « déformations » poétiques de la chaîne signifiante et de la structure de la signification : elles cèdent sous l'assaut des « restes des premières symbolisations » (Lacan), c'est-à-dire des pulsions que la phase thétique n'a pas pu relever pour les enchaîner en signifiant/signifié. [...] C'est précisément ce dont témoignent les pratiques artistiques, et notamment le langage poétique. A partir de et après (logiquement et chronologiquement) la position phallique et la castration que la sous-tend, c'est-à-dire après l'Œdipe et surtout après le réglage de la génitalité par la rétroaction de l'Œdipe et lors de la puberté, la *chora* sémiotique se donne à lire non pas comme une défaillance par rapport au thétique mais comme sa condition." (Kristeva 1974, 47–48)

139 "Ich ertrugs nicht, neigte mich auf ihre Hand und küßte sie unter den wonnevollsten Thränen." (54)

become a symbol of tragic love, replacing a symbol of God's providence with an emblem of 18th century literature.

These transgressions triggered by the literary medium reveal its efficacy, and its danger. Literature as a medium for the weathery forces presents itself as comparable to the famous bag of Aeolus, known from the tenth book of Homer's *Odyssey*: the force and violence of the winds, of the weathery forces are banned into it – and whenever this bag is opened, that is, when the literary text is read, these weathery forces are set free again, bringing forth incalculable effects.

3 Well and hut – idyll and prison

In the preceding sections my focus on the weathery forces and their conflicting interaction with the concentric constellation has led to a slight misrepresentation of what is taking place in the novel; this is now due to be corrected. My emphasis on the events of breaking out and on the pleasure set free by these events must have obscured the fact that the novel presents us with not one, but two, diametrically opposed tendencies of "desire" or "inner drive". A complex, conflicting situation structures the whole novel and is made explicit in an early letter:

> Dear Wilhelm, I have thought about this and that, about man's desire to expand, make new discoveries, roam; and then again on his inner drive to submit willingly to limitations, to carry on in the rut of habit, looking neither right nor left. (44)[140]

There is thus not only "man's desire to expand", but also an "inner drive to submit willingly to limitations" that both motivate actions and account for bliss and pleasure. As we have already seen, "limitations" play an important role for the concentric constellation and the contemporary understanding of what the human being is. The passage quoted emphasises the impression that it is difficult to evaluate this notion of 'limitations'. Whereas the "desire to expand, make new discoveries" is much more easily connected with 'positive' associations of freedom and adventure, the willing submission to limitations appears to be ambivalent from the beginning. Its being linked to "the rut of habit" and the rather ignorant behaviour of "looking neither right nor left" violate important values of the enlightenment and thereby indicate its difficult ambiguity. As

---

[140] "Lieber Wilhelm, ich habe allerley nachgedacht, über die Begier im Menschen sich auszubreiten, neue Entdekkungen zu machen, herumzuschweifen; und dann wieder über den innern Trieb sich der Einschränkung willig zu ergeben, und in dem Gleise der Gewohnheit so hinzufahren, und sich weder um recht noch links zu bekümmern." (56)

we learn from this early letter, it is, however, the paradoxical interplay of both desires or drives (the one to expand as well as the one to submit to limitations) that accounts for bliss:

> It is marvelous how I came here and gazed down from the hills into the beautiful valley, how everything all around me attracted me – The little stand of trees over there! – Oh, if you could see over the whole wide region from up there! – The enchained hills and the gentle valleys! – Oh, if I could lose [*verliehren*] myself in them! – I hurried to be there, and returned, and had not found what I had hoped to find. Oh, distance is like the future! A vast twilit whole looms before our soul, our feeling blurs [*verschwimmt*] in it like our eyesight, and we long, oh, to surrender our whole being, to let ourselves be filled to the brim, blissfully [*mit all der Wonne*], with a single, great, glorious emotion. – And alas! when we rush to be there, when there becomes here, everything is as it was before, and we stand there as poor and limited as before, and our soul craves the balm that has slipped away.
>
> Thus, in the end, the most restless vagabond longs once more for his homeland, and in his cottage, at his wife's breast, in the circle of his children, in the occupations that provide for them, he finds the bliss that he sought in vain in the whole wide world. (44–45)[141]

In this early passage we find everything I have written about so far: the concentric constellation defined by limitations, the centrifugal impulse to break out and the notion of "surrendering" one's individual being to become part of something bigger, something unlimited. Here again two more verbs are added to the series of 'ecstatic' verbs marked by the prefix *ver-* ("verliehren", "verschwimmt"), signifying what David Wellbery calls the "transcendence of human corporeal limitation" (1994, 184) and the "absorption into the fluid and unconstrained unity of the absolute body" (1994, 197). However, this passage introduces the important observation that the "desire to expand" and the "drive to submit willingly to limitations" differ markedly in one central aspect: whereas the drive to submit can lead to and realise its goal, can make present and

---

141 "Es ist wunderbar, wie ich hierher kam und vom Hügel in das schöne Thal schaute, wie es mich rings umher anzog. Dort das Wäldchen! Ach könntest du von da die weite Gegend überschauen! Die in einander gekettete Hügel und vertraulichen Thäler. O könnte ich mich in ihnen verliehren! – Ich eilte hin! und kehrte zurük, und hatte nicht gefunden was ich hoffte. O es ist mit der Ferne wie mit der Zukunft! Ein grosses dämmerndes Ganze ruht vor unserer Seele, unsere Empfindung verschwimmt sich darinne, wie unser Auge, und wir sehnen uns, ach! unser ganzes Wesen hinzugeben, uns mit all der Wonne eines einzigen grossen herrlichen Gefühls ausfüllen zu lassen. – Und ach, wenn wir hinzueilen, wenn das Dort nun Hier wird, ist alles vor wie nach, und wir stehen in unserer Armuth, in unserer Eingeschränktheit, und unsere Seele lechzt nach entschlüpftem Labsale.

Und so sehnt sich der unruhigste Vagabund zulezt wieder nach seinem Vaterlande und findet in seiner Hütte, an der Brust seiner Gattin, in dem Kreise seiner Kinder und der Geschäfte zu ihrer Erhaltung, all die Wonne, die er in der weiten öden Welt vergebens suchte." (56)

liveable what it is aiming for, the desire to expand is not to be satisfied, proves unattainable, cannot be translated into a liveable present. It rather 'opens up' this present: towards an (unreachable) future, or towards itself, making the bliss possible that would not have been felt without the vain attempt to realise a liveable expansion. It is thus not Werther's fault that his and Lotte's ecstatic moments cannot be transformed into a stable, blissful existence. Abstractly speaking, expansion and submitting to the limitations are not located on the same categorical level. The one answers the question of the *real*, of the liveable, of the factual coordinates (submission), of the 'what is' and 'what can be' in the present; the other is concerned with the question of the *virtual*, of the future-to-come, of becoming, of the (always relational) intensity that fills the factual coordinates (expansion).[142] As a consequence, the drive (to the real) of submitting to the limitations and the desire of (the virtual of) expansion are not alternatives ('either ... or') – they are supplements, one supplementing the other.

It is the task of this section to explain these abstract and perhaps incomprehensible, philosophical terms. There is, however, no need to resort to philosophy since the novel itself provides us with precise characterisations of these two 'movements'; movements that are central for a reading of the novel, since, as we will see, they play a decisive role for the self-reflection of the novel as an aesthetic medium. Goethe's *Werther* connects specific aesthetic traits and practices to both of these movements, to the desire to expand as well as to the inner drive to submit willingly to limitations. It is therefore important to take both of these supplementary movements and their complex relation to each other seriously in order to shed some light on the novel's own stance in these aesthetical debates, and to develop an idea of the novel's self-conceptualisation as a novel in a certain field of aesthetic practices that it so extensively keeps citing and alluding to.

The novel repeatedly stages the bliss that the passage quoted above described in an abstract way, this simple bliss experienced in the "cottage, at [the] wife's breast, in the circle of [the] children", which is the bliss of submitting to the limitations. This happens, for example, in the quite well-known peas-and-cabbage-episode that follows in the same letter that contained the abstract meditation on expansion and submission:

> When mornings at sunrise I leave for my Wahlheim, and in the garden of the inn I pick my own sugar peas, sit down, snip off their strings, and in between read my Homer; when in the little kitchen I choose a saucepan, baste the peapods with a little butter, set them on the fire, cover them, and sit there to shake the pan from time to time; then I feel vividly how Penelope's boisterous suitors slaughter, carve up, and roast oxen and swine. Nothing

---

[142] For the conceptual distinction between 'virtual', 'possible' and 'real', see Deleuze 1968, 272–276.

fills me with such serene, genuine feeling as the features of patriarchal life, which, thank God, I can weave into my way of life without affectation.

How happy I am that my heart can feel the simple, innocent bliss of the man who brings to his table the head of cabbage he has grown himself and who now, in a single moment, enjoys not only the cabbage but all the fine days, the beautiful morning he planted it, the lovely evenings he watered it, and the pleasure he took in watching it grow continuously – all rolled into one. (45)[143]

Here the domestic circle, with its daily, basic cares of supplying and preparing food are addressed and affirmed. More than that, the passage affirms the limitations of experiencing "simple, innocent bliss" in satisfying these fundamental needs of life. Strikingly, the domestic circle finds an unmistakable centre, as the accumulation of first person pronouns shows: all the activities that 'the I', Werther, undertakes ("I leave", "I pick", "[I] read", "I feel") are re-appropriated in a second step: "my Wahlheim", "my own sugar peas", "my Homer", "my way of life", "my heart". This pattern is confirmed and even explained in Werther's generalisation of his current situation, formulated as a sort of planting-parable in the third person, attributed to an exemplary "man": the cabbage that "he planted", "he watered" and "watch[ed]" can finally be brought to the table and "enjoy[ed]" "in a single moment". The movement of this "simple, innocent bliss" is a double movement of concentration: (1) It condenses the pleasures of the different stages of planting, watering, growing and picking, that is to say the stages of a temporal series. The pleasures are, as the novel puts it, "all rolled into one" "single moment". (2) This condensed, concentrated bliss of a moment can then be appropriated by the centre of the domestic constellation, by the subject who literally incorporates all the pleasures concentrated in the cabbage head or the peas in the moment of eating.

---

143 "Wenn ich so des Morgens mit Sonnenaufgange hinausgehe nach meinem Wahlheim, und dort im Wirthsgarten mir meine Zukkererbsen selbst pflükke, mich hinsezze, und sie abfädme und dazwischen lese in meinem Homer. Wenn ich denn in der kleinen Küche mir einen Topf wähle, mir Butter aussteche, meine Schoten ans Feuer stelle, zudekke und mich dazu sezze, sie manchmal umzuschütteln. Da fühl ich so lebhaft, wie die herrlichen übermüthigen Freyer der Penelope Ochsen und Schweine schlachten, zerlegen und braten. Es ist nichts, das mich so mit einer stillen, wahren Empfindung ausfüllte, als die Züge des patriarchalischen Lebens, die ich, Gott sey Dank, ohne Affektation in meine Lebensart verweben kann.

Wie wohl ist mir's, daß mein Herz die simple harmlose Wonne des Menschen fühlen kann, der ein Krauthaupt auf seinen Tisch bringt, das er selbst gezogen, und nun nicht den Kohl allein, sondern all die guten Tage, den schönen Morgen, da er ihn pflanzte, die lieblichen Abende, da er ihn begoß, und da er an dem fortschreitenden Wachsthume seine Freude hatte, alle in einem Augenblikke wieder mit geniest." (58)

The "simple, innocent bliss" that Werther experiences in this episode is modelled on the precarious life of simple people like the woman and mother of three children that Werther encounters in the streets of Wahlheim:

> I tell you, my dear friend, when my mind will not rest, all my turmoil is soothed by the sight of such a creature who, calm and happy, moves through the narrow circle of her existence, making the best of things from one day to the next, watches the leaves fall, and thinks no more about it than that winter is coming. (32)[144]

It is this "creature['s]" "calm and happy", "narrow circle" of existence, her state of intense, exclusive concentration on her existential affairs that fascinates Werther. The woman's so stable and strong organisation of her limited life appeals to Werther's "inner drive to submit willingly to limitations". The sight of the simple woman's existential care for herself and her children soothes his restlessness and unquenchable thirst for excess. Her way of reading the signs of falling leaves is significant for several reasons. First of all, she refers these signs to nothing but her own life: "the narrow circle of her existence" is the only horizon on which the signs of the falling leaves take on meaning. In this, her way of interpreting is strikingly similar to Lotte's, who will give us an explicit explanation of her hermeneutics only few letters later. The fact that Lotte and the woman share a very specific way of understanding is certainly no coincidence: the novel presents them, in a more general sense, as important parallel figures. They are both introduced as emblems of the domestic circle, of its bliss and its affirmation. It is above all the children they care for that constitute this circle – precisely as the vagabond's domestic sphere (in Werther's abstract musing on the drives of expansion and limitation) was defined by the "circle of his children". However, the woman's reading of the falling leaves indicates an important function that she fulfils as a parallel figure to Lotte: her thinking "no more about it than that winter is coming", as Werther puts it, sits uneasily with Werther's impression of the woman's being "calm and happy". In fact, Werther appears to be so much savouring the momentary sight's soothing effect that he is not aware of the woman's all-too justified worries about the future. Her seeing the winter come foreshadows the miseries the novel later tells us have ruptured her life. Her husband returns home poor and without his heritage, her youngest child dies, the happiness of the picture that Werther had drawn himself of this woman and of "the narrow circle of her existence" is

---

144 "Ich sage dir, mein Schatz, wenn meine Sinnen gar nicht mehr halten wollen, so linderts all den Tumult, der Anblick eines solchen Geschöpfs, das in der glücklichen Gelassenheit so den engen Kreis seines Daseyns ausgeht, von einem Tag zu dem andern sich durchhilft, die Blätter abfallen sieht, und nichts dabey denkt, als daß der Winter kömmt." (32)

retrospectively qualified. She serves as a corrective to the idea of the universality of simple, domestic bliss, a corrective independent from the events around Werther's and Lotte's love. The idyllic picture of domestic bliss is thus very early questioned and revealed to be misleading in its deceptive momentariness.

The affirmation of the domestic circle's limitation is not a privilege of simple people. As already noted, Lotte features as the novel's central representative of this "simple, innocent bliss" and also Werther, imitating Lotte's world (Müller 1969, 157), aspires to the organisation of life in the limited, "narrow circle" of a hut:

> You've long known my habit of planting myself down, setting up a little hut at some cozy spot, and settling in there with all limitations. Here, too, I've once again come across a spot that attracted me. (29; transl. altered)[145]

The famous peas-and-cabbage episode quoted above narrates the "settling" in this "cozy spot", which not only includes gardening and preparing food but also, and significantly, the consumption of literature that Werther "can weave into [his] way of life without affectation". As the metaphor of weaving, topical for the production of (literary) texts, indicates, the affirmation of the domestic circle and the connected notion of a particular way of reading literary texts is also of special metapoetical importance. It is therefore not astonishing that critics have carefully scrutinised Werther's apparently odd way of reading Homer. They have come to astonishingly different conclusions, which in many cases appear to be symptomatic of the critics' general attitude towards the novel as a whole. Heinz Schlaffer and Bruce Duncan share the view that Werther's reading of Homer unmasks the protagonist's "self-deception" (Schlaffer 1978, 216; my transl.). As Bruce Duncan writes, "Werther's reading of Homer – he himself says 'mein Homer' – is so eccentric that it can be viewed only as a projection of his own psyche" (1982, 44), which implies that the deviance of Werther's reading from a 'correct', 'appropriate' reading of Homer calls for an ironic distancing of "the figure/character Werther and the novel Werther" that, according to Heinz Schlaffer, is "still underestimated today" (1978, 217; my transl.). However, as strange and inappropriate as Werther's identification with Penelope's "boisterous suitors" might seem, his way of reading Homer cannot be called "eccentric", at least not if we take this notion seriously in its literal sense. As Robert Stockhammer has observed, the novel presents us with two modes of reading: an "ego-strengthening centripetal identification that reduces the Other

---

[145] "Du kennst von Alters her meine Art, mich anzubauen, irgend mir an einem vertraulichen Orte ein Hüttchen aufzuschlagen, und da mit aller Einschränkung zu herbergen. Ich hab auch hier wieder ein Plätzchen angetroffen, das mich angezogen hat." (26)

[*Fremde*] to the own"; and a second "centrifugal" way of reading that "abandons the own to the other" (1991, 159; my transl.). Without doubt, Robert Stockhammer is right in categorising Werther's reading of Homer (in contrast to Lotte's and his reading of Ossian) as centripetal: it is a reading that affirms the narrow circle of the hut, making sense of what is read on the narrow horizon of one's own life and position. In this, it is similar to the poor woman's reading of the falling leaves. The fact that Werther's reading is intrinsically likened to the savouring of peas and cabbage is telling: according to Robert Stockhammer, Werther's reading of Homer is "dietetic [*diätetisch*]" (1991, 168; my transl.). He enjoys his peas and he enjoys his Homer in the most 'centripetal' way possible, in the most extreme way of referring the story to himself, as the centre: by eating, by incorporating in order to give himself a treat, or even use his reading as a medicine, as Peter Pütz argues (cf. 1983, 63). As with the woman's reading, Werther's identification with Penelope's "boisterous suitors" contains the implicit prophesy of a doomed future: the suitors will all be cruelly slaughtered by Ulysses, of which Werther, savouring the idyllic moment, again remains completely unaware.

It is however Lotte who gives the most encompassing description or characterisation of this centripetal, domestic way of reading:

> But since I have so little time to read, it has to be something completely to my taste. And I do love best of all that author in whom I rediscover my own world, in whose books things happen the way they do all around me, and whose story is as interesting and heartfelt as my own domestic life, which, of course, is no paradise and yet all in all is a source of inexpressible happiness. (38)[146]

What Lotte evokes here is the concentric constellation's theory of reading. As with Werther's "cozy spot" and his cooking and savouring of peas, the world is organised "all around" a subjective centre that refers to its surroundings in an appropriating fashion. The "things" happening in a 'good' book (i.e. a book that is to the taste of Lotte as a representative of the concentric constellation) fit this concentric organisation, they are readily appropriated as part of the domestic experience, as a part of 'the own'. Moreover, a book like this mirrors and promotes the concentric, domestic organisation of life so that one's "own world" can be "rediscover[ed]" in it. In its evaluation of books and authors this theory

---

146 "Doch da ich so selten an ein Buch komme, so müssen sie auch recht nach meinem Geschmakke seyn. Und der Autor ist mir der liebste, in dem ich meine Welt wieder finde, bey dem's zugeht wie um mich, und dessen Geschichte mir doch so interessant so herzlich wird, als mein eigen häuslich Leben, das freylich kein Paradies, aber doch im Ganzen eine Quelle unsäglicher Glükseligkeit ist." (44)

of reading thus also includes a corresponding theory of writing that is of greatest importance for the metapoetical conception of the novel. Despite its censuring the titles and authors of the books that suit Lotte's taste, the novel does not refrain from giving us one paradigmatic example: Oliver Goldsmith's *The Vicar of Wakefield*. The impression that whenever a novel names and affirmatively discusses another, existing novel this novel must be of formative importance for it is underlined by the fact that Goethe's autobiography *Poetry and Truth* contains a passage on *The Vicar of Wakefield* (cf. Pabst 2009, 136) in the section that relates the events preceding his work on *Werther*. The following sentences extracted from a much longer section provide us with two or three key words that will help to understand the metapoetical negotiations at work in *Werther*:

> A Protestant country clergyman is, perhaps, the most beautiful subject for a modern idyl; he appears, like Melchizedek, as priest and king in one person. [...] But at the same time add the necessary limitation, so that he must not only pause in a small circle, but may also perchance pass over to a smaller; [...] – then you will have put together pretty well the image [*Bild*] of our excellent Wakefield. (Goethe 1848, 368–369)[147]

Goethe's description of Goldsmith's novel lists several traits that must look familiar to us with regard to his *Werther*: above all the "limitation" of a "small" or even "smaller" "circle", also the comparison to a patriarchal figure of the Old Testament, as will presently be seen. What has been called the concentric constellation in *Werther*, the drive to submit to the limitations of a domestic, small circle of life, may even have been modelled on Goldsmith's *Vicar of Wakefield*. In his autobiographic retrospect Goethe quite famously attaches a label to this novel that will turn out to be of highest interest for our endeavour: the label "modern idyl". The way Goethe ends his description of the Protestant clergyman of Goldsmith's novel has to be read as an allusion to this label: if you have followed the descriptions, Goethe writes, "then you will have put together pretty well the image [*Bild*] of our excellent Wakefield". The metaphor of painting is here employed against the background of the etymological roots of the word *idyll*: from Greek εἰδύλλιον, the diminutive of εἶδος, signifying 'small picture'. As Stephan Pabst (2010) has shown, the notion of the idyll with its media-theoretical implications going back to its "purely pictorial foundation" (2010, 21; my transl.) plays an important role in Goethe's *Werther*. This observation

---

[147] "Ein protestantischer Landgeistlicher ist vielleicht der schönste Gegenstand einer modernen Idylle; er erscheint, wie Melchisedech, als Priester und König in Einer Person. [...] Zugleich füge man die nötige Beschränktheit hinzu, daß er nicht allein in einem kleinem Kreise verharren, sondern auch allenfalls in einen kleineren übergehen möge [...]: so hat man das Bild unseres trefflichen Wakefield so ziemlich beisammen." (FA 14, 465)

is not limited to the impression that the novel is divided in a first idyllic and a second catastrophic part, as Peter U. Hohendahl (1972, 199) suggests. The novel rather links one of the poles it identifies as being structural for the contemporary organisation of life, the inner drive to submit willingly to limitations, to the genre of the idyll, popular throughout the 18th century, influenced by the huge success of Salomon Geßner. The idyll as a rich discursive, intertextual reservoir as well as an intermedial link to the visual arts, is thus established as corresponding to what I have called the concentric constellation.

Werther's reading of Homer is a case in point for the idyllic attitude: as Erdmann Waniek notes, "his understanding of the *Odyssey* as an archetype of idyllic-patriarchal circumstances matches with [the understanding] of his time" (1982, 62; my transl.). Klaus Scherpe adds, also commenting on the 18th century view of "Homer's world", that the "longing for earthiness [*Urtümlichkeit*] and naivety dominates the imaginary world of the fashionable-sentimental idyllicists [*Idylliker*] as well as the ingenious-powerful *Sturm-und-Drang*-poet" (1970, 58; my transl.).

Lotte's domestic world, Werther's "cozy spot[s]" – these are idyllic *loci amoeni* that the novel 'paints' with words before our eyes. It is here (and only here) that Achim Aurnhammer's thesis of Werther as a painter (1995) has its place in the novel; it is here that the novel's protagonist and the art of painting meet in an affirmative way. Werther not only moves through and enjoys the idyll's *loci amoeni* that are delivered to the readers in a pseudo/quasi-ekphrastic fashion, scenes that we then find 're'-translated into the famous etchings of illustrated editions of the novel, Lotte feeding the circle of her children, ... Emblematically, Werther once even draws an idyllic scene himself, and it is important to note that this takes place when he has finally found his "cozy spot" in Wahlheim, sitting in the middle of this idyll, drawing it, unsurprisingly, with quite some success:

> I was charmed by the sight. I sat down on a plow that stood opposite them and was greatly delighted to sketch the pose of the two brothers. I put in the nearby hedge, a barn door, and some broken wagon wheels, everything the way each stood behind the other, and after an hour I found that I had produced a well-composed, very interesting drawing [...]. (30)[148]

---

[148] "Mich vergnügte der Anblik, und ich sezte mich auf einen Pflug, der gegen über stund, und zeichnete die brüderliche Stellung mit vielem Ergözzen, ich fügte den nächsten Zaun, ein Tennenthor und einige gebrochne Wagenräder bey, wie es all hintereinander stund, und fand nach Verlauf einer Stunde, daß ich eine wohlgeordnete sehr interessante Zeichnung verfertigt hatte [...]." (26)

Curiously enough, the story of Werther's drawing is linked from the beginning to meta-artistic reflections: Werther immediately emphasises that he has produced this drawing "without having introduced the slightest bit of [him]self" (30),[149] only to be led to a longish digression on the role of rules with regard to art. The credo of his little lecture is simple: "rules will destroy the true feeling of nature and the genuine expression thereof" (30).[150] Werther's musing on meta-artistic reflections hardly fits however his own artistic work and the circumstances of its production. His "wohlgeordnete" (that is not only "well-composed", but also "well-organised", "well-arranged", "orderly") drawing does not seem to comply at all with the aesthetics of genius that his reflections outline. Werther does not seem to realise that the conventionality of his drawing, the meticulous order of the idyllic scene is a result of his previous careful selection of this "cozy spot" – tellingly situated in *Wahl*heim [choice-home]. It is not rules that Werther imposes on himself when drawing that "suppl[y] limits, prune[ ] the rampant vines" (30),[151] but the very idyllic scenery that he had chosen: As shown above, the *loci amoeni* of the concentric constellation follow strict rules, all being topologically constructed in the very same way, all alluding to the same markers of the domestic, the patriarchal, the earthy, all being initially portrayed as places of simple, innocent bliss.

As usual, Werther enjoys the idyllic bliss, without paying attention to the little signs depicted in the idyllic image which may indicate that what he is rejoicing in is not a stable world or life, but a momentary picture, merely an *eidyllion*. In Werther's drawing it is the "broken wagon wheels" (used and seen by Werther from a purely aesthetic point of view) that may be read as representing past and perhaps also future mishaps and suffering. They at least call into question the unqualified bliss that Werther experiences when he is "charmed by the sight". This minor sign may be negligible; others, however, are to follow in a much more manifest way.

The parable of love that Werther relates to explain the role of rules in the arts is one of the instances that cast severe doubt on his perception of the blissfulness of the idyllic sight. Here the contradictions between what Werther is describing and the actual idyllic setting and the drawing this setting has produced and that has triggered the parable, cannot be overlooked. The parable tells the story of an excessive lover:

---

[149] "[...] ohne das mindeste von dem meinen hinzuzuthun [...]." (26–28)
[150] "[...] dagegen wird aber auch alle Regel, man rede was man wolle, das wahre Gefühl von Natur und den wahren Ausdruk derselben zerstören!" (28)
[151] "[Alle Regel] schränkt nur ein, beschneidet die geilen Reben [...]." (28)

> A young heart gives itself entirely to a girl, spends every waking hour of every day with her, squanders all his energies, his entire fortune, so as to let her know at every moment that he gives himself entirely to her. (30; transl. altered)[152]

The excessive lover, characterised by his tendency to give everything, to "give[ ] himself entirely" and thereby lose himself in the end, serves as the model for the true artist, who does not follow the rational rules that would urge him to manage his resources in order to live a liveable life, but equals the lover in his actualisation of excess:

> Oh, my friends! Why does the torrent of genius gush out so rarely, so rarely come rushing in on a spring tide to shatter your amazed soul? – Dear friends, these sedate gentlemen dwell on the banks of the stream, where their little summer houses, their tulip beds and cabbage patches would be ruined, and who therefore have the sense in good time to use dams and flood channels to ward off the impending threat of danger. (30–31)[153]

The figure of the excessive genius looks as familiar to the readers of the novel, as the weathery "torrent [...] rushing in on a spring tide". Both will dominate later parts of the plot, parts that Peter U. Hohendahl regards as being attuned to catastrophe rather than to the idyll (cf. 1972, 199). The decisive question thus has to be what this aesthetics of the torrent of genius, this aesthetics of excess has to do with Werther's idyll, and his "well-composed drawing" that initially inspired this excursus on rules and art. At first glance, the answer seems to be straightforward: Werther's "cozy spot", selected following an "inner drive to submit willingly to limitations" and his drawing the bliss of simple life are opposed to the lover's or the artist's excess. Werther's "little hut", his enjoying his "cozy spot" and "settling in there [...] with all limitations" rather appear to approximate him to the "sedate gentlemen" of whom the passage speaks with some disdain. Werther's later idyllic joy that he ascribes to the planting, growing and savouring of cabbage even increases this impression. There is however one decisive difference between him and the "sedate gentlemen": as we have seen in several of the idyllic scenes, Werther does not share their cautious care for the future. He does not "have the sense in good time to use dams and flood

---

152 "[...] ein junges Herz hängt ganz an einem Mädchen, bringt alle Stunden seines Tages bey ihr zu, verschwendet all seine Kräfte, all sein Vermögen, um ihr jeden Augenblick auszudrükken, daß er sich ganz ihr hingiebt." (28)
153 "O meine Freunde! warum der Strom des Genies so selten ausbricht, so selten in hohen Fluthen hereinbraust, und eure staunende Seele erschüttert. Lieben Freunde, da wohnen die gelaßnen Kerls auf beyden Seiten des Ufers, denen ihre Gartenhäuschen, Tulpenbeete, und Krautfelder zu Grunde gehen würden, und die daher in Zeiten mit dämmen und ableiten der künftig drohenden Gefahr abzuwehren wissen." (28)

channels to ward off the impending threat of danger". In this his meta-artistic statement that his savouring goes "without having introduced the slightest bit of [him]self" (not even some measures of protection!) proves true and problematic, at the same time.

The contrast between Werther's idyllic reality and the aesthetics of weathery excess he talks about thus undermines the idyll's bliss. Although Werther is not aware of his own naivety of indulging in the only momentary joys of simple life and limitation, the contrast of limitation and excess, of fixation on the moment and the weathery "impending threat of danger", indicates the idyll's limitations and the impossibility of detaching the idyll's *locus amoenus* from the rest of the stormy world. As Robert H. Brown rightly observes, the "stream of genius that roars in high floods threatens to inundate Werther's own idyllic nature spots and destroy the patriarchal ideal associated with them" (1991, 92). Furthermore, the novel even stages the realisation of this threat when an inundation floods Werther's beloved valley and his "cozy spot" – as it stages the unhappy future of the siblings that his idyllic drawing depicts. Werther's not warding off the weathery dangers illustrates the complex stance that the novel takes in the aesthetic debates of its day: it neither takes sides with the popular idyllic tradition that forecloses the threatening reality of a weathery world, nor does it refrain from the idyll. It rather upholds the idyllic tradition, participates in its aesthetic bliss and the ideals it transports, but only to situate it in a world that does not respect these limitations, that is not ideal but weathery.

It is not adequate to read the novel as a renunciation of the idyll. The idyll does not fail in the strict sense. It is however not blindly affirmed either. The novel rather, from the beginning, displays the sweet deception that is at the heart of the idyll, a deception that demands a different, less ideal aesthetics to account for the reality of the world. The suspicion of the idyll's fundamental ambiguity is introduced in one of the earliest and perhaps the most prominent idyllic scenes of the novel, and one already discussed above. Against the background of what has been said about the idyll, the famous scene at the well certainly deserves a second reading:

> I do not know whether deceitful spirits hover around this region or whether it is the warm, divine fantasy in my heart that makes everything around me appear like paradise. Just outside the town there is a well, a well that holds me spellbound like Melusine and her sisters. – You walk down a little hill and find yourself before a stone vault from which some twenty steps go down to where the clearest water spurts from marble blocks. The low wall above, which forms the surrounding enclosure, the tall trees that cast their shade all around, the coolness of the place; all this has something so attractive, so awesome about it. Not a day goes by that I do not sit there for an hour. The girls come from the town to fetch water, the most innocent occupation and the most essential, which in olden

times the daughters of kings performed. When I sit there, the patriarchal idea comes to life so vividly around me; they are there, all our forebears, meeting others and courting at the well, while benevolent spirits hover around the fountains and the springs. (24; transl. altered)[154]

This scene at the well assembles a rich intertextual web. As Erdmann Waniek (1982, 69) and Clayton Koelb (2008, 50) have noted, it alludes to a biblical tradition of encounters taking place at wells: Isaak's servant and Rebecca (Gen 24, 11–14), Jacob and Rachel (Gen 29, 1–8) in the Old Testament, prefiguring the New Testament encounter of Jesus and the Samaritan woman (Jh, 4,5). The fact that Werther's letter of the 12th of May does not tell any story but rather draws the picture of a scene ties in well with Erdmann Waniek's suggestion that it may not be the biblical stories but Rembrandt's two etchings of Jesus and the Samaritan woman at the well that establish the link of the bible and this letter. The pictorial, quasi-ekphrastic mode is certainly typical for this idyllic emblem, and so is the association of "the patriarchal idea" that seems to come to Goethe's mind whenever the notion of idyll is present: not only with regard to *Werther* where the patriarchal is evoked in Werther's idyll of eating peas and thinking of Homer, but also in Goethe's musing on Oliver Goldsmith's "modern idyl", where the Vicar of Wakefield is described as resembling the patriarchal figure of Melchizedek. To complete the list of obvious idyllic intertextual and intermedial allusions, it should be mentioned that the scenery of the well also actualises one of Salomon Geßner's popular idylls, known as 'Daphne. Chloe' (1973, 87–90), a link that the story of Werther helping a "young servant girl" (25) to lift her jug (narrated in the letter of May 15th) substantiates.

With regard to the scenery's dense intertextual web, its framing is of extreme interest: Werther's not knowing "whether deceitful spirits hover around this region or whether it is the warm, divine fantasy in [his] heart that makes everything around [him] appear like paradise" betrays a certain awareness of the

---

154 "Ich weiß nicht, ob so täuschende Geister um diese Gegend schweben, oder ob die warme himmlische Phantasie in meinem Herzen ist, die mir alles rings umher so paradisisch macht. Da ist gleich vor dem Orte ein Brunn', ein Brunn', an den ich gebannt bin wie Melusine mit ihren Schwestern. Du gehst einen kleinen Hügel hinunter, und findest dich vor einem Gewölbe, da wohl zwanzig Stufen hinab gehen, wo unten das klarste Wasser aus Marmorfelsen quillt. Das Mäuergen, das oben umher die Einfassung macht, die hohen Bäume, die den Platz rings umher bedecken, die Kühle des Orts, das hat alles so was anzügliches, was schauerliches. Es vergeht kein Tag, daß ich nicht eine Stunde da sizze. Da kommen denn die Mädgen aus der Stadt und holen Wasser, das harmloseste Geschäft und das nöthigste, das ehmals die Töchter der Könige selbst verrichteten. Wenn ich da sizze, so lebt die patriarchalische Idee so lebhaft um mich, wie sie alle die Altväter am Brunnen Bekanntschaft machen und freyen, und wie um die Brunnen und Quellen wohlthätige Geister schweben." (16)

scene's ambiguous, doubtful character. No matter whether it is produced by "deceitful spirits" or the heart's "warm, divine fantasy", the scene surrounding Werther is somehow not quite real. It is, we could say, a projection, resulting from idyllic literary and pictorial predecessors, or, as Clayton Koelb puts it:

> The revivified life [...] that Werther feels around the spring therefore comes from acts of reading – his reading of old books, to be sure, but then more directly his reading of this actual place as a literary place, a topos that belongs figuratively in the same world with the springs and wells of literature. (2008, 50)

This world's appearing "like paradise" and its being ordered around a well are not to be separated. As already discussed above, the well episode also functions as a metaphor for the concentric constellation. For this metaphor the symbolism of water, identified by Ilse Graham (1974, 281) as one of the key features of the novel, plays an important role. In contrast to the weathery "torrent of genius [...] rushing in on a spring tide", the well's water does not appear to represent "immoderateness and lability" (1974, 282), but constitutes a constant and moderate reservoir. Rolf Zimmermann has identified precisely this opposition of the rainstorm's weathery, overpowering water and the constant, moderate water of the well in his reading of Goethe's *Zwo wichtige bisher unerörterte biblische Fragen, beantwortet von einem Landgeistlichen in Schwaben*, a short text that appeared only a year before *Werther* (cf. 1968, 281). It is the absence of the troubling weather, the constant stasis of the well and its "clearest water" feeding this idyllic world that accounts for its paradisiac character.

The idea of a central source filling the concentric structure with life will reoccur in later idyllic scenes: for example when Lotte describes her "own domestic life, which, of course, is no paradise [...][,] a source of inexpressible happiness" (38), or when "the features of patriarchal life" "fill[ ] [Werther] with such serene, genuine feeling" (45). It is no coincidence that these two scenes reflect on the need for 'sources' to feed the seemingly stable reservoirs by connecting literal to literary 'sources': they reflect on the effect of reading (Goldsmith for Lotte, Homer for Werther). The well-scene, with its intertextual background, explicates this analogy of sources. Its two analogical centres – Werther and the water reservoir – are the sources that bring about the life grouped around them: as an intertextual space of resonances projected by Werther, as a social place of assemblage by the water of the well that supplies the village. The intertextual, the literary side of the analogy however indicates a fundamental instability: the "benevolent spirits" (which are also, and perhaps mainly, literary products) "hover[ing] around" and conjuring up a "paradise" cannot hide the fact that they are "deceitful". As spirits, they cannot claim the ontological stability one would wish for this paradise to be a liveable place. With these spirits, benevolent but deceitful, the paradisiac world around the well, this *locus amoenus*, is from the beginning haunted by a characteristic uncannyness: the danger is in the air that these spirits could suddenly disappear, that the oasis of the well could finally turn out to be but a mirage.

If the well dries up the people formally living in paradise would face a serious problem: Werther has not only been attracted to this paradisiac place; the well, as he writes, rather "holds [him] spellbound like Melusine and her sisters". In other words, he is trapped in this world, the "stone vault" harbouring the spring of "clearest water" turns into a deserted prison, a dungeon, once the deceitful spirits cease to create paradise. In the words of Lilian R. Furst, "the self-imposed captivity is regarded as a felicitous state, an enclosure that insulates from the assaults of a hostile world", but later, "[t]hough self-created and conceived as a means of liberation, it nonetheless proves a prison in the conventional, negative sense of the word" (1990, 150). David Wellbery calls this movement the "morphism of the incarcerated body", "the source of a kind of claustrophobic torment" that produces Werther's "impulse to get out" (1994, 197), the impulse that my first sections have focused on.

It is important to keep the dialectics of the protective but limiting walls in mind, also with regard to the aesthetic and generic questions linked to the constellation. The transformation of the idyll into a prison is a problem that is inherent in the very conception of the idyll. Its being sealed off from the weathery rest of the world is not a weakness, but the condition for a 'good', for an aesthetically 'well-composed' idyll; nevertheless, it also exhibits the narrow limitations of the genre, as Goethe's critique of one of Salomon Geßner's idylls articulates in clear words:

> Who will deny select passages true feeling of the poet? Nobody. Select passages are excellent, and of the little poems each makes a neat whole. However the larger ones; as splendid as the detail may be, as little as there is to deny that it is well-composed/well-ordered [*wohl geordnet*] to reach certain purposes, you do miss the spirit weaving the parts together so that each becomes an essential part of the whole. He cannot conflate scene, plot and sentiment either. As early as in the first scene the moon appears, and the whole idyll is sunshine. The storm is therefore unbearable. Voltaire from his bed at Lausanne cannot have watched the storm of the Lake Geneva more calmly in his mirror than the people on the rock, around which the weather is raging, detail to themselves, vice versa, what they both see. (FA 18, 48; my translation)[155]

---

[155] "Wer wird aber einzelnen Stellen wahres Dichtergefühl absprechen? Niemand. Einzelne Stellen sind vortrefflich, und die kleinen Gedichte machen jedes ein niedliches Ganze. Hingegen die Größern; so trefflich das Detail sein mag, so wenig zu leugnen ist, daß es zu gewissen Zwecken wohl geordnet ist, so mißt ihr doch überall den Geist, der die Teile so verwebt, daß

Viewed closely, Goethe's criticism does not aim at an author's individual achievements and weaknesses, but at the genre that he, Salomon Geßner, stands for: as its name already suggests, the idyll – the *eidyllion*, the little picture – is a genre of the little, of detail. Goethe lauds the "little poems" that each make "a neat whole"; "the detail" can be splendid and, using a formulation that, as we have seen, reoccurs in *Werther*, "wohl geordnet" [well-composed, well-ordered].[156] It is no coincidence that these two words, here characterising Salomon Geßner's idylls, are employed in the novel as an adjective describing Werther's drawing of an idyllic scene: in both cases it expresses the generic limits of the idyll, the neatness and orderliness of the limited, as a consequence of its being limited. Goethe's review may be said to be unfair, failing to do justice to its actual subject: in a way it is not a review, because it points beyond the genre of the text it discusses. It rather envisions a genre that is capable of surpassing the idyll's limits, a genre that does not merely focus on the 'little', the detail, but that tackles the whole, the essential "weaving" of the details together (again a metaphor of/for the (literary) text). Its rather abrupt turn to what looks like a specific idyll's problem with the weather has to be read as a reformulation of the question of genre and the idyll's limitedness: "the whole idyll is sunshine" – the fact that the "storm is therefore unbearable" demands a different genre, a genre capable of situating the idyll's sunshine in the storm and weatheriness of the world in order to capture 'the whole'.

Goethe's *Werther* writes the story of the creation of this 'new' genre. It thereby narrates and performs its own genealogy. It takes the idyll's sunshine as a start, demonstrates that its sealing off turns it into a suffocating prison and develops aesthetic means to transgress the idyll's limitations and get in touch with the weathery forces storming outside and urging inside. As Stephan Pabst writes, the idyll fails with regard to the human being and the storm (2010, 18), a shortcoming that Goethe's novel sets out to amend. The world of the novel therefore does not comply with the idyllic consciousness (Pabst 2010, 19), it rather supplements it with an aesthetics of the weather. The novel's challenge is, however, not a purely aesthetic enterprise: as we have already seen, the aesthetic, the social and the epistemic are closely interwoven. The idyll as an

---

jeder ein wesentliches Stück vom Ganzen wird. Ebensowenig kann er Szene, Handlung und Empfindung verschmelzen. Gleich in der ersten tritt der Mond auf, und die ganze Idylle ist Sonnenschein. Der *Sturm* ist unerträglich daher. Voltaire kann zu Lausanne aus seinem Bette dem Sturm des Genfer Sees im Spiegel nicht ruhiger zugesehen haben, als die Leute auf dem Felsen, um die das Wetter wütet, sich vice versa detaillieren, was sie beide sehn." (FA 18, 48)

156 "[...] und fand nach Verlauf einer Stunde, daß ich eine wohlgeordnete sehr interessante Zeichnung verfertigt hatte [...]." (26)

aesthetic affirmation of the concentric constellation corresponds to the enlightened [*aufgeklärt*] subject and to a knowledge of the world that is centred around the human sphere of control. As a consequence, the project of writing a weathery novel is inseparable from critically questioning the dominant ideology of the time.

The novel pursues this project in an astonishingly systematic and consistent fashion. Starting from its first pages, it takes several steps to sketch a model that reflects on the constellation that the novel is working on. As we have already seen in our reading of the well-scene, the model attempts to give an account of the two decisive traits that structure the concentric constellation of modern subjectivity: (1) the deceitfulness, the illusoriness induced by its narrow limitations, shutting out the weathery world (including, excess, human passion, love, etc.); (2) its inescapability, its necessity, as a protection, as a condition of the liveability of life. During the process of exploring and problematising this constellation, the novel evokes several images or metaphoric explanations that fill with life the abstract characterisations I have given of this constellation in an earlier section. Perhaps the richest of these images actualises a topos (it may even have substantially contributed to the success story of this topos) that can claim to have traversed modernity from the 18th to the 20th century, and thus apparently has something essential to say of it:

> That human life is but a dream is something that has already occurred to many, and this feeling forever haunts me as well. When I observe the narrow limits in which man's powers of action and investigation are confined; when I see how all our activity aims at satisfying needs that once again have no purpose beyond prolonging our wretched existence; and that all our satisfaction with certain aspects of our investigations is only dreamy resignation, since we merely paint colored shapes and brilliant prospects on the walls that hold us captive – all this, Wilhelm, stuns me into silence. I turn back into myself and discover a world! (27–28)[157]

What had been the deceiving spirits in the well-scene is now replaced by a notion of the dream, both representing the doubtful ontological status of the apparitions, their deceitfulness. The translator's use of the verb *to haunt* to render

---

[157] "Daß das Leben des Menschen nur ein Traum sey, ist manchem schon so vorgekommen, und auch mit mir zieht dieses Gefühl immer herum. Wenn ich die Einschränkung so ansehe, in welche die thätigen und forschenden Kräfte des Menschen eingesperrt sind, wenn ich sehe, wie alle Würksamkeit dahinaus läuft, sich die Befriedigung von Bedürfnissen zu verschaffen, die wieder keinen Zwek haben, als unsere arme Existenz zu verlängern, und dann, daß alle Beruhigung über gewisse Punkte des Nachforschens nur eine träumende Resignation ist, da man sich die Wände zwischen denen man gefangen sizt, mit bunten Gestalten und lichten Aussichten bemahlt. Das alles, Wilhelm, macht mich stumm. Ich kehre in mich selbst zurük, und finde eine Welt!" (22)

Werther's impression that he cannot get rid of the feeling that life is a dream is therefore a happy choice: it emphasises the close connection between these two scenes, one being merely a variation of the other. The variation we get here introduces the topos of 'our painting the walls of our prison' and adds the important observation that the structure of this constellation is intrinsically linked to (an idea of) the constitution of the human being. The "narrow limits" in which we find ourselves "confined" are not outer, oppressive measures violently shutting us in, measures from which we could emancipate ourselves, from which we could break free. The longing for liberation is qualified by the fact that it is "man's" capacities, his "powers of action and investigation" that impose or define these limits. The prison Werther bemoans is the prison of human existence, the very same "narrow circle of [...] existence" (32) that he praised in so affirmative words in the idyllic scene when he encountered the woman and her children in Wahlheim. Man's "wretched existence" that Werther here so desperately complains about will be admired again only a few letters later, when Werther writes of the "simple, innocent bliss of the man who brings to his table the head of cabbage he has grown himself and who now, in a single moment, enjoys [it]" (45). The "inner drive to submit willingly to limitations" is here reformulated as "dreamy resignation". This ambiguity, this oscillating between prison and paradise is not merely a sign for Werther's deranged state of mind; he cannot be blamed for a distorted perception of reality. The topos of man painting the walls of the prison that constitutes his existence provides us with the model that gives an account of this seemingly contradictory oscillation: the idyllic pleasures, these paradisiac moments are nothing but the "colored shapes and brilliant prospects" that we paint "on the walls that hold us captive". Moreover, it is worth noting that this really insightful metaphor of modern human existence, here again, closely associates the idyll's pictorial roots.

The insight involving the deceitfulness of mere "shapes", the insight that our life is but a dream and that our human perceptions do not reach the essence of the world "has already occurred to many", as Werther admits. In fact, his vision of our illusorily living in a prison (without us really noticing it) bears unmistakable resemblances to Plato's famous allegory of the cave. There are, however, two decisive deviations: (1) the shapes are not representations of ideas, are not the shadows of 'something' of a 'truer' nature; they are products of art without a true, verifiable ideal; (2) the basic structure on which the whole constellation is founded is not that of an ascending or descending order of 'things' that teleologically leads towards a highest good as in Plato, but that of a concentric order with man occupying the centre. These two deviations from the Platonic model are obviously closely connected, and they show that the two models come to stand for two completely different views of the world:

Plato's answering the question of knowledge, situating the human being in a cosmological order of truth; and a modern interpretation of the problem of human existence that considers this existence as the very centre, where the human has become the world, without any access to transcendent truth whatsoever.

For our purposes, the question of the source that feeds these models, the instance from where the energy issues that drives the whole thing, is of major interest. In the case of Plato, it is the sun, standing for the highest good, truth; its energy, so to speak, descends the ladder of the order, and finally reaches the humans chained to the rocks, deflected, driving the game of shadows that they take for real. Human art would, according to this linear scheme, be of an even more distant, degraded order, even further away from the sun's pure truth, being merely the shadow's shadow. In Werther's model of man painting his own prison, the source of the deceitful "colored shapes" is man himself. He is not passively watching and, perhaps, imitating what he has seen – it is his painting, his art that brings forth the (deceitful) world. He *is* the captivating prison and the source of "brilliant prospects on the walls that hold [him] captive", at the same time – both form part of the concentric constellation that the novel reconstructs as the constitutive structure of modern subjectivity. In order to emphasise this constellation's seemingly paradoxical unity Werther resorts to an apparatus extremely popular in Goethe's age called the *laterna magica*:

> Wilhelm, what is the world to our heart without love! What a magic lantern is without light! No sooner have you set the little lamp inside than the most colorful pictures glow on your white wall! And if it were nothing more than that – fleeting phantoms – we are always happy when we stand before them like expectant boys and are charmed by these wondrous apparitions. (55–56)[158]

The model of the magic lantern very intuitively helps to understand why the concentric constellation needs limitations for its functioning, how limit and centre intrinsically belong together. In order to produce the "colorful pictures", the idyll, the narrow circle of our world, a "white wall" is needed as a screen on which the centre can project its images. Without a wall at a reasonably short distance from the centre, there are no pictures, that is to say, no objective world, no environment perceivable for the subject, as there are no "colorful pictures" without the subject's emitting energy, without its overflowing, so to speak. This

---

158 "Wilhelm, was ist unserm Herzen die Welt ohne Liebe! Was eine Zauberlaterne ist, ohne Licht! Kaum bringst Du das Lämpgen hinein, so scheinen Dir die buntesten Bilder an deine weiße Wand! Und wenn's nichts wäre als das, als vorübergehende Phantomen, so machts doch immer unser Glük, wenn wir wie frische Bubens davor stehen und uns über die Wundererscheinungen entzükken." (78)

leads to a second important observation. The model of the magic lantern answers a question that came to Werther's mind in the well-scene, the question of "whether deceitful spirits hover around this region or whether it is the warm, divine fantasy in my heart that makes everything around me appear like paradise" (24). In a way, it is both: the "colorful pictures" are indeed "wondrous apparitions", "fleeting phantoms", they are of a ghostly, ontologically doubtful nature; and they are products of our heart, issuing from the centre of the constellation. Moreover, they are products of love – an insight that changes a lot. Had not love and art been paradigmatically associated with the weather's excess, disturbing the idyllic calmness and its constancy of perpetual sunshine? They now turn out to be, literally, at the heart of the constellation. The weather haunts even the most idyllic, weather-free, *aufgeklärte* situation, because its forces fuel the apparatus bringing about the idyll's "colorful pictures", no matter whether painted (art) or projected (love).

This thought is not new to us: in our abstract characterisation of the concentric constellation we have already seen that there is not only an outer limitation warding off the weather, but also a second, inner limitation holding the 'weather' at bay. What Werther however realises in the course of the novel is that the distinction between calm idyll and violent weather does not hold. Both are intrinsically linked: the idyllic calmness is fuelled by the weather's forces – and abruptly ceases to be idyllic calmness when the weather changes. In other words, the well's constant supply of water, independent of the weather that seems to be sealed off from the constellation, is a delusion. That is not say that the idyllic bliss is not 'real'. The "expectant boys[']" being "charmed" does not question the authenticity of that feeling, on the contrary. It, however, indicates the naivety of their limited view of the world: their relation to the world is 'idyllic'. In contrast to Goethe's criticising the genre of the idyll, they do not care for "the spirit weaving the parts together so that each becomes an essential part of the whole", they simply rejoice in the momentary beauty of the detail. For them these beautiful "colorful pictures" are not "fleeting phantoms"; the observation of these "wondrous apparitions[']" fleetingness betrays knowledge of the hidden weatheriness of these seemingly weather-free phenomena. The characteristic uncannyness that is so intrinsically linked to the concentric constellation thus in an astonishingly precise Freudian way indicates the return and the presence of something more than familiar that has been repressed, that has been constitutively banned from the sphere of phenomenal life: the weather. It haunts, as the driving force behind the phenomena, the weather-free world of the idyll, perceivable only in the transitoriness of the world, in its instability, suggesting that with regard to the fleetingness of the idyll's apparitions ontology might better be called 'hauntology' (cf. Derrida 2006, 10).

There are, obviously, two sorts of changing weather that set an end to the (phantoms of) idyllic paradise, heavy weather or draught, too much water, or too little, as Werther very revealingly writes in his only letter addressed to Lotte that reaches her in his lifetime:

> If you could see me, my dearest, in this torrent [*Schwall*] of distractions! How parched [*ausgetrocknet*] my senses are becoming! Not One moment of fullness of the heart, not One blessed hour! nothing! nothing! I stand as if in front of a peep show and see the manikins and tiny horses jerk around in front of me, and I often ask myself whether it is not an optical illusion. (84–85; transl. altered)[159]

At first glance, the dominant water imagery of this passage might appear contradictory: the notion of Werther's senses becoming "parched", their becoming dried up [*ausgetrocknet*], like a well or a reservoir of water can dry up, supported by the idea of the missing "fullness" of his heart, does not seem to comply with the "torrents of distraction" disturbing his life. However, both weathery interventions stop the working of the apparatus: the torrent of distraction troubles the outer limitation from without, thereby preventing it from working as the white wall, the screen for the projections; the drying up of Werther's heart robs the magic lantern of its light, there are no "colorful pictures" without the overflowing "fullness of the heart". Werther's letter thus very well explains the fleetingness of the apparitions, the fact that this apparatus is not an autarkic perpetuum mobile but intimately involved in a complex net of a paradigmatically unstable, weathery world. The idyllic sunshine – that is to say, the functioning of the concentric constellation's apparatus – turns out to be only one, lucky constellation of weather, produced by and corresponding to other constellations and forces, it is part of an ever shifting process of (im)balances.

The passage's changing from the imagery of water to the imagery of optics, once again the suspicion of an "optical illusion", is indicative. It emphasises the fact that the novel resorts to a whole web of images and imagery in order to sketch the complex model of the concentric constellation, consisting of: (1) the notion of the hut whose narrow limitations produce a certain innocent bliss; (2) the notion of the prison, as the underside of the hut; (3) the notion of the *laterna magica*, explaining the connection between the hut's bliss and the prison's suffering; (4) the notion of the well, being a variation of the *laterna magica* image, but closer to the question of weather and nature, thereby also tying in

---

[159] "Wenn Sie mich sähen meine Beste, in dem Schwall von Zerstreuung! Wie ausgetroknet meine Sinnen werden, nicht Einen Augenblik der Fülle des Herzens, nicht Eine selige thränenreiche Stunde. Nichts! Nichts! Ich stehe wie vor einem Raritätenkasten, und sehe die Männgen und Gäulgen vor mir herumrükken, und frage mich oft, ob's nicht optischer Betrug ist." (134)

with the hut's function of providing necessary protection against the weather. Despite the manifold and disparate dimensions of this web, it presents an astonishingly consistent and precise model that is a problematisation (cf. Foucault 1984, 16) of both social and epistemic as well as aesthetic issues and their inseparable interweaving.

As claimed above, Goethe's novel participates with this model in a topos that has established itself as important and influential for the aesthetics of what is called 'modernity': the period of time starting with the middle of the 18th and reaching to the 20th century, at least. In order to grasp the aesthetic dimension of this model and the novel's over-all stance in these debates I would like to quote extensively from quite a late version of this topos, developed by David Henry Lawrence for a foreword he wrote introducing another poet's collection of poems. The closeness to Goethe's *Werther* is remarkable, despite the fact that Lawrence writes about poetry and Werther's reflections on art are very likely to be self-reflectively aiming at the genre of the novel. Lawrence's claim that "[t]he essential quality of poetry is that it makes a new effort of attention and 'discovers' a new world within the known world" (2005, 109) strikingly resonates with Werther's "I turn back into myself and discover a world!" (28), all the more so since this sentence from *Werther* is the last sentence of the passage where the novel develops the topos that we find again in Lawrence. It therefore appears very likely that Lawrence was directly inspired by Goethe's novel. For my purposes here, however, I do not want to pursue the question of influence but take Lawrence's version of the topos as a text that sheds light on Werther's reflections concerning the world, especially with regard to the connection of poetics/aesthetics and the weather. In other words, I treat Lawrence's text as a way of reading Goethe's novel, no matter whether it actually is a reading and rewriting of it, or whether I make it into one by grouping the two versions of the topos together in my reading of *Werther*. The foreword from which the following passage is taken is titled "Chaos in Poetry":

> Man, and the animals, and the flowers, all live within a strange and forever-surging chaos. The chaos which we have got used to, we call a cosmos. The unspeakable inner chaos of which we are composed we call consciousness, and mind, and even civilisation. But it is, ultimately, chaos, lit up by visions, or not lit up by visions. Just as the rainbow may or may not light up the storm. And like the rainbow, the vision perisheth.
>
> But man cannot live in chaos. The animals can. To the animal, all is chaos, only there are a few recurring motions and aspects within the surge. And the animal is content. But man is not. Man must wrap himself in a vision, make a house of apparent form and stability, fixity. In his terror of chaos, he begins by putting up an umbrella between himself and the everlasting whirl. Then he paints the under-side of his umbrella like a firmament. Then he parades around, lives and dies under his umbrella. Bequeathed to his descendants, the umbrella becomes a dome, a vault, and men at last begin to feel that something is wrong.

> Man fixes some wonderful erection of his own between himself and the wild chaos, and gradually goes bleached and stifled under his parasol. Then comes a poet, enemy of convention, and makes a slit in the umbrella; and lo! the glimpse of chaos is a vision, a window to the sun. But after a while, getting used to the vision, and not liking the genuine draught from chaos, commonplace man daubs a simulacrum of the window that opens on to chaos, and patches the umbrella with the painted patch of the simulacrum. That is, he has got used to the vision, it is part of his house-decoration. So that the umbrella at last looks like a glowing open firmament, of many aspects. But alas, it is all simulacrum, in innumerable patches. Homer and Keats, annotated and with glossary.
>
> This is the history of poetry in our era. Some-one sees Titans in the wild air of chaos, and the Titan becomes a wall between succeeding generations and the chaos they should have inherited. The wild sky moved and sang. Even that became a great umbrella between mankind and the sky of fresh air; then it became a painted vault, a fresco on a vaulted roof, under which men bleach and go dissatisfied. Till another poet makes a slit on to the open and windy chaos. (Lawrence 2005, 109–110)

Lawrence's allegorical myth of (modern) man first of all claims the human necessity of building himself a hut: man cannot live within chaos; he must "make a house of apparent form and stability, fixity". The similarity to Werther's "setting up a little hut at some cozy spot" (29) is emphasised by the fact that man not only lives "within" chaos, that is to say, is surrounded by chaos, but that there is also an "inner chaos" of which he is "composed". The vision of calmness, of "stability, fixity", is therefore standing in-between chaos, limited by chaos from two sides, as it is in Goethe's novel. The fact that man "begins by putting up an umbrella between himself and the everlasting whirl" or a parasol against the sun's forces tells us that for Lawrence chaos and weathery forces are one and the same thing: throughout the myth weathery forces are used to convey what he calls "open and windy chaos", no matter whether it is standing for the dangerous dimension of chaos, its "wild air" against which one has to be protected, or its "fresh air" that is so much longed for. It is this complex encounter with the weather, the fact that it proves a double, dialectical driving force for the emergence of culture that accounts for the culture-theoretical potential of the myth. Lawrence narrates a double story of cultural production: on the one hand, by protecting against the weather a productive force is unleashed, "the umbrella becomes a dome, a vault", or rather a "painted vault, a fresco"; on the other hand, the claustrophobic fear, or rather awareness, arises that by protecting against the weather man is in fact "completing [his] own painted prison" (Lawrence 2005, 110).

Lawrence has not invented this culture-theoretical idea that focuses on the contact-zone of man and weather: it had already been discussed and was even very likely to have been developed in the Straßburg circle of Herder and Goethe. The most concise summary of these reflections, revolving around writing the myth of the origins of northern art and culture, is given by Goethe in his autobiographical retrospect on this period of his life:

> If [the Greeks and Romans], living under a more favourable sky, allowed their roof to rest upon columns, a wall, broken through, arose of its own accord. We, however, who must always protect ourselves against the weather, and everywhere surround ourselves with walls, have to revere the genius who discovered the means of endowing massive walls with variety, of apparently breaking them through, and of thus occupying the eye in a worthy and pleasing manner on the broad surface. (1848, 441)[160]

Goethe here summarises his text called "Von Deutscher Baukunst" that appeared in Herder's collection *Von Deutscher Art und Kunst* (1773c). It is surrounded there by Herder's famous essays on Ossian and Shakespeare that both pursue the same project of founding a 'northern' style of art, and both also resort decisively to the role of the weather. In order to testify to this observation and to give evidence of the important connection to weather and Shakespeare, here is the famous beginning of Herder's essay on 'the Bard':

> If any man brings to mind that tremendous image of one "seated high atop some craggy eminence, whirlwinds, tempest, and the roaring sea at his feet, but with the flashing skies about his head," that man is Shakespeare! (Herder 2006, 291)[161]

Furthermore, the idea of the differences of Greek and northern architecture that Goethe has worked out in his essay seems to be alluded to in Herder's essay as well, when he writes: "You would say to Sophocles: 'Paint the sacred panels of this altar! And you, O northern bard, cover every side and every wall of this temple with your immortal fresco!'" (Herder 2006, 298)[162] It is therefore not surprising to find this debate continued in Goethe's *Werther*, a novel heavily imbued with the intellectual debates kindled in Straßburg. The project involved here is, however, much more radical than Goethe's retrospective summary or Herder's praise of Shakespeare: the novel is not content with creating the illusion

---

[160] "Wenn jene [Griechen und Römer], unter einem glücklicheren Himmel, ihr Dach auf Säulen ruhen ließen, so entstand ja schon an und für sich eine durchbrochene Wand. Wir aber, die wir uns durchaus gegen die Witterung schützen, und mit Mauern überall umgeben müssen, haben den Genius zu verehren, der Mittel fand, massiven Wänden Mannigfaltigkeit zu geben, sie dem Scheine nach zu durchbrechen und das Auge würdig und erfreulich auf der großen Fläche zu beschäftigen." (FA 14, 553)

[161] "Wenn bey einem Manne mir jenes ungeheure Bild einfällt: 'hoch auf einen [sic] Felsengipfel sitzend! zu seinen Füssen, Sturm, Ungewitter und Brausen des Meers; aber sein Haupt in den Strahlen des Himmels!' so ists bey Shakespear!" (Herder 1773b, 74)

[162] "Würdest zu Sophokles sagen: mahle das heilige Blatt dieses Altars! und du o nordischer Barde alle Seiten und Wände dieses Tempels in dein unsterbliches Fresko!" (Herder 1773b, 92)

of "breaking [...] through" "the massive walls with variety [*dem Scheine nach zu durchbrechen*]". On the contrary, as we have seen, the novel dismantles and bemoans this illusion: "we merely paint colored shapes and brilliant prospects [*lichte Aussichten*] on the walls that hold us captive" (28), Werther writes. In contrast to architecture, the medium of literature promises to allow for a 'real' 'breakthrough', replacing "dreamy resignation" with the adventure of facing the weather, of facing uncontrollable chaos. Again, in a rather qualifying and distanced fashion, Goethe describes this awakening or new aesthetic impulse in his autobiography, looking back at the years of his *Sturm und Drang* period:

> More than ever was I directed to the open world and to free nature. On my way I sang to myself strange hymns and dithyrambics, of which one entitled "The Wanderer's Stormsong" (*Wanderer's Sturmlied*) still remained. This half-nonsense I sang aloud, in an impassioned manner, when I found myself in a terrific storm, which I was obliged to meet. (1848, 453)[163]

This being "directed to the open world" is not merely a personal habit of the young Goethe, for a period of time preferring outdoor experiences to the calmness of the reading chair, but also, and more importantly, a poetological principle; a poetological principle whose 'strangeness' or rather radicalism and high costs the novel *Werther* sets out to explore. The re-discovery of the weather, of the unruly, the chaotic does not merely invite a simple re-appropriation: the story of excess and its deadly consequences that *Werther* relates must be read as an expedition that brings home troubling, but certainly unclear results. Venturing beyond the walls of the prison implies a split that separates aesthetics from the sphere of the ideal, from the sphere of the moral and even from the sphere of the liveable.

To be sure, the distinction between "commonplace man" and the poet, or the artist, the genius that Lawrence's myth is based on can be found already in Goethe's novel: with the "sedate gentlemen" using "dams and flood channels to ward off the impending threat of danger" countered by the "torrent of the genius". However, Goethe's later skepticism towards his early novel and the critical reactions of many readers indicate that for him and his contemporaries the role of the artist (and that is to say the role of art) in society is still far from being solely defined as "mak[ing] slits in the umbrella", creating weathery visions. As we have seen, Goethe also participates in the "paint[ing] [of] the

---

[163] "Mehr als jemals war ich gegen offene Welt und Natur gerichtet. Unterwegs sang ich mir seltsame Hymnen und Dithyramben, wovon noch eine, unter dem Titel Wanderers Sturmlied, übrig ist. Ich sang diesen Halbunsinn leidenschaftlich vor mich hin, da mich ein schreckliches Wetter unterwegs traf, dem ich entgegen gehn mußte." (FA 14, 567)

under-side of [this] umbrella": he contributes to the idyllic, despite dismantling its status as a "simulacrum". These are the important historical differences separating Goethe's 18th century novel from Lawrence's 20th century essay. However, the comparison of the two versions of the same topos specifies the role that the novel plays for the development of a modern aesthetics, leading the way towards the 19th and 20th century, towards a new, a different distribution of the sensible (cf. Rancière 2000), towards a different understanding of art. As the topos we have been looking at underlines, the weather and art's relation to it play a decisive role for this shift of paradigms. Again, an affinity of art and the weather develops and is realised – an affinity, however, that could not differ more from the alliance of weather and theatre that Shakespeare spells out in *The Tempest*. In the early modern age the weather had been a most familiar phenomenon: culturally, theologically and also epistemically a well established central category of life and of the organisation and conceptualisation of the world. This changes fundamentally with the rise of the Enlightenment: in a world grouped around the human being, 'his' ratio and control, the weather becomes a problem, repressed, 'othered', driven to the margins or even effaced. Literature, discovering the weather for itself thus sets out to reach beyond the familiar, beyond the accessible, beyond the human sphere, that is, beyond the controllable.

In order to shed some light on the historical differences of the weather's role in the understanding of the world and the status of human or artistic reference to it, I would like to introduce a visual engagement with this problem. The wood engraving I have in mind has had a remarkable career as a mysterious emblem for many different purposes, but has, to my knowledge, not yet been read in the way I would like to present it: as another manifestation of the topos of the idyllic prison we found in *Werther* and in Lawrence's essay. Despite being often considered as stemming from the Middle Ages, it in fact first appeared as one of around three hundred illustrations in Camille Flammarion's monograph *L'atmosphère. Météorologie populaire* (1888). It features in the chapter called "La forme du ciel", where it illustrates a short passage that relates the story of a medieval anchorite reaching the point where the sky and earth touch, a story that Flammarion uses to refute this sort of superstitious knowledge. I reproduce it here, including the caption that accompanies it in Flammarion's book.

Although the technique of wood engraving, invented at the end of the 18th century for the purposes of printing, establishes a definitive frame for dating this illustration, speculations about a medieval or Renaissance predecessor have not decreased. These speculations are nurtured by two indicators: (1) the style and iconography of the engraving, which is clearly modelled on pre-modern precursors; (2) the conception of the world depicted that looks so medieval to our eyes. The second aspect, however, should have revoked these speculations, once

Un missionnaire du moyen âge raconte qu'il avait trouvé le point
où le ciel et la Terre se touchent...

Figure 1: "Un missionaire du moyen âge raconte qu'il avait trouvé le point où le ciel et la Terre se touchent...". Taken from Camille Flammarion, *L'atmosphère. Météorologie populaire* (1888), page 163. Photo Deutsches Museum Munich.

and for all: the worldview represented on the engraving is not at all medieval, for several reasons. We are given here, on the contrary, a characteristically modern world projected back into a medieval iconography. The idea that the world is flat, a disk, and that the firmament covers it like a cheese dome is not medieval. Since antiquity the conception of the earth as a sphere, surrounded by several other spheres had been well established, and it is only modernity that invents this 'medieval', unenlightened 'other'. The following Renaissance woodcut depicting a medieval conception of the cosmos testifies to this assertion.

The first visual impression already makes us aware of a fundamental difference to Flammarion's wood edging: Cortes's model of the cosmos does not know an outside. The degree of perfection increases from the centre to the outer spheres: the earth and the elemental spheres of "Aer" and "Fyer" are imperfect,

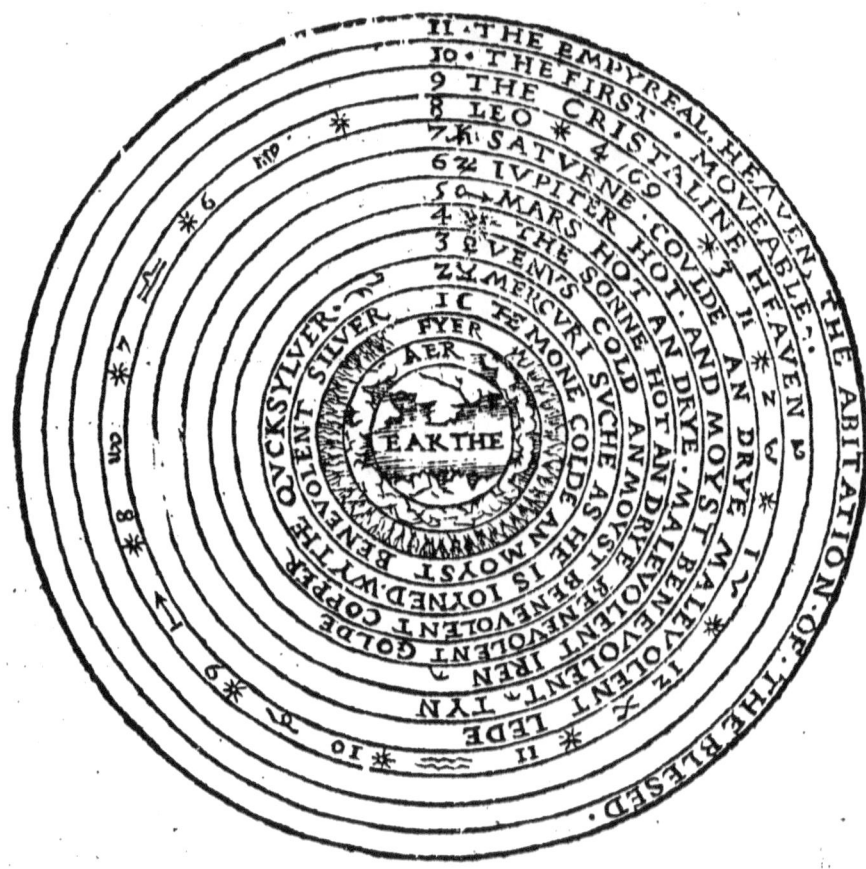

Figure 2: Taken from Martin Cortes, *The Arte of Navigation* (1572), fol. viii.

indicated by the non-spherical patterns (i.e. the oceans, clouds and flames) filling these 'locations', the sphere of the "Moone" serves as a liminal sphere, followed by the perfect planetary and celestial spheres. Against the background of this Renaissance model that depicts a conception of the world compatible with Aristotle's thinking and therefore also reflects the medieval state of the art, the organisation of the world in Flammarion's wood engraving must appear odd: Why should there be this apparent 'chaos' 'behind' the firmament? Where does this limit, this distinction between an inside and an outside, come from? What about the earthly, elemental imperfection and the heavenly perfection?

The picture's composition is dominated by the boundary/limitation whose transgression the story narrates. Inside the boundary/limitation, we find the stars, the moon and the sun shining on a beautiful landscape settled by humans, as the houses, fields and churches indicate. The opulent plants in the foreground of the right corner and especially the central, oversized tree give this rural scenery not only an idyllic, but also a paradisiac appearance. It seems to be much more difficult to characterise the realm beyond the boundary/limitation. As the missionary's groping gesture of the right hand might signal, this realm appears to be still waiting for exploration; it is at least not easily recognisable for the viewer. What we do see is the organisation of parallel or concentric strata, clearly not oriented towards the same centre as the firmament. The patterns of these strata are much more abstract than the rather iconic representation of stars, moon and sun on the other side of the boundary/limitation. Some of the patterns look familiar: the stratum close to the missionary's hand seems to consist of icicles, the most dominant icons of this realm are the clouds in the middle of the strata and also to the left of the missionary's head. These icons, icicles and clouds, betray what the ominous realm is actually all about: paradoxically enough, this is the part of the picture imbued with the most detailed references to medieval knowledge, knowledge that has become obscure to our modern eyes. What we tend to read as chaos actually depicts the strata of the air (in Martin Cortes's model the first sphere surrounding what he calls "Earthe"). This realm of the air, as the place where the weather was engendered (and with the weather, the circulation of life in general) was not conceptualised as homogenous:

> Th'Aire, hoste of Mistes, the bounding Tennis-ball.
> That stormie Tempests tosse and play with-all,
> Of winged Clouds the wide inconstant House,
> Th'un-setled Kingdome of swift *AElous*,
> Great Ware-house of the Winds, whose traffike gives
> Motion of life to every thing that lives,
> Is not through-out all one: our Sages
> Have fitly parted it into three Stages:
> [...]
> Whereof, because the Highest still is driven
> With violence of the *First-moving* Heaven,
> [...]
> And also seated next the Fierie vault,
> It by the learned very hot is thought.
> That, which we touch, with Times doth variate,
> Now hot, now cold, and sometimes temperate;
> [...]
> But now, because the middle-Region's set
> Farre from the Fierie feelings flagrant heat,
> And also from the warme reverberation
> Which aye the Earth reflects in divers fashion;
> That Circle shivers with eternall cold: (Sylvester 1605, 45–46)

With this knowledge in mind, the seemingly chaotic realm beyond the limitation reveals some sort of organisation: the lowest "Stage[ ]" that the missionary literally "touch[es]" is indeed the least homogeneous, the white area there appears to be similar to the temperate region on the other side of the boundary/limitation; however, the cloud at the missionary's chin disrupts the picture. Is it moving vertically, as indicated by the parallel perpendicular lines, is it raining? Does it represent the rising vapours and exhalations? The icicles mark the beginning of the middle region of the air, a circle "shiver[ing] with eternall cold" that is responsible for the condensation of clouds and the brewing of hail and thunderstorms. The rays issuing from the half-circle in the upper region of that realm apparently indicate the hotness close to the "Fiery vault". In other words, what we see to the left of the boundary/limitation is exactly what Cortes tries to depict in his model with the strange, irregular patterns that fill the elemental spheres of "AER" and "FYER". Flammarion's engraving thus bans the irregularity of the imperfect, elemental spheres beyond the boundary of the firmament; the spheres that according to the ancient and medieval system of the world are actually the spheres closest to the human being, himself composed of elements and subjected to the processes of time, weather and death. Quiet, unchangeable perfection seems to govern the paradisiac, idyllic landscape on the right side of the picture: the whole idyll is sunshine, as Goethe would say. There are no clouds, no weather, just the celestial bodies of stars, moon and sun all grouped together in one, single moment, in an unreal ideality.

Perfection on earth, imperfect chaos, the weather, the elemental beyond the firmament – all this is an absurd inversion of the medieval conception of the world. So either the engraving goes back to a fantastic, parodying medieval predecessor, dislocating the contemporary worldview, turning it upside down, mixing it up in a carnivalesque spirit, or, and that is what I would argue for, the wood engraving does not depict a medieval world at all. It is a decisively modern world we get to see. A world that our reading of Goethe's *Werther* has made us familiar with. So much so that I think Flammarion's illustration could stand as an emblem for the project of this novel.

We see the construction of a perfect world, an idyll that is defined by a limitation/boundary that bans the forces of imperfection, of the weather and chaos beyond its defining limitation. In Flammarion's engraving this boundary indeed "looks like a glowing open firmament" (Lawrence 2005, 110) – but rather fulfils, again confirming Lawrence's myth, the function of an "umbrella": *écran* and *écrin* at the same time (cf. Derrida 1972, 380), *Schirm* [umbrella/screen], shielding off the weathery chaos that storms without, protecting the precious idyllic inside, and serving as a screen for the idyllic projection of glittering stars within. The distribution of light inside the idyllic sphere emphasises its concentric organisation: the source of light, here the sun, occupies a central position, the light radiating from there fades the more it approaches the firmament's dark boundary. Geometrically, it is, however, not the sun, but the human settlement, the village with the spire near the picture's right corner, that occupies the place closest to the centre of this concentric constellation. The pious Christian is to choose this centre as 'his' 'Wahlheim', there to savour the bliss of this paradisiac 'world' and thank God for his benevolence. The missionary whose story the engraving 'relates', is obviously not content with living a calm life at the blissful centre. Something, probably his curiosity or a "desire to expand, make new discoveries" (44), drives him to the margin, to the 'point where the sky and the earth touch each other'. The paradisiac world seems to be too narrow to him.

On whose mission is this missionary? He is, for certain, not a philosopher. His point of interest could not be more distant from the sun's light of truth; it is at his back, shining from where he had departed. In fact, Flammarion's edging presents us with a sort of inversion of Plato's allegory of the cave: although both, Plato's philosopher and Flammarion's missionary (that is to say Lawrence's artist and Goethe's Werther) discover their familiar world as "all simulacrum" (Lawrence 2005, 110), as painted "colored shapes and brilliant prospects on the walls that hold us captive" (28), their points of departure and their destination are mixed up. The missionary does not aspire to sighting the perfect, the highest of goods, the stable and everlasting sphere of ideas. On the contrary, it is the stable, the idyll's eternal sunshine that he leaves behind, poking his nose into the "fresh air" of "forever-surging chaos", discovering the weather's imperfect, whirling forces banned behind the umbrella of the firmament. Despite the engraving's caption, Flammarion's missionary does not settle for finding the point where sky and earth touch; his aim obviously consists in reaching beyond the boundary. Has he used his hiking stick to "make[ ] a slit on to the open and windy chaos"? He is at least not merely peeping through a crevice in the firmament, but has forced head and shoulders through an opening that indeed looks as if the firmament's parchment had been violently broken through, as if it had been torn. As his groping right hand indicates (and as we, as viewers, can vividly co-experience) this realm beyond the boundary, in contrast to the idyll world, cannot merely be viewed, regarded. What he 'sees' (and what we see) is of a different order. In fact, there is nothing to see, really, nothing to represent, nothing to bring back to the idyll in the form of pictures or postcards to be marvelled at. The "Great Ware-house of the Winds, whose traffike gives | Motion of life to every thing that lives," is rather to be encountered – a troubling, upsetting encounter: the windy "traffike" of this weathery realm, giving "Motion of life to every thing that lives" has not been banned beyond the enlightened sphere of the human, idyllic world, beyond this sphere of knowledge and control, without reason. The outer realm's weathery forces, driving life, driving generation, bringing forth the opulent, idyllic beauty of nature, also uncontrollably drive corruption, change and death; they undermine the illusion of control, of everlasting sunshine. The message that the missionary Werther brings home from his eccentric explorations to the weathery realm (despite the ecstatic joys of his weathery waltz) is pessimistic and disillusioning, at best:

> It is as if a curtain had been drawn back from my soul, and the spectacle of infinite life is transformed before my eyes into the abyss of an ever-open grave. Can you say: This is what is! since everything passes, since everything rolls on with the swiftness of a passing storm [*mit der Wetterschnelle vorüber rollt*], so rarely does the entire force of its existence last, oh! torn along into the river and submerged and shattered on the rocks? There is no moment that does not consume you and those near and dear to you, no moment when you are not a destroyer, must be one. (70)[164]

Werther's insistence on the fact that "[t]here is no moment" not also haunted by the weather, by time and corruption is important: it qualifies "the simple, innocent bliss" he had described as "all rolled into one", "single moment" when describing the joy of eating the cabbage grown by man himself (45). The missionary's impressions from beyond the boundary/limitation do therefore not *complete* the picture of nature that the idyll, for its pictorial foundation, could not adequately draw. The problem is not a problem of representation, the task does not consist in representing the negativity or the movement of nature, as Stephan Pabst claims (2010, 23). It is also not primarily a problem of the artistic medium (Lawrence's artist can be poet or painter), although the literary medium seems to be well suited for the task, perhaps better than the visual arts. What the missionary discovers beyond the boundary is a supplement, in the strict Derridean understanding of this concept (cf. Derrida 1967). An element is missing, shut out, barred, unrepresented; an element, or rather an open set of forces that cannot be represented, that is of a different, deeper, more fundamental order than the world of representations. These forces, without anyone taking notice, are rather doing something, working, behind the scenes; without which, however, the phenomenal, representable present inside the boundary would not be there, would not function. All the missionary can do is give testimony of these

---

[164] "Es hat sich vor meiner Seele wie ein Vorhang weggezogen, und der Schauplatz des unendlichen Lebens verwandelt sich vor mir in den Abgrund des ewig offnen Grabs. Kannst du sagen: Das ist! da alles vorübergeht, da alles mit der Wetterschnelle vorüber rollt, so selten die ganze Kraft seines Daseyns ausdauert, ach in den Strom fortgerissen wird. Das ist kein Augenblick, der nicht dich verzehrte und die Deinigen um dich her, kein Augenblick, da du nicht ein Zerstöhrer bist, seyn mußt." (106–108)

supplementary forces: a difficult task, since this is not a question of widening the sphere of representation, that is to say the human, enlightened sphere of control, but demands an art beyond the simulacrum. This art does not primarily *represent* the weather: it is impossible to control and to capture the "swiftness of a passing storm" without taming it, without missing what it essentially is all about. To put it in an exaggerated way: the weather, as weather cannot be represented; as a representation it turns into landscape, no matter whether idyllic, sublime or terrifying. An art beyond the simulacrum therefore is rather 'doing' this weather, acting as a supplement to the ordered, enlightened sphere of human control.

As Gilles Deleuze, an emphatic reader of Lawrence's myth, writes, "[i]n order to have seen Life in the living or the Living in the lived, the novelist or painter returns with reddened eyes, short of breath" (1991, 163; my transl.).[165] To these reddened eyes, once they have been exposed to the weathery realm beyond the boundary, the "splendid nature" of the idyll looks different:

> oh! when this splendid nature stands before me as rigid as a lacquered miniature, and all the glory cannot pump one drop of happiness from my heart into my brain, and this fellow here stands before the countenance of God like a well run dry, like a broken pail. I have often thrown myself on the ground and begged God for tears, like a farmer for rain when the heavens loom iron-colored above him and the earth all around him is dying of thirst. (107)[166]

The "glory" of "splendid" nature cannot cure the missionary from his insight into the fatal "swiftness of a passing storm" present in every moment of natural proceedings. On the contrary, against this background the illusion of idyllic stability can only dismantle itself as a "lacquered miniature", again clearly alluding to the genre of the idyll that stands paradigmatically for this narrow and naïve view of the world. In other words, the absence, the lack of the weather's enlivening forces becomes tangible, the weather's forces as a repressed, silenced supplement cannot be denied any longer. The supplement makes itself felt, at the latest when the feeding of the wells and pails of the concentric constellation fails and the working of the apparatus comes to a halt.

---

165 "[…] pour avoir vu la Vie dans le vivant ou le Vivant dans le vécu, le romancier ou le peintre reviennent les yeux rouges, le souffle court" (Deleuze and Guattari 1991, 163).
166 "o wenn da diese herrliche Natur so starr vor mir steht wie ein lakirt Bildgen, und all die Wonne keinen Tropfen Seligkeit aus meinem Herzen herauf in das Gehirn pumpen kann, und der ganze Kerl vor Gottes Angesicht steht wie ein versiegter Brunn, wie ein verlechter Eymer! Ich habe mich so oft auf den Boden geworfen und Gott um Thränen gebeten, wie ein Akkersmann um Regen, wenn der Himmel ehern über ihm ist und um ihn die Erde verdürstet." (178)

And yet, despite the seemingly catastrophic consequences, the missionary has accomplished his mission. It would not have been better to leave the margins of the human sphere alone, not at all. More than that, I would assert that the novel as a whole affirms this mission, although the costs for the missionary turn out to be high. The novel has not only set the readers' circulation of bodily fluids into motion – most of them, certainly, did not have to throw themselves "on the ground and beg[ ] God for tears"; it has also developed an artistic relation to the world that is not merely "lacquered miniature", but takes a broader, an emphatically aesthetic perspective, a perspective that markedly differs from established social or moral, worldly perspectives. This perspective is 'weathery' not only because it moves its readers, as Shakespeare's theatre moved its audience. It is weathery, because it critically supplements the established organisation of life and world, it reaches beyond the sphere of human control and order. It discovers, experiments with and exposes its readers to forces that have increasingly been banned from human life, that have almost ceased to exist in the modern organisation of the human sphere. The role of the weather as the most intuitive of these forces surely has to do with the development of art as an autonomous realm, that is to say as a realm with a specific, differentiated perspective on the world that can then even be attributed a social function:

> What about the poets, then, at this juncture? They reveal the inward desire of mankind. What do they reveal? – They show the desire for chaos, and the fear of chaos. The desire of chaos is the breath of their poetry. The fear of chaos is in their parade of forms and technique. (Lawrence 2005, 111)

Viewing the reactions to the novel, it has indeed raised fears. Not only in the majority of its audience, but apparently also in its author. With regard to Goethe, Lawrence might have a point, listing the "parade of forms and technique" as a poetological response to this "fear of chaos". Werther, however, lived his desire: "he does not search for a roof that protects him from tempests, nor some earth where he could take roots, his dream is flying" (Neppi 2010, 316; my transl.).

4 At the limits of human nature – the novel's storm and urge

The novel's resonances with Flammarion's engraving or D. H. Lawrence's modern myth of the poet (both cultural phenomena emerging quite some time later than Goethe's *Werther*) have made us aware of a central problem that Goethe addresses with his novel as early as the last third of the 18th century:

the problem of the human sphere, and more precisely, the human sphere as it is defined by its limitations. As I have attempted to demonstrate in the preceding sections, this problem is almost omnipresent, at least implicitly, through the important topology of what I have called the concentric constellation, a topology that structures the novel's proceedings from the first to the last page. Besides this latent configuration, its topological structuring and the questions of transgression and restitution that are acted out in the novel, there is, however, also another dimension of addressing this central problem of the human: Werther's letters assemble some very pertinent, explicit reflections on the topic, whether in the form of reported conversations (or rather arguments) with Albert, or as Werther's private reflections on life and the world that he brings to paper and passes on to the letters' addressees. These reflections revolve around one decisive question:

> What is man, the celebrated demigod! Does he not lack strength precisely where he needs it most? And if he soars upward in joy or sinks down in sorrow, will he not be arrested in both, just there, just then, brought back to dull, cold consciousness when he was longing to lose himself in the fullness of the infinitude? (115)[167]

With the question, 'What is man?' Werther raises an issue that is at the heart of contemporary epistemological debates. According to Michel Foucault's famous distinction of three epistemes (cf. Foucault 1966), Goethe's novel is written in a time when the most recent of the three, the modern episteme that takes 'man' as its focal point for organising knowledge, is about to emerge. The role of the question 'What is man?' in Werther's reflections confirms Foucault's observation. As we will see, Werther very clearly argues his point as part of an on-going contemporary discussion, he refers to opposing standpoints and takes a very individual, poetologically interesting stance.

In order to trace Werther's argument and situate it in the contemporary debates, I would like to introduce a passage from a philosophical classic, from Immanuel Kant's *Critique of Pure Reason*. Kant's so-called first critique appeared seven years after *Werther* so that taking it as a background for contrasting Werther's position must certainly face reproaches of anachronism. Kant's whole critical project can, however (and this is a well established topos for attempts to

---

[167] "Was ist der Mensch? der gepriesene Halbgott! Ermangeln ihm nicht da eben die Kräfte, wo er sie am nöthigsten braucht? Und wenn er in Freude sich aufschwingt, oder im Leiden versinkt, wird er nicht in beyden eben da aufgehalten, eben da wieder zu dem stumpfen kalten Bewusstseyn zurük gebracht, da er sich in der Fülle des Unendlichen zu verliehren sehnte." (192)

locate Kant in the history of philosophy) be understood as emerging from these debates about the role of man, debates that precede his book by at least a decade if not much longer. With his critical project Kant provides a 'late' response to the question 'What is man'; he, in hindsight, so to speak, develops an impressively consistent answer to the issues of a debate that he observes and comprehends from some distance. It is, one could argue, this 'belatedness' that makes such an elaborate, complex, all-encompassing, and, most of all, conclusive answer possible. Kant's position therefore very well sums up the solutions that these debates have brought forward, and that have given birth to the view of the world that is still formative for our self-understanding today. Here is the passage that introduces the important distinction of *phaenomena* and *noumena* and thus holds an important architectonic place in the book:

> We have now not only traveled through the land of pure understanding, and carefully inspected each part of it, but we have also measured it, and determined the place for each thing in it. This land, however, is an island, and enclosed in unalterable boundaries by nature itself. It is the land of truth (a charming name), surrounded by a broad and stormy ocean, the true seat of illusion, where many a fog bank and rapidly melting ice pretend to be new lands and, ceaselessly deceiving with empty hopes the voyager looking around for new discoveries, entwine him in adventures from which he can never escape and yet also never bring to an end. (Kant 1998 [1787], 338–339; transl. altered)[168]

As is typical for Kant, he employs a topographic metaphor for explaining a complicated philosophical problem. The basic structure that Kant sketches must look familiar to readers of Goethe's novel: the image of the island surrounded by the sea takes up the same circular structure we so often encounter in *Werther*. As Kant emphasises, the decisive, the defining element for this sort of organisation is the limit, the fact that this island is "enclosed in unalterable boundaries by nature itself". It is these boundaries and their acknowledgement that grant stability to the sphere enclosed by them (this is, in one sentence, Kant's ingenious philosophical insight). The topography that he maps out is divided into two parts: (1) the inner sphere of the island with its stable ground that can be subjected

---

[168] "Wir haben jetzt das Land des reinen Verstandes nicht allein durchreiset und jeden Theil davon sorgfältig in Augenschein genommen, sondern es auch durchmessen und jedem Dinge auf demselben seine Stelle bestimmt. Dieses Land aber ist eine Insel, und durch die Natur selbst in unveränderliche Grenzen eingeschlossen. Es ist das Land der Wahrheit (ein reizender Name), umgeben von einem weiten und stürmischen Oceane, dem eigentlichen Sitze des Scheins, wo manche Nebelbank, und manches bald wegschmelzende Eis neue Länder lügt und, indem es den auf Entdeckungen herumschwärmenden Seefahrer unaufhörlich mit leeren Hoffnungen täuscht, ihn in Abenteuer verflechtet, von denen er niemals ablassen, und sie doch auch niemals zu Ende bringen kann." (Kant 1968 [1787], 202)

completely to the mastery of pure understanding and (2) the "broad and stormy ocean" that lacks this stability and must thus be regarded as dangerous. What makes Kant's topographic metaphor so interesting for our purposes is the fact that 'the weather' takes a leading role in this metaphorical layout. As in Goethe's novel, it is the defining feature of the outer realm beyond the boundary, no matter whether in the shape of the "stormy ocean", the "fog bank" of illusion or the melting ice. It comes to signify the dynamics, the changeability of this region that contradicts the island's stability of truth. Viewed from the safe soil of the island with the expectancy of stable, solid, timeless truth, this region must appear as "the true seat of illusion". This region of illusion, however, cannot merely be viewed from safe soil – that is what makes it so dangerous. As Kant emphasises, it exerts a strong attracting force that lures the mariner, "deceiving [him] with empty hopes", "entwin[ing] him in adventures from which he can never escape". Astonishingly enough, the force that draws the mariner, the adventurer, the human being beyond the realm of pure understanding, beyond the realm where he is in control, is regarded by Kant to be almost as fundamental, as stable and invincible as the "unalterable boundaries" set by nature.

Is not Werther an incarnation of this centrifugal force? The passage where he muses upon the question of 'what is man?' clearly articulates his disdain for the safe soil of Kant's island of pure understanding: will man not be "brought back to dull, cold consciousness when he was longing to lose himself in the fullness of the infinitude?"

There is, however, a decisive difference between what Kant is aiming at with his topographic metaphor and what Werther is striving for: Kant's question is the question of truth and knowledge of the truth, he focuses on the epistemological foundations of human life, whereas Werther's longing for the infinite is of a more general nature. The limits Kant speaks of are limits of secure knowledge, whereas for Werther, these limits encompass all sorts of different, normalising limits of 'experience'. As his critique of the "cold consciousness" already indicates, the perhaps most important limit he experiences concerns the sentiments and passions: "Human nature [...] has its limits: it can endure joy, sorrow, pain up to a certain degree, and it perishes the minute *it* is exceeded." (65)[169] Werther however does not merely explicate these limits given by nature and bemoans the limited sphere of human life. Despite the fact that these limits seem to be inscribed in human nature, transgressions do take place, they form part of human life as well: not only as the calculated transgressions of the adventurer who follows the longing for the beyond, like Kant's mariners; transgressions can

---

[169] "Die menschliche Natur, fuhr ich fort, hat ihre Gränzen, sie kann Freude, Leid, Schmerzen, bis auf einen gewissen Grad ertragen, und geht zu Grunde, sobald der überstiegen ist." (98)

also involve the human being without his or her consent, suddenly he or she finds him/herself overwhelmed by uncontrollable forces:

> Look at a man within his limitations, the way impressions affect him, ideas become entrenched in him, until finally a growing passion robs him of all his powers of calm reflection and destroys him. (65)[170]

The excessive cannot be evaded; as Kant so unreservedly admits, man "can never escape" coming into contact with these excessive, uncontrollable forces as he can "never bring [this adventure] to an end". In other words, these forces cannot be colonised, cannot be appropriated by the stable realm of pure understanding. Kant has found a creative way of dealing with these forces, whose efficacy he nevertheless acknowledges as part of reality: he divides the waters from the land, the stable from the weathery dynamics of the fluid, thereby creating a realm controllable by reason, banning the untameable rest beyond the "unalterable boundaries". It is this move that establishes the stable distinction between (secure knowledge of) truth and illusion. Kant's idea of using the inaccessible side of the distinction to find philosophical space for making human freedom possible and thinkable must be regarded as both original and ingenious; the production of stability by introducing a limiting distinction, that is to say by a movement of exclusion, belongs, however, to the basic toolbox of modern thinking.

As Michel Foucault has shown in his early book *Histoire de la folie à l'âge classique* (1972), this constitutive move of excluding and banning from view and influence is not limited to the abstract sphere of producing a realm of pure understanding, as it is in the case of Kant. It is also realised in the social world, most prominently in the case of madness (but also concerning disease (Foucault 1963) and delinquency (Foucault 1975)): from a certain point in time (Foucault locates it somewhere in the 17th century) 'the mad' (as well as 'the diseased', and 'the delinquent') cease to be habitual parts of human life with a place among all the others and are excluded from the rest, secluded in an institution that bans them from the visibility of human society. According to Foucault, these exclusions and seclusions are constitutive for the specifically modern formation of a realm of reason, of a realm of normality. Although, with regard to Kant, this act of exclusion and banning beyond a boundary operates 'only' on the level of the abstract architectonics of his philosophical system, his so influential project clearly participates in this characteristic constitution of the

---

[170] "Sieh den Menschen an in seiner Eingeschränktheit, wie Eindrükke auf ihn würken, Ideen sich bey ihm fest sezzen, bis endlich eine wachsende Leidenschaft ihn aller ruhigen Sinneskraft beraubt, und ihn zu Grunde richtet." (98)

modern world. He may be said to have written the philosophical foundation of it. The metaphor he employs for reflecting upon the architecture of his system (in the view of many philosophical readers a very 'literary', somewhat loose and uncontrolled passage) betrays that his thinking is situated much more strongly in the debates of the 18th century than his argument might indicate. His distinguishing the stable land of pure understanding from the "stormy ocean", taking sides with the stable land that can be "measured", where one can "determine[ ] the place for each thing in it", participates in a general epistemological trend that Michel Serres has famously worked out in several of his books. Starting from the middle of the 17th century, he observes a clear 'scientific' bias for the "order of the world. [...] This order is that of a system, stable through its periodic variations, the solar system" (1977a, 228; my transl.).[171] This bias constitutively implicates the exclusion and foreclosure of the weather: "the meteorological chaos: the winds, the lightnings, the clouds. Not one word of it since the classical period [middle of the 17th century]" (1977a, 228; my transl.).[172] Immanuel Kant is indeed a paradigmatic case for what Michel Serres calls the "normal philosopher, of the Copernican or Galilean revolution, for example" (1977a, 228; my transl.),[173] for which the following characterisation (the importance of the concept of 'law' for Kant's thinking is well known) holds true:

> [...] philosophers, historians, the masters of science, are concerned only with the ancient idea of the law. With exact determination or rigorous over-determination, and with the god of Laplace. With absolute control, and thus with mastery without vacillation or the ambiguity of margins. With power and order. The weather now and the weather to come infinitely surpass our account of them, so they are of no account. Because it is the place of disorder and the unforeseeable, of local danger, of the formless. (Serres 2000, 67)[174]

The weather is thus banned from the philosophical and, more than that, from the human sphere, despite still driving the unforeseeable movements of the

---

171 "[...] l'ordre du monde. [...] Cet ordre est celui d'un système, stable par ses variations périodiques, le système solaire." (Serres 1977a, 228)
172 "[...] le chaos météorologique : les vents, les éclairs, les nuages. Pas un mot sur lui, depuis l'âge classique [...]." (Serres 1977a, 228)
173 "Le philosophe normal, celui, par exemple de la révolution copernicienne ou galiléenne [...]." (Serres 1977a, 228)
174 "[...] les philosophes, les historiens, les maîtres de la science, n'ont souci que de l'ancienne idée de loi. De la détermination exacte ou de la surdétermination rigoureuse, et du dieu de Laplace. Du contrôle absolu, et donc de la maîtrise sans marge ni tremblé. De la puissance et de l'ordre. Le temps qu'il fait ou le temps qu'il fera excède infiniment leur compte, dont il ne compte pas. Parce qu'il est le lieu de désordre et de l'imprévisible, du hasardeux local, de l'informe." (Serres 1977b, 86)

atmosphere, and with that, the life of nature. The mechanisms that this philosophical and ideological trend must develop, no matter whether on the abstract level of concepts as for Kant, or on the level of everyday, social life, are mechanisms of 'confinement'. As Serres writes: "It is enough to send the children to school and the workers to the factory in order to forget [the weather]" (1977a, 229; my transl.).[175] For the philosopher with his claim of universality and stable truth ignoring the weather demands a more direct disavowal: "Philosophy watches the sky, the eclipses and the ellipses and never says that, sometimes, the clouds hinder its seeing them." (Serres 1977a, 9; my transl.)[176] 'Philosophy' – this term being rather a placeholder for a complicated web responsible for developing a new, modern view of the world – was in need of fabricating a serviceable 'microclimate' in its realm so that the weather's disorder and changeability did not conceal or threaten the view of stable truth. This is at least what the German term for 'enlightenment', *Aufklärung*, suggests: a (stable, universal) clearing up of the sky, so that no illusory "fog banks" delude or detract from the essential and eternal, so that no clouds cover up the view on the stable course of the planets. As we have seen, Flammarion's engraving illustrates this fantasy of an enlightened world, with a clear sky granting an open view on the firmament and the weather's chaos of clouds and imperfect elements banned beyond the limitation of the firmament. However, Flammarion's engraving also, and primarily, depicts the longing for the beyond that goes along with the constitution of this world. The central role of this longing cannot be denied: we encounter it in Flammarion's edging as well as, rather in passing, in Kant's metaphor – and, most outspokenly, in Goethe's *Werther*. It is inherent in the constitution of this modern world; positing a limit, introducing a finitude, creates a longing for transgression, a longing for "the fullness of the infinitude", as Werther puts it. This longing, however, finds no place in the official grid of the modern world. How could it? Since it longs for a beyond that has been banned in order to constitute the order that our control over the world we are living in is based on. As Michel Serres almost tautologically writes: "This confinement is also a repression of this disorder." (Serres 1977a, 229; my transl.)[177]

It is here that the tragedy begins. Kant's metaphor (representative for his whole project) illustrates this very well. He admits the longing, but only to

---

[175] "Il suffit de mettre les enfants à l'école et les ouvriers à l'usine pour l'oublier." (Serres 1977a, 229) Cf. Goethe's transformation of the failed weather observatories into schools of observation (160), that appears to confirm Serres's claim in a very interesting way.
[176] "La philosophie regardait le ciel, les éclipses et les ellipses, et ne disait jamais que les nuages, quelquefois, l'empêchaient de les voir." (Serres 1977a, 9)
[177] "Cet enfermement-là est aussi une répression de ce désordre-là." (Serres 1977a, 229)

characterise it as dangerous, vain, as an aberration from truth to "illusion". Ideally, there were no mariners following the hope for some new land; ideally, we would all, like the sober philosopher, stay on the stable rocks at the shore, viewing the unknown only to see a conceptual chance to found human freedom on this inaccessible beyond. However, there is, somehow, this longing that man "can never escape". Despite the fact that he posits this longing almost as apodictically as the existence of the realm of pure understanding, Kant will not tell us more about this longing. We learn a lot about illusion and the chances that positing this limit produces; not a word, however, about the questions of why the human being obviously somehow, sometimes, against good judgment, longs to leave this island of order and understanding. A part of reality, we could say, is neglected, silenced, even. As we have seen, for 'good' reasons: a world that constitutes itself as 'confinement' is threatened by the longing for transgression, for breaking out, that appears to be constitutively created by this world's very formation. It is therefore no surprise that, at some point, "disorder", the unruly that has been suppressed by this confinement, raises its voice against the domination of human understanding:

> Oh, you rationalists! I exclaimed, smiling. Passion! Drunkenness! Madness! You stand there, so calmly, without any empathy [*Theilnehmung*], you moral men! You chide the drinker, despise the man bereft of his senses, pass by like the priest, thank God like the Pharisee that He did not make you as one of these. I have been drunk more than once, my passions were never far from madness, and I regret neither: for in my own measure I have learned to grasp how all extraordinary men who have achieved something great, something seemingly impossible, have inevitably been derided as drunkards or madmen. (64)[178]

Goethe's *Werther* takes sides with those non-rational 'phenomena' that, although silenced, excluded, covered up, are still part (and a characteristic part) of the modern world. Far from idealising these unruly, transgressing phenomena of excess or making them appear harmless, the novel lends them a voice so that the 'side-effects' of the constitution of this modern world can be problematised. As Werther's complaint indicates, the 'other' of the 'true', solid soil of human

---

[178] "Ach ihr vernünftigen Leute! rief ich lächelnd aus. Leidenschaft! Trunkenheit! Wahnsinn! Ihr steht so gelassen, so ohne Theilnehmung da, ihr sittlichen Menschen, scheltet den Trinker, verabscheuet den Unsinnigen, geht vorbey wie der Priester, und dankt Gott wie der Pharisäer, daß er euch nicht gemacht hat, wie einen von diesen. Ich bin mehr als einmal trunken gewesen, und meine Leidenschaften waren nie weit vom Wahnsinne, und beydes reut mich nicht, denn ich habe in meinem Maase begreifen lernen: Wie man alle ausserordentliche Menschen, die etwas grosses, etwas unmöglich scheinendes würkten, von jeher für Trunkene und Wahnsinnige ausschreien müßte." (94–96)

understanding is not merely weathery 'illusion', as it must have appeared to the philosopher Kant with his epistemological interest. "Passion! Drunkenness! Madness!" represent an 'other' of human understanding and reason that cannot merely be abandoned as false illusion, but that confronts the "rationalists", as Werther does, with a critical, ethical question: How is it that this evident part of reality, of human life does not deserve "empathy" from those that present themselves as "moral men"? What is at stake here is the normativity that the limit/limitation/boundary with its favouring of order and rationality exercises – against all the unruly, weathery forces that are still existing in this world, but existing as dislocated, existing to be eliminated, vanquished and driven out. What is finally questioned is the dominant role of reason in the organisation of the world:

> My friend, I exclaimed, a man is a man, and the modicum of reason he might have counts for little or nothing when passion rages [*wüthet*] and the limits of human being press against [*drängen*] him! (67)[179]

It is exactly here, I would like to suggest, that the novel finds and defines its place, or rather, its point of interest: at the limits of human being, where these limits are felt, because uncontrollable forces press and urge [*drängen*], from within and from without, a place, as Michel Serres has taught us, that is left unoccupied by "the philosophers, the historians, the masters of science" all aiming at the rational, the stable and the well-ordered. Werther's choice of words tellingly characterises these forces at work when "the limits of human being press against him": the passion "rages" [*wüthet*], he says, using a verb that, in German as well as in the English translation, denotes the uncontrollable, violent and excessive quality of these forces. For the German verb *wüten*, the *Deutsches Wörterbuch* lists the basic meaning of "being seized with a violent [*heftig*] agitation [*erregung*] that evades the governance [*lenkung*] of reason and will and being driven, by that, to certain irresponsible action" (*DWB*, wüten, v.; my transl.).[180] This modern use of the word is informed by older meanings that betray a different worldview, a worldview that our first chapter on Shakespeare and the early modern weather has made us familiar with. *Wüten* is another example of a word that had been conceptualised according to the analogy of microcosm and macrocosm: as the *Deutsches Wörterbuch* tells us, it can, on

---

[179] "Mein Freund rief ich aus, der Mensch ist Mensch, und das Bißgen Verstand das einer haben mag, kommt wenig oder nicht in Anschlag, wenn Leidenschaft wüthet, und die Gränzen der Menschheit einen drängen." (102)

[180] "[...] *von heftiger, sich der lenkung durch verstand und willen entziehender erregung ergriffen und durch sie zu bestimmtem, nicht verantwortbarem tun getrieben sein* [...]." (*DWB*, wüten, v.)

the microcosmic side, be used as a "signification of raging, raving, being-beside-oneself [*auszer-sich-sein*] in the state of obsession [*besessenheit*]" (*DWB*, wüten, v. A.; my transl.);[181] it can denote madness as well as sickness (i.e. a tumult of the humours). It is, however, also used with reference to phenomena of heavy weather: "of the stormy movement, of the raging of the unleashed elements (water, fire, air)" (*DWB*, wüten, v. F. 1.; my transl.)[182] The only indication that we find in the *Deutsches Wörterbuch* of this verb's analogical conceptualisation is the brief remark that this transference between the verb's reference to inner as well as outer phenomena is "encountered already in ancient and medieval Latin (ignis, fretum, tempestas furit; pontus, ventus saevit)" (*DWB*, wüten, v. F. 1.; my transl.).[183]

Goethe, however, is well aware of this old, analogical link. As we have seen in our analysis, the famous ball-scene makes this analogy of violent outer weather and the erupting passion of love visible on the level of the narrated world. It is therefore not astonishing that in Werther's letter to Lotte, the verb *wüten* is used not only to signify the raging of passion, but also to denote the raging of the weather:

> [A]nd now, in this hovel, in this solitude, in this confinement, with snow and hailstones raging [*wüthen*] against the windowpane, here you were my first thought. (84; transl. altered)[184]

As in the ball-scene, the window represents the limit of the human sphere, so that there is weather from without, "snow and hailstones", as well as passion from within that both "rage[ ]" against "the limits of human being". By resorting to this old and anachronistic analogy that only the memory of language has preserved, Goethe has thus found an interesting way of questioning the limit, the boundary on which the constitution of the modern world is based. He has found a connection (be it an atavistic one) that transgresses the limit by approximating what has come to be thought of as incomprehensible: inner and outer forces, the non-human weather and the human passions. Taking this

---

181 "[...] bezeichnung des rasens, tobens, auszer-sich-seins im zustande der besessenheit [...]." (*DWB*, wüten, v. A.)
182 "[...] von der stürmischen bewegung, dem rasen der entfesselten elemente (wasser, feuer, luft) [...]." (*DWB*, wüten, v. F. 1.)
183 "[...] eine übertragung, die bereits im antiken und mittelalterlichen latein (ignis, fretum, tempestas furit; pontus, mare, ventus saevit) begegnet [...]." (*DWB*, wüten, v. F. 1.)
184 "Und jetzt in dieser Hütte, in dieser Einsamkeit, in dieser Einschränkung, da Schnee und Schlossen wider mein Fenstergen wüthen, hier waren Sie mein erster Gedanke." (134)

stance offers huge strategic advantages: (1) the "unalterable boundaries" that, according to Kant, nature herself has erected, enclosing the human being on his island, have obviously not always been there – they therefore cannot be as natural as Kant claims, their modern historical index reappears; (2) with these forces raging from the inside as well as from the outside, perfectly sealing off the human island from the "broad and stormy ocean" does not help: it merely increases the urging from within, increases the longing to break out, the longing for "fresh air".

Goethe's strategic use of the old analogy of passions and other inner tumults and the outer weather that we have observed in *Werther* not only legitimates my talking of 'weathery forces' when referring to all the unruly phenomena that do not comply with the contemporary bias for the stable and the rational. It has shown itself to be a strategic, critical position of an efficacy that has surpassed the limits of this novel and has become emblematic for a whole intellectual 'movement': a movement known in German as *Sturm und Drang*, which translates into English as 'storm and urge'.

The genealogy of this label has not contributed to its being taken seriously in literary criticism. On the contrary, as Jörg-Ulrich Fechner, the editor of the drama that has lent its name to the movement, *Sturm und Drang* by Friedrich Maximilian Klinger, writes: "'Sturm und Drang' does not express a self-understanding held by the group, but an arbitrary, tendentious, poster-like [*plakatartig*] label attached to it." (1998, 158; my transl.) Klinger's friend Christoph Kaufmann has become famous for having advised his friend to change the name of a play originally titled *Der Wirrwarr* to the name it now so famously bears. With respect to Klinger's play, Kaufmann's new title appears indeed arbitrary. Except for its very first speech, which is of an overtly Shakespearean type, there is not much that justifies this choice. It is however no coincidence that Kaufmann's title made its career as a label for the group or movement. The label might "not express a self-understanding held by the group", it might not have been coined by one of the prominent personalities of this movement, it is a label attached to the group from 'without'. However, all these characteristics might, paradoxically, be responsible for the label's aptness and precision. Jörg-Ulrich Fechner has followed up the two components of the label in the intellectual debates of the time and discovered an interesting net of references and directions, reaching from Lavater to Klopstock's and Herder's religious thinking, without finding any original coining or any dominant specification of the terms in question (cf. 1998). Goethe's *Werther* holds a central place in Fechner's sketch of a reconstruction, because it makes prominent use of the keyword *Drang* [urge] already in its dedication to the reader: "And you, good soul, who feel the same urge [*Drang*] as he, take comfort from his sufferings [...]" (19; transl. altered).[185] Nevertheless, tracing the terms does not do justice to Kaufmann's label, because, as we have seen, it is the characteristic conceptual combination of these two words, resorting to old analogical thinking, that accounts for the label's conceptual force. Kaufmann's title *Sturm und Drang* is not the creation of a genius; above all, it has to be read as a promotion coup of someone who really had a feeling for the market. Despite its apparent arbitrariness, it communicates an important philological or cultural-historical insight. Kaufmann's *Sturm und Drang* testifies to a happy moment of literary criticism rather than of poetological self-understanding. His familiarity with the major players (Rousseau, Lavater, Herder, Goethe) of the intellectual movement that has become classified under this label surely facilitated its coinage.

The fact that Klinger's play was not a particularly good example of the alliance of weather and the human passions that Kaufmann's label actually evokes may have contributed decisively to the label's rather ambiguous success, especially in literary history. The weathery component of this label (and with it, its conceptual force) was very soon forgotten. Instead, the youthful urge became the emblem of this movement, as exemplified by Georg Gottfried Gervinus 19th century literary-historical summary of that period:

> This time has been named *Sturm und Drang* after one of [Klinger's] plays, because its characteristic signal is the inner fight, in which youth found itself in-between ideal and world, heart and reason, freedom and convention [*Convenienz*], nature and culture. (1844, 122; my transl.)

The fact that the notion of youthfulness takes the weather's place as a second characteristic at the side of 'the urge' retrospectively curbs the social extension of the intellectual movement. As we have seen in our reading of Goethe's *Werther*, the weather had served to connect the urge's unruly, uncontrollable forces to the undeniably objective and equally uncontrollable 'outer' forces of the weather and had thus provided an ontological foundation that emphasises their reality and impact. When the notion of youthfulness takes over this role, it refers these forces back to their supposed place of origin, that is to say it qualifies them as subjective and only temporary phenomena. As a consequence, the urge no longer questions the constitution of our modern world, but rather the problematic phases of a subject's formation, its way to the safe harbour of maturity with its rational calmness and "cold consciousness". As is well known, Goethe himself had, very successfully, advocated this reading of his

---

185 "Und du gute Seele, die du eben den Drang fühlst wie er, schöpfe Trost aus seinen Leiden [...]." (10)

early works. His *Werther*, however (as many readers, Goethe among them as we will see, have noticed) resists this qualification.

Werther is well aware that he himself, his state of mind and situation, could be to blame for the "raging [*tobende*], endless passion" that torments him:

> Wretched creature! Are you not a fool? Aren't you deluding yourself? What is the meaning of this raging [*tobende*], endless passion? I have no prayers other than those directed to her; no shape appears to my imagination other than hers, and I see everything in the world around me only in relation to her. (72)[186]

His attempts to make sense, or at least to give an account of this "raging [*Toben*]" fail. It cannot be categorised among the phenomena of human life. All that Werther can do is, again and again, resort to stressing the analogy of these forces with the forces of the weather:

> At times it takes hold of me; it is not terror, not lust – it's an unfamiliar inner raging [*Toben*] that threatens to rip my breast apart [*zerreissen*], that constricts my throat! Woe! Woe! and then I roam through the frightful night scenes of this hostile season. [...]
>
> Oh, Wilhelm! How gladly I would have given up my human existence to be with that stormy wind and rip the clouds apart [*zerreissen*] and seize the floodwaters! Ha! And might that bliss not be bestowed on this imprisoned creature one day? (123; transl. altered)[187]

The reference of Werther's "inner fight", as Gervinus calls it, to the processes of the outer weather is a constant in Goethe's novel. In this respect it complies very well with the label *Sturm und Drang* – or, to put it the other way round, it well illustrates the constellation that this term conceptualises. However, the decisive, critical question that my argument raises concerns the 'ontological status' of this 'transference' from 'urge' to 'weather': Does Werther's 'urge' have, in fact, anything to do with 'the weather'? Does he really refer to the weather as weather, as 'a reality', or is his talking about it merely metaphorical, figurative, a projection of his deranged mind?

---

[186] "Unglücklicher! Bist du nicht ein Thor? Betrügst du dich nicht selbst? Was soll all diese tobende endlose Leidenschaft? Ich habe kein Gebet mehr, als an sie, meiner Einbildungskraft erscheint keine andere Gestalt als die ihrige, und alles in der Welt um mich her, sehe ich nur im Verhältnisse mit ihr." (112)

[187] "Manchmal ergreift mich's, es ist nicht Angst, nicht Begier! es ist ein inneres unbekanntes Toben, das meine Brust zu zerreissen droht, das mir die Gurgel zupreßt! Wehe! Wehe! Und dann schweif ich umher in den furchtbaren nächtlichen Scenen dieser menschenfeindlichen Jahrszeit. [...]

O Wilhelm, wie gern hätt ich all mein Menschseyn drum gegeben, mit jenem Sturmwinde die Wolken zu zerreissen, die Fluthen zu fassen. Ha! Und wird nicht vielleicht dem Eingekerkerten einmal diese Wonne zu Theil!" (194)

The vast majority of critics read the weather in *Werther*, if it is given any attention at all, as metaphorical, as illustrative of Werther's state of mind. This is not astonishing; they make sense of what they read according to the way of the world they are living in, the world in which they have been socialised, is organised. To us, the idea that the weather and the passions are somehow connected appears to be even more remote than to the 18th century reader, for whom the idea of humours flowing through the body was yet of some, already old-fashioned, but still practiced medical reality. Reading the weather as a projection, as metaphorical, is undertaken from the island, to resort once more to Kant's metaphor. It is spoken from a point of view from which phenomena of weather (fog banks, clouds, melting ice) cannot be 'real' subjects of interest in themselves. Either they are mere illusions, delusions, agents of darkness, or simulacra. They are merely figurative, standing for something different, something that can claim a stronger ontological stance, something that is 'more real', so to speak: something that is located on the island's safe soil. In this, the critics are following Michel Serres's dictum: not a word on the weather since the middle of the 17th century. If we speak of the weather, then it must be an indirect way of mentioning something else, say the human passions, the deranged mind of a poor human being, the "inner fight" of youth.

Werther himself, however, provides us with an ontological link that connects his "inner fight" to the realities of "outer nature". In his letter of August 18th, he sketches a theory that bases the changeability of bliss and misery on the constitutively instable, weathery character of nature itself. Despite being quite an early letter, located in the first half of the novel, it nevertheless relates a comprehensive story of different stages of bliss and misery that reads like an elaborated reflection on the novel as a whole – with its decisive parts still to come! It thereby offers to the reader an important conceptual background that counters the intuition of reading Werther's sufferings as an idiosyncratic affair, as the pathology of a single individual that has nothing to do with the modern world that Werther and his readers share.

In its very first sentence, the letter raises the decisive question to which the rest of the letter attempts to develop an answer: "Does it have to be this way, that whatever it is that makes a man blissfully happy in turn becomes the source of his misery?" (68)[188] It is his experience, and a specific observation while reflecting on this experience that triggers this question:

---

[188] "Mußte denn das so seyn? daß das, was des Menschen Glükseligkeit macht, wieder die Quelle seines Elends würde." (104)

> The full, warm feeling of my heart for living nature, which flooded me with such joy, which turned the world around me into a paradise, has now become an unbearable torturer, a tormenting spirit that pursues me wherever I turn. (68)[189]

"[L]iving nature" will thus be the subject of this letter's ponderings, a subject to which Werther seems to be exposed as one is to the weather in open nature. The passage that follows narrates the first of the stages that the course of this letter will traverse: it looks back on the happy times, the times of bliss. Three longish periods, all starting with "when ..." paint the idyllic picture of Werther who finds himself "surrounded" by the abundant life of "the fruitful valley". Werther praises the "sprouting and swelling" around him in a hymnic tone clearly inspired by Brockes's and Klopstock's religious poetry. This enthusiasm is however burdened by the demonstrative relegation of this bliss to a period of time that has passed. The parallelism of these sentences, all being introduced by "when", emphasise the reference to a certain, irrevocable point in time, and the insistent use of the past tense prepare for the turn of fortunes that is to follow. Before that, however, Werther raises the stakes by linking a reflection of the corresponding human self-understanding to this paradisiac natural experience:

> when I heard the birds around me lend life to the forest while a million swarms of gnats boldly danced in the last red rays of the sun, [...] and the whirring and weaving around me made me look to the ground and to the moss that wrests its nourishment from these hard rocks, and the shrubbery that grows along the barren sand dunes revealed to me the innermost glowing sacred life of nature: how I enfolded all that with warm heart, lost myself in the infinite abundance, and the glorious shapes of the infinite world moved all-living in my soul. (69; transl. altered)[190]

On the one hand Werther's losing himself "in the infinite abundance" marks a moment of mystical excess that mirrors his bliss when dancing with Lotte. On the other hand, his enfolding "all that with warm heart", the fact that "the infinite world moved all-living in [his] soul" also elevates him as the actual

---

189 "Das volle warme Gefühl meines Herzens an der lebendigen Natur, das mich mit so viel Wonne überströmte, das rings umher die Welt mir zu einem Paradiese schuf, wird mir jetzt zu einem unerträglichen Peiniger, zu einem quälenden Geiste, der mich auf allen Wegen verfolgt." (104)

190 "[...] wenn ich denn die Vögel um mich, den Wald beleben hörte, und die Millionen Mükkenschwärme im lezten rothen Strahle der Sonne muthig tanzten, [...] und das Gewebere um mich her, mich auf den Boden aufmerksam machte und das Moos, das meinem harten Felsen seine Nahrung abzwingt, und das Geniste, das den dürren Sandhügel hinunter wächst, mir alles das innere glühende, heilige Leben der Natur eröfnete, wie umfaßte ich das all mit warmen Herzen, verlohr mich in der unendlichen Fülle, und die herrlichen Gestalten der unendlichen Welt bewegten sich alllebend in meiner Seele." (104–106)

place or agent of a sort of *unio mystica*, establishing a union between infinite (pantheistic) nature and the human soul. In his later reworking of the text in 1787 Goethe disambiguated this passage by replacing the phrase "lost myself in the infinite abundance [*verlohr mich in der unendlichen Fülle*]" by the words "felt like a god among the overflowing abundance [*fühlte mich in der überfließenden Fülle wie vergöttert*]" (cf. FA 8, 106–107). He thereby weakened the excessive, the uncontrollable aspect of this bliss (a typical move of his classicist reworking) in favour of emphasising the (hubris of the) peak that this experience marks. This peak is however present in both versions, which is indicated by a turn of register. Directly following the quoted passage the register all of a sudden changes, the picturesque description of a *locus amoenus* makes way for the sublime:

> Enormous mountains surrounded me, chasms lay before me, and swollen brooks plunged downward, streams rushed beneath me, and woods and mountains resounded; and I saw them, all the unfathomable forces, entwined in their hustle and bustle in the depths of the earth; and now, above the earth and under the skies swarm all the species of the manifold creatures, and everything, everything is populated with a thousand shapes; (69)[191]

Despite the change from the picturesque to the sublime, Werther finds himself still in the centre of the scene, the "[e]normous mountains surround[ ] [him]", and in an elevated position, looking down on the violent forces of nature, as the "streams rush[ing] beneath [him]" indicate. His position seems to be reminiscent of the emblem that Herder had painted for Shakespeare that we have quoted above, "'seated high atop some craggy eminence, whirlwinds, tempest, and the roaring sea at his feet, but with the flashing skies about his head'". Werther however only evokes this association in order to refute it with another sudden turn: instead of towering above nature's violent forces, occupying an intermediary position between nature and god (that is to say instead of using the power and violence of nature to glorify the human position that is still superior to 'mere nature', as Kant will do and others have done before him), he emphasises human vulnerability and need of protection:

> and then men shelter together [*zusammen sichern*] in their little houses and build their nests and think they govern the whole wide world! Poor fool, who thinks so little of everything because you are so little. (69)[192]

---

[191] "Ungeheure Berge umgaben mich, Abgründe lagen vor mir, und Wetterbäche stürzten herunter, die Flüsse strömten unter mir, und Wald und Gebürg erklang. Und ich sah sie würken und schaffen in einander in den Tiefen der Erde, all die Kräfte unergründlich. Und nun über der Erde und unter dem Himmel wimmeln die Geschlechter der Geschöpfe all, und alles, alles bevölkert mit tausendfachen Gestalten […]." (106)

[192] "[…] und die Menschen dann sich in Häuslein zusammen sichern, und sich annisten, und herrschen in ihrem Sinne über die weite Welt! Armer Thor, der du alles so gering achtest, weil du so klein bist." (106)

The contrast to Immanuel Kant's use of the sublime for his critical endeavour sixteen years after *Werther* is striking. For Kant, "the mind feels itself elevated in its own judging" (Kant 2000 [1790], 139) when watching "shapeless mountain masses towering above one another in wild disorder with their pyramids of ice, or the dark raging sea" (Kant 2000 [1790], 139):[193]

> Bold, overhanging, as it were threatening cliffs, thunder clouds towering up into the heavens, bringing with them flashes of lightning and crashes of thunder, volcanoes with their all-destroying violence, hurricanes with the devastation they leave behind, the boundless ocean set into rage, a lofty waterfall on a mighty river, etc., make our capacity to resist into an insignificant trifle in comparison with their power. But the sight of them only becomes all the more attractive the more fearful it is, as long as we find ourselves in safety, and we gladly call these objects sublime because they elevate the strength of our soul above its usual level, and allow us to discover within ourselves a capacity for resistance of quite another kind, which gives us the courage to measure ourselves against the apparent all-powerfulness of nature. (Kant 2000 [1790], 144–145)[194]

Kant, watching the sublime from the safe soil of the island, discovers, through the experience of the sublime, "another, nonsensible standard [...] against which everything in nature is small" (Kant 2000 [1790], 145), that is to say, the human being finds in his/her "own mind a superiority over nature itself even in its immeasurability" (Kant 2000 [1790], 145).[195] Werther, in contrast, stresses the point that the human being does not live "in safety"; there is no safe soil that would make her/him independent from nature's overpowering violence.

---

[193] "Wer wollte auch ungestalte Gebirgsmassen, in wilder Unordnung über einander gethürmt, mit ihren Eispyramiden, oder die düstere tobende See, u.s.w. erhaben nennen? Aber das Gemüth fühlt sich in seiner eigenen Beurteilung gehoben [...]." (Kant 1968 [1790], 256)

[194] "Kühne überhängende, gleichsam drohende Felsen, am Himmel sich aufthürmende Donnerwolken, mit Blitzen und Krachen einherziehend, Vulcane in ihrer ganzen zerstörenden Gewalt, Orkane mit ihrer zurückgelassenen Verwüstung, der grenzenlose Ocean, in Empörung gesetzt, ein hoher Wasserfall eines mächtigen Flusses u.d.gl. machen unser Vermögen zu widerstehen in Vergleichung mit ihrer Macht, zur unbedeutenden Kleinigkeit. Aber ihr Anblick wird nur um desto anziehender, je furchtbarer er ist, wenn wir uns nur in Sicherheit befinden; und wir nennen diese Gegenstände gern erhaben, weil sie die Seelenstärke über ihr gewöhnliches Mittelmaß erhöhen, und ein Vermögen zu widerstehen von ganz anderer Art in uns entdecken lassen, welches uns Muth macht, uns mit der scheinbaren Allgewalt der Natur messen zu können." (Kant 1968 [1790], 261)

[195] "Denn so wie wir zwar an der Unermeßlichkeit der Natur und der Unzulänglichkeit unseres Vermögens einen der ästhetischen Größenschätzung ihres *Gebiets* proportionirten Maßstab zu nehmen unsere eigene Einschränkung, gleichwohl aber doch auch an unserm Vernunftvermögen zugleich einen andern, nicht-sinnlichen Maßstab, welcher jene Unendlichkeit selbst als Einheit unter sich hat, gegen den alles in der Natur klein ist, mithin in unserm Gemüthe eine Überlegenheit über die Natur selbst in ihrer Unermeßlichkeit fanden [...]." (Kant 1968 [1790], 261)

On the contrary, the "little" human being exists in the middle of this immensity of nature. S/he cannot escape its violence and just stand by, calmly watching and savouring its sublime phenomena. Instead of governing "the whole wide world", s/he has to desperately erect some shelter against nature's threatening forces, has to build "little houses", "nests" in order to secure his/her place in the world. We here encounter the 'other' side of the prison walls that Werther so often dreams of breaking through. Lilian R. Furst has best summed up this situation (I have already quoted this passage above) writing that "the self-imposed captivity" is built as "an enclosure that insulates from the assaults of a hostile world" (1990, 150). There is no island of human mastery and control, "enclosed by nature herself within unchangeable limits" as Kant claims. Mankind has to erect these boundaries/limitations/limits in order to attain a 'human sphere'. The human being rationally creates for himself a realm of relative independence from the 'outer' forces, from disorder and chaos. As a consequence, these limits are not mere givens, they are heavily contended – this is what Goethe's *Werther* is all about. As a novel, it situates itself exactly at the limits of human nature.

Having contrasted men's "littleness", their little houses and nests with "the spirit of the eternally creative One" that "wafts" from "the inaccessible mountains across the desert where no one has set foot, to the ends of the unexplored oceans" (69),[196] the constellation where human longing is produced is then described:

> Oh, then, how often did I long to have the wings of the crane soaring above me to fly to the shores of the uncharted oceans, to drink that surging joy of life from the foaming beaker of infinity, and to feel for even a moment in the confined power of my breast a drop of the bliss of that Being that brings forth everything in and through Itself. (69)[197]

Werther's (exemplary) longing is thus not only an impulse to break free from the prison that confines him; it cannot tell a story of emancipation, because this longing is not to be separated from the dialectics of confinement and shelter. It always refers back to the "confined power of [Werther's] breast" that does not allow a 'solution' to the problem that causes both Werther's bliss and his suffering. Werther's excess, his transgression of the limits of the human being is thus not sublated by the discovery of (some different kind of) securing order beyond

---

[196] "Von unzugänglichen Gebürge über die Einöde, die kein Fuß betrat, bis ans Ende des unbekannten Ozeans, weht der Geist des Ewigschaffenden und freut sich jedes Staubs, der ihn vernimmt und lebt." (106)
[197] "Ach damals, wie oft hab ich mich mit Fittigen eines Kranichs, der über mich hinflog, zu dem Ufer des ungemessenen Meeres gesehnt, jene schwellende Lebenswonne zu trinken, und nur einen Augenblick in der eingeschränkten Kraft meines Busens einen Tropfen der Seligkeit des Wesens zu fühlen, das alles in sich und durch sich hervorbringt." (106)

the limit: unlike Hegel, who questions and tries to overcome Kant's limits thirty years later, Werther's longing for "something that goes beyond limits, and since these limits are its own, [...] something that goes beyond itself" (Hegel 1977 [1807], 51),[198] his "Bacchanalian whirl [*Taumel*] in which there is no link which is not drunk" (Hegel 2005 [1807], 153–154)[199] does not 'realise' that it is truth itself, that was "with us, in and for itself, all along, and of its own volition" (47).[200] It is not an imperialistic enterprise, expanding the human or spirit's or the concept's realm of sovereignty to the all-encompassing totality that has actually always been 'the own', that only has to be re-appropriated. On the contrary, what Werther discovers behind the limit's curtain, is as far from the reign of understanding, reason and spirit as possible:

> It is as if a curtain had been drawn back from my soul, and the spectacle of infinite [*unendlich*] life is transformed before my eyes into the abyss of an ever-open [*ewig offnen*] grave. Can you say: This is what is! since everything passes, since everything rolls on with the swiftness of the weather [*mit der Wetterschnelle vorüber rollt*], so rarely does the entire force of its existence last, oh! torn along into the river and submerged and shattered on the rocks? There is no moment that does not consume you and those near and dear to you, no moment when you are not a destroyer, must be one; the most innocent stroll costs the lives of thousands and thousands of tiny creatures; one footstep shatters the laboriously erected structures of the ant and pounds a tiny world into a miserable grave. Ha! I am not moved by the great, rare disasters of this world, those floods that wash away your villages, those earthquakes that swallow your cities; my heart is undermined by the destructive force that is concealed in the totality of nature; which has never created a thing that has not destroyed its neighbor or itself. And so I stagger about in fear! heaven and earth and their interweaving forces around me: I see nothing but an eternally [*ewig*] devouring, eternally [*ewig*] regurgitating monster. (70; transl. altered)[201]

---

[198] "[...] das Hinausgehen über das Beschränkte und, da ihm dies Beschränkte angehört, über sich selbst [...]." (Hegel 1986 [1807], 74)
[199] "[...] der bacchantische Taumel, an dem kein Glied nicht trunken ist [...]." (Hegel 1986 [1807], 46)
[200] "[...] an und für sich schon bei uns wäre und sein wollte [...]." (Hegel 1986 [1807], 69)
[201] "Es hat sich vor meiner Seele wie ein Vorhang weggezogen, und der Schauplatz des unendlichen Lebens verwandelt sich vor mir in den Abgrund des ewig offnen Grabs. Kannst du sagen: Das ist! da alles vorübergeht, da alles mit der Wetterschnelle vorüber rollt, so selten die ganze Kraft seines Daseyns ausdauert, ach in den Strom fortgerissen, untergetaucht und an Felsen zerschmettert wird. Da ist kein Augenblick, der nicht dich verzehrte und die Deinigen um dich her, kein Augenblick, da du nicht ein Zerstöhrer bist, seyn mußt. Der harmloseste Spaziergang kostet tausend tausend armen Würmgen das Leben, es zerrüttet ein Fustritt die mühseligen Gebäude der Ameisen, und stampft eine kleine Welt in ein schmähliches Grab. Ha! nicht die große seltene Noth der Welt, diese Fluthen, die eure Dörfer wegspülen, diese Erdbeben, die eure Städte verschlingen, rühren mich. Mir untergräbt das Herz die verzehrende Kraft, die im All der Natur verborgen liegt, die nichts gebildet hat, das nicht seinen Nachbar, nicht sich selbst zerstörte. Und so taumele ich beängstet! Himmel und Erde und all die webenden Kräfte um mich her! Ich sehe nichts, als ein ewig verschlingendes, ewig wiederkäuendes Ungeheur." (106–108)

Behind the curtain, Werther discovers time as the principle of nature. His idea of "infinite life" had been a spatial conception: nature and life as a vast expansion of something that 'is there' [*unendlich*], that is stable, that can be admired and appropriated, of which one can be a part. This idea is now transformed into the idea of "the ever-open grave", a temporal conception of generation and corruption where nothing but 'time' itself proves stable and infinite. 'Time' is here explicitly linked to its obsolete meaning of 'weather' (cf. *OED*, time, *n.* †20): the fact that "everything rolls on with the swiftness of the weather" is the basic characteristic of nature at the heart of Werther's discovery. The weather here serves as the paradigmatic illustration, or rather 'instance', of an 'ontological' foundation that does not take stable substance but the process of generation and corruption, changeability, a notion of 'the fluid', of 'time' as its principle. An insight that Michel Serres two hundred years later puts in the following words: "The *meteora* are neither stable nor completely unstable, they are the visible models of existence itself, this world of statics outside statics." (2000, 88)[202] The "destructive force that is concealed in the totality of nature" thus does not consist of rare weather events, from time to time hitting and disturbing the ontological substance of the world from without; it is inherent in nature, nature is itself nothing but the totality of these weathery, "interweaving forces".

The formulation that Werther's "heart is undermined" by his discovery of the weathery character of nature has to be taken at face value: it is not a discovery that can be added to the archive of knowledge without some significant consequences. On the contrary, it "undermines" the limit, the boundary that constitutes the modern world: the boundary/limit/limitation that separates disorder from order, the weather from the rational and stable, illusion from truth, good from bad, misery from bliss. Werther's "stagger[ing] about in fear" is the staggering of Flammarion's missionary or Lawrence's artist, returning from their missions with "reddened eyes, short of breath". Werther has indeed "seen Life in the living or the Living in the lived" and his letter of August 18th gives an account of this insight.

What he has, above all, discovered is the fact that "the innermost glowing sacred life of nature" is supplemented by death. When he returns to the island of pure understanding, Werther does however not return to the same island he had left when heading out for his explorations. Death is an irrefutable part of human existence and therefore also of the human sphere. It is no coincidence that philosophy so successfully banned it from their island, or repressed it,

---

[202] "Les météores ne sont ni stables ni complètement instables, ils sont les modèles évidents de l'existence même, ce mot de statique hors statique." (Serres 1977b, 110)

rather (until Heidegger famously re-discovered it as late as the 20th century), for death indicates that time and the weathery changeability cannot be separated from human existence.

In contrast to Kant, Hegel and the other philosophers of idealism, Werther is violently confronted with death. Death makes an appearance as the most incommensurable, the most uncontrollable part of human existence:

> Oh, man is so transitory that even there, where he has a genuine certainty of his existence, there, where his presence makes its one truthful impression in the memory, in the soul of his dear ones, there too he must be extinguished, must vanish, and so soon! (69)[203]

His thoughts on death are certainly a contribution to the contemporary moral debate on suicide; they are, however, more than that. Death, for Werther, is a paradigmatic case of a phenomenon that is beyond the reach of human control, beyond the horizon of reason but still undeniably part of the human sphere, a reality of human existence. With death the limitedness of the human being enters the human sphere itself, is given a face that can be recognised, and signals a permanent threat against which one cannot build houses or flood dams. Death is the paradigmatic case of 'an other' of reason and eternal truth against which understanding is a blunt weapon:

> To die! what does that mean? See, we are dreaming when we speak of death. I have seen more than one person die; but mankind is so limited that it cannot conceive of the beginning and end of its existence. [...] How can I pass away? How can you pass away? We are, yes! – pass away! – what does that mean? There is merely another phrase! an empty noise, which my heart cannot feel. [...] To die! Grave! I do not understand these words! (141)[204]

"[M]ankind is so limited", one could rephrase Werther's insight, that it cannot give a true, objective, scientific or philosophical account of its limits. On the other hand, phenomena like death (or being born!) cannot merely be banned from the human sphere, because they so obviously form a defining part of human existence. In other words, there are realities, liminal realities, that

---

[203] "O so vergänglich ist der Mensch, daß er auch da, wo er seines Daseyns eigentliche Gewißheit hat, da, wo er den einzigen wahren Eindruk seiner Gegenwart macht; in dem Andenken in der Seele seiner Lieben, daß er auch da verlöschen, verschwinden muß, und das – so bald!" (174)

[204] "Sterben! Was heist das? Sieh wir träumen, wenn wir vom Tode reden. Ich habe manchen sterben sehen, aber so eingeschränkt ist die Menschheit, daß sie für ihres Daseyns Anfang und Ende keinen Sinn hat. [...] Wie kann ich vergehen, wie kannst du vergehen, wir sind ja! – vergehen! – Was heißt das? das ist wieder ein Wort! ein leerer Schall ohne Gefühl für mein Herz. [...] Sterben! Grab! Ich verstehe die Worte nicht!" (248)

demand a different mode of 'knowledge' or recognition than rational understanding with its characteristic of human control. Death is only one, perhaps the most radical and therefore intuitive of these liminal realities that exceed the limits of human understanding: Werther's triad of "Passion! Drunkenness! Madness!" surely also belongs to the 'phenomena' that are both 'real', part of human experience and yet somehow beyond the limits we accept as 'normal' or rationally graspable. As Werther demonstrates with regard to death in the passage quoted above, the status of language changes when speaking of these phenomena: we can and we do speak of them, but as we do language becomes opaque, it ceases to transparently communicate propositions. There is speech beyond understanding, language to a certain extent exceeds the limits of the human, controlled sphere: "we are dreaming when we speak of death". I do not think that Werther dismisses these dreams as mere illusion, as Kant dismisses the fog banks of the wide ocean as misleading mirages. He rather marks a field of reality opening up at the limits of the human being, a field of reality that does not speak to us in rational words.

As we have already seen with the notion of the uncanny, the *(un)heimlich*, haunting Werther's cosy spots, the spectre of psychoanalysis looms in this field long before Freud will discover and develop it into a 'science' (*Wissenschaft*). The opacity of 'dreamy' language is, however, in Goethe's novel first and foremost the language of – the novel. It is literature that discovers this liminal realm of reality (and that is to say the weathery nature of the human being and his surroundings) for itself. Life (human and non-human, as the letter of August 18th has taught us) consists of more than the sciences of enlightened reason can cover. There is more to it than the stability and the eternal truth that the island of human understanding accounts for. There is more to the world than enlightenment's cleared up sky, as Moses Mendelssohn, one of the representatives of this intellectual movement, seems to have been well aware, as early as the year 1755:

> If we want to quell the storm of an unpleasant passion, reason commands us to reflect on the causes of our displeasure and to clarify [*aufzuklären*] the concepts. Only out of these dark clouds does the violent storm arise, and the furor of the passion vanishes as soon as it becomes sunny in our soul. But is the makeup of things different for pleasant sentiments? By no means! They have the same fate. As soon as we think, we no longer feel. The emotion vanishes as soon as concepts are elucidated [*aufgeklärt*]. (Mendelssohn 1997 [1755], 12)[205]

---

205 "Wenn wir den Sturm einer unangenehmen Leidenschaft besänftigen wollen; so befiehlt uns die Vernunft, über die Ursachen unsres Mißvergnüges nachzudenken und die Begriffe aufzuklären. Nur diese finstere Wolken sind es, aus denen das Ungewitter entsteht; und so

This is however only an early position of "Euphranor", one of the two fictional protagonists of the dialogue that Mendelssohn's text titled *Briefe über die Empfindungen* stages, from which I quote. It is the position of a "youthful ethics [*jugendliche Sittenlehre*]" (Mendelssohn 1997 [1755], 12) that will be contested and tamed in the course of the letter exchange. In Mendelssohn's text, perfection [*Vollkommenheit*] will remain the enlightened frame and telos towards which all the observations will be bundled and oriented. Nevertheless, Euphranor's observation is an important one for our interest in Goethe's *Werther* and for situating this novel in the intellectual context of its time. Euphranor sketches 'an other' of reason, that is passion or more broadly 'sentiments', no matter whether pleasant or unpleasant. The two cannot actively coexist, once reason starts to think, the sentiments vanish. Thus far, there seems to be nothing spectacular about this argumentation. What makes it quite special is its extensive use of weather 'imagery' that exhibits the enlightenment's investment in the weather. The passage's weather 'imagery' is not brought to it from without, it is not the result of a creative finding of remote similarities that can be made fruitful for illustrative or rhetorical purposes. It is already there in the linguistic material of what is being talked about: in English as well as in German, the raging storm of a passion or the dark clouds of a bad mood are idiomatic. Furthermore, listening closely to the German word for enlightenment, *Aufklärung*, Euphranor discovers its weathery meaning, signifying a clearing of the sky. The passage's argument is carried by the interplay linking the two phenomena of weather: enlightenment's clearing up the sky makes the phenomena of 'bad', 'heavy weather', the "raging" "storm" of the passions, the "dark clouds" disappear. At first glance, there seems to be no problem with that. However, *Aufklärung*, enlightenment, tends to forget about its weathery implications, tends to forget that it is only one part of an interplay that stops being an interplay and fundamentally changes its nature once one of the constitutive forces – clouding or clearing – ceases to exist. This happens when the clear sky assumes the status of the ideal, of truth and the weathery side is reduced to illusion: "The emotion vanishes as soon as concepts are elucidated [*aufgeklärt*]".

It is exactly at this point that Goethe's early novel (and with it, I would suggest, modern literature) intervenes; not as a protest or appeal against 'enlightenment' – but in its wake, supplementing the clear sky of reason and concepts with its weathery, stormy underside without which the concept of *Aufklärung* loses an

---

bald es in unsrer Seele heiter wird, so verschwindet das Toben der Leidenschaft. Hat es aber mit den angenehmen Empfindungen ein andre Beschaffenheit? O nein! sie haben eben dasselbe Schicksal: wir fühlen nicht mehr, so bald wir denken. Der Affekt verschwindet, sobald die Begriffe aufgekläret werden." (Mendelssohn 1780 [1755], 8–9)

important dimension. *Aufklärung* signifies more than the emancipation from the 'dark' middle ages, which is, as we all know, a rather blunt, self-securing myth of modernity. As the label's verbal and therefore rather process-like, 'active' morphology suggests (*Aufklär-ung* signifies a process, rather than a state), it stands for the on-going, interminable struggle of the solid and the fluid, of stability and changeability. This struggle takes place at the margins, at the limits, and is defined by its dialectic nature. As we have seen, philosophy and the growing sciences took sides with solidity and thereby brought forth the hegemony of the (paradoxically) weather-free, clear sky. As a consequence, its dialectical counterpart, the incontrollable, the non-rational, the fluid, which had once been at the very centre of the characteristically imperfect, elemental world) was left in need of a voiced proponent. Albrecht Koschorke has written the history of literature taking over this task in the 18th century in his book *Körperströme und Schriftverkehr. Mediologie des 18. Jahrhunderts* [Streams of the Body and the Correspondence of Letters. Mediology of the 18th Century] (2003) whose findings our reading of the *Werther* confirms. Language takes over the part of the fluid, as Koschorke writes (2003, 133), the theory of the humours is delegated to literature (2003, 215). With the theory of humours, literature also inherits the analogical connection of the humours with the macrocosmic weather, a connection with which our reading of Shakespeare has made us familiar. In other words, the "streams of the bodies" Koschorke writes about are inseparably linked with the streams storming through Klopstock's poetry or characterising Ossian's songs. Goethe's *Werther* is a prime example for this supplementary role that modern literature takes over in an enlightened world. It is situated at the very knot of sentimentalism and *Sturm und Drang*, it unfolds the old analogical link of the passions and the weather, both located at the weathery, and thus constitutive, underside of the *Aufklärung*.

"Does it have to be this way, that whatever it is that makes a man blissfully happy in turn becomes the source of his misery?" – Werther obviously agrees with Mendelssohn's Euphranor. Sentiments, no matter whether 'positive' or 'negative' are of a weathery nature. They are changeable and instable and of an origin beyond the control of reason. They form an important part of human existence, but are, nevertheless not at home in the cosy hut or on the stable island of human understanding. "Is it, however, any different with our pleasant sentiments? Oh no! they have the same fate: as soon as we start to think we do not feel any longer." Euphranor and Werther both know well enough that they cannot hope for a rational backing of their observation, not in an enlightened world:

> Why is it that you people, I exclaimed, whenever you speak about anything, immediately find yourself saying: this is foolish, this is clever, this is good, this is bad! And what is that supposed to mean? Have you investigated the deeper circumstances of an action to that end? Are you able to explain the causes definitively, why it happened, why it had to happen? If you had done so, you would not be so hasty with your judgments. (63)[206]

The investigation of "the deeper circumstances of an action" therefore has to focus on the weathery limits of the human being, the limits from where language speaks beyond our understanding. Werther has plunged his head into this weathery chaos – and has returned to us with more than reddened eyes. We surely cannot "explain the causes definitely, why it happened, why it had to happen", however, we continue to listen to his story with eager ears.

5 Werther's *passio* – and his Ossianic resurrection

Allusions to the Bible form a constant part of the novel's so characteristically rich and dense intertextual web (cf. Goethe 1996, 591–593). They pervade the novel from the beginning, here and there adding to the text a rather loose association. Towards its end, however, things change: the biblical allusions crystallise into a consistent image that dominates the last quarter of the novel. Here we encounter Werther's "re-enactment of Christ's passion" (Molnar 1984, 79), a rather distorted, almost mocking "imitatio Christi" (Grimm 1999, 61, Neumann 2000, 523). The fact that this parallel is of importance for the novel is indicated by its title: "*Die Leiden des jungen Werthers*", 'The sufferings of young Werther'. This title approximates Werther's passions to Christ's and adds a decisive dimension to the passions (and sufferings) of the lover: the dimension of redemption and resurrection.

As Werther writes in his letter of November 15th, his relation to religion and the Christian dogma is rather uneasy and complicated. It is the role of a "perverted Jesus Christ" (Jackson 2004, 44) that Werther assumes when his decision to leave the world approaches reality. What must appear as the most profane and even blasphemous trait of Werther's '*imitatio*' is that although he in a way re-enacts Christ's passion, he does not follow Christ, he does not acknowledge and confirm Christ's role in the dogma:

---

[206] "Daß ihr Menschen, rief ich aus, um von einer Sache zu reden, gleich sprechen müßt: Das ist thörig, das ist klug, das ist gut, das ist bös! Und was will das all heissen? Habt ihr deßwegen die innern Verhältnisse einer Handlung erforscht? Wißt ihr mit Bestimmtheit die Ursachen zu entwickeln, warum sie geschah, warum sie geschehen mußte? Hättet ihr das, ihr würdet nicht so eilfertig mit euren Urtheilen seyn." (94)

> Does not the Son of God himself say that those shall be around him [um ihn] whom the Father has given to him? Now, what if I have not been given? Now, what if the Father wants to keep me for Himself, as my heart tells me? (108; transl. altered)[207]

Werther's *imitatio* is thus rather a *substitutio*: he imagines himself and Jesus Christ sharing the same father, the same structural position of mediation between the earthly and the heavenly, with the same direct contact to the father. In other words, he imagines himself to be Christ's secular, his profane, but also his excessive brother.

What motivates Werther's re-enactment of Christ's passion is not only the suffering that exceeds the limits of human existence and raises the question of death. Above all, Werther seeks to give his suffering and death a meaning, to render it effective beyond the boundaries of his death. It is Christ's 'afterlife', his sacrificial role in the Christian plan of salvation, transforming suffering into meaning, that fascinates Werther. He is driven by the abstract idea that there is another world for him and his weathery experiences, for him and Lotte. He believes that his death will bring about the transformation towards this world.

The most important 'prop' for Werther's re-enactment of Christ's passion is the chalice:

> What is it except man's fate to suffer his measure to the end, drain his cup to the dregs? – And if the chalice was too bitter on the human lips of the God from Heaven, why should I boast and pretend that it tastes sweet to me? And why should I be ashamed in the dreaded moment when my whole being trembles between being and not-being, when the past flashes like lightning over the gloomy abyss of the future and everything around me sinks to the bottom [versinkt] and the world goes to ruin with me? (109)[208]

Werther's drinking from the chalice marks the moment when the limit of human existence is crossed once and for all. As Werther's choice of words emphasises, he conceives of this transgression as a last, an ultimate act of excess: "everything around me sinks to the bottom", Werther writes, using a formulation that

---

[207] "Sagt nicht selbst der Sohn Gottes: daß die um ihn seyn würden, die ihm der Vater gegeben hat. Wenn ich ihm nun nicht gegeben bin! Wenn mich nun der Vater für sich behalten will, wie mir ein Herz sagt!" (180)

[208] "Was ist's anders als Menschenschiksal, sein Maas auszuleiden, seinen Becher auszutrinken. – Und ward der Kelch dem Gott vom Himmel auf seiner Menschenlippe zu bitter, warum soll ich gros thun und mich stellen, als schmekte er mir süsse. Und warum sollte ich mich schämen, in dem schröklichen Augenblikke, da mein ganzes Wesen zwischen Seyn und Nichtseyn zittert, da die Vergangenheit wie ein Bliz über dem finstern Abgrunde der Zukunft leuchtet, und alles um mich her versinkt, und mit mir die Welt untergeht." (180)

echoes his earlier blissfully ecstatic moments. Death is situated at the junction of bliss and catastrophe, it expresses the peak of ambivalence when the notion of 'passion' is brought to its extremes. Werther is well aware of this ambivalence:

> She does not see, she does not sense that she is preparing poison [*Gift*] that will destroy both her and me; and I, with lustful pleasure, sip from the cup she hands me, to my ruination. (109)[209]

> Here, Lotte! I do not shudder to take the cold, terrible chalice from which I shall drink the ecstasy of death! You handed it to me, and I do not waver. (148)[210]

Drinking the "ecstasy of death" is reminiscent of the ecstasy of dance, as well as of Werther's Dionysian excesses with wine (cf. the letter of November 8th). This time, however, Lotte does not reproach Werther for his excesses. On the contrary, Werther imagines her to be preparing and to finally hand the chalice to him, it is from her hands (or is it her lips?) that he receives the "lustful pleasure" of his "ruination". The ambivalence at the heart of Werther's passion very precisely stages the logic of the gift/*Gift* that Jacques Derrida has coined (1991, 25). Werther's self-stylisation as a Christ figure however adds another turn to this paradoxical logic of giving and taking: receiving the fatal gift is the precondition for giving (and receiving) something greater. Werther's receiving is, according to his own blasphemous re-enactment of Christ's passion, sacrificial; it is essentially done *for* a certain goal, that he, in a phallocentric way, imagines to be connected with Lotte:

> It is not despair, it is the certainty that I have borne my suffering to the end and am sacrificing myself for you. Yes, Lotte! Why should I keep silent? One of the three of us must go, and I want to be the one! (128)[211]

Werther's male heroic self-stylisation is as desperate as it is illusory. He did not really have a choice. It is not his heroic courage, but the problem of his excesses that drive him from this world. Werther's suicide paradigmatically

---

[209] "Sie sieht nicht, sie fühlt nicht, daß sie einen Gift bereitet, der mich und sie zu Grunde richten wird. Und ich mit voller Wollust schlurfe den Becher aus, den sie mir zu meinem Verderben reicht." (182)
[210] "Hier Lotte! Ich schaudere nicht den kalten schröklichen Kelch zu fassen, aus dem ich den Taumel des Todes trinken soll! Du reichtest mir ihn, und ich zage nicht." (262)
[211] "Es ist nicht Verzweiflung, es ist Gewißheit, daß ich ausgetragen habe, und daß ich mich opfere für Dich, ja Lotte, warum sollt ich's verschweigen: eins von uns dreyen muß hinweg, und das will ich seyn." (224)

represents the experience of a world that has no place for excess, that has no place for the weathery forces that disturb the calm, cloudless order of human control. Behind the façade of heroic self-sacrifice Werther senses that his dying for a higher purpose is not as simply realised as he had thought:

> That I might have had the happiness of dying for you! Lotte, of sacrificing myself for you! I would die courageously, I would die joyously if I could restore to you the calm, the bliss of your life. But alas! it has been given to only a few noble souls to spill their blood for their loved ones and by their death to kindle a new hundredfold life for their friends. (148)[212]

As the novel tells us, Werther's suicide did not at all "restore to [Lotte] the calm, the bliss of [her] life". It is not the bliss of calmness for which Werther dies. His leaving this world indeed removes a troubling, dislocated agent of weathery forces, but only as a superficial side effect, which for Lotte and Albert does not even work: "Albert was unable [to walk behind the body]. They feared for Lotte's life." (150)[213] Like Christ, he envisages another world, a world where eternity and the transitory, weathery bliss of his love to Lotte, where, more generally, eternity and "glowing life" can somehow be reconciled:

> Do you recall the flowers you sent me [...]? All that is fleeting, but no eternity shall snuff out the glowing life that I savored yesterday on your lips, that I feel in me! She loves me! This arm embraced her, these lips trembled on her lips, this mouth stammered on hers. She is mine! You are mine! Yes, Lotte, for all eternity. [...] I will lead the way! going to my Father, to your Father. To him I will lament, and He will comfort me until you come and I fly to meet you and hold you and stay with you in never-ending embraces before the countenance of the Infinite Being. (141–142)[214]

The drastic description of Werther's cruel, not at all heroic or divine death undermine the harmonious fantasy of a paradisiac 'afterlife' shared with Lotte

---

[212] "Für dich zu sterben, Lotte, für dich mich hinzugeben. Ich wollte muthig, ich wollte freudig sterben, wenn ich dir die Ruhe, die Wonne deines Lebens wieder schaffen könnte; aber ach das ward nur wenig Edlen gegeben, ihr Blut für die Ihrigen zu vergiessen, und durch ihren Tod ein neues hundertfältiges Leben ihren Freunden anzufachen." (262)

[213] "Nachts gegen eilfe ließ [der Amtmann] ihn an die Stätte begraben, die er sich erwählt hatte, der Alte folgte der Leiche und die Söhne. Albert vermochts nicht. Man fürchtete für Lottens Leben." (266)

[214] "Erinnerst du dich der Blumen die du mir schiktest [...]. Alles das ist vergänglich, keine Ewigkeit soll das glühende Leben auslöschen, das ich gestern auf deinen Lippen genoß, das ich in mir fühle. Sie liebt mich! Dieser Arm hat sie umfast, diese Lippen auf ihren Lippen gezittert, dieser Mund am ihrigen gestammelt. Sie ist mein! du bist mein! ja Lotte auf ewig! [...] Ich gehe voran! Geh zu meinem Vater, zu deinem Vater, dem will ich's klagen und er wird mich trösten biß du kommst, und ich fliege dir entgegen und fasse dich und bleibe bey dir vor dem Angesichte des Unendlichen in ewigen Umarmungen." (250)

that Werther dreams of when his death draws near. Do we readers believe in this harmonious vision? Having read the description of Werther's death it is not hope for another, better world as preached by the Christian dogma, but empathy with his earthly suffering that I think dominates our reactions to the text:

> When the physician came to the wretched man, he found him on the ground, beyond saving, there was a beating pulse, all his limbs were paralyzed. He had shot himself in the forehead above his right eye, his brain was extruded [*herausgetrieben*]. A vein in his arm had been opened unnecessarily [*zum Ueberflusse*], the blood ran, his breath was still coming in gasps. (149)[215]

The circumstances of Werther's dying translate his ultimate excess into drastic, bodily terms. Instead of a spiritual liberation from the limits of human existence, instead of Werther's "losing [himself] in the infinite abundance" we face the transgression of his bodily limits 'taken literally': it is not the Father he is meeting when leaving this world, but a physician. The act of excess, of transgressing the boundaries takes place in the form of the extrusion of his brain and his blood's running from his body. In the German original the notion of overflowing finds its way into the text ("zum Ueberflusse") when the editor comments on the rather senseless medical endeavour of opening a vein of the dying man. On a symbolic level, however, this opening of a vein is revealing: the physician supports Werther's ultimate excess; obviously not because he thinks this endeavour particularly blissful, but, inadvertently or not, he shortens the insufferable 'spectacle' of Werther's slow death. The whole scene tragically puts on display Werther's role in (and for) society: his excesses confront the human world with parts of itself that do not fit its self-understanding, that are to be covered up, hidden, not spoken about. His excesses bring to light realities of human existence that repression has relegated to darkness: here it is the bodily reality of dying in all its brutality and the human powerlessness in the face of this cruel 'spectacle'. The human reaction to it is as understandable as it is significant: no matter whether it is the characters of the fictional world, like the physician, or the readers of the novel, one wishes this scene, and with it, Werther's as well as our empathetic sufferings would end. This is exactly what the novel is about – and why Werther's suicide concerns us all, why it is no individual, idiosyncratic pathology but a tragic diagnosis of the world we are living in. Having "investigated the deeper circumstances of [Werther's] action" with the

---

[215] "Als der Medikus zu dem Unglüklichen kam, fand er ihn an der Erde ohne Rettung, der Puls schlug, die Glieder waren alle gelähmt, über dem rechten Auge hatte er sich durch den Kopf geschossen, das Gehirn war herausgetrieben. Man ließ ihm zum Ueberflusse eine Ader am Arme, das Blut lief, er holte noch immer Athem." (264)

help of the novel we, as representatives of a world that is governed by human reason and control, we, who have been socialised in a normalised, modern world, can only acknowledge our share in Werther's fate.

In other words, there is more to this scene than drastic corporeality. This dimension cannot be a spiritual 'afterlife', as the novel's famous last sentence unmistakably underlines: "No clergyman attended" (150). Paradoxically, Werther's 'afterlife', his redeeming resurrection, is inherent in the scene's drastic corporeality. It is a different, but still a 'worldly' world that emerges in the scene of Werther's death, because what the editor confronts us with is not only a cruel spectacle, but a sight of signs, left to be read:

> From the blood on the back of the armchair it could be inferred that he had accomplished the deed while sitting at the desk, had then slumped over and thrown himself convulsively around the chair. He lay feebly on his back, against the window, he was fully dressed, his boots on and wearing a blue dress coat with a yellow waistcoat. (149)[216]

In this description Werther has already taken on the stability of an object. His exact position in the room can be determined, his appearance can be described in the present tense, without any notion of time or change. Despite Werther's being "paralyzed", despite his having long lost the ability to speak, the so stable setting does however not transform Werther's unrest, his unruly urge for (eccentric) movement into a more or less peaceful or at least tragic calmness. The absence of outer movement does not absolve him from his disturbing past. Despite his having to a large extent already left this world, despite his having been transformed into a mere material presence in space, to a gasping corpse, the circumstances of Werther's last paralyzed moments do not contrast to his past life. On the contrary, as the editor's 'reading' of this setting shows, it makes these final moments readable, it tells the story of a fall, of violent "convulsive[ ]" movements. It is not just any traces that Werther's death struggle has left behind, as Werther is not wearing just any outfit for his worldly 'afterlife'. His lethal suffering, that is his fall from the chair to the ground, his "throw[ing] himself convulsively around the chair" echo the centrifugal, excessive movement of the waltz, they are all iconic for Werther's life as a whole. It is no coincidence that the 'afterlife' that the editor's description narrates is the 'afterlife' of Werther's body, not of his soul. This body, as a body, comes to lie on the interior side of the window, facing it, being directed "against" [*gegen*] it; it, however, does not

---

216 "Aus dem Blut auf der Lehne des Sessels konnte man schliessen, er habe sizzend vor dem Schreibtische die That vollbracht. Dann ist er herunter gesunken, hat sich konvulsivisch um den Stuhl herum gewälzt, er lag gegen das Fenster entkräftet auf dem Rükken, war in völliger Kleidung gestiefelt, im blauen Frak mit gelber Weste." (264)

cross this symbolical threshold, it does not indulge in any spiritual vision, but keeps the same position that Werther held as a living human being.

It is a brutal, earthly, but still a meaningful, a 'positive' and 'productive' transformation that is taking place, I would suggest. In a certain way, and only in this certain way, against his own naïve hopes, Werther does not fail. His unstable, unruly, weathery self transforms into a stable set of signs, into an icon, an emblem, that affirms and conserves his former weathery self. This material remainder, this 'afterlife', like the corpse "against the window", remains a part of this world. It gives a readable, a mediated presence to the weathery, excessive forces that unmediated, in their brutal, troubling material power could not find representation in the dominant order of the world, and therefore had to be sacrificed.

The sight of signs presents us with yet another important detail that critics who argue for Werther's ultimate failure have not hesitated to read as pleading their case: Werther has "accomplished the deed while sitting at the desk". The place and posture of writing, "sizzend vor dem Schreibtische", is used for killing oneself, so that a proximity is established that seems to be one of substitution: "Werther kills himself, because he has nothing to write, at least nothing that lives up to his standards" (Pütz 1983, 55; my transl.). With regard to the narrated world, Werther is indeed "the paradigmatic dilettante" (Vaget 1983, 13). If he were an artist figure one would have to see him as a failed one (cf. Zimmermann 1968, II, 197–198) – but he is not. His *imitatio Christi* is no *imitatio poetae* (cf. Dumiche 2000, 135), Werther not an author figure, because in the narrated world he is never in the position of coexisting with a literary work that he conceives himself of having authored (except for his translation of Ossian, perhaps). Literary work and life do not coexist in Goethe's novel, so that Peter Pütz can rightly claim that, at the end of the novel, "Werther escapes from his life into literature" (Pütz 1983, 59; my transl.). This is the transformation, the resurrection that Werther's *passio* as an '*imitatio Christi*' was directed toward: Werther becomes what he, for us, has been all the time, "a figure transmissible through text" (Edmunds 1996, 45). He turns into the protagonist of *Werther*, the performance is a complex, paradoxical, actually impossible narratological operation. This operation, although similar, does not follow the pattern of the conventional metalepsis (cf. Genette 1972), popular and unproblematic (though still breathtaking) at least since Sterne's *Tristram Shandy*. It does not connect the pragmatically incompatible narrated world and the readers' world and thus is not 'merely' metafictional in a narrower sense. This operation does not aim at fiction alone, it does not exhibit its conventions and illusions. It is the relation of fiction and world, and a special historical constellation of these two, that Goethe's novel focuses on. To put it in abstract terms: Werther's *passio* narrates the re-entry of the form of the literary medium into the form of the literary medium itself (Luhmann 1997, 102). It thereby not only gives testimony to the birth or the emergence of an 'autonomous' literary medium, it also gives an account of the historical 'necessity', or more aptly, the historical demand for such a medium, it gives reasons why there is need for mediation, and that is to say, for literature.

At first glance, Werther's *passio*, death and 'resurrection' resemble rather an Ovidian metamorphosis than an '*imitatio Christi*': he kills himself and "becomes a set of dead letters in need of a spirit, friendly or unfriendly, to guide him and give him life" (Koelb 2008, 67). He turns into (the protagonist of) a novel so that "[h]is life-after-death will be as a textualized remainder that holds forever open the space that he no longer occupies" (Koelb 2008, 66). It is, however, exactly here that the redeeming, the productive and meaningful dimension of his death and resurrection/'afterlife' as a phenomenon of literature emerges: The space Werther occupied as a living person, his weathery eccentricity could not claim any stability in the dominant order in which he was living. On the contrary, it proved to be incompatible, an unlivable space so that Werther could only feel dislocated, driven from this world by restorative forces, only free to leave this world for another. This 'other' world turns out not to be a world beyond the threshold of the window, but a mediated world that emerges inside the 'old world'. His death is thus the "ultimate expression of his acceptance of mediation" (Edmunds 1996, 49): it is mediation, that is to say the emergence of the medium of literature that "holds forever open" a space that without mediation would have remained covered up, repressed and would thus factually cease to find representation under the reign of the dominant, enlightened order of the world. If Werther, in a blasphemous analogy to Jesus Christ, can be said to 'redeem' this somehow corrupted or at least insufficient order of the world, then not by leading the way towards a transcendent beyond, but by causing to emerge a supplementary medium inside this order of the world, as part of this world, that resists and keeps questioning the reigning order's almost universal dominance.

The openly phallocentric character of Werther's heroic self-stylisation, 'his' redeeming self-sacrifice has rightly been criticised by Béatrice Dumiche and others as a desperate attempt to patriarchally appropriate the agency of a failing patriarchy. As we have seen, it is in fact Lotte who initiates the decisive moments – she even voices Werther's 'death sentence': "This is the last time! Werther! You will never see me again." (139)[217] and hands him the means to

---

[217] "Das ist das leztemal! Werther! Sie sehn mich nicht wieder." (246)

carry it out. However, the structural dimension behind these processes is even more important than the questions of categorising agency according to the gender of the acting persons: "the symbolical rescue of patriarchy through literary authorship fails", Béatrice Dumiche (Dumiche 2000, 140; my transl.) notes. It fails, I would suggest, because the phenomenon that Werther's myth is about has nothing to do with authorship. The transformation of Werther into the novel *Werther*, that is to say, the relocating of the weathery forces from an impossible, unmediated space to the medium of literature is not the question of an author's authority. On the contrary, the still excessive, uncontrollable weathery forces now captured in the literary medium resist authorial attempts to appropriate these forces for any intentional, strategic purposes.

Goethe's *Werther* is, inadvertently, perhaps one of the best examples of the failure of authorial control over these forces: Goethe could never agree with the reception of his novel, despite the fact that it was a huge success. His own reading differed markedly from the readings of the masses, and it is the readings of the masses that account for the fame of the novel. As Robert Stockhammer has pointed out, the form as a monological epistolary novel already reflects the fact that mediation puts the act of reading in the centre of literary discourse (1991, 165). Once literature (or art, in general) begins to form an autonomous, aesthetic medium as part of a social system characterised by differentiation, a literary text can no longer be simply regarded as an author's enunciation, expressive of his or her wit, intentions, ideas, worldviews. It has to be read – a fact that, paradoxically, also makes the question of the mysterious, opaque links to the (person of the) author that also have to be read, that are not transparent, much more interesting than before. In a way Goethe's *Werther* even stages this problem of the author/writer: the writer of the letters, Werther, has to die in order to bring about the transformation that turns the letters into a novel and himself into a protagonist. The connection of writer and novel is irreducibly divided by the gap of death. There is no link. The reading begins, when Werther's slow death leaves behind a sight of signs – and it is from there that we begin our reading of Werther's letters.

Is Werther now one of the "few noble souls" who have "spill[ed] their blood for their loved ones and by their death [have] kindle[d] a new hundredfold life for their friends"? Certainly not in a way that lives up to the heroics of this formulation. The product brought about in Werther's metamorphosis, the "little book" called *The Sufferings of Young Werther*, can however be understood as being 'good' or of use *for* someone, it fulfils, on a more humble scale, the meaningfulness that Werther wanted to ascribe to his self-sacrifice. According to its dedication to the readers this is what this book is for:

> And you, good soul, who feel the same urge [*Drang*] as he, take comfort from his sufferings and let this little book be your friend if by fate or your own fault you can find none closer to you. (19; transl. altered)[218]

As Erdmann Waniek notes with some astonishment, it is not the human being named Werther that the editor (or the one in charge of the paratext) offers to the reader as a friend, but a product of art, "this little book" (1982, 55). The 'service' that this book can do is thus not of the order of identification: Werther is neither an inspiring example nor is his story merely a cautionary tale. Our new, odd friend, the little book, asks to be read. The distance introduced through this process of mediation seems to account for the comforting effect that this friend can produce: neither identification with the character 'Werther', nor taking his story as an instruction not to follow his way seem to be comforting. Reading this book, however, which certainly combines both identification and a certain aesthetic distance in a way that cannot be further theorised, seems to have a special effect.

The logic of the novel's dedication to the readers implies that a friend like that cannot easily be found. It cannot be found "closer to you" than as a novel, a little book – otherwise the book at hand could easily be replaced by 'real', 'genuine', living friends and would not be read at all. Millions of readers, however, indeed took this book as a friend, and thereby confirmed the dedication's subtle but not quite humble logic. Viewed more closely, the dedication voices a confident self-assertion of the novel, claiming for it a place in social life that it holds exclusively, a social role somehow necessary, but necessarily filled, "held open" by literature, by the little book of a novel. What informs this 'role', this 'place'? The dedication gives us an unmistakable hint: it is the "urge" that links the reader and the book's hero, an urge for which the book (not the hero!) via reading appears to provide a comforting space. As was made clear above, this urge is not to be separated from the weather; it is inscribed in the analogy of *Sturm und Drang*, so that the problem at stake here, the problem for which the literary medium provides a solution concerns the weathery forces and their relation to enlightened society.

All this would remain utterly abstract and speculative if the novel itself had not provided us with an exemplary instance of a literary text taking the role of a friend. We watch this text being read and can observe the effect that it has.

---

[218] "Und du gute Seele, die du eben den Drang fühlst wie er, schöpfe Trost aus seinem Leiden, und laß das Büchlein deinen Freund seyn, wenn du aus Geschick oder eigner Schuld keinen nähern finden kannst." (10)

We watch the famous bag of Aeolus being opened and see the weathery forces being unleashed. In other words: we also get to experience that "tak[ing] comfort", as the dedication suggests, does not have to be a harmonious vision, but can also consist in the violent manifestation that one is not alone with one's weathery urges, that there is still a source of excess, of resisting or breaking out of the dominant order, despite the weather's forces being framed by mediation. Literature thus testifies to the fact that these forces are still real and effective although being enclosed in a medium, that they transcend the medium through the act of reading.

This takes place in the famous Ossian reading scene. In the logic of Werther's *'imitatio Christi'* one could say that this scene holds the structural place of the Last Supper, an event to which Werther later explicitly alludes when "[h]e had bread and wine brought to him" (146)[219] shortly before his death. The assertion that it is rather the reading scene than Werther's lonely meal of wine and bread that takes the place of the Last Supper, as far-fetched as it might seem, has to do with its relation to Werther's 'transformation': like the Eucharist that Jesus Christ celebrates with his disciples, Werther's reading his translation of Ossian to Lotte anticipates his transformation. In both cases, the 'surrogate' (i.e. bread and wine or the book) is, paradoxically, co-present with the seemingly 'real' person that is to leave this world, the scenes depict the rare moment of 'overlapping' that is used for instruction. In both cases the person to leave demonstrates a ritual that is to become important once this person has died – or rather, has been transformed into what he really is, (son of) God, or (the literary character of) a book. In both cases this ritual (the Eucharist, reading) teaches how to 'animate' a seemingly dead 'surrogate' and gives an account of the unexpected forces that can be released from the "dead set of letters" or mere bread and wine.

The scene of reading Ossian also contains a hidden relation to the novel's dedication to the readers, with its approximation of book and friend. It is triggered by Werther's surprisingly visiting Lotte despite her request (following her husband's demand for more distance between her and Werther) not to see her until Christmas. Albert, trusting that Werther and his wife comply with this arrangement, is absent overnight, so that Werther's visit puts Lotte in an awkward situation: she is alone with someone she should not at all be alone with, according to her husband. She has an idea how to solve this problem:

---

[219] "Er ließ sich Brod und Wein bringen [...]." (258)

You did not keep your word. – I promised nothing, was his answer. – Then you should at least have granted me my wish, she replied; I asked you for the sake of both our peace of mind. When saying that she had thought by herself to send for some friends. They should be testimonies of her talk with Werther, and in the evening, because he had to walk them home, she would get rid of him at the right time. (131; transl. altered to the 1774 version)[220]

Unfortunately (it is by fate rather than by Lotte's own fault) her friends cannot come, visiting relatives and the bad weather prevent their testifying presence. This is the moment when Lotte, fully in the spirit of the novel's dedication to the readers, resorts to another friend:

She became thoughtful for some minutes, until the feeling of her innocence revolted with some pride. She resisted Albert's maggots and the purity of her heart gave her firmness so that she did not call her maid into the parlour, as she initially intended, but after playing some minuets on the piano to recover and allay the confusion of her heart, she sat down calmly next to Werther on the settee.

Do you have nothing to read? she said. – He had nothing. – There in my drawer, she began, is your translation of some of the songs of Ossian. [...] He smiled, he fetched the songs, a tremor went through him as his hands held them, and his eyes filled with tears as he glanced at the pages. He sat back down and read: (132; transl. altered to the 1774 version)[221]

It is a piece of literature she resorts to, and even before a word has been read both Lotte's thoughts and Werther's emotional reaction betray that this 'friend's' company is different from the company of the friends Lotte initially had wished for. Nevertheless, this 'friend' also acts as a witness: however not facilitating and testifying to their chastity, to their appropriate and limited interaction but, on the contrary, facilitating and testifying to their love, to the weathery urge that links the two and resonates with the weathery piece of literature they

---

220 "Sie haben nicht Wort gehalten! rief sie ihm entgegen. Ich habe nichts versprochen, war seine Antwort. So hätten Sie mir wenigstens meine Bitte gewähren sollen, sagte sie, es war Bitte um unserer beyder Ruhe willen. Indem sie das sprach, hatte sie bey sich überlegt, einige ihrer Freundinnen zu sich rufen zu lassen. Sie sollten Zeugen ihrer Unterredung mit Werthern seyn, und Abends, weil er sie nach Hause führen mußte, ward sie ihn zur rechten Zeit los." (230)
221 "Darüber ward sie einige Minuten nachdenkend, bis das Gefühl ihrer Unschuld sich mit einigem Stolze empörte. Sie bot Alberts Grillen Truz, und die Reinheit ihres Herzens gab ihr eine Festigkeit, daß sie nicht, wie sie anfangs vorhatte, ihr Mädgen in die Stube rief, sondern, nachdem sie einige Menuets auf dem Clavier gespielt hatte, um sich zu erholen, und die Verwirrung ihres Herzens zu stillen, sich gelassen zu Werthern auf's Canapee sezte. Haben Sie nichts zu lesen, sagte sie. Er hatte nichts. Da drinne in meiner Schublade, fieng sie an, liegt ihre Uebersezzung einiger Gesänge Ossians [...]. Er lächelte, holte die Lieder, ein Schauer überfiel ihn, als er sie in die Hand nahm, und die Augen stunden ihm voll Thränen, als er hinein sah, er sezte sich nieder und las:" (230)

are reading. From a structural point of view, the text by Ossian holds the same place that Klopstock's *Frühlingsfeyer* had occupied in the ball scene. It is again Lotte who establishes the important connection to literature and thereby opens up the decisive dimension for the project of productively transgressing the current order (cf. Pütz 1983, 64), a project that Werther so heroically claims for himself. There is, however, one important contrast to the scene at the window and the invocation of Klopstock: whereas in this early scene the resonance that their love found in literature could still be read merely as a sign for something other, real, existing or at least something to be realised outside and independent from literature, Werther knows by the time of their reading Ossian that there is no place in reality available for their love, except in and via literature. The weathery urge that links him to Lotte cannot be lived out in an unmediated fashion between human beings of this society. The weather has found a space in enlightened society, but it is inseparably connected with the ritual of reading; it is relegated to the medium of literature.

As many critics have noted, there is, however, a fundamental problem with this passage of the book, which is indeed "one of its principal climactic scenes" (Koelb 2008, 47): it "almost always bores or mystifies modern readers almost to the point of ruining their pleasure in the story" (Koelb 2008, 47), it is tearful, but tedious and banal so that it is likely to be the passage most often skipped over (Anderegg 1997, 122). The modern readers just cannot share Lotte's and Werther's enthusiasm and must thus rather trudge through the long and lengthy translation of Ossian (Waniek 1982, 72). Does it have to be understood ironically, then, as Bruce Duncan claims (cf. 1982, 45–46)?

There is no evidence of irony. On the contrary, the translation of some of Ossian's songs that Werther reads to Lotte marks a very complex narratological point that stands out in the novel's fictional world and touches on the circumstances of the novel's production: the translation that inside the fictional world is ascribed to Werther is in fact a montage of two passages of Goethe's own translation of the songs of Ossian. The passage thus cannot be read as creating ironic distance, it is rather the novel's point of least distance, a point where the levels of the fictional world and the real world cease to be distinguishable. For several pages there is hardly any mediating narratological instance separating Werther's voice from Goethe's. The typographical layout of inserted headlines undermines even the fact that this passage is read by Werther, a fact that would very soon be forgotten if there were not the fictional reader's and the listener's emotional reaction to the text, abruptly interrupting their (and our) reading. Furthermore, it is not just any text that Goethe inserts into his novel: Ossian's songs are a programmatic text for the time, especially for the intellectual circle of which Goethe was a member. And it is, above all, a programmatic text for the novel in which it is featured, into which it re-enters, quoted verbatim over several pages. One does not so much have to wonder "what possessed Goethe to divert our attention from the characters for whom he has worked so diligently to kindle our interest to these literary ghosts translated from a translation?" (Koelb 2008, 47), but rather what it is that keeps us modern readers at a distance, so that we are not moved, as Lotte and Werther are, but tend to look for signals of irony instead. This is an important question, because it does not aim at rescuing the few 'boring' pages of the Ossian, but concerns the novel as a whole.

The climactic reading of Ossian is a key scene of the novel because it outlines a theory of the literary medium: it is a theory of the relation of literature and the world, a theory of reception and reading. In other words, "these literary ghosts" are not mere spectres of a negligible, obsolete event in literary history (Macpherson's forgeries of 'Ossian'), but are what haunts the novel called *Werther*. They are at the heart of its project. The fact that we feel "our attention" "diverted" "from the characters" may lead us towards an answer to the question of the mysterious distance that separates us from the 18th century enthusiasm for Ossian, and from the 18th century reception of Goethe's novel that participates in the same enthusiasm. This novel is not about characters (as so many others are, as this genre 'in general' is said to be) – it is about forces that surpass or transgress the limits of the human being. Like the company at the ball after Lotte's game we, reading novels focussing on characters, have "forgot [ten] weather and all". Reading the novel as a novel about a character, Werther, we concentrate our attention on the restorative game, and tend to overlook why this game was actually started, what it is holding at bay. Goethe's novel is complex enough to work for both readings, for the one interested in characters as well as for a reading focussing on the weathery forces. This does not hold true for the Ossian passage: there are no 'characters', and if we look for them, we might, like Clayton Koelb, merely find ghosts. For our enlightened mind-set this discovery confirms the judgment that the passage is of little substance, about nothing really, and worth skipping. Goethe, however, has inserted this passage, a carefully composed and reworked selection of his own translations of Ossian (Schmidt 1875, 227), at the climax of the novel – in an overtly metamedial scene about reading and the relation between fiction and the world. With regard to the structural place of the passage in the novel, as well as to the important role that *Ossian* plays for Goethe and his intellectual contemporaries it is impossible to neglect this passage. On the contrary, however 'boring' and aesthetically questionable it might be, understanding or giving meaning to the Ossian passage is an intrinsic part of giving meaning to the novel as a whole.

Consequently, in a way, the inserted songs of Ossian serve as an important indicator: they indicate the distance of the modern reader to the intellectual climate of the time when the novel was written. It also makes us aware of the fact that any reading that cannot account for this, admittedly, 'odd' passage has missed something important in the novel – and might even have missed 'the gist' of it.

So what is this ominous passage that is read out aloud by Werther about, if it is not about characters? It is, to the most extreme degree possible, about weather. It presents a world that is composed of weather, a world, for which the weather and its manifold phenomena form the constitutive foundation. Consequently, when a character is introduced this is done by a series of weather similes:

> Thou wert swift, O Morar! as a roe on the desert; terrible as a meteor of fire in the sky. Thy wrath was as the storm. Thy sword in battle, as summer lightning on the heath. Thy voice was as a stream in the forest after rain; like thunder on distant hills. [...] Thy face was like the sun after a thunderstorm; like the moon in the silence of night; thy breast calm as the lake when the blustering of the wind has abated. (136; transl. altered)[222]

> Daura, my daughter! thou wert fair; fair as the moon on the hills of Fura; white as the fallen snow; sweet as the breathing air. [...]

> Arindal, thy bow was strong. Thy spear was swift on the field, thy look was like mist on the wave; thy shield, a cloud of fire in a storm! (137; transl. altered)[223]

These characters are, however, not introduced to praise their heroic deeds. Despite the tragic story of Daura and Arindal that parts of the passage relate, I would like to suggest that it is not stories that this passage of Ossian is centring on; but one, single theme: through its varying constellations of characters and singers, it rather describes and elaborates on the pragmatic situation of the song. This pragmatic situation is composed of several characteristic elements, of which the singer's loneliness in the middle of rough weather is one:

---

[222] "Du warst schnell o Morar, wie ein Reh auf dem Hügel, schreklich wie die Nachtfeuer am Himmel, dein Grimm war ein Sturm. Dein Schwerdt in der Schlacht wie Wetterleuchten über die Haide. Deine Stimme glich dem Waldstrohme nach dem Regen, dem Donner auf fernen Hügeln. [...]. Dein Angesicht war gleich der Sonne nach dem Gewitter, gleich dem Monde in der schweigenden Nacht. Ruhig deine Brust wie der See, wenn sich das Brausen des Windes gelegt hat." (238)

[223] "Daura, meine Tochter, du warst schön! schön wie der Mond auf den Hügeln von Fura, weiß wie der gefallene Schnee, süß wie die athmende Luft. [...] Arindal, dein Bogen war stark, dein Speer schnell auf dem Felde, dein Blik wie Nebel auf der Welle, dein Schild eine Feuerwolke im Sturme." (240)

> It is night; I am alone, forlorn on the stormy hill. The wind is singing in the mountain. The torrent howls down the rock. No hut protects me from the rain; forlorn on the stormy hill. (133; transl. altered)[224]
>
> Here I must sit alone! (134)[225]

As this allusion to the hut, which, as we have seen, plays an important role in Goethe's novel, indicates, the situation that the Ossian passage spells out is beyond the dialectics of protection and excess. It is therefore not concerned with the human being and its limits, but is located beyond these limits, where there is no protection, only weather. The weather is not threatening the singer's existence – it is the only company the singer finds, a company, "singing" and "howl[ing]" that, from the beginning, uncannily resembles the singer's song: S/he is part of this weather. Sitting in the middle of the loud weather, it is not easy to establish a communicative situation, to hear others and make oneself heard:

> The stream and the wind roar aloud. I hear not the voice of my love! (133)[226]
>
> Hush a little while, O wind! stream, be thou silent awhile! let my voice be heard around! Let my wanderer hear me! (133; transl. altered)[227]

This is however no accident, it is the second element of this special pragmatic situation of the song. There is no counterpart at whom the songs could be directed, no one answers the singer, a loner on the hill is desperately looking for an interlocutor:

> Speak to me, O my friends! To Colma they give no reply. Speak to me; I am alone! My soul is tormented with fears! Ah, they are dead! (134)[228]
>
> Speak to me; hear my voice; hear me, sons of my love! They are silent; silent for ever! (134)[229]

---

[224] "Es ist Nacht; – ich bin allein, verlohren auf dem stürmischen Hügel. Der Wind saust im Gebürg, der Strohm heult den Felsen hinab. Keine Hütte schüzt mich vor dem Regen, verlassen auf dem stürmischen Hügel." (232)
[225] "Hier muß ich sizzen allein." (234)
[226] "Der Strohm und der Sturm saust, ich höre nicht die Stimme meines Geliebten." (234)
[227] "Schweig eine Weile o Wind, still eine kleine Weile o Strohm, daß meine Stimme klinge durch's Thal, daß mein Wandrer mich höre!" (234)
[228] "Redet o meine Freunde! Sie antworten nicht. Wie geängstet ist meine Seele – Ach sie sind todt!" (234)
[229] "Hört meine Stimme, meine Geliebten. Aber ach sie sind stumm. Stumm vor ewig." (234)

> Speak, I will not be afraid! [...] No feeble voice is on the gale; no answer half-drowned in the storm! (134)[230]
>
> [...] but thy son heareth thee not. (136)[231]
>
> [S]he called on Armar. Nought answered, but the voice of the rock. (137; transl. altered)[232]

No one answers. There are different reasons for the absence of an interlocutor (Daura is separated by the sea, her complaints are heard by her father who can do nothing, but listen; in most cases, the singers' friends and family are dead). However, the communicative situation produced by the absence is always the same: The singer does not share a world with those that may be listening; an insurmountable gap separates singer and listener. Only the song can traverse this gap, and only in one direction, as a song, as a 'mediation' that is not to be re-translated into life.

The realm from where the song is sung, the realm beyond the hut's protection, is a realm of weather – and it is a realm of death. The song, with its strange pragmatic character of not being 'answerable' testifies to death, death is inherent in it. It is not dependent on life:

> My life flies away like a dream! why should I stay behind? here shall I rest with my friends, by the stream of the sounding rock. When night comes on the hill; when the winds arise on the heath my ghost shall stand in the wind, and mourn the death of my friends. The hunter shall hear from his little hut. He fears my voice and loves it, for sweet shall my voice be for my friends; they were both so dear to me. (134; transl. altered)[233]

No one answers, but the song is heard. It makes its way from the weathery realm, where "[n]o hut protects" the singer to the hunter's "little hut". It is indeed ghostly: it speaks from the realm of death, testifying to death and mourning, but reaches the world of the living, the world where there is still protection, and something to protect. The song is spectral, of an insubstantial nature, it is but a voice reaching the hunter's ear like the howling of the wind is heard from within the hut. It is hardly astonishing that he "fears [this] voice and loves it": like the rough, the violent weather of Ossian's world, the songs

---

[230] "Redet! [...] Keine schwache Stimme vernehm ich im Wind, keine wehende Antwort im Sturme des Hügels." (234)

[231] "[...] aber dein Sohn hört dich nicht." (238)

[232] "Sie [...] rief nach Armar. Nichts antwortete als die Stimme des Felsens." (242)

[233] "Mein Leben schwindet wie ein Traum, wie sollt ich zurük bleiben. Hier will ich wohnen mit meinen Freunden an dem Strohme des klingenden Felsen – Wenns Nacht wird auf dem Hügel, und der Wind kommt über die Haide, soll mein Geist im Winde stehn und trauren den Tod meiner Freunde. Der Jäger hört mich aus seiner Laube, fürchtet meine Stimme und liebt sie, den<n> süß soll meine Stimme seyn um meine Freunde, sie waren mir beyde so lieb." (236)

themselves are of a sublime register. They are (and that is the decisive characteristic) nothing but a weather phenomenon: it is not only that the world we hear about is composed of weather; the song itself is consistently characterised as weather. All is based on the basic equation: song equals voice equals breath equals wind or related weather phenomena. As simple as this old equation (as we have seen in the first chapter) might appear, the spectrum of nuances that the passage from Ossian sketches for this analogy of song and weather is immense:

> How are ye changed, my friends, since the days of Selma's feast? when we contended for the honor of song, like gales of spring, as they fly along the hill, and bend by turn the feebly whistling grass. (133; transl. altered)[234]
>
> All night I heard her cries. Loud was the wind; the rain beat hard on the hill. Before morning appeared her voice became weak; it died away like the evening breeze among the grass of the rocks. (138; transl. altered)[235]
>
> Sweet are thy murmurs, O stream! but more sweet is the voice I hear. (135)[236]
>
> [W]hy complainst thou, as a blast in the wood, as a wave on the lonely shore? (135)[237]
>
> The song comes with its music, to melt and please the soul. It is like soft mist, that, rising from a lake, pours on the silent vale; the green flowers are filled with dew, but the sun returns in his strength, and the mist is gone. (136–137)[238]
>
> When shalt thou awake with thy songs? with all thy voice of music?
>
> Arise, winds of autumn, arise; blow along the heath! streams of the mountains, roar! roar, tempests, in the groves of my oaks! Walk through broken clouds, O moon! show thy pale face, at intervals! bring to my mind the night when all my children fell; when Arindal the mighty fell, when Daura the lovely failed! (137)[239]

---

[234] "Wie verändert seyd ihr meine Freunde seit den festlichen Tagen auf Selma! da wir buhlten um die Ehre des Gesangs, wie Frühlingslüfte den Hügel hin wechselnd beugen das schwach lispelnde Gras." (232)

[235] "[D]ie ganze Nacht hört ich ihr Schreyn. Laut war der Wind, und der Regen schlug scharf nach der Seite des Bergs. Ihre Stimme ward schwach, eh der Morgen erschien, sie starb weg wie die Abendluft zwischen dem Grase der Felsen." (244)

[236] "Süß ist dein Murmeln Strohm, doch süsser die Stimme, die ich höre." (236)

[237] "[...] warum jammerst du wie ein Windstoß im Wald, wie eine Welle am fernen Gestade." (236)

[238] "Klingt nicht Lied und Gesang, die Seele zu schmelzen und zu ergözzen. Sind wie sanfter Nebel der steigend vom See auf's Thal sprüht, und die blühenden Blumen füllet das Naß, aber die Sonne kommt wieder in ihrer Kraft und der Nebel ist gangen." (240)

[239] "Wann erwachst du mit deinen Gesängen, mit deiner melodischen Stimme? Auf! ihr Winde des Herbst, auf! Stürmt über die finstre Haide! Waldströhme braust! Heult Stürme in dem Gipfel der Eichen! Wandle durch gebrochene Wolken o Mond, zeige wechselnd dein bleiches Gesicht! Erinnere mich der schröklichen Nacht, da meine Kinder umkamen, Arindal der mächtige fiel, Daura, die liebe, vergieng." (240)

This song's "blast in the wood", its "mist [...] rising from a lake", its "tempest [...] walk[ing] through broken clouds" not only reach the hunter in his hut. They also enter Lotte's parlour and are not without effect:

> A stream [*Strohm*] of tears pouring from Lotte's eyes and freeing her anguished heart checked Werther's song. He threw the pages down, grasped her hand, and wept the bitterest tears. [...] The emotions [*Bewegung*] of both were agonizing. They felt their own misery in the fate of those noble figures, felt it together, and their tears united them. (138–139; transl. altered)[240]

With regard to the weathery nature of this song, Lotte's and Werther's reaction is 'appropriate': their being moved continues the logic of the weather and its analogies. Lotte's (and Werther's) "stream of tears" mirror the song's macrocosmic streams and their murmurs. Similar to the Klopstock episode, the literary medium opens up a space that did not exist before, that somehow takes the pressure off the readers' and listeners' non-literary existence: the literary and its reception provide room for the weathery and for the fluid. It establishes a space of streams, a space that transgresses the fixity of the individual, a space of feeling, a space facilitating processes of melting, of togetherness. Although the tears are said to have "free[d] [Lotte's] anguished heart", they are not merely signs of romantic bliss. On the contrary, like the hunter who "fears [the singer's] voice and loves it", the effect that the song has on Lotte and Werther is ambiguous: there is also agony and misery. The weathery logic of the passage resists being morally categorised as either good or bad; it is the reality of this weathery space, the reality of this fluidity of moving and being moved, constituting a realm of togetherness beyond the human individual and his limits, that is affirmed by these sentences.

The most difficult, confusing or astonishing words describing Lotte's and Werther's reaction to the songs are certainly the ones articulating the fact that "[t]hey felt their own misery in the fate of those noble figures". They address the key question of the relation between the intradiegetic level of Ossian's songs and the diegetic world of Lotte, Werther and their fate. Reading these words in the most 'direct' way, that is to say, relating them to the level of characters and plot, produces unsatisfying results: there is a tragic love story between Daura and Armar in the passage quoted from Ossian, but no further structural similarities can be found, so that an identification on this level must be regarded as

---

[240] "Ein Strohm von Thränen, der aus Lottens Augen brach und ihrem gepreßten Herzen Luft machte, hemmte Werthers Gesang, er warf das Papier hin, und faßte ihre Hand und weinte die bittersten Thränen. [...] die Bewegung beyder war fürchterlich. Sie fühlten ihr eigenes Elend in dem Schiksal der Edlen, fühlten es zusammen, und ihre Thränen vereinigte sie." (244)

superficial and weak. What looks like a Freudian slip in the passage quoted above reveals the more complex connection of the diegetic layers: "A stream [*Strohm*] of tears pouring from Lotte's eyes and freeing her anguished heart checked *Werther's song*", the editor writes, oddly confusing or identifying the act of Werther's reading with *what* he has translated, with what he is actually reading out loud, *Ossian*'s Songs. This is however not a Freudian slip but a sign for something that has, silently, already shaped the text of his letters for some time: as scholars interested in the connection between *Ossian* and *Werther* have explained, long before the episodes from *Ossian* are read, there is a lot of 'Ossian' to be found, sung by Werther, so to speak. Especially his letters of October 12th and December 8th are consistently quoted as prime examples for the Ossianic nature of Werther's writing (cf. Niggl 2000, 52–54, Edmunds 1996, 51–53, Klein 2011, 69–71). Erich Schmidt, one of the pioneers of this field of study goes so far as to claim that towards the novel's end, Werther's and Macpherson's diction cease to be distinguishable (1875, II, 771). Sonja Klein shares this observation, but reads it psychologically: as a sign of Werther's perspective on the world being irretrievably distorted through literature, for his having ultimately lost any possibility of experiencing the world (2011, 69–71). I think her reading misjudges the role that Ossian (this also holds true for Homer) plays for Goethe's novel, and more generally, for the intellectual climate that has brought forth the novel we are reading. Werther, although an enthusiastic reader of literature, is no Don Quijote and no Emma Bovary. The text he reads is dear to him (it is 'his own translation'), as it is dear to Goethe (it is in fact his own translation!). There is no ironic distance, at all. On the contrary, the fact that *Werther* resonates with *Ossian* is a sign of aspiration. Goethe's novel does not qualify or judge *Ossian*'s Songs, quite the reverse, it approximates itself to it. Werther follows Ossian: this is what the odd formulation of "Werther's song" expresses, and this is also what the mysterious phrase that "[t]hey felt their own misery in the fate of those noble figures" suggests. Werther and Lotte feel that their weathery love is not realisable, not liveable in the 'real' world. Their fate is to be the tragic protagonists of a song, this is the fate they share with Ossian's "noble figures". In other words, we face a complex, paradoxical narratological operation: characters in a novel feel that they have no future but as characters in a novel. The literary medium re-enters the literary world. More than that, their story makes them read a literary text and they identify with it, because they find themselves to be the subject of the next song. "Moving up through the embedded songs, this brings us to Werther", writes Kathryn Edmunds (1996, 51), giving, I think, a very precise description of the relation between the diegetic levels, between the text read out aloud, and the diegetic world of Werther and Lotte.

When the editor depicts the effects that "Werther's song" has on the reader and the listener, the strange ambiguity of this 'label' is no coincidence. "Thou has left no son, but the song shall preserve thy name. Future times shall hear of thee; they shall hear of the fallen Morar!" (136; transl. altered),[241] Werther reads, and what he reads will also hold true for himself, and his love story with Lotte. There is another world for him and Lotte, where they will lead a long and famous afterlife; following his passions there is 'resurrection', as "noble figures" of a literary world, in a 'song' whose title indeed "preserves [his] name": *Die Leiden des jungen Werthers*.

Sonja Klein is right, Werther in a way loses contact with the world and is swallowed up by literature. This is however not to be understood as criticism of the estranging and therefore dangerous effect of reading (how could the dedication to the readers suggest the book as a friend, if the book itself then criticised reading as dangerous, even lethal?), but as a story devoted to the formation of a literary medium. The 'other world' that Werther envisages and that turns out to be the novel bearing his name in its title is a closed world, a world with its own rules and ways of access, a world that is different from the social reality of daily life; a world that does not communicate directly with the 'real world'. It is beyond the limits of the liveable, beyond the limits of the rational and also beyond the limits of life. Nevertheless, it also paradoxically forms part of the enlightened social order. As a medium it takes over important social and societal functions, opening up a space for the weathery, the fluid and the irrational. It produces a space for practices and notions that have been repressed or driven into the dark with the rise of the enlightenment and the epistemological dominance of the human being and ratio: all the weathery forces, the streams, the analogy of microcosm and macrocosm, the concepts of being moved by uncontrollable 'outer' forces...

The passage from *Ossian* that Goethe inserted in his novel offers an exaggerated but paradigmatic example of this relatively new literary medium. The fact that these songs turned out not to be testimonies of a glorious past of 'Nordic literature' (as Goethe and his contemporaries thought) but fabrications of their own age only emphasises my argument. They attest to the contemporary imaginary of what literature was forming to be at this crucial point in the middle of the 18th century: a medium with its own code, a world of its own within the world, a world that is different, that supplements the enlightened world – a world that is functional in a functionally differentiated society (cf. Luhmann 1987) precisely for this being 'different', for its opening up new spaces and dealing

---

241 "Du hinterliesest keinen Sohn, aber der Gesang soll deinen Nahmen erhalten. Künftige Zeiten sollen von dir hören, hören sollen sie von dem gefallenen Morar." (240)

with repressed realities. There is certainly no more extreme (and therefore perhaps no more banal and boring) example for the role the weather, the weathery forces and the notion of the fluid plays in this supplementary relation of the literary medium and the world than *The Songs of Ossian*. The sterility of its construction, depicting a pure counter-world of weather, reveals that it serves stereotypically a contemporary intellectual or socio-cultural demand. In this, it is in fact not dissimilar to Kaufmann's coining of "*Sturm und Drang*". Goethe's *Werther* is certainly much more interesting than the *Ossian*, because it scrutinises the medium's relation to the world, observes and narrates both the processes of repression of weather and weathery forces in enlightened society and their being integrated into the medium that is created to give space to these forces.

Inserting a selection from *The Songs of Ossian* follows however a clever strategy: it enables Goethe to close the circle of the novel's complex metamedial project. The text read out aloud articulates a (simplified) model of the literary medium: a weathery world, that is itself working as weather, that moves its readers, who participate in this unique weathery community with their streams of tears. It is an atavistic community, resembling an order of the world that has once been dominant, as we have seen in the first chapter, but has now found a new, particularised space in a society that works very differently.

In this medium, as Ossian's songs insistently emphasise, the dominant, the speaking voice does not receive an answer, and constitutively so. This medium's speech-act is not the speech-act of communication. The structural correspondence to the characteristically monological nature of Werther's letters is obvious: the lonely, ghostly singers without interlocutors, Werther or the Ossianic ones, are emblems of the literary medium and its characteristic pragmatic asymmetry. There is an insurmountable gap between the production, the 'singing' of the literary and its reception, that makes the process of reading the most important part of it all. By inserting a paradigmatic, exaggerated example of this new medium into his novel, Goethe can expose and demonstrate this process of reading. He thereby illustrates the medium's efficacy: the fact that it not only tames the weathery forces by delegating them to the medium of literature (providing a container for the weathery), but also that it has the capacity of unleashing these forces when 'Aeolus' bag' is opened by the act of reading:

> The full force of these words fell upon the unhappy man. He threw himself down before Lotte in complete despair, grasped her hands, pressed them to his eyes, to his brow, and a foreboding of his terrible resolve appeared to fly through her soul. Her senses became confused, she squeezed his hands, pressed them against her breast, bent over him with a plaintive gesture, and their glowing cheeks touched. The world faded from them [*vergieng ihnen*]. He flung his arms around her, pressed her to his breast, and covered her trembling, stammering lips with furious kisses. – Werther! she cried in a choked voice, turning away,

> Werther! – and with a weak hand pushed his breast away from hers; – Werther! she cried in the collected tone of the loftiest feeling. – He did not resist, released her from his arms, and, insensate, threw himself down before her. – She tore herself upward, and in anxious confusion, trembling between love and fury, she said – This is the last time! Werther! you will never see me again. – And with the fullest look of love at the wretched man, she hurried into the next room and locked the door behind her. (139)[242]

Are we here becoming testimonies of a successful, an exemplary act of reading? The difference from the innocent, weathery tears of the first interruption of Werther's reading cannot be missed. The song's 'weather' has definitely become more violent, the "full force of these words" makes itself felt on both Werther and Lotte. As again indicated by the typical formulation – "The world faded from them [*vergieng ihnen*]" – the reading finally initiates a moment of ecstasy. The weathery forces break from the literary medium and lead to the novel's ultimate transgression: "furious kisses" pressed on the lips of a married woman. Is this moment of excess now to be read as a sign for the medium's failing, because, like the medium of the waltz, it cannot contain the weathery forces? Or does it testify to the medium's efficacy, because it shows the capacity of the medium to unleash the forces it harbours, to have an impact on reality?

First and foremost the scene's transgression has to be read according to the logic of Werther's *passio*. It serves the same structural purpose as Judas's betrayal in the context of Jesus Christ's last days. The transgression is certainly scandalous – at the same time, it is calculated, programmed, it is necessary for the transformation that is to come. Werther knew before he went to Lotte that he was going to die, but he could not die without this transgression occurring between them. As Judas' betrayal (also performed via a kiss) is essential for the Christian plan of salvation, Lotte's contribution to the transgression is necessary for the birth of the literary medium, for Werther's (and her?) death and their

---

[242] "Die ganze Gewalt dieser Worte fiel über den Unglüklichen, er warf sich vor Lotten nieder in der vollen Verzweiflung, faßte ihre Hände, drukte sie in seine Augen, wider seine Stirn, und ihr schien eine Ahndung seines schröklichen Vorhabens durch die Seele zu fliegen. Ihre Sinnen verwirrten sich, sie drukte seine Hände, drukte sie wider ihre Brust, neigte sich mit einer wehmüthigen Bewegung zu ihm, und ihre glühenden Wangen berührten sich. Die Welt vergieng ihnen, er schlang seine Arme um sie her, preßte sie an seine Brust, und dekte ihre zitternde stammelnde Lippen mit wüthenden Küssen. Werther! rief sie mit erstikter Stimme sich abwendend, Werther! und drükte mit schwacher Hand seine Brust von der ihrigen! Werther! rief sie mit dem gefaßten Tone des edelsten Gefühls; er widerstund nicht, lies sie aus seinen Armen, und warf sich unsinnig vor sie hin. Sie riß sich auf, und in ängstlicher Verwirrung, bebend zwischen Liebe und Zorn sagte sie: Das ist das leztemal! Werther! Sie sehn mich nicht wieder. Und mit dem vollsten Blik der Liebe auf den Elenden eilte sie in's Nebenzimmer, und schloß hinter sich zu." (246)

'resurrection' in 'the literary'. It is she who initiates the intimate body contact, "she squeezed his hands, pressed them against her breast, bent over him with a plaintive gesture, and their glowing cheeks touched", and it is she who speaks his death sentence: "This is the last time! Werther! you will never see me again".

However, Goethe's decision to combine this necessary act of transgression with the act of reading (adding his novel to the prominent history of a literary topos, writing the names of Werther and Lotte next to Abelard and Héloïse, or Dante's Francesca and Paolo) has an important side effect. Although it is, according to the logics of the *passio*, the last, decisive step in closing the literary circle, in separating the worlds and driving the weathery Werther from the enlightened world into the literary medium, where he belongs, it nevertheless leaves a constitutive gap for the weather to continue troubling the world: the act of reading is given the power to unleash the weathery forces from the literary medium, the aesthetic is thereby granted a rather ambiguous, because uncontrollable, social and political impact.

This constitutive gap haunted Goethe and his later attempts to reflect on *Werther*, its circumstances of production and its reception. What is interesting to see is that he very explicitly and consistently thinks about this novel in terms of weather:

> The resolution to let my internal nature do according to its peculiarities, and to let external nature influence me [*auf mich einfließen zu lassen*] according to its qualities, impelled me to the strange element in which *Werther* is designed and written. (Goethe 1848, 470; transl. altered)[243]

Goethe's reference to his exposing himself to the forces of the "internal" and the "external nature" can only be read as an alternative formulation of Kaufmann's label *Sturm und Drang*. The fact that the famous "strange element [*wunderliche Element*]", in which *Werther* was written, is later in the book characterised as having been of a meteorological nature, underlines my argument that the weather plays a key role for understanding this novel – and with it, the development of a literary medium:

> [...] for by this composition, more than by any other, I had freed myself from that stormy element [*stürmischen Elemente*], upon which through my own fault and that of others, through a mode of life both accidental and chosen, through design and thoughtless precipitation, through obstinacy and pliability, I had been driven about in the most violent manner. I felt, as if after a general confession, once more happy and free, and justified in beginning

---

[243] "Jener Vorsatz, meine innere Natur nach ihren Eigenheiten gewähren, und die äußere nach ihren Eigenschaften auf mich einfließen zu lassen, trieb mich an das wunderliche Element in welchem Werther ersonnen und geschrieben ist." (FA 14, 588)

a new life. The old domestic remedy had been of excellent service to me on this occasion. But while I felt myself eased and enlightened [*aufgeklärt*] by having turned reality into poetry, my friends were led astray by my work, for they thought that poetry ought to be turned into reality, that such a moral was to be imitated, and that at any rate one ought to shoot oneself. What had first happened here among a few, afterwards took place among the larger public, and this little book, which had been so beneficial to me, was decried as extremely injurious. (Goethe 1848, 511–512; transl. altered)[244]

The story that Goethe here relates is the story of the novel's production. It takes its point of departure from a 'meteorological situation', the "stormy element" and finally arrives at another situation that, less obviously, has to do with the weather: "I felt myself eased and enlightened [*aufgeklärt*]", resorting to the weathery connotation of the German word for enlightenment, *Aufklärung*. The way to achieve this 'change of weather', or rather, to get rid of the weather and establish the eternal sunshine of enlightenment, is the "old domestic remedy" of cathartic literary writing, "turn[ing] reality into poetry". As we have seen, this is also exactly the paradoxical story that Werther tells and undergoes with his *passio* and 'resurrection' as a literary "noble figure": he dies, so to speak, to redeem his author and his weathery troubles. Furthermore, Goethe's situation is not idiosyncratic but rather an emblem of an epistemological and cultural constellation. The movement towards enlightenment, towards the eternal sky of sun and stars without troubling clouds, has to deal with the weather, it somehow has to get rid of it. 'Turning reality into poetry' is the appropriate slogan for the strategy employed to cope with this 'problem': it gives birth to a new medium of literature assembling the weathery forces that do not find a place in the eternal sunshine of the enlightened world.

Goethe's story of the novel's production is, however, from the beginning haunted by the problem of its reception. The very words he finds for explaining his own difficult, weathery situation, his being driven about in a stormy element "through my own fault and that of others", echo the novel's dedication to the readers that suggest the novel as a friend "*if by fate or your own fault* you can

---

[244] "[...] denn ich hatte mich durch diese Komposition, mehr als durch jede andere, aus einem stürmischen Elemente gerettet, auf dem ich durch eigne und fremde Schuld, durch zufällige und gewählte Lebensweise, durch Vorsatz und Übereilung, durch Hartnäckigkeit und Nachgeben, auf die gewaltsamste Art hin und wider getrieben worden. Ich fühlte mich, wie nach einer Generalbeichte, wieder froh und frei, und zu einem neuen Leben berechtigt. Das alte Hausmittel war mir diesmal vortrefflich zu statten gekommen. Wie ich mich nun aber dadurch erleichtert und aufgeklärt fühlte, die Wirklichkeit in Poesie verwandelt zu haben, so verirrten sich meine Freunde daran, indem sie glaubten, man müsse die Poesie in Wirklichkeit verwandeln, einen solchen Roman nachspielen und sich allenfalls selbst erschießen; und was hier im Anfang unter wenigen vorging, ereignete sich nachher im großen Publikum, und dieses Büchlein, was mir so viel genutzt hatte, ward als höchst schädlich verrufen." (FA 14, 639–640)

find none closer to you". It however remains unclear how the act of reading could possible emulate the cathartic effect of Goethe's act of writing, how the readers could "take comfort from Werther's sufferings", as the dedication calls on them to do. All the more so since the readers get to observe an act of reading that performs the opposite, that initiates a moment of excessive ecstasy, an unheard of transgression. The question is not so much about the myth of the '*imitatio Wertheri*', of people following Werther and committing suicide (a myth that Goethe himself has contributed to establishing with this statement), but rather about the 'weather's fate' in this process of mediatisation. Are the weather and its troubling forces merely driven from the enlightened order of the world, are they turned into poetry and thereby ultimately tamed and silenced, or is there also a reverse movement: can the act of reading again unleash these troubling forces, are they capable of re-confronting reality with its repressed part of itself?

With the Ossian reading scene, the novel perhaps inadvertently answers this question in the positive. The novel's reception, as Goethe has to admit, comes to the same conclusion. And, surprisingly enough, Goethe himself testifies to the uncontrollable forces set free by reading his novel, in one of his famous conversations with Eckermann:

> [...] I have only read the book once since its appearance, and have taken good care not to read it again. It is a mass of Congreve-rockets [*Brandraketen*]. I am uncomfortable when I look at it; and I dread lest I should once more experience the peculiar mental state from which it was produced." (Eckermann, Goethe, and Soret 1850, 117)[245]

Unfortunately, the elder Goethe's use of the metaphor of the "Congreve-rockets" does not continue his so consistent reference to the weather that, as we have seen, had shaped his earlier discourse on the issue. Nevertheless, he could as well have resorted to a weather metaphor to express the very same idea, because what he says confirms the fact that the act of reading has the capacity of reversing the taming of forces undertaken by the act of writing: Goethe has eased, 'enlightened' his "peculiar mental state", the "stormy element", by transforming reality into poetry – reading threatens to undo this taming transformation, threatens to bring this "stormy" state back to the world. As Klaus Scherpe notes, this is the uncanny and threatening effect that Goethe experiences when, late in his life, he turns back to his early work: he learns that the weathery forces which literature discovers as its very own material resist any attempt at harmonisation

---

[245] "'[...] Übrigens habe ich das Buch, wie ich schon öfter gesagt, seit seinem Erscheinen nur ein einzigesmal wieder gelesen und mich gehütet, es abermals zu tun. Es sind lauter Brandraketen! – Es wird mir unheimlich dabei und ich fürchte, den pathologischen Zustand wieder durchzuempfinden, aus dem es hervorging.'" (Goethe 1986, 490)

(Scherpe 1970, 106). Nevertheless, for his early novel, and the intellectual climate that had contributed to its production, the literary medium's uncontrollable forces that threatened to trouble the enlightened status quo did not constitute a problem. On the contrary, the "storming", the "tempestuous" character of literature was programmatic: "Our poetry does not emerge from a living world, nor exist in the storm and confluence of such objects and feelings. Instead we force either our theme or our treatment or both" (Herder 1985 [1773], 159),[246] Herder complains, calling for poetry to become "the most storming, confident daughter of the human soul" (Herder 1985 [1773], 159; transl. altered).[247] In his review of Sulzer's *Die schönen Künste in ihrem Ursprung, ihrer wahren Natur und besten Anwendung*, which appeared two years before the *Werther*, Goethe ascribes to Herder's point of view:

> Are the raging storms, floods of water, rain of fire, subterranean blaze and death in all elements not equally true testimonies of their eternal life as the magnificently rising sun above the vineyards and fragrant orange groves? (FA 18, 98; my translation)[248]

His early novel *Werther* is Goethe's strongest statement towards this constitutively weathery character of literature that does not merely tame these forces, but cultivates them in the literary medium; that gives them a social reality in enlightened society and thereby also the capacity to be set free to work its often troubling effects.

Werther's transformation to *Werther* would not be complete, if we deny this book to set free the weathery forces that he and Lotte are able to unleash from *Ossian*. *Werther* is (at least!) as moving and compelling and as stormy a song as is the one sung by his Scottish 'ancestor'. This novel's exciting and indeed turbulent history of reception has shown that through his transformation, Werther achieves what he wished to achieve: when opening the book "preserving his name" we open Aeolus' bag: and experience, in the 21st century, 'Werther's' "roaring away like the waves! [*dahin zu brausen wie die Wellen*]" (123), moving readers to tears and troubling a world, even though it has had more than another two hundred years to forget the weather and all.

---

[246] "[...] wir dichten nicht über und in lebendiger Welt, im Sturm und im Zusammenstrom solcher Gegenstände, solcher Empfindungen; sondern erkünsteln uns entweder Thema, oder Art, das Thema zu behandeln, oder gar beydes [...]." (Herder 1773a, 42)
[247] "Die Dichtkunst, die die stürmendste, sicherste Tochter der menschlichen Seele sein sollte, ward die ungewisseste, lahmste, wankendste [...]." (Herder 1773a, 42)
[248] "Sind die wütenden Stürme, Wasserfluten, Feuerregen, unterirdische Glut, und Tod in allen Elementen nicht eben so wahre Zeugen ihres ewigen Lebens, als die herrlich aufgehende Sonne über volle Weinberge und duftende Orangenhaine." (FA 18, 98)

III *Les Rougon-Macquart*. Describing the Weather – and a Changing Climate

1 From weather to climate

This third chapter differs from the two chapters preceding it in one central aspect. In contrast to the readings of Shakespeare and Goethe, it is not dedicated to the study of one single, exemplary literary text but instead attempts to tackle a complete, voluminous cycle of novels: Émile Zola's *Les Rougon-Macquart*. With my decision not to pick out one particularly pertinent novel but to focus on the cycle as a whole I am not merely adopting the intended scope of Zola's literary project or his own ambitions or reflections on it. Viewed more closely, this 'decision' is not at all of a methodological or strategic nature. It is rather guided by the findings which reading the cycle with my interest in the relation of weather and literature has brought to light.

In contrast to its role in Goethe's *Werther*, the weather does not break into Zola's world as an unexpected event, as a foreign force that disrupts the dominant regime of representation and order. It does not make itself felt as a forgotten or, rather, repressed force at the underside of the enlightened world that turns out to be constitutive. In the novels of the *Rougon-Macquart* the weather and its defining notions – temperature, humidity, precipitation, cloudage and with it changing conditions of light, but also the movement of water and the general notion of (seasonal) changeability – are omnipresent. As the analyses of the following sections will show, the world of the *Rougon-Macquart* is not haunted by the weather as the world of Goethe's *Werther* was, it *is* in actuality a world of weather.

Nevertheless, weather events play an important role in quite a number of the novels of the *Rougon-Macquart*: the hailstorm in *La Terre*, the snowstorms of *L'Assommoir* and *La Bête humaine*, the pouring rain in the climactic scenes of *L'Argent* and *Une page d'amour*, only to name some examples of a much longer list. However, despite their primarily catastrophic nature, these instances of heavy weather are not alien to the world they seem to haunt. On the contrary, they characteristically correspond to it: Mouche dies while the hailstorm destroys the fields outside; the snowstorm of *L'Assommoir* resonates with Gervaise's misery, with her haunting the streets, being driven by her hunger to prostitute herself; the snowstorm of *La Bête humaine* that causes damage to the locomotive 'metaphorically' prepares the catastrophe of the disastrous accident that will follow; in *L'Argent* the wet weather accompanies the crash of the stock exchange, mirroring the relentless flood of sales; the pouring rain of *Une page d'amour* corresponds to Hélène's finally succumbing to her passion and at the same time resonates with Jeanne's jealousy and corrupted health, which leads to her death.

However, Zola does not merely garnish his stories with 'fitting' weather – the 'banal' phenomena of the weather are not only artistic devices [*Kunstmittel*] at the author's disposal to underline what s/he actually talks about, as Friedrich Christian Delius (1971) would have it. The relation between the weather events and the narrated stories is not merely metaphorical; it is not motivated by a deliberate, arbitrary authorial decision that fulfils an aesthetic function. As paradoxical as it might seem, the field of the weather is not alien to the social processes and circumstances on which the novels focus and that the weather appears merely to emphasise or illustrate. With regard to Zola's novels, the distinction between the weather as an artistic device and the 'actual' subject that the novels 'treat' is impossible to ascertain: the famous weather events are but a metonymical extension of a narrated world that is itself essentially governed by the logics of the weather.

We can illustrate this with an example. The neat correspondences that *Une page d'amour* establishes between Hélène's passions and the varying, seasonal weather of the Paris tableaus is not a clever method Zola has introduced for the sake of aesthetic composition. It is the result of his literary analysis of the subject of passion: passion follows a weathery, a seasonal logic. The individual is subjected to it as a person is subjected to the forces of the weather. Although not predictable or controllable, passion, like the weather, is not pure chaos. It has its rules, its seasonal organisation for example. It is essentially instable, deriving its beauties as well as the misery it causes from sudden changes. Moreover, it is neither good nor bad in itself, it cannot simply be evaded or eradicated. It is part of the world, a condition constitutive of bliss as well as of catastrophe. In short, the weather is not a metaphor for passion. The novel rather posits an intrinsic connection between two complex phenomena. Therein consists its very particular epistemological stance: no matter whether we tend to dismiss this literary knowledge – calling it 'pseudo-scientific' or 'mythic' – or not, as readers of Zola's novels we cannot refuse to share in the narrated world, in Zola's reconstruction of the Second Empire, which is essentially weathery. In this world, according to the premises it is build upon, the pouring rain and the violent weather that coincide with Hélène's falling for Henri are metonymic – not metaphoric. An ontological, factual link exists between the two. Theoretically, Zola could have accompanied their encounter with any weather, also with the most beautiful sunshine. However, by doing so he would have offended against the rules and logic of the diegetic world he depicts: The novel as a whole, with its strict, symmetric composition erects a central correspondence of seasonal weather and passion. According to the narrated world Zola has constructed, Hélène's fall has its own weather, or rather, it is itself weathery: climactic, catastrophic rain, a mythical deluge.

The same holds true for all the other weather 'events'. They only appear to be unforeseeable occurrences, unexpectedly breaking into the daily routine and causing disastrous consequences. In fact, the narration reveals them to be an integral, recurrent, 'natural' and governing part of the world: hailstorms and death, as well as the rainy collapse of the stock exchange do not happen to the world – they are examples of the weathery nature of this world. As we have seen, in Goethe's *Werther* the world cannot cope with the intruding weather, not until the literary medium assigns a place to it. The weathery hero and the weathery love lose out to the neat and orderly, weather-free organisation of the enlightened world. In Zola's universe resistance to the weathery world of the Second Empire seems to be pointless: the weather wins over it all. This holds true for the unstoppable capitalistic success of the weather machine called 'Le Bonheur des Dames' as well as for the weathery debacles towards which the society as a whole is said to be sliding.

What makes the 'epistemology', the specifically literary knowledge of Zola's cycle so peculiar, and perhaps so difficult, is the fact that he does not give himself a level of meta-language to explain and present the results of his observations. He does not, 'metaphorically', transfer knowledge from a secure epistemological field to a field that he is examining. His narrated universe – or rather the universe of his narration – is essentially monistic: the fields he links 'metaphorically' are settled on the same plane. They are part of the same world, they are all objects of observation. The knowledge he produces consists in establishing links, using the observations he made of one field – the weather – to create and formulate the observations of the other fields, no matter whether the object of description is a department store, a strike, or a war. At first glance this might look like a metaphorical procedure; however, the 'metaphor' is characteristically held in suspense: as a consequence of Zola's monistic world's renunciation of a level of meta-language and secure knowledge, vehicle and tenor, *proprium* and *improprium* remain instable and are fundamentally interchangeable. Notions of war 'metaphorically' explain an observation of the weather – notions of the weather 'metaphorically' explain an observation of war. There seem to be only metaphors and no passage is left to the literal.

This may, however, be misleading. Zola's epistemological procedure is not at all an ingenious, witty game of building a world from *tertia comparationis*. It is ontological rather than rhetorical. For the historical and cultural formation that he examines he observes, or, rather, proposes, an actual, a characteristic interpenetration of fields: war is not *like* the weather, because they would share the abstract notion of forces fighting against each other. That would be a rhetorical link, a link established by an authorial agent. War *is* weather, and weather *is* war. Capitalism is weather and weather is capitalism. Life is a torrent and a torrent is life. Zola does not explain capitalism via his profound meteorological knowledge. He rather posits a 'metaphorical' link between the two – a link that turns out to be metonymic, because it is the actual interpenetration of fields that makes it possible, and not a third, abstract entity connecting the fields. This link holds the status of an ontological truth in the narrated world; Zola not only believes in it, this link even determines the way his narrated world turns, it determines what is natural, logical and inevitable in his fictional universe. That is perhaps why Zola's novels are so often and rightfully conceived of as 'mythical' – which, paradoxically, describes his specifically literary 'epistemology'.

As a consequence, it is not possible and not desirable to distinguish between the 'actual', the diegetic weather of Zola's narrated world and the 'metaphorical', figural use Zola's narration makes of the various phenomena of the weather. Both contribute to the impression that his famous descriptions are characteristically saturated with weather: undoubtedly, Zola quite extensively takes the weather, the state of the atmosphere, as an object for his descriptions (in his famous, recurring panoramas of Paris, for instance). He, however, also uses weather descriptions as a source of linguistic and semantic material for all of his descriptions, no matter whether of the urban topography, of the clients and merchandises in the warehouse or of the masses going on strike.

In order to demonstrate the oscillation between (weather) imagery and the 'actual' state of the 'weathery' world that is so characteristic for Zola I would like to compare three passages selected from three different novels of the *Rougon-Macquart*. The first draws on perhaps the most famous of 'pure' weather descriptions, a prime example of "detailed concrete and meteorological notation" (Nelson 1973, 14), it is the fourth of the Paris tableaus that forms the climactic centre of *Une page d'amour*:

> At that moment the tempest broke out. [...] For a moment chaos reigned. Some enormous clouds, grown like blots of ink, swept through a host of smaller ones, which were scattered and floated like shreds of rag which the wind tore to pieces and carried off thread by thread. A moment later two clouds attacked one another other, and rent one another with crashing reports, sowing the copper coloured expanse with wreckage; and every time the hurricane thus veered, blowing from every point of the compass, there was the crashing of armies in the air [...].
>
> Away in the background, over Notre-Dame, the cloud divided and poured down such a torrent of water that the island of La Cité was submerged; [...] one might have imagined

that the heavens were precipitating themselves on the earth; streets vanished, sinking into the depths, and swimming on the surface, amidst tremors [*secousses*] whose violence seemed to foretell the end of the city. A prolonged roar ascended – the voice of all the swollen streams, the thunder of the water falling into the drains. However, above muddy-looking Paris, which the showers had soiled with a yellow hue, the livid clouds spread themselves out in uniform fashion, without a rift or stain. (*PA*, II 1031–1032; my transl.)[249]

For my purposes here, I would like to bracket the role that this scene plays in the novel. The description of the weather is not focalised by the scene's protagonist Jeanne, who is actually looking out of the open window and who serves as the focaliser for large parts of the scene, but by the narrator. For his very detailed description of the meteorological phenomena – it actually covers several pages – the narrator resorts to a considerable amount of figurative speech; what we are faced with is in fact far from being a 'pure' weather description. The passage I have selected begins with two similes, "like blots of ink" and "like shreds of rag", which the narrator uses to characterise the shape of the clouds. The field of warfare serves as a dominant metaphorical isotopy accounting for the weather's violent processes and forces: the clouds "attack one another", "the crashing of armies" is "in the air", the violence of the roar and "the end of the city" could as well belong to the battlefield as to a mythical catastrophe. The 'natural' weather phenomena that the tableau describes, the "torrents of water" showering from breaking clouds, the heavy wind, the "swollen streams" overflowing the city, the weather's noise and its violent tremors are all inflated to mythical dimensions. It is the narrator, not a character, who establishes the connection of heavy weather with the biblical Deluge, with the mythical debacle of an "end of the city"; he thereby lends it authorial weight that cannot simply be dismissed. However, notwithstanding its seemingly wild and 'idealistic' associations, despite this scene's mythical impact, the tableau of Paris that dominates the scene remains a detailed, very exact and exceptionally meticulous –

---

[249] "A ce moment, la tempête éclatait. [...] Pendant un instant, ce fut le chaos. D'énormes nuages, élargis comme des taches d'encre, couraient au milieu de plus petits, dispersés et flottants, pareils à des haillons que le vent déchiquetait, et emportait fil à fil. Un instant, deux nuées s'attaquèrent, se brisèrent avec des éclats, qui semèrent de débris l'espace couleur de cuivre ; et chaque fois que l'ouragan sautait ainsi, soufflant de tous les points du ciel, il y avait en l'air un écrasement d'armées [...]. Au fond, sur Notre-Dame, le nuage se partagea, versa un tel torrent, que la Cité fut submergée ; [...] on eût dit que le ciel se jetait sur la terre ; des rues s'abîmaient, coulant à fond et surnageant, dans des secousses dont la violence semblait annoncer la fin de la cité. Un grondement continu montait, la voix des ruisseaux grossis, le tonnerre des eaux se vidant aux égouts. Cependant au-dessus de Paris boueux, que ces giboulées salissaient du même ton jaune, les nuages s'effrangeaient, devenaient d'une pâleur livide, également épandue sans une fissure ni une tache." (*PA*, II 1031–1032)

a naturalistic? – account of meteorological phenomena. It is artfully staged as a sort of dialogue with the protagonist's desperate train of thoughts. The violent, mythical story that the changing meteorological conditions narrate is aptly brought to an end by a sober description of the return of 'quiet' weather, of the conditions from where the 'meteorological story' started: "the livid clouds spread themselves out in uniform fashion, without a rift or stain."

The second passage that I would like to relate to the first is taken from *Au Bonheur des Dames*. It narrates the end of a successful day at the department store, after the last customers have left:

> Inside, beneath the flaming gas jets which, burning in the dusk, had illuminated the supreme tremors [*secousses*] of the sale, it was like the battlefield still hot from the massacre of materials. The salesmen, harassed and exhausted, were camping amidst the havoc [*débâcle*] of their shelves and counters, which looked as if they had been wrecked by the raging blast of a hurricane. [...] Liénard was dozing on a sea of materials in which some half-destroyed stacks of cloth were still standing, like ruined houses about to be carried away by an overflowing river [*un fleuve débordé*]; further along, the white linen had snowed all over the ground, and one stumbled against ice-flows of table-napkins and walked on the soft flakes of handkerchiefs. (*eLP*, 117; transl. altered)[250]

In this passage rich with weather imagery the violent weather phenomena thatōwere raging over Paris in the previous description now return as figural speech: the store looks as if "the raging blast of a hurricane" has swept through it, we encounter the same dominant notion of wreckage ("wrecked", "half-destroyed", "ruined") and uncanny "tremors" as in the tableau of *Une page d'amour*. What had been "swollen streams" inundating the streets of Paris have become here an "overflowing river" – and we will return to this most frequent of weather themes that is perhaps the trademark of the *Rougon-Macquart*. On the whole, the scene seems to invert metaphorically the previous passage's weather description of Paris: in *Une page d'amour* imagery of cloth had served to describe the weather phenomena over Paris (the clouds floating "like shreds of rag") – in *Au Bonheur des Dames* it is now weather phenomena that serve to characterise pieces of cloth ("the white linen had snowed all over the ground",

---

[250] "A l'intérieur, sous la flamboiement des becs de gaz, qui, brûlant dans le crépuscule avaient éclairé les secousses suprêmes de la vente, c'était comme un champ de bataille encore chaud du massacre des tissus. Les vendeurs, harassés de fatigue, campaient parmi la débâcle de leurs casiers et de leurs comptoirs, que paraissait avoir saccagés le souffle furieux d'un ouragan. [...] Liénard sommeillait au-dessus d'une mer de pièces, où des piles restées debout, à moitié détruites, semblaient des maisons dont un fleuve débordé charrie les ruines ; et, plus loin, le blanc avait neigé à terre, on butait contre des banquises de serviettes, on marchait sur les flocons légers des mouchoirs." (*BD*, III 499–500)

"ice-flows of table-napkins", "soft flakes of handkerchiefs"). Moreover, the fact that the passage's 'figural' weather is connected to the characteristic microclimate of the shop is noteworthy: it is no coincidence that the passage sets out with an isotopy of heat and fire and ends on notions of polar cold. The two paradoxically coexist within one and the same location, more than that, they both contribute decisively to the shop's atmosphere and the way it works. We will examine this in detail in a later section, but for the moment it is important to underline that the shop's heat and fire, its "flaming gas jets" "burning in the dusk" are not only metonymically linked to the preceding figural heavy weather (they had "illumined the supreme tremors of the sale") but are held together by the familiar metaphor of warfare: the fact that the "battlefield" is conceived of as "hot" associates the store's artificial, characteristically hot and fiery microclimate with the violence of the raging figural weather. There is, I would claim, a rather disconcerting passage from the store's 'actual', non-figural microclimate to the 'figural' weather events taking place inside that unsettles the stable distinction between metaphorical and literal. In other words, in Zola's narrative universe, the "hurricane" might, after all, not be as metaphorical as it seems.

The movement of 'metaphorical' inversion that we observed between the two passages, the weather phenomena being the *proprium* of the description in one passage, turning into the *improprium* for the description of phenomena in the second (phenomena which, in turn, had served as *impropria* for the weather description), is stabilised and seems to be sublated by an astonishingly constant meta-metaphor: by imagery of war. We have seen that the metaphoric field of clashing armies and the mythical end of a city figured prominently in the Paris tableau; we encounter the very same imagery in the description of the department store after a day of sales: the store resembles a "battlefield still hot from the massacre of materials", the salesmen are "camping" as if the "havoc [*débâcle*]" was not "of their shelves and counters" but of a war scenario's "ruined houses". It is obviously the disastrous forces unleashed by both the 'real' weather raging over Paris and the 'figural' weather of the mass of clients in the department store that enables the meta-metaphor of war to hold together the 'figural' and 'literal' weather, that makes them point in the same semantic, rather mythical and 'idealistic' direction. However, "the end of the city", the "crashing of armies", "ruined houses", "massacre" and "battlefield" do not remain an esoteric vision of a chronic pessimist's hallucinating about a mythical catastrophe. It is not a rather arbitrary projection of a reader blending his observations with fantasies that reveal a rather bourgeois and darkly romantic education: the meta-metaphor of war, so closely connected to the weather, 'figural' and 'literal', is not exempt from the instability of the literal and the figural that characterises Zola's metaphors. The 'metaphoric' debacle of war, all the notions quoted above metaphorically characterising the 'real' as well as the 'figural' weather, become reality;

they all prefigure *La Débâcle*, towards which Zola makes the whole cycle move. It might not come as a surprise that this catastrophic world is a weathery world, a world where "a terrifying storm br[eaking] out, a truly diluvian downpour" "soak[ing] the men to the skin" (*eD*, 69)[251] and "a hailstorm, a hurricane of bullets and shells" (*eD*, 223; transl. altered)[252] coincide, where 'figural' and 'literal' weather become indistinguishable:

> [...] ferocious yells which the crackling bullets accompanied with the noise of hailstorm, rattling down upon everything metal, mess-tins, water bottles, the copper trim on their uniforms and on the harnesses. Through the hail came the hurricane blast of wind and thunder that set the ground trembling, leaving a smell of scorched [*brûlée*] wool and sweating beasts rising up into the sunlight. (*eD*, 266; transl. altered)[253]

This passage exemplarily illustrates what the novel stages as a whole: the fields of weather and war, and that is also to say the fields of natural phenomena and the socio-cultural formation of the Second Empire, interpenetrate, are located on the same (mythical) plane. We encounter the familiar semantic material that was used for metaphorical descriptions of the Second Empire's cultural and social processes, the "trembling" of the ground, the weathery noise, we encounter catastrophic weather phenomena that were part of the weather events 'haunting' the narrated world, like the hailstorm that makes us think of *La Terre*. Furthermore, the isotopy of heat and fire resurfaces: the battlefield indeed turns out to be hot, as the "scorched wool" and the "sweating beasts" indicate. It is however not clear whether the sunlight (that forms part of this isotopy) or the violence of the battle is responsible for this heat. The same undecidability is at work when a "hurricane blast of wind and thunder" comes through the hail: is this wind an 'actual' meteorological phenomenon or is it brought about by the blasting shells? These 'weathery' phenomena coincide, they are of the same ontological nature, one as real and as much a defining part of the same world as the other. *La Débâcle* contradicts all attempts to free Zola's naturalism of its metaphorical, peculiarly mythical imagery and turn it into a sober, hyper-realistic, 'scientific' observation of an 'objective' world. With *La Débâcle* Zola underlines that the connections he has established between different semantic fields (weather and social processes, weather and war, etc.) are not mere rhetorical

---

[251] "Et le pis, ce fut qu'un épouvantable orage éclata, dix minutes à peine après le départ, une pluie diluvienne qui trempa les hommes jusqu'aux os [...]." (*D*, V 461)

[252] "« [...] Une grêle, un ouragan de balles et d'obus ! [...] »" (*D*, V 618)

[253] "[...] ces hurlements féroces, que le crépitement des balles accompagnait d'un bruit de grêle, en tapant sur tout le métal, les gamelles, les bidons, le cuivre des uniformes et des harnais. Dans cette grêle, passait l'ouragan de vent et de foudre dont le sol tremblait, laissant au soleil une odeur de laine brûlée et de fauves en sueur." (*D*, V 660)

ballast, but ontologically motivated: In this novel all the semantic fields that were oscillating between figural use and phenomena of the narrated world are assembled, they all coincide as closely related parts of the fictional world. The 'metaphors', even the most 'mythic' ones, come true, so to speak, and what looked like 'bold' imagery is revealed to be in fact metonymic, ontologically co-present: Jean and Maurice are exposed to heavy weather as well as to the massacre of war; the inhabitants of Paris illuminate their city with flaming fire, however, not as a metaphor of excessive party and 'hot' city life, but literally, this time, in order to make "the end of the city" a reality.

It is not astonishing that this assemblage of semantic fields and images in the narrated world of *La Débâcle* not only incorporates the isotopy of heat, weather events like a hailstorm or a hurricane and the ominous tremors (are they of 'real' or 'figural' thunder?), but also, and almost too frequently, the key motive of 'overflowing' [*débordement*]. No matter whether it is the overpowering presence of the enemy, or the masses of fugitives, the debacle is characteristically shaped by this notion:

> [...] the enemies received reinforcements, flowing [*débordaient*] from all directions (*eD*, 246; transl. altered)[254]
>
> All around them the tail-end of the crowd of fugitives was still pouring down the middle of the road, gathering speed like an overflowing torrent [*torrent débordé*]. (*eD*, 311)[255]

I do not emphasise the importance of this notion merely because I will soon come back to it; my aim here is mainly to point out the astonishing degree of consistency with which the field of weather – consisting of weather events and their narratological role, weather phenomena and their semantic connections, as well as weather imagery – permeates the whole cycle of novels.

It is especially with regard to certain motifs or imagery that this consistency has not gone unnoticed in criticism: Lewis Kamm noticed quite early the role that "the elements of earth, air, fire, and water" play in *The Rougon-Macquart*, "enclosing, suffocating, crushing, and destroying man" (1975, 225). Brian Nelson pursues a closely related argument, claiming that "the coherence of Zola's novels rests on their dense metaphorical structures" (1977, 11). The metaphors of heat and fire, of the aquatic and of liquidity that he holds responsible for this coherence are confirmed as dominant by Gabrielle Maryse Rochecouste's study of the "Catamorphic Systems in the structure of the *Rougon-Macquart*"

---

[254] "[...] les ennemies recevaient des renforts, débordaient de partout [...]." (*D*, V 641)
[255] "Autour d'eux, la queue extrême des fuyards coulait toujours à pleine route, d'un train sans cesse accru de torrent débordé." (*D*, V 705)

(1988), which comes to very similar results, adding weather imagery to Brian Nelson's list.

However, as long as the consistency permeating the novels is conceptualised as a more or less loose ensemble of imagery or motifs it must remain rather vague and intuitive. I think that understanding this consistency as a semantic, conceptual and narratological field of weather, one that transgresses the distinctions of imagery and object in the narrated world, of signifier and signified, of artistic devices and diegetic events, suggests an important approach to the cycle. It allows us to demonstrate that of the cycle's novels each is not, as Clayton R. Alcorn claims, "set in a specific well-defined milieu, a kind of 'air-tight cell'" (1969, 105). On the contrary, our findings support Brian Nelson's argument that "the surface diversity of the *Rougon-Macquart*, Zola's division of the world into categories and social groups, is belied by the strong unifying impression given by the dominant themes and characteristic imagery of his novels" (1977, 11).

The field of the weather that I have attempted to sketch with my reading of the three passages seems to be one example of what Brian Nelson holds responsible for the cycle's "strong unifying impression". It is not any example, but a particularly pertinent one, because the weather not only contributes fundamentally to the dominant themes and the characteristic imagery of the cycle, as we have seen, it even bridges the distinction between theme and imagery. The aim of this chapter is thus to turn the vagueness of an "impression" – although strong and, as Gumbrecht states, manifestly shared by the majority of critics (1978, 63) – into hypotheses. What is it, that the cycle as a whole narrates? How does the "intimate fusion of the various constituents of each novel" (Kamm 1975, 233) come about? What is responsible for the fact that despite their extreme diversity and the diversity of the milieus surrounding the characters of the *Rougon-Macquart*, "[c]haracter after character suffers similar sensations" (Kamm 1975, 234)? How does the cycle as a whole integrate the descriptions of specific milieus in a synchronic tableau of the Second Empire (Gumbrecht 1978, 69)?

It is these questions that lie behind Brian Nelson's notion of "the strong unifying impression". In the end, examining this impression boils down to finding an answer to one central question that encompasses all the others: what does it mean to narrate "the Second Empire"?

"I have taken the whole of society for my subject", Zola writes in his essay "Du roman" (1893b, 260).[256] At first glance, this poetological statement looks quite straightforward. What exactly 'is' however "the whole" of a society? What 'is' the Second Empire? What defines or characterises this complex conglomerate of a historical, socio-cultural formation, of a specific political regime, and also

---

256 "J'ai pris pour sujet la société tout entière [...]." (*RE, OC* IX 438)

of a certain 'mentality' – or, as Zola would call it, of a 'temperament'? Zola's narrative project is, I would claim, dedicated to this question and arrives at a specifically literary answer to it. Despite its epic proportions of twenty novels Zola's cycle does not content itself with an encyclopaedic approach to the 'whole' of the Second Empire: the 'whole' is not to be captured by a meticulous description of all of its parts (all of its milieus, for example) but emerges transversally 'from' these descriptions as the "strong unifying impression" that Brian Nelson talks of. In other words, Zola's innovative answer to the question of 'what the Second Empire' 'is' lies beyond his 'science' of a positivistic, detailed description of 'reality'; it is through "theme" and "imagery" that Zola's answer has to be approached; the knowledge that his cycle of novels produces is intrinsically literary. The 'Second Empire' (whatever this term might stand for) cannot be described, it has to be *narrated*. It is, according to Zola's reconstruction, not a static constellation of elements or relations, not an abstract ensemble of characteristics, but a process, a historical development – a story? As our reading of the three passages has already indicated, Zola claims that the laws governing this historical process can very aptly be revealed and reconstructed by means of literary narration. It is a logic of transition from the metaphoric to the 'real' or the metonymic; it is, also, a project of discovering 'the truth' of literary metaphor and the story that it entails. Paris's burning of *jouissance* and party leads over to Paris burning. All the ensuing sections will attempt to provide evidence to substantiate these claims.

Insisting on the literary character of Zola's knowledge and on the assertion that his answer to the question of 'The Second Empire' is only to be approached via the literary means of dominant themes and imagery – that is to say via the weather – obliges us to take the concrete realisation of theme and imagery seriously. Why is it the weather that pervades the cycle, dominant both as a theme and as a far-reaching web of imagery? A first hypothesis forces itself upon us: This complex 'subject', the 'Second Empire', with its "strong unifying impression" – caused by all that weather – could in the end itself be 'weathery'. Does it integrate the cycle's diverse milieus as notions of weather under an overarching notion, under, perhaps, the notion of climate? Do the *Rougon-Macquart* narrate the history of the Second Empire as the history of a climate?

At first glance this must look like an arbitrary and perhaps not too well-founded choice of metaphor. However, we have already seen the role the weather plays: it oscillates between weather events of the narrated world and imagery, it permeates the Zolian universe and determines its course, it drives the cycle's story. Against this background, it appears sensible and consistent to read the "strong unifying impression" emerging from the literal or figural weather of the diverse milieus and social groups as 'the climate' of this world.

All the more since Zola's one, central statement about the "great characteristic" of the Second Empire resorts to a weather concept that must seem familiar to us. In Brian Nelson's English translation the famous sentence of the first novel's preface reads: "The great characteristic of the Rougon-Macquarts, the group or family I propose to study is their ravenous appetites." (eFR, 3)[257] Only a few lines later Zola underlines the metonymic role of this exemplary family. Their "ravenous appetites" represent "the essentially modern impulse that sets the lower classes marching through the social system" (eFR, 4)[258] so that the members of the family in fact "tell the story of the Second Empire" (eFR, 4)[259] – and, perhaps, more than that, reveal certain traits of what we conceive of as 'modern'. The familiar weather concept I am speaking of is concealed by Brian Nelson's adjective "ravenous": In the French original Zola speaks of the characteristic "débordement des appétits", the 'overflowing of the appetites'. This weather metaphor of overflowing is not an arbitrary figure of speech; it connects the cycle's plot-generating proto-motif (Blaschke 2005, 41) to the surely most prominent of weather themes and imagery that, as our three short passages have already shown, keeps recurring throughout the whole cycle. More than twenty years later Zola resorts to the very same metaphor: When Docteur Pascal in the final novel of the cycle resumes the findings of his research, which is an intradiegetic, metaleptical double of Zola's narrative project, he repeats the formulation of the first novel's preface verbatim.[260] The notion of "overflowing appetites" thus not only frames the whole project, but also resonates strikingly with the cycle's insistent theme and imagery of the weather.

The metaphor of an overflowing of appetites makes a difference. Brian Nelson's rendering the characteristic trait as a "ravenous appetite" makes it appear a deviance of morals, it implies a de-humanisation, a tendency towards the animalistic or the bestial that can easily be ascribed to the more or less 'human' members of this society. Put in this way, the novels raise the rather conventional question of ethics for which it is human beings who remain the agents of this sort of 'social' history. They have lost track of their true humanity – and, it

---

[257] "Les Rougon-Macquart, le groupe, la famille que je me propose d'étudier, a pour caractéristique le débordement des appétits, le large soulèvement de notre âge, qui se rue aux jouissances." (FR, I 3)
[258] "[...] cette impulsion essentiellement moderne que reçoivent les basses classes en marche à travers le corps social [...]." (FR, I 3)
[259] "[...] et ils racontent ainsi le second Empire [...]." (FR, I 3)
[260] "[...] les nôtres sont partis du peuple, se sont répandus parmi toute la société contemporaine, ont envahi toutes les situations, emportés par le débordement des appétits, par cette impulsion essentiellement moderne, ce coup de fouet qui jette aux jouissances les basses classes, en marche à travers le corps social [...]." (DP, V 1015)

seems, it is in their hands to defeat the beasts in them and regain their humanity, their balance and contentment, their temperance. Zola might write this kind of story in his late works that follow the *Rougon-Macquart*, especially in his *Les Quatre Évangiles*. His *Rougon-Macquart*, however, focus on something quite different. As the metaphor of 'overflowing' indicates, the determining factor behind the characteristic behaviour of this family and era is beyond the realm of 'the human(e)', even beyond the negotiations of what is still human and what not. In the *Rougon-Macquart*, Brian Nelson writes, "the natural order of things is reversed: objects and things become the real protagonists of his novels, and the human element is only incidentally mentioned" (1978, 63). The 'overflowing' of appetites points to forces governing human behaviour and, with it, the socio-cultural formation organising human life, that are beyond the reach of ethical or rational considerations. It is these 'quasi-natural' forces (Kaiser 1990, 35) that are actually the agents of this world, acting 'through' the human beings as well as acting upon them as forces of the milieu they are living in – forces that they themselves at times contribute to produce and reproduce. It is the rules, the logic of these forces that the narrative project of the *Rougon-Macquart* ultimately pursues.

As we have seen in the second chapter, the notion of 'overflowing' had already been central for Goethe's *Werther*. The use of the same motif provides us with a good opportunity to mark the difference separating Goethe's and Zola's projects. Goethe's is a novel of weather. The overflowing of his torrents, no matter whether the literary "torrent of the genius" (30–31) or its later 'literal', 'real' counterpart inundating the "dear valley" (122), are local, singular events: they happen to a world that does not know about the weather, that has characteristically repressed the weather, driven it beyond its boundaries. They stake out the weather's claims in an enlightened, 'supposedly weather-free' world. They expose the weather to be this world's constitutive underside and create a modern harbour for these seemingly alien, but actually constitutive forces in the form of literature. Goethe's *Werther* tells the story of a weather event overcharging the world by confronting it with a repressed part of itself.

Zola's cycle of novels is not primarily concerned with the weather. It does not tell the story of weather events disturbing a 'weather-free' world. The world it finds itself confronted with is all but weather-free. On the contrary, it is essentially weathery. In Zola's universe 'overflowing' does not merely feature as a local event, but constitutes the "strong unifying impression" characterising the (weathery) processes of a whole society. Zola writes the 'natural history' of the coherence holding together the Second Empire's different local milieus and social groups, holding together its diverse states of the atmosphere – he writes the 'natural history' of the Second Empire's climate.

In contrast to Goethe, Zola thus does not narrate the weather, he narrates a climate. His project does not aim for the local event, it aims for a *total* (Gumbrecht 1978, 63, Jennings 1980, 396), a "global" (Kamm 1975) vision of a 'world', the world of the Second Empire. In other words, Zola reconstructs the world of the *Second Empire* as an essentially weathery world in order to give an account of it, of its laws, of the logic that regulates and determines the processes of this world. He evokes the Second Empire's characteristically modern *climate*.

2 Milieu

In our reading of Goethe's *Werther* we have observed a structural pattern that reoccurred with striking frequency throughout the text. The 'concentric constellation', as I have termed it, manifested itself in the novel's topography, in the way the world was grouped around the central protagonist. The trees, houses or walls surrounding the human individual are not merely instances of a peculiar state of topography that characterises Goethe's narrated world, they are the literary materialisation of an abstract, 'philosophical' 'phenomenon' that the novel *Werther* represents: modern subjectivity. We have seen that the human subject with its inseparable notion of autonomy and control is a phenomenon of limitation. Goethe's novel exhibits how the core of the enlightened worldview is brought about by drawing boundaries, by driving uncontrollable, weathery forces beyond the horizon of human autonomy. The notion of 'environment' is born as a Siamese twin of the modern subject; it is thought of as surrounding this subject, as being constructed around the subject at the centre. As Goethe's *Werther* so impressively illustrates, the environment works as a wall enclosing the subject; it reflects the idyllic projections and bliss of autonomy, it wards off the unruly forces that have been driven from this world, but also always both imprisons the world and is in danger of being destroyed by the very forces it attempts to ward off. *Environment* thus paradoxically connotes both bliss and the danger of fatal destruction, without a calm in-between. It is a phenomenon of boundary. Goethe's novel deconstructs this boundary, showing that the boundary is necessarily permeable, and constitutes a supplement: literature.

We do not find this structural pattern in Zola's *Rougon-Macquart*. The notions of centre and circular peri-phery that featured so prominently in Goethe's *Werther*, all these 'arounds' and 'surroundings', play no significant role in the collection of novels written about a hundred years later. Instead, a rather disconcerting trait emerges from Zola's novels with astonishing constancy: a metonymic correspondence of protagonist and 'surroundings', a very special relation that holds together the individual and the world s/he is living in.

This observation can be made on the macro-level of the novels, on the level of theme and protagonist. We have already seen that in Une page d'amour Hélène's passions seem to be linked to the changing views of Paris, so that the novel's examination of 'passion' in fact tells (at least) two stories: one of an individual fall, one of the city's weather. A similar strong resonance or reciprocal determination can be claimed for Saccard and the world of speculation, for Jacques Lantier and his locomotive, for both Denise and Octave Mouret and the department store, for Lisa and the covered market, for Pauline and the sea, and for most of the other protagonists of Zola's novels.

However, this metonymic correspondence can also be traced on the novels' micro-level, and this might be the more promising approach to attain an insight into its workings. Especially the way Zola sets out to construct his narrative world at the beginning of his novels seems to me to say a lot about the rules and logics governing his universe and the poetics of the whole project.

The opening paragraph of *Une page d'amour* does not introduce the reader to the novel's protagonist, at least not directly. It describes a room. The "bourgeois harmony of the room" (*PA*, II 801; my transl.)[261] with its characteristic blue wallpaper metonymically introduces us to the novel's protagonist, Hélène, who lives in this room together with her daughter Jeanne. Hélène, a widow, has been leading a very quiet, secluded life – and it is this life that the room represents, or rather embodies. Beginning the novel with a description of this room before panning to Hélène, whose "good sleep, peaceful and strong" (*PA*, II 801)[262] resonates with the room's "bourgeois harmony", and emphasises their metonymic connection, is however not merely a narrative device that indicates Zola's prowess in the art of narration; the metonymy that links this room and the protagonist's life and temperament remains a dominant theme throughout the novel. In fact, the initial scene of Jeanne's nocturnal crisis that disturbs the room's harmony emblematically anticipates the story the novel is going to tell. Hélène is forced to leave her beloved room in the middle of the night, dressed inappropriately, exposing herself to the "coldness of this icy night of February" (*PA*, II 803),[263] and walks right into the arms of her future lover, the doctor Henri. To the blue room, the metonymic point of departure – cool, silent, bourgeois, peaceful – a counterpart will be added in the course of the novel: the pink room in the house of Mother Fetu. Over-heated, furnished with bad taste, the location of moral corruption, it is here that Hélène will finally fall for Henri. The story develops between these two contrasting rooms. It is impossible to say whether these

---

261 "L'harmonie bourgeoise de la pièce [...]." (*PA*, II 801)
262 "Elle sommeillait d'un beau sommeil, paisible et fort [...]." (*PA*, II 801)
263 "[...] le froid de cette glaciale nuit de février [...]." (*PA*, II 803)

rooms represent Hélène's passions, or whether Hélène's passions are evoked by the atmosphere of the rooms surrounding her. She is not responsible for the furnishing of either of the rooms: 'her' blue room is of M. Rambaud's make, Malignon has built himself the pink chamber for his amorous adventures.

Although very different in terms of composition, *Pot-Bouille* is structured by a quite similar metonymic theme that becomes evident in the very first scene of the novel. Here it is not a characteristic room, but a whole bourgeois house to which the readers' attention is directed. To be more precise, it is a very telling part of that house that is focused on: its staircase. Octave Mouret, the future boss of the department store 'Le Bonheur des Dames' has just arrived in Paris, he is still a young man. We do not learn anything about him – but a lot about the house he will be living in. The tour of the house introduces us to the novel's narrated world: the novel, known as Zola's brutal and provocative study of the 19th century urban bourgeoisie, is in fact all about this house. It is about looking behind its façade and the "grand air of chilly cleanliness" (*ePL*, 4)[264] issuing from its courtyard. The abundance of ornaments (for example the "female heads" (*ePL*, 3)[265] supporting a balcony) and the mass of "imitation marble [*faux marbre*]" (*ePL*, 5),[266] which define its design, almost ostentatiously betray this world's hypocrisy. The staircase and the novel's protagonist Octave Mouret seem to share a narrative function for Zola's fictional universe: they connect the little episodes Zola narrates which all contribute to the grand picture he draws of the bourgeois world. More than that, a closer look reveals a striking number of correspondences between staircase and protagonist.

In contrast to the "chilly cleanliness" which the bourgeois house radiates on the outside, an unexpected warmth surprises Octave when he comes into the building: "But what struck Octave most on entering was the hothouse temperature, a warm breath which seemed puffed by some mouth into his face." (*ePL*, 5)[267] The fact that "'the staircase is heated'" (*ePL*, 5)[268] is not extraordinary, his guide, the architect Campardon, tells him. On the contrary, "'[a]ll self-respecting landlords go to that expense nowadays'" (*ePL*, 5).[269] The resonance between Octave and the staircase makes itself felt rather quickly: "Little by little the staircase had filled him with awe; he felt quite flattered at the thought of living

---

[264] "La cour, au fond, pavée et cimentée, avait un grand air de propreté froide [...]." (*PB*, III 4)
[265] "[...] des têtes de femme soutenaient un balcon [...]." (*PB*, III 3)
[266] "[...] faux marbre [...]." (*PB*, III, 5)
[267] "Mais ce qui frappa surtout Octave, ce fut, en entrant, une chaleur de serre, une haleine tiède qu'une bouche lui soufflait au visage." (*PB*, III 5)
[268] "[...] l'escalier est chauffé [...]." (*PB*, III 5)
[269] "[...] tous les propriétaires qui se respectent font cette dépense [...]." (*PB*, III 5)

in such a fine house, as Campardon had termed it." (*ePL*, 6)²⁷⁰ It does not take long for the reader and Octave to find out that the heated staircase forms part of the deceptive bourgeois façade: behind the doors that it connects a characteristic coldness reigns. "'Oh, the cold in our room!'" (*ePL*, 31),²⁷¹ Berthe Josserand complains; their dining room, however, is in this respect not any different from their neighbours', the Pichons' "chilly little dining-room" (*ePL*, 65).²⁷² This coldness also metonymically characterises the people living there. Most iconically the "coldness of little Madame Pichon" (*ePL*, 71)²⁷³ and the recurring motif of her "icy lips" (*ePL*, 110), her "lips [...] cold as ice" (*ePL*, 74),²⁷⁴ represent this metonomy. Mme Duveyrier and her former boarding school friend Mme Hédouin, though situated in much more comfortable financial circumstances, share this bourgeois coldness: in their youth they were already known as "'the polar bears', because they were always twenty degrees below zero" (*ePL*, 81).²⁷⁵ As the novel tells us, they still live up to this (c)old nickname. M. Duveyrier suffers so intensely from this coldness that he tries to kill himself, once his "other hot-water bottle" (*ePL*, 81; transl. altered),²⁷⁶ his affair Clarisse, emancipates herself from him and he is robbed of the "snug corner where one lives warmly [*niche où vivre chaudement*]" (*ePL*, 348; transl. altered)²⁷⁷ that her apartment had been to him.

Although the "respect" that the heated staircase had raised in Octave turns out to be unfounded, created by deceit, by a false façade, by another instance of "imitation marble", his resonance with the staircase does not suffer. On the contrary: the house might not be "such a fine house" in a moral sense, it, however, turns out to be a very fine house for the young Octave's fortune. All the coldness surrounding him, this lack of warmth, favours his one central talent: He almost unwittingly knows how to transport some (false?) warmth into the chronically cold bourgeois rooms. Soon the young arrival advances from "'[...]

---

270 "L'escalier, peu à peu, l'avait empli de respect ; il était tout ému d'habiter une maison si bien, selon l'expression de l'architecte." (*PB*, III 7)
271 "« [...] ce qu'il fait froid, chez nous ! » dit Berthe en grelottant. « Ça vous gèle les morceaux dans la bouche... [...]. »" (*PB*, III 32)
272 "[...] la petite salle à manger froide [...]." (*PB*, III 65)
273 "[...] la froideur de la petite Mme Pichon [...]." (*PB*, III 73)
274 "[...] ses lèvres toujours froides" (*PB*, III 112); "Les lèvres de la jeune femme étaient glacées." (*PB*, III 75)
275 "« [...] on les appelait les ours blancs, parce qu'elles étaient toujours à vingt dégrées au-dessous de zéro... [...]. »" (*PB*, III 83)
276 "« [...] Si Duveyrier n'avait pas d'autre boule d'eau chaude à se mettre aux pieds, l'hiver ! »" (*PB*, III 83)
277 "Alors, chassé, n'ayant plus de niche où vivre chaudement, Duveyrier, après avoir battu les trottoirs, était entré dans une boutique perdue acheter un revolver de poche." (*PB*, III 355)

the person'" (ePL, 4)[278] to the ladies' favourite "hot-water bottle", most of them falling for him very quickly, making the resistance of others appear 'unnatural' and mean: "He did not know what to think; these bourgeois women, whose virtue had frozen him at first, seemed now as if they would surrender at a mere sign, and when one of them resisted it filled him with surprise and vexation." (ePL, 110)[279] It is a servant he overhears that makes him aware of the opportunities that his talent opens up for him: "'I tell you Monsieur Hédouin died last night. If only the handsome Octave had foreseen that, he would've gone on warming Madame Hédouin, 'cos she'll be worth a lot now." (ePL, 264; transl. altered)[280] This is exactly what Octave does: he heats up the bourgeois coldness, he meets the structural demand of warmth, and profits from this deep longing. He melts the bourgeois ice and introduces circulation to the bourgeois affected seclusiveness. In the end, he will successfully heat up Mme Hédouin, which is also an instrumental step to his gaining control over the 'Le Bonheur des Dames'. As we will see in a later section, the very same talent that made him ascend in the bourgeois house is also responsible for the capitalistic success of his department store. His talent in heating up the bourgeois coldness resonates with the Second Empire society – and it is this resonance that the emblematic staircase embodies: The novel does not tell of curing the bourgeois society from its chronic coldness, it is about exploiting this coldness and the longings it produces. The reason why "[a]ll self-respecting landlords go to that expense nowadays" is not moral or humane; as the financial connotations of "expense" already indicate, it is an investment that promises profits.

The heated staircase is thus not only an 'image' that illustrates Octave's role in the house, his introducing warmth, circulation and his ascendency. Zola very clearly erects it as emblematic for the Second Empire's society as a whole: "[a]ll self-respecting landlords go to that expense nowadays". Octave Mouret's metonymic correspondence with his immediate surroundings, with the heated staircase and the bourgeois house he is living in is a prime example for the way Zola narrates the Second Empire. So much so that against the background of what we have just seen, the emblematic staircase even shines through the famous programmatic sentence about the Rougon-Macquarts in the preface of *La Fortune des Rougon*:

---

[278] "« Monsieur Campardon, est-ce la personne? » « Oui, monsieur Gourd, c'est M. Octave Mouret [...]. »" (*PB*, III 4)

[279] "Il ne savait plus : ces bourgeoises, dont la vertu le glaçait d'abord, lui semblaient maintenant devoir céder sur un signe ; et, lorsqu'une d'elles résistait, il restait plein de surprise et de rancune." (*PB*, III 112)

[280] "« Je vous dis que M. Hédouin est mort hier soir... Si le bel Octave avait prévu ça, il aurait continué à chauffer Mme Hédouin, qui a le sac. »" (*PB*, III 270)

Historically the Rougon-Macquarts originate in the common people, spread through the whole of contemporary society, and *rise to all sorts of positions* because of the essentially modern impulse that sets the lower classes marching through the social system. Thus the dramas of their individual lives tell the story of the Second Empire [...]. (*eFR*, 3; emph. J.U.)[281]

Pot-Bouille exemplarily relates the "rise to all sorts of positions", it tells of the "essentially modern impulse that sets the lower classes marching through the social system." However, it does not simply narrate the story of an individual's rise to a certain unexpected social status – the novel's episodic composition and the multiplicity of little, non-linear stories betrays this argument. In contrast to *Au Bonheur des Dames* it is not even focusing mainly on Octave's success. It rather narrates the heated staircase. Its subject is the protagonist's resonance with a certain social configuration. The conditions for this "rise" and its relation with this "essentially modern impulse" (which is not an abstract trait, but a complicated phenomenon of resonance) are what it means to express. The characteristic metonymic connection of protagonist and his surroundings provide the key for Zola's project of narrating the Second Empire through the stories of the Rougon-Macquarts' "individual lives".

Perhaps the most extreme metonymic correspondence of a protagonist with her 'surroundings', the most special relation that holds together the individual and the world she is living in is, literally, staged at the beginning of *Nana*. With regard to this novel's title, Zola deviates from his habit of combining a somehow emblematic, thematic concept or phenomenon with the direct article: *La Fortune*, *La Curée*, *Le Ventre de Paris*, *La Terre*, *Le Rêve*, *L'Argent* ... Instead, he opts to name his novel after its protagonist. This is a conventional choice, connecting the novel to the genre's 18th century birth and development, emulating predecessors like Richardson's *Clarissa*, Chateaubriand's *René* or – Goethe's *Werther*. However, with *Nana* Zola not only adds his name to a list of famous predecessors, he also, and mainly, uses the connection to work out the differences that distinguish his novelistic project from the tradition.[282] The way Nana enters the novel that carries her name marks this difference from the very beginning.

The novel opens with an account of a theatre performance. Two minor characters focalise the scene, beginning with their early arrival at the empty auditorium and ending with the crowd leaving after the performance. It is the

---

281 "Historiquement, ils partent du peuple, ils s'irradient dans toute la société contemporaine, ils montent à toutes les situations, par cette impulsion essentiellement moderne que reçoivent les basses classes en marche à travers le corps social, et ils racontent ainsi le second Empire [...]." (*FR*, I 3)
282 As Janet Beizer rightly claims, *Nana* is a "metanovel" (1989, 56).

atmosphere of the place that the scene tries to capture. Nana is merely the epitome of this atmosphere. Although she "kept the audience well waiting" (*eN*, 12; transl. altered),[283] although it is not until quite late in the scene that she eventually enters the stage, she is somehow 'present' from the beginning. She is 'in the air' so to speak – and this quite literally. Bordenave, the theatre director, has good reasons to be "delighted". He has indeed successfully "kindled his public" (*eN*, 6; transl. altered):[284] Nana is the subject of every conversation, she is the reason why the audience goes to the theatre. Long before anyone has seen her play or heard her sing, her name repeatedly fills the theatre building:

> In front of them a queue of people was crushed at the box-office, an uproar of voices was growing louder and louder, in which the name 'Nana' sounded with the singing liveliness of its two syllables. (*eN*, 6; transl. altered)[285]

> But now, like an echo, Nana resounded from the four corners of the foyer more and more loudly, in a desire increased by the time of waiting. (*eN*, 7; transl. altered)[286]

Nana 'is', 'essentially', one could say, nothing but hot air. Or, warm words, as it is not only the sound of her name that fills the building: "tall yellow posters were spread violently all over the place with the name 'Nana' in large black letters" (*eN*, 3; transl. altered).[287] The colour-code of these violent posters that are uncannily proliferating is telling: 'Nana' is warm words, indeed, or rather, *fiery* words – Bordenave quite literally has "kindled" or 'fired', 'inflamed' [*allumé*] his public. This is his job, this is what he makes a living from. Like Octave Mouret, he has discovered the exploitation of heating. In fact, the whole first scene narrates the success story of this job.

When the journalist Fauchery and his cousin La Faloise enter the auditorium, early, well before the beginning of the performance, it is not a particularly hot or

---

[283] "Cette Nana se faisait bien attendre." (*N*, II 1106) Douglas Parmée's English translation unfortunately does not listen too carefully to the French wording. As my working with the text aims at nuances of imagery that very often are not rendered by Parmée's English text, I have seen myself forced to quite extensively alter the translations. Sometimes, as in this particular case, hardly one of Parmée's words is left untouched by these 'alterations'. Nevertheless, I have decided to 'quote' from his translation in order to enable the reader to situate the 'quote' and read up on its surroundings.
[284] "Il disparut, enchanté d'avoir allumé son public." (*N*, II 1100)
[285] "Devant eux, une queue s'écrasait au contrôle, un tapage de voix montait, dans lequel le nom de Nana sonnait avec la vivacité chantante de ses deux syllabes." (*N*, II 1100)
[286] "Mais à présent, comme un écho, Nana sonnait aux quatre coins du vestibule sur un ton plus haut, dans un désir accru par l'attente." (*N*, II 1101)
[287] "[…] hautes affiches jaune s'étalaient violemment, avec le nom de Nana en grosses lettres noires." (*N*, II 1097)

heated place. They find themselves in "the dawn of the chandelier's turned down fire" (*eN*, 1; transl. altered).[288] However, the narration's insistency on "the small flames of the grand chandelier" (*eN*, 2; transl. altered)[289] already establishes the isotopy of fire and prepares for the great 'inflammation' that is to follow. When half an hour later the "the theatre was resplendent[, h]igh flames of gas lighted the grand crystal chandelier with a flooding of yellow and pink fire, breaking into a rain of clarity from the proscenium arch to the pit" (*eN*, 8; transl. altered),[290] this is not merely the result of someone having opened the gas tap. In fact, the main energy of the heating comes from the outside, as an effect of Bordenave's kindling: he manages to channel "the fiery life of the boulevards, which swarmed and flamed under this lovely April evening" (*eN*, 2; transl. altered)[291] into his theatre, to concentrate and work with its flaming, fiery energy. No wonder that "[i]t was already hot" (*eN*, 8; transl. altered)[292] in the theatre before Nana even comes on stage; the whole theatre event is about managing the energies that it receives from the outside. Bordenave seems to be a master of this dramaturgy of heating: "the public heated itself up/warmed [*s'échauffa*]" (*eN*, 12; transl. altered)[293] and "became cold again" (*eN*, 12; transl. altered),[294] only to burst into flames when the waiting has an end and Nana finally appears on stage. Zola illustrates the striking, 'thermic' effect of Nana's appearance with the help of a "cherub, the schoolboy playing truant" whose "fair face [is] set on fire [*enflammée*] at the sight of Nana" (*eN*, 14; transl. altered).[295] Nana is surely the central ingredient of Bordenave's dramaturgy of heating, not only because "a flame passed over her cheeks" (*eN*, 14; transl. altered)[296] spreading the fire among the audience. Although she cannot sing, although her movements are neither elegant nor skilled, every little gesture, especially her "famous flick of the hips" is answered by a shock of heat proliferating in the audience: "the stalls caught fire [*s'allumait*], a warmth [*une*

---

[288] "[…] le petit jour du lustre à demi-feux […]." (*N*, II 1095)
[289] "[…] les flammes courtes du grand lustre […]." (*N*, II 1096)
[290] "Maintenant la salle resplendissait. Des hautes flammes de gaz allumaient le grand lustre de cristal d'un ruisselement de feux jaunes et roses, qui se brisaient du cintre au parterre en une pluie de clarté." (*N*, II 1102)
[291] "[…] la vie ardente des boulevards, qui grouillaient et flambaient sous la belle nuit d'avril […]." (*N*, II 1096)
[292] "Il faisait déjà chaud." (*N*, II 1102)
[293] "[…] le public s'échauffa […]." (*N*, II 1106)
[294] "[…] le public redevint froid […]." (*N*, II 1106)
[295] "[…] le chérubin, l'échappé de collège sa face blonde enflammée par la vue de Nana […]." (*N*, II 1107)
[296] "[…] une flamme passait sur ses joues […]." (*N*, II 1108)

chaleur] was spreading upwards from one gallery to another, right up to the arch." (*eN*, 19–20; transl. altered)[297] Nana in fact unleashes weathery forces that seem to be familiar to us from Goethe's *Werther*, bringing about the same ecstasy, the same excess of frenzy:

> It was as if a wind had very sweetly passed through, charged with a muffled menace. This good-natured girl had suddenly become a disturbing woman, bringing with her the fit of frenzy of her sex, opening up desire's unknown. (*eN*, 25; transl. altered)[298]

> The entire hall was trembling, having slid into a frenzy [*vertige*], weary and excited, taken in by these lovers' beds. (*eN*, 27; transl. altered)[299]

The staging of her nudity is surely a provocative act, and, in a certain sense, a singular event: "Never before had one dared a hotter [*plus chaude*] seduction scene" (*eN*, 26; transl. altered).[300] However, this hottest of seduction scenes is but part of Bordenave's dramaturgy of heating, it is not alien to the world of viewers that hold their breaths watching it; on the contrary, as the dominant isotopy of fire and heat that pervades this scene clearly indicates, it unleashes the forces that the audience itself has brought to the theatre. The public encounters the condensed essence of "the fiery life of the boulevards" they have led before they entered the theatre, and which they will lead the very same way after leaving it. The scene thus ends as it has begun:

> The cry "Nana! Nana!" had thundered furiously. Then, the hall was not even empty, when it was plunged into darkness; the footlights went out, the chandelier was lowered, long, grey canvas covers slid out from the proscenium and hid the guilt of the galleries; and this hall, so hot, so noisy, suddenly fell into a heavy sleep [...]. (*eN*, 28; transl. altered)[301]

This first chapter (and I would claim the same for the whole novel) does not merely tell the story of an individual character. "'Nana is an invention of

---

[297] "Quand elle donnait son fameux coup de hanche, l'orchestre s'allumait, une chaleur montait de galerie en galerie jusqu'au cintre." (*N*, II 1113)
[298] "Un vent semblait avoir passé très doux, chargé d'une sourde menace. Tout d'un coup, dans la bonne enfant, la femme se dressait, inquiétante, apportant le coup de folie de son sexe, ouvrant l'inconnu du désir." (*N*, II 1118)
[299] "La salle entière vacillait, glissait à un vertige, lasse et excitée, prise de ces alcôves." (*N*, II 1120)
[300] "Jamais encore on n'avait osé une scène de séduction plus chaude." (*N*, II 1119)
[301] "Le cri : « Nana ! Nana ! » avait roulé furieusement. Puis, la salle n'était pas encore vide qu'elle devint noire ; la rampe s'éteignit, le lustre baissa, de longues housses de toile grise glissèrent des avant-scènes, enveloppèrent les dorures des galeries ; et cette salle, si chaude, si bruyante, tomba d'un coup à un lourd sommeil [...]." (*N*, II 1120)

Bordenave'" (*eN*, 3; transl. altered),[302] Fauchery says, and of Zola, we could hasten to add. However, she is not just any invention. Bordenave follows a clear commercial interest with this invention, the interest of exploiting a particular social constellation and development. Like Octave Mouret, he has sniffed a certain available energy among the masses, a certain resonance that somehow transcends the diversity of their social background, of their age, of their gender even. Nana is not a character, she is an embodiment of this resonance. She *is* "an echo" "resound[ing] from the four corners" of the Second Empire, "more and more loudly". In the novel's first scene Zola quite artfully stages Bordenave's success by framing the account of the theatre performance with the crowd's recurring and intensifying acclamations of 'Nana'. Bordenave has indeed 'struck a chord' with his 'invention': the resonance obviously works, it brings the audience into his theatre, where it warms to his dramaturgy. The interest of Zola's invention of Nana is not too different from Bordenave's: he is in pursuit of the same resonance, certainly not primarily to profit from it (which is a welcome by-product) but to narrate it. Despite the so conventional title, *Nana* does not "go[ ] back to 'La Nouvelle Heloise,' to 'Werther,' to 'René,' which are but the analyses of a psychological fact" (Zola 1893b, 261);[303] it is rather a prime example of what it means "to study, not characters, but temperaments" (*eTR*, 1).[304] Comparable to the role the correspondence of Hélène's passions to the Paris panoramas plays in *Une page d'amour*, Zola includes the crowd's shouting in unison as a key motif for structuring the novel. It not only frames the novel's first scene, it also frames the novel as a whole. In *Nana* Zola even takes the time to stage the fact that his interest in 'temperaments' can be detached from his novel's protagonist. When at the occasion of a horse race the crowd once again acclaims the familiar 'Nana! Nana!', Zola's protagonist, Nana, rightfully feels herself confirmed in her former triumph; she feels herself to be the reigning queen of the masses:

> It was the noise of the rising tides. Nana! Nana! Nana! The cry thundered in ever-increasing waves, with the violence of a storm, gradually filling the horizon [...].
>
> And from the other side of the track the enclosure of weighing answered, an agitation moved the grandstands, though the only thing that could be clearly seen was a sort of quivering in the air, like the invisible flame of a brazier above this living pile of tiny,

---

[302] "Nana est une invention de Bordenave." (*N*, II 1096)
[303] "Sans remonter à *La Nouvelle Héloïse*, à *Werther*, à *René*, qui ne sont que des analyses d'un fait psychologique [...]." (*RE, OC* IX, 438)
[304] "Dans *Thérèse Raquin*, j'ai voulu étudier des tempéraments et non des caractères." (*TR, OC* III 27)

> hysterical figures with writhing arms and open mouths and eyes like black pin-points. [...] Nana! Nana! Nana! The cry rose in the glory of the sun, whose golden rain beat down on the frenzy [*vertige*] of the crowd. (*eN*, 336; transl. altered)[305]

The details in wording and imagery, the isotopy of heat and fire ("like the invisible flame of a brazier"), the weather forces ("rising tides", "thundered", "violence of a storm", "golden rain") and the result of "the frenzy of the crowd" very clearly indicate that we are dealing with the same resonance that Bordenave had sensed and that Nana embodies. It does, paradoxically, not matter too much that the novel's protagonist, Nana, is not actually the 'correct reference' of the crowd's shouting: it was the triumph of the outsider horse called 'Nana' that had inflamed the watchers. 'Nana', for Bordenave as for Zola is but a name for the phenomenon that both the diegetic theatre director and Zola are after: a striking resonance characterising a crowd.

Zola even goes a further step at the end of his novel. Nana's death is accompanied by another instance of the crowd's shouting in unison. It is, I would claim, the very same resonance making itself heard, a resonance that survives its metonymic embodiment:

> [...] this frenzy [*vertige*], these confused masses, streaming with the flood [*roulées par le flot*], exhaled a terror, an immense pity for the massacres to come. They were bewildered, their voices cracking in the drunkenness of their fever as they rushed towards the unknown, there, beyond the dark wall of the horizon.
>
> 'On to Berlin! On to Berlin! On to Berlin!' (*eN*, 420; transl. altered)[306]

Very conventionally, the novel called *Nana* ends with the death of its protagonist. However, by taking up the structuring motif of the crowd's collective shouting, which had from the beginning defined Nana's role and life, and by shifting this motif towards the 'historical' (from 'Nana' to 'On to Berlin!') Zola, in retrospect, points out that the novel narrates more than an individual life.

---

[305] "Ce fut comme la clameur montant d'une marée. Nana ! Nana ! Nana ! Le cri roulait, grandissait, avec une violence de tempête, emplissant peu à peu l'horizon [...]. Et de l'autre côté de la piste, l'enceinte du pesage répondait, une agitation remuait les tribunes, sans qu'on vît distinctement autre chose qu'un tremblement de l'air, comme la flamme invisible d'un brasier, au-dessus de ce tas vivant de petites figures détraquées, les bras tordus, avec les points noirs des yeux et de la bouche ouverte. [...] Nana ! Nana ! Nana ! Le cri montait dans la gloire du soleil, dont la pluie d'or battait le vertige de la foule." (*N*, II 1404)

[306] "[...] ce vertige, ces masses confuses, roulées par le flot, exhalait une terreur, une grande pitié de massacres futurs. Ils s'étourdissaient, les cris se brisaient dans l'ivresse de leur fièvre se ruant à l'inconnu, là-bas, derrière le mur noir de l'horizon. « A Berlin ! à Berlin ! à Berlin ! »" (*N*, II 1480–1481)

He lays bare the metonymic link, the correspondence that connects the novel's protagonist with the world surrounding her. Even more importantly, it reveals that the novel has been, all the while, not interested in the character's idiosyncrasies, but in this metonymic link, in this correspondence.

Nana is surely the most extreme, or the most explicit case of Zola's indicating his narratological focus and subject. However, it is an exemplary case that exposes the mechanisms that are at work in all the other novels of the cycle as well. Although the metonymic link between the protagonist and his or her surroundings might be on a different scale in the different novels, it is doubtless the characteristic trait of Zola's cycle. Against the background of the beginnings with which we are already familiar from *Une page d'amour*, *Pot-Bouille* and *Nana*, we can now attempt to describe this trait and contrast it to the concentric constellation, to the role of the 'environ-ment' we found dominant in Goethe's *Werther*.

Zola himself has provided us with some indications concerning the relationship with his predecessors and the innovations of his novelistic enterprise. We have already quoted from his dictum that the naturalistic novel does not 'merely' aim at analysing "a psychological fact" (Zola 1893b, 261), as, according to Zola, "*La Nouvelle Héloïse*, [...] *Werther*, [...] *René*" do. This implies, as we will presently see, that it is not psychology, but rather physiology that serves as the conceptual background or framework for Zola's narrative project. Before turning to this implication I would suggest focusing on another, a rather basic, but important aspect of Zola's 'dismissal' of psychology: with psychology Zola rejects the centring of the novel on the individual. Famously his novels do not narrate "characters, but temperaments", which is a bold poetological statement. The genre of the novel is traditionally inseparable from the notion of modern subjectivity, its birth in the early 18th century coincides with and contributes to the developing 'modern' conception of a world ordered around the individual. In our second chapter we have noted how closely Goethe's *Werther* adhered to this conception. The handful of brief readings undertaken so far already allows us to form an idea of how Zola deviates from this traditional orientation on the individual. Even one of the more conventional, less 'sociological' or 'socio-critical' novels of the series, *Une page d'amour*, finds ways of transcending the individual and the story of her biography: despite the limited circle of personages and the novel's quite exclusive focus on Hélène's sensations and fate, it does not merely tell 'her' story by telling her story. It is the mechanism of metonymic correspondences that links her environment (be it her friends, neighbours, fellow citizens, but also the things surrounding her, the architectonics of the city, the institutions of that particular society) to her fate and impressions, to her passions. M. Rambaud and the *abbé* belong to the blue room, whereas the hypocritical salon society of Mme Deberlé somehow all contribute to the pink nest of love. The institution of the church with its religious feverish passion is inseparable from Hélène's passion, as it is from the symptomatic constitution of Jeanne's health. It is this net of metonymical relations that extends the novel's focus, moving it beyond the story of a character, towards a narration of 'temperaments' – whatever that might exactly signify. To be sure, Zola's novels do not narrate the individual, they do not focus on one particular character that is to be scrutinised in his or her characteristic traits, his or her 'existential' unity. Instead, as I have just tried to suggest with *Une page d'amour* and as we have already seen in our exemplary readings of *Pot-Bouille* and *Nana*, Zola rather aims for an account of 'the masses', of a resonance somehow emerging from the masses, a resonance that determines or at least influences the life of the individual.

Zola however also underlines the continuities that link his narrative project to his 18th century predecessors. Despite the obvious differences, which are of indisputable poetological weight, it is important to take these continuities seriously. Goethe and Zola do not live in a world governed by completely different paradigms. The model Goethe elaborates, the model of the individual and his/her blissful and threatening environ-ment, has not become alien to Zola and his 19th century contemporaries. On the contrary, this model is not foreign and difficult to decipher (as Shakespeare's world must appear to the 'modern' eye), it is still very much shaping the perception of the world, whether in Zola's 19th century, or still today. Zola simply poses a question different from Goethe's. It is a shift in question, a 19th century question, so to speak, which, however, is unthinkable without the 18th century's foundation. Zola's question builds on this very foundation.

In Zola's words, the 18th century novel has seen "nature shooting forth [...] in philosophical dissertations" (Zola 1893b, 231),[307] whereas his naturalistic novel excels in the "scientific employment of description" (Zola 1893b, 231).[308] According to this rough scheme, the 18th century novel and the naturalistic novel share the fact that they do not narrate their stories "on a neutral, indeterminate, and conventional ground" (Zola 1893b, 231);[309] 'nature' enters the scene, "shoot[s] forth", and asks for literary representation. For our interest in the weather this claim is more than pertinent. As we have seen in Goethe's *Werther* the weather can be regarded as the paradigm of natural forces making themselves felt, breaking into a world that has neglected their role. In fact, *Werther*

---

[307] "Puis, avec les romans du dix-huitième siècle, nous verrions poindre la nature, mais dans des dissertations philosophiques [...]." (*RE, OC* IX 424)
[308] "[...] l'emploi scientifique de la description [...]." (*RE, OC* IX 425)
[309] "[...] sur un fond neutre, indéterminé, conventionnel [...]." (*RE, OC* IX 424)

can indeed quite appropriately be called a "philosophical dissertation[ ]". It narrates the fact *that* the weathery forces are part of the world and confronts the conceptual core of the enlightened world, the autonomous individual, with this shock. The novel's quite surprising finding, the recognition that the weathery forces turn out to be inseparable from the constitution of the subject, that they are the return of what has been repressed and driven beyond the boundaries, operates on the very same, abstract and philosophical level. These are all negotiations taking place on the conceptual level, on the level of the abstract model, examining the core of the 'modern', enlightened world: the subject being the foundation of a worldview, its birth, its stability.

Zola's "scientific employment of description" takes a further step that shifts the question. The fact *that* nature's weathery forces are part of the world has ceased to be questionable, has ceased to be problematic (cf. Foucault 1984, 16). As Zola's intrinsically weathery world shows, the co-presence of the weather/weathery forces and the modern, 'autonomous' subject has become reality in the world of the late 19th century: the weather does not break into the world as a disturbing event, it has become a defining part of the world. Zola's new question testifies to this co-presence. It is not the fact *that* the weather is part of the world, but the question of *how* this co-presence of subject and nature, of subject and weathery forces works that Zola raises with his cycle of novels. This does not only imply leaving the abstract, philosophical level of the model and of "philosophical dissertations" and turning towards the concrete, towards the phenomena of exchange and interaction that characterise the 19th century society. Zola's "scientific employment of description" also suggests a conceptual shift. Goethe's question aiming at the fact *that* the weather forms part of the world, at the fact *that* human life and human society as an organisation of autonomous subjects do not take place "on a neutral, indeterminate, and conventional ground" assumes a '*digital*' attitude towards nature and its weathery forces. As we have seen with regard to the concentric constellation, the constitution of the modern subject is a project of drawing boundaries. With boundaries, there are always only two possibilities: either they hold or they do not hold. Either the weather remains on the outside (or in the 'inner inside'), repressed, and all is bliss and fine inside, enlightened sunshine; or the boundaries leak and break, the weather disturbs the order and chaos and death reign. Although Goethe's *Werther* deconstructs and complicates this dual, digital attitude towards the weather, showing that it is the weathery forces themselves that drive the process of building boundaries, its project of constituting a literary supplement, a literary harbour for these forces in the end works towards strengthening the boundaries. Although his novel acknowledges and represents the weathery forces of nature, the question of the 'environment' remains for Goethe a question of a boundary, a question of life and death, with nothing but literature in-between.

Zola's approach to the weathery forces is 'analog'. Instead of *boundary*, it takes *interaction, communication, correspondence* as its paradigms. Whereas Goethe was 'digitally' concerned with *'environ-ment'* (which is a phenomenon of boundary), Zola focuses on *milieu*.

Milieu – this is what the "scientific employment of description" is all about. As Zola himself puts it in an attempt to "define description: 'An account of the milieu which determines and completes man.'" (Zola 1893b, 233; transl. altered)[310] It is significant that I had to overrule the translator, Belle M. Sherman, who rendered the French *milieu* with the English *environment*. With regard to this sentence, *environment* is surely not a wrong semantic choice, all the more because there does not seem to be a better, 'genuinely English' alternative available. However, the translation (and the English word *environment* in general) blurs the conceptual difference that, I would claim, actually distinguishes Zola's narrative project from Goethe's. The semantic and etymological difference between *milieu* and *environment* may even distinguish the 18th century's thinking of 'nature' and its weathery forces from the 19th century's.

The conceptual difference manifests itself in the very words that represent the two conceptual possibilities, so that it is important to examine closely their semantic implications and their provenance. As we have seen in the second chapter, *environment* was coined in the proximity and with reference to the birth of the modern individual, it testifies to the subject's being in the centre, and the world grouped 'around' it. The French *milieu* tells of a very different semantic history. An all-too hasty look into the *Petit Robert* might find this word to be merely a synonym of *environment*: we encounter a group of meanings labelled "ce qui entoure" ('that which surrounds') (*PetRob*, milieu, n. III.). This group of meanings assembles all the 'scientific' references concerning the notion of 'milieu' that are of importance for Zola: biological, physiological, sociological references, even a quotation from Claude Bernard. This is obviously the path Belle M. Sherman followed when translating *milieu* with *environment*. However, the equivalence of the two is limited and superficial. The emergence date of *milieu* meaning 'ce qui entoure' should attract our attention: this specific use of *milieu* is clearly a product of the 19th century. It appears initially in specialised, scientific discourses, in very young discourses that are themselves children of the 19th century, like physiology, ecology and sociology. For these young sciences *milieu* is a key concept – it is their very foundation. As a result, an

---

[310] "Je définirai donc la description : un état du milieu qui détermine et complète l'homme." (*RE, OC* IX 425)

important discrepancy is established between Goethe's 18th century concentric constellation, its notions of the 'um-herum', the 'arounds' and 'surroundings' that manifest themselves in the word *environment* and the 19th century notion of *milieu*. This 19th century notion seems to denote the same 'thing', 'ce qui entoure' ('that which surrounds') but with one central modification.

The modification concerns the older, 'original' meanings of *milieu*. As the *Petit Robert* points out, the emergence of the word *milieu* dates back to the twelfth century. It is formed by combining two semantic elements: *lieu*, 'place', and *mi-*, 'middle' – *milieu*, literally, is the 'middle-place' (*PetRob*, milieu, *n.*). The two other, older groups of meanings that the *Petit Robert* lists for *milieu*, apart from its signifying 'ce qui entoure', reflect its etymological origins much more explicitly: "ce qui est à mi-distance dans l'espace ou le temps" ('that which is in mid-distance in space or time') and "position moyenne" ('average position') (*PetRob*, milieu, *n.* I., II.). *Milieu* signifying 'that which surrounds' inherits this semantic and etymological legacy: if it conveys the meaning of something being surrounded by, being in *the middle of* other things, then this is not a statement of its abstract topographical or geometrical relations; the *milieu*'s *mi-* does not refer to the hierarchy of centre and periphery but underlines the notion of *mediation*, communication, interaction, correspondence. Whereas *environment* 'originally' signifies a constellation (before serving as a translation for *milieu*!), *milieu* signifies the processes of interaction taking place. This is the decisive conceptual rupture that separates the 18th and the 19th century's thinking of 'that which surrounds' – a rupture that is obliterated by the English word *environment*.

We have arrived at the point where the results of our exemplary readings of *Une page d'amour*, *Pot-Bouille* and *Nana* can be fused with the epistemological background setting off Zola's 19th from Goethe's 18th century. The metonymic correspondences of the protagonist and his or her 'surroundings' that we have observed, the special relation holding together the individual and the world s/he is living in, which we have identified as the characteristic trait of Zola's *Rougon-Macquart*, are rooted in the notion of milieu. Zola's narrative project does not discuss the boundaries separating 'the own' from 'the other', the autonomous human individual from its environment; it focuses on the passages, on the interactions and correspondences traversing these boundaries: "we are into the exact study of the milieu", Zola writes, "into the observation of the conditions of the exterior world, which correspond to the interior conditions of the characters." (Zola 1893b, 233; transl. altered)[311]

---

[311] "[...] nous sommes dans l'étude exacte du milieu, dans la constatation des états du monde extérieur qui correspondent aux états intérieurs des personnages." (*RE*, *OC* IX 425)

The "scientific employment of description" can be called "scientific" because it is the concept of the milieu that serves as its epistemological foundation. Catherine Bordeau's claim that the "[b]elief in the power of the milieu pervades nineteenth-century thought" (1998–1999, 96) is supported by the entries that the *Petit Robert* lists for *milieu* signifying 'that which surrounds': *milieu* is indeed a concept brought forward by the nascent sciences of the 19th century, by physiology, ecology and sociology. With his famous poetological essay "Le Roman expérimental" Zola has rather covered up than exposed the points of contact linking his literary project to the sciences of his time: the analogy he constructs between Claude Bernard's "experimental method" (Zola 1893a, 14)[312] and his own poetics has set his readers on the wrong track. With few exceptions (for example Gamper 2005) the critics agree that this analogy is merely a stylisation (Cryle 2004, 56), a "rhetorical move" (Counter 2014, 198), "maladroit" (Woollen 1985, 59), all in all a "famously 'unconvincing' application of the experimental method to the novel" (Counter 2014, 198). Unfortunately, the dismissal of Zola's pseudo-scientific "experimental method" most often accompanies dismissing any notion of the proximity of Zola's literary project with 19th century science. This is inadequate, since science sheds important light on one of the poetological foundations of Zola's project. It is not the "experimental method", but the notion of milieu that Zola has borrowed from 19th century scientific discourse. It is, I would suggest, also this notion of milieu that connects Zola's project to Claude Bernard's physiological studies. Although concealed by the explicit analogy of method that Zola develops for his readers, the important concept of the milieu and its characteristics nevertheless shine through the famous testimony of Zola's enthusiasm towards his colleague.

Claude Bernard's scientific innovation, laying the cornerstone for the nascent discipline of physiology, is one of milieu, more exactly, one of the capacity of communication and correspondence that the concept of milieu creates. This innovation marks the point of departure of Zola's essay:

> The difference is simply that an inanimate body finds itself in the external and common milieu, while the elements of the superior organisms bathe in an internal and perfected milieu, however gifted with constant physico-chemical properties, like the exterior milieu. (Zola 1893a, 3; transl. altered)[313]

---

[312] "[…] méthode expérimentale […]." (*RE*, OC IX 329)
[313] "La différence vient uniquement de ce qu'un corps brut se trouve dans le milieu extérieur et commun, tandis que les éléments des organismes supérieurs baignent dans un milieu intérieur et perfectionnée, mais doué de propriétés physico-chimiques constantes, comme le milieu extérieur." (*RE, OC* IX 325)

Bernard's discovery cannot be captured by his coinage of the term *milieu intérieur* alone. His distinction of internal and external milieu simply mirrors the traditional distinction of animate and inanimate bodies. It is the transition that the concept of the milieu opens that revolutionises the scientific world: it discovers/establishes a correspondence between animate and inanimate bodies; internal and external milieu are both "gifted with constant physico-chemical properties". One of the oldest ontological boundaries, the one of animate and inanimate bodies, is crossed by this correspondence. We encounter here the textbook example of what the concept of milieu does: it connects the distinct, makes the separated and disparate communicate. It erects correspondences crossing the boundaries and making interaction possible and thinkable ("The living body [...] never falls into chemical or physical indifference with the external milieu" (Zola 1893a, 21; transl. altered)[314]). From an epistemological point of view Bernard's discovery is important, because it allows animate bodies to become the subject of scientific research. Zola quotes here[315] from Bernard: "'With living beings as well as inanimate, the conditions of the existence of each phenomenon are determined in an absolute manner'" (Zola 1893a, 16),[316] implying that "[t]he end of all experimental method, the boundary of all scientific research, is then identical for living and for inanimate bodies" (Zola 1893a, 3).[317] "[E]xperimental method" is just a name for the science that has become possible by the transition that the concept of milieu has created; being "determined" is the trademark for belonging to the realm of scientific truth. The science Zola observes operating in Bernard's work transcends the boundary of the animate and the inanimate, because its approach to the world takes the route of the *milieu*. The realm of the living bodies is not governed by transcendent, ideal forces that would place it beyond the reach of science. Life is not "'a mysterious and supernatural agent, which acts arbitrarily'" (Zola 1893a, 15);[318] external and internal milieu correspond, the passage from knowledge of the one to knowledge of the other is possible: "For the physiologist, the external milieu and the internal milieu are purely chemical and physical, and this aids

---

314 "« Le corps vivant [...] ne tombe jamais en indifférence physico-chimique avec le milieu extérieur [...].»" (*RE, OC* IX 333)
315 The quotations inside the quotations following all refer to Claude Bernard.
316 "« Chez les êtres vivants aussi bien que dans les corps bruts, les conditions d'existence de tout phénomène sont déterminés d'une façon absolue. »" (*RE, OC* IX 330)
317 "Le but de la méthode expérimentale, le terme de toute recherche scientifique, est donc identique pour les corps vivants et pour les corps bruts [...]." (*RE, OC* IX 325)
318 "« [...] la vie comme une influence mystérieuse et surnaturelle qui agit arbitrairement [...]. »" (*RE, OC* IX 330)

him in finding the laws which govern them easily" (Zola 1893a, 20; transl. altered).[319]

Having reconstructed Bernard's innovation, Zola emulates Bernard's move that has revolutionised science and takes it one step further: Bernard had found a passage from the realm of the inanimate bodies to the animate bodies; Zola aspires to bridge another traditional and fundamental gap, the gap between 'the natural' and 'the social':

> In one word, we should operate on the characters, the passions, on the human and social data, in the same way that the chemist and the physicist operate on inanimate beings, and as the physiologist operates on living beings. Determinism dominates everything. (Zola 1893a, 18)[320]

As neat and logical as Zola's emulation of Bernard's innovation looks, extending the scientific reach beyond yet another boundary, there is one fundamental difference: in contrast to Bernard, Zola cannot base the correspondence of the milieus on knowledge of their factual similarity. Although the "constant physicochemical properties" linked Bernard's external and internal milieu, Zola and his contemporaries "are not yet able to prove that the social milieu is also physical and chemical" (Zola 1893a, 20; transl. altered)[321]. In other words, Zola's project of crossing the boundary of 'the natural' and 'the social', declaring the social milieu to be another realm where the laws of science, where "determination" reigns, relies completely on the milieu's 'promise' of correspondence. The concrete realisation and 'nature' of the correspondence of 'the social' and 'the natural' remains yet unknown; it has yet to be discovered. This is why Zola's project is neither physiological nor sociological, why his narrative project is, as he states, not quite scientific: it is literary. According to its author, it paves the road for future science as a pioneering forerunner.

Zola's cycle of novels already bears the task that Zola formulates in "Le Roman expérimental" in its name: *Les Rougon-Macquart. Histoire naturelle et sociale d'une famille sous le Second Empire*. Against the background of this dogmatic, fundamental divide between the social and the natural, writing the 'natural and social history' of a family, or even of a historical formation seems to be a para-doxical endeavour. However, this is exactly what Zola attempts to do: establishing a passage between these two realms. The concept of *milieu*

---

[319] "Pour le physiologiste, le milieu extérieur et le milieu intérieur sont purement chimiques et physiques, ce qui lui permet d'en trouver les lois aisément." (*RE, OC* IX 332)
[320] "En un mot, nous devons opérer sur les caractères, sur les passions, sur les faits humains et sociaux, comme le chimiste et le physicien opère sur les corps bruts, comme le physiologiste opère sur les corps vivants. Le déterminisme domine tout." (*RE, OC* IX 331)
[321] "Nous n'en sommes pas à pouvoir prouver que le milieu social n'est, lui aussi, que chimique et physique." (*RE, OC* IX 332)

serves as the conceptual backbone for this challenge: "finally to exhibit man living in the social milieu produced by himself, which he modifies daily, and in the heart of which he himself experiences a continual transformation" (Zola 1893a, 21; transl. altered).[322] The terms according to which this interaction between "man" and "social milieu" is taking place cannot yet be classified or proven, as stated above; they remain part of what Zola's literary project tries to find out. All that Zola's conceptual framework of "social milieu" makes sure, or rather posits, is *that* there is correspondence and interaction that crosses the boundary of surrounding and centre, of environment and man. *How* this correspondence or interaction works is what the project sets out to examine.

Although pioneering, Zola's literary project is not the first to tackle the social milieu. Whosoever works on a theory of milieu in the 1860s or 70s (as Zola does in the preface to the *Rougon-Macquart*) cannot deny the influence of Hippolyte Taine, writes Hans Wiegler (1905, 35). Taine's influence on Zola has been researched, even with regard to small details (Schor 1978, 137, Camarani 1990, 184, Chalhoub 1993, 601). One of Zola's most famous poetological formulations of "Le Roman expérimental" , right in the middle of his discussion of Claude Bernard, plagiarises from Hippolyte Taine:

> *Man is not alone*; he lives in society, in a social milieu; and consequently, for us novelists, this social condition unceasingly modifies the phenomena. Indeed our great study is just there, in the reciprocal effect of society on the individual and the individual on society. (Zola 1893a, 20; transl. altered; emph. J.U.)[323]

The passage that Zola has in mind forms part of Hippolyte Taine's famous introduction of *Histoire de la littérature anglaise*:

> Having thus outlined the interior structure of a race, we must consider the milieu in which it lives. For *man is not alone* in the world; nature envelops him, and his fellow-men surround him; accidental and secondary folds spread over the primitive and permanent fold, and physical or social circumstances disturb or confirm the character [*le naturel*] committed to their charge. (Taine 1920, 19; transl. altered; emph. J.U.)[324]

---

322 "[...] puis montrer l'homme vivant dans le milieu social qu'il a produit lui-même, qu'il modifie tous les jours, et au sein duquel il éprouve à son tour une transformation continue." (*RE, OC* IX 332)

323 "L'homme n'est pas seul, il vit dans une société, dans un milieu social, et dès lors pour nous, romanciers, ce milieu social modifie sans cesse les phénomènes. Même notre grande étude est là, dans le travail réciproque de la société sur l'individu et de l'individu sur la société." (*RE, OC* IX 332)

324 "Lorsqu'on a ainsi constaté la structure intérieure d'une race, il faut considérer le milieu dans lequel elle vit. Car l'homme n'est pas seul dans le monde ; la nature l'enveloppe et les autres hommes l'entourent ; sur le pli primitif et permanent viennent s'étaler les plis accidentels et secondaires, et les circonstances physiques ou sociales dérangent ou complètent le naturel qui leur est livré." (Taine 1863, XXV–XXVI)

As this short excerpt shows, the milieu in which the human being lives and which forms his 'character' or 'nature' is not itself 'social' or 'natural': it encompasses both, "nature" and "fellow-men", "physical or social circumstances", without introducing any hierarchy or categorisation. Taine's monistic concept of milieu erects a plane that lies transversal to the traditional distinctions of nature and culture, of the natural and the social, the physical and the moral – a plane that is all about the communication of causes, all about interaction:

> No matter if the facts be physical or moral, they all have their causes; there is a cause for ambition, for courage, for truth, as there is for digestion, for muscular movement, for animal heat. Vice and virtue are products, like vitriol and sugar; and every complex datum arises from other more simple data on which it depends. (Taine 1920, 10-11; transl. altered)[325]

Although Zola only speaks of "social milieu" and society in the passage quoted above, his project of a "social and natural history" is substantially indebted to Taine's thinking about milieu: for Taine as for Zola milieu is a plane, a dense web (Belgrand 1987, 25) that transcends ontological distinctions and regroups all the elements according to the paradigm of universal communication and interaction. As Anna Belgrand emphasises, Zola constantly proclaims that there is a profound connection between all the elements that are constitutive for the human existence: physiology, space and time, historical and social situation, psychology and others (1987, 25). Zola's "monistic levelling" not only affects the distinction between "man and beast" (Woollen 1985, 49), it affects the distinction between nature and culture as a whole: with regard to milieu and surrounding, the distinction between social and biological constituents is missing, writes Hans Ulrich Gumbrecht (1978, 25); according to Elke Kaiser the relation between culture and nature is not one of similarity, but of identity (1990, 37). For Zola, the historical subject has become a natural element (Vibert 2007, 6).

However, despite good reasons (to which we will return presently) and a strong tendency in criticism (Wiegler 1905, Camarani 1990), I think that calling Zola's transversal concept of milieu a 'physiological monism' (Kaiser 1990, 37) is rather misleading. As we have seen in our reading of Zola's essay "Le Roman expérimental", the science physiology is for Zola inseparably linked to Claude

---

[325] "Que les faits soient physiques ou moraux, il n'importe, ils ont toujours des causes ; il y en a pour l'ambition, pour le courage, pour la véracité, comme pour la digestion, pour le mouvement musculaire, pour la chaleur animale. Le vice et la vertu sont des produits comme le vitriol et le sucre, et toute donnée complexe naît par la rencontre d'autres données plus simples dont elle dépend." (Taine 1863, XV)

Bernard and very distinct scientific coordinates. I see no reason why we should doubt Zola's concession that he and his contemporaries "are not yet able to prove that the social milieu is also physical and chemical." All the more so since it is this 'concession' that legitimises Zola's project as a literary – and not a physiological – endeavour. The coordinates that the project of the *Rougon-Macquart* follows are different from the coordinates of Bernard's physiology: it is not "constant physico-chemical properties" that mediate the correspondence and interaction between the milieus; Zola's concept of the milieu rather opens up a field of universal metonymy, an 'unstriated' field (cf. Deleuze and Guattari 1980, 592–625) without categorical boundaries. The openness of this field for metonymical or analogical connections defines the base-structure, the axiomatics of Zola's poetics. The "correspondence between man and things" (Kamm 1974, 100) that is so important for the *Rougon-Macquart* cannot be reduced to physiology, no matter how broadly we define this term. Zola's narrative project is social, natural and historical at the same time – exactly as its extensive title announces.

In spite of the characteristic heterogeneity of 'forces', causes and results involved in Zola's metonymic nets of relations, the correspondences and interactions that Zola relates, are far from arbitrary, incoherent or chaotic. We have again arrived at the "unifying impression" holding together the cycle of novels, with its descriptions covering the diversity of a whole society. The conceptual background of the milieu has however equipped us with the decisive tool that lends support to some of the hypotheses formulated in the preceding section.

More or less in passing Philip Walker notes Zola's tendency "to break down traditional distinctions between the natural kingdoms, to depict everything in his fictional world as caught up in the same tempestuous action" (1982, 262). Philip Walker's speaking of "tempestuous action" is an interesting way of formulating the "unifying impression" emerging from and holding together Zola's descriptions and metonymical correspondences. It correlates strikingly with all our readings undertaken so far: "tempestuous" is not a metaphorical expression that Walker has come up with, it merely adopts the isotopy of weather that permeates Zola's characteristic metonymical net. Is Zola's monism, enacted by the notion of the milieu, "tempestuous" rather than "physiological"?

All the metonymical links that we have so far examined were intrinsically connected to the weather and its phenomena, especially with temperature and heavy wind and rain: Hélène's passions and the seasonal weather of Paris, the cold blue room associated with calm harmony and the hot pink room associated with heavy weather; Octave Mouret, the ladies' favourite hot water-bottle, the heated staircase and the bourgeois coldness, the weather-machine 'Le Bonheur des Dames', with its tempestuous clients, heated by Octave in the same way he had heated his chilly neighbours; Nana and Bordenave's successfully heating up the theatre, producing the same 'tempest' that the horse race and the crowd's war enthusiasm will bring forth; finally, the weathery nature of this war itself, telling of the catastrophic weather metaphors' coming true.

Zola's tendency "to break down traditional distinctions between the natural kingdoms" and his inclination "to depict everything in his world as caught up in the same tempestuous action" thus approximate two notions: *milieu* and *weather/climate*. This raises an inevitable question: Why does Zola narrate the monistic plane of milieu, the plane of the correspondence of the surrounding with the surrounded, of the interaction of the disparate, as a plane of weather/climate?

There are good reasons why Zola's narration of milieu follows the paradigm of weather/climate. "The notion of climate is part of the notion of milieu" (*PetRob*, milieu, n. III. 2.; my transl.)[326] – on this sentence the *Petit Robert*'s first entry, dedicated to the biological meaning of *milieu* ends. The climate here serves as a *pars pro toto* for the other conditions surrounding and interacting with the living organism: physical, chemical conditions, as well as the ensemble of material objects and living beings.[327] The dictionary's entry for the everyday, "Common [*Courant*]" meaning of *milieu*, "material and moral surrounding of a person", again refers to the weathery notions of "climate" and "atmosphere" (*PetRob*, milieu, n. III. 5.; my transl.).[328] In Hippolyte Taine's introduction to *Histoire de la littérature anglaise* the climate plays a very similar, paradigmatic role, and it is here that we come to know why. Having introduced the notion of milieu with the passage I have quoted above, it is the climate that serves as Taine's first example, or rather as the first instance of "physical or social circumstances disturb[ing] or comfirm[ing] the character [*le naturel*] committed to their charge". It is no coincidence that Taine considers the effects of the climate before turning to the political circumstances and social conditions. The climate establishes his approach to the notion of (social) milieu, it provides him with an available conceptual model on which his notion of the milieu builds, that makes his notion of milieu conceivable. The tripartite list of the milieu's modes of articulation, climate, political circumstances and social condition, is thus not as symmetrical as its parallel construction (*Tantôt le climat* [...] *Tantôt les*

---

[326] "La notion de climat est comprise dans celle de milieu [...]." (*PetRob*, milieu, n. III. 2.)
[327] "(1831) BIOL. Ensemble des objets matériels, des êtres vivants, des conditions physiques, chimiques, climatiques qui entourent un organisme vivant et interagissent avec lui. *Le milieu naturel*." (*PetRob*, milieu, n. III. 2.)
[328] "(1846) COURANT Entourage matériel et moral d'une personne (→ ambiance, atmosphère, cadre, climat, décor, environnement) [...]." (*PetRob*, milieu, n. III. 5.)

circonstances politiques [...] *Tantôt les conditions sociales*) suggests. It rather takes its point of departure from a field of knowledge that secures the thinking of a correspondence or an interaction between the surrounding circumstances and the 'character' (the passage from climate to temperament to which we will soon come back) and transfers this conceptual framework analogically to the fields of the political and the social.

The same implicit hierarchy haunts Taine's second famous tripartite coordination of the "[t]hree different sources contribut[ing] to produce this elementary moral state – RACE, MILIEU, and MOMENT" (Taine 1920, 17; transl. altered).[329] Although Taine's analysis of race sets out with the classical, racist statement that "[t]here is a natural variety of men, as of oxen and horses, some brave and intelligent, some timid and dependent" (Taine 1920, 17),[330] it soon leaves the essentialist foundations of race and turns towards an explanation of the formation of racial differences:

> For as soon as an animal begins to exist, it has to reconcile itself with its milieu; it breathes and renews itself differently, is differently affected according to the difference in air, food, temperature. Different climate and situation bring it different needs, and consequently a different course of activity; and this, again, a different set of habits; and still again, a different set of aptitudes and instincts. Man, forced to accommodate himself to circumstances, contracts a temperament and a character corresponding to them; and his character, like his temperament, is so much more stable, as the external impression is made upon him by more numerous repetitions, and is transmitted to his progeny by a more ancient descent. (Taine 1920, 18; transl. altered)[331]

Race is but 'sedimented' milieu, racial difference the result of repeated and enduring external impression. Against this background, we get an idea of the conceptual arrangement of Taine's famous triad of 'race, milieu and moment': whereas 'race' is located on the level of phenomenon that is to be explained

---

[329] "Trois sources différent contribuent à produire cet état moral élémentaire, la race, le milieu et le moment." (Taine 1863, XXII–XXIII)

[330] "Il y a naturellement des variétés d'hommes, comme des variétés de taureaux et de chevaux, les unes braves et intelligentes, les autres timides et bornées [...]." (Taine 1863, XXIII)

[331] "Car dès qu'un animal vit, il faut qu'il s'accommode à son milieu ; il respire autrement, il se renouvelle autrement, il est ébranlé autrement, selon que l'air, les aliments, la température sont autres. Un climat et une situation différente amènent chez lui des besoins différents, par suite un système d'actions différentes, par suite encore un système d'habitudes différentes, par suite enfin un système d'aptitudes et d'instincts différents. L'homme, forcé de se mettre en équilibre avec les circonstances, contracte un tempérament et un caractère qui leur correspond, et son caractère comme son tempérament sont des acquisitions d'autant plus stables, que l'impression extérieure s'est enfoncée en lui par des répétitions plus nombreuses et s'est transmise à sa progéniture par une plus ancienne hérédité." (Taine 1863, XXIV–XXV)

and examined, 'milieu' is the main pattern of explanation, the formative mechanism effective behind the phenomena, responsible for bringing forth the phenomena. The notion of "moment" introduces the important conceptual tool of historicity, accounting for the processes of sedimentation, opening up the historical perspective and locating this perspective on the level of the phenomena themselves: the processes of interaction operate with a sort of memory, past impressions and influences exert an influence on present influences.

However, this very telling passage even extends its equation: race is not only sedimented milieu, it is, in the end, sedimented climate. The passage introduces a chain of causes and effects leading from climate to aptitude and instinct: "[d]ifferent climate" causes "a different course of activity", which again causes "a different set of habits", which finally causes "a set of aptitudes and instincts". It is not difficult to see through the manoeuvre that Taine stages with reference to "an animal": his chain of causes and effects describes the passage from the natural ("air, food, temperature", "climate") to the social ("habits"), cultural ("aptitudes") and psychological ("instincts"). Taine then leaps from the animal to the human without any mediation, quietly transferring this chain of causes and effects, and with it the passage from the natural to the cultural, social and psychological. His one climactic sentence that suddenly refers to "Man", summarises and bundles what the lengthy chain of causes and effects has spelled out for "an animal": "Man, forced to accommodate himself to circumstances, contracts a temperament and a character corresponding to them". Here Taine drops the two keywords of his concept of milieu: the notion of man's *corresponding* to the surrounding circumstances, and the notion of *temperament*.

Once again we see why thinking *milieu* also always implies thinking *climate*, why the notion of milieu must remain "strange and incomprehensible to one who has not studied the climate and the race" (Taine 1920, 9):[332] with the correspondence of climate and temperament (these are the two concepts framing the whole passage) Taine buys into the core of ancient natural philosophy. It is ancient natural philosophy and its concept of humoral pathology that provide the conceptual model for Taine's thinking of milieu. In my first chapter I have discussed this conception of the world, dominant from antiquity to the early modern age, a system of correspondences, grouped around the central correspondence of micro- and macrocosm. The epistemological framework has become alien to Taine's world – and this is the reason why it is of interest for Taine: The theory of the humours paradigmatically establishes correspondences between

---

[332] "[...] étrange et incompréhensible pour quiconque n'a pas étudié le climat et la race [...]." (Taine 1863, XII)

what the modern world would reconstruct as disparate realms. Abstracting from the very different epistemological frameworks, Taine uses natural philosophy to pave the way for his 19th century project of milieu: ancient thought constructs a passage from the natural to the social that allows observing 'modern' interaction. What Taine is aiming for, in a way, has been thought before him – although, we should hasten to emphasise this point, the epistemological problems Taine is tackling are of a decisively modern pedigree. The fact that Taine imports ancient philosophemes of humoral theory into his thinking of milieu is obvious: the initial parameters of "difference in air, food, temperature" stem from the same repertoire of Hippocratic, humoral thinking as his theory of race and its connection to the climate. Taine's shifting the characteristic of the milieu into the realm of 'physiology', as Hans Wiegler (1905, 51) and Ana Luiza Silva Camarani (1990, 184) claim is thus not a move motivated by contemporary science: on the contrary, it fills a gap. The science of modern physiology had not yet established a monism extending beyond the divide of the natural and the social. Taine thus has to analogically ground his study (examining the correspondences of milieu, crossing this boundary) on the atavistic notions of humoral pathology and its correspondence of climate and temperament. The humoral correspondence of temperament and climate is an auxiliary structure Taine introduces to approach the phenomena of interaction that he is after. As a consequence, the notion of the climate oscillates in Taine's text between a metaphorical model and the basis of a 'physiological' or rather humoral, tempestuous monism: on the one hand, we find a metaphorical model whose functioning analogically explains all the other phenomena of interaction and correspondence present in Taine's milieu; on the other, we have a 'physiological' or rather humoral, tempestuous monism of which all other phenomena are only superficial effects. In fact, no matter whether metaphorical model or monistic plane, the correspondence of climate and temperament is of heuristic value for Taine's project. It renders conceivable what Taine intends, it promises access to the phenomena of interaction that are foreclosed by the rigid epistemological boundaries erected by enlightenment, phenomena that, however, increasingly shape the realities of modern life. As paradoxical as it might seem, the innovative concept of milieu is made possible by the atavistic, ancient theory of humoral pathology, explaining the omnipresence of 'archaic' notions of temperament and climate.

Zola's project is intrinsically indebted to Taine's. There is a reason for Zola's setting out "to study not characters, but temperaments" (*eTR*, 1).[333] As for Taine, Zola's central question is "dual" because it concerns "temperaments and milieus"

---

[333] "Dans *Thérèse Raquin*, j'ai voulu étudier des tempéraments et non des caractères." (*TR, OC* III 27)

(Zola 1893a, 3; transl. altered), or rather, because it concerns the correspondences and interactions between the two that had once formed the central notion of humoral pathology. Like Taine's, Zola's "study of the temperaments and the profound modifications brought about in the human organism by the pressure of milieus and circumstances" (*eTR*, 5; transl. altered)[334] is based on the auxiliary construction of a humoral correspondence between temperament and the surrounding climatic conditions. For Taine, it had been "with a people as with a plant" (Taine 1920, 22);[335] Zola uses the same image with reference to personage: "The character has become the product of the air and the soil, like a plant; this is the scientific conception." (Zola 1893b, 233; transl. altered).[336] For this kind of analysis 'character' is "no longer a psychological abstraction" (Zola 1893b, 233)[337] but conceptualised as interacting and corresponding with its 'milieu' – the description therefore deserves the label "scientific". The conceptual basis, however, that makes this correspondence or interaction of the human being and its surrounding conceivable is for Zola as heuristic as for Taine. Both pursue an intuitive approach to the interactions crossing the nature/culture divide via the atavistic notions of the climate's influence on plant or temperament.

It is therefore not astonishing that Zola narrates the monistic plane of milieu, the plane of the correspondence of the surrounding with the surrounded, of the interaction of the disparate, as a plane of weather or climate. In fact, the literary nature of his project enables him to use this heuristic platform of the correspondences of climate and temperament for thinking of interaction even more boldly and innovatively than Taine has done: his project being a literary project, Zola explicitly and extensively plays with the oscillation of the climate's role being both metaphoric and 'real'. The climate's net of correspondences, 'metaphorical' and 'non-metaphorical', its range of affecting everything that is exposed to its weathery forces, proliferates far beyond the initial humoral correspondences of macro- and microcosm. Zola's novels not only stage an interactive combinatorics of temperament and milieu (Ventarola 2010, 315) that has become intelligible against the background of humoral pathology; they metonymically expand the climate's net of interactions to pervade the world, to encompass everything. It is not only the individual character, or the temperament of a 'race' that corresponds to the climate of a region. As *Une page d'amour* so impressively illustrates, a whole city and its life seem to be narratable in weathery terms, as corresponding to the atmospheric processes of the skies:

---

[334] "[…] l'étude du tempérament et des modifications profondes de l'organisme sous la pression des milieux et des circonstances […]." (*TR*, *OC* III 30)
[335] "Il en est ici d'un peuple, comme d'une plante […]." (Taine 1863, XXIX)
[336] "Le personnage y est devenu un produit de l'air et du sol, comme la plante ; c'est la conception scientifique." (*RE*, *OC* IX 425)

> For eight days it had been Hélène's diversion to gaze on that mighty expanse of Paris, and she never wearied of doing so. It was as unfathomable and varying as the ocean, fair in the morning, ruddy with fire at night, borrowing all the joys and sorrows of the skies reflected in its depths. A flash of sunshine came, and it would roll in waves of gold; a cloud would darken it and raise a tempest. It always renewed itself [*Toujours, il se renouvelait*]. A complete calm would fall, and all would assume an orange hue; gusts of wind would sweep by from time to time, and turn everything livid; in keen, bright weather there would be a shimmer of light on every housetop; whilst when showers fell, blurring both heaven and earth, all would be plunged in the debacle of chaos [*débâcle d'un chaos*]. At her window Hélène experienced all the hopes and sorrows that pertain to the open sea. As the keen wind blew in her face she imagined it wafted a saline fragrance; even the ceaseless noise of the city seemed to her like that of a surging tide beating against a rocky cliff. (*PA*, II 846–847; my transl.)[338]

Zola's weathery re-construction of Paris and the Second Empire does not know the difference of the social and the natural. The city's ocean is a "sea of houses with blue roofs, like surging billows [*flots*] that filled the horizon" (*eK*, 67),[339] a city, characterised by "the rising tide [*flot montant*] of speculation, whose foam was to cover [it as a whole]" (*eK*, 49; transl. altered)[340] as by the "cascades [*flots*]" of vegetables "flooding across the footpaths" (*eBP*, 26)[341] near the covered markets. No matter whether the "vast stream [*flot*] of people" protesting for war against Prussia (*eN*, 413),[342] or "the uninterrupted stream [*flot ininterrompu*] of men, animals, and carts, an endless march of workers going

---

337 "Le personnage n'y est plus une abstraction psychologique [...]." (*RE, OC* IX 425)
338 "Hélène, depuis huit jours, avait cette distraction du grand Paris élargi devant elle. Jamais elle ne s'en lassait. Il était insondable et changeant comme un océan, candide le matin et incendié le soir, prenant les joies et les tristesses des cieux qu'il reflétait. Un coup de soleil lui faisait rouler des flots d'or, un nuage l'assombrissait et soulevait en lui des tempêtes. Toujours, il se renouvelait : c'étaient des calmes plats, couleur orange, des coups de vent qui d'une heure à l'autre plombaient l'étendue, des temps vifs et clairs allumant une lueur à la crête de chaque toiture, des averses noyant le ciel et la terre, effaçant l'horizon dans la débâcle d'un chaos. Hélène goûtait là toutes les mélancolies et tous les espoirs du large ; elle croyait même en recevoir au visage le souffle fort, la senteur amère ; et il n'était pas jusqu'au grondement continu de la ville qui ne lui apportait l'illusion que la marée montante, battant contre les rochers d'une falaise." (*PA*, II 846–847)
339 "[...] sur Paris, sur cet océan de maisons aux toits bleuâtres, pareils à des flots pressés emplissant l'immense horizon." (*C*, I 387)
340 "[...] ce flot montant de la spéculation, dont l'écume allait couvrir Paris entier." (*C*, I 367)
341 "On déchargeait toujours ; des tombereaux jetaient leur charge à terre, comme une charge de pavés, ajoutant un flot aux autres flots, qui venaient maintenant battre le trottoir opposé." (*VP*, I 628)
342 "[...] le flot humain s'enflait de minute en minute, dans une coulée énorme de la Madeleine, à la Bastille [...]." (*N*, II 1474)

to work" (eA, 7; transl. altered),[343] no matter whether the "endless flow [*flot*]" of "silks from Lyons, woollens from England, linens from Flanders [...] streaming like rain from some spring higher up" (eLP, 36–37),[344] "the growing cascade [*flot montant*] of pillow lace, Mechlin lace, Valenciennes, Chantilly" (eLP, 110)[345] or "the stream of customers [*flot des clientes*], flowing through the entrance hall" of the 'Le Bonheur des Dames', "drinking in the population from the four corners of Paris" "[a]s rivers draw together the stray of waters of a valley" (eLP, 240–241):[346] all these streams and cascades communicate and interact, they belong to the same climatic constellation. They draw a coherent picture despite their huge differences in 'actual' substance. The "rising tides [*flot qui montait*]" (JV, III 816; my transl.)[347] of *La joie du vivre* cannot be separated from "the surging flood [*flot grossissant*]" of strikers (eG, 320),[348] from "the endless stream [*continuel flot*]" of railway passengers (eBH, 51),[349] from "the growing flood [*flot montant*] of strollers [*promeneurs*]" (eM, 182; transl. altered),[350] the "flow [*flot*] of gold pouring over Paris" (eM, 44)[351] or the war refugees' "streams [*flot*] of carts and foot travellers", their "swollen, irresistible torrent" (eD, 39–40).[352] All these descriptions of highly diverse milieus resonate through their weathery character – a weathery character that integrates them in a sort of meta-milieu: the climate of the Second Empire.

Zola's literary expansion of the old humoral correspondence of temperament and climate to a monism encompassing everything, the whole universe of a society, is a bold, hardly intuitive enterprise: his radical conception of a climatic

---

343 "[...] le flot ininterrompu d'hommes, de bêtes, de charrettes, un défilé sans fin d'ouvriers allant au travail, leurs outils sur le dos, leurs pains sous le bras ; et la cohue s'engouffrait dans Paris où elle se noyait, continuellement." (A, II 377)
344 "[...] un flot intarissable, les soieries de Lyon, les lainages d'Angleterre [...] ruisseler en pluie d'une source supérieure [...]." (BD, III 422)
345 "[...] ce flot montant de guipures, de malines, de valenciennes, de chantilly [...]." (BD, III 493)
346 "Comme les fleuves tirent à eux les eaux errantes d'une vallée, il semblait que le flot des clientes coulant à plein vestibule, buvait les passants de la rue, aspirait la population des quatre coins de Paris." (BD, III 618)
347 Here and in the following, the translations of *La Joie de vivre* are my own, based on Ernest Alfred Vizetelly's translation published by Chatto & Windus (1901). "[...] flot qui montait [...]." (JV, III 816)
348 "[...] ce flot grossissant qui envahit le carreau [...]." (G, III 1410)
349 "[...] tout ce monde qui passait, le continuel flot [...]." (BH, IV 1042)
350 "[...] le flot montant des promeneurs [...]." (Ar, V 199)
351 "[...] ce flot d'or qui coulait sur Paris [...]." (Ar, V 55)
352 "[...] le flot des voitures et des piétons passait toujours, gênant la marche des troupes, si compact aux approches de Belfort, d'un tel courant irrésistible de torrent élargi, que des haltes, à plusieurs reprises, devinrent nécessaires." (D, V 433)

milieu that dissolves the traditional distinctions of the natural and the social/cultural/moral and integrates the diverse milieus of an era not only foreshadows future sociological knowledge and provides its contemporary readers with valid interpretations of their living environment, as Hans Ulrich Gumbrecht (1978, 80) claims. At the cost of his narrative universe's *vraisemblance*, its losing credibility as a 'scientific' description and rather taking on a 'mythic' appearance, Zola's radical layout of universal correspondence and interaction opens up conceptual possibilities that must be called anachronistic. In contrast to Taine, for whom "the change of climate" is always the result of a race's migration (the climate itself is thought as stable) leading to an alteration of "the whole economy, intelligence, and organisation of society" (Taine 1920, 16),[353] Zola conceptualises the guiding correspondence of climate and temperance as radically interacting, one influencing the other, both open to change: "Indeed our great study is just there, in the reciprocal effect of society on the individual and the individual on society." (Zola 1893a, 20)[354] In other words, Zola's *Natural and Social History of a Family under the Second Empire* narrates the story of a changing 'climate' that is both brought about by the human agents of a modern society and, at the same time, shaping these agents' perceptions and actions. To be sure, Zola's novels are not ecocritical in any narrower sense of this concept; he does not know about carbon dioxide and the scientific concept of the greenhouse effect. It is, however, no coincidence that his novels resonate so intensely with 20th and 21st century notions of climate change. Zola's construction of a milieu that abandons the divide between the natural and the social, his positing a radical correspondence and interaction of the modern human being and the 'climate' surrounding it led him to more or less metaphorically project or anticipate what science, still believing in the old division between nature and culture, started to reconstruct a hundred years later, only because data became available that demanded an explanation.

The metaphorical links that Zola constructs between the mentality of an era, the galloping forces of industrialisation and speculation, the employment of the steam engine with its combustion of fossil fuel and a 'general heating up' turning into a weathery catastrophe cannot but strike the modern reader. However, the 'climate change' that Zola narrates is not merely an anticipation of a fact that would challenge generations after him. In fact, Zola's story of a 'climate change' always oscillates between the metaphorical and the 'real'. For

---
353 "La race a émigré, comme l'ancien peuple aryen, et le changement de climat a altéré chez elle toute l'économie de l'intelligence et toute l'organisation de la société." (Taine 1863, XXI)
354 "Même notre grande étude est là, dans le travail réciproque de la société sur l'individu et de l'individu sur la société." (*RE*, *OC* IX 332)

Zola, 'climate change' is not the description of a certain fact of nature ('average temperature is rising') but a societal diagnosis: it is the answer to a complicated question, a question similar to the one that Hippolyte Taine had raised: Zola is searching for "certain general traits, certain characteristics of the intellect and the heart common to men of one race, age, or country" (Taine 1920, 13),[355] in Zola's case, those of the Second Empire. 'Climate' stands for the forces behind the voluntary or the rational. His natural and social history of the Second Empire goes beyond the human agent; that is why it is natural and social. The kind of history that Zola pursues does not assemble the historical events of a certain historical period, it does not paint "the picture of a whole epoch" (Zola 1893b, 269) by puzzling together the descriptions of all of its 'milieus'. Zola captures the "whole" of an epoch by capturing its 'historical *a priori*', as Michel Foucault (cf. 1969, 174) would say. The "general traits", the "certain characteristics", common to the Second Empire find expression in a meta-milieu that shapes the temperament and actions of the human agents and is, at the same time, itself shaped and brought about by these temperaments and actions. This meta-milieu that, as we have seen, Zola conceptualises as a resonance in 'climate' (always fluctuating between weather imagery and this imagery's becoming 'real' weather) gives an account of the 'unconscious' impetus behind the voluntary action of the individual, of phenomena of human behaviour that are inaccessible to individual consciousness and the will (Gumbrecht 1978, 91).

Zola's novels exhibit that this 'unconscious' is not the most intimate and personal secret of the individual, not a remnant of its upbringing and family situation; the unconscious forces that determine or at least influence the human agents' actions and thoughts are not to be separated from "the general tendency of the whole" (*eFR*, 3).[356] They testify to an embeddedness in the collective. They express a historical tendency rather than an individual fate. Zola's natural and social history does not narrate historical events, it does not relate characters, it tells of the mass's characteristic, historical resonances.

Even on the basis of the few exemplary readings presented up to this point it is not difficult to identify the most important of the "general traits" that Zola observes as shaping the Second Empire's 'climate'. No matter whether it is the cold blue room and the over-heated pink room in *Une page d'amour*, or the hottest of seduction scenes in *Nana*; no matter whether it is Octave Mouret's heating up his neighbours and customers that are concerned – they all tell the story of "a difference [...] in temperature", as Taine would say. And we

---
[355] "[...] certains traits généraux, certains caractères d'esprit et de cœur communs aux hommes d'une race, d'un siècle ou d'un pays [...]." (Taine 1863, XVII)
[356] "[...] la poussée générale de l'ensemble [...]." (*FR*, I 3)

remember well that "[d]ifferent climate and situation bring [...] different needs, and consequently" ...

3 Global warming – the old and the new Paris

Quite early in the *Rougon-Macquart* a rupture appears in the narrated world; a rupture that splits Zola's universe into two contrasting parts. When in *La Curée* Saccard and his wife Renée go to visit Renée's father, they leave the homogenous Second Empire world with its busy activity for some moments and enter a very different environment:

> Sometimes the husband and wife, feverish devotees of money and pleasure, would penetrate the icy mists of the Île Saint-Louis. They felt as if they were entering a city of the dead. [...]
>
> There, in the depths of the courtyard, cold and silent as a well, lighted with a pale, wintry light, one would have thought oneself a thousand miles away from the new Paris, ablaze with every form of ardent [*chaudes*] enjoyment and among the clamour of millions. (*eK*, 78–79; transl. altered)[357]

The contrast between the two worlds is carefully composed along the lines of several isotopies that combine for a description of a difference in 'climate': the "new Paris" represented by "husband and wife" is hot ("feverish", "chaudes jouissances"), bright ("ablaze") and thus full of sparkling, fiery life and its noises ("enjoyment", "vacarme"), whereas the Île Saint-Louis seems to be cold ("icy", "cold", "wintry"), damp ("mists", "as a well"), dark ("pale, wintry light") and thus "silent" like "a city of the dead". This difference of 'worlds' is both metonymically embodied by its inhabitants, the Saccards and Renée's father, as by the buildings they live in. The description of the Hôtel Béraud that the Saccards visit, especially of the "austere bareness of the façade[, which] was heightened by the complete absence of awnings or shutters, for at no season of the year did the sun shine on those pale, melancholy stones" (*eK*, 79),[358] must

---

[357] "Parfois, le mari et la femme, ces deux fièvres chaudes de l'argent et du plaisir, allaient dans les brouillards glacés de l'île Saint-Louis. Il leur semblait qu'ils entraient dans une ville morte. [...] Là, au fond de cette cour fraîche et muette comme un puits, éclairée d'un jour blanc d'hiver, on se serait cru à mille lieues de ce nouveau Paris où flambaient toutes les chaudes jouissances, dans le vacarme des millions." (*C*, I 399–400)
[358] "Et ce qui augmentait encore la nudité austère de la façade, c'était l'absence absolue de persiennes et de jalousies, le soleil ne venant en aucune saison sur ces pierres pâles et mélancoliques." (*C*, I 400)

call to mind the description of the Hôtel Saccard, with which the novel opens. The houses and their façades could not differ more clearly: The Hôtel Saccard, built in "the Napoleon III style, that opulent bastard of so many styles" (eK, 17)[359] is characterised by its "sumptuous" (eK, 15)[360] façade, by its being "hidden under its sculpture". In contrast to the Hôtel Béraud, it certainly does not at all lead a shadowed existence:

> On summer evenings, when the rays of the setting sun lit up the gilt of the railings against its white façade, the strollers in the gardens would stop to look at the crimson silk curtains behind the ground floor windows; and through the sheets of plate glass so wide and clear that they seemed like the window-fronts of a big modern department store, arranged so as to display to the outside world the wealth within, the petty bourgeoisie could catch glimpses of the corners of tables and chairs [...] with envy and admiration. (eK, 17)[361]

The contrast between the Hôtel Saccard and the Hôtel Béraud, much discussed in criticism (cf. Joly 1977, 70, Nelson 1977, 6, Berthier 1987, 116, Leduc-Adine 1987, 130, Best 1989, 110, Kaiser 1990, 137, Warning 2005, 156), is however not only one of architecture. These buildings stand for two ages: for the "new Paris" as the narrator calls it, and for its counterpart, the 'old Paris'. The Saccards' house is set in the new quarter, it is excited by the wind of fashion, on one of the margins toppled by innovation and speculation, where Paris invents itself a new face (Berthier 1987, 116). The other, the "Hôtel Béraud, built at the beginning of the seventeenth century" (eK, 78; transl. altered),[362] is just there, immutable and faithful to itself, in the heart of the old capital, calmly moored on its island, which isolates but also protects it from passing follies (Berthier 1987, 116). Clearly, the Hôtel Béraud belongs to the "vestiges of the past" (Walker 1986, 7) that the novel uses as a contrastive background against which it paints the picture of the new quarters that are in the middle of deep transformations like that of the *plaine Monceau* (Joly 1977, 77). As Rainer Warning (2005) has shown, Zola's text employs a literary technique that Michael Bakhtin has called 'chronotopos': the contrasting houses translate a difference in chronology (past vs. present/future) into a difference of locale. The contrast of old age and new age, of permanence/stability and transformation/changeability (Berthier 1987,

---

[359] "[...] style Napoléon III, ce bâtard opulent de tous les styles [...]." (C, I 332)
[360] "[...] somptueuse [...]." (C, I 331)
[361] "Les soirs d'été, lorsque le soleil oblique allumait l'or des rampes sur la façade blanche, les promeneurs du parc s'arrêtaient, regardaient les rideaux de soie rouge drapés aux fenêtres du rez-de-chaussée ; et, au travers des glaces si larges et si claires qu'elles semblaient, comme les glaces des grands magasins modernes, mises là pour étaler au-dehors le faste intérieur, ces familles de petits bourgeois apercevaient des coins de meubles [...] dont la vue les clouait d'admiration et d'envie au beau milieu des allées." (C, I 332)
[362] "L'hôtel Béraud, bâti vers le commencement du dix-septième siècle [...]." (C, I 399)

116, El Kettani 2010, 211) indicates, however, only one aspect of the opposition. As we have already seen with regard to the brief passage quoted above, the other aspect consists of the dominant characteristic of these two opposing locations, in their contrasting 'climates': the comforting heat of Renée's private rooms, the oppressive heat of the hothouse, the luxury of heat and of light opposed to the asceticism, to the coldness of the walls where her father lives (Joly 1977, 130, Leduc-Adine 1987); the overheated atmosphere of the Hôtel Saccard (Warning 2005, 156) is contrasted with the constant coldness (Berthier 1987, 117), hostile to life (Warning 2005, 156), of the Hôtel Béraud.

For *La Curée* the importance of the "antithesis of heat and cold" (Hemmings 1969, 37) has not gone unnoticed in criticism. It plays the role of a guiding difference that structures the narrated world, that creates the characteristic specificity of the Second Empire, its being associated with heat, intelligible and narratable. This climatic opposition is however not just an idiosyncratic trait of *La Curée*. It structures the world of the *Rougon-Macquart* as a whole. In order to fully understand the role of this binary it is important to broaden the focus and disclose how other novels resonate with the contrasting atmospheres of the Hôtel Saccard and the Hôtel Béraud of *La Curée*. Another pair of houses and protagonists, this time in Zola's *Nana*, will make us aware of the fact that the difference in 'climate' we have diagnosed is not simply antithetical; cold vs. hot does not merely *refer* to the binary of old vs. new. The climatic realisation of this opposition opens up the possibility of communication, of passage, of crossing the boundary between the two worlds: the cold world can, and will be heated up. It does not have to remain as isolated, apart and protected as the Île Saint-Louis and Renée's father in *La Curée*. The warmth of the new world is spreading – this is the story of the Second Empire and its transformations that Zola tells in his *Rougon-Macquart*.

The residences of the Muffats, writes Jean-François Tonard, cannot but remind us of the severe architecture of the Hôtel Béraud (Tonard 1994, 201). Located in the "Rue Miromesnil, on the corner of the Rue de Penthièvre",

> [t]his huge, square building had been occupied by the Muffat family for more than a century; the tall, sombre façade with its large slatted shutters, rarely opened, looked asleep, as melancholy as a convent; in the tiny, damp back garden the trees had grown so tall and puny in their search for sun that their branches were visible above the slate roof. (*eN*, 54)[363]

---

[363] "C'était un vaste bâtiment carré, habité par les Muffat depuis plus de cent ans ; sur la rue, la façade dormait, haute et noire, d'une mélancolie de couvent, avec d'immenses persiennes qui restaient presque toujours fermées : derrière, dans un bout de jardin humide, des arbres avaient poussé, cherchant le soleil, si longs et si grêles, qu'on en voyait les branches, par-dessus les ardoises." (*N*, II 1144)

As with the Hôtel Béraud, the reader is immediately made aware of this building's history, reaching back into the past: the Hôtel Muffat is another remnant of a different century. Its façade, "tall" and "sombre", very unlike the splendour of the heavily ornamented Hôtel Saccard, testifies to this, as well as its "convent"-like atmosphere, its quasi monastic severity (Tonard 1994, 201) that reminds one of the courtyard of the Hôtel Béraud and its "cloistral coldness" (eK, 262).[364] The first few sentences describing the place already carefully establish a specific 'climate' that must look familiar to us: the place is characterised by the absence of sunlight ("search for sun", "sombre") accompanied by the typical dampness that we know from the Hôtel Béraud. These impressions are confirmed and intensified by the following descriptions that transport the characteristics of the building's exterior into its interior, starting from

> the garden, which on this rainswept evening was making its damp presence felt despite a big log-fire. The sun never managed to penetrate down to this room and the greenish light of day did little to relieve the gloom; but at night, when the chandelier and the lamps were lighted, it was but solemn, with its solid mahogany Empire furniture, its hangings, and chairs in yellow-patterned velvet boldly embroidered in gold. One entered a cold dignity, bygone customs, a vanished age exhaling an odour of devotion. (eN, 54; transl. altered)[365]

The place's characteristic "cold dignity" is one of Zola's typical labels for a milieu: it is both a metaphorical label for its "customs" and "morality", but also, literally, refers to its specific 'climate'. This climate, damp, dark and cold affects the inhabitants of the house, especially countess Sabine, who, as the narrator tells us, is shaken by "a slight shudder" which makes her "go pale" (eN, 55),[366] adapting herself to the pale "greenish light" of her environment. She herself provides the reader with an explanation of her little indisposition: "'I felt a sudden chill [*J'ai eu un peu froid*] ... This drawing-room takes so long to warm up.'" (eN, 55)[367]

Although the metonymic relation of house and inhabitant, the relation between temperament and the climate of the environment is obvious, the question of whether it is Sabine's temperament that accounts for the house's "cold

---

[364] "La cour avait sa froideur de cloître." (C, I 597)
[365] "[...] le jardin, dont on sentait l'humidité par cette pluvieuse soirée de la fin d'avril, malgré les fortes bûches qui brûlaient dans la cheminée. Jamais le soleil ne descendait là ; le jour, une clarté verdâtre éclairait à peine la pièce ; mais, le soir, quand les lampes et le lustre étaient allumés, elle n'était plus que grave, avec ses meubles Empire d'acajou massif, ses tentures et ses sièges de velours jaune, à larges dessins satinés. On entrait dans une dignité froide, dans des mœurs anciennes, un âge disparu exhalant une odeur de dévotion." (N, II 1144)
[366] "[...] la comtesse prise d'un léger frisson, qui la pâlissait [...]." (N, II 1145)
[367] "« J'ai [Sabine de Muffat] eu un peu froid ... ce salon est si long à chauffer ! »" (N, II 1145)

dignity" or the other way round (does the cold house affect Sabine's temperament?) seems to be difficult to determine:

> Some people in her set thought she was of the coldness of a pious person [*d'une froideur de dévote*] and others felt sympathy for her, remembering her cheerfulness and laughter, the glow in her large, dark eyes [*yeux de flamme*], before she'd been shut up in the depths of this old mansion. (*eN*, 58)[368]

It is not Zola's purpose to give a definitive answer to this question (rather the old hen-and-egg problem) but to underline the close and reciprocal interaction of temperament and the environment's climate. By pointing to an allegedly repressed glimmer/spark of fire slumbering deep inside the countess that resists her adaptation to the environment, Zola prepares the ground for a transformation: the "cold dignity" of the Muffats' residence might have changed Sabine's "cheerfulness and laughter, the glow in her [...] eyes" into her assuming the appearance of a cold, pious person. Why should it not be possible to revert this process of cooling down and extinguishing the fire, why should not a re-kindling of Sabine's fiery temperament heat up the house's damp, cold walls?

This is indeed the trajectory for the story that Zola tells in *Nana*. It is a double story, in which Sabine takes a part in the background. However, it is an important part, because it mirrors and generalises the story of her husband's falling for Nana. In fact Sabine's transformation is less predictable and therefore more striking than her husband's. In the first scene that we have already analysed above, her coldness seems to be hardly challenged by Bordenave's heating spectacle. Watching the "hottest of seduction scenes" she keeps her "pale, earnest face" (*eN*, 26–27), whereas her husband "was standing, open-mouthed, his cheeks mottled with purple spots" (*eN*, 27).[369] However, she does warm a bit when they meet the journalist Faucherey – who is to become her future lover. Here her husband, in turn, exhibits his familiar cold appearance, greets "very distantly [*se montra très froid*]" (*eN*, 21)[370] and maintains "a dignity so icy [*dignité si glacée*] that you might have thought him at a sitting of the Legislative Body" (*eN*, 22; transl. altered).[371] Like his wife, he metonymically shares and

---

[368] "Dans le monde, les uns la disaient d'une froideur de dévote, les autres la plaignaient, en rappelant ses beaux rires, ses grands yeux de flamme, avant qu'on l'enfermât au fond de ce vieil hôtel." (*N*, II 1148)

[369] "[...] derrière la comtesse, blanche et sérieuse, le comte se haussait, béant, la face marbrée de taches rouges [...]." (*N*, II 1119)

[370] "La Faloise présenta son cousin au comte Muffat de Beuville, qui se montra très froid." (*N*, II 1114)

[371] "Le comte gardait une dignité si glacée, qu'on l'aurait cru à quelque séance du Corps législatif." (*N*, II 1115)

embodies the "cold dignity" of the house he is living in. His coldness seems to be part of the family tradition that had been passed on to him in his youth: "His nursery had been dreadfully cold. Later on, at the age of 16, every evening when he kissed his mother goodnight, her icy kiss [la glace de ce baiser] would pursue him even during his sleep." (eN, 128)[372] As with his wife a spark of fire slumbers deep inside him that, finding fuel to spread, creates the possibility of a deep transformation. This is the story Zola tells us: "His youth was stirring from its sleep; a voracious puberty of the adolescent, suddenly burning in his coldness of the catholic and in his dignity of the mature man." (eN, 144; transl. altered)[373] The resonances not only with his wife's disposition, but also with that of his house are striking: we have only to remind ourselves of the Hôtel's "tall, sombre façade" that "looked asleep" (cf. "stirring from its sleep") and "melancholy as a convent" (cf. "coldness of the catholic"), as well as of the interior's "cold dignity" (cf. "dignity of the mature man"). The transformation that Zola's novel narrates is thus not merely the conventional one of a man falling for a woman. The system of 'climatic' resonances connecting Muffat to his wife, to his house and the "vanished age" of the old Paris renders his story the metonymic example of a transformation that transcends his individual fate.

The novel relates the encounter of two worlds: the cold, old world embodied by the Muffats, in their "icy look" (eN, 28)[374] and house and the new, hot world represented by Nana. Apart from its first scene in the theatre that already brings the two worlds into contact and exposes the process of societal transformation as a process of heating, the beginning of the novel is characterised by a rhythmical oscillation between these two contrasting worlds. Similar to the iterative narration of the Saccards' visit to the Île Saint-Louis in *La Curée* this narrative strategy helps Zola establish the difference between these worlds – which is, as we have seen, essentially a difference in 'climate' reflected by temperament. As the novel's emblematic first scene has however already indicated, Zola is not content with just contrasting the old and the new age as he had done in *La Curée*. His focus is now on the process of transformation, on the spreading of the new world. The new world affects the old world and incorporates it, winning it over to be assimilated and become part of it.

The model for the astonishing proliferation of this 'new Paris' that the novel itself repeatedly exhibits is a model of infection. Fauchery's famous newspaper article representing Nana as "'The Golden Fly'" spells out the basic traits of this model: Nana is "a golden fly, the colour of the sunshine, escaping from its

---

[372] "Sa chambre d'enfant était toute froide. Plus tard, à seize ans, lorsqu'il embrassait sa mère, chaque soir, il emportait jusque dans son sommeil la glace de ce baiser." (*N*, II 1213)

[373] "C'était sa jeunesse qui s'éveillait enfin, une puberté goulue d'adolescent, brûlant tout à coup dans sa froideur de catholique et dans sa dignité d'homme mûr." (*N*, II 1227)

[374] "[...] les Muffat passèrent, l'air glacial." (*N*, II 1121)

dung-heap and bringing with it the deadly germs [*prenait la mort*] of the carrion allowed to fester by the roadside" (*eN*, 190).³⁷⁵ Douglas Parmée's English translation leaves little doubt that the model Zola uses for conceptualising this infection is the 'modern' model of "germs" and contamination: Nana is said to "carry this pollution upwards to contaminate the aristocracy" (*eN*, 190). However, when paying close attention to the French wording, it is clear that Zola resorts to a different, much older model of infection. "With [Nana], the putrefaction [*pourriture*] that one had let ferment in the people, re-mounted [the social ladder] and putrefied [*pourrissait*] the aristocracy".³⁷⁶ Nana does not carry and transmit "germs"; similar to the sun in Shakespeare's *Tempest* which "sucks up" "[a]ll the infections" "[f]rom bogs, fens, flats" and makes them fall on Prospero, infecting him with "disease" (cf. 2.2.1–3), this "golden fly, the colour of the sunshine" merely transports putrefaction, an intemperance, which in turn causes further intemperance. We have discussed this ancient model of infection in the first chapter on Shakespeare and have located it epistemologically in the weathery conceptualisation of the world according to humours, elements and the correspondence of micro- and macrocosm.³⁷⁷ It is important to note this difference in concept with regard to infection, because it is only against the background of this specific concept of infection that the passage unfolds its consistency and is appropriately situated in the web of Zola's narrative universe. The claim that Nana's "very scent spoiled the world" (*eN*, 192; transl. altered)³⁷⁸ must appear an inappropriate, metaphorical exaggeration when assuming the model of infection as the transmission of germs. According to the older conceptualisation of infection, however, smell was one of the key indicators of contact with corruptive material that threatened one's health. Mary Donaldson-Evans has shown that this notion of a corrupt, smelly atmosphere plays an important role in the *Rougon-Macquart*, especially in *L'Assommoir*, and is closely connected to Zola's conception of milieu (1992). As we have seen in our readings of the novel's first chapter in the theatre and of the horse-race scene, Nana has been 'in the air'. Not only as an acoustic phenomenon of resonance, but also as a certain "contaminated condition or unhealthy quality (of air, water, etc.)" (*OED*, infection, *n*. 2. I.). She metonymically embodies and spreads this unwholesome atmosphere or 'climate' which is not her idiosyncratic 'quality' but a phenomenon of the 'new Paris': this is what turns her "into a force of nature and, without any

---

375 "[...] une mouche couleur de soleil, envolée de l'ordure, une mouche qui prenait la mort sur les charognes tolérées le long des chemins [...]." (*N*, II 1270)
376 "Avec elle, la pourriture qu'on laissait fermenter dans le peuple, remontait et pourrissait l'aristocratie." (*N*, II 1269)
377 Cf. chapter I, 5.
378 "C'était la bête d'or, inconsciente comme une force, et dont l'odeur seule gâtait le monde." (*N*, II 1271)

intention on her part, a ferment of destruction" (*eN*, 190).³⁷⁹ Like the "southwest" that Caliban wishes to "blow on [Prospero and Ariel] | And blister [them] all o'er" (1.2.324–325) Nana's scent and the atmosphere surrounding her threaten to infect and harm everyone who comes close. Not by transmitting germs, but by being hot, which resonates with the focal difference of heat and coldness: "Nana shot through like a cloud of invading locusts, a devastating fire flattening a whole province. Wherever she set her little foot, there was burnt earth." (*eN*, 393)³⁸⁰

The measures for avoiding an infection are perfectly obvious: above all, avoid contact with this unwholesome atmosphere. Count Muffat has experienced the effect that Nana on stage, in the "hottest of seduction scenes", had on him and his coldness: an intense inner movement illustrated by the "purple spots" mottling his face. When he sees Nana a second time, this time in person and in her apartment, it is hardly surprising that the same thing happens again. Accompanied by his father-in-law, the elderly Marquis de Chouard, he goes to see Nana as part of a charity project, asking her to donate for the amelioration of the quarter's "'misery: children with not even a crust of bread to eat, women ill, completely helpless, dying from cold...'" (*eN*, 46–47)³⁸¹ In the words that the Marquis addresses to Nana, alleging that she "'cannot imagine'" this misery, lies a bitter irony: Nana can more than imagine this misery; she has grown up in this misery, her mother will, a short time after this encounter, supposedly die of cold. And more than that, as Zola insinuates with the picture of the 'Golden Fly', the unwholesome atmosphere surrounding Nana and characterising her apartment, although seemingly different as can be from misery's coldness (i.e. tropically hot), is intrinsically connected to her miserable past: "It was too hot in this little room, a sultry heat like a tropical hothouse. The roses were wilting, the scent of patchouli was overpowering." (*eN*, 47)³⁸² Despite Nana's actually donating all she has, even creating financial problems for herself, this encounter in the name of charity does not distribute wealth down the social ladder. On the contrary, Nana's unwholesome atmosphere, originating in the misery's "dung-heap", in the "carrion" that the elite had "allowed to fester by the roadside", carries the "pollution" of misery upwards to infect the aristocracy. This infection is an infection involving heat: it is this room's "tropical", "sultry"

---

379 "Elle devenait une force de nature, un ferment de destruction, sans le vouloir elle-même, corrompant et désorganisant Paris entre ses cuisses de neige [...]." (*N*, II 1269)

380 "Nana passait, pareille à une invasion, à une de ces nuées de sauterelles dont le vol de flamme rase une province. Elle brûlait la terre où elle posait son petit pied." (*N*, II 1455)

381 "« Vous ne vous imaginez pas une pareille détresse : des enfants sans pain, des femmes malades, privées de tout secours, mourant de froid... »" (*N*, II 1138)

382 "Il faisait trop chaud dans ce cabinet, une chaleur lourde et enfermée de serre. Les roses se fanaient, une griserie montait du patchouli de la coupe." (*N*, II 1138)

atmosphere – again scents form an intrinsic part of that atmosphere (cf. that Nana's "very scent spoiled the world") – and an involuntary, seductive gesture that brings the aristocrats' cold blood to boil: "A patch of blood brought a flush to the marquis's ashen cheeks. Count Muffat, who'd been about to speak, dropped his eyes." (eN, 47)[383] It takes some moments, and the ringing of a bell, for the two to master "their embarrassment" and regain "their stance of cold formality [ils redevinrent froids]" (eN, 47).[384]

Against the background of this disquieting experience it is not astonishing that Muffat refuses the invitation to Nana's supper party. He thereby avoids contact with an atmosphere that contrasts sharply with the Muffats' way of receiving, coldly, reservedly, hardly a dozen elderly guests. At Nana's apartment, the same infecting hotness reigns that had affected Muffat in the earlier encounters:

> The room was growing warmer and warmer from the candelabra, the food in the dishes, and the whole tableful of thirty-eight people struggling to breathe. (eN, 89)
>
> It was too hot, and the smoky light of the candles on the table was becoming more and more yellow. (eN, 94)[385]

The dinner scene depicts the gradual warming of the room – and the corresponding increasing noise, drunkenness and frenzy: "[p]eople were starting to let themselves go" (eN, 94),[386] in the end, "the hullabaloo was deafening" (eN, 98).[387] Although the count does not form part of the excessive party, it nevertheless emblematically foreshadows the story of his feverish, demeaning fall for Nana. A little detail, one of the most ridiculous incidents of the party, may underline this claim: the youthful and very drunk George's idea "of crawling on all-fours under the table and nestling at Nana's feet, like a little dog" (eN, 95).[388] It will not take too long until Nana makes Muffat her "dog",

---

[383] "Un peu du sang parut aux joues terreuses du marquis. Le comte Muffat, qui allait parler, baissa les yeux." (N, II 1138)
[384] "Ils se gênaient, ils redevinrent froids, l'un carré et solide, avec sa chevelure fortement plantée, l'autre redressant ses épaules maigres, sur lesquelles tombait sa couronne de rares cheveux blancs." (N, II 1138)
[385] "Une chaleur montait des candélabres, des plats promenés, de la table entière où trente-huit personnes s'étouffaient [...]." (N, II 1176)
 "Il faisait trop chaud, la clarté des bougies jaunissait encore, épaissie, au-dessus de la table." (N, II, 1181)
[386] "On finissait par se moins bien tenir." (N, II 1181)
[387] "Maintenant, le bousin était à ne pas s'entendre, histoire de dire qu'on pouvait tout se permettre, quand on soupait chez Nana." (N, II 1184)
[388] "Et Georges, très gris, très excité par la vue de Nana, hésita devant une idée qu'il mûrissait gravement, celle de se mettre à quatre pattes, sous la table, et d'aller se blottir à ses pieds, ainsi qu'un petit chien." (N, II 1182)

not only to nestle at her feet: "She'd throw her scented handkerchief to the other side of the room and he had to scamper over and retrieve it with his teeth, crawling on his hands and knees." (*eN*, 398–399)[389]

It however proves impossible for the Count to keep the necessary distance from Nana and avoid contact with the unwholesome atmosphere she embodies. The fact that everyone around him seems already infected by her hotness does not prevent his succumbing in this endeavour. Thus it is again as part of a group of people, in the train of the prince of Scotland, and again in the theatre, that he is to meet Nana a third time. Bordenave, the theatre director, leads his prominent guests through the mazes of the theatre to meet Nana backstage:

> Count Muffat, who still had his hat on, had broken into a sweat; in particular, he was feeling stifled by the heavy, overheated, backstage atmosphere, with its strong underlying stench of gas, stage-set glue, squalid dark corners, and the smell of the female extras' unwashed underwear. The passageway was even more suffocating; from time to time the sharp scent of toilet-water and soap drifting down from the dressing-rooms blended with the pestilential odour of human breath. As he went by, the count raised his eyes and glanced up the stair-well, startled by the sudden burst of heat and light which struck the back of his neck from above. (*eN*, 121)[390]

The foreign, "heavy, overheated, backstage atmosphere" to which Muffat is exposed and against which his hat offers no protection affects him; he sweats. The tour through the parts of the theatre usually hidden from its audience gives an idea of the 'unwholesomeness' of its overheated atmosphere, an atmosphere, as we have seen, that also characterised the auditorium: backstage quite a disgusting mix of scents, "the smell of the female extras' unwashed underwear", the "sharp scent of toilet-water and soap" and the "pestilential odour of human breath" clearly indicates the infectious (in its old, atavistic sense) nature of the theatre's 'climate'. Despite all these disgusting markers Muffat is nevertheless caught, taken in [*saisi*], by "the sudden burst of heat and light" on the stair-well. Like the trees in the "damp back garden" of his house, he is irresistibly attracted to this "heat and light" luring "from above" – he, as well, is in "search for sun" and finds it in Nana.

---

[389] "D'autres fois, il était un chien. Elle lui jetait son mouchoir parfumé au bout de la pièce, et il devait courir le ramasser avec les dents, en se traînant sur les mains et les genoux." (*N*, II 1461)
[390] "Le comte de Muffat, pris de sueur, venait de retirer son chapeau ; ce qui l'incommodait surtout, c'était l'étouffement de l'air, épaissi, surchauffé, où traînait une odeur forte, cette odeur de coulisses, puant le gaz, la colle des décors, la saleté des coins sombres, les dessous douteux des figurantes. Dans le couloir, la suffocation augmentait encore ; des aigreurs d'eaux de toilette, des parfums de savons descendus des loges, y coupaient par instants l'empoisonnement des haleines. En passant, le comte leva la tête, jeta un coup d'œil dans la cage de l'escalier, saisi du brusque flot de lumière et de chaleur qui lui tombait sur la nuque." (*N*, II 1206)

When Nana in her dressing room finally takes his hand for a few seconds, he is ultimately infected: he "quiver[s] with emotion [*frissonnant*] at the touch of her tiny hand, so cool and scented, on his own, which was burning" (*eN*, 124).[391] The fact that his hand is burning indicates that his characteristic coldness has yielded to the hot atmosphere that surrounds him. The importance of this clash of climates and temperaments, the hot winning over the aristocrats' "cold dignity", seems to occupy Muffat's unconscious. It is highly indicative that in a state of complete disturbance, all at sea in the tropical, odoriferous air and Nana's touch, Zola makes him speak about the place's climate and Nana's ability to cope with it:

> To cover his confusion, the only thing Muffat could think of was to comment on the heat.
>
> 'My goodness, it's hot here', he said. 'How do you manage to survive in such a temperature, madame?' (*eN*, 124)[392]

Muffat cannot believe that the sultry atmosphere does not drive Nana beyond her comfort zone; how can her hand be cool, whereas his is burning, whereas he is soaked with sweat? He cannot understand that this tropical heat *is* her comfort zone and that it is rather fresh air, the alleged fact that "someone's just opened a window" (*eN*, 133)[393] that threatens to 'kill' Nana. Muffat is affected by the "sudden burst of light and heat", Nana fears the "sudden gusts of cold air" (*eN*, 133).[394]

However, once infected by this hot, tropical atmosphere, Muffat very quickly acclimates himself. More than that, mirroring *Pot-Bouille*'s Duveyrier, he develops a tragic dependency on the warmth of this climate:

> So, like a robot, he went back to Nana's flat. [...] No, he really was too tired, he had got too much of the rain, he suffered too much from the coldness. The thought of going home to his gloomy mansion in the Rue Miromesnil was even more chilling [*le glaçait*]. [...] As he went upstairs he was smiling in anticipation of the cosy warmth of this little love nest where he could lie down and sleep. (*eN*, 205; transl. altered)[395]

---

391 "[...] frissonnant d'avoir tenu une seconde, dans sa main brûlante, cette petite main, fraîche des eaux de toilette." (*N*, II 1209)
392 "Muffat, pour cacher son trouble, ne trouva qu'une phrase sur la chaleur.
  « Mon Dieu ! qu'il fait chaud ici, dit-il. Comment faites-vous, madame, pour vivre dans une pareille température ? »" (*N*, II 1209)
393 "[...] qu'on vient d'ouvrir une fenêtre [...]." (*N*, II 1217)
394 "Les artistes se plaignaient toujours des courants d'air. Dans la chaleur lourde du gaz, des coups de froid passaient, un vrai nid à fluxions de poitrine, comme disait Fontan." (*N*, II 1217–1218)
395 "Et, machinalement, il retourna chez Nana. [...] A la fin, il était trop las, il avait reçu trop de pluie, il souffrait trop du froid. L'idée de rentrer dans sons hôtel sombre de la rue Miromesnil le glaçait. [...] En montant, il souriait, pénétré déjà par la chaleur molle de cette niche, où il allait pouvoir s'étirer et dormir." (*N*, II 1283)

It is this dependency that accounts for his fall; Nana's humiliations may reach a degree far beyond the bearable, he, like Duveyrier, will endure them patiently, as he cannot live without this dubiously cold source of heat.

Muffat's fall for Nana, his complete self-abandonment for this woman and her air of hotness, distances him from his wife, separating the couple formerly united by their "icy look". Zola however uses this distance in an ingenious way that makes Muffat's story transcend the story of an individual's fate and that underlines the fact that Nana is not merely morally debasing 'bad company', but the impersonation of something that is in the Second Empire's air: all the while that the novel has focused on the count's adventures and transformations, Sabine's "coldness of a pious person" has undergone the same process of warming without being exposed to the infecting contact of Nana. Thus in the end, Sabine and her husband, side by side, as it were, united in their new hotness, receive guests for a party in their newly renovated house:

> The party took place in a setting full of gentle, spring-like charm; mild June weather had made it possible to open up the double doors of the large drawing-room and to extend the dancing out on to the sandy garden terrace. The first guests, greeted at the door by the count and countess, were quite dazzled; they could remember the icy cold Countess Muffat and the old-fashioned drawing-room full of stern piety and solid mahogany Empire furniture, with its yellow velvet hangings and its damp [*trempé d'humidité*], musty green ceiling. Now on entering the front hall you saw glittering mosaics picked out in gold, with the marble staircase and its delicately carved banisters gleaming under the high candelabra. [...] In this room the chandeliers and crystal sconces lit up a luxurious array of mirrors and fine furniture; Sabine's former single *chaise longue*, with its red silk upholstery which had looked so much out of place in the old days, seemed now to have spawned and expanded, filling the whole grand residence with a mood of idle pleasure and eager enjoyment which had broken out with the violence of a fire that had long been smouldering. (*eN*, 353)[396]

---

[396] "C'était une de ces fêtes de printemps, d'un charme si tendre. Les chaudes soirées de juin avaient permis d'ouvrir les deux portes du grand salon et de prolonger le bal jusque sur le sable du jardin. Quand les premiers invités arrivèrent, accueillis à la porte par le comte et la comtesse, ils eurent un éblouissement. Il fallait se rappeler le salon d'autrefois, où passait le souvenir glacial de la comtesse Muffat, cette pièce antique, toute pleine d'une sévérité dévote, avec son meuble Empire d'acajou massif, ses tentures de velours jaune, son plafond verdâtre, trempé d'humidité. Maintenant, dès l'entrée, dans le vestibule, des mosaïques rehaussées d'or se moiraient sous de hauts candélabres, tandis que l'escalier de marbre déroulait sa rampe aux fines ciselures. Puis le salon resplendissait [...]. Les lustres, les appliques de cristal allumaient là un luxe de glaces et de meubles précieux. On eût dit que la chaise longue de Sabine, ce siège unique de soie rouge, dont la mollesse autrefois détonnait, s'était multipliée, élargie, jusqu'à emplir l'hôtel entier d'une voluptueuse paresse, d'une jouissance aigue, qui brûlait avec la violence des feux tardifs." (*N*, II 1419–1420)

The Muffats' residence, the emblem of the old Paris, with its characteristic atmosphere or 'climate', cold, humid, dark, is transformed. It has suddenly become a place of warm light: "candelabra" and "crystal sconces" making the formerly sober and gloomy rooms "gleam[...]" and "glitter[...] in gold". The fire imagery that Zola had, as we have seen, long prepared by indicating sparks glimmering in the old "cold dignity" (the "glow in [Sabine's] large, dark eyes", her somehow misplaced *chaise longue*) is here taken up again. The narrator not only resorts to the metaphor of the "smouldering" fire that finally breaks out with violence; the whole place is of a fiery character, hot, illumined by artificial, flaming light. This sort of 'climate' is familiar to the readers of the novel: the atmosphere of the Muffats' renovated residence is not distinguishable from the fiery atmosphere in the variété theatre or at Nana's supper-party. The very same fiery hotness reigns: the new Paris's air has heated up the old Paris, adopting it, transforming it into a part of itself. The name for this transformative hot air is 'Nana'. Zola leaves no doubt that it is this very air that has infected and changed the Muffats' residence:

> The waltz being played by the orchestra was the vulgar little dance-tune from *The Blonde Venus*, and as its cheerful, saucy rhythm flowed into the house it seemed to send a thrill warming the old walls, like a wind of the flesh [*vent de la chair*] sweeping away a bygone age [*un âge mort*] in the haughty Muffat residence and dispersing their past, a hundred years of honour and Christian belief which had been sleeping in the dark corners of its lofty ceilings. (*eN*, 353; transl. altered)[397]

Again 'Nana' is in the air, metonymically, through the tune of the waltz that had already warmed up the atmosphere in the "hottest of seduction scenes". This process of warming is indeed a process of 'climate' change, a process of a "wind of the flesh" "warming the old walls", "sweeping away" the "cold dignity" of the damp, dark old Paris.

With the party at the Muffats' Zola brings the novel's different threads together: the new 'climate' merges the impressions of the theatre performance and of Nana's supper-party, it expands the circle of this 'hot' new Paris to convert and encompass even its most distant, contrasting other, the old and high, 'icy' aristocracy. More than that, the Muffats' party carries the characteristic heat of the new Paris to extremes that still astonish and affect guests who are used and therefore surely already acclimatised to this kind of atmosphere:

---

[397] "Cette valse, justement la valse canaille de *La Blonde Vénus*, qui avait le rire d'une polissonnerie, pénétrait le vieil hôtel d'une onde sonore, d'un frisson chauffant les murs. Il semblait que ce fût quelque vent de la chair, venu de la rue, balayant tout un âge mort dans la hautaine demeure, emportant le passé des Muffat, un siècle d'honneur et de foi endormi sous les plafonds." (*N*, II 1420)

> The gusts of air from the garden were making the candles flare up very high. Each time a ball-gown swept by to the rhythmical tapping of the dance, a puff of fresher air cooled the glow from the chandeliers above.
>
> 'It's pretty hot in there, by Jove!' muttered la Faloise. (*eN*, 357–358)[398]

Zola uses the party's "peak of glittering revelry" to prognosticate the catastrophic consequences of the extreme warming/heating transforming the climate of Paris:

> The waltz swirled voluptuously on and on, battering at the old house in a rising tide of pleasure. The thrills of the piccolos were shriller, the sighs of the violins more and more rapturous; amidst the gilt and the paintings and the Genoa velvet, the chandeliers were glowing like hazy suns and the throng of guests, amplified by the mirrors, seemed to be growing larger and larger, the buzz of their voices louder and louder. [...] In the garden, the Venetian lanterns looked like the glowing embers of a fire which lit up the shadowy figures of the men and women strolling off to take a breath of air in the remoter oaths, with a gleam as if from some distant conflagration. And these quaking walls [*tressaillement des murs*] and this red haze were like a final holocaust [*flambée dernière*] consuming the honour of the whole of this ancient house. Those timid bursts of laughter which were just vaguely audible in that night in April in the past when Fauchery had mentally compared them to the tinkle of broken crystal, had become bolder and wilder to culminate in this peak of glittering revelry [*éclat de fête*]. Now, the crack [*la fêlure*] was widening and soon the whole house would crumble. In working-class slums, families dragged down by drunkenness finish up in utter destitution, with larders emptied and mattresses stripped to satisfy the mad craving for alcohol; in this house, where a vast accumulation of wealth was suddenly about to go up in flames and collapse in ruins, the knell of this ancient family was being tolled with a waltz, while poised over the dancers, loose-limbed and invisible, with the smell of her body fermenting in the stuffy air [*ferment de son odeur flottant dans l'air chaud*], Nana was turning this whole society putrid to the rhythm of her vulgar tune. (*eN*, 363–364)[399]

---

[398] "Sous les souffles venus du dehors, les bougies brûlaient très hautes. Quand une robe passait, avec de légers claquements de la cadence, elle rafraîchissait d'un petit coup de vent la chaleur braisillante tombante des lustres.

« Fichtre ! ils n'ont pas froid, là-dedans ! » murmura La Faloise." (*N*, II 1423–1424)

[399] "Mais la valse déroulait toujours son balancement de rieuse volupté. C'était une reprise plus haute du plaisir battant le vieil hôtel comme une marée montante. L'orchestre enflait les trilles de ses petites flûtes, les soupirs pâmés de ses violons ; sous les velours de Gênes, les ors et les peintures, les lustres dégageaient une chaleur vivante, une poussière de soleil ; tandis que la foule des invités, multipliée dans les glaces, semblait s'élargir, avec le murmure grandi de ses voix. [...] Dans le jardin, une lueur de braise, tombée des lanternes vénitiennes, éclairait d'un lointain reflet d'incendie les ombres noires des promeneurs, cherchant un peu d'air au fond des allées. Et ce tressaillement des murs, cette nuée rouge, étaient comme la flambée dernière, où craquait l'antique honneur brûlant aux quatre coins du logis. Les gaietés timides, alors à peine commençantes, que Fauchery, un soir d'avril, avait entendues sonner avec le

The scenario that Zola anticipates is not only a sort of apocalypse, staging the end of a world; it is, as the imagery shows, also a climate catastrophe: "a rising tide of pleasure" "batter[s] at the old house", the "red haze" testifies to the overheated, fiery atmosphere finally turning into real fire, consuming the house and all. We will examine this theme of climate catastrophe towards which the changing, warming climate is, according to Zola, destined to lead in a later section. What is of interest for us here, however, concerns the somehow surprising generalising or comparative note on which Zola closes the quoted passage.

The last sentences open up the perspective of class: "working class" families are ruined by alcohol, whereas the old aristocracy is brought to fall by Nana's 'air', by waltz and smell, by her "smell floating in the hot air". It is however not the contrast of different 'lethal' vices that this generalising move intends, but the overarching integration of these ruins: one and the same *fêlure* destroys the working class and kills the old aristocracy. This *fêlure* is a heat damage, induced by the energy of a blatant difference in temperature, and it is precisely this *fêlure* that is the concern of Zola's *Rougon-Macquart*, as a "natural and social history" of the Second Empire (cf. Deleuze 1969). *Nana*, I would like to claim, does not merely tell of the old, cold aristocratic world being infected and incorporated/assimilated by the hot milieu of the demi-monde (cf. Tonard 1994, 201). The change of climate, the warming transcends the classes. The problem of alcohol and the problem of the ruin of the aristocracy belong together, as Nana's biography already underlines. Furthermore, they can, as we will see, both be referred to the same problematic transformation of climate, a warming induced by social circumstances and developments that Zola diagnoses as paradigmatic for the Second Empire.

In order to grasp the range of this transformation of 'the old' to 'the new Paris' that Zola reconstructs as a warming of 'climate' that is not specific for a certain class or milieu it is necessary to turn to a third example: the world of retail trade. When Denise arrives at Paris with her two younger siblings, what she finds in the quarter of retail trade where her uncle lives and has his small shop is a world split in two. Her brothers as well as Denise herself are immediately taken in by the sheer grandness of a department store, "the windows

---

son d'un cristal qui se brise, s'étaient peu à peu enhardies, affolées, jusqu'à cet éclat de fête. Maintenant, la fêlure augmentait ; elle lézardait la maison, elle annonçait l'effondrement prochain. Chez les ivrognes des faubourgs, c'est par la misère noire, le buffet sans pain, la folie d'alcool vidant les matelas, que finissent les familles gâtées. Ici, sur l'écroulement de ces richesses, entassées et allumées d'un coup, la valse sonnait le glas d'une vieille race ; pendant que Nana, invisible, épandue au-dessus du bal avec ses membres souples, décomposait ce monde, le pénétrait du ferment de son odeur flottant dans l'air chaud, sur le rythme canaille de la musique." (*N*, II 1429–1430)

of which were bursting with bright colours" (*eLP*, 3).⁴⁰⁰ More than that, it seems to them "as if the shop were bursting and throwing its surplus stock into the street" (*eLP*, 4–5).⁴⁰¹ When the three finally arrive at their destination, uncle Baudu's shop, right opposite the department store, the contrast could not be more striking. "The door, which was ajar, seemed to lead into the dark gloom of a cellar." (*eLP*, 7)⁴⁰² A glance inside the house's "inner courtyard which communicated with the street by means of a dark alley" best summarises its 'climate':

> This yard, sodden and filthy, was like the bottom of a well, a sinister light fell into it. In the winter the gas had to be kept burning from morning to night. When the weather allowed them to do without it, the effect was even more depressing. (*eLP*, 13)⁴⁰³

This court's climate must appear familiar to us; although it is situated in a very different quarter, although it is part of a very different building and architecture, reflecting a very different social milieu, it shares a climate with the Hôtel Béraud, in whose depths, as we have seen,

> cold and silent as a well, lighted with a pale, wintry light, one would have thought oneself a thousand miles away from the new Paris, ablaze with every form of ardent [*chaudes*] enjoyment and among the clamour of millions. (*eK*, 78–79; transl. altered)⁴⁰⁴

Dark, damp, and cold, like a well – this seems to be the climate that Zola associates with the 'old Paris', no matter whether the 'old' aristocracy or the 'old' trade are concerned. This characteristic 'climate' metonymically spreads from the Baudus' courtyard to the house's interior and further to the atmosphere of the shop: "The shop retained its musty smell, its half-light, in which the old-fashioned way of business, good-natured and simple, seemed to be weeping at its neglect." (*eLP*, 15)⁴⁰⁵ Despite her family ties, her being well aware of the looming threat that the gigantic competitor poses for her uncle's business and

---

400 "[...] dont les étalages éclataient en notes vives [...]." (*BD*, III 390)
401 "[...] le magasin semblait crever et jeter son trop-plein à la rue [...]." (*BD*, III 391)
402 "La porte, ouverte, semblait donner sur les ténèbres humides d'une cave." (*BD*, III 394)
403 "[...] une petite cour intérieure, communiquant avec la rue par l'allée noire de la maison ; et cette cour, trempée, empestée, était comme un fond de puits, où tombait un rond de clarté louche. Les jours d'hiver, on devait allumer le gaz du matin au soir. Lorsque le temps permettait de ne pas allumer, c'était plus triste encore." (*BD*, III 399)
404 "Là, au fond de cette cour fraîche et muette comme un puits, éclairée d'un jour blanc d'hiver, on se serait cru à mille lieues de ce nouveau Paris où flambaient toutes les chaudes jouissances, dans le vacarme des millions." (*C*, I 400)
405 "La boutique gardait son odeur de vieux, son demi-jour, où tout l'ancien commerce, bonhomme et simple, semblait pleurer d'abandon." (*BD*, III 402)

her feeling with her uncle and his family, Denise cannot resist being attracted to the neighbouring department store:

> But what fascinated Denise was the Ladies' Paradise on the other side of the street [...]. The sky was still overcast, but the mildness brought by rain was warming the air in spite of the season; and in the clear light, dusted with sunshine, the great shop was coming to life, and business was in full swing.
>
> Denise felt that she was watching a machine working at high pressure; its dynamism seemed to reach to the display windows themselves. [...] But the furnace-like heat with which the shop was ablaze [*la chaleur d'usine dont la maison flambait*] came above all from the selling, from the bustle at the counters, which could be felt behind the walls. (*eLP*, 15–16)[406]

It is no coincidence that Zola uses a weather phenomenon, "the mildness brought by rain" which "was warming the air in spite of the season" to lead to the department store and its contrasting climate. "[W]arming the air in spite of the season", this is what the department store does. As we will see in greater detail in the next section, it is a weather machine: "a machine working at high pressure", producing a specific "furnace-like heat". We know this fiery heat to be the characteristic trait of the 'new Paris', no matter whether of Bordenave's theatre, Nana's or the Muffats' party or the Saccards' passions: "the new Paris, ablaze with every form of ardent enjoyment [*où flambaient toutes les chaudes jouissances*] and among the clamour of millions".

The case of Denise in *Au Bonheur des Dames* introduces an important new dimension to the narration of the Second Empire's warming of the climate: in contrast to Saccard or Nana, she is an almost unrestrictedly appealing figure; she is not falling for an obviously morally corrupted order, she is not seduced by the 'false', or 'ill' historical tendency that she ought to have resisted or rejected. Though "irrational" and "instinctive", her attraction to the 'Le Bonheur des Dames' and her "disdain" for her uncle's shop are 'genuine', and suggest a new perspective on the warming of the climate so characteristic for the Second Empire:

---

[406] "Mais, de l'autre côté de la rue, ce qui la passionnait, c'était le *Bonheur des Dames* [...]. Le ciel demeurait voilé, une douceur de pluie attiédissait l'air, malgré la saison ; et, dans ce jour blanc, où il y avait comme une poussière diffuse de soleil, le grand magasin s'animait, en pleine vente.
  Alors, Denise eut la sensation d'une machine, fonctionnant à haute pression, et dont le branle aurait gagné jusqu'aux étalages. [...] Mais la chaleur d'usine dont la maison flambait, venait surtout de la vente, de la bousculade des comptoirs, qu'on sentait derrière les murs. Il y avait là le ronflement continu de la machine à l'œuvre, un enfournement de clientes, entassées devant les rayons, étourdies sous les marchandises, puis jetées à la caisse." (*BD*, III 402)

> At the same time her uncle's shop made her ill at ease. She felt an irrational disdain, an instinctive repugnance for this icy little place where the old-fashioned methods of business still prevailed. [...] And in spite of her kind heart, her eyes kept turning back to the Ladies' Paradise, as if the salesgirl in her felt the need to go and warm herself before the blaze of this huge sale. (eLP, 16–17)[407]

The novel shows this "need to go and warm herself" to be the same need that made the trees in the Muffats' "tiny, damp back garden" grow "tall and puny in their search for sun": it is "a passionate desire for life and light" (eLP, 16).[408] Denise, despite her being entangled in the Rougon-Macquarts' hereditary web, is like Caroline of L'Argent included as a neutral figure experiencing and illustrating the decisive ambivalence of the Second Empire's warming: the 'new Paris' is not only the result of a corruptive debauchery, of a *débordement des appétits*; Zola also unmistakably places it on the side of life, as its imagery of light, warmth, fire and passion shows (Parkhurst-Ferguson 1993, 81). With the 'old Paris' being associated with death ("un âge mort" (N, II 1420), "a city of the dead" (eK, 78)) there is also, besides the excessive, a 'natural' tendency towards the 'new Paris', introducing an anti-bourgeois, vitalistic axiology (Kaiser 1990, 140): life itself, for reasons of self-preservation, is attracted to the 'new Paris'. Denise, who, like Caroline, is not at all prone to excess and "ravenous appetites" embodies this 'natural', "irrational" but "instinctive" attraction to life. She is drawn towards and decides for the new Paris, because the climate of the "old neighbourhood" does not seem to be compatible with her affirmation of life:

> Night had fallen, and she found the street quite dark, soaked with fine, dense rain which had been falling since sunset. A surprise greeted her: a few moments had sufficed for the roadway to become filled with pebbles, for the gutters to be running with dirty water and the pavements to be covered in thick, sticky mud; and through the driving rain she could see nothing but a confused stream of umbrellas, jostling each other, swelling out like great gloomy wings in the darkness. She drew back at first, struck by the cold, feeling even more depressed because of the badly lit shop, which had a particularly dismal appearance at this time of night. A damp breeze, the breath of the old neighbourhood, came in from the street; it seemed as if the water streaming from the umbrellas was running right up to the counters and the pavement, with its mud and puddles, was coming into the old shop's ground floor, white with saltpetre rot, giving it a final coat of mildew. It was a vision of

---

[407] "En même temps, la boutique de son oncle lui causait un sentiment de malaise. C'était un dédain irraisonné, une répugnance instinctive pour ce trou glacial de l'ancien commerce. [...] Et malgré son bon cœur, ses yeux retournaient toujours au *Bonheur des Dames*, comme si la vendeuse en elle avait eu le besoin de se réchauffer au flamboiement de cette grande vente." (*BD*, III 403)

[408] "[...] une passion de la vie et da la lumière [...]." (*BD*, III 403)

old Paris, soaked through, and it made her shiver, surprised and dismayed to find the great city so cold and ugly.

But on the other side of the road the deep rows of gas burners at the Ladies' Paradise were being lit. She drew nearer, once more attracted and, as it were, warmed by this source of blazing light. The machine was still humming, still active, letting off steam in a final roar [...]. (*eLP*, 27–28)[409]

Again Zola approximates a milieu's 'social climate' with a phenomenon of the weather, with the 'actual' meteorological state of the atmosphere: This time it is not "the mildness brought by rain", "warming the air in spite of the season" that represents the 'new Paris', but a "damp breeze, the breath of the old neighbourhood" establishing a "cold and ugly" "vision of old Paris" that makes Denise "shiver". She is "struck by the cold", appalled by the darkness of her uncle's shop. Despite the monstrosity of the department store's machine it is most likely that the reader feels with her and shares her "passionate desire for life and light".

However, *Au Bonheur des Dames* does not only narrate Denise's individual choice for the 'new Paris', her decision to leave her uncle and family in order to work for the hated representative of the 'new retail trade'. Like *Nana* it tells the story of the fall and transformation of this old world, of its being 'eaten up' by the proliferating 'new Paris'. Octave Mouret's 'Le Bonheur des Dames' grows and grows, devouring one little shop after the other, whose walls literally fall in order to become integrated in the new warm and shiny universe of the department store. The "old neighbourhood" with its "old-fashioned methods of business", cold, dark and damp, is transformed into a new quarter dominated by the gigantic department store, its "furnace-like heat" and its flaming light: *Au Bonheur des Dames*, as well, tells the story of a warming climate.

---

[409] "Ce fut pour elle une surprise : quelques instants avaient suffi, la chaussée était trouée de flaques, les ruisseaux roulaient des eaux sales, une boue épaisse, piétinée, poissait les trottoirs ; et, sous l'averse battante, on ne voyait plus que le défilé confus des parapluies, se bousculant, se ballonnant, pareils à de grandes ailes sombres, dans les ténèbres. Elle recula d'abord, prise de froid, le cœur serré davantage par la boutique mal éclairée, lugubre à cette heure. Un souffle humide, l'haleine du vieux quartier, venait de la rue ; il semblait que le ruissellement des parapluies coulât jusqu'aux comptoirs, que le pavé avec sa boue et ses flaques entrât, achevât de moisir l'antique rez-de-chaussée, blanc de salpêtre. C'était toute une vision de l'ancien Paris mouillé, dont elle grelottait, avec un étonnement navré de trouver la grande ville si glaciale et si laide.

Mais, de l'autre côté de la chaussée, le *Bonheur des Dames* allumait les files profondes de ses becs de gaz. Et elle se rapprocha, attirée de nouveau et comme réchauffée à ce foyer d'ardente lumière. La machine ronflait toujours, encore en activité, lâchant sa vapeur dans un dernier grondement [...]." (*BD*, III 413–414)

Against the background of our readings of *La Curée*, *Nana* and *Au Bonheur des Dames* a specific resonance or consistency cannot be denied: a symbolic opposition between the old Paris and the modern city (Capitanio 1987, 183) emerges from all of these novels, an opposition that is established by "[c]ontrasting images of old and new, cold and heat, silence and noise, total immobility and dynamic movement" (Nelson 1977, 25). The world of Zola's *Rougon-Macquart* is structured by the guiding difference of two contrasting climates: the damp, dark, icy climate of the 'old Paris', and the warm, fiery, passionate atmosphere of the new (1).

Zola's narrative universe does however not merely statically oppose two contrasting climates. It narrates the transpersonal development from an old to a new societal order (Warning 2005, 153), it is a "vision [...] of the metamorphosis of a civilization" (Walker 1986, 6). We here encounter the historical perspective of Zola's *Natural and Social History of a Family under the Second Empire*. Zola's concept of history is Tainean to the core: he unfolds a history of conditions (social, natural, cultural) that "combined with [the humans'] renewed effort, produces another condition, sometimes good, sometimes bad, sometimes slowly, sometimes quickly, and so forth" (Taine 1920, 16). History thus examines the "mechanism of human history" (Taine 1920, 16), that is to say the interaction of forces of the milieu and human (re)action, bringing forth "a permanent force": "we may regard the whole progress of each distinct civilisation as the effect of a permanent force which, at every stage, varies its operation by modifying the circumstances of its action." (Taine 1920, 16)[410] In the *Rougon-Macquart* this permanent force finds expression as a changing, a warming climate. On the one hand, this warming is "a product of the *débordement des appétits* which characterizes the Empire" (Warning 1998, 723), that is to say of the warming of the temperaments; on the other hand, it is an effect of modern developments, industrialisation, architecture, financial speculation etc., a 'warming of the world'. The two interact, increase and result from it each other, producing the permanent force of a warming 'climate'. Zola's narrative project presents the 'history' of this 'climatic' change (2).

---

[410] "En tout cas, le mécanisme de l'histoire humaine est pareil. Toujours on rencontre pour ressort primitif quelque disposition très-générale de l'esprit et de l'âme, soit innée et attachée naturellement à la race, soit acquise et produite par quelque circonstance appliquée sur la race. Ces grands ressorts donnés font peu à peu leur effet, j'entends qu'au bout de quelques siècles ils mettent la nation dans un état nouveau, religieux, littéraire, social, économique; condition nouvelle qui, combinée avec leur effort renouvelé, produit une autre condition, tantôt bonne, tantôt mauvaise, tantôt lentement, tantôt vite, et ainsi de suite ; en sorte que l'on peut considérer le mouvement total de chaque civilisation distincte comme l'effet d'une force permanente qui, à chaque instant, varie son œuvre en modifiant les circonstances où elle agit." (Taine 1863, XXII)

As we have seen, this warming climate, transforming the old, cold, dark and damp Paris to the hot and fiery new Paris is not limited to a certain specific social milieu, but transcends social hierarchies and geographical boundaries. The warming that the *Rougon-Macquart* relate is not local or regional – it is 'global', it affects Zola's narrative universe as a whole (3).

The object of the *Rougon-Macquart*'s text is constantly some *pot-bouille*, writes Michel Serres (1975, 181), and, indeed, for many of the novels the theme of heating plays an obviously important role. *La Curée*, for example, not only exposes the difference of the old and the new Paris by contrasting Saccard's residence to the Hôtel Béraud. Primarily it tells the story of the speculation in the process of the Haussmannisation of Paris. As Saccard himself explains to his first wife Angèle in the famous scene on the Montmartre, real estate speculation intrinsically has to do with warming and *pot-bouille*:

> At one moment a ray of sunlight gliding from between two clouds was so resplendent that the houses seemed to catch fire and melt like an ingot of gold in a crucible.
>
> 'That's the Vendôme Column, isn't it, glittering over there? And over there, to the right, you can see the Madeleine. A wonderful district, where there's much to be done. Ah! Now it's all going to flare up [*tout va brûler*]! Can you see? You'd think the whole neighbourhood was bubbling away in a chemist's retort.' [...]
>
> 'Yes, yes, that's what I said, whole neighbourhoods will be melted down, and gold will stick to the fingers of those who heat and stir the mortar. [...]' (*eK*, 68)[411]

Also those far away from the gold of speculation that sticks to the fingers of the heaters are exposed to an atmosphere of warming and to a bubbling retort. Surprisingly, "the conditions of sweated toil and poverty" which "ruins" the "ignorant" (*eA*, 18)[412] protagonists of *L'Assommoir* turn out to participate in this process of heating as well. The heating that affects the lower classes is however not produced by a warming air of passion or by the fire of the capital's steam engine, but by an 'artificial' substitute: the alcohol emblematically produced in the *Assommoir*'s "booze-machine" (*eA*, 344).[413]

---

411 "Il vint un moment où le rayon qui glissait entre deux nuages, fut si resplendissant, que les maisons semblèrent flamber et se fondre comme un lingot d'or dans un creuset.

« C'est la colonne Vendôme, n'est-ce pas, qui brille là-bas ?... Ici, plus à droite, voilà la Madeleine... Un beau quartier, où il y a beaucoup à faire... Ah ! cette fois, tout va brûler ! Vois-tu ? ... On dirait que le quartier bout dans l'alambic de quelque chimiste. » [...]

« Oui, oui, j'ai bien dit, plus d'un quartier va fondre, et il restera de l'or aux doigts des gens qui chaufferont et remueront la cuve. [...] »" (*C*, I 388)

412 "[...] ils ne sont qu'ignorants et gâtés par le milieu de rude besogne et de misère où ils vivent [...]." (*A*, II 374)

413 "[...] l'alambic, la machine à soûler [...]." (*A*, II 704)

The "search for sun", the "passionate desire for life and light", the need to go and warm [oneself] before the blaze" familiar to us from *Nana* and *Au Bonheur des Dames* is here substituted and perverted by the need for alcohol, for the *eau-de-vie*, as the character with the telling name Boit-sans-Soif [Drinks-without-Thirst] exhibits:

> Perhaps it was true that for other men strong drink [*l'eau-de-vie*] weakened the muscles, but he needed booze [*l'eau-de-vie*], not blood, in his veins; the drop he'd just had was warming his body like a boiler, he felt as powerful as a bleeding steam-engine. (*eA*, 167)[414]

The alcohol's warming is not a placebo, it is 'real'. It factually leads to the tragic end that we know from *La Bête humaine* or *L'Argent*: overheating. The locomotive Lison is deadly damaged in its fight against the snowdrift that urges the engineer to exceed the limits of pressure and power, the stock exchange crashes as a consequence of Saccard's excessive heating of 'the machine' 'L'Universelle', Coupeau dies from warmth induced by alcohol. Again resorting to atavistic medical knowledge, Zola describes Coupeau's frenzy that has brought him to an asylum as being accompanied or even caused by an increase in body temperature:

> His skin, which shone like polished hide, was so hot that the air round him was steaming, and heavy sweat poured off him constantly. (*eA*, 425–426)[415]
>
> 'And the temperature's still a hundred and four, is it?' (*eA*, 431)[416]

Zola uses Coupeau's hallucinations to underline the connection to the logic of heating or overheating by bringing up the theme of the steam engine, a theme that links the alcohol's warmth unmistakably to the warming narrated in *Au Bonheur des Dames*, *La Bête humaine* and *L'Argent* (cf. Noiray 1981): "Then he started to hurry and, believing he had a steam engine in his belly, he puffed steam out of his wide open mouth, thick steam that filled the cell and went out of the window" (*eA*, 434).[417] Before his body, bereft of all humanity, uncannily comes to a final rest, resembling the Lison's last tremors, his frenzy makes him pronounce some important truths: about himself, about the fact that his

---

[414] "Peut-être bien que l'eau-de-vie amollissait les bras des autres, mais lui avait besoin de l'eau-de-vie dans les veines, au lieu de sang ; la goutte de tout à l'heure lui chauffait la carcasse comme une chaudière, il se sentait une sacrée force de machine à vapeur." (*A*, II 532)

[415] "[Coupeau] avait la peau si chaude, que l'air fumait autour de lui ; et son cuir était comme verni, ruisselant d'une sueur lourde qui dégoulinait." (*A*, II 783)

[416] "« Et la température, toujours quarante degrés, n'est-ce pas ? " (*A*, II 788)

[417] "Alors, en se dépêchant, il crut qu'il avait une machine à vapeur dans le ventre ; la bouche grande ouverte, il soufflait de la fumée, une fumée épaisse qui emplissait la cellule et qui sortait par la fenêtre [...]." (*A*, II 791)

madness and death are induced by the alcohol – and about the future of the society that he has been living in. He anticipates the holocaust of Paris aflame that will mark the fatal end of the Second Empire's historical process of warming:

> The scumbags have gone an' stuck a machine [*une machine*] behind the wall, I can hear it rumblin' away, they're gonna blow us up ... Fire, fire! Jesus Christ, fire! There's a fire, What a blaze! Oh, it's so bright, so bright! The sky's all on fire, there's red flames, an' green, an' yellow ... Help, help! Fire! (*eA*, 431; transl. altered)[418]

Although depicting a very distinct social milieu, a milieu as different as can be from the glamour of the new Paris that we encounter in most of Zola's other city novels, *L'Assommoir* is perfectly well integrated in the meta-story of a global warming that Zola narrates of the Second Empire.

This holds true for the other novels of the cycle as well. We have already seen that *Une page d'amour* relates the movement from the cold blue to the overheated pink room. *La Faute de l'abbé Mouret* tells the story of the chilly, sickening atmosphere of the church (only feverishly warming to the licensed excitation towards the Virgin Mary) that is challenged by the Paradou's warmth of life. This warmth, however, is not a place of constant bliss; the biblical fall is re-enacted as a process of unpreventable passionate warming, a warming that happens under the perfect conditions of the laboratory, so to speak. Far away from the corruptive conditions of the city, this process of warming examines the backbone, as it were, of all the stories of warming and indicates that tragedy is part of the game, that suffering cannot be eliminated. *Le Rêve* dreams of this elimination, it tries to make up or fabricate a story of 'pure' warming, which must be tragic as well, because it diminishes life in favour of morals and replaces a corrupted life with pure death. The icy kisses of *Pot-Bouille*'s little bourgeoisie link this story of Octave Mouret's heating with the heating of the old aristocracy narrated in *Nana* and show that the warming climate indeed transcends the social hierarchies.

Germinal must look like an exception, or at least a special case: Zola's exploration of the milieu of the coal mining very literally turns to the material foundation of the city's and the modern steam engine's heating. However, not only the coal pit, as we will see later in greater detail, proves to be a place of "sudden changes in temperature" (*eG*, 36),[419] also the social world above

---

[418] "« [...] Et ils ont mis une machine derrière le mur, ces racailles ! Je l'entends bien, elle ronfle, ils vont nous faire sauter... Au feu ! nom de Dieu ! au feu. On crie au feu ! Voilà que ça flambe. Oh ! ça s'éclaire, ça s'éclaire ! Tout le ciel brûle, des feux rouges, des feux vertes, des feux jaunes... A moi ! Au secours ! Au feu ! »" (*A*, II 788)
[419] "Mais ce qui l'étonnait surtout, c'étaient les brusques changements de température." (*G*, III 1161)

ground is decisively structured by a difference in warmth: the freezing world of the hungry miners opposes the comfortable warmth of the capitalists. When La Maheude, miner and mother of seven children, enters with some of her offspring at the Grégoires', who are stakeholders of the coal pit, to beg for something to eat, the huge, unbridgeable distance separating these two worlds becomes apparent, also as a difference in temperature:

> And in came La Maheude and her children. They were frozen and famished, and were stricken with panic to find themselves standing in such a room, which was so warm, with its lovely smell of brioche. (eG, 85)[420]

Like La Maheude and her children, who are "dazed by the sudden heat [*brusque chaleur*]" (eG, 92)[421] of the Grégoires' house, the delegates of the strikers are overcome by "the heat from the stove, filling the room so evenly it took them by surprise" (eG, 216),[422] when they enter the house of the coal company's director, M. Hennebeau.

It is this significant difference in temperature that both illustrates and drives the miners' social upheaval. Michel Serres very rightly points to the fact that the revolt itself is a process of heating, of people catching fire [*l'incendie de la révolte*] (Serres 1975, 181). This becomes evident when Étienne assembles the strikers on a clearing of the woods, speaks to them and incites them to fight the social injustice:

> They forgot the cold as his burning words had warmed their guts. A religious fervour lifted them towards the heavens, the fever of hope that the early Christians nourished, waiting for the coming reign of justice. (eG, 284; transl. altered)[423]

When the protests finally escalate and change into atrocious violence it is a result of the "hot fever of revenge" "carry[ing] away and "intoxicat[ing]" (eG, 324; transl. altered)[424] Étienne and his comrades. The catastrophe had been prepared by a long process of warming: "All the old Flemish blood was there, in these heavy, placid people; it took months for it to warm up, but then they

---

[420] "Alors, la Maheude et ses petits entrèrent, glacés, affamés, saisis d'un effarement peureux, en se voyant dans cette salle où il faisait si chaud, et qui sentait si bon la brioche." (G, III 1203)
[421] "[...] étourdis par la brusque chaleur [...]." (G, III 1210)
[422] "Mais ce qui les suffoquait surtout, c'était la chaleur, une chaleur égale de calorifère, dont l'enveloppement les surprenait, les joues glacées du vent de la route." (G, III 1319)
[423] "Ils ne sentaient plus le froid, ces ardentes paroles les avaient chauffés aux entrailles. Une exaltation religieuse les soulevait de terre, la fièvre d'espoir des premiers chrétiens de l'Église, attendant le règne prochain de la justice." (G, III 1380)
[424] "Lui-même [Étienne] se grisait, emporté dans cette fièvre chaude de revanche." (G, III 1414)

threw themselves into the most abominable savagery" (*eG*, 356).⁴²⁵ Despite the very distinct social milieu that *Germinal* sets out to examine, and despite its geographical distance to the fashions of the old and the new Paris, the story narrated in this novel clearly forms part of the meta-narration of the warming climate at the heart of the *Rougon-Macquart*.

Even the farmers of *La Terre*, although pursuing the most earthy and everlasting of businesses, are not exempt from the changing climate that haunts the world of the Second Empire. Their greedy fights for every little patch of soil makes them blind to the real threat looming over their business, as the schoolmaster tells them:

> "And you think you can compete with all that with your puny equipment," he went on, "when you don't know anything and don't want to, stuck as you are in the same old rut. Yes you're already knee-deep in wheat from America! And there'll be a lot more of it, it'll be up to your waist, up to your shoulders, up to your mouths and then over your heads! A river, a torrent, a flood [*débordement*]! It'll swallow the whole lot of you!" (*eE*, 387)⁴²⁶

The warming that Zola's *Rougon-Macquart* narrate can be called nothing but global.

There is, however, a decisive complication characterising the Second Empire's global warming. It does not simply, for whatever exterior reason, convert a cold state of atmosphere and temperament into a warmer (and rather too warm!) one. Such a univocal movement would be quite easy to evaluate: there must be some sane, healthy temperature, (cold, or warm, probably somewhere in the middle) so that a process of warming could be classified as either good or bad, and perhaps even be balanced so that a 'temperate' atmosphere would be achieved in the end. In Zola's narrative universe, however, the atmosphere of overheating is intrinsically linked to a certain chill or coldness that cannot be 'heated' away.

As we have seen, despite the excessive heat in her changing room, Nana's hand is surprisingly "cool" and makes Muffat "quiver with emotion [*frissonnant*]" (*eN*, 124). This surprising coldness resisting the hot surrounding is a common, recurring trait of the *Rougon-Macquart*: Bijou, Nana's dog, "lying in her skirts

---

425 "Tout le vieux sang flamand était là, lourd et placide, mettant des mois à s'échauffer, se jetant aux sauvageries abominables, sans rien entendre, jusqu'à ce que la bête fût soûle d'atrocités." (*G*, III 1442)

426 "« Et vous espérez lutter avec vos outils de quatre sous, continua-t-il, vous qui ne savez rien, qui ne voulez rien, qui croupissez dans votre routine !... Ah ! ouiche ! vous en avez jusqu'aux genoux, du blé de là-bas ! et ça grandira, les bateaux en apporteront toujours davantage. Attendez un peu, vous en aurez jusqu'au ventre, jusqu'aux épaules, puis jusqu'à la bouche, puis par-dessus la tête ! Un fleuve, un torrent, un débordement où vous crèverez tous ! »" (*T*, IV 767–768)

trembled with cold in spite of the warmth" (eN, 307; transl. altered);[427] Marie Pichon, despite Octave's passionate warming, has "lips that are always cold" (ePL, 110; transl. altered);[428] despite finding herself alone with her lover in the overheated pink room, Hélène feels cold, her "feet of snow" are as "icy" as they have always been, despite having changed the over-chilled atmosphere for an overheated one (PA, II 1022; my transl.).[429] The abbé Mouret's dictum that, after leaving the garden where he has succumbed to Albine and which has by now become dead to him, he is "still cold" (eSAM, 270),[430] seems to be true to the Rougon-Macquart's postlapsarian world as a whole: even the most hot-tempered and passionate characters are haunted by a strange coldness. Saccard, as Bernhard Joly points out, has something cold and icy about him that makes his first wife Angèle shiver (1977, 64). Renée explicitly says about herself that she is "always so cold" (eK, 236),[431] a characteristic that Bernhard Joly very convincingly calls the key to her personality (1977, 56) and the knot of her tragedy (1977, 60), which is a tragedy of desperate heating (Berthier 1987, 115). It is no coincidence that the place before the fire is so regularly frequented, by Renée, by Nana, by Hélène and Henri, by Jeanne and M. Rimbaud. There is a necessary connection between coldness and overheating, a connection for which, as Naomi Schor suggests, the relation between Hélène and her little daughter Jeanne offers exemplary insight: there is, Schor writes, a necessary connection between Hélène's coldness and Jeanne's lethal illness (1976, 189). Jeanne does not die of a cold, neither does she die of overheating. Like Gervaise of L'Assommoir one could say that she dies of both, of "hot and cold" (eA, 439; transl. altered).[432] The concept of fever seems to be very adequate for capturing this uncanny ambivalence of heating that is intrinsically linked to the notion of essential coldness. Zola consistently resorts to 'images' of "fever and freneticism to evoke Saccard's frenzied speculative activity and the wild promiscuity of the age" (Nelson 1978, 64); these two notions of fever and frenzy also play an important role in his building up a scenario of catastrophe (Stöber 2005, 35).

However, fever is not only a characteristic of certain characters in La Curée (Joly 1977, 61) and other novels; the process of warming or heating is basically connected to the notion of fever. Paris is itself "feverish" (DP, V 1011; my

---

[427] "Le chien, couché dans ses jupes, tremblait de froid, malgré la chaleur [...]." (N, II 1377)
[428] "[...] ses lèvres toujours froids [...]." (PB, III 112)
[429] "« Oui, c'est vrai, j'ai froid », murmura-t-elle avec un frisson, malgré la grosse chaleur. Ses pieds de neige étaient glacés." (PA, II 1022)
[430] "« Le jardin est mort, j'ai toujours froid », murmura-t-il." (FaM, I 1503)
[431] "« [...] Moi qui ai toujours froid [...] »." (C, I 569)
[432] "Même on ne sut jamais au juste de quoi elle était morte. On parla d'un froid et chaud." (A, II 796)

transl.),[433] it is both driven by "its violent fever" (*eK*, 96) and suffers from it; the Empire is "'proud of this hot fever of the industry'" (*eG*, 208; transl. altered),[434] which is at the same time responsible for a severe crisis when the demand ceases and the coal-pits and factories become unprofitable. The notions of tremor and shivering [*secousse, frisson, tressaillement*] associated with the notion of fever belong to the key vocabulary of Zola's descriptions: it is "a thrill [*frisson*]" that is "warming the old walls" (*eN*, 353; transl. altered)[435] of the Hôtel Muffat, whose "quaking walls [*tressaillement des murs*] and this red haze were like a final holocaust [*flambée dernière*] consuming the honour of the whole of this ancient house" (*eN*, 364).[436] Angélique, the protagonist of *Le Rêve*, having been rescued from the snow and brought into the Huberts' house, suffers from "great shiver[s] [when she is] exposed to the oven's heat which started to penetrate her" (*R*, IV 820; my transl.);[437] in *Le Docteur Pascal* the overheated sky itself displays a "last shiver" (*DP*, V 935; my transl.)[438] at the end of a very hot day. These shivers mark, as Bernhard Joly has observed, a transition between the cold and the hot (Joly 1977, 57). More than that, according to Michel Serres, they are a sign for the energy set free from the transition between hot and cold, a sign for the thermodynamic process fed from this thermal difference between two sources, one hot, one cold (Serres 1975, 210).

Zola's association of the process of warming with fever should not too hastily be read as a clear-cut moral judgement. And, in fact, a feverish warming prevents an all-too affirmative, vitalistic reading: warmth is not simply healthy and sane, not simply a step towards a more intense modern life. It is, however, not simply sick and damnable either. Fever, in the Hippocratic tradition, is not sickness: it marks the moment of crisis, where the destructive and the restorative forces coexist and the fight between the two is brought to a decision. The feverish crisis is a necessary stage for restoring the health of the patient, but it is also always dangerous, because there is only one alternative to health: death. We

---

433 Here and in the following, the translations of *Le Docteur Pascal* are my own, based on Mary J. Serrano's translation published by Macmillan (1898). "[...] au milieu de Paris enfiévré [...]." (*DP*, V 1011)
434 "« [...] Et l'Empire qui était si fier dans cette fièvre chaude de l'industrie ! »" (*G*, III 1311)
435 "[...] un frisson chauffant les murs [...]." (*N*, II 1420)
436 "Et ce tressaillement des murs, cette nuée rouge, étaient comme la flambée dernière, où craquait l'antique honneur brûlant aux quatre coins du logis." (*N*, II 1429)
437 "Et elle eut de nouveau un grand frisson, sous la chaleur du fourneau qui commençait à la pénétrer [...]." (*R*, IV 820)
438 "L'ardent pluie de braise avait cessé, il n'y avait plus, tombant de haut, que le dernier frisson du ciel surchauffé et pâlissant ; et, de la terre brûlant encore, montaient des odeurs chaudes, avec la respiration soulagée du soir." (*DP*, V 935)

will come back to the notion of crisis and Zola's affirmation of it in a later section. For now, it is important to emphasise the fundamental ambivalence of the global warming that Zola narrates in his *Rougon-Macquart*. The paradoxical, feverish heat, carrying an essential coldness deep inside itself, is reflected by the moral ambivalence of this process of warming.

The critics' striking disagreement with regard to the evaluation of the cold Hôtel Béraud and its owner, Renée's father, provides us with a good example of this characteristic ambivalence. "Renée's father", writes Brian Nelson, "survivor from a former age, is the only character in *La Curée* whom Zola describes in unambiguously positive terms" (1977, 7). For Philippe Berthier, the Hôtel Béraud is a little lost paradise, a patrimonial space of dignity, of a genuinely full and human life nourished by lasting values, the only true house, resisting to the vain fashions outside (1987, 116–117). Elke Kaiser agrees with Philippe Berthier and Brian Nelson that the novel's evaluations favour the Hôtel Béraud, not only with regard to morals (1990, 139) – she however also contends that neither the Hôtel Béraud, nor Renée's father are free of ambivalences (1990, 139). Béraud du Châtel is no positive role model, Elke Kaiser concludes, sharing Bernhard Joly's opinion that, despite everything, Zola is more attracted to Renée than to her father (Joly 1977, 79). It is the first impression of coldness and death (Joly 1977, 74), these associations of death sticking to the climate of the old Paris (Kaiser 1990, 140) that makes the chronotopical basis opposition of cold and hot appear in a new light (Kaiser 1990, 140): as we have already seen with Denise and *Au Bonheur des Dames* the global warming of Zola's narrative universe is not merely a movement of moral corruption and fall, it is at the same time a necessary and inevitable 'natural' movement towards life, towards the sun's light and warmth. The new Paris is placed on the side of life (Parkhurst-Ferguson 1993, 81), the ancient virtues of the Île Saint-Louis do not provide any solution to the dilemmas produced by modernisation (Parkhurst-Ferguson 1993, 81). Rainer Warning very rightly claims that Zola's denunciation of the new comes to stand immediately next to a secret fascination for it (2005, 159).

The process of warming is thus not a unifying one: it leads towards corruption and catastrophe, and it is, at the same time, life's 'natural' and only way of progress. For Zola, there does not seem to be any less radical alternative available, but the one of escaping the dead (damp, dark and cold) old Paris, and taking the path of warming, towards a feverish crisis of overheating. If there is hope for a sane, healthy, temperate state, then it must be patient: temperance may, if at all, only be located beyond the Second Empire's fever crisis, beyond the inevitable catastrophe. Zola in a way has to affirm the ambivalent warming climate, not as a particularly decent, but as a necessary era of transition, preparing the ground for an open, perhaps for a better future.

With this diagnosis of a deeply ambivalent warming climate of the 19th century, feverish rather than positively passionate, Zola was not alone:

> 248. Our era is not an excited era, and that is why it is not an era of passion; it continually heats up, because it senses that it is not warm – it feels cold, at bottom. I do not believe in the greatness of all these "great events", of which you are talking. (Nietzsche 1988b, 82–83; my transl.)[439]

4 Meteorotopoi – the proliferation of the hothouse

The importance of the paradigm of space for the *Rougon-Macquart* has been examined in an impressive number of publications (cf. Jennings 1973, Kamm 1975, Best 1989, Tonard 1994, Warning 2005, Kaczmarek 2011 and others). The reading I would like to add to this list takes as its point of departure two concepts that especially Rainer Warning (cf. 2005, 2009) has made fruitful for interpreting Zola's novels: the Bakhtinian concept of chronotopos (cf. also Best 1990) and the Foucauldian concept of heterotopos (cf. Foucault 2001). It is however not primarily time, *le temps qui passe*, that the spaces or locations that I would like to analyse embody, but *le temps qu'il fait*, a certain climate or weather. In other words, the *Rougon-Macquart* assemble a remarkable number of locations or enclosed spaces that I would like to call 'meteorotopoi': these are spaces that are characterised by their very own climate that, apparently, differs from the climate outside their boundaries. Although constructed and managed by human beings, these locations are particularly 'weathery' places. Their atmosphere is not only dominantly described in meteorological terms, it also acts upon the human beings exposed to their atmosphere in the very 'bodily' way that the weather does. The 'meteorotopoi' are therefore emblematic locations for Zola's analysis of milieu. Being shaped by modern technology, architecture and organisation, they bring together the historical and social specificities of locations that play an important role in the daily life of the Second Empire. They thereby embody the interaction of the social/cultural and the 'natural': they are, at the same time, products of human technology and progress *and* produce an inescapable, quasi-meteorological atmosphere that subjects the human beings and shapes their behaviour and temperament. The

---

439 "248. Unser Zeitalter ist ein aufgeregtes Zeitalter, und eben deshalb kein Zeitalter der Leidenschaft; es erhitzt sich fortwährend, weil es fühlt, daß es nicht warm ist – es friert im Grunde. Ich glaube nicht an die Größe aller dieser ‚großen Ereignisse', von denen ihr sprecht." (Nietzsche 1988b, 82–83)

human beings that frequent the meteorotopoi are therefore exposed to forces that they themselves have caused, but that nevertheless exert an uncontrollable and inescapable influence on them. The fact that the climate 'strikes back' is however concealed by the 'naturalness' of the atmosphere that rather encompasses than represses. The meteorotopoi, built by human beings, envelop its creators and make them part of their intense weathery activity.

In order to demonstrate what I mean by speaking of 'meteorotopoi' I would like to direct attention to an example that is surely not the most prominent one, but may serve for a first impression, to the washhouse from the beginning of *L'Assommoir*:

> It was an enormous shed with a level ceiling, exposed beams resting on cast-iron pillars, and big clear glass windows. Pallid daylight shone freely through the hot steam hanging in the air like a milky fog. Clouds of vapour rose up here and there and spread out, their bluish haze blotting out what lay beyond. The place was filled with a clinging dampness, like fine rain, smelling of soap, a stale, dank, persistent smell overpowered at times by the sharper fumes of bleach. (*eA*, 16)[440]

The washhouse is certainly, as Patricia Carles claims, above all, 'an atmosphere' (1989, 125). As the dominance of meteorological vocabulary shows, this 'atmosphere' is also to be understood in a narrow, weathery sense: Zola begins this initial scene in the washhouse with a meteorological description of the place's characteristic weather conditions. The interplay of the washhouse's modern architecture, its "big clear glass windows" allowing the daylight to enter and of its "steam[y]" business, setting free all kinds of "vapour" and "fumes" creates a weather spectacle very similar to the ones that fascinated Zola in the panoramas of Paris, known from *Une page d'amour* or *Le ventre de Paris*: "[c]louds" and "fog" form and dissolve, veil the vision and interact with the sunlight, producing sometimes colourful, sometimes pallid tinges. A damp, almost tropical heat dominates the climate of the washhouse. It however remains unclear whether it is the sunlight that enters through the windows from outside, or the washhouse's 'own' heat, produced by the steam engine or steaming from the buckets of hot water that account for the intolerable conditions:

---

[440] "C'était un immense hangar, à plafond plat, à poutres apparentes, monté sur des piliers de fonte, fermé par de larges fenêtres claires. Un plein jour blafard passait librement dans la buée chaude suspendue comme un brouillard laiteux. Des fumées montaient de certains coins, s'étalant, noyant les fonds d'un voile bleuâtre. Il pleuvait une humidité lourde, chargée d'une odeur savonneuse, une odeur fade, moite, continue ; et, par moments, des souffles plus forts d'eau de javel dominaient." (*A*, II 386)

> The heat was becoming unbearable; rays of sunlight streaming through the high windows on the left lit up the steamy vapour with opalescent bands of the softest rosy-grey and blue-grey. And, since people were beginning to grumble, the attendant, Charles, went from window to window pulling down the heavy canvas blinds, and then crossed to the other side, the shady side, and opened some fanlights. (eA, 21)[441]

The fact, however, that the washhouse's atmosphere is all but healthy lies beyond doubt. The air's "smelling of soap, a stale, dank, persistent smell overpowered at times by the sharper fumes of bleach" signals the corruptive quality of the tropical climate. Mary Donaldson-Evans has dedicated a whole article to the unwholesomeness of this climate, arguing for "the importance of atmosphere, conceived in a physical sense, on the heroine's destiny" (1992, 161). She emphasises that the washhouse gathers together all the Second Empire's filth, also the most private and intimate filth usually hidden from view. The novel's text provides convincing evidence for Mary Donaldson-Evans's hypothesis that the deplorable climate somehow contaminates the washer women:

> Washing tubs lined either side of the central aisle and rows of women stood at them, their sleeves rolled right up to their shoulders [*les bras nus jusqu'aux épaules*], their necks bare [*le cou nu*], their skirts hitched up showing their coloured stockings and heavy laced boots. They were beating away like mad, laughing, leaning back to yell something above the uproar, then bending low over their tubs again, a foul-mouthed, coarse, ungainly lot, soaking wet as if they'd been in a downpour, with red, steaming skin. (eA, 16)[442]

It is not only the women's having become "soaking wet" (exposed not to "a downpour" but to the washhouse's "fine rain" of water that is everywhere) and 'infected' by the tropical heat, as their "red, steaming skin" testifies; they also seem to act under the spell of the filth they are in contact with. The washhouse appears to be a public place where the norms of decency and moral conduct are suspended, a fact for which the pragmatic necessities dictated by the hard manual labour that has to be done there do not fully account. The description (a prime example for Zola's overtly male and fetishist perspective (cf. Vinken

---

[441] "La chaleur devenait intolérable ; des rais de soleil entraient à gauche, par les hautes fenêtres, allumant les vapeurs fumantes de nappes opalisées, d'un gris rose et d'un gris bleu très tendres. Et, comme des plaintes s'élevaient, le garçon Charles allait d'une fenêtre à l'autre, tirait des stores de grosse toile ; ensuite, il passa de l'autre côté, du côté de l'ombre, et ouvrit des vasistas." (*A*, II 391)

[442] "Le long des batteries, aux deux cotés de l'allée centrale, il y avait des files de femmes, les bras nus jusqu'aux épaules, le cou nu, les jupes raccourcies montrant des bas de couleur et de gros souliers lacés. Elles tapaient furieusement, riaient, se renversaient pour crier un mot dans le vacarme, se penchaient au fond de leurs baquets, ordurières, brutales, dégingandées, trempées comme par une averse, les chairs rougies et fumantes." (*A*, II 386)

1996)) clearly marks that the washer women display naked skin, body parts and pieces of clothing that ought to be covered up. Zola paints a rather obscene picture of the women, "a foul-mouthed, coarse, ungainly lot", "yell[ing]" and "laughing", "beating away like mad". Especially the women's ostentatiously loud demeanour points to the fact that they not only suffer from the climate of the washhouse, they also decisively form part of it, of its "noise of tempest":

> And, amidst the shouts and the rhythmic thumping and the gentle patter of rain, in that noise of tempest [*clameur d'orage*] muffled by the wet ceiling, the steam engine, covered with a fine white dew, puffed and snorted away over on the right without ever stopping, as if the frenzied vibration of its fly-wheel was regulating the whole outrageous din. (*eA*, 17; transl. altered)[443]

The climate of the meteorotopos washhouse is thus brought about by the interaction of heterogeneous elements: the modern architecture of the building, the sun, the steamy and filthy business inside, the washing women's demeanour. Zola emphasises the fact that this climate, despite involving human agents, is somehow beyond human control: it is the "steam engine" that seems to be "regulating the whole outrageous din", subjecting the washing women to its monotone rhythm and its damp atmosphere. Although it plays only quite a marginal role for Gervaise's use of the washhouse, Zola nevertheless describes it as being at the heart of this meteorotopos: "it was like the very breathing of the washhouse, a scalding breath that blew the ever-present steam into a cloud which hovered in the air beneath the rafters." (*eA*, 21)[444] The steam engine, with its furnace of fiery heat, turning cold water into clouds of hot steam seems to be emblematic for the idea of a climate produced by progressive 'human' technology that in turn retroacts on human temperament and behaviour.

Although the washhouse obviously produces a tropical, 'artificial' climate inside its walls that differs markedly from the state of the atmosphere outside, it is not hermetically 'heterotopic'. On the contrary, Zola carefully indicates that it is intrinsically linked to the proceedings taking place in the seemingly more temperate and decent world that surrounds it. He does so by ingeniously interweaving the novel's narrative threads with the scene of washing. It is no coincidence that Gervaise learns about her partner Lantier's infidelity in the washing

---

[443] "Et, au milieu des cris, des coups cadencés, du bruit murmurant de pluie, de cette clameur d'orage s'étouffant sous le plafond mouillé, la machine à vapeur, à droite, toute blanche d'une rosée fine, haletait et ronflait sans relâche, avec la trépidation dansante de son volant qui semblait régler l'énormité du tapage." (*A*, II 386–387)

[444] "[...] c'était [le machine à vapeur] comme la respiration même du lavoir, une haleine ardente amassant sous les poutres du plafond l'éternelle buée qui flottait." (*A*, II 391)

house, the place where the filth of the world comes to light. As Gervaise's neighbour and interlocutor Mme Boche expresses it quite frankly: "Boche hardly dirties his things at all ... How about you?" (*eA*, 17).⁴⁴⁵ The little heap of laundry Gervaise has to deal with turns out to be in a much bigger mess, literally and metaphorically, especially when her children suddenly appear to tell her that their father has just moved out, leaving Gervaise and her young family alone and penniless. Her conversation with Mme Boche and the story of Lantier's infidelity and departure tie the washhouse atmosphere to events past and present; Gervaise's ensuing fight with Virginie associates it with events to come in the future.

The battle taking place between Gervaise and Virginie, whose sister is Lantier's new mistress and who overtly and provocatively enjoys Gervaise's misery, must appear like an almost comical exaggeration of the washhouse's characteristic, steamy and brutal atmosphere: The two woman soak each other with pails of water, and "[s]houts and screams accompany[y] every drenching [*déluge*]" (*eA*, 27).⁴⁴⁶ In a quasi-ritualistic way, they re-enact the washing procedure, soil each other with verbal filth before rinsing it away with a shower of water, not sparing each other the suds and the bleaching: "The foul exchanges [*leurs ordures*] continued while they waited [for the buckets to be filled again]" (*eA*, 27).⁴⁴⁷ In the end both look as if the washhouse's characteristic "fine rain" "of clinging dampness" had developed into a heavy "downpour" to which they have been exposed:

> Soon it was impossible to keep track of the score. Both were shivering and streaming with water from head to foot, their bodices sticking to their backs, their skirts clinging to their buttocks; they seemed to have grown stiffer and skinnier, as they stood there dripping all over like a pair of umbrellas in a downpour. (*eA*, 27)⁴⁴⁸

Not only the dampness, also the obscenity of the scene has increased: the laundry boy – and Zola as well – seem to be very much "enjoying the bits of naked flesh the two women [are] displaying" (*eA*, 29):⁴⁴⁹

---

445 "« [...] Boche ne salit presque pas son linge... Et vous ? [...] »" (*A*, II 387)
446 "Et chaque déluge était accompagné d'un éclat de voix." (*A*, II 397)
447 "Et, en attendant qu'ils fussent pleins, elles continuaient leurs ordures." (*A*, II 397)
448 "Bientôt, d'ailleurs, il ne fut plus possible de juger les coups. Elles étaient l'une et l'autre ruisselantes de la tête aux pieds, les corsages plaqués aux épaules, les jupes collant sur les reins, maigries, roidies, grelottantes, s'égouttant de tous les côtés ainsi que des parapluies pendant une averse." (*A*, II 397)
449 "[Le garçon du lavoir] riait, il jouissait des morceaux de peau que les deux femmes montraient." (*A*, II 399)

> The tall brunette's red ribbon and blue chenille net went flying; her bodice had split at the neck, showing a lot of skin and most of one shoulder, while the blonde was half naked, one sleeve of her white bodice ripped off somehow or other and a tear in her chemise revealing the naked curve of her waist. (eA, 28–29)[450]

Although the fight is so clearly staged as belonging to the atmosphere of the washhouse, it anticipates the battles fought on the streets of Paris. It anticipates, too, Virginie's taking over Gervaise's shop and her regained lover Lantier, as well as her humiliating Gervaise, who, in her misery will be reduced to cleaning the floor for her rival, crawling on her knees, while Virginie watches and commands her around.

The meteorotopos washhouse thus seems to be a place governed by rules and conditions hardly different from the rules and conditions that determine the rest of the world. On the contrary, it appears to be a place where an atmosphere, a climate, is playing an important role in directing the way things go in a certain 'world', and it emerges here in its most intense, its most elemental manifestation. The washhouse is a meteorotopos, a particularly weathery place, which, however, is no exception within the world surrounding it; it is however a zone of intensity, whose so dominantly exhibited climate exceeds the boundaries of this location.

In *L'Assommoir* we encounter another meteorotopos that is closely related to the washhouse: Gervaise's laundry shop. It is part of the place's climate that "[t]he heat in the place knocked you back" (eA, 137),[451] that "the laundry hanging up to dry steamed" (eA, 137).[452] A stove is fired to heat up the irons and produces a feverish, unbearable temperature in the room:

> They'd refilled the stove with coke and as a ray of sunlight, stealing between the sheets, fell directly on to it, you could see the fierce heat rising up in the sunbeam, like an invisible flame that quivered in the tremulous air [*dont le frisson secouait l'air*]. The heat became so stifling under the skirts and tablecloths hung up to dry near the ceiling that cross-eyed Augustine ran out of spit and let a bit of her tongue dangle from her mouth. (eA, 150)[453]

---

450 "Le ruban rouge et le filet en chenille bleue de la grande brune furent arrachés ; son corsage, craqué au cou, montra sa peau, tout un bout d'épaule ; tandis que la blonde, déshabillée, une manche de sa camisole blanche ôtée sans qu'elle sût comment, avait un accroc à sa chemise qui découvrait le pli nu de sa taille." (A, II 398)
451 "Il faisait là [dans la boutique de Gervaise] une température à crever." (A, II 503)
452 "[…] les pièces qui séchaient en l'air, pendues aux fils de laiton, fumaient […]." (A, II 503)
453 "On avait encore empli de coke la mécanique, et comme le soleil, glissant entre les draps, frappait en plein sur le fourneau, on voyait la grosse chaleur monter dans le rayon, une flamme invisible dont le frisson secouait l'air. L'étouffement devenait tel, sous les jupes et les nappes séchant au plafond, que ce louchon d'Augustine, à bout de salive, laissait passer un coin de langue au bord des lèvres." (A, II 515)

The shop's atmosphere not only transforms Augustine into a sort of animal, displaying her tongue like a dog; its "fierce heat" also makes Coupeau, Gervaise's lover, who has just returned home drunk from another tour around the quarter's bars, "tipsier still": the alcohol and the unbearable temperature in the room seem to have put him 'in rut' – were he female he would, literally, be 'in heat'. He is generally horny, turned on by every female person nearby.

As claimed above, the *Rougon-Macquart* assemble dozens of meteorotopoi, of locations where the forces of the milieu thicken, where the hot, damp atmosphere literally condenses into clouds and thereby becomes visible. Instead of the washhouse or Gervaise's laundry shop we could have chosen the kitchen of the Quenus of *Le Ventre de Paris*, where "there was not a single nail from floor to ceiling that was not dripping with grease" , which is a result of "the continuous evaporation from the three big pots, in which pork was boiling and melting [*où fondaient les cochons*]", producing a haze of "ever-rising steam" (*eBP*, 78).[454] It is no coincidence that the climate of this "devil's kitchen" (*eBP*, 78)[455] so closely matches the terrible, tropical climate of Cayenne which Zola has Florent describe in this very kitchen whilst Quenu and his employee are preparing the boudin. Florent had been deported to Cayenne on a false accusation of having participated in the revolutionary uprisings. He manages to escape, having suffered from the climate there – and finds himself in another debilitating climate, which is unbearably tropical for more human-made reasons and which finally incites him to plan a revolutionary act. In the case of the Quenu kitchen it is not a steam engine but a paradigmatic 'pot-bouille', the "three big pots", that serve as the source of heat and energy for the weathery processes in this meteorotopos. They distribute the steamy air of "cochon" that must surely be regarded as pestilent or filthy, especially against the background of Zola's having famously ended his critique of the Paris bourgeoisie in *Pot-Bouille* on the provocative note: "C'est cochon et compagnie" (*PB*, III 386).

These examples of meteorotopoi (washhouse, Gervaise's shop and the kitchen of the Quenus, all hot, tropical, intensifying the passions) already provide us with a first idea of the "strong unifying impression" (Nelson 1977, 11) that Brian Nelson and Hans Ulrich Gumbrecht vaguely but rightly diagnosed as holding the *Rougon-Macquart* together. Instead of completing this rather random survey of meteorotopoi I would like to elaborate on four specific meteorotopoi in greater detail. These examples are of an even more emblematic nature than the

---

454 "Et, au milieu de cette buée amassée goutte à goutte, de cette évaporation continue des trois marmites, où fondaient les cochons, il n'était certainement pas, du plancher au plafond, un clou qui ne pissât pas la graisse." (*VP*, I 683)
455 "[…] cuisine de l'enfer […]." (*VP*, I 682)

washhouse, the shop or the kitchen: their milieus come to stand metonymically for a whole novel or, as we will see, even transcend the novels' boundaries to characterise a certain trait of the atmosphere that pervades the cycle. At the same time, these four meteorotopoi appear at first glance much more diverse than the rather similar washhouse, kitchen and shop: the bar, the coal-pit, the department store and the hothouse do not seem to be comparable in terms of their climate. However, it is exactly this apparent dissimilitude that will help us to discover the "strong unifying impression" that Brian Nelson talks about. For a start we will return to *L'Assommoir*, and shift our attention from Gervaise's shop towards the equally noxious atmosphere (cf. Donaldson-Evans 1992, 151) of the bar.

4.1 The bar – Paris inebriated

Zola does not introduce the atmosphere, the climate of the bar as he proceeded to do with the climate of the washhouse or the shop: instead of confronting a protagonist with specific conditions and describing the interplay taking place between the 'local' weather and the human temperament exposed to it, he chooses first to exhibit the bar's quasi-mythical centre, in a sober, abstract way, without any climate or atmosphere obscuring the view:

> The still, with its weirdly-shaped containers and its endless coils of piping, had a gloomy look about it; there was no steam escaping from it, and you could just hear a kind of breathing, like a subterranean rumbling, coming from deep within; it was as if some midnight task were being glumly performed in broad daylight by a strong, taciturn worker. (*eA*, 42)[456]

The famous still is of an uncanny nature, especially as it seems to hide the essential 'something' deep in its interior. Although its outward appearance does not resemble anything familiar to the readers, the narrator very quickly but latently associates it with a machine we know from another meteorotopos: the still's "breathing" reminds us of the steam engine's "scalding breath" that "was like the very breathing of the washhouse". The unfulfilled expectation of "steam escaping from it" is a product of this identification of the still with the washhouse's steam engine. The novel continues to use this technique of 'identification by negation':

---

[456] "L'alambic, avec ses récipients de forme étrange, ses enroulements sans fin de tuyaux, gardait une mine sombre ; pas une fumée ne s'échappait ; à peine entendait-on un souffle intérieur, un ronflement souterrain ; c'était comme une besogne de nuit faite en plein jour, par un travailleur morne, puissant et muet." (*A*, II 411)

> The still worked silently on, with no flame visible, no cheerful play of light on its lack-lustre copper surface, sweating out its alcohol like a slow-flowing but relentless spring which would eventually flood the bar-room, spill over the outer boulevards and inundate the vast pit that was Paris. Gervaise gave a shudder and stepped back; trying to smile, she murmured:
>
> 'I know it's silly, but that machine really makes me feel cold [*ça me fait froid*] ... Drink always makes me feel cold [*me fait froid*] ...' (*eA*, 42; transl. altered)[457]

Although "there was no steam escaping from it", although "no flame", "no cheerful play of light" is "visible", the still is a machine similar to the steam engine [*machine à vapeur*] of the washhouse: a "booze-machine [*machine à soûler*]", as the novel later calls it (*eA*, 344).[458] We all know that the "breathing" and "subterranean rumbling" "coming from deep inside" the still indicate that this machine is indeed fired by "flames" and produces "steam", that there are, not dissimilar to a steam engine, a source of heat and a source of cold water at work concealed by its gloomy and weird copper surface. More than that, the still is also a weather-machine: a "relentless spring which would eventually flood the bar-room, spill over the outer boulevards and inundate the vast pit that was Paris." There is, however, one decisive difference between the bar's *machine à soûler* and the washhouse's *machine à vapeur*: The still, "with its weirdly-shaped containers and its endless coils of piping" is not in itself a workable weather machine. Unlike the steam engine or Gervaise's stove its process of distillation, silent but effective, like "a strong, taciturn worker", does not bring forth any spectacular, unwholesome or tropical atmosphere *of itself*. The fact that soberly observing the machine work "makes [Gervaise] feel cold [*ça me fait froid*]" clearly marks the absence of any troubling or unwholesome 'climate'. Gervaise is not under the spell of the apparatus when she judges the machine, and drink in general, to be worrying. Her unchallenged moral indignation signals the dysfunction of the *machine à soûler* at that point of the story. The bar's weather-machine is not complete, a decisive part is still missing, a part that has to be attached to the still. An agent that converts the potential weather (the steam, the flames) condensed in the trickling, "slow-flowing" stream into the powerful, heavy weather of the deluge-like dimensions that Zola prophesies, "flood[ing]

---

[457] "L'alambic, sourdement, sans une flamme, sans une gaieté dans les reflets éteints de ses cuivres, continuait, laissait couler sa sueur d'alcool, pareil à une source lente et entêtée, qui à la longue devait envahir la salle, se répandre sur les boulevards extérieurs, inonder le trou immense de Paris. Alors, Gervaise, prise d'un frisson, recula ; et elle tâchait de sourire, en murmurant :
« C'est bête, ça me fait froid, cette machine... la boisson me fait froid... »" (*A*, II 411–412)
[458] "[...] l'alambic, la machine à soûler [...]." (*A*, II 704)

the bar-room, spill[ing] over the outer boulevards and inundat[ing] the vast pit that was Paris". The weather-machine that brings forth the characteristic atmosphere of the bar has an important human component. It is the drinkers who convert the alcohol's potential weathery energy into actual, catastrophic weather:

> It was very warm, pipe-smoke swirled up like a cloud of dust in the blinding gas-light, engulfing the customers in a slowly thickening fog; and out of this fog came a din, a deafening, chaotic din, of cracked voices, clinking glasses, oaths, and fists banging on tables with a sound like guns going off. So Gervaise had a snooty expression on her face because that kind of place isn't very nice for a woman, especially when she's not used to it; she was suffocating, her eyes were smarting and her head already throbbing from the reek of alcohol that the whole room gave off [*l'odeur d'alcool qui s'exhalait de la salle entière*]. Then, suddenly, she sensed there was something yet more disturbing behind her back. She turned round and saw the still, the booze-machine, working away under the glass roof of the narrow little court-yard, its devil's kitchen vibrating deep inside it. (eA, 344)[459]

With customers, drinkers, peopling the bar the situation changes radically. The "booze-machine" starts functioning as a weather-machine that produces a typical climate. We now see why it is another "devil's kitchen", like that of the Quenus (cf. eBP, 78): the bar's climate seems familiar to us, the room is very warm, blazingly lighted and the air filled with all sorts of pestilent vapours, here it is "a slowly thickening fog" of pipe-smoke and the penetrant "reek of alcohol that the whole room gave off". This time the human actants' share in the creation of this climate is not only limited to their orchestrating it with all kinds of noises ("a deafening, chaotic din") as was the case in the washhouse; factually, all the climatic influences that Gervaise suffers from have been produced by the drinkers themselves: the fog of pipe-smoke that make Gervaise suffocate and her eyes smart, the "reek of alcohol" from which her head throbs. Zola's speaking of the room's "reek [*l'odeur d'alcool qui s'exhalait de la salle entière*]" is not merely metaphorical or metonymic trim, it underlines the boozers'

---

[459] "Il faisait très chaud, la fumée des pipes montait dans la clarté aveuglante du gaz, où elle roulait comme une poussière, noyant les consommateurs d'une buée, lentement épaissie ; et, de ce nuage, un vacarme sortait, assourdissant et confus, des voix cassées, des chocs de verre, des jurons et des coups de point semblable à des détonations. Aussi Gervaise avait-elle pris sa figure en coin de rue, car une pareille vue n'est pas drôle pour une femme, surtout quand elle n'en a pas l'habitude ; elle étouffait, les yeux brûlés, la tête déjà alourdie par l'odeur d'alcool qui s'exhalait de la salle entière. Puis, brusquement, elle eut la sensation d'un malaise plus inquiétant derrière son dos. Elle se tourna, elle aperçut l'alambic, la machine à soûler, fonctionnant sous le vitrage de l'étroite cour, avec la trépidation profonde de sa cuisine d'enfer." (A, II 704)

essential contribution to the bar's climate. The bar thus presents an exemplary picture of a milieu, of a climate that is both somehow produced by human beings and at the same time affects those exposed to it; they both contribute decisively to it and, at the same time, suffer from it.

Yet despite the weather-machine's important human component, the driving force behind it all, the reason the customers frequent the bar, is the flow of alcohol produced by the still. The washhouse's "whole outrageous din" seemed to have been "regulat[ed]" by the steam engine and "the frenzied vibration of its fly-wheel"; in the case of the bar, it is surely the emblematic still that sets the rhythm for the bar's "chaotic din". Although the circumstances are now different, Gervaise is still aware of her moral condemnation of the still and its devilish workings. However, the "bloody great pot" that has now turned into a weather-machine no longer makes her feel cold. *In concreto*, exposed to the bar's atmosphere produced by its weather-machine, which is now functioning properly, Gervaise's 'moral' cold has turned into an ambivalent "shiver [*frisson*]":

> And she kept casting sidelong glances at the boozing machine behind her. That bloody great pot, as round as the belly of a fat tinker's wife, with its thrusting, twisting snout, sent shivers [*frisson*] down her back, shivers of fear mixed with longing. Yes, it was like the metallic innards of some gigantic whore, of some sorceress who was distilling, drop by drop, the fire that burned in her gut. A pretty source of poison, an operation so shameless, so foul, it should have been buried away deep down inside a cellar! But in spite of what she felt, Gervaise would have liked to get her nose right in it, to sniff the smell and taste the filthy stuff [*goûter à la cochonnerie*], even if it burned her tongue and made it peel like an orange. (*eA*, 345–346)[460]

As the shiver indicates, the still not only radiates the coldness of moral worry, of "fear", it also promises to set something free that nurtures a "longing": a certain warmth. Gervaise's associations of the "fire" that is somehow contained in the alcohol's drops and that threatens to "burn[ ] her tongue" (a risk that she is ready to take) clearly marks that she, like the others, is falling for the warmth that the alcohol promises to produce: "'[…] let's keep each other's tootsies

---

[460] "Et elle jetait des regards obliques sur la machine à soûler, derrière elle. Cette sacrée marmite, ronde comme un ventre de chaudronnière grasse, avec son nez qui s'allongeait et se tortillait, lui soufflait un frisson dans les épaules, une peur mêlée d'un désir. Oui, on aurait dit la fressure de métal d'une grande gueuse, de quelque sorcière qui lâchait goutte à goutte le feu de ses entrailles. Une jolie source de poison, une opération qu'on aurait dû enterrer dans une cave tant elle était effrontée et abominable ! Mais ça n'empêchait pas, elle aurait voulu mettre son nez là-dedans, renifler l'odeur, goûter à la cochonnerie, quand même sa langue brûlée aurait dû en peler du coup comme une orange." (*A*, II 706)

warm'" (eA, 43),⁴⁶¹ Coupeau had told her to encourage her to drink. We remember that "the drop [Boit-Sans-Soif]'d just had was warming his body like a boiler, he felt as powerful as a bleeding steam-engine" (eA, 205);⁴⁶² in short, the alcohol "put[s] fire in the idlers' guts" (eA, 216; transl. altered).⁴⁶³ This longing for warmth is not too dissimilar from the longing that haunts the grand Paris of a very different social milieu, the longing of the Muffats, of Renée and of the bourgeoisie. And, in fact, Zola uses the youthful Nana to underline that it is one and the same:

> Pale with desire, she'd stop in her tracks, feeling the warmth of the Paris paving stones creeping up her thighs, feeling a fierce urge to taste all the pleasures that pressed in upon her in the crowded street. (eA, 366)⁴⁶⁴

> When Nana went past the Assommoir and caught sight of her mother sitting in the back there with her nose stuck in her glass, looking like a slut with all those bawling men round her, she'd be furiously angry, because the young are greedy for a different kind of pleasure and don't understand about drink. (eA, 367)⁴⁶⁵

As we have already seen above, Zola comes back to this point in *Nana* to emphasise the point that the "kind of pleasure" might differ between the social classes and milieus – the general trend, the longing for warming, is however essentially the same: "[i]n working-class slums, families dragged down by drunkenness finish up in utter destitution", whereas "in [the Muffats'] house, where a vast accumulation of wealth was suddenly about to go up in flames and collapse in ruins", it is Nana and "the smell of her body fermenting in the stuffy air [*ferment de son odeur flottant dans l'air chaud*]" that "turn[ ] this whole society putrid" (eN, 364).⁴⁶⁶

---

461 "« […] nous nous chaufferons les petons. »" (A, II 412)
462 "[…] la goutte de tout à l'heure lui chauffait la carcasse comme une chaudière, [Boit-Sans-Soif] se sentait une sacrée force de machine à vapeur." (A, II 532)
463 "Le vin décrassait et reposait du travail, mettait le feu au ventre des fainéants ;" (A, II 579)
464 "Elle s'arrêtait toute pâle de désir, elle sentait monter du pavé de Paris une chaleur le long de ses cuisses, un appétit féroce de mordre aux jouissances dont elle était bousculée, dans la grande cohue des trottoirs." (A, II 726)
465 "Lorsque Nana, en passant devant l'Assommoir, apercevait sa mère au fond, le nez dans la goutte, avachie au milieu des engueulades des hommes, elle était prise d'une colère bleue, parce que la jeunesse, qui a le bec tourné à une autre friandise, ne comprend pas la boisson." (A, II 727)
466 "Chez les ivrognes des faubourgs, c'est par la misère noire, le buffet sans pain, la folie d'alcool vidant les matelas, que finissent les familles gâtées. Ici, sur l'écroulement de ces richesses, entassées et allumées d'un coup, la valse sonnait le glas d'une vieille race ; pendant que Nana, invisible, épandue au-dessus du bal avec ses membres souples, décomposait ce monde, le pénétrait du ferment de son odeur flottant dans l'air chaud, sur le rythme canaille de la musique." (N, II 1429–1430)

As is well known, the novel does not shy from demonstrating very explicitly the disastrous, the fatal consequences of resorting to the source of warmth available to the working-class. We have already discussed Coupeau's brutal death in an asylum, literally reduced to a component of the Assommoir's weather-machine, "puff[ing] steam out of his wide open mouth, thick steam that filled the cell and went out of the window" (eA, 434),[467] the steam that the still concealed behind its copper surface. Gervaise – we remember the "shivers" that the still sent "down her back" – eventually dies of "hot and cold" (eA, 439; transl. altered).[468] The two are however not exemplary victims who merely represent all their comrades who have, like them, fallen for the alcohol and drowned their lives in one of Paris' working-class bars. The weather-machine 'bar' functions in a different, in a more indirect or mediated way than all the other weather-machines, and it is exactly this trait that makes it so powerful. Zola's prophecy that the still's "relentless spring [of alcohol] [...] would eventually flood the bar-room, spill over the outer boulevards and inundate the vast pit that was Paris" holds true, because the human component of the machine spreads the pestilent atmosphere beyond the boundaries of the meteorotopos 'bar'. It is the drunkards breath that carries this weather beyond the walls of the bar and thus "there is a fume of brandy and wine in the streets of Paris" (eA, 312; transl. altered).[469] This "hot, foul breath" is contagious, as Zola shows with regard to the teenagers Nana and Pauline:

> [Nana's and Pauline's] bare arms, their bare necks, their bare heads were warmed by hot, foul breath, and bathed in a stench of wine and sweat. And they'd laugh, finding it great fun, not in the least disgusted, their faces a little pinker, as if on their natural dung. (eA, 353; transl. altered)[470]

With their uncovered arms and necks Nana and Pauline resemble the women in the washhouse, mirroring their obscenity; they are however not bathed in the steam of laundry and rinsing, but "in a stench of wine and sweat", "warmed by

---

[467] "Alors, en se dépêchant, il crut qu'il avait une machine à vapeur dans le ventre ; la bouche grande ouverte, il soufflait de la fumée, une fumée épaisse qui emplissait la cellule et qui sortait par la fenêtre [...]." (A, II 791)
[468] "Même on ne sut jamais au juste de quoi elle était morte. On parla d'un froid et chaud." (A, II 796)
[469] "On ne se doute pas combien ça désaltère les pochards, de quitter l'air de Paris, où il y a dans les rues une vraie fumée d'eau-de-vie et de vin." (A, II 673)
[470] "Leurs [Nana et Pauline] belles robes fraîches s'écrasaient entre les paletots et les bourgerons sales. Leurs bras nus, leur cou nu, leurs cheveux nus, s'échauffaient sous les haleines empestées, dans une odeur de vin et du sueur. Et elles riaient, amusées, sans un dégoût, plus roses et comme sur leur fumier naturel." (A, II 713)

hot, foul breath". Although Nana does not drink, although she, as we have seen, does not even "understand about drink", she nevertheless exemplarily spreads the pestilent atmosphere, the climate in which she has grown up. *Nana* narrates this story of infection precisely, frequently resorting to the keyword "dung [*fumier*]" to underline that the decadence of the upper class and the aristocracy is linked to the working class's misery of alcohol; both form part of the same changing, warming climate as it steers towards catastrophe.

Nana's biographical story is however only one example of a much more encompassing general trend. The atmosphere of the bar spreads beyond its boundaries, it "inundat[es]" the world. As *Le Ventre de Paris* spells out with regard to its protagonist Florent, it is no coincidence that the revolutionary movements or uprisings that *Les Rougon-Macquart* tell of take their origins in the bar's climate:

> Florent began to spend more and more time at Monsieur Lebigre's, until he hardly stirred from the place. He found there an overheated atmosphere [*un milieu surchauffé*] in which his passion for politics [*fièvres politiques*] could be freely indulged. [...] The atmosphere of the little room, reeking with the smell of spirits and warm with tobacco smoke, transported him, prompting a kind of abandonment of himself which made him willing to acquiesce in the wildest ideas [*choses très grosses*]. (eBP, 136–137)[471]

The same could be said of the three revolutionary figures in *Germinal*, Étienne, Rasseneur and Souvarine. They meet at the bar of the former worker and strike leader Rasseneur, who has become a pub-owner. They are all three associated with the bar's specific climate, without being drunkards. The revolutionary ideas are engendered in an atmosphere (overheated, intoxicated with alcohol and the fumes of tobacco) that resembles the atmosphere brought about by the masses that these leaders assemble; it is a climate of a certain, of a characteristic drunkenness or intoxication: "a kind of intoxication [*ivresse*]" of a crowd "drunk with their own cries, courage and confidence [*grisée de broit, de courage et de foi*]" (eFR, 28)[472] like the rebels standing up against the coup d'état in *La Fortune des Rougon*; it is the "hot fever of revenge" developing amongst the striking mob and lastly also infecting Étienne, who, too, "felt intoxicated [*se grisait*],

---

[471] "Florent, peu à peu, venait davantage, ne quittait plus le cabinet. Il y trouvait un milieu surchauffé, où ses fièvres politiques battaient à l'aise. [...] L'odeur du cabinet, cette odeur liquoreuse, chaude de la fumée du tabac, le grisait, lui donnait un béatitude particulière, un abandon de lui-même dont le bercement lui fait accepter sans difficulté des choses très grosses." (*VP*, I 745)

[472] "Une ivresse singulière montait de cette foule grisée de brout, de courage et de foi." (*FR*, I 31)

carried away" (*eG*, 324; transl. altered)[473] in *Germinal*. As we will see in a later section, the weather of the masses is a sort of extension of the weather of the bar; it is the crowd that represents not only the alcohol's "flood[ing] the bar-room", but also its "spill[ing] over the outer boulevards and inundat[ing] the vast pit that was Paris".

Intoxication or drunkenness is thus associated with revolution, and the climate of the bar metonymically represents the pestilent milieu in which intoxication and revolution are breeding. It, however, also epitomises the trend of warming as a whole. In addition to the revolutionary intoxication/drunkenness, there is shopping fever, an "intoxication [*griserie*] exuded by the materials which were being handled" (*eLP*, 267)[474] that is produced by the atmosphere of sales in the 'Le Bonheur des Dames'; the "intoxication [*griserie*]" of speculation, "a passion which would grow and carry away all common sense" (*eM*, 154)[475] in *L'Argent*; the hot atmosphere in Nana's apartment with its wilting roses and its emblematically metonymic "intoxication [*griserie*] which the patchouli in the bowl set free" (*eN*, 47; transl. altered).[476] To make things a bit more complicated, intoxication or drunkenness is not merely a sign of decadence or misguided overheating; Zola makes clear that it radiates from life itself: when Pauline in *La Joie de vivre* manages to save the life of Louise's new-born, weak child, she breathes in a "hot harshness/bitterness [*âpreté chaude*] of life, which intoxicated her [*qui la grisait*]" (*JV*, III 1102; my transl.).[477]

The alcohol's intoxication, which is the characteristic trait of the meteorotopos bar thus forms an inherent part of the cycle's overarching meta-climate of a global warming. It is therefore not astonishing that it also features prominently in one of Zola's most impressive emblems of this global warming that leads to catastrophe, the train racing along without an engine driver at the end of *La Bête humaine*:

> And on the machine raced, now out of control, onward and onward. At last this restive, temperamental thing could yield to the wild energy of youth, like a young filly, still unbroken, who has slipped the clutches of her groom, and gone galloping off across the

---

[473] "Lui-même [Étienne] se grisait, emporté dans cette fièvre chaude de revanche." (*G*, III 1414)
[474] "Cette fièvre, depuis le matin, avait grandi peu à peu, comme la griserie même qui se dégageait des étoffes remuées. La foule flambait sous l'incendie du soleil de cinq heures." (*BD*, III 644)
[475] "[...] de grandes affiches jaunes, collées dans tout Paris, annonçant la prochaine exploitation des mines d'argent du Carmel, achevaient de troubler les têtes, y allumaient un commencement de griserie, cette passion qui devait croître et emporter toute raison." (*Ar*, V 170)
[476] "Il faisait trop chaud dans ce cabinet, une chaleur lourde et enfermée de serre. Les roses se fanaient, une griserie montait du patchouli de la coupe." (*N*, II 1138)
[477] "Des glaires, des mucosités lui souillaient les lèvres, mais sa joie de l'avoir sauvé emportait son dégoût : elle aspirait maintenant une âpreté chaude de vie, qui la grisait." (*JV*, III 1102)

open plain. There was water in the boiler, and the firebox, which had just been stoked, was all ablaze; and as the pressure rose wildly during the first half hour, so the engine reached a terrifying speed. The chief guard must have succumbed to exhaustion and dropped off to sleep. The soldiers, whose drunkenness was increased by their being thus piled on top of each other, suddenly grew merry at this furious onrush and sang even more loudly. (*eBH*, 366)[478]

4.2 The coal-pit – battle of weathers

Germinal is a 'weather novel', even though considerable parts of it take place in the coal-pit hundreds of meters below the surface of the earth and as far away and as independent of the processes of the atmosphere, of the 'home' of meteorology as one can imagine. The "storm theme", Philip Walker writes, pervades the novel "from beginning to the end", telling a story with "two great climaxes – the human flood thundering across the plain in Part v and the catastrophic, apocalyptic descriptions of the inundated mines in Part vii" (Walker 1959, 449). I will discuss both these climaxes in great detail in two later sections; in the present section the focus will be on the location itself, the coal-pit, and its weather. It is here, I would like to claim, that the catastrophic events of the human flood and the inundated mine both originate, it is from here that these catastrophic weather events derive their energy.

The coal-pit is an exemplary meteorotopos. It is obviously not designed as a place creating its 'own' weather; its specific climate rather inadvertently results from the needs and necessities that the exploitation of coal generates. Dug deep into the earth, the coal-pit's isolation from the weather 'outside', the weather of the world, is iconic; so much so that the pit seems to be a parallel world, almost invisible from the world above ground. When Étienne errs around in search of work at the beginning of the novel, suffering from the "icy cold" "March wind, blowing in wide swathes as if sweeping across the sea" (*eG*, 5),[479] all he sees is a vague impression of fires that he hopes belong to some kind of heavy industry

---

[478] "Et la machine, libre de toute direction, roulait, roulait toujours. Enfin, la rétive, la fantasque, pouvait céder à la fougue de sa jeunesse, ainsi qu'une cavale indomptée encore, échappée des mains du gardien, galopant par la campagne rase. La chaudière était pourvue d'eau, le charbon dont le foyer venait d'être rempli, s'embrasait ; et pendant la première demi-heure, la pression monta follement, la vitesse devint effrayante. Sans doute, le conducteur-chef, cédant à la fatigue, s'était endormi. Les soldats, dont l'ivresse augmentait, à être ainsi entassé, subitement s'égayèrent de cette course violente, chantèrent plus fort." (*BH*, III 1330)

[479] "Devant lui, il ne voyait même pas le sol noir, et il n'avait la sensation de l'immense horizon plat que par les souffles du vent de mars, des rafales larges comme sur une mer, glacées d'avoir balayé des lieues de marais et de terres nues." (*G*, III 1133)

that could provide him with a job. Although forming part of the coal-pit, the fires burning at the surface obviously do not represent its parallel underground world. There is only one typical signal of this world perceivable that Étienne cannot yet identify: "a lone voice, the prolonged, loud breathing of a steam engine exhaust valve, hidden somewhere out of sight" (*eG*, 6; transl. altered).[480] Having recognised this place as a coal-pit, it does not take long for Étienne to locate and understand the strange sound: it is produced by "the pump letting off steam, with its long, raucous, repetitive breathing, like the hoarse snorting [*l'haleine engorgée*] of some monster" (*eG*, 52; transl. altered).[481] Zola's choice of words for this machine must look familiar to us: we remember the steam engine that had been described as "the very breathing of the washhouse [*la respiration même du lavoir*]" (*eA*, 21);[482] and indeed, the "drainage pump" – *la machine d'épuisement* – fulfils a similar function for the coal-pit. "[T]he heavy, slow breathing of the drainage pump, panting away day after day and night after night" (*eG*, 132; transl. altered),[483] recurring frequently throughout the novel, is the 'very breathing' of the coal-pit. It is at the heart of this meteorotopos that Zola paints, on the one hand, as a monstrous creature, devouring the miners that it swallows in its enormous shaft and, on the other hand, as a location brought about by human technology. The "breathing", the "hoarse snorting" belongs to a machine without which the pit's underground world would not be accessible to human life and work. In addition to the wooden "shaft linings" the pump serves to "contain the gushing springs, and insulate the shafts from the surrounding lakes, whose dark unseen waters lapped up against their walls" and that gathers at the bottom of the pit (*eG*, 454–455).[484] In other words, the climate of the coal-pit is not to be mixed up with the 'natural' conditions one finds when digging a shaft of considerable depth; as Zola explains by pointing to the notorious 'Torrent', the 'natural' 'weather' underground would rather be 'nautical', a place for diving rather than for exploiting coal:

---

480 "[…] de cette apparition fantastique, noyée de nuit et de fumée, une seule voix montait, la respiration grosse et longue d'un échappement de vapeur, qu'on ne voyait point." (*G*, III 1134)
481 "Il s'expliquait jusqu'à l'échappement de la pompe, cette respiration grosse et longue, soufflant sans relâche, qui était comme l'haleine engorgée du monstre." (*G*, III 1136)
482 "[…] c'était [la machine à vapeur] comme la respiration même du lavoir, une haleine ardente amassant sous les poutres du plafond l'éternelle buée qui flottait." (*A*, II 391)
483 "Peu à peu, la nuit se noyait, la pluie tombait maintenant, lente, continue, abîmant ce néant au fond de son ruissellement monotone ; tandis qu'une seule voix s'entendait encore, la respiration grosse et lente de la machine d'épuisement, qui jour et nuit soufflait." (*G*, III 1247)
484 "Seule, la construction des cuvelages, de ces pièces de charpente jointes entre elles comme les douves d'un tonneau, parvenait à contenir les sources affluentes, à isoler les puits au milieu des lacs dont les vagues profondes et obscures en battaient les parois." (*G*, III 1528)

> That was where they had encountered the Torrent, an underground sea, the terror of the coalfields in the Nord Department, a sea with its storms and shipwrecks, an unknown, unfathomable sea, whose black waves broke more than 300 metres underground. (eG, 455)[485]

The coal-pit is thus a meteorotopos not only because it is underground, isolated from the meteorological weather-conditions reigning on the earth's surface. It must also be isolated, protected from the 'natural' conditions, especially all the water that surrounds it. Its climate is artificial, a product of human technology battling against the conditions that prevail underground.

The weather phenomena that Étienne encounters in the pit are thus produced by the layout of the construction and by the necessities of coal exploitation. The first of these unusual and unexpected phenomena already waits for the miners in the shaft: they are exposed to a "driving rain which was showering down the black hole" (eG, 57).[486] This rain is a mixture of water leaking through the shaft linings and a phenomenon of condensation induced by the shaft's cold air. However, the pit's thermic conditions are even more astonishing for Étienne, who enters the pit for the first time:

> But what surprised him most were the sudden changes in temperature. Down at the pit bottom it was very cold, and in the haulage road, where all the air ventilating the mine was channelled, there was an icy wind, which started blowing at gale force as the tunnel walls got narrower. Afterwards, as they plunged deeper into the byways, which received only a meagre ration of ventilation, the wind dropped, and the heat rose, a suffocating, leaden heat. (eG, 36)[487]

The sudden changes in temperature are to some degree geological and physical phenomena. They are however also, and mainly, produced by one of the basic necessities of mining: ventilation. Oxygen has to be brought into the pit, dust and noxious gases have to be diluted and removed. The German expression for underground mine ventilation, 'Bewetterung', literally 'weathering', tells a lot about the meteorotopos coal-pit: the exploitation of coal is made possible by a sort of artificial weather, a technology of producing winds that distribute

---

[485] "[...] c'était là que se trouvait le Torrent, cette mer souterraine, la terreur des houillères du Nord, une mer avec ses tempêtes et ses naufrages, une mer ignorée, insondable, roulant ses flots noirs, à plus de trois cents mètres du soleil." (G, III 1528)
[486] "[...] la pluie battante qui tombait du trou noir [...]." (G, III 1180)
[487] "Mais ce qui l'étonnait surtout, c'étaient les brusques changements de température. En bas du puits, il faisait très frais, et dans la galerie du roulage, par où passait tout l'air de la mine, soufflait en vent glacé, dont la violence tournait à la tempête, entre les muraillements étroits. Ensuite, à mesure qu'on s'enfonçait dans les autres voies, qui recevaient seulement leur part disputée d'aérage, le vent tombait, la chaleur croissait, une chaleur suffocante, d'une pesanteur de plomb." (G, III 1161–1162)

fresh air and transport dust, noxious air and also heat out of the pit. In the case of 'Le Voreux' the main ventilation air flow, the "icy wind", is produced by the technology of an air furnace (in German a 'Wetterofen', a 'weather-furnace'). An air furnace works as an 'exhausting system', meaning that a coal-fire draws all the air it needs for burning from the pit (it is fed by the pit's exhaust air) and produces a continuous air-flow providing the ventilation that is needed. The air furnace of 'Le Voreux' is located in an old neighbouring pit connected to 'Le Voreux' by galleries: "there blazed the enormous, hellish coal furnace whose powerful blast drew in tempestuous draughts of air right through the neighbouring pit." (eG, 269).[488] The meteorotopos coal-pit is a good example for the extremeness of the 'weather' that has to be produced in these locations in order to fulfil the function it serves: although the ventilation wind is "tempestuous", "blowing at gale force", it hardly suffices to reach the byways where the actual mining is taking place. The technology of 'weathering' the pit, ventilation and drainage, makes the exploitation of coal possible; it has, however, to employ more and more extreme measures the more the process of exploitation progresses. The equation is quite simple: the most effective exploitation demands the most extreme technological efforts – and that is to say, to produce the most extreme weather conditions. Comparable, as we will see, to the department store and the stock exchange, the meteorotopos coal-pit is a hyper-weathery location: its capitalistic success demands extreme conditions, conditions without which the exploitation would not be possible at all. It is thereby a privileged place to show the dialectic of a world savouring the fruits of technological progress that at the same time subjects the human species to inhuman conditions brought about by their own, 'progressive' technology.

Étienne, like all the others suffers from the pit's extreme climate: At the coal-face "the temperature reached thirty-five degrees, and there was no air, so in time you could die of suffocation" (eG, 39).[489] Water leaks from the rocks so that "[a]fter a quarter of an hour, [Étienne] was soaked, covered in his own sweat as well, giving off a stream of dirty, warm vapour" (eG, 39).[490]

---

[488] "[...] on avait délaissé les galeries supérieures, pour ne surveiller que la galerie du fond, dans laquelle flambait le fourneau d'enfer, l'énorme brasier de houille, au tirage si puissant, que l'appel d'air faisait souffler le vent en tempête, d'un bout à l'autre de la fosse voisine." (G, III 1366–1367)
[489] "En haut, la température montait jusqu'à trente-cinq degrés, l'air ne circulait pas, l'étouffement à la longue devenait mortel." (G, III 1164)
[490] "[...] il était trempé, couvert de sueur lui-même, fumant d'une chaude buée de lessive." (G, III 1164)

> [A]nd what he suffered from most was the cold, a growing cold which had gripped him as they left the coal-face, and was making him shiver more and more as they approached the shaft. Between the narrow walls, a rushing wind whistled stormily past. (eG, 57)[491]

In contrast to the horse called "Trompette", who, "[s]ince he had gone underground, [...] had never been able to become acclimatized" and eventually dies in the mine (eG, 420),[492] Étienne seems to be very talented in adapting to the extreme weather of the pit. The experienced miner Maheu finds in him "the first casual worker who became acclimatized so quickly" (eG, 137; transl. altered).[493] It is this talent (a special relation to extreme weather), I would like to suggest, that privileges him to become the leader of the strike: in this function he manages to carry the violent weather from the coal-pit to the surface, where, as we will see, it rages brutally as an uncontrollable weather of the masses. Étienne thus successfully makes the violence of the weather transgress the boundaries of the meteorotopos coal-pit, which is an important step, because the boundaries of the pit also guarantee the functioning of a cruel system of exploitation and unfair distribution: it is only the class of the miners working in the pit that suffers from the extreme climate there; the warmth and riches, the fruit of modern progress fuelled by the mining of coal are enjoyed by another class. A "pineapple, cut into slices and served in a crystal bowl" is emblematically served at the Hennebeaus' house, "which seemed as warm as a greenhouse" when they receive their capitalist friends, while the strikers outside are suffering from the "bitter north-east wind" of a cold December day (eG, 206).[494] As we will see in the section on the weather of the masses, Étienne, however, proves unable to guide or control the weathery energy he has managed to set free from the pit, that he has managed to transfer above ground. This weathery energy of the striking mob resists any appropriation for the goals of class struggle, so that, in the end, it even strengthens the monopole of the syndicate that owns 'Le Voreux' by driving the little competitor of the neighbouring mine into bankruptcy.

Nevertheless, Étienne is not the only character in the novel who resists the subjection to the technological weather of the pit. Zola also portrays a rather

---

[491] "[...] et ce dont il souffrait surtout, c'était du froid, un froid grandissant qui l'avait pris au sortir de la taille, et qui le faisait grelotter davantage, à mesure qu'il se rapprochait du puits. Entre les muraillements étroits, la colonne d'air soufflait de nouveau en tempête." (G, III 1180)
[492] "C'était Trompette, en effet. Depuis sa descente, jamais, il n'avait pu s'acclimater." (G, III 1499)
[493] "C'était le premier ouvrier de rencontre qui s'acclimatait si promptement." (G, III 1250)
[494] "Dehors, la journée de décembre était glacée par une aigre bise du nord-est. Mais pas un souffle n'entrait, il faisait là une tiédeur de serre, qui développait l'odeur fine d'un ananas, coupé au fond d'une jatte de cristal." (G, III 1310)

marginal figure who pursues a very different strategy: whereas Étienne tries to channel the weathery energy of the pit and direct it against the system of exploitation in a great, public action, Jeanlin – a child of eleven years, severely handicapped after an accident in the pit – rather parasitically and clandestinely appropriates the best of what can be gotten from this gigantic weather machine. He has found an old gallery of the neighbouring pit that has been out of use for years, a location where he secretly lives. When Étienne surprises Jeanlin in his underground retreat, he is immediately taken in by the temperate climate he encounters there:

> And in fact he did appreciate the comfort at the bottom of this hole: the heat was bearable, with an even temperature in all seasons, rather like a warm bath, while up above the ground the sharp December cold was freezing his wretched comrades rigid. (eG, 272)[495]

Jeanlin is surely not a morally exemplary human being: he steals, tyrannises and abuses his comrades and in the end even kills a soldier just for fun. Nevertheless, he is an interesting outlaw figure, premature and beast-like, that instinctively understands the role the weather or climate (and the power over them) plays for questions of social hierarchy and subjection. On the one hand, he embodies the cruel effects of the mining milieu: Zola portrays him as the degenerate offspring of a family of miners, who has both inherited and suffered from the traces that working in the pit from the early years of childhood imprint on the body. He is the epitome of the victims that the milieu of mining produces. On the other hand, he is the only character who finds a way to escape the so distinct 'class-climates': when all the miners on strike suffer from the wintery cold, starving, while the capitalists meet at the Hennebeaus', enjoying their dinner and the warmth of the central heating, Jeanlin sits in his underground nest, temperate "like a warm bath", with lots of provisions that he even offers to share with his unexpected guest Étienne. Although Jeanlin is not entitled to be where he is, although all the provisions are stolen and even violently taken from his accomplices, Jeanlin's little paradise (a place not subjected to the seasons, supplied with provisions for which Jeanlin has not really worked) is described with a certain sort of sympathy, despite Jeanlin's corrupt, perverse morals. It is a location of ambivalent resistance: both a brigand's lair and a re-appropriation of the weather-machine coal-pit that defies the goals of exploitation and capitalism. Without doubt, Jeanlin is an ambivalent character; he however comes to embody the individual, very concrete desire to regain agency

---

[495] "Et, en effet, il goûtait un bien-être, au fond de ce trou : la chaleur n'y était plus trop forte, une température égale y régnait en dehors des saisons, d'une tiédeur de bain, pendant que le rude décembre gerçait sur la terre la peau des misérables." (G, III 1369)

over the climate in which one lives and that proves to be so important not only for one's prosperity, but also fundamentally shapes the human being that is exposed to it. Jeanlin has been deformed, morally and physically, by the climate (and that is to say by the milieu) of the pits; his desire of and joy over re-appropriating the power over the weather, and be it for moments only, when the striking mob attacks and in parts destroys the overground buildings of the pit of 'Le Voreux' should be viewed against this background:

> The jets blew out as violently as gunshots, and the five boilers emptied with a tempestuous blast, whistling with such a thunderous roar that it made their ears bleed. Everything was drowned in steam, the coal seemed white, the women looked like ghosts, making dream-like gestures. Only the boy showed up clearly, standing on the overhead platform where he had clambered, beyond the spirals of white vapour, looking delighted, with his mouth cracked open by the pleasure of having unleashed this hurricane. (*eG*, 324; transl. altered)[496]

Jeanlin does not pursue any concerted strategy backed by an elaborate ideology like Souvarine. His participation in the destruction of the pit's plant cannot be called anarchic in the stricter sense of the word: what he does is not revolutionary, it is not motivated politically; he acts instinctively. It is "the pleasure" of appropriating the agency of weather-making that drives Jeanlin. Like the weather-god, like Shakespeare in Herder's famous praise,[497] Jeanlin is positioned high atop some craggy, industrial eminence (he is "standing on the overhead platform"), looking down on the heavy weather he has created, the "tempestuous blast", the "thunderous roar", "the spirals of white vapour", the "hurricane" at his feet. For generations his family had been exposed to and had to suffer from the artificial heavy weather produced to increase the exploitation of coal, he had suffered from tempestuous weather unchained for the benefit of others. For moments Jeanlin now enjoys the violent weather he himself has created for his very own sake, for his pleasure.

Germinal stages a battle of and over the weather(s). The weather of the pit, produced by human technology continuously struggles with the natural weather of Le Torrent and the underground springs and gases (in German: 'schlagende Wetter'), while the miners carry the heavy weather brewing among them from the pits to the surface in order to fight their exploitation and direct their violence

---

[496] "Les jets partirent avec la violence de coups de feu, les cinq chaudières se vidèrent d'un souffle de tempête, sifflant dans un tel grondement de foudre, que les oreilles en saignaient. Tout avait disparu au milieu de la vapeur, le charbon pâlissait, les femmes n'étaient plus que des ombres aux gestes cassés. Seul, l'enfant apparaissait, monté sur la galerie, derrière les tourbillons de buée blanche, l'air ravi, la bouche fendue par la joie d'avoir déchaîné cet ouragan." (*G*, III 1413–1414)
[497] Cf. chapter II, 2.

against the overground representation of the pit's weather technology. The anarchist Souvarine manages to short-circuit this tripartite fight over the weather in order to create the most devastating destruction of the pit: he uses the natural power of Le Torrent for his anarchic action. By manipulating the shaft lining, causing the waters of Le Torrent to enter the pit, he unchains enormous forces that bring about a catastrophe, flooding and collapsing the coal-pit and killing many miners. Were it not for Jeanlin's little (be it morally corrupted and beastly) paradise and his embodying the desire for and instinct of re-appropriating *some* agency over the climate to which one is exposed, the novel would tell a rather disillusioning story. Both the strikers' violent weather and Souvarine's anarchic and quite cynical unchaining of the natural forces underground lead to an outbreak of blind violence, a violence fuelled by resentment that Zola shows apparently leads nowhere, as it brings about no changes for a better future. The battle of weathers has, however, no final winner: on the contrary, the very notion of weather contains the instability of forces fighting against each other. Balances are always shifting, without being predictable nor controllable: neither for the revolutionists nor the capitalists.

4.3 The department store – a weather machine

When Denise risks a first glance into the interior of the department store called 'Le Bonheur des Dames', into this bright and attractive place that differs so markedly from the gloomy and damp neighbourhood of the old little boutiques, it is not so much the luxury of the commodities that draws her attention; the manifold impressions rather condense into one metaphoric and perhaps quite surprising 'vision':

> Through windows dimmed with condensation she could make out a vague profusion of lights, the confused interior of a factory. Behind the curtain of rain this vision, distant and blurred, seemed like some giant stokehold, in which the black shadows of the stokers could be seen moving against the red fire of the furnaces. (*eLP*, 27–28)[498]

This vision ties in well with the climatic difference between the old and the new Paris we have analysed above, one cold, damp and dark, the other of a fiery heat. The "vision" of the department store as a factory or a great machine, whose furnaces have to be constantly heated in order to ensure its working properly is however of greater importance: Zola keeps coming back to this vision all the

---

498 "C'était, à travers les glaces pâlies d'une buée, un pullulement vague de clartés, tout un intérieur confus d'usine. Derrière le rideau de pluie qui tombait, cette apparition, reculée, brouillée, prenait l'apparence d'une chambre de chauffe géante, où l'on voyait passer les ombres noires des chauffeurs, sur le feu rouge des chaudières." (*BD*, III 414)

way through the novel, it is established as the store's emblematic metaphor. For instance, the last procedures at the end of a day of sales are described as the "final movement of the overheated machine [*dernier branle de la machine surchauffée*]" (*eLP*, 117),[499] and during the "summer slack season" (*eLP*, 153)[500]

> the factories lay idle, the workers were deprived of their daily bread; and this took place with the unfeeling motion of a machine [*le branle indifférent de la machine*] – the useless cog was calmly thrown aside, like an iron wheel to which no gratitude is shown for services rendered. (*eLP*, 154)[501]

The protagonist and owner of the store Octave Mouret is constantly haunted by the worst of his fears, the fear of feeling "his great machine coming to a standstill and growing cold beneath him." (*eLP*, 95)[502] Although Octave does all he can to heat his store's furnaces, he, like the theatre manager Bordenave in *Nana*, is dependent on his 'audience', which brings in the essential heat from the streets of Paris. Only when he hears the crowd of shoppers arrive, can he be sure that during this day his machine will reach its perfect operating temperature:

> And he could no longer have any doubt about the sounds arriving from outside, the rattle of cabs, the banging of doors, the growing babble of the crowd. Beneath his feet he felt the machine being set in motion, warming up and coming to life again [...]. (*eLP*, 99)[503]

Octave has, like Bordenave, certainly contributed to this swarming in of the crowd: "Newspapers and walls were plastered with advertisements, and the public was assailed as if by a monstrous brass trumpet relentlessly amplifying the noise of the great sales to the four corners of the globe" (*eLP*, 392);[504] the crowd that the store attracts is "a crowd warmed [*une foule chauffée*] by a month of advertising" (*eLP*, 390; transl. altered).[505] This strategy of metaphorical heating

---

[499] "[...] dernier branle de la machine surchauffée [...]." (*BD*, III 500)
[500] "Quand la morte-saison d'été fut venue, un vent de panique souffla au *Bonheur des Dames*." (*BD*, III 534)
[501] "L'usine chômait, on supprimait le pain aux ouvriers ; et cela passait dans le branle indifférent de la machine, le rouage inutile était tranquillement jeté de côté, ainsi qu'une roue de fer à laquelle on ne garde aucune reconnaissance des services rendus." (*BD*, III 535)
[502] "Mouret, indigné d'avoir peur, croyait sentir sa grande machine s'immobiliser et se refroidir sous lui." (*BD*, III 479)
[503] "Et il ne se trompait plus aux bruits qui lui arrivaient du dehors, roulements de fiacres, claquement de portières, brouhaha grandissant de foule. Il sentait, à ses pieds, la machine se mettre en branle, s'échauffer et revivre [...]." (*BD*, III 482)
[504] "C'était l'envahissement définitif des journaux, des murs, des oreilles du public, comme une monstrueuse trompette d'airain, qui, sans relâche, soufflait aux quatre coins de la terre le vacarme des grandes mises en vente." (*BD*, III 763)
[505] "[...] une foule chauffée par un mois de réclame [...]." (*BD*, III 761)

is accompanied by the quite excessive 'real' heating of the building: "It was very warm under the covered galleries; the heat was that of a hothouse, moist and close, laden with the insipid smell of the materials [...]." (eLP, 242)[506] The economic calculus behind the store's temperature management seems to work out, as Zola shows with regard to a group of shoppers whose experiences and emotions he describes during a day of sales:

> But a feeling of well-being was stealing over them; they felt they were entering spring after leaving the winter of the street. Whereas outside the icy wind of sleet storms was blowing, in the galleries of the Paradise the warm summer months had already arrived, with the light materials, the flowery brilliance of soft shades, and the rustic gaiety of summer dresses and parasols. (eLP, 241)[507]

As Edward Welch writes, "the store creates a parallel universe to the world outside. It has its own distinct climate, shoppers leaving a wintry breeze to enter a realm of perpetual spring or summer" (2003, 44). With regard to its constantly warm temperature the store thus lives up to its paradisiac name.

The climate that Octave Mouret creates in his store is however not limited to the generous use of the building's central heating. Octave ingenuously adds commodities to the store's assortment that have an effect on the store's climate, that transport the exotic warmth and even the sunny smell of the Orient to the wintry Paris and that distinguish the interior of his *Paradise* from its cold and damp surroundings:

> Turkey, Arabia, Persia, the Indies were all there. Palaces had been emptied, mosques and bazars plundered. Tawny gold was the dominant tone in the worn antique carpets, and their faded tints retained a sombre warmth, the smelting of some extinguished furnace, with the beautiful burnt hue of an old master. Visions of the Orient floated beneath the luxury of this barbarous art, amid the strong odour which the old wools had retained from lands of vermin and sun. (eLP, 88)[508]

---

506 "Sous les galeries couvertes, il faisait très chaud, une chaleur de serre, moite et enfermée, chargée de l'odeur fade des tissus, et dans laquelle s'étouffait le piétinement de la foule." (*BD*, III 620)

507 "Mais un bien-être les envahissait, il leur semblait entrer dans le printemps, au sortir de l'hiver de la rue. Tandis que, dehors, soufflait le vent glacé des giboulées, déjà la belle saison, dans les galeries du *Bonheur*, s'attiédissait avec les étoffes légères, l'éclat fleuri des nuances tendres, la gaieté champêtre des modes d'été et des ombrelles." (*BD*, III 619)

508 "La Turquie, l'Arabie, la Perse, les Indes étaient là. On avait vidé les palais, dévalisé les mosquées et les bazars. L'or fauve dominait, dans l'effacement des tapis anciens, dont les teintes fanées gardaient une chaleur sombre, un fondu de fournaise éteinte, d'une belle couleur cuite de vieux maître. Et des visions d'Orient flottaient sous le luxe de cet art barbare, au milieu de l'odeur forte que les vieilles laines avaient gardée du pays de la vermine et du soleil." (*BD*, III 471)

Furthermore, Mouret has also found a way to make the less exotic, the traditional range of goods contribute to the store's very own, spectacular climate. He and his employees arrange these commodities to form artful compositions, creating weather phenomena like the "wild cataract" of the silk department that crowns the sales of winter fashion:

> At the far end of the hall, around one of the small cast-iron columns which supported the glass roof, material was streaming down like a bubbling sheet of water, falling from above and spreading out on to the floor. First, pale satins and soft silks were gushing out: royal satins and renaissance satins, with the pearly shades of spring water; light silks as transparent as crystal – Nile green, turquoise, blossom pink, Danube blue. Next came the thicker fabrics, the marvellous satins and the duchess silks, in warm shades, rolling in great waves. And at the bottom, as if in a fountain-basin, the heavy materials, the damasks, the brocades, the silver and gold silks, were sleeping on a deep bed of velvets – velvets of all kinds, black, white, coloured, embossed on a background of silk or satin, their shimmering flecks forming a still lake in which reflections of the sky and of the countryside seemed to dance. Women pale with desire were leaning over as if to look at themselves. Faced with this wild cataract, they all remained standing there, filled with the secret fear of being caught up in the overflow of all this luxury [*le débordement d'un pareil luxe*] and with an irresistible desire to throw themselves into it and be lost. (*eLP*, 103–104)[509]

With this composition of materials Mouret does not merely reproduce or simulate a classical weather phenomenon, a phenomenon found in nature that is now represented in a different setting. This "wild cataract" of materials has the very same effect on the shoppers as the rushing waters of the inundated valley had on Goethe's Werther: "the desire to throw themselves into it and be lost", "the bliss of [...] roaring away like the waves!" (123)[510] Obviously this is what

---

[509] "A la soie, la foule était aussi venue. [...] C'était, au fond du hall, autour d'une des colonnettes de fonte qui soutenaient le vitrage, comme un ruissellement d'étoffe, une nappe bouillonnée tombant de haut et s'élargissant jusqu'au parquet. Des satins clairs et des soies tendres jaillissaient d'abord : les satins à la reine, les satins renaissance, aux tons nacrés d'eau de source ; les soies légères aux transparences de cristal, vert Nil, ciel indien, rose de mai, bleu Danube. Puis, venaient des tissus plus forts, les satins merveilleux, les soies duchesse, teintes chaudes, roulant à flots grossis. Et, en bas, ainsi que dans une vasque, dormaient les étoffes lourdes, les armures façonnées, les damas, les brocarts, les soies perlées et lamées, au milieu d'un lit profond de velours, tous les velours, noirs, blancs, de couleur, frappés à fond de soie ou de satin, creusant avec leurs taches mouvantes un lac immobile où semblaient danser des reflets de ciel et de paysage. Des femmes, pâles de désirs, se penchaient comme pour se voir. Toutes, en face de cette cataracte lâchée, restaient debout, avec la peur sourde d'être prises dans le débordement d'un pareil luxe et avec l'irrésistible envie de s'y jeter et de s'y perdre." (*BD*, III 487)
[510] "Ach! Mit offenen Armen stand ich gegen den Abgrund, und athmete hinab! hinab, und verlohr mich in der Wonne, all meine Quaalen all mein Leiden da hinab zu stürmen, dahin zu brausen wie die Wellen." (194)

Octave Mouret indeed wants his customers to do: he wants them to be "caught up in the overflow of all this luxury", he wants them to lose control and drown in the mass of items they buy and carry home – despite the fact that they often neither need nor are really able to afford what they acquire. Octave's store is not only a machine that has to be metaphorically heated to work properly and to produce the best of results; it is a weather-machine: the customers are exposed to the well-calculated violence of the store's climate which is not as cosy as it looks. It rather aims at infecting the shoppers with the store's excessive weather conditions, at inducing them to become part of this weather, to give in to the desire of losing themselves in "the overflow of all this luxury" and to fall prey to the excesses of shopping fever.

Mouret's composition of the cataract of materials is topped once more by an arrangement he comes up with for the re-opening of the store after its extension:

> It was the stupendous sight of the great exhibition of white which had caused the ladies to stop. First of all, surrounding them, there was the entrance hall, with bright mirrors, and paved with mosaics, in which displays of inexpensive goods were drawing the voracious crowd. Then there were the galleries, dazzling in their whiteness like a polar vista, a snowy expanse unfolding with the endlessness of steppes draped with ermine, a mass of glaciers lit up beneath the sun. It was the same whiteness as that displayed in the outside windows, but heightened and on a colossal scale, burning from one end of the enormous nave to the other with the white blaze of a conflagration at its height. There was nothing but white, all the white goods from every department, an orgy of white [...]. (*eLP*, 397; transl. altered)[511]

The climate of the "polar vista", of the "snowy expanse" into which Mouret has turned the complete building tells us a lot about the working of the meteorotopos department store. As this short introductory paragraph already insinuates (pages of detailed description are to follow) the climatic conditions inside Octave Mouret's store are highly paradoxical: extreme cold and extreme heat seem to coexist without any problems. The phenomenon of "a mass of glaciers lit up beneath the sun", although already containing both notions of hot and cold,

---

511 "Ce qui arrêtait ces dames, c'était le spectacle prodigieux de la grande exposition de blanc. Autour d'elles, d'abord, il y avait le vestibule, un hall aux glaces claires, pavé de mosaïques, où les étalages à bas pris retenaient la foule vorace. Ensuite, les galeries s'enfonçaient, dans une blancheur éclatante, une échappée boréale, toute une contrée de neige, déroulant l'infini des steppes tendues d'hermine, l'entassement des glaciers allumés sous le soleil. On retrouvait le blanc des vitrines du dehors, mais avivé, colossal, brûlant d'un bout à l'autre de l'énorme vaisseau, avec la flambée blanche d'un incendie en plein feu. Rien que du blanc, tous les articles blancs de chaque rayon, une débauche de blanc, un astre blanc dont le rayonnement fixe aveuglait d'abord, sans qu'on pût distinguer les détails, au milieu de cette blancheur unique." (*BD*, III 768)

may still evoke the semblance of a phenomenon to be found in nature; the narrator's associations of all the whiteness with a "burning [...] white blaze of a conflagration at its height [*la flambée blanche d'un incendie en plein feu*]", however, upsets the understanding of Mouret's arrangements as quasi-realistic representations of 'nature'. He does not bring 'pieces of nature', weather phenomena, from elsewhere to Paris in order to make his meteorotopos emulate the effect these phenomena have on the human beings exposed to them. He does not want his customers to marvel and freeze at the sight of the sublime "polar vista" he has created for them. He does not want them to share the polar explorers' "fear of being caught up" in the icy desert. On the contrary, his project is paradoxically to use the "polar vista" to fire up his customers "irresistible desire to throw themselves into it and be lost". As the imagery of the "burning white blaze" signifies, Octave stokes up his machine with this icy arrangement, and it is thus not marring his project at all that the store's temperature does not seem to fit the decorations:

> Along the fretwork of the iron frames, all up the staircases, and on the suspension bridges, there was an endless procession of little figures, as if lost among snowy mountain peaks. The suffocating hothouse heat which confronted them on those glacial heights came as a surprise. The buzz of voices made a deafening noise like a swiftly flowing river. (*eLP*, 399)[512]

On the contrary, the customers' reaction, their "buzz of voices" shows that Octave's seemingly paradoxical weather-machine is working perfectly well: it does not represent or copy weather as realistically as possible, its purpose is to make the weather. The store's arrangement, with its polar vista presented in a "suffocating hothouse heat" successfully draws the customers into its climate, makes them lose themselves and become part of the meteorotopos, signalled by the "deafening noise" they are producing, the noise of "a swiftly flowing river".

It is however not only the customers that are infected by the weather Octave Mouret creates in his department store. Zola himself can be said to have fallen for it. Defying the notion of narrative economy he dedicates several pages of orgiastic description to prove that, indeed, the "orgy of white" includes "all the white goods from every department". It is not just "lengths of linen, calico, and

---

[512] "Dans les découpures des charpentes de fer, le long des escaliers, sur les ponts volants, c'était ensuite une ascension sans fin de petites figures, comme égarées au milieu de pics neigeux. Une chaleur de serre, suffocante, surprenait, en face de ces hauteurs glacées. Le bourdonnement des voix faisait un bruit énorme de fleuve qui charrie." (*BD*, III 770)

muslin, hanging in sheets, like falls of snow" (*eLP*, 393),[513] but also "infants' vests made of fluffy quilting, flannel hoods, chemises, and bonnets no bigger than toys, and christening robes, and cashmere shawls, the white down of birth like a shower of fine white feathers." (*eLP*, 410)[514] The silk department, decorated "like a huge bedroom dedicated to love, hung with white by the whim of a woman in love who, snowy in her nudity, wished to compete on whiteness" (*eLP*, 413)[515] forms part of the grand composition of the snow expanse as well as the silk department:

> The department had been transformed into a white chapel. Tulle and guipure lace were falling from above, forming a white sky, as if veiled by clouds, its flimsy gossamer paling the early morning sun. Round the columns flounces of Mechlin and Valenciennes lace were hanging down like the white skirts of ballerinas, falling to the ground in a shiver of whiteness. And everywhere, on all the counters, there was a snowy whiteness, Spanish blond-lace as light as air, Brussels appliqué with large flowers on fine mesh, needle-point and Venetian lace with heavier designs, Alençon and Bruges lace of regal and almost religious richness. (*eLP*, 419–420)[516]

Zola surely unmasks Octave Mouret's seemingly paradoxical strategy of seducing his customers by using the colour of innocence and purity to celebrate an "orgy of white" (cf. Vinken 1995, 258–259). Doubling his heating with ice and snow, Mouret seduces with innocence and purity, by merging bedroom and chapel, religion and sensuality. Zola vividly suggests the 'insincerity' of this arrangement, which itself quite ostentatiously exposes the fact that it does not and cannot refer to anything real or substantial behind its alluring façade with its composition of opposing extremes. Despite its obvious 'falseness' (there is neither 'authentic' pureness, nor 'authentic' coldness 'behind' the signifier 'white'), Octave Mouret's tempting weather simulation works: so much so that Zola's 'unmasking' glance beyond the 'façade' of the attractive arrangement, unveiling that the 'white' is part of the seductive strategy, that it contributes to

---

[513] "[…] des pièces de toile, de calicot, de mousseline, tombant en nappe, pareilles à des éboulements de neige […]." (*BD*, III 764)

[514] "[…] des brassières en piqué pelucheux, des béguins en flanelle, des chemises et des bonnets grands comme des joujoux, et des robes de baptême, et des pelisses de cachemire, le duvet blanc de naissance, pareil à une pluie fine de plumes blanches […]." (*BD*, III 781)

[515] "Le rayon des soieries était comme une grande chambre d'amour, drapée de blanc par un caprice d'amoureuse à la nudité de neige, voulant lutter de blancheur." (*BD*, III 784)

[516] "On avait changé le rayon en une chapelle blanche. Des tulles, des guipures tombant de haut, faisaient un ciel blanc, un de ces voiles de nuages dont le fin réseau pâlit le soleil matinal. Autour des colonnes, descendaient des volants de malines et de valenciennes, des jupes blanches de danseuse, déroulées en un frisson blanc, jusqu'à terre. Puis, de toutes parts, sur tous le comptoirs, le blanc neigeait […]." (*BD*, III 790)

the infecting weather, draws on the very energy that entangles the customers in the weathery violence of the meteorotopos. Were it not a narratological, metaleptic paradox, we could say that Mouret's weathery arrangement also heats up Zola's narration, bringing about an "orgy in white" in the form of an endless description of all sorts of white materials. The narrator is seized by the weathery power that his descriptions narrate and attribute to an intradiegetic, calculated simulation. The gesture of uncovering turns into an act of self-infection (Pellini 2003, 22), carrying the contamination on to his readers and – on to us. The luring fascination (Vinken 1997, 615) kindled by narrating and disclosing the fascination that others fall prey to opens up an intricate mise-en-abîme trap. Zola's buying into the aesthetic excitation of Octave Mouret's weathery arrangements cannot but show the inevitability of and the helplessness with which one encounters this fetishistic fascination. It supports Barbara Vinken's dictum that the core of naturalism is actually fetishism (Vinken 1996, 221).

Octave Mouret's weathery installations (the "wild cataract" of materials or the "polar vista") form part of the meteorotopos department store, they are an important cog in the weather-machine. The fact, however, that the weather-machine is working, cannot be demonstrated by merely analysing these installations: regarded by themselves, they are static; the weather they *represent* is not to be mixed up with the actual weather this meteorotopos *produces* (cf. Deleuze and Guattari 1972). The weather Octave Mouret tries to create by heating up his store, by firing its furnaces (and that is also to say by arranging its items in the spectacular way he does) is characterised by a violent dynamic that brings all that is present in the shop into the fastest of circulations and thereby maximises turnover. It is thus the crowd itself that has to be observed in order to get an idea of the weather in the store:

> A compact mass of heads was surging through the arcades, spreading out like an overflowing river [*fleuve débordé*] into the middle of the hall. [...] The great afternoon rush-hour had arrived, when the overheated machine led the dance of customers, extracting money from their very flesh. (*eLP*, 108)[517]

Zola here exhibits an association that is at the centre of my whole argument: the heating of the machine is thermodynamically linked to the violent movement of the weather. In other words, by (over)heating the machine Octave Mouret produces the violent weather of the crowd "spreading out like an overflowing river". It is this important juncture that links the *Rougon-Macquart*'s dominant

---

[517] "Une houle compacte de têtes roulait sous les galeries, s'élargissant en fleuve débordé au milieu du hall. [...] L'heure était venue du branle formidable de l'après-midi, quand la machine surchauffée menait la danse des clientes et leur tirait l'argent de la chair." (*BD*, III 491–492)

theme and the imagery of the steam engine and of heating in general (examined extensively by Michel Serres (1975) and Jacques Noiray (1981)) with the theme of (violent) weather that we are investigating in this study. The association of heat with the weather's dynamic is one of the basic intuitions from which the theory of thermodynamics departed:

> To heat also are due the vast movements which take place on the earth. It causes the agitations of the atmosphere, the ascension of clouds, the fall of rain and of meteors, the currents of water which channel the surface of the globe, and of which man has thus far employed but a small portion. Even earthquakes and volcanic eruptions are the result of heat. (Carnot 1897, 37–38)[518]

This passage is taken from the first pages of Sadi Carnot's ground-breaking study entitled *Réflexions sur la puissance motrice du feu et sur les machines propres à développer cette puissance*, which can be regarded as the foundation of the theory of thermodynamics. I would maintain that the thermodynamic discovery of the transformability of thermic energy into motive power is of crucial importance for Zola's *Rougon-Macquart*. This discovery forms the juncture between the 'warming global climate' that Zola, as we have seen, diagnoses for the Second Empire and this world's increasing "dynamism" (Nelson 1977, 30, Rochecouste 1988, 121), and consequently its increasingly heavy weather that in turn leads towards climate-catastrophe, to the apocalyptic end of this world.

Octave Mouret's store, as a weather-machine, emblematically exemplifies this thermodynamic procedure: Octave stokes the furnace of this machine (metaphorically by promotion and spectacular installations, literally by heating up the store's air) and what he, thermodynamically, "causes" are indeed "agitations of the atmosphere", "ascension of clouds" and "currents of water which channel the surface of the globe":

> the eddy of the crowd continued endlessly, its dual stream of entry and exit making itself felt as far as the silk department [...]. This sea of multi-coloured hats, of bare heads, both fair and dark, was flowing from one end of the gallery to the other [...]. (*eLP*, 250)[519]

---

[518] "C'est à la chaleur que doivent être attribués les grands mouvements qui frappent nos regards sur la terre ; c'est à elle que sont dues les agitations de l'atmosphère, l'ascension des nuages, la chute des pluies et des autres météores, les courants d'eau qui sillonnent la surface du globe et dont l'homme est parvenu à employer pour son usage une faible partie ; enfin les tremblements de terre, les éruptions volcaniques reconnaissent aussi pour cause la chaleur." (Carnot 1878 [1824], 1–2)

[519] "[...] le remous de la foule, dont le double courant d'entrée et de sortie se faisait sentir jusqu'au rayon de la soie [...]. Et cette mer, ces chapeaux bariolés, ces cheveux nus, blonds ou noirs, roulaient d'un bout de la galerie à l'autre [...]." (*BD*, III 627)

By focalising on a customer, Mme Desforges, fighting her way through the store during a day of sales, Zola illustrates that it is almost impossible "to avoid being carried away by the stream of people" (*eLP*, 253).[520] The story of the sales is a story of the weathery natural forces that Octave releases in his store. The nautical topos of "flowing" streams, of a "sea of hats" or an "ocean of heads" (*eLP*, 253)[521] is dominant for relating the violent dynamic of the crowd. Moreover, the crowd cannot only be described as a weathery phenomenon: this is how it feels to be in the middle of it. When Mme Desforges, tossed about amidst it, closed her eyes, "she found herself even more conscious of the crowd because of the muffled sound of a rising tide it was making, and the human warmth it gave off" (*eLP*, 254).[522] The violent forces at work in the crowd spread throughout the whole building: "In the living vibration of the whole shop, the iron supports were perceptibly moving underfoot, as if trembling at the breath of the crowd." (*eLP*, 253)[523] This is important to note because the weather produced in the meteorotopos department store is not merely a phenomenon of a socio-psychical dynamic; it is not only human beings that get caught up in the violent weather of flows, streams and oceans but also the commodities of the shop:

> The counter was overflowing [*débordait*]; [Mme de Boves] was plunging her hands into the growing cascade of pillow lace, Mechlin lace, Valenciennes, Chantilly, her fingers trembling with desire, her face gradually warming with sensual joy; while Blanche, by her side, possessed by the same passion, was very pale, her flesh soft and puffy. (*eLP*, 110)[524]

The imagery used to narrate the circulation of the materials is exactly the same as that found in the description of the dynamic of the crowd. The crowd's "dual stream of entry and exit" finds a mirroring counterpart in the "endless flow" of commodities circulating mostly behind the scenes, entering the building through a "yawning trap" in order to be sold and carried out of the shop again as quickly as possible:

---

[520] "Alors, précédée de Denise, Mme Desforges monta lentement l'escalier. Il lui fallait s'arrêter toutes les trois secondes, pour ne pas être emportée par le flot qui descendait." (*BD*, III 630)
[521] "[...] un océan de têtes [...]." (*BD*, III 631)
[522] "[...] c'était, lorsqu'elle fermait les paupières, de sentir davantage la foule, à son bruit sourd de marée montante et à la chaleur humaine qu'elle exhalait [...]." (*BD*, III 631)
[523] "Dans la vibration vivante de la maison entière, les limons de fer avaient sous les pieds un branle sensible, comme tremblant aux haleines de la foule." (*BD*, III 630)
[524] "Le comptoir débordait, [Mme de Boves] plongeait les mains dans ce flot montant de guipures, de malines, de valenciennes, de chantilly, les doigts tremblants de désir, le visage peu à peu chauffé d'une joie sensuelle ; tandis que Blanche, près d'elle, travaillée de la même passion, était très pâle, la chair soufflée et molle." (*BD*, III 493)

Everything entered through this yawning trap; things were being swallowed up all the time, a continual cascade of materials falling with the roar of a river. During big sales especially, the chute would discharge an endless flow into the basement, silks from Lyons, woollens from England, linens from Flanders, calicoes from Alsace, prints from Rouen [...] streaming like rain from some spring higher up. (*eLP*, 36–37)[525]

The "roar of a river" of materials clearly equals the crowd's "deafening noise" of "a swiftly flowing river", the "overflowing river" of shoppers corresponds to the "overflowing counter" and the "cascade of materials". The flow of materials and the flow of customers (the flow of money would have to be added!) are not only similar, they are not only narrated in an analogous manner, they form part of the same setting. Furthermore, the similarity of the weather imagery indicates that both flows or streams are to be located on the same plane; neither of the two can claim a privileged position with regard to the other. Both are parts and products of Octave Mouret's weather machine. The meteorotopos department store thus provides us with a perfect example of Zola's weathery conception of milieu and the role that 'the human' plays in this constellation: the shop's milieu brings together different elements (human beings, commodities, money) and makes these disparate elements communicate and interact. Instead of resorting to the physico-chemical conditions that his idol Claude Bernard uses to bridge the boundary between the animate and the inanimate, Zola constructs a different medium: a medium of weather, of flows, streams, cascades, of weathery forces. In a way this choice, on the one hand, favours the abstract, it is as alien to the commodities (that are 'things') as to the human beings and their motivations and intentions. On the other hand, it is the seeming abstractness of the medium that makes the observation of the communication or interaction possible. By abstracting from the privileged access via the human individual and its instrumental, rational or psychological approach to the world and its objects Zola introduces an approach to the interaction of the disparate and to the mutual effects brought about when the disparate communicates. It is, for example, not desire that drives the customers into the store and that can consequently be singled out as the actual, the anthropological, individual or trans-individual starting point, as the 'Ur-Sache' of the whole dynamic process. The narrator makes it quite clear that Mme de Bove's pleasure is an effect of her contact with the flow of materials: she "was plunging her

---

[525] "Tous les arrivages entraient par cette trappe béante ; c'était un engouffrement continu, une chute d'étoffes qui tombait avec un ronflement de rivière. Aux époques de grande vente surtout, la glissoire lâchait dans le sous-sol un flot intarissable, les soieries de Lyon, les lainages d'Angleterre, les toiles des Flandres, les calicots d'Alsace, les indiennes de Rouen [...] ruisseler en pluie d'une source supérieure." (*BD*, III 422)

hands into the growing cascade of pillow lace, Mechlin lace, Valenciennes, Chantilly, her fingers trembling with desire, her face gradually warming with sensual joy". This is the way the meteorotopos department store and its milieu work: it is a place of intensive interaction, where a "growing cascade" has an effect of "gradually warming" the customers, who, themselves, flow through the shop with the increasing violence of flows and streams. Octave Mouret's capitalistic success feeds upon these violent forces set free in the shop, because increasing the violence and the speed of circulation increases his turnover.

The way Zola reconstructs how the department store works allows him to show that its success is not due to a superior economic calculus that would ensure its functioning to the end of time. The interaction of disparate forces that produces this success (interaction of human beings in a crowd, interaction with commodities) does not provide a stable or rational ground. The department store is a phenomenon of its time; even more so, it is a weather phenomenon that derives its relative stability from the climate of the Second Empire.

Of all the *Rougon-Macquart*'s meteorotopoi, the department store exhibits the most obvious and the most aggressive relation to its surroundings. Octave Mouret very calculatedly locates some of the selling beyond the shop's boundaries: "bargains and remnants [...] were displayed right into the street" (*eLP*, 239).[526] The strategy is obviously successful since "[i]n spite of the cold weather, the assistants who were selling to the crowd on the pavement could not serve fast enough." (*eLP*, 240)[527] It is obviously not the profit he draws from selling cheap goods on the pavement that Mouret is after; he aims at attracting people to the proximity of his shop. Once the potential customers have been lured close enough to the actual building, they enter the store's sphere of influence, which exceeds its architectonic boundaries. Irresistibly, the prospective customers will be "caught up and carried away by the wind of the crowd" (*eLP*, 240; transl. altered):[528]

> Caught in the current, the ladies were no longer able to turn back. As rivers draw together the stray waters of a valley, so it seemed that the stream of customers, flowing through the entrance hall, was drinking in the passers-by from the street, sucking in the population from the four corners of Paris. They were advancing very slowly, jammed so tightly that

---

[526] "Mouret ait calculé juste : toutes les ménagères, une troupe serrée de petites bourgeoises et de femmes en bonnet, donnaient assaut aux occasions, aux soldes et aux coupons, étalés jusque dans la rue." (*BD*, III 617)

[527] "Malgré le temps froid, les commis qui vendaient au plein air du pavé ne pouvaient suffire." (*BD*, III 617)

[528] "Cependant, leurs yeux ne quittaient pas la porte, [Mme de Boves, Mme Marty and their daughters] elles étaient prises et emportées dans le vent de la foule." (*BD*, III 618)

they could hardly breathe, held upright by shoulders and stomachs, whose flabby warmth thy could feel; and their satisfied desire revelled in this painful approach, which inflamed their curiosity even more. (*eLP*, 240–241)[529]

The weathery forces seize the customers and immediately make them become part of the climate of the place, part of the crowd whose interaction (the warmth, the touch) incites the shopping-fever for which there is no rational explanation: the weather works by self-strengthening loops, cause and effect, victim and culprit cannot be clearly separated. In a way "the monster" (*eLP*, 49)[530] of the shop thus swallows its customers as the monstrous mine 'Le Voreux' does the miners. Its prosperous functioning is however not without consequences: the "monster" shop continually and rapidly devours and grows: like the desperate competitors of the old, small boutiques the readers see "the rival [i.e. the 'Le Bonheur des Dames'] gradually growing, at first disdained, then equal in importance, then overflowing [*débordante*], threatening" (*eLP*, 26; transl. altered).[531] The weather of the meteorotopos department store is thus not only exceeding its boundaries in order to draw buyers, inside, its excessive forces are also violently directed against its rivals outside, 'colonising' them (Vedder 2013, 361), with the same goal of devouring. As noted above, the department store is itself a weather phenomenon of violent natural force that is familiar to all its competitors: they have all felt "the breath/wind [*souffle*] of the new way of business", and secretly they all know that it is useless "to resist such a powerful current, which would carry all before it" (*eLP*, 195; transl. altered).[532]

The novel relates the violent force of this weather-machine that grows continuously, "overflowing" the world around it, that feeds on what it draws into its circulation, on what it infects, ruins and devours. "[T]his force which was transforming Paris" (*eLP*, 199)[533] acts indeed, as Zola's so consistent weather

---

[529] "Ces dames, saisies par le courant, ne pouvaient plus reculer. Comme les fleuves tirent à eux les eaux errantes d'une vallée, il semblait que le flot des clientes, coulant à plein vestibule, buvait les passants de la rue, aspirait la population des quatre coins de Paris. Elles n'avançaient que très lentement, serrées à perdre haleine, tenues debout par des épaules et des ventres, dont elles sentaient la molle chaleur ; et leur désir satisfait jouissait de cette approche pénible, qui fouettait davantage leur curiosité." (*BD*, III 618)

[530] "[...] le monstre [...]." (*BD*, III 434)

[531] "[Mme Baudu] avait eu la continuelle souffrance de voir grandir peu à peu la maison rivale, d'abord dédaignée, puis égale en importance, puis débordante, menaçante." (*BD*, III 412)

[532] "Souvent [Robineau] avait senti ce souffle du commerce nouveau, cette évolution dont parlait [Denise] ; et il se demandait, aux heurs de vision nette, pourquoi vouloir résister à un courant d'une telle énergie, qui emportait tout." (*BD*, III 374–375)

[533] "[...] cette force qui transformait Paris [...]." (*BD*, III 579)

imagery suggests, as a natural force. Its "powerful current" sweeps away the old boutiques and expands the reach of its influence to transform a city. It acts as a natural force because it is not subjected to any sort of controlling human agency. This is the main message in Zola's description of this force in terms of weather; although Octave Mouret successfully exploits this irresistible force, he cannot control it, he will never have an instrumental relation to these forces. On each day of sales he anxiously waits for the crowd to flood his store – the 'weather-event' has to just happen, Octave can neither be sure *that* it will happen nor can he on this very day do anything about it. Certainly, he knows about or rather senses the Second Empire's special climate, he very expertly creates the best conditions to profit from this climate. The weather of his meteorotopos is, however, not at all in his hands. On the contrary, Octave Mouret is, like his rivals, at the mercy of this indomitable force, only his strategic alliance with it distinguishes his position from that of his rivals. He is less a creator of weather, sitting, like Shakespeare in Herder's famous words high atop some craggy eminence, than a cunning meteorologist, using his astonishing capabilities of reading the current climatic trend to profit from it, to exploit it in the most effective way.

Zola's literary project of a "natural and social history" of the Second Empire rests on the supposition of this natural, elemental force driving the transformations that are taking place in this historical period. Rita Schober's reproach that Zola did not take the decisive step from nature to society, from the reign of nature to the reign of mankind (1979, 70) thus misses Zola's central point. In his *Rougon-Macquart* Zola does not share her simple nature/society divide. The violent, 'natural force' driving the transformations emerges, as we have seen, from a complex interaction of all kind of forces, including influences that are to a certain extent products of the 'reign of mankind', like technology or architecture. The complexity of these interactions cannot simply be theorised away. The dominant natural force emerging from these interactions is rather a product of that 'reign of mankind' than an atavistic remnant of a 'reign of nature' that could be overcome by human agency and the rational construction of a world.

For Zola there is no agency or alternative standpoint available that would escape this natural force. His novel is however not a gloomy and pessimistic complaint about a lost world. On the contrary, despite the violence and the suffering that this natural force of the new commerce brings about, the novel vehemently pleads for an affirmation of this force. Denise, the sympathetic protagonist, both affected by the suffering and at the same time fascinated by the attractive innovation, repeatedly weighs its pros and cons, finally becoming "full of enthusiasm [*se passionner pour*] for this force which was transforming

Paris" (eLP, 199):[534] "Wasn't she once more going to assist the machine which was crushing the poor? But it was as if she was being swept along by some invisible force; she felt that she was not doing wrong." (eLP, 231)[535] What must at first glance look like her simply giving in to this "invisible" force and losing her good judgment is quite early in the novel backed by an authorial comment by the narrator: "With her instinctive love of logic and life, she was secretly on the side of the big shops." (eLP, 194)[536] The weathery forces that Octave Mouret's department store sets free and that are transforming Paris are not an epiphenomenon that one could criticise as an aberration, a wrong development that would have to be steered against as Rita Schober would have it. These forces are not only of a violence that exceeds human control, they are also supported by "logic and life". In other words, according to the novel, both the 'reign of nature' and the 'reign of mankind' stoke the machine that produces the ominous weather. The historical development which it represents is therefore of such fundamentality that there seems to be only one, unattractive alternative: seclusion and waiting for death. The desperate struggle of the old boutiques must resemble Renée's father in his house, the Hôtel de Béraud. They resist – and although the moral intuition is on their side, their resistance against the historical transformation is in vain; it is but a representation of death.

4.4 The hothouse (effect)

Zola's second novel of the cycle, *La Curée*, is dominated by a meteorotopos that, at first glance, appears to differ markedly from those analysed thus far. In contrast to the washhouse, the bar, the coal-pit and the department store that are all public or workplaces, the hothouse of *La Curée* is part of a 'private' building, of the ominous Hôtel Saccard: "On the right was an enormous hothouse, built on to the side of the house and communicating with the ground floor through the glass door of a drawing room." (eK, 16)[537] It is therefore not a location characterised by the weather of flowing masses, but the location of the intimate encounter of the novel's protagonist Renée and her stepson Maxime:

---

[534] "Ce fut là qu'elle acheva de comprendre la puissance du nouveau commerce et de se passionner pour cette force qui transformait Paris." (*BD*, III 579)
[535] "N'allait-elle pas remettre la main à la machine qui écrasait le pauvre monde ? Mais elle se trouvait comme emportée par une force, elle sentait qu'elle ne faisait pas le mal." (*BD*, III 610)
[536] "Elle était secrètement pour les grands magasins, dans son amour instinctif de la logique et de la vie." (*BD*, III 574)
[537] "A droite, se trouvait une vaste serre, scellée a flanc même de l'hôtel, communiquant avec le rez-de-chaussée par la porte-fenêtre d'un salon." (*C*, I 332)

"the hothouse and its exotic flora provide a milieu in which incestuous passion is first imagined and then realized" (Braswell 2013, 81).

It is indeed at the moment when Renée for the first time explicitly imagines her incestuous passion for Maxime that the readers get an initial, extensive impression of the hothouse. Renée is standing in the middle of it, watching Maxime flirt with Louise in the neighbouring drawing room:

> Around her the hothouse, like the nave of a church with a domed glass roof supported by slender iron columns, displayed its rich vegetation, its mass of lush greenery, its spreading rockets of foliage. (eK, 37)[538]

In one of his characteristically endless and artful descriptions, Zola suggests that the milieu of the hothouse plays a decisive role for the love and the "keen, specific desire" that Renée feels growing within her:

> Endless love and voluptuous appetite pervaded this stifling nave in which seethed the ardent sap of the tropics. Renée was wrapped in the powerful bridals of the earth that gave birth to these dark growths, these colossal stamina; and the acrid birth-throes of this hotbed [mer de feu], of this forest growth, of this mass vegetation aglow with the entrails that nourished it, surrounded her with disturbing odours [chargés d'ivresse]. At her feet was the steaming tank, its tepid water thickened by the sap from the floating roots, enveloping her shoulders with a mantle of heavy vapours, forming a mist that warmed her skin like the touch of a hand moist with desire. Overhead she could smell the palm trees, whose tall leaves shook down their aroma. And more than the stifling heat, more than the brilliant light, more than the great dazzling flowers, like faces laughing or grimacing between the leaves, it was the odours that overwhelmed her. An indescribable perfume, potent, exciting, composed of a thousand different perfumes, hung about her; human exudation, the breath of women, the scent of hair; and breezes sweet and swooningly faint were blended with breezes coarse and pestilential, laden with poison. But amid this strange music of odours, the dominant melody that constantly returned, stifling the sweetness of the vanilla and the orchids' pungency, was the penetrating, sensual smell of flesh, the smell of lovemaking escaping in the early morning from the bedroom of newlyweds. (eK, 39)[539]

---

[538] "Autour d'elle, la serre chaude, pareille à une nef d'église, et dont de minces colonnettes de fer montaient d'un jet soutenir le vitrail cintré, étalait ses végétations grasses, ses nappes de feuilles puissantes, ses fusées épanouies de verdure." (C, I 354)

[539] "Maintenant un désir net, aigu, l'emplissait. Un amour immense, un besoin de volupté, flottait dans cette nef close, où bouillait la sève ardente des tropiques. La jeune femme était prise dans ces noces puissantes de la terre, qui engendraient autour d'elle ces verdures noires, ces tiges colossales ; et les couches âcres de cette mer de feu, cet épanouissement de forêt, ce tas de végétations, toutes brûlantes des entrailles qui les nourrissaient, lui jetaient des effluves troublants, chargés d'ivresse. A ses pieds, le basin, la masse d'eau chaude, épaissie par les sucs des racines flottantes, fumait, mettait à ses épaules un manteau de vapeurs lourdes, une buée qui lui chauffait la peau, comme l'attouchement d'une main moite de volupté. Sur sa tête, elle

The love and the appetite she feels is the "[e]ndless love and [the] voluptuous appetite" of the hothouse surrounding her. The hothouse is shown to be a location of 'hyper-nature', a "hotbed" of proliferating "growth" that the narrator connects with the theme of reproduction and sexuality: the scenery is one of the "powerful bridals of the earth", of conception and of giving birth. It is however not the highly suggestive imaginary power of the place that awakens Renée's desire; she is affected in a much more corporeal and immediate way. The climate of the hothouse approaches her, she is quickly "wrapped in the powerful bridals of the earth" and finds her shoulders "envelop[ed]" "with a mantle of heavy vapours, forming a mist that warmed her skin like the touch of a hand moist with desire". The climate of the hothouse infects her. It is characterised by "heavy vapours", "stifling heat" and "brilliant light", and thus resembles the tropical heat of the 'new Paris' that we already encountered in the washhouse, the kitchen of the Quenus, Bordenave's theatre, Nana's apartment or the re-decorated house of the Muffats.

The interaction taking place between Renée and the milieu of the hothouse surrounding her once more spells out the communication of the disparate that Zola's conceptualisation of milieu makes possible: the place's weather and the world of plants somehow metamorphose, bringing about 'human' affects[540] like "the touch of a hand moist with desire", "faces laughing or grimacing" and, most importantly, "human exudation, the breath of women, the scent of hair", "the penetrating, sensual smell of flesh, the smell of lovemaking". Before making love with her stepson Maxime in this hothouse, Renée makes love with the milieu of the hothouse itself, with its climate and its plants. The fact that the categorical difference between the human and the vegetal or even the meteorological does not prevent this encounter, that it does not even play any role for this encounter, is due to Zola's thinking of milieu as suspension of these boundaries. As the shoppers' desire in Octave Mouret's department store was provoked by the touch of the materials, Renée's love and appetite is kindled by

---

sentait le jet des Palmiers, les hauts feuillages secouant leur arôme. Et plus que l'étouffement chaud de l'air, plus que les clartés vives, plus que les fleurs larges, éclatantes, pareilles à des visages riant ou grimaçant entre les feuilles, c'étaient surtout les odeurs qui la brisaient. Un parfum indéfinissable, fort, excitant, traînait, fait de mille parfums : sueurs humaines, haleines de femmes, senteurs de chevelures ; et des souffles doux et fades jusqu'à l'évanouissement, étaient coupés par des souffles pestilentiels, rudes, chargés de poisons. Mais, dans cette musique étrange des odeurs, la phrase mélodique qui revenait toujours, dominant, étouffant les tendresses de la Vanille et les acuités des Orchidées, c'était cette odeur humaine, pénétrante, sensuelle, cette odeur d'amour qui s'échappe le matin de la chambre close de deux jeunes époux." (*C*, I 357)

540 For the Spinozist/Deleuzian way of conceptualising affects, see chapter three of my *Sexes of Winds and Packs* (2014).

her contact with the tropical climate of the hothouse. The speaking of the plants' and the weather's metamorphosis and their assuming some sort of 'human shape' must remain a rhetorical construction only; a construction that serves to formulate the interaction of the disparate which proves to be very difficult to conceive of and put into words. Zola emphasises the heuristic quality of this rhetorical construction by underlining that this interaction cannot merely be examined as a pseudo-human interaction, as a becoming-human of plants and weather, but also has to be regarded as a becoming-plant of Renée:

> Renée sank back slowly, leaning against the granite pedestal. In her green satin dress, her head and breast covered with the liquid glitter of her diamonds, she was like a great flower, green and pink, one of the water-lilies in the tank, swooning from the heat. In this moment of insight all her new resolutions vanished, the intoxication of dinner returned, imperious, triumphant, strengthened by the flames of the hothouse. She thought no longer of the soothing freshness of the night, of the murmuring shadows of the gardens, whose voices had whispered to her of the bliss of serenity. In her were aroused the senses of a woman who desires, the caprices of a woman who is satiated [blasée]. (eK, 40)[541]

The fact that Renée, and later also her stepson and lover Maxime, are related to have effectively become plants of the hothouse (Couillard 1978, 403) is no coincidence; it draws on one of the basic intuitions that had generated the notion of milieu and of its influence on 'beings' from the beginning. Hippolyte Taine's attempts to show the susceptibility of a people to the milieu surrounding it repeatedly comes back to the image of a plant and the climatic conditions in which it grows: "Thus it is with a people as with a plant" (Taine 1920, 22),[542] he writes and concludes that "[h]istory must search now-a-days for [the] rules of human vegetation" (Taine 1920, 33; transl. altered).[543] Zola repeatedly resorts to this image (also for both Albine and Désirée in *La Faute de l'abbé Mouret* (cf. Bertrand-Jennings 1980–1981, 96)), in order to emphasise and make intuitive the influences that the milieu (conceptualised as climate) exerts on the protagonists.

---

[541] "Renée, lentement, s'était adossée au socle de granit. Dans sa robe de satin vert, la gorge et la tête rougissantes, mouillées des gouttes claires de ses diamants, elle ressemblait à une grande fleur, rose et verte, à un des Nymphéa du bassin, pâmé par la chaleur. A cette heure de vision nette, toutes ses bonnes résolutions s'évanouissaient à jamais, l'ivresse du dîner remontait à sa tête, impérieuse, victorieuse, doublée par les flammes de la serre. Elle ne songeait plus aux fraîcheurs de la nuit qui l'avaient calmée, à ces ombres murmurantes du parc, dont les voix lui avaient conseillé la paix heureuse. Ses sens de femme ardente, ses caprices de femme blasée s'éveillaient." (C, I 357–358)
[542] "Il en est ici d'un peuple, comme d'une plante [...]." (Taine 1863, XXIX)
[543] "Ce sont ces règles de la végétation humaine que l'histoire à présent doit chercher." (Taine 1863, XLIII)

The hothouse as a meteorotopos confronts the lovers with an extreme, a tropical weather:

> The heat was suffocating, a sultry heat that did not fall from the sky in a rain of fire, but trailed on the ground like a poisonous exhalation, its steam rising like a storm-laden cloud. A warm dampness covered the lovers with dew, with burning perspiration. (*eK*, 157)[544]

The little detail on which this quotation ends, the fact that the "warm dampness" that covers the lovers oscillates ambivalently between "dew" (coming from 'without', from the climate of the hothouse) and "burning perspiration" (coming from 'within' the lovers) is telling: the warm dampness, like the incest itself, is a genuine product of an interaction of the lovers and the climate. Both dampness and incest are brought about by the specific conditions of the hothouse that are, as with all the other meteorotopoi, not independent from the actions and desires of the human beings that move and act there, and thereby contribute to the very conditions that they are subjected to:

> It was then, in the depths of this glass cage, boiling in the summer heat, lost in the keen December cold, that they relished their incest, as if it were the criminal fruit of an overheated soil, with the dull fear of this terrifying hotbed. (*eK*, 160)[545]

Zola very carefully stages the incest scene; he makes it occur in the winter season when the contrast of the weather outside, where "it was freezing terribly" (*eK*, 157; transl. altered), and the conditions inside the hothouse, which "was heated to such a point that Maxime fainted on the bearskin" (*eK*, 157),[546] is most obvious. As a consequence, there can be little doubt that the incest is the "fruit" of the hothouse's tropical climate, which seems to bring about another sort of 'perversion' as well: "It was in the hothouse especially that Renée assumed the masculine role." (*eK*, 158)[547] Gender trouble and incest must appear indeed as "the criminal fruit of an overheated soil", which associates the hothouse and its climate with pure negation, as Olivier Got writes, with moral, psychological

---

[544] "La chaleur était suffocante, une chaleur sombre, qui ne tombait pas du ciel en pluie de feu, mais qui traînait à terre, ainsi qu'une exhalaison malsaine, et dont la buée montait, pareille à un nuage chargé d'orage. Une humidité chaude couvrait les amants d'une rosée, d'une sueur ardente." (*C*, I 485)

[545] "C'était alors au fond de cette cage de verre, toute bouillante des flammes de l'été, perdue dans le froid clair de décembre, qu'ils goûtaient l'inceste, comme le fruit criminel d'une terre trop chauffée, avec la peur sourde de leur couche terrifiante." (*C*, I 488)

[546] "Au-dehors, il gelait terriblement, par un clair de lune limpide. Maxime était arrivé frissonnant, les oreilles et les doigts glacés. La serre se trouvait chauffée à un tel point, qu'il eut une défaillance, sur la peau de bête." (*C*, I 485)

[547] "Et c'était surtout dans la serre que Renée était l'homme." (*C*, I 486)

and sexual negation (Got 2002, 159). The striking difference between the lovers' overheated *hortus conclusus* and the Siberian coldness outside (Rochecouste 1987, 44) thus serves to underline the hothouse's share in the artificial and the confined (Berthier 1987, 113). In other words, the hothouse appears to be and has been read by many critics as a place of aberration from 'the natural', a witch's cauldron where evil influences seethe (Got 2002, 166): the artificial climate of the hothouse that grows the "criminal fruit" of incest and perversion is thus interpreted as representing the Second Empire's decadence, the decadence of a world addicted to luxury (Gumbrecht 1978, 70).

At first glance the novel seems to confirm this coincidence of the difference in weather with a difference in morality, outside cold, silent and natural, inside hot, perverted and aberrated:

> Through the little panes of the hothouse they could catch glimpses of the Parc Monceau, clumps of trees with fine black outlines, lawns white as frozen lakes, a whole dead landscape whose exquisiteness and light, even tints were reminiscent of Japanese prints. And this burning piece of earth, this blazing couch on which the lovers lay seethed strangely in the midst of the great, silent cold. (*eK*, 157–158; transl. altered)[548]

The aesthetic "exquisiteness" of the landscape outside, its black and white, calm beauty seems to underline the clear-cut and morally biased opposition between natural outside and perverted, devilish inside. There is however one little detail that undermines this opposition and introduces another pair of opposites that significantly complicates the evaluation of the hothouse: as beautiful, calm and silent as the December landscape might appear, it is a "dead landscape". The association of moral integrity, of seemingly exemplary conditions with death is not new to us: we have seen that Zola has developed this theme with regard to Renée's father and his house. In fact, the whole cycle repeatedly comes back to this theme whenever resistance is attempted against the historical development of 'the new Paris'. Coldness, as the opposite of the warming Second Empire, is associated with death, meaning, on the other hand, that warmth and warming come to stand on the side of life.

The hothouse of *La Curée* is thus not at all the anti-Paradou, as Philippe Berthier claims (1987, 114). On the contrary, Zola's *La Faute de l'abbé Mouret*

---

[548] "Au-dehors, par les petites vitres de la serre, on voyait des échappées du parc Monceau, des bouquets d'arbres aux fines découpures noires, des pelouses de gazon blanches comme des lacs glacés, tout un paysage mort, dont les délicatesses et les teintes claires et unies rappelaient des coins de gravures japonaises. Et ce bout de terre brûlante, cette couche enflammée où les amants s'allongeaient, bouillaient étrangement au milieu de ce grand froid muet." (*C*, I 485)

(often regarded as one of the cycle's few odd ones out) spells out the very argument that the hothouse of *La Curée* posited: nature, life and especially 'enhanced' life are in themselves highly ambivalent, as Elke Kaiser formulates this claim (1990, 161). The Paradou of *La Faute* is a place of hyper-nature, a place where the forces of nature reign without being bridled or limited by human standards, be they moral or social, economic or enlightened. Similar to the hothouse of *La Curée*, the Paradou is well-confined, it is surrounded by a high brick wall. With his highly 'artificial' construction of a world within the world that suspends all cultural and social norms, a world that re-enacts the biblical myth of Paradise and the Fall, Zola has surely broken all the rules of 'naturalistic' narration. With regard to his naturalistic cycle, however, this 'odd one out' proves necessary: the abbé's fall (taking place outside society, with no or little remembrance of his former life, in the middle of unbridled nature) can surely not be called a decadent aberration; it cannot be read as the cultural product of a perverted society. It has to be ascribed to nature itself and therefore cannot simply be blamed and eradicated as a naïvely understood cultural criticism would do. With *La Faute* Zola thus provides against an all-too naïve reading of his cycle: he complicates the nature/culture divide by including a fundamental, ineluctable contradiction or dissent between a vitalistic and a moralistic principle. Life and morality are not to be reconciled in an easy way; life without morality is cruel – morals without life are dead. As a consequence, there is no secure ground of 'good nature' to be found beneath the proliferation of decadent culture. Decadent nature, towards which even the paradisiac idyll of the Paradou tends, is a product of 'natural forces'. The nature/culture divide does not help to evaluate or disentangle the historical developments on which the *Rougon-Macquart* focus. This is why the cycle understands itself as a *Natural* and *Social History*.

The elaboration of this argument that is already present, I would assume, in the hothouse scene of *La Curée* retroacts on this very scene: the Paradou and the hothouse share the experience of plenitude, and they share the ambivalence of life that is enhanced with regard to procreation and sexuality (Kaiser 1990, 160). Whereas perversion and incest (the "criminal fruit" growing in the hothouse of *La Curée*) rather put the emphasis on the moral 'aberration' taking place, the paradisiac setting of the Paradou focuses on the vitalistic plenitude of nature; both, however, tell of the same ineluctable ambivalence of moralising discourse and vitalistic axiology (Kaiser 1990, 161).

The abbé's fall and the incest in the hothouse are incited by intense forces of nature. Both couples, Albine and Serge as well as Renée and Maxime, are infected by the voluptuous nature surrounding them. In the case of *La Faute*, the neo-mythical framing with its 'artificial' absence of society assures that it is nature itself that produces some sort of perverting, sexual heat; as the many readings that blame cultural decadence as the reason for the aberration taking place in the hothouse show, things are not so clear with Renée and Maxime. The novel however repeatedly and very explicitly describes the atmosphere in the hothouse by resorting to the fundamental natural principle of "the earth itself": the scenery gives the impression "as if the earth itself had burst into voluptuous sobs in a paroxysm of satisfied desire" (*eK*, 160; transl. altered)[549] and resembles "an alcove in which the earth itself was giving birth" (*eK*, 160).[550] What we encounter here is not an imagery that projects cultural decadence onto exotic nature but, the other way round, the linking of cultural decadence and excess to excessive forces of nature, which undercuts the simplistic 'good nature'/'bad culture' divide. Zola very consistently upholds this line of 'imagery' throughout the incest scene in the hothouse:

> Maxime and Renée, their senses perverted, felt carried away in these mighty nuptials of the earth. The ground burnt their backs through the bearskin, and drops of heat fell upon them from the lofty palms. The sap that rose in the tree-trunks penetrated them, filling them with a mad longing for the immediate growth, for gigantic procreation. They joined the copulation of the hothouse. (*eK*, 159)[551]

The lovers quite literally join the "mighty nuptials of the earth" – without deviating from nature. On the contrary, they are infected by the hothouse's hypertrophy, by its "immediate growth", its "gigantic procreation". It is no coincidence that the narrator resorts to the notion of penetration to describe the encounter of the lovers and their surroundings. It all blends into one sex scene, into one joined "copulation of the hothouse":

> The hothouse loved and burnt with them. In the heavy atmosphere, in the pale light of the moon, they saw the strange world of plants moving confusedly around them, exchanging embraces. [...] At their feet the tank steamed, full of a thick tangle of plants, while the pink petals of the water-lilies opened out on the surface, like virgin bodices, and the tornelias let their bushy tendrils hang down like the hair of swooning water-nymphs.

---

549 "[...] comme si la terre elle-même, dans une crise d'assouvissement, eût éclaté en sanglots voluptueux [...]." (*C*, I 487–488)

550 "Et ils restaient ivres de cette odeur de femme amoureuse, qui traînait dans la serre, comme dans une alcôve où la terre enfantait." (*C*, I 488)

551 "Maxime et Renée, les sens faussés, se sentaient emportés dans ces noces puissantes de la terre. Le sol, à travers la peau d'ours, leur brûlait le dos, et, des hautes palmes, tombaient sur eux des gouttes de chaleur. La sève qui montait aux flancs des arbres les pénétrait, eux aussi, leur donnait des désirs fous de croissance immédiate, de reproduction gigantesque. Ils entraient dans le rut de la serre." (*C*, I 487)

Around them the palm trees and the tall Indian bamboos rose up towards the domed roof, where they bent over and mingled their leaves with postures of exhausted lovers. (*eK*, 158)[552]

Remembering that Renée had been associated with "a great flower, green and pink, one of the water-lilies in the tank, swooning from the heat" it is not difficult to decipher the erotic scene that Zola metonymically narrates as an encounter of anthropomorphic plants.

In conclusion, the hothouse, as a meteorotopos, produces a characteristic climate that differs markedly from its surrounding. Like the climate of the department store or the coal-pit its climate is artificial, it is brought about by the use of technology. Nevertheless, the hothouse is not an 'unnatural' or 'counter-natural' place. On the contrary, its atmosphere is hyper-natural, hypertrophic – the technology of heating does not mar but enhance the natural proceedings of growth and procreation. It thereby also reveals the moral ambivalence inherent in the notions of life, growth and procreation, an ambivalence that the proliferation of the department store, its nurturing on the ruins of the old boutiques come back to.

Critics have complained that these "celebrated descriptions of the hothouse and its monstrous tropical flora are not successful because they have an excessively lurid flavour and are not satisfactorily absorbed into the novel's thematic structure" (Nelson 1977, 10), and that in contrast to Balzac, Zola does not prove capable of linking the two thematic complexes of the novel, financial speculation and the Renée plot (Warning 2005, 151). However, Zola has provided his readers with sufficient clues that the hothouse, this cage of iron and glass, is not as hermetically protected from the least of contacts with the outside world (Campmas 2003, 49) as it seems.

The first indication that the hothouse transcends its boundaries of glass and iron and that its world is not a world of its own, unconnected to the rest of the narrative universe, consists in its metonymic connection with the Hôtel Saccard that is underlined by the latter's architecture: the "house was hidden under its sculpture", under "volutes of flowers and branches", "there were balconies

---

[552] "La serre aimait, brûlait avec eux. Dans l'air alourdi, dans la clarté blanchâtre de la lune, ils voyaient le monde étrange des plantes qui les entouraient se mouvoir confusément, échanger des étreintes. [...] A leurs pieds, le bassin fumait, plein d'un grouillement, d'un entrelacement épais des racines, tandis que l'étoile rose des Nymphéa s'ouvrait, à fleur d'eau, comme un corsage de vierge, et que les Tornélia laissaient pendre leurs broussailles, pareilles à des chevelures de Néréides pâmées. Puis, autour d'eux, les Palmiers, les grands Bambous de l'Inde, se haussaient, allaient dans le cintre, où ils se penchaient et mêlaient leurs feuilles, avec des attitudes chancelantes d'amants lassés." (*C*, I 486)

shaped like baskets full of blossoms, and supported by tall, naked women with wide hips and jutting breasts" as well as "fanciful escutcheons, clusters of fruit, roses, every flower it is possible for stone or marble to represent". The fact that, in short, "the building burst into blossom" (*eK*, 16)[553] approximates it to the hypertrophic proliferation of plants that we have encountered in the hothouse. The richness of the decoration and the architecture of the Hôtel Saccard mirror the vegetation of the hothouse, writes Jean-Pierre Leduc-Adine (1987, 131), a reading underlined by Sarah Capitanio's observation that the flowers of the hothouse see themselves assimilated to the flowers of the house's façade (1987, 183). This metonymic connection of the hothouse and the Hôtel Saccard forms an important juncture, because the house, its architecture and ostentatious function, emblematically represent the Second Empire and Saccard's economic success in the wild speculations of the age. The hothouse as a place for Renée's 'private' intimate adventures is thus, via this juncture, linked to the greater societal processes in which her husband finds himself entangled.

Zola however also finds a more direct way of exhibiting the link between the two "thematic complexes": Commenting on Saccard's role in the fever of speculation that was brought about in the wake of 'Haussmann's renovation of Paris' the narrator comes up with a curious but telling image:

> [His partners] refused, moreover, to entertain the subsidiary speculative schemes that sprouted in [Saccard's] head each morning: the building of concert halls and immense baths on the building-ground bordering their boulevards; of railways along the line of the new boulevards; arcades [*galeries vitrées*] which would increase the rent of the shops tenfold and allow people to walk about Paris without getting wet. [...] They wisely continued to sell [their ground]. Saccard built on his. His brain teemed with extravagant ideas. He would have proposed in all seriousness to put Paris under an immense bell-glass, so as to transform it into a hothouse for forcing pineapples and sugar-cane. (*eK*, 98)[554]

---

[553] "L'hôtel disparaissait sous les sculptures. Autour des fenêtres, le long des corniches, couraient des enroulements de rameaux et de fleurs ; il y avait des balcons pareils à des corbeilles de verdure, que soutenaient de grandes femmes nues, les hanches tordues, les pointes des seins en avant ; puis, çà et là, étaient collés des écussons de fantaisie, des grappes, des roses, toutes les efflorescences possibles de la pierre et du marbre. A mesure que l'œil montait, l'hôtel fleurissait davantage." (*C*, I 331)

[554] "Ils refusèrent également les spéculations secondaires qui poussaient chaque matin dans sa tête : construction de salles de concert, de vastes maisons de bains, sur les terrains en bordure ; chemins de fer suivant la ligne des nouveaux boulevards ; galeries vitrées, décuplant le loyer des boutiques, et permettant de circuler dans Paris sans être mouillé. [...] Eux continuèrent à vendre sagement leurs lots. Lui fit bâtir. Son cerveau bouillait. Il eût proposé sans rire de mettre Paris sous une immense cloche, pour le changer en serre chaude, et y cultiver les ananas et la canne à sucre." (*C*, I 419)

Putting Paris "under an immense bell-glass", "transform[ing] it into a hothouse" cannot only be read as the most extreme of Saccard's "extravagant ideas". It is also a very adequate way of describing how speculation, so characteristic for the Paris of the Second Empire, works. As the novel makes clear, speculation is not to be separated from a notion of weather, or of a special climate that announces itself for the experienced observer:

> From the beginning Aristide Saccard could sense the rising tide of speculation, which was soon to engulf the whole of Paris. He found himself in the midst of the hot rain of crown-pieces that fell thickly on the city's roofs. (*eK*, 49)[555]

Meteorological talent is thus a precondition for becoming a successful speculator. It does however not suffice to know "that the shower of gold beating down upon the walls would fall more heavily every day" (*eK*, 67)[556] – the correct analysis of the weather makes up but half the job. The second (and the more demanding) half of the art of speculation consists in the art of making the weather, of bringing "the radiant cloud" to "burst over [one's] own courtyard", so that it is oneself, and not some competitor, who will in the end "pick up the twenty-franc pieces" (*eK*, 71).[557] All the successful 'speculators' of the *Rougon-Macquart* are meteorological talents, who sense the changing climate of the age and try to exploit it for their own profit. Like Bordenave and Octave Mouret Saccard is however well aware that merely picking up the twenty-franc pieces that the 'natural' climate of the age brings along ('natural' meaning produced by others, by the sum of interactions that lies beyond one's own control) does not do the job. Speculation is about creating this "hot rain" or at least about enhancing the violence of the age's weather – by heating:

> 'Oh! Look!' said Saccard, laughing like a child. 'It's raining twenty-franc pieces in Paris!'
>
> '[...] A wonderful district, where there's much to be done. Ah! Now it's all going to flare up! Can you see? You'd think the whole neighbourhood was bubbling away in a chemist's retort.' [...]

---

[555] "Aristide Saccard, depuis les premiers jours, sentait venir ce flot montant de la spéculation, dont l'écume allait couvrir Paris entier. Il en suivit les progrès avec une attention profonde. Il se trouvait au beau milieu de la pluie chaude d'écus tombant dru sur les toits de la cité." (*C*, I 367–368)

[556] "[...] il savait que la pluie d'or qui en battait les murs tomberait plus dru chaque jour." (*C*, I 387)

[557] "[...] il pensa que le nuage radieux avait crevé chez lui, dans sa cour, et qu'il allait ramasser les pièces de vingt francs." (*C*, I 391)

'Yes, yes, that's what I said, whole neighbourhoods will be melted down, and gold will stick to the fingers of those who heat and stir the mortar. [...]' (eK, 68)[558]

Like Octave Mouret with his department store and Bordenave with his theatre Saccard runs a weather machine that dreams of enhancing life, of enhancing circulation, of creating a hypertrophic atmosphere that produces growth, transformation, progress – and profit. Speculation is a weather machine and there is no more adequate image for it than the dream of "put[ting] Paris under an immense bell-glass, so as to transform it into a hothouse". It might not be "pineapples and sugar-cane" that this machine forces; the "immediate growth", the "gigantic procreation" it brings about might above all concern the proliferation of new buildings sprouting in Paris which rapidly transforms its cityscape.

As Zola emphasises with regard to Saccard, this fever of speculation that causes a building boom is not even limited by economic calculations of profits: Saccard does not "wisely" sell his ground: he builds (and will thereby ruin himself). As with Bordenave and Mouret, the climate of the Second Empire and its fever are not to be instrumentalised. It does therefore not come as a surprise that enhancing the "hot rain of crown-pieces" also conjures up less agreeable rain, a rain of vice haunting the gigantic hothouse of Paris:

> Meanwhile the Saccards' fortune seemed to be at its height. It blazed in the heart of Paris like a huge bonfire. [...] The city had become an orgy of gold and women. Vice, coming from on high, flowed through the gutters, spread out over the ornamental waters, shot up in the fountains of the public gardens, and fell on the roofs as fine rain. [...] Then, amid the feverish sleep of Paris [...] one felt a growing sense of madness, the voluptuous nightmare of a city obsessed with gold and flesh. (eK, 112; transl. altered)[559]

The hothouse with its ambivalence of hypertrophic, enhanced nature and moral aberration thus turns out to be emblematic for both protagonists, for Renée as

---

[558] "« Oh ! vois, dit Saccard, avec un rire d'enfant, il pleut des pièces de vingt francs dans Paris ! »

« [...] Un beau quartier, où il y a beaucoup à faire... Ah ! cette fois, tout va brûler ! Vois-tu ? ... On dirait que le quartier bout dans l'alambic de quelque chimiste. » [...]

« Oui, oui, j'ai bien dit, plus d'un quartier va fondre, et il restera de l'or aux doigts des gens qui chaufferont et remueront la cuve. [...] »" (C, I 388)

[559] "Cependant la fortune des Saccard semblait à son apogée. Elle brûlait en plein Paris comme un feu de joie colossal. [...] La ville n'était plus qu'une grande débauche de millions et de femmes. Le vice, venu de haut, coulait dans les ruisseaux, s'étalait dans les bassins, remontait dans les jets d'eau des jardins, pour retomber sur les toits, en pluie fine et pénétrante. [...] Alors, dans le sommeil fiévreux de Paris [...] on sentait le détraquement cérébrale, le cauchemar doré et voluptueux d'une ville folle de son or et de sa chair." (C, I 435)

for Saccard. It links their characteristic 'passions' in a way that makes it adequate to call them "these two hot fevers of money and pleasure" (*eK*, 78; transl. altered).[560]

The overarching or integrating function of the hothouse is not limited to *La Curée*; on the contrary, the hothouse serves as a constant point of reference that emerges in nearly all of the novels of the *Rougon-Macquart*. *La Faute de l'abbé Mouret* talks of a "natural hothouse" (*eSAM*, 140),[561] a notion that will again come up in *Germinal* where the so-called Côte-Verte also forms "a natural greenhouse, warmed by the fires from the lower regions" (*eG*, 304).[562] We encounter "a sort of hothouse transformed into a Japanese pavilion" (*PA*, II 833; my transl.)[563] in *Une page d'amour* and "a small dilapidated glass-house" (*eBH*, 47)[564] in *La Bête humaine*. There are, of course, also 'real', actual, proper hothouses, for example the one that Nana sees as part of a place they visit in the countryside: "And there's a greenhouse over there! Isn't it huge!" (*eN*, 150),[565] which probably incites in her "a major whim" that she later satisfies by having "a winter-garden [built] in part of her house" (*eN*, 394).[566] In *L'Argent* the story of a "little greenhouse" (*eM*, 169)[567] is told: the Maugendres had been madly longing for this little greenhouse to be constructed in their garden until Monsieur Maugendre one day wins the money for it at the stock exchange. Unfortunately, this 'happy' incident infects his wife with the fever of speculation, which will eventually ruin the couple. One way or another, all these 'actual' hothouses, as marginal as they might seem, are connected to the main stories of the novels. Nevertheless, Zola's use of the notion of the hothouse to describe the atmosphere, the 'climate', of 'ordinary' places seems to be still more important than the actual hothouses: "a sultry heat like a tropical hothouse [*une chaleur lourde et enfermée de serre*]" (*eN*, 37)[568] characterises Nana's apartment; in *Germinal*

---

560 "[...] le mari et la femme, ces deux fièvres chaudes de l'argent et du plaisir [...]." (*C*, I 399)
561 "On entrait en pleine terre ardente, dans une serre naturelle, où le soleil tombait d'aplomb." (*FaM*, I 1362–1363)
562 "C'était une serre naturelle, chauffée par l'incendie des couches profondes." (*G*, III 1396)
563 "Au fond du jardin, dans une sorte de serre transformée en pavillon japonais, elles trouvèrent Mme Deberle." (*PA*, II 833)
564 "Mais, tout de suite, comme [Jacques] longeait une petite serre en ruines, la vue d'une ombre [=Flore], accroupie à la porte, l'arrêta." (*BH*, IV 1038)
565 "« Zoé, je vois, je vois !... [...] C'est une serre, là-bas ! Mais c'est très vaste... Oh ! que je suis contente ! Regarde donc, Zoé, regarde donc ! »" (*N*, II 1233)
566 "[...] elle contenta un gros caprice, un jardin d'hiver dans un coin de son hôtel [...]." (*N*, II 1456)
567 "Pourtant, une occasion s'était présentée, tous deux [les Maugendre] depuis longtemps avaient la folle envie de faire construire, dans leur jardin, une petite serre de cinq ou six mille francs [...]." (*Ar*, V 186)
568 "Il faisait trop chaud dans ce cabinet, une chaleur lourde et enfermée de serre." (*N*, II 1138)

the Hennebeaus' house "seemed warm as a greenhouse [*une tiédeur de serre*]" (*eG*, 206),[569] while the strikers were freezing in the cold December day outside. When Caroline in *L'Argent* attempts to visit the broker Mazaud in his apartment only to find him dead, having committed suicide, the climate of the room is identical to the climate at the Hennebeaus': a "hothouse warmth [*tiédeur de serre*]" (*eM*, 333).[570] The "covered galleries" of 'Le Bonheur des Dames' and the staircase of *Pot-Bouille* share the same "*chaleur de serre*" ("heat [...] of a hothouse" (*eLP*, 242);[571] "hothouse temperature" (*ePL*, 5)[572]). The fact that in the home of Doctor Pascal (Zola's mouthpiece and representation in the fictional world) called the Souleiade, the great room also "form[s] a sort of hothouse, creating the sweetness of a lovely temperature" (*DP*, V 1036; my transl.)[573] underlines the ambivalence of the notion of the hothouse: it can be 'natural' or 'artificial', it can create both unbearable as well as lovely climatic conditions.

Regarded from an architectural point of view, many of the places that I have suggested calling 'meteorotopoi' are 'hothouses', meaning that they are constructed of the 'new' materials iron and glass: the washhouse, "an enormous shed with a level ceiling, exposed beams resting on cast-iron pillars, and big clear glass windows" (*eA*, 16)[574] provides a prime example of this architectural link. The construction of 'Le Bonheur des Dames', for which Zola consulted his friend and architect Frantz Jourdain (cf. Welch 2003, El Kettani 2010), is another. Saccard's bank (a meteorotopos that we have not yet talked about) is established by "simply mak[ing] a glass roof for the courtyard" (*eM*, 98),[575] and grows, taking the same measure, by "glazing over the courtyard of the adjoining house" (*eM*, 155).[576] With this architectural characteristic the 'Banque Universelle' not only mirrors the "devil's kitchen" of *L'Assommoir*'s booze-machine, "working

---

[569] "[...] il faisait là [chez les Hennebeau] une tiédeur de serre, qui développait l'odeur fine d'un ananas [...]." (*G*, III 1310)

[570] "Mais il faisait très chaud, de grosses bûches achevaient de se consumer dans la cheminée [...] Sur une table, une gerbe de roses, un royal bouquet pour la saison, que, la veille encore, l'agent de change avait apporté à sa femme, s'épanouissait dans cette tiédeur de serre, embaumait la pièce." (*Ar*, V 358)

[571] "Sous les galeries couvertes, il faisait très chaud, une chaleur de serre [...]." (*BD*, III 620)

[572] "Mais ce qui frappa surtout Octave, ce fut, en entrant, une chaleur de serre, une haleine tiède qu'une bouche lui soufflait au visage." (*PB*, III 5)

[573] "[...] à la Souleiade, les fenêtres de la salle, tournées au midi, formaient serre, entretenaient là une douceur de température délicieuse." (*DP*, V 1036)

[574] "C'était un immense hangar, à plafond plat, à poutres apparentes, monté sur des piliers de fonte, fermé par de larges fenêtres claires." (*A*, II 386)

[575] "On se contenterait de vitrer la cour, pour servir de hall central ;" (*Ar*, V 111)

[576] "[...] une nouvelle idée d'agrandissement [...], celle de vitrer aussi la cour de la maison voisine [...]." (*Ar*, V 171–172)

away under the glass roof of the narrow little court-yard" (*eA*, 344),[577] it also mirrors the central weather-machine of the novel, the stock exchange, whose hectic action, as we will see, takes place under an enormous "glass roof" (*eM*, 301).[578] There can be no doubt that Zola establishes a significant link between the architectural resemblances of these meteorotopoi with the 'archi'-meteorotopos hothouse and their functioning *as* meteorotopoi. This link can be studied best by focussing on a last meteorotopos. We could have investigated this meteorotopos on its own, like the department store, the coal-pit or the bar, but instead, I would suggest examining it as a giant hothouse. It is the covered markets called 'Les Halles' that I am talking about:

> Florent watched Les Halles emerge slowly from the shadows, from the dreamland in which he had seen them, stretching out like an endless series of open palaces. Greenish-grey in colour, they looked more solid now, and even more gigantic, with their amazing [*prodigieuse*] mast-like columns supporting the great expanse of roofs. They rose up in geometrically shaped masses; and when all the inner lights had been extinguished and the square, uniform buildings were bathed in the light of dawn, they seemed like some vast modern machine, a steam engine or a cauldron supplying the digestive needs of a whole people, a huge metal belly, bolted and riveted, constructed of wood, glass and iron, with the elegance and power of a machine working away with fiery furnaces and wildly turning wheels. (*eBP*, 25)[579]

With regard to its architecture, 'Les Halles' are a hothouse. The elaborate technique of their construction, "their amazing mast-like columns supporting the great expanse of roofs" and the 'modern' material, the fact that they are "constructed of wood, glass and iron", dominate the description of this "forest of ironwork" (*eBP*, 24).[580] Florent's impression of the buildings is however not of a purely technical nature. On the contrary, it is the covered markets' very own

---

577 "[...] l'alambic, la machine à soûler, fonctionnant sous le vitrage de l'étroite cour, avec la trépidation profonde de sa cuisine d'enfer [...]." (*A*, II 704)
578 "[...] il ne tombait du toit vitré qu'un jour bas et roussâtre, d'une désespérée mélancolie." (*Ar*, V 323)
579 "Et Florent regardait les grandes Halles sortir de l'ombre, sortir du rêve, où ils les avait vues, allongeant à l'infini leurs palais à jour. Elles se solidifiaient, d'un gris verdâtre, plus géantes encore, avec leur mâture prodigieuse, supportant les nappes sans fin de leurs toits. Elles entassaient leurs masses géométriques ; et, quand toutes les clartés intérieures furent éteintes, qu'elles baignèrent dans le jour levant, carrées, uniformes, elles apparurent comme une machine moderne, hors de toute mesure, quelque machine à vapeur, quelque chaudière destinée à la digestion d'un peuple, gigantesque ventre de métal, boulonné, rivé, fait de bois, de verre et de fonte, d'une élégance et d'une puissance de moteur mécanique, fonctionnant là, avec la chaleur du chauffage, l'étourdissement, le branle furieux des roues." (*VP*, I 626)
580 "[...] cette forêt de fonte [...]." (*VP*, I 625)

aesthetics that strike him. The description touches upon the typical aesthetical categories of colour ("[g]reenish-grey in colour"), shape ("geometrically shaped") and material ("constructed of wood, glass and iron") to express a hardly veiled fascination for this complex of buildings: 'Les Halles', "gigantic" and "amazing", with all their "elegance and power" clearly provide for a sublime encounter. The description leaves no doubt that this powerful aesthetics is of a decidedly modern nature: the elegant, the beautiful appearance is, perhaps quite surprisingly, likened to "some vast modern machine". Florent experiences the sublime fascination before "the elegance and power of a machine". The machine's "fiery furnaces and wildly turning wheels" foreshadow the machine-imagery of *Au Bonheur des Dames*; the association of "cauldron" and "steam engine" make us think of the other meteorotopoi that were all, one way or another, connected with heating technology. Doubtlessly, 'Les Halles' form an exemplary meteorotopos. The "huge metal belly" fulfils its societal function ("supplying the digestive needs of a whole people") in the typically 'meteorotopical' way: it enhances nature and speeds up circulation by providing hypertrophic conditions (cf. Noiray 1981, 288) with the help of technology. The violent 'weather' of the greenery and of all the other goods that the meteorotopos brings into circulation produces a 'weather spectacle' as spectacular and sublime as the architecture of the place. This time it is the painter Claude, Florent's first new friend in Paris, through whose eyes we are watching the scene:

> Claude had enthusiastically jumped onto the bench. He urged his companion to admire the effect of the day dawning over the vegetables. It was like an ocean spreading between the two groups of markets from the Pointe Saint-Eustache to the Rue des Halles. In the two open spaces at either end the flood of greenery rose even higher, submerging the footpaths. Dawn came slowly, a soft grey that spread light watercolour tints everywhere. The piles of greenery were like waves, a river of green flowing along the roadway like an autumn torrent; and they assumed delicate, shadowy hues – pale violet, milky pink, and greenish yellow, all the soft, light hues that turn the sky into a canopy of shot silk as the sun rises. (*eBP*, 25)[581]

---

[581] "Mais Claude était monté debout sur le banc, d'enthousiasme. Il força son compagnon à admirer le jour se levant sur les légumes. C'était une mer. Elle s'étendait de la pointe Saint-Eustache à la rue des Halles, entre les deux groupes de pavillons. Et, aux deux bouts, dans les deux carrefours, le flot grandissait encore, les légumes submergeaient les pavés. Le jour se levait lentement, d'un gris très doux, lavant touts choses d'une teinte claire d'aquarelle. Ces tas moutonnants comme des flots pressés, ce fleuve de verdure qui semblait couler dans l'encaissement de la chaussée, pareil à la débâcle des pluies d'automne, prenaient des ombres délicates et perlées, des violets attendris, des roses teintés de lait, des verts noyés dans des jaunes, toutes les pâleurs qui font du ciel une soie changeante au lever du soleil [...]." (*VP*, I 626–627)

The similarities of this "ocean" of green, of this "flood of greenery" to the department store's cascades of materials are obvious; the aesthetical fascination that Zola shares with his focalising characters might here be even more explicit than in *Au Bonheur des Dames*. As in the department store, the flow of goods has its counterpart in a flow of people: once Florent enters this violent 'ocean' of the crowd, "he was nothing but a piece of flotsam tossed about by the incoming tide" (*eBP*, 31).[582]

'Les Halles' are a hothouse, not only because the sun, pouring down a "rain of fire", "heat[s] them as if they were a great boiler" (*eBP*, 121);[583] not only because the "masses of food" (*eBP*, 121)[584] assembled there literally create a hypertrophic atmosphere; not only because this "vast Babylonian structure of metal" (*eBP*, 170)[585] conjures up exotic associations; this gigantic hothouse is also characterised by a deep ambivalence. On the one hand, its hypertrophic atmosphere brought about by its modern, technical design, and the weather-like violent circulation that nourishes a whole city radiate a sublime, an aesthetic fascination; on the other hand, these very same hyper-natural, over-saturated processes reek of death and putrefaction. Especially in the evenings they spread, like the hothouse of *La Curée*, the nauseating smell of ephemeral nature: "Les Halles now seemed to [Florent] like a huge ossuary, a place of death, littered with the remains of things that had once been alive, a charnel house reeking with foul smells and putrefaction." (*eBP*, 189)[586]

In conclusion, the covered markets are an exemplary meteorotopos, because they most obviously refer to the emblematic archetype, the Platonic 'idea' of all meteorotopoi, to the hothouse. The hothouse, I would maintain, with Aude Campmas (2003, 53), is the symbol of the Second Empire. Not only a symbolic space of its corruption (Couillard 1978, 403), but a space that captures the complexity and the ambivalence of the historic developments and the radical transformations of this age. In other words, I agree with Jean-Pierre Leduc-Adine (1987, 132) that it is a comprehensive and powerful architectural trace of the Second Empire's society. I think that Zola in his *Rougon-Macquart* very

---

[582] "Alors, stupide, il s'arrêta, il s'abandonna aux poussées des uns, aux injures des autres ; il ne fut plus qu'une chose battue, roulée, au fond de la mer montante." (*VP*, I 632)
[583] "[…] une pluie de feu tombait sur les Halles, les chauffait comme un four de tôle […]." (*VP*, I 729)
[584] "[…] cet entassement de nourriture […]." (*VP*, I 730)
[585] "[…] une babylone de métal, d'une légèreté hindoue, traversée par des terrasses suspendues, des couloirs aériens, des ponts volants jetés sur le vide." (*VP*, I 781)
[586] "Alors, les Halles qu'il avait laissées le matin, lui parurent un vaste ossuaire, un lieu de mort où ne traînait que le cadavre des êtres, un charnier de puanteur et de décomposition." (*VP*, I 803)

extensively and consistently makes use of this trace; his cycle may even be regarded as an elaborate reading of this trace and its implications.

What renders this symbol so powerful, so telling and also so interesting is the fact that, as Maarten van Buuren (1987, 159) puts it, the hothouse is associated with the idea of progress. The fashion of constructing public and private hothouses hit Paris in the middle of the 19th century, probably in the wake of the construction of the famous Chrystal Palace for the Great Exhibition in London 1851 (cf. Maione 1980, 112, Buuren 1987, 159, Braswell 2013, 70). Hothouses can thus be regarded as a characteristic trait of the age (Berthier 1987, 113) which obviously has to do with its typical architecture: constructing with iron and glass was not only fashionable in the Second Empire (Pellini 2003, 37), its also relies on scientific and technical progress (Noiray 1981, 237). The new architecture, with its functional character and its main employment for public buildings like hothouses, train stations, libraries or covered markets (Noiray 1981, 237) also introduced new, modern architectural 'virtues': it defines itself as an architecture of transparency, of openness and of light (Leduc-Adine 1987, 131). Jacques Noiray claims that this cast-iron architecture represents for Zola the archetype of a modern and authentic art (Noiray 1981, 237); the aesthetic fascination that the construction of meteorotopoi like 'Les Halles', or the department store exert on his characters may support this claim. Critics have also looked for indications outside his novels, finding clear evidence for Zola's "désir de modernité" (Leduc-Adine 1987, 134), his fascination for "[m]odernity and its uses of light" (LeGouis 1993, 430) in the *Notes préparatoires* (Leduc-Adine 1987, 134) or in the later photographs that he took himself of the Crystal Palace (cf. Buuren 1987, 159, LeGouis 1993, 430).

If Jean-Pierre Leduc-Adine is right that Zola saw in the 'new Paris' the germs of an urban modernity, architectural and decorative, that announces the aesthetical methods and procedures of the future (Leduc-Adine 1987, 136), then this is surely due to the fact that the architecture of iron and glass, with its ideals of clarity and elucidation also bears a poetological potential (Leduc-Adine 1987, 131, Tonard 1994, 67). Many critics refer to Zola's letter to Valabrègue (cf. Walker 1959, Schor 1969, Saint-Gérand 1986, Beizer 1989) when it comes to his naturalistic agenda; a letter, Phillip Walker claims, that gives "a more exact description of Zola's art during his best creative period than *Le roman expérimental*" (1959, 448). The letter's famous poetological metaphor of the realist screen [*écran réaliste*] that is neither whitened, depicting the world as black schemes like its classical predecessor, nor a bit blurred and coloured like the romantic prism, but a simple, thin piece of glass, clearly admires the ideals of transparency that we have discovered as the defining characteristic of the new architecture of iron and glass that fascinated Zola. Pierluigi Pellini (2003, 10) refers us to a passage of *Les Romanciers naturalistes* where this connection of modern, cast-iron architecture and naturalistic novel becomes even more explicit: "I would well like a simple composition", writes Zola, "a clear language, something like a glass house that lets us see the ideas of its interior." (*RN*, *OC* X 499; my transl.)[587]

The hothouse is however not only of interest for Zola as an abstract, an aesthetical apparition that enters the cityscape of Paris and points towards possible artistic futures. It is, as we have already seen, deeply entangled in the age's societal and cultural developments: not only as an aesthetic idea, but as expressive of its very function and characteristics. The hothouse therefore offers itself as a privileged object for a critical analysis of the Second Empire. Walter Benjamin's *Passagen-Werk* [*Arcades Project*] (obviously focussing on the arcades rather than the hothouse) may in this respect be understood as a successor of Zola's narrative project. It is here that Elke Kaiser (1990, 162) has found a fragment, or rather a quotation from a contemporary play which shows that the idea of putting "Paris under an immense bell-glass, so as to transform it into a hothouse", (*eK*, 98) which Zola ascribes to Saccard, the protagonist of *La Curée* and *L'Argent*, is not the idea of an idiosyncratic fantasist; it rather articulates the spirit of an age: "'I hear they want to roof all the streets of Paris with glass. That will make for lovely hothouses; we will live in them like melons.' (p. 19)" (Benjamin 1999, 56)[588]

What is it that makes the hothouse so attractive and so characteristic for the 19th century?

Firstly, its hypertrophic climate resonates with a society that is more and more shaped by the forces of industrialisation and the triumph of capitalism. With its tropical proliferation of plants, their excessive growth, in short, with its violent 'enhancement of nature' it provides a very apt image for the enhancement of circulation, for the acceleration of production (destruction, transformation) and of life that characterises the Second Empire.

Secondly, its architectural and technological association with modern scientific and technological achievements links the hothouse and its violently prolific climate to the idea of progress. The hothouse illustrates, or rather exemplifies, how technology is capable of transforming living conditions and of literally creating a climate that strongly affects the world subjected to it.

Thirdly, the hothouse redefines or rather paradoxically dissolves the boundary of inside and outside (Leduc-Adine 1987, 131, Kaiser 1990, 138, Vedder 2013, 360):

---

[587] "Je voulais bien une composition simple, une langue nette, quelque chose comme une maison de verre laissant voir les idées à l'intérieur [...]." (*RN*, *OC* X 499)
[588] "« Apprenez que l'on veut faire couvrir toutes les rues de Paris avec des vitres, ça va faire de jolies serres chaudes ; nous vivrons là-dedans comme des melons. » (p 19)" (Benjamin 1983, 104)

although this might at first glance not seem intuitive (in the hothouse scene of *La Curée*, the hothouse appears to produce a contrast in climate of outside and inside) the hothouse is yet a prime example for the development of turning the interior of the house into a sort of exterior space. The difference in season and temperature might accentuate the artificiality of the climate that is created with the help of technology; it should, however, not be forgotten that transparency, openness and light are all ideals or characteristics taken from open nature and applied to the construction of indoor space. The idea of protection from the weather as the fundamental principle of architecture that had been still of great importance for Goethe's and Herder's reflections on architecture seems to have lost its relevance. The dialectics of protection and imprisonment, crucial for Goethe's reconstruction of modern subjectivity are suspended. Instead, it is glass and permeability that dominate the discussion. At this point we see again the difference between a concentration on boundaries, on environ-ment and a concentration on milieu; the one is concerned with imprisoning, but protecting walls and a longing for the weather beyond these walls, the other with glass, and with the weather on both sides of the glass. The observation that, in contrast to traditional techniques of building with stone, the outside and the inside form coincides when constructing with iron and glass (Leduc-Adine 1987, 131) is important; it expresses the characteristic suspension of internal and external and underlines the fact that the same sort of forces are working inside and out.

Our readings of the *Rougon-Macquart*'s meteorotopoi confirm Rainer Warning's impression (resonating with the architectural observations) that what happens inside and what happens outside the buildings is essentially the same (2005, 157). Instead of being protected from the weather and from violent natural forces, there is interior and exterior weather: violent flows, oceans, winds and proliferating 'nature'. In addition to that, the inside and the outside 'weather' communicate. None of the meteorotopoi we analysed prove capable of keeping their 'own' weather inside boundaries. Their violent 'weather' spreads and infects the neighbourhood, like the reeking exhalations of the gigantic hothouse called 'Les Halles':

> All these exhalations formed into a single great cloud over the rooftops, spread to the neighbouring houses, and seemed to fill the sky over the whole of Paris. It was as if Les Halles were bursting out of their iron belt and enveloping the gorged city with their foul breath. (*eBP*, 249)[589]

---

[589] "Le nuage de toutes ces haleines s'amassait au-dessus des toitures, gagnait les maisons voisines, s'élargissait en nuée lourde sur Paris entier. C'étaient les Halles crevant dans leur ceinture de fonte trop étroite, et chauffant du trop-plein de leur indigestion du soir le sommeil de la ville gorgée." (*VP*, I 868)

Fourthly, the suspension of inside/outside also affects the principal difference of nature/culture. Technology and progress do not work against the weather, they work with and they works *as* weather. Technology and nature do not form an opposition. In fact, Zola generalises the principle of the hothouse and its intense interaction of technology and nature, which brings forth an 'artificially' enhanced nature, a hyper-nature of accelerated life and circulation.

He obviously could not know that his literary ('metaphorical/metonymical') assumption, or rather fabrication of a 'hothouse effect' would, about a hundred years later, be supported by a scientific counterpart, called the 'greenhouse effect'. Certainly, this 'greenhouse-effect' receives its name from a different source; it is not the extrapolated product of a socio-critical observation of cultural and historical developments like Zola's 'hothouse effect', but an image for a physical phenomenon. To be sure, the 'greenhouse effect' with its layer of carbon dioxide and other greenhouse gases differs from the idea of 'literally' roofing all the streets with glass. The one may seem to happen by accident, behind 'man's back', the other may be said to be voluntarily brought about by 'man'. However, the way that Zola describes the historical and cultural developments of the Second Empire suspends this distinction. His cycle does not refer to itself as a 'natural and social history' without a reason: the 'social' developments of the age, the 'human' achievements, progress in science and technology, as well as the human passions and desires are all related. They act and interact as natural forces: forces brought about by the anonymous crowd, forces that are beyond rational or voluntary control.

In fact, Zola's assumed 'hothouse effect' quite closely approximates the 'greenhouse effect' that since, let us say, the turn of the millennium dominates our perception of the world. He certainly short-circuits the 'actual', the physical reason by metonymically assuming the hothouse as emblematic for the age. For the rest, his analysis is astonishingly pertinent. As we have seen, he diagnoses a 'global warming' as the primary effect of the hothouse. This warming causes secondary effects, like violent weather, that threaten to be of catastrophic dimension. This 'warming', this 'weather' always oscillates between the 'metaphorical' and the 'actual', and its foundation is essentially literary and not physical. For Zola's central insight, however, there is no qualification: he had a clear intuition that human progress and the transformation of society into modern mass society that is nourished and equipped by booming capitalism had reached a stage where it had grown into a natural force. It had become a natural force that interacted with other natural forces, effecting changes in balance. The Second Empire's 'climate' describes a human-induced natural force that is beyond human control. Human society has developed the power to collectively change the climate, to enhance or shift the balances of nature for their profit – that is what the hothouse and its proliferation represent. It chronotopically condenses this atmosphere, as Rainer Warning writes (2005, 156). This is the story that all the meteorotopoi and their spreading beyond their boundaries tell. With his observation, Zola anticipates Bruno Latour's critique of the nature/society divide (cf. Latour 1993) as well as the notion of the anthropocene that Dipesh Chakrabarty has elaborated on (cf. Chakrabarty 2009).

Zola sensed the ambivalence of this development, a horror mixed with fascination, as Marie Couillard (1978, 404) calls it. As we have seen, he is, on the one hand, attracted to modernity and its aesthetics, but, on the other, well aware of the cruel subjection to the violent and uncontrollable climate that modern 'progress' and its attempted enhancement of life and nature force on the human being. I do not think that Zola evaluates modern progress as a 'progress backwards', as Maarten van Buuren seems to imply (1987, 159); Zola rather spells out the deep and inevitable dialectics of progress, of a historical and cultural development for which there seems to be no alternative; of a 'natural' development even, that cannot but be overcome by its own tendency towards crisis. The only hope that remains is the hope for the purging effect of a catastrophe.

5 The weather of the masses

In the course of the previous sections we have repeatedly come across crowds (or masses of people, as I prefer to call them) that were somehow linked to notions of the weather. Our reading of *Au Bonheur des Dames*, with its flows, oceans and torrents of customers streaming through the department store, perhaps made us most familiar with this phenomenon. We encountered yet other masses: the theatre audience, the spectators at the horserace and the crowd celebrating the declaration of war in *Nana*, the masses shopping in the covered markets in *Le Ventre de Paris*, the miners of *Germinal* and the boozers of *L'Assommoir*, to name only the ones that immediately come to mind. Undoubtedly, these masses appear in the *Rougon-Macquart* with a certain insistency. My readings, however, have so far treated them as rather marginal: as either the products or fuel of meteorotopoi or as resonating with the protagonist Nana. With regard to Zola's narrative project, the masses are, however, not at all marginal. On the contrary, I propose it is in fact they that are the actual 'subject' of the *Rougon-Macquart*.

The observation that Zola's novels break with the novelistic tradition of centring on the human individual is not new. Zola is the first French novelist in whose writings the human personage seems to have lost the central place that it had occupied before, Chantal Jennings (1980, 396) notes. In his novels "the individual is replaced by the crowd, the *amorphe Masse*" (Rennie 1996, 400), which, according to Olivier Lumbroso, relegates Zola to the Baudelairean tradition of a 'Peintre de la vie moderne', whose domain is the crowd (2012, 9). One may regret the increasing dehumanisation of the personages (Jennings 1980, 400), or, in contrast, provocatively ask, as did his friend and fellow writer Henry Céard, why Zola did not concentrate exclusively on the crowd (cf. Chevrel 1985, 448). His 'choice' of subject, however, can surely not be regarded as an autonomous aesthetic decision. We rather observe a socio-cultural factor retroacting on the aesthetic production: Zola's literary subject is clearly influenced by the fact that the historical subject is characterised by a depersonalisation of the individual and thus favours the anonymous masses (Vibert 2007, 6). His novels therefore have to be read as a diagnosis of a specific historical state and development of society. As Nicholas Rennie has shown, Zola's novelistic project is definitely in agreement with Walter Benjamin's observation that crowds are the 'proper' subject of 19th century literature (1996, 396). Since the Republican Zola conceptualises the *Rougon-Macquart* as a historical as well as a political project, an understanding of the role and the functioning of the masses promises to lead us to the core of the cycle's view of 19th century society.

With regard to the cycle's synchronous, 'sociological' reconstruction of different milieus and the living conditions that these milieus create (in the cases of the decadent aristocracy, the poor working class, the miners, etc.) the crowd as the 'historical subject' does not immediately appear at the centre of the stage. Here, above all, the experiences of individuals provide appropriate access to the conditions of the time, which can be analysed and generalised, and which add up to a more or less complete and adequate picture of the Second Empire. It is however no coincidence that the masses keep emerging in these analyses at one point or another as a necessary driving force of all of these milieus, no matter whether they are firing up the circulation of the 'Le Bonheur des Dames', the heating of Bordenave's theatre and Saccard's bank or whether the voices of the crowd resonate, all shouting the name of a high-society courtesan. The crowd is not merely a product of the milieus; it is a necessary agent in their production, which is affected by complex interactions.

With regard to the cycle's diachronic dimension, the central importance of the masses cannot be overlooked. Although Zola somewhat masks this fact by calling his project the "natural and social history of a family", it is very clear that the agents of this history, which spans the period from the *coup d'état* in 1851 to the defeat of the French troupes that marks the end of the Second Empire in 1870, cannot be located in a family setting; they are not individuals. "[B]oth Marx and Zola view history as a process determined by super-individual, material forces", writes Gerhard Gerhardi (1974, 150), and it is these forces that the successful members of the family know how to use for their own profit. It is also these forces, I maintain, that Zola sets out to examine in his *Rougon-Macquart*.

With her analysis of the mythic substrata pervading Zola's texts Barbara Vinken (2015a) has worked out the axiological framework in which the historical events take place and according to which they are evaluated. The coordinates organising Zola's view on history follow a figure of *translatio*: Paris is the new Rome, the decadent Second Empire with its fruitless but excessive sexuality, embodied by Nana, mirrors the Roman Empire and its (Babylonian) cult of Venus. The effeminate and barren empire has to perish in order to make possible the advent of a new republic, virile and fertile, true and hardworking, that Zola will later attempt to fabricate with his *Les Quatre Évangiles*.

This is the axiological framework that the *Rougon-Macquart* transport via their mythic substrata. The question I am concerned with in this and the next section involves this frame, or rather what fills it: the aim is to analyse the historical process that is to bring about change. What drives, what makes history? I think that the classical *translatio imperii* scheme Zola employs and his clear-cut and rather simplistic axiology of opposing a bad empire and a good republic is supplemented by a conceptualisation of history that clearly 'translates' this *translatio* itself into the 19th century. To put it differently, with his *Rougon-Macquart* Zola feels the need to paradoxically supplement the figure of *translatio imperii* with a concept of historicity. The "super-individual, material forces" determining the historical process are not theologically stabilised, at least not in any direct, dogmatic way. These forces are radically secular and above all, they are forces of the masses.

Zola is "one of the great virtuosi of modern crowd depiction" writes Nicholas Rennie (1996, 396), confirming Naomi Schor's earlier statement that Zola has more successfully than any other modern novelist integrated the crowd into his novelistic universe (1982, 27). And yet, despite these eulogies and despite the academic work undertaken to tackle the question of the crowd in the *Rougon-Macquart* (cf. Schor 1978, 1982, Rennie 1996, Laville 2012, Lumbroso 2012), I think that the central role the masses play for Zola's history of the Second Empire has not yet been adequately elucidated.

In the introduction to her landmark study of this very subject called *Zola's Crowds* Naomi Schor identifies a reason for this shortcoming in critical discourse: "a *poetics* of the novel founded on the structural analysis of myth, which decomposes characters into bundles of qualifications and functions" forecloses insight into the relations of the crowd and the individual (1978, xiii). By choosing for her analysis a Girardian frame that takes the notion of the scapegoat for "Zola's founding myth" (Schor 1978, 4), enables Schor to examine the "hard and fast distinctions between crowd and individual" and their movements of mediation and interplay. Despite the insights Naomi Schor produces, I find that her study of the crowd, in the end, falls prey to the same, inevitable historicity of methods and their blind spots that she censured with regard to the "structural analysis of myth": her approach of analysing the masses via the interplay of individual and crowd is not well suited to the way the masses function in the *Rougon-Macquart*. As Nicholas Rennie so felicitously put it in referring to Walter Benjamin, "the individual is replaced by the crowd, the *amorphe Masse*" (1996, 400), implying that there is an unbridgeable gap between this "*amorphe Masse*" and all the familiar notions of the human individual, of its mimetic desires and its ideas about economy and functionality. I assume that the reason Zola's crowds have not yet been discovered as crucial for the cycle's interpretation of history has to do with the fact that Zola radically conceptualises 'the crowd' as a Benjaminian "*amorphe Masse*".

It has not gone unnoticed that "Zola's recurrent crowd metaphor [...] is oceanic" (Schor 1978, 84): "the crowd itself, like the fabrics, is identified through aquatic imagery", writes Gabrielle Maryse Rochecouste (1988, 144), and Philip Walker has observed that the "mob of strikers [is] described in terms of a steadily mounting storming tide" (1959, 449). However, these observations of motif or theme strikingly fail to be integrated into some sort of systematic reading of the crowd and its far-reaching implications. Philipp Walker's article on "Prophetic Myths" in *Germinal* senses and even formulates the importance of the weather theme for the crowd: "The storm theme is thus, as Zola has developed it, a major expression of his thought – and particularly of his vision of history." (Walker 1959, 449). Unfortunately he did not find any alliance for his project amongst his readers. There are structural reasons for the divergence of the observations made in the text (Zola's 'weathery' descriptions of the crowd) and the critical reconstructions' of the crowd not listening to the text, but rather resorting to Girardian or another methodology. A detail in an article by Michael Gamper inadvertently may indicate why: Gamper, like many of his colleagues, is well aware of the masses being depicted in Zola as an ambivalent, a 'quasi-natural' [*naturförmige*] force (2005, 168). Nevertheless, he reads 'tide' [*Flut*] and 'torrent' [*Strom*] as stereotypes, like 'savage' [*Wilde*] and 'horde' [*Herde*], which serve as semantic signals and merely express the exceptionality [*Außerordentlichkeit*] of the procedures (Gamper 2005, 162). In other words: Zola's radical depiction of the "super-individual, material forces", of history as an interplay of natural forces, his telling the story of the historical subject becoming a natural element (Vibert 2007, 6), has triggered a reflex of 'othering' these historical forces in the world of criticism. They are banned from the discussion of historicity by being labelled 'extraordinary' – animals like the weather, or natural forces, do not make history. If their effect cannot be denied, then the impact works as history's 'other'. Obviously, the vast majority of critics are not willing to follow Zola's suspending the neat nature/culture divide, so that "the striking absence of any human agent or subject, [...] suggest[ing] total *débandade* – the lack of any controlling or directing human consciousness" (Nelson 1978, 63) cannot be taken seriously as a concept of history. Although the textual evidence is overwhelming, it still seems to be provocative to insist that Zola's "natural and social history" rests on this very concept of history; on history not as an arena of great human actions or the struggle of convictions and beliefs, nor of unifying processes of scapegoating that at least somehow refer to the 'social', that is the cultural and not the 'natural' realm, but on history as the processes of the *amorphe Masse*, of the brewing weather of the masses.

The previous sections provide us with the necessary background against which we can read and make sense of this weather of the masses. In my opinion, there is no need to bring any analytical instruments, any methodological support, any structural, functional or psychological theory of the masses to this text; Zola's conceptualising them as 'weathery' is itself a theory of the masses that deserves to be examined in detail. For the analysis that is to follow I have selected three exemplary crowds that explicitly carry a political and historical meaning.

In *La Fortune des Rougon* the teenage lovers Miette and Silvère spend a romantic day in the country, at the river Viorne outside the town of Plassans, when their intimate activity is suddenly disrupted by strange noises:

> For the last few moments, muffled sounds had been coming from behind the hills through which the Nice road disappears from view. It was like the distant jolting of a procession of carts. These sounds, as yet vague, were muffled further by the roar of the Viorne. Gradually, however, the noise grew louder, and became like the tramping of an army on the march. Then, in the growing rumble, shouting could be heard, strange rhythmical blasts, as if a gale was blowing. They sounded like the thunderclaps of a rapidly gathering storm that was already disturbing the stillness of the air as it approached. Silvère strained his ears, but was unable to make out the words being shouted by this tempest of voices, which the hillsides prevented from reaching him clearly. Suddenly a dark mass appeared round the bend, and the formidable sound of the *Marseillaise*, sung with vengeful fury, burst upon the air. (*eFR*, 23–24)[590]

---

[590] "Depuis un instant, des bruits confus venaient de derrière les coteaux, au milieu desquels se perd la route de Nice. C'étaient comme les cahots éloignés d'un convoi de charrettes. La Viorne, d'ailleurs, couvrait de son grondement ces bruits encore indistincts. Mais peu à peu ils s'accentuèrent, ils devinrent pareils aux piétinements d'une armée en marche. Puis on distingua, dans ce roulement continu et croissant, des brouhahas de foule, d'étranges souffles d'ouragan cadencés et rythmiques ; on aurait dit les coups de foudre d'un orage qui s'avançait rapidement, troublant déjà de son approche l'air endormi. Silvère écoutait, ne pouvant saisir ces voix de tempête que les coteaux empêchaient d'arriver nettement jusqu'à lui. Et, tout à coup, une masse noire apparut au coude de la route ; *la Marseillaise*, chantée avec une furie vengeresse, éclata, formidable." (*FR*, I 26)

The "dark mass" breaking into the couple's idyllic world is a mass of republican insurgents, mainly craftsmen and farmers of the region, who are marching against the *coup d'état* of Napoléon III. Zola artistically stages the arrival of this mass by fading in their noise, first "muffled" by the "roar" of the river, then growing more and more distinct. What Miette and Silvère hear is an approaching heavy weather: "strange rhythmical blasts, as if a gale was blowing", "thunderclaps of a rapidly gathering storm", a "tempest of voices". The "dark mass" they finally see appearing "round the bend" resonates with the couple's perception of the crowd as a weather event:

> The crowd descended the slope in one long, marvellous, irresistible rush. There could have been no more majestic sight than the irruption of these few thousand men into that cold, still landscape. The road became a torrent, rolling with living waves that seemed never to end; again and again, yet more dark throngs came round the bend, their singing continually swelling the great voice of this human tempest. (*eFR*, 24)[591]

Watching from "the top of the bank", standing "in the shadow of the bushes" Miette and Silvère form part of a setting that could be cited as a textbook example of the sublime: the "majestic sight" of the "marvellous, irresistible rush" is both overwhelming, and too large to be perceived, fulfilling both Kantian categories of the sublime at once (cf. Kant 1968 [1790]). As typical for the sights associated with the sublime and like many of Kant's examples, it is a view of a powerful, a violent natural spectacle: the "irruption of these few thousand men" is perceived as a weather event, "a torrent, rolling with living waves". As the formulation "living waves" already indicates, the crowd of insurgents not only sounds *like* and looks *like* a phenomenon of weather, it is indeed performing, it is constituting such an event. Zola uses their singing of the *Marseillaise* as the symbol for the insurgents' active participation in moving the air: "their singing continually swelling the great voice of this human tempest" emphasises that the weathery noises of the crowd are not just secondary effects of their marching, noises that happen to remind bystanders of the familiar noises of heavy weather; on the contrary, the notion of thousands of voices sounding together, "swelling the great voice" of the "dark mass" is indicative of how this mass is conceived, how it holds together, how it forms a mass: it is no coincidence that the notion of "swelling" ties in so neatly with the aquatic 'imagery' of the "torrent, rolling

---

[591] "La bande descendait avec un élan superbe, irrésistible. Rien de plus terriblement grandiose que l'irruption de ces quelques milliers d'hommes dans la paix morte et glacée de l'horizon. La route, devenue torrent, roulait des flots vivants qui semblaient ne pas devoir s'épuiser ; toujours, au coude du chemin, se montraient de nouvelles masses noires, dont les chants enflaient de plus en plus la grande voix de cette tempête humaine." (*FR*, I 27)

with living waves". The weather imagery that, over several pages, so consistently and insistently pervades the scene is not merely a metaphorical means employed for the description of an unfamiliar phenomenon: it very precisely tells of the way that the mass individuates itself as a mass, and the way it works: the mass is, ontologically, a "human tempest". The narrator's authorial voice even explicitly speaks out that it is weathery forces that hold this political crowd together (a notion unfortunately lost in Brian Nelson's English translation): "There were probably about three thousand of them, united and borne along by a wind of anger [*unis et emportés d'un bloc par un vent de colère*]." (eFR, 25; transl. altered)[592]

What breaks into the "cold, still landscape" of the narrative world is thus indeed a formation of heavy weather. Zola makes his protagonists instantly feel that this event is of importance, that it introduces a rupture that irreversibly distances them from the previous story of their love:

> When they had reached the top of the bank and stood in the shadow of the bushes, Miette, now quite pale, gazed sadly at the procession of men whose distant singing had been enough to snatch Silvère from her arms. It was as if the whole procession had thrust itself between them. They had been so happy a few minutes before, so tightly locked in their embrace, so alone, so cut off amidst the great silence and the soft light of the moon. (eFR, 24)[593]

With this sudden intrusion of the "human tempest" happening towards the end of the first chapter of the cycle's first novel, the pastoral, idyllic world of the lovers comes to an end. For Miette this rupture means an important and tragic biographical turn; for the readers of the cycle these lines contain a clear poetological message: the literary world of the *Rougon-Macquart* will not be the pastoral one of a couple "cut off" from the rest of the world, living their lives in "the soft light of the moon" surrounded by a "cold, still landscape". With the tempestuous weather of the "dark mass", disturbing the lovers' intimate togetherness, the 'actual' world of the *Rougon-Macquart* arrives. A world that could not differ more from the pastoral idyll: it is not the world of (two) individuals, characterised by the absence of external influences, surrounded by silence. The world arriving is a world of the weather: a world of masses interacting without any clear, human agent coordinating the proceedings, a world that consists merely

---

[592] "Il pouvait y avoir là environ trois mille hommes unis et emportés d'un bloc par un vent de colère." (*FR*, I 28)

[593] "Quand ils furent sur le talus, dans l'ombre des broussailles, l'enfant, un peu pâle, regarda tristement ces hommes dont les chants lointains avaient suffi pour arracher Silvère de ses bras. Il lui sembla que la bande entière venait se mettre entre elle et lui. Ils étaient si heureux, quelques minutes auparavant, si étroitement unis, si seuls, si perdus dans le grand silence et les clartés discrètes de la lune !" (*FR*, I 27)

of 'external influences' and the effects of their interaction, a world of loud noise and violent energy.

Our reading of *Au Bonheur des Dames* and other novels has made us familiar with the consequences of "the gust of wind of the century" (*eLP*, 374; transl. altered)[594] that rages violently against the 'old world': it is not only destroyed, but also 'devoured' by the violent weather, infected and drawn into it. This is exactly what happens to Miette and Silvère:

> His voice was choking with emotion as he finished naming the men, who seemed to be borne away by a whirlwind as fast as he enumerated them. Leaning forward, his face glowing, he feverishly pointed out the various contingents. Miette followed his gestures. The road below attracted her like the depths of a precipice. To avoid slipping down the slope, she clung to the young man's neck. From the men below there rose a kind of intoxication; and the men themselves were drunk with their own cries, courage and confidence. (*eFR*, 28)[595]

Silvère's "glowing", feverish face indicates that the "intoxication" rising from the mass has already reached and infected him. All the characteristics of this crowd of republican insurgents look familiar to us: the contagious warmth and intoxication they spread, their fever and glowing faces had been amongst the phenomena of the meteorotopoi we analysed in the last section. Miette's attraction towards the crowd resembles the forces drawing the customers of *Au Bonheur des Dames* into the shop: "the depths of a precipice" and the image of an attraction reminding us of "rivers draw[ing] together the stray waters of a valley" (*eLP*, 240–241)[596] both refer to the physical force of gravity that is responsible for the energy of violent natural phenomena. This is how the "irresistible rush" of the "human tempest" works, and how it is fed: although Silvère shares the mass's political, republican attitude, his and his girlfriend's joining the mass of insurgents cannot be explained by a rational or ideological decision. They are rather drawn into it by forces that cannot be captured with reference to the autonomous human individual. The sublime constellation, with its necessary distance between the watchers and the spectacle collapses and the watchers suddenly become part of the spectacle, contributing to its sublime violence.

---

594 "[…] le coup de vent du siècle […]." (*BD*, III 747)
595 "Et il acheva, d'une voix étranglée par l'émotion, le dénombrement de ces hommes, qu'un tourbillon semblait prendre et enlever à mesure qu'il les désignait. La taille grandie, le visage en feu, il montrait les contingents d'un geste nerveux. Miette suivait ce geste. Elle se sentait attirée vers le bas de la route, comme par les profondeurs d'un précipice. Pour ne pas glisser le long du talus, elle se retenait au cou du jeune homme. Une ivresse singulière montait de cette foule grisée de bruit, de courage et de foi." (*FR*, I 31)
596 "Comme les fleuves tirent à eux les eaux errantes d'une vallée, il semblait que le flot des clientes, coulant à plein vestibule, buvait les passants de la rue […]." (*BD*, III 618)

The observation that Zola's description makes the political belief and agenda of the republican insurgents fade against their forming a violent natural force is important: All the more so since, if my argument is correct, Zola paradoxically chooses a *republican* crowd to introduce the decadent world of the Second Empire into his narrative universe! The message of this astonishing move is clear: history and historical developments are not primarily driven by political beliefs and their struggle, but by a dynamic that is more complex, less foreseeable and controllable: the "wind of the century" rather than its spirit or belief, the masses' weathery force rather than a rational, political agenda. That is why Zola, despite of his being himself a republican, is not interested in portraying the insurgents' political cause: it is their natural force, their exerting an irresistible attraction, their producing a feverish drunkenness and dynamic that he is after. It is also as a 'blind' natural force, developing their own dynamic that is not guided by a rational strategy that the masses inadvertently, and against their political beliefs, contribute to the "wind of the century": Pierre Rougon very effectively uses the terror that the crowd exerts to stage his own coup. By streaming through the region without any strategy (that is to say, by blindly following, like a river, the way with the smallest resistance instead of developing an effective plan), by staying in Plassans only to eat and rest, the insurgents are easy prey for Pierre Rougon: he stylises himself as the hero who protects the town against (weathery) chaos. Without any reason the crowd leaves the town to the self-declared saviour, only to be slaughtered by the army's bullets on the open field:

> [T]he men from the towns and villages that the woodcutter had called to arms gathered together under the elms, forming a dark, uneven mass, grouped without regard to any of the rules of strategy, simply placed there like a block [bloc], as it were, to bar the way or die. (*eFR*, 198; transl. altered)[597]

It is no coincidence that when the soldiers begin to fire "[i]t seemed to Silvère as if a great gust of wind was passing over his head, while a shower of leaves, lopped off by the bullets, fell from the elms" (*eFR*, 199);[598] the mass of the insurgents, breaking into the world as a heavy weather perishes through heavy weather – in a debacle of natural forces annihilating each other. Miette, who

---

[597] "[L]es villes, les villages que le bûcheron avait appelés à l'aide se réunissaient, formaient sous les ormes une masse sombre, irrégulière, groupée en dehors de toutes les règles de la stratégie, mais qui avait roulé là, comme un bloc, pour barrer le chemin ou mourir." (*FR*, I 214–215)

[598] "Il lui sembla qu'un grand vent passait sur sa tête, tandis qu'une pluie de feuilles coupées par les balles tombaient des ormes." (*FR*, I 215)

has become the symbol of the insurgents and carries their red banner, is killed. Silvère will follow her a little later, when a gendarme he has injured during the insurgents' stay in Plassans recognises him after their defeat and executes him on the lovers' favourite place, the tombstone of the old graveyard.

A scene in *Germinal* strikingly resembles the sudden appearance of the republican "dark mass" experienced by the lovers Miette and Silvère in *La Fortune des Rougon*. Négrel, the engineer of the coal-pit, has embarked with Mme Hennebeau and some bourgeois daughters on a little day trip through the region on the very day that the colliers' violent protests break out. The inevitable happens: the ways of the bourgeois day trip company and of the rebelling colliers cross. When Négrel and his company spot "a great black crowd of people pouring like a flood down the road towards Vandame and yelling fiercely" (*eG*, 356)[599] they take shelter in the farm they were about to visit. Having hid their horses and the carriage, and having barricaded the entrance gate, all the party can do is wait. 'Fortunately', the "double doors" behind which Négrel and the ladies have taken position "didn't shut at all well" and "were so full of cracks that they could see the road between the rotten planks" (*eG*, 347).[600] In other words, Zola has equipped his characters with perfect places (hidden, but close to the 'scene', with good sight) for watching the spectacle that announces itself. Like Miette and Silvère standing at "the top of the bank", "in the shadow of the bushes", Négrel and the ladies serve as focalisers with whose ears and eyes the readers experience the approach of the rebelling mob; and like the two lovers, what the party behind the "double doors" perceive first is the approach of weathery noises:

> The noise increased, although there was nothing to be seen as yet, and it seemed as if a violent storm wind were blowing up along the empty road, like the sudden gusts which precede a great thunderstorm. (*eG*, 347)[601]

Only moments later "[t]he thunderous noise came nearer, they felt the ground vibrate beneath their feet" (*eG*, 347)[602] and the mob finally enters their view. What they encounter is clearly another "human tempest", "a hurricane of shouting and

---

[599] "Déjà, les jeunes filles, allongeant la tête, s'étonnaient de ce qu'elles distinguaient à gauche, un flot noir, une cohue qui débouchait en hurlant du chemin de Vandame." (*G*, III 1434)
[600] "La porte charretière, pourtant, fermait très mal, et elle avait de telles fentes, qu'on apercevait la route entre ses bois vermoulus." (*G*, III 1435)
[601] "Le bruit grandissait, on ne voyait rien encore, et sur la route vide un vent de tempête semblait souffler, pareil à ces rafales brusques qui précèdent les grands orages." (*G*, III 1435)
[602] "Le roulement de tonnerre approchait, la terre fut ébranlée et Jeanlin galopa le premier, soufflant sa corne." (*G*, III 1435)

gesticulating" (eG, 348)⁶⁰³ that drowns any possibility of communication even behind the farm's double doors.

> Then the men hove into view, a raging mob 2,000 strong, pit boys, hewers, and wastemen, a compact mass rolling forwards like a single body [*une masse compacte qui roulait d'un seul bloc*], whose discoloured breeches and ragged woollen jerseys merged into a single mud-coloured mass [*effacés dans la même uniformité terreuse*]. Only their burning eyes and the dark holes of their gaping mouths could be seen as they sang the 'Marseillaise' [...]. (eG, 348; transl. altered)⁶⁰⁴

Even though the crowd's individuation and functioning as a weather event or a natural force is not as explicitly spelled out as it had been with regard to the mass of insurgents in *La Fortune des Rougon*, the few precise allusions that Zola weaves into this description suffice to continue the conceptualisation of the crowd that he had initiated in the first novel of the cycle. The "compact mass" takes up the notion of the "dark mass" that Miette and Silvère saw coming round the bend; its "rolling forwards like a single body", "a single mud-coloured mass" is a variation of the "torrent, rolling with living waves". In fact, the passage concentrates on the uncanny individuation of the mass, its forming "a single body [*d'un seul bloc*]" that is not simply an ensemble of angry individuals, but merges them into something new, something that is not a group of human beings, but a mass, something that is governed by different laws. Against this background Négrel's shouting out "'I'm damned if I recognize a single one of them! Where on earth do these thugs come from?'" (eG, 348),⁶⁰⁵ has to be understood: We know him to be very close to the miners, he regularly inspects the pits and works underground; the fact that even he strikingly feels unable to recognise "a single" miner of the mob evokes the singular quality of the mass, its dissolving the individual to form a new, a "compact", "singular body", not a group of individuals, but a torrent, a "human tempest".

In fact, the attribute "human" of this "human tempest" is rather misguiding: tellingly Négrel does not see human individuals, but their "discoloured breeches and ragged woollen jerseys" merge into the mass. It is this dehumanization that

---

603 "Mais son [Négrel] mot spirituel fut emporté dans l'ouragan des gestes et des cris." (G, III 1435)

604 "Et les hommes déboulèrent ensuite, deux mille furieux, des galibots, des haveurs, des raccommodeurs, une masse compacte qui roulait d'un seul bloc, serrée, confondue, au point qu'on ne distinguait ni les culottes déteintes, ni les tricots de laine en loques, effacés dans la même uniformité terreuse. Les yeux brûlaient, on voyait seulement les trous des bouches noires, chantant *La Marseillaise* [...]." (G, III 1436)

605 "« Le diable m'emporte si j'en reconnais un seul ! D'où sortent-ils donc, ces bandits-là ? »" (G, III 1436)

frightens him most, as his brutal, bourgeois vision of revolution indicates, which is triggered by the view of the mass rolling along the road:

> It was a scarlet vision of the revolution that would inevitably carry them all away, on some blood-soaked *fin de siècle* evening. That was it, one night the people would rise up, cast caution aside, and run riot like this far and wide all over the countryside; and there would be rivers of bourgeois blood, their heads would be waved on pikes, their strong-boxes hacked open, and their gold poured all over the ground. The women would scream, and the men would look gaunt as wolves, their fangs drooling and gnashing. Yes, these same rags and the same thunder of clogs, the same terrifying pack of animals with dirty skins and foul breath, would sweep away the old world, as their barbarian hordes overflowed and surged through the land. There would be blazing fires, not a stone of the towns would be left standing, and they would become savages again, living out in the woods, once the poor had enjoyed their great orgy and garnered their harvest, sucked the women dry and sacked the cellars of the rich. There would be nothing left, not a sou of inherited wealth, not a line of legal entitlement, until the day when, perhaps, a new order might at last spring up from the earth. And that was the future out there, tearing down the road like a force of nature, and the terrible wind was blowing in their faces. (*eG*, 349; transl. altered)[606]

Overwhelmed by the "force of nature" and the "terrible wind" he sees unchained by a mass of poor people streaming along the road Négrel fabricates a revolutionary scenario. His obvious bourgeois fear of losing his privileges makes him fill the dehumanization he observed with a vision of brutal, 'barbarian' bestiality. It is important to note that the spectacle on the road did not display any evidence of this register. Négrel's vision gives testimony to a movement leading from the observation of a violent "force of nature" to the association of brutal bestiality and savagery. Very consistently the two isotopies are mixed: "rivers of bourgeois blood", "the same thunder of clogs, the same terrifying pack of animals", "the barbarian hordes overflowed". I insist on this difference

---

[606] "C'était la vision rouge de la révolution qui les emporterait tous, fatalement, par une soirée sanglante de cette fin de siècle. Oui, un soir, le peuple lâché, débridé, galoperait ainsi sur les chemins ; et il ruissellerait du sang des bourgeois, il promènerait des têtes, il sèmerait l'or des coffres éventrés. Les femmes hurleraient, les hommes auraient ces mâchoires de loups, ouvertes pour mordre. Oui, ce seraient les mêmes guenilles, le même tonnerre de gros sabots, la même cohue effroyable, de peau sale, d'haleine empestée, balayant le vieux monde, sous leur poussée débordante de barbares. Des incendies flamberaient, on ne laisserait pas debout une pierre des villes, on retournerait à la vie sauvage dans les bois, après le grand rut, la grande ripaille, où les pauvres, en une nuit, efflanqueraient les femmes et videraient les caves des riches. Il n'y aurait plus rien, plus un sou des fortunes, plus un titre des situations acquises, jusqu'au jour où une nouvelle terre repousserait peut-être. Oui, c'étaient ces choses qui passaient sur la route, comme une force de la nature, et ils en recevaient le vent terrible au visage." (*G*, III 1436–1437)

between the observation of the rebelling mass and Négrel's vision of revolution, because the vision does transport some truth as a vision for the narrative world: the "blazing fires", the overflowing and the complete destruction foreshadow the fate of Paris and France at the end of the Second Empire. Négrel does however not merely serve as a prophetic mouthpiece. The class distinction he introduces between the poor animals and the bourgeois human beings is not Zola's. The othering of violent forces, be they natural or bestial, that Négrel attempts is shown to be futile and deceptive by Zola: the bourgeois as well as the aristocracy are shown to contribute to this "human tempest", to this brutal "wind of the century" at least as much as the poor do. In Zola's narrative vision of the *Rougon-Macquart*, they all uncannily merge into the "single mud-coloured mass", the "force of nature" and "terrible wind" of the historical development leading towards the final debacle.

Viewed from the wayside, the republican mass of insurgents and the rebelling mob of colliers can hardly be distinguished. Announced by the noises of "a rapidly gathering storm", "thunderclaps", "sudden gusts, which precede a great thunderstorm", their "dark" and "compact" "mass[es]" roll along the road like an overflowing torrent, exerting the natural force of a "human tempest". Their singing of the Marseillaise underlines the two masses' similarity. In contrast to the crowd of insurgents where we only get to know about the process of Miette's and Silvère's 'infection', of their joining the crowd, *Germinal* gives us insight into the actual formation of the mob's violent weather. Étienne initiates a gathering of the miners that takes place in a clearing in the woods:

> Nearly 3,000 colliers had come to the meeting, and a teeming crowd of men, women, and children gradually filled the clearing and spilled over into the edge of the wood; but still latecomers kept arriving, until the sea of heads, swimming in darkness, poured into the neighbouring copses. A murmuring sound arose like a stormy wind from the still, frozen forest. (*eG*, 279; transl. altered)[607]

As the aquatic 'imagery' of the "sea of heads", "spill[ing] over the edge" and "pour[ing] into the neighbouring copses", indicates, the mass is from the beginning conceptualised as a natural phenomenon. All that Étienne does by his speaking to this liquid, aquatic mass is load it with energy, warming it, bringing these waters to move:

---

[607] "Près de trois mille charbonniers étaient au rendez-vous, une foule grouillante, des hommes, des femmes, des enfants, emplissant peu à peu la clairière, débordant au loin sous les arbres ; et des retardataires arrivaient toujours, le flot des têtes, noyé d'ombre, s'élargissait jusqu'aux taillis voisins. Un grondement en sortait, pareil à un vent d'orage, dans cette forêt immobile et glacée." (*G*, III 1376)

> And beneath the chill air there rose a furious mass of faces, with gleaming eyes and open mouths, a tumult of people, men, women, and children, driven by starvation to demand restitution of the heritage which had been stolen from them. They forgot the cold as his burning words lit a fire in their hearts. A religious fervour lifted them towards the heavens, with the urgency that inspired the early Christians to hope that the reign of justice was about to materialize. (eG, 284)[608]

It is still in the clearing that his warming, heating words release the forces of violent weather from this mass of strikers in one of the cycle's so crucial thermodynamic transformations: "He was answered by a thunderous round of cries and exclamations" (eG, 280).[609] "Voices were raised again, in a tempestuous blast: 'Death to all cowards!'" (eG, 288).[610] "The tempest of their 3,000 voices fill[ing] the heavens" (eG, 291)[611] seem to mark Étienne's complete success as a demagogue. However, the moment that the violent weather of the mass is released, he at once loses control of the situation:

> He was applauded wildly in his turn, and from then on Étienne lost control of the meeting [Étienne lui-même fut débordé]. Speaker after speaker stood on the tree trunk, gesticulated amid the uproar, making wild proposals. They were possessed with the divine folly of inspired believers, the impatience of a religious sect which, tired of waiting for the promised miracle to happen, decides to accomplish it unaided. (eG, 290)[612]

As the French original puts it more precisely, Étienne himself is 'overflowed' [débordé] by the dynamics of the situation, by the violent forces that he himself has conjured up. The mass's 'natural force' is not a metaphor; it is not merely a name for the immense power to which the forces of three thousand individuals add up. The forces that Étiennne sets free are indeed 'natural forces', forces of a violent weather: the laws governing the course of this crowd and its rebellion do not have anything to do with regulating, guiding or taming human behaviour,

---

608 "Et c'était sous l'air glacial, une furie de visages, des yeux luisants, des bouches ouvertes, tout un rut de peuple, les hommes, les femmes, les enfants, affamés et lâchés au juste pillage de l'antique bien dont on les dépossédait. Ils ne sentaient plus le froid, ces ardentes paroles les avaient chauffés aux entrailles. Une exaltation religieuse les soulevait de terre, la fièvre d'espoir des premiers chrétiens de l'Église, attendant le règne prochain de la justice." (G, III 1380)
609 "Un tonnerre lui répondit, des cris, des exclamations." (G, III 1377)
610 "Les voix reprirent, avec leur souffle de tempête : « Mort aux lâches ! »" (G, III 1384)
611 "L'ouragan de ces trois mille voix emplit le ciel et s'éteignit dans la clarté pure de la lune." (G, III 1386)
612 "On l'applaudit furieusement à son tour, et dès lors Étienne lui-même fut débordé. Des orateurs se succédaient sur le tronc d'arbre, gesticulant dans le bruit, lançant des propositions farouches. C'était le coup de folie de la foi, l'impatience d'une secte religieuse, qui, lasse d'espérer le miracle attendu, se décidait à le provoquer enfin." (G, III 1385)

with ethical standards, rationality, strategic thinking or with governing human beings. The forces that the mass develops are genuinely natural forces. This is exactly the story that Zola's account of the rebellion tells at great length. The guiding 'metaphor' for this story is again the familiar one of river that has overflowed:

> Miners were arriving from all sides, the Maheus from the highway, the women from across the fields, all in dribs and drabs [*tous débandés*], with no leaders, and no weapons, flooding in like some natural stream that had overflowed its banks [*une eau débordée*] and was pouring downhill. (*eG*, 319)[613]

> More and more comrades kept arriving, until there were nearly a thousand of them, spilling chaotically [*sans ordre*] down the road like a swollen stream bursting its banks. (*eG*, 326)[614]

This 'metaphor' characterises several dimensions of the crowd. (1) Its formation and organisation: there are no leaders, there is no abstract principle of formation except for one gravitational force drawing it together. (2) Its course: the mass does not follow a strategic plan, the events seem to happen by chance. "The flood [*le flot*] was already surging on its way towards the next pit." (*eG*, 332; transl. altered)[615] (3) Its principle of gathering power:

> They arrived at Gaston-Marie in a mass that had still grown [*en une masse grossie encore*], now counting 2,500 of the desperadoes, smashing or sweeping aside everything in their path, with the accumulated force of a rolling torrent. (*eG*, 336; transl. altered)[616]

It is important to underline again that Zola's characterisation of the rebelling mass as an overflowing river is not a simple metaphor. The mass is perfectly well individuated, despite its lack of abstract organisation and leaders. Although not following any strategy, its course (like the course of a river) is not 'pure coincidence', but the result of a complex interplay of factors, gravitation, topography, resistance of the materials it encounters, etc. The image of the "swollen stream" does therefore not merely indicate the fact that the mass is chaotic and violent. It gives a very precise account of the mass (probably more precise than any

---

[613] "De partout, des mineurs débouchaient, les Maheu par la grande route, les femmes à travers champs, tous débandés, sans chefs, sans armes, coulant naturellement là, ainsi qu'une eau débordée qui suit les pentes." (*G*, III 1410)

[614] "D'autres camarades arrivaient toujours, on était près de mille, sans ordre, coulant de nouveau sur la route en un torrent débordé." (*G*, III 1416)

[615] "Déjà, le flot s'éloignait, roulait sur la fosse voisine." (*G*, III 1421)

[616] "On arriva à Gaston-Marie, en une masse grossie encore, plus de deux mille cinq cents forcenés, brisant tout, balayant tout, avec la force accrue du torrent qui roule." (*G*, III 1425)

reading of this 'metaphor' could be), because the mass *is* a swollen stream. This is the way it is individuated, this is the way that it works and brings destruction.

Facing this natural force, this violent weather, Étienne's role changes quickly from the leader who unleashes this force to the one watching and experiencing a weather event. In fact, the novel uses Étienne's previous central role to stage the powerlessness of the individual trying to command or at least tame the mass once its forces have been set free. Instead of regaining control, Étienne, like Miette and Silvère, finds himself infected by the fever of the crowd:

> Even he felt intoxicated, carried away by the hot breath of revenge. [...] But still they wouldn't listen to him, and his voice was about to be smothered again [*il allait être débordé de nouveau*], when they heard a commotion outside, coming from a little low door, where the ladder well emerged. (*eG*, 324)[617]

Since "nobody obeyed Étienne any more" (*eG*, 356),[618] all he can do is desperately watch the violence of the mass rage against everything that comes in their way. A new level of brutality is reached when the increasing fever of the mass is thermodynamically transformed into the heavy weather of hailing stones:

> Despite his orders, the stones continued to fly [*continuaient à grêler*], and he was astonished and dismayed to see these brutes that he had unleashed, so slow to be roused, and yet so terrible afterwards, with their vicious and implacable fury. All the old Flemish blood was there, in these heavy, placid people; it took months for it to warm up, but then they threw themselves into the most abominable savagery, and were incapable of listening to reason, until the beast had drunk its fill of atrocities. (*eG*, 356)[619]

His attempt to divert the mass from attacking the bourgeois house they are already covering with their violent hail of stones only provokes the "most abominable savagery" that happens in *Germinal*: the shop-owner Maigrat (known for having sexually exploited his customers' poverty, sharing sexual services for credit) is killed and castrated, his chopped off penis is shown around as a trophy.

---

617 "Lui-même [Étienne] se grisait, emporté dans cette fièvre chaude de revanche. [...] On ne l'écoutait toujours pas, il allait être débordé de nouveau, lorsque des huées s'élevèrent dehors, à une petite porte basse, où débouchait le goyot des échelles." (*G*, III 1414)

618 "Personne, du reste, n'obéissait plus à Étienne." (*G*, III 1442)

619 "Les pierres, malgré ses ordres, continuaient à grêler, et il s'étonnait, il s'effarait devant ces brutes démuselées par lui, si lentes à s'émouvoir, terribles ensuite, d'une ténacité féroce dans la colère. Tout le vieux sang flamant était là, lourd et placide, mettant des mois à s'échauffer, se jetant aux sauvageries abominables, sans rien entendre, jusqu'à ce que la bête fût soûle d'atrocités." (*G*, III 1442)

Against the raging of this "blind force" (eG, 446)[620] Étienne feels and proves utterly powerless:

> But he felt that he was running out of courage, that he no longer even had any fellow feeling for his comrades, he was afraid of them, of their enormous numbers, of the blind, irresistible force of the people, sweeping onwards like some natural disaster, ignoring all rules and theories. (eG, 447)[621]

Neither "rules and theories", nor strategic thinking, nor human pity can stop this "natural disaster". If these natural forces are to be stopped, then by clashing with other mighty natural forces, in a moment of crisis. In the case of the mob attacking Maigrat, it is the appearance of gendarmes that has the effect of a hurricane dispersing the "human tempest" of the rebellion: "It was a debacle [*une débâcle*], a stampede [*un sauve-qui-peut*] so frenzied that in only a couple of minutes the road was empty, swept absolutely clear as if by a hurricane." (eG, 369; transl. altered)[622]

When somewhat later a mass of miners again rages against the class enemy, releasing another "storm of giant hailstones" (eG, 429),[623] this time throwing stones at soldiers that are protecting the mine of 'Le Voreux', the "hurricane" that answers the protesters' "hail of stones" (eG, 429)[624] is less metaphorical than the appearance of the gendarmes: a "storm of bullets" (eG, 432)[625] executes a massacre against the raging mob, killing and injuring dozens of miners – and bringing the heavy weather of the rebellion to an end. In other words, the "compact mass" of rebelling colliers is stopped the same way that the "dark mass" of insurgents had been brought to a halt: by the bullets of soldiers. Both times the violent intervention of the army that answers the raging "human tempest" of protesters or insurgents is itself related to be a weathery event: we have seen that the bullets passing over Silvère's head seemed like "a great gust of wind"; the "storm of bullets" fired at the colliers very precisely takes up this conceptualisation, which is not merely metaphorical, but, again, describes the

---

620 "[…] une force aveugle […]." (*G*, III 1520)
621 "Mais il se sentait à bout de courage, il n'était même plus de cœur avec les camarades, il avait peur d'eux, de cette masse énorme, aveugle et irrésistible du peuple, passant comme une force de la nature, balayant tout, en dehors des règles et des théories." (*G*, III 1521)
622 "Ce fut une débâcle, un sauve-qui-peut si éperdu, qu'en deux minutes la route se trouva libre, absolument nette, comme balayée par un ouragan." (*G*, III 1455)
623 "C'était une grêle, des grêlons énormes, dont on entendait les claquements sourds." (*G*, III 1507)
624 "Sous cette rafale de pierres, la petite troupe disparaissait." (*G*, III 1508)
625 "Tout semblait terminé, l'ouragan des balles s'était perdu très loin, jusque dans les façades du coron, lorsque le dernier coup partit, isolé, en retard." (*G*, III 1510)

events, their logic and their interaction. Heavy weather is only to be answered and stopped by heavy weather, leading to a catastrophic moment, to a debacle – to a moment of crisis that proves to be necessary for the world to renew.

When all the atrocities, the sufferings and religious fervours of the strikers' rebellion have come to a catastrophic end without any of the colliers goals having been reached, Étienne poses an important question: "So who was the guilty party then?" (eG, 447)[626] The strike has brought incredible suffering to the colliers, poverty, starvation, violence and death. Étienne is well aware that he has facilitated the brewing and the outbreak of the strike's heavy weather. Nevertheless, he feels that he cannot take responsibility for the natural forces he seems to have set loose. The question of guilt on which the novel ends does not distribute responsibility for the horrible events among the characters and parties involved. Strikingly, it does not undertake a political evaluation of what has been narrated. Zola brings up this important question only to qualify it: he refutes the notion that history consists of 'parties' fighting for their interests and beliefs and which can, in the end, be made responsible for the damages their strife has caused. That is why *Germinal*, in a certain sense, is not primarily a political novel – although attempted repeatedly, it cannot be convincingly appropriated for a distinct ideological position. It is futile to ask whether Zola is on the side of the strikers or, on the contrary, staging their complete failure. Zola is interested in the greater historical development of which these events (strike and exploitation, outbreak of violence and crisis) form a part.

It is the question of the "guilty party" that Zola uses to make this point. Étienne is not the only person to reflect on the events, his role and responsibility; Deneulin, the owner of the pit located next to 'Le Voreux', who is ruined by the strikers' rebellion, also ponders the question of guilt and historical agency:

> And as he knew that disaster was inevitable, he felt no more hatred for the bandits from Montsou; for he felt that they were all in it together, he and they, all guilty accomplices from time immemorial [*une faute générale, séculaire*]. Doubtless they were brutes, but they were illiterate, starving brutes. (eG, 327)[627]

Surprisingly, La Maheude, who has hosted Étienne in her family of miners when he newly is arrived at the pit and whose tragic story gives perhaps the most pitiable account of the suffering caused by the strike and rebellion, ends in a similar situation. She has lost the majority of her family during the strike,

---

[626] "Qui donc était le coupable ?" (*G*, III 1521)
[627] "Et, dans cette certitude de son désastre, il n'avait plus de haine contre les brigands de Montsou, il sentait la complicité de tous, une faute générale, séculaire. Des brutes sans doute, mais des brutes qui ne savaient pas lire et qui crevaient de faim." (*G*, III 1416)

a child starved, her husband killed by a soldier's bullet, three other children come to death in the wake of the events. When life returns to 'normality' after the strike, she is herself forced to work again in the pit under the most cruel conditions to nourish her remaining children, despite her forty years of age and her frail health. Nevertheless, when she meets Étienne a last time before he leaves the region, the man who has spread the idea of the strike that had turned out so disastrously for her, she surprisingly does not blame him for the events:

> '[...] There was a time when I wanted to kill you, after all that butchery. But then you think it over, don't you? You realize that in the end it's not really anyone's fault ... No, it's really not your fault, it's everyone's fault.' (eG, 518)[628]

What does it mean that the fault is "general" [*générale*], "ancient" [*séculaire*], that not "anyone" but "everyone" has to be blamed? It is certainly no coincidence that Zola puts this verdict in the mouths of both a miner and a capitalist: their surprisingly univocal judgment rejects any naïve Marxist reading of the novel. History, according to Zola, cannot be understood by delegating historical agency to the classes and the logics of class struggle only. Neither the violent natural force of the rebelling mass that Étienne helped to unleash nor the soldier's "storm of bullets" that stopped this rebellion can be understood without the overarching historical situation and development in which these events are embedded: they contribute and form part of the "wind of the century", of the Second Empire's catastrophic warming climate. To be sure, there are class struggle, brutal exploitation and violent excesses during the rebellion. It cannot be my aim to merely displace the responsibility for the events by shifting it from individuals or groups to an abstract 'natural' force. Strikingly, it is not only not "anyone's fault", it is also, at the same time, "everyone's fault", meaning that the contribution to the historical situation is more complex than can be captured by the concept of individual or group agency that presupposes rational and intentional behaviour.

With his consistent reference to weather and climate Zola conceptualises an alternative way of reconstructing historical development and analyses how social interaction, the influence of technological progress and political circumstances add up to a historical force. Speaking of "natural forces" instead of class struggle, of the 'climate of an age' instead of individual intentions and guilt does

---

[628] "« [...] Un moment, je t'aurais assommé, après toutes ces tueries. Mais on réfléchit, n'est-ce pas ? on s'aperçoit qu'au bout de compte ce n'est la faute de personne... Non, non, ce n'est pas ta faute, c'est la faute de tout le monde. »" (*G*, III 1586)

not mean to switch to an abstract, metaphorical mode that disavows contact with the 'actual' historical events and responsibilities. On the contrary, resorting to the complex logic of climate and weather accounts for the complexity of human interaction, of culture and society, of a modern world. The course that the world of the anthropocene takes is not determined by powerful individuals or groups, but by the complex, stochastic interaction of the disparate.

The third and last mass of people I would like to examine is 'composite but continuous'. It resurfaces in different novels and always tells the story of the Second Empire's desire to march towards the debacle. It enters the world of the *Rougon-Macquart* in the last scene of *Nana* and is significantly interwoven with the horrible scenes of Nana's dying from smallpox. From the windows of her hotel room, high above the city, a group of courtesans visiting Nana at her deathbed witness two spectacles, one inside the room, one outside, in the streets of Paris:

> The light was fading fast, and in the distance the gas-jets were coming on one by one. People could now be seen watching the scene from their windows while the human stream [*le flot humain*] under the trees was swelling every minute, powerfully rolling from the Madeleine to the Bastille; carriages were having to crawl along. From this solid mass [*masse compacte*] a dull rumble was rising; they were still silent, attracted by a need to pile up, tramping round like a herd of animals, but they were heating themselves up of a shared fever. (*eN*, 413; transl. altered)[629]

It is not difficult to spot that this mass of people is related in the same way that the mass of insurgents and the mass of rebelling miners have been described. The concept of the "swelling" stream is used, familiar words serve to individualise the mass ("masse compacte", "masse compacte qui roulait d'un seul bloc" (*G*, III 1436)), it is again associated with the notion of a growing fever. Every time that the courtesans' view switches from the inside of the room, from their talking about Nana's sad fate and the circumstances of her last hours, to the spectacle on the streets, the 'theme' of the 'weathery' character of the mass that is celebrating the declaration of the war with Prussia is re-actualised:

> There were more and more people crowding in the streets. In the bright lights from the shop-windows and the flickering patches of the gas-jets you could see the double stream flowing on the pavements, sweeping along hats [*le double courant des trottoirs, qui*

---

[629] "La nuit grandissait, des becs de gaz dans le lointain s'allumaient un à un. Cependant, aux fenêtres, on distinguait des curieux, tandis que, sous les arbres, le flot humain s'enflait de minute en minute, dans une coulée énorme, de la Madeleine à la Bastille. Les voitures roulaient avec lenteur. Un ronflement se dégageait de cette masse compacte, muette encore, venue par un besoin de se mettre en tas et piétinant, s'échauffant d'une même fièvre." (*N*, II 1474)

charriait des chapeaux]. The fever was beginning to spread and people were constantly dashing into the road to join the gangs of men in smocks, a continuous thrust sweeping the road [*une poussée continue balayait la chaussée*]; and the shout rising from all the breasts, jerky, obstinate:

'On to Berlin! On to Berlin! On to Berlin!' (*eN*, 416; transl. altered)[630]

In fact, the theme of the mass as an overflowing stream flooding the streets of Paris keeps reappearing, it dominates the descriptions and mirrors the insistency of the crowd's shouting "'On to Berlin!'". It is its sublime dimension that makes this spectacle so "amusing to watch": "Down below it was very amusing [*amusant*] to watch the crowd roll like a torrent on the pavements and the roadway" (*eN*, 418; transl. altered).[631] However, the courtesans are only insufficiently aware of the fact that this "amusing" side forebodes the ultimate catastrophe. Like the violent natural force of the insurgents or the strikers, the "human stream" of war-enthusiasts cannot be stopped but in a clima(c)tic disaster; like the torrent of the insurgents and the rebelling strikers, the stream of patriots is blindly but surely rushing towards a debacle. Zola's narratological construction of the scene, paralleling it with Nana's dying, leaves no doubt about this fate: As already noted above, the crowd's shouting "'On to Berlin! On to Berlin! On to Berlin!'" echoes the crowd's univocally shouting "'Nana! Nana!'" (*eN*, 28) during the horserace. Nana's cruel death is emblematic, it is a prophesying symbol for the catastrophe towards which the torrent of the enthusiastic mass is inevitably and unstoppably flowing. Only one of the courtesans senses that the torches of the crowd, producing the stunning spectacle of a "a red gleam, like a burning fuse glowing its way through the crowd and spreading out over them in a broad sheet of flame" (*eN*, 418),[632] portend the future disaster of the lost war and the burning city: "'[…] And now war's been declared and the Prussians are going to come and set fire to everything … […]'"

---

[630] "La foule augmentait toujours. Dans le coup de lumière des boutiques, sous les nappes dansantes du gaz, on distinguait le double courant des trottoirs, qui charriait des chapeaux. A cette heure, la fièvre gagnait de proche en proche, des gens se jetaient à la suite des bandes en blouse, une poussée continue balayait la chaussée ; et le cri revenait, sortait de toutes les poitrines, saccadé, entêté :

« A Berlin ! à Berlin ! à Berlin ! »" (*N*, II 1477)

[631] "Puis, au-dessous, c'était très amusant, on voyait les coulées de la foule rouler comme un torrent sur les trottoirs et la chaussée […]." (*N*, II 1479)

[632] "Mais la bande qui arrivait en vociférant avait des torches ; une lueur rouge venait de la Madeleine, coupait la cohue d'une traînée de feu, s'étalait au loin sur les têtes comme une nappe d'incendie." (*N*, II 1479)

(*eN*, 421).⁶³³ The narrator, however, does not leave the readers in the dark concerning the disastrous course of the crowd's torrent:

> Torches were still being carried past, throwing out sparks; in the distance, the groups of people were rippling in the gloom like long flocks of sheep being led by night to the slaughter, and this confused, whirling mass of people streaming by [*ce vertige, ces masses confuses, roulées par le flot*] created a feeling of terror and immense pity for the massacres to come. They were bewildered, their voices cracking in the frenzy of their intoxication as they hurtled towards their unknown fate beyond the dark wall of the horizon.
>
> 'On to Berlin! On to Berlin! On to Berlin!' (*eN*, 420)⁶³⁴

Zola has dedicated a novel to the fate of this "whirling mass of people" so enthusiastically affirming the war with Prussia, a novel programmatically titled *La Débâcle*. Dealing with the war of 1870/71 between France and Prussia, this penultimate novel of the cycle narrates the end of the Second Empire and thereby also closes the cycle's historical frame. Maurice, one of the novel's protagonists, a soldier of the French army that tries to fight back the Prussian attack, embodies the link between the enthusiastic crowd on the streets of Paris we encountered at the end of *Nana* and the mass of French soldiers that are marching through the north of France in *La Débâcle*:

> To Berlin! To Berlin! The savage cry from the crowds teeming through the boulevards, on that night of wild enthusiasm which had made Maurice decide to join up, rang again in his ears. The wind had just changed, whipped by a stormy breeze [*Le vent venait de tourner, sous un coup de tempête*]; and there was a terrible lurch, the whole temperament of the race was there in his over-excited confidence, which went plunging so precipitously into deep despair at the first sign of defeat, taking him off as it galloped away, among these soldiers who wandered, vanquished scattered, without even having seen action. (*eD*, 32–33)⁶³⁵

---

633 "« [...] Et voilà la guerre déclarée, les Prussiens vont venir, ils brûleront tout... [...] »" (*N*, II 1481)

634 "Des torches passaient encore, secouant des flammèches ; au loin, les bandes moutonnaient, allongées dans les ténèbres, pareilles à des troupeaux menés de nuit à l'abattoir ; et ce vertige, ces masses confuses, roulées par le flot, exhalaient une terreur, une grande pitié des massacres futurs. Ils s'étourdissaient, les cris se brisaient dans l'ivresse de leur fièvre se ruant à l'inconnu, là-bas, derrière le mur noir de l'horizon.

« A Berlin ! à Berlin ! à Berlin ! »" (*N*, II 1480–1481)

635 "A Berlin ! à Berlin ! Maurice entendit ce cri hurlé par la foule grouillante des boulevards, pendant la nuit de fol enthousiasme, qui l'avait décidé à s'engager. Le vent venait de tourner, sous un coup de tempête ; et il y avait une saute terrible, et tout le tempérament de la race était dans cette confiance exaltée, qui tombait brusquement, dès le premier revers, à la désespérance dont le galop l'emportait parmi ces soldats errants, vaincus et dispersés, avant d'avoir combattu." (*D*, V 426)

"The wind had just changed, whipped by a stormy breeze" – this is what *La Débâcle* relates in a detailed and extensive fashion. The "swelling" "human stream" violently rumbling along the Paris boulevards, feverishly demonstrating the strength of the Empire, very soon experiences 'a weather' that changes it all: "the wind of panic" (*eD*, 39)[636] hits the mass of soldiers "at the first sign of defeat, [...] without even having seen action." Zola had conceptualised the dynamic of the "over-excited confidence" of the mass streaming through Paris as a weather phenomenon; his description of the "deep despair" spreading amongst the mass of soldiers continues this conceptualisation. The fact that "the wind had just changed" thus does not merely metaphorically signify a turn of fortunes: it is a precise way of describing the dynamic that takes place in the mass and that accounts for the course it takes.

The first gust of the changing wind hitting the mass of soldiers consists of a "wind of panic" emerging from a mass of fugitives they encounter. This wind is narrated to literally "ruffle[ ] [the fugitives'] hair and set hastily buttoned garments flapping about wildly" (*eD*, 39),[637] it is a sort of corporeal, physical force that spreads over to the soldiers when the two masses, soldiers and fugitives, clash:

> [...] back on the road, the streams of carts and foot travellers flowed steadily past, hindering the troops' onward march. They swept along so thick and fast as they neared Belfort that it was like battling against a swollen, irresistible torrent, and more than once, the soldiers were obliged to a halt. (*eD*, 39–40)[638]

A second, similar gust of the changing wind arrives when the soldiers around Maurice hear of the "debacle of a crushed army", of "the main roads teeming with [*roulant*] a dreadful confusion of men, horses, carts, and cannon", all "lashed by the mad winds of panic" (*eD*, 59–60).[639] The "storm of stupefaction" that blew, "carrying off both conquered and conquerors" (*eD*, 60)[640] very early also captures Maurice's company, without having yet become involved in

---

[636] "[...] vent de panique [...]." (*D*, V 432)

[637] "[...] ce vent de panique qui échevelait les têtes et fouettait les vêtements attachés à la hâte." (*D*, V 432)

[638] "[...] sur la route, le flot des voitures et des piétons passait toujours, gênant la marche des troupes, si compact aux approches de Belfort, d'un tel courant irrésistible de torrent élargi, que des haltes, à plusieurs reprises, devinrent nécessaires." (*D*, V 433)

[639] "[...] les grands chemins roulant une affreuse confusion d'hommes, de chevaux, de voitures, de canons, toute la débâcle d'une armée détruite, fouettée du vent fou de la panique [...]." (*D*, V 452)

[640] "Mais les généraux galopaient, dans l'effarement, et une telle tempête de stupeur soufflait, emportant à la fois les vaincus et les vainqueurs [...]." (*D*, V 452)

any battle, at the latest, when they finally catch "sight of a crowd rushing headlong, with officers wounded, soldiers scattering and unarmed, convoy wagons galloping along, men and beasts fleeing, the wind of disaster behind them." (eD, 126)[641] One might be tempted to read all these winds and storms ("of panic", "of stupefaction", "of disaster") as extensions of the "wind that had just changed" that all metaphorically signify the change of a group's psychological state of mind, plunging from "confidence" "into deep despair". However, this 'metaphor' of winds forms part of a larger complex of 'weather imagery' that is all grouped around the central 'image' of the overflowing river:

> On 7 August, the remains of the 1st Corps began crossing Saverne, like an overflowing, silt-lade river, sweeping the wreckage along. At Sarrebourg, on the 8th, the 5th Corps ran straight into the 1st like one runaway torrent meeting another, in full flight, defeated without a battle, dragging its poor commander – General de Failly – down with it. (eD, 60)[642]

Zola's use of weather imagery, and especially of the theme of the overflowing river is so consistent and insistent that I would suggest speaking of a 'conceptualisation *as* weather' rather than of the employment of weather metaphors. The weathery character of the masses does not only *illustrate* their behaviour, their spirit, their change of psychological state and their defeat – it rather *explains* it.

The brewing of the heavy weather in Paris, the wind and the warming of the century, its growing fever, have given an account of the way that led to this war: the swelling torrent of the mass that gathered in Paris (gathering power the way that a swelling torrent does) has blindly but surely swept towards this final debacle. More than that, the mass's following the blind, complex logic of the weather, the absence of any instance of control and of strategic guidance, also explains the debacle itself. In other words, *La Débâcle* does not tell the story of a historical event, of two armies clashing and fighting each other until one is defeated – with an open, unforeseeable outcome; it rather traces a natural phenomenon that follows the course that the natural laws governing this phenomenon provide for. Chaos does not happen to the French army as a surprising event, it rather follows from the 'ordinary', the 'natural' run of things. It is the

---

641 "Tout d'un coup, par un chemin de traverse, on aperçut une cohue qui se précipitait, des officiers blessés, des soldats débandés et sans armes, des voitures du train galopant, les hommes et les bêtes fuyant, affolés sous un vent de désastre." (*D*, V 519)
642 "Le 7, les débris du 1er corps traversaient Saverne, ainsi qu'un fleuve limoneux et débordé, charriant des épaves. Le 8, à Sarrebourg, le 5e corps venait tomber dans le 1er, comme un torrent démonté dans un autre [...]." (*D*, V 452)

same principles that had made this torrent of the Second Empire's masses swell and gather violence, the same principles that had also fired up and driven the meteorotopoi, that now cause the total breakdown: its being individualised and organised as a torrent, its weathery character and dynamic that does not follow a strategy and cannot be controlled, but just blindly flows according to the resistance and circumstances that it encounters. When the mass of French soldiers collide with the Prussian army (well-organised, disciplined, guided by a rational strategy) this torrent hits an obstacle that it cannot just incorporate and make part of itself. It hits a rock of solidity that disperses the torrent's natural force, makes it seek another path of less resistance, turning its forces against itself. Zola writes the natural history of this 'natural' spectacle: he gives a 'natural' account of what must be called the 'self-defeat' or at least the 'self-weakening' of the French army. The phenomenon of "one runaway torrent meeting another, in full flight, defeated without a battle" is not a phenomenon of coincidence and pure chaos; it rather follows the inevitable laws of fluid mechanics. Zola merely observes and narrates what happens when a torrent hits a solid body, a body that is not organised and individuated in this fluid, weathery fashion.

Very quickly "the wind had [...] changed", meaning that as a result of this resistance the torrent (that is to say the mass) of French soldiers has found a new course. A mighty "crowd of fugitives" has formed and is "pouring down the middle of the road, gathering speed like an overflowing torrent" (eD, 311):[643]

> This was what a rout looked like, a muddy river of men rolling down toward the ditches of Sedan, like the mass of soil and stones that a storm buffeting the high ground sends tumbling down into the valley. And from all the neighbouring plains, in a panic, at a gallop, down every slope, along every fold of land, down the Floing road, through Pierremont, through the graveyard, over the Champ de Mars, and through Fond de Givonne came the same crowd, swelling with every minute, streaming down. (eD, 302)[644]

The dynamic that this "muddy river of men", this torrent of "deep despair" develops is not any different from the torrent of "over-excited confidence" of which Maurice had been a part in the streets of Paris, except for its not heading "To Berlin!", but fleeing from it. As "on that night of wild enthusiasm" Maurice is again infected by the crowd, drawn into it and loses himself in it: "Even

---

[643] "Autour d'eux, la queue extrême des fuyards coulait toujours à pleine route, d'un train sans cesse accru de torrent débordé." (D, V 705)

[644] "C'était la déroute roulant vers les fossés de Sedan, en un flot bourbeux, pareil à l'amas de terres et de cailloux qu'un orage, battant les hauteurs, entraîne au fond des vallées. De tous les plateaux environnants, par toutes les pentes, par tous les plis de terrain, par la route de Floing, par Pierremont, par le cimetière, par le Champ de Mars, aussi bien que par le Fond de Givonne, la même cohue ruisselait en un galop de panique sans cesse accru." (D, V 696)

though he knew the countryside, Maurice didn't know where he was heading, unable to stop, caught up in the overflowing torrent, the terror-stricken crowd coursing down the road." (*eD*, 149)[645] His senses do not find a point of reference any more outside the crowd: "Like a drowning man, all he could hear was a dull, droning sound, all he could distinguish was the continuous, babbling flood of men and beasts sweeping him along." (*eD*, 151)[646] In short, Maurice, once he has become part of the "muddy river of men", ceases to be an individual:

> He no longer knew whether he was afraid or not, but just ran, carried along by the galloping of the others, with no will of his own, his only desire being to get it all over with there and then. Such was the extent to which he'd been reduced to a mere drop in this surging torrent, that when there was a sudden recoiling movement at the far end of the trench [...] he at once felt panic overwhelm him and was ready to take flight. (*eD*, 252)[647]

It is only logical that all these "surging torrents" following their own 'natural' course, uninformed by knowledge of the countryside or tactical considerations, accumulate in the hollow around the town of Sedan: "the muddy river of men [is] rolling *down* towards the ditches of Sedan, like the mass of soil and stones that a storm buffeting the high grounds sends tumbling *down* into the valley", "the same crowd" is coming down from the "neighbouring plains", "swelling with every minute", "streaming *down*". Their natural course sends them into a trap, they are easily empocketed by the Prussian army, which fires down from the hills – the defeat of the French is sealed.

However, the Second Empire does not get "swept away in the debacle of its sins and vices" (*eD*, 405)[648] at Sedan, it is not merely symbolically defeated in a decisive military battle. The fact that the enthusiastic stream heading "To Berlin!" comes to a tragic halt there does not affect the source of this stream back in Paris. Although the frontline is continually pushed back, and the Prussians finally besiege Paris, the weather that had led the "whirling mass of people" "to the slaughter" (*eN*, 420), to the massacre at Sedan, is, against all sanity and reason, still brewing:

---

[645] "Maurice, qui connaissait pourtant le pays, ne savait plus où il roulait, incapable de se reprendre, dans le torrent débordé, la cohue affolée qui coulait à pleine route." (*D*, V 543)

[646] "Comme un homme qui se noie, il n'entendait que le bourdonnement sourd, il ne distinguait que le ruissellement continu du flot d'hommes et de bêtes dans lequel il était charrié." (*D*, V 544)

[647] "Il ne savait plus s'il avait peur, il courait emporté par le galop des autres, sans volonté personnelle, n'ayant que le désir d'en finir tout de suite. Et il était à ce point devenu un simple flot de ce torrent en marche, qu'un brusque recul s'étant produit, [...] il avait aussitôt senti la panique le gagner, prêt à prendre la fuite." (*D*, V 646)

[648] "[...] le second Empire emporté dans la débâcle de ses vices et de ses fautes [...]." (*D*, V 801)

> While the army, its courage drained and sensing that the end was near, was asking for peace, the people were still clamouring for a massive breakout, like a great flood, in which the entire population, including women and even children, would charge at the Prussians like a river bursting its banks, overturning everything, sweeping it all away. (eD, 466)[649]

The world of the Second Empire cannot "crumble[ ]" (eD, 405) without the "wind of fury" (eD, 476)[650] reaching and completely destroying the core of the Empire. In order to annihilate this world, the heavy weather has to be turned back on itself and annihilate the very climate of its production. The Second Empire thus literally gets "swept away in the debacle of its sins and vices", in the ultimate catastrophe, the conflagration of Paris that we will examine in greater detail in the following section.

In conclusion, the mass of republican insurgents, the mass of rebelling colliers and the enthusiastic mass of patriotic 'defenders' of the Empire are carbon copies of each other, despite their strikingly different political agendas and aims. It is impossible to tell them apart with regard to the descriptions that we get of them. They are related with interchangeable words, conceptualised the very same way, as torrents, overflowing rivers, that sweep along, follow their natural course and inevitably lead to a debacle. The same laws govern their formation, individuation and course, and it is this impression of their striking resemblance that relegates their actual political aim or agenda to a question of secondary importance. If it is true that the *amorphe Masse* has become the actual agent of history (and I think it quite obvious that Zola shares this view), then the relation between history and politics has shifted. Zola's crowds, despite their political 'denomination', are not parties of a political struggle that fight with each other in order to shape the future. They are not vehicles of beliefs and convictions, they are, as crowds, as masses of de-individualised, de-humanised human beings symptoms of one and the same historical climate. More than that, the fact that natural forces have become the subject of history introduces its own apocalyptic historicity: as we have seen, all the crowds unstoppably take the course of their own destruction. The mass of insurgents as well as the mass of rebelling colliers in fact pre-perform or prefigure, they foreshadow the final great debacle, the "appalling holocaust" (eD, 509)[651] as Zola has his protagonist

---

649 "Tandis que l'armée à bout de courage et sentant venir la fin, demandait la paix, la population réclamait encore la sortie en masse, la sortie torrentielle, le peuple entier, les femmes, les enfants eux-mêmes, se ruant sur les Prussiens, en un fleuve débordé qui renverse et emporte tout." (D, V 863)
650 "[…] [le] vent de fureur soufflant partout." (D, V 873)
651 "[…] l'abominable holocauste […]." (D, V 907)

call it, that annihilates the world of the Second Empire. To be more precise, it is the fatal climate that annihilates itself.

If the *Rougon-Macquart* are a 'political' cycle of novels then not on the level of the narrated world, not in the way that it secretly adheres to one of the political movements (republican insurgents, socialists, Bonapartists, the International, anarchists, ...) portrayed there. Zola's political stance remains beyond the horizons of the narrated world, a world that is, as we have seen, conceived of as complicit as a whole in its catastrophic tendency. However, Zola's projecting the historic developments of the modern, industrialised world into a vision of the Second Empire, connecting it to a certain political regime, has made the label 'Republican' available for a stance that already the *Rougon-Macquart*'s view of the modern world and its processes reveals to be at least one of "conservatism" (Nelson 1982, 74) and "latent authoritarianism" (Nelson 1982, 79). The radicalism behind the idea of the modern world, a world of the natural forces of the crowd, a world that must annihilate itself in order to make a 'better future' possible, carries so overtly "protofascist" (Warning 1998, 714) traits that one can be happy that the *Rougon-Macquart* stay within their historical frame, that they focus on the analysis and reconstruction of this modern world, its logic and aesthetics, and hold the concrete realisation of a 'better world' that follows the debacle at bay, postponing it to the "unreadable" (Warning 1998, 733) *Quatre Évangiles*.

6 Climate catastrophes, climate crises – the seasons and life

The world of the *Rougon-Macquart* tends towards catastrophe. The Second Empire is to perish in a final debacle, and it is the process culminating in this disastrous 'event' that constitutes the subject of Zola's cycle. The catastrophe does not intrude into the narrative universe; it does not strike this world unexpectedly. On the contrary, as we have seen in the last section, it is its 'natural' course that leads the Second Empire directly and necessarily to its own collapse. With his cycle of novels Zola analyses the conditions leading to the catastrophe, he works out the 'natural' laws and the logic behind this 'historical' and 'social' evolution. In the previous sections I attempted to show that Zola conceptualises the complex web of the Second Empire's characteristic developments (technological, social, cultural, economic and political) as a changing climate: as a process of 'global' warming, of speeding up circulation, of developing and exploiting 'weathery forces', of mass formation and its intrinsic connection to the weather. I think that these reflections provide a necessary background for understanding the way that Zola conceptualises the "débâcle": the Second Empire falls prey to its own characteristic climate. It perishes in a climate catastrophe, that is to say by an eruption of exceptionally heavy weather that results from the era's changing climate.

It is not only "La Débâcle", the one big and final disaster that Zola narrates in the penultimate novel of the cycle that bears this very name. In fact, the *Rougon-Macquart* repeatedly foreshadow and anticipate the epochal 'event': 'local' calamities pervade the cycle, almost every novel has its clima(c)tic catastrophe. They all emblematically follow and exhibit the logic and rules that also govern the 'global' historical development which overarches and embeds the single milieus. This holds true especially for the meteorotopoi, for these spots of intensified weather, for these paradigmatic places of the Second Empire's climate: here the weathery logic leading from heating and over-heating towards the final, fatal explosion of the weather-machine becomes most manifest. In order to approach the phenomenon of the "débâcle" and the role it plays in the *Rougon-Macquart* I will therefore analyse two 'local' debacles of meteorotopoi – the collapsing coal-pit of *Germinal* and the crumbling of Saccard's bank on the stock market of *L'Argent* – before turning to *La Débâcle* itself and the collapse of the Second Empire.

Germinal assembles a whole series of 'debacles': we have already followed the course of the mass of rebelling strikers that attack and partly destroy the coal-pit only to be massacred by the soldiers' bullets in the end. We have seen that both these 'debacles' are narrated as the blind violence of natural forces crashing against each other, as natural phenomena, as events of heavy weather, as a hailstorm or a heavy tempest that hit a world. However, although the damage is considerable (dozens of colliers have been killed and wounded, the overground facilities of the pits are in need of repair), these incidents are not fatal, the world they attack is hit, but does not perish. Shortly after life and work in the pits have resumed their daily routine, shortly after the strike and the rebellion have come to an end, a third calamity shatters the world of the colliers: This time the events take on the scale of a catastrophe. It is the work of a single person, Souvarine, who 'finishes off' what the violence of the mass has not managed to 'achieve': He brings about the destruction of a 'local' world, the destruction of the meteorotopos coal pit.

At first glance Souvarine's act of sabotage does not seem to fit into the dynamic that the novel narrates; it seems to be alien to the tragedy of the rebelling miners. Souvarine is a minor character, whose biography and anarchist political attitudes the readers get to know, but who does not feature in the description of the colliers' miserable fate. He is an outsider who does not form part of the social dynamics of suffering and rebellion. Descending from a noble Russian family, he followed his political views and learned the profession of a mechanic to get in touch with the crowd. After participating in a failed assassination of the Russian Emperor, and having watched his wife be hanged, he flees to France and begins to work as a mechanic at the coal-pit. One night, completely out of the blue, he ropes down the shaft of the pit and saws a hole into its wooden lining. The intruding water floods and at last collapses the pit; many of the miners that work down there are entrapped and killed.

At second glance, however, Souvarine's cold-blooded act of sabotage does turn out not to be merely the deed of a politically deluded psychopath, a psychopath who even says goodbye to the miners he watches descend into the pit (only pitying and trying to warn Catherine) – despite knowing that it is unlikely they will ever leave it again. His act in fact uncannily mirrors Étienne's unleashing of the natural forces of the mass of colliers against the pit. There is one, decisive difference: Souvarine does not take the 'detour' of the human crowd. The natural forces he unleashes are genuinely 'natural'; the 'torrent' he sets free does not have to be formed by excited speeches, it does not merge thousands of suffering and angry colliers into one, de-humanised earth-brown mass. The "Torrent, an underground sea, the terror of the coalfields in the Nord Department, a sea with its storms and shipwrecks, an unknown, unfathomable sea, whose black waves broke more than 300 metres underground" (eG, 455)[652] had been there all the time, behind the shaft's lining, as if waiting to destroy the pit one day.

This is also why the catastrophe triggered by Souvarine does form part of the plot and why it does not happen to the pit as an unforeseeable event. As we have seen in the section on the pit as a meteorotopos, all sorts of technology are needed to protect the pit against the natural forces of its surroundings. A milieu, a climate, has to be created and defended against the neighbouring conditions and forces: drainage, airing and temperature management determine the daily routine of the pit. In fact, the progressing exploitation of the pit demands ever more extreme measures. A continuous battle of weather is taking place in the belly of the earth: human hubris and 'weather technology' against nature's natural forces. In fact, it was this battle, its risks and costs that sparked the miners' strike: when the company tries to force the miners to invest more time in stabilising the galleries (thereby effectively diminishing their wages) they are easily persuaded to go on strike. Neither the company nor the miners, the ones

---

[652] "[...] c'était là que se trouvait le Torrent, cette mer souterraine, la terreur des houillères du Nord, une mer avec ses tempêtes et ses naufrages, une mer ignorée, insondable, roulant ses flots noirs, à plus de trois cents mètres du soleil." (G, III 1528)

whose lives are threatened by collapsing galleries, have any interest in paying for the pit's battle against nature. Damage to the shaft's lining that is only cosmetically repaired by the company, with water of the Torrent leaking in, becomes the symbol for the fact that nothing has changed after the strike; it is this symbol that Souvarine reads and uses as an opportunity for sabotage.

As a result of the well-known problem with the lining and with leaking water, the sabotage is not even realised at first. The fact that the cage hardly passes the deformed lining is conceived of as 'normal', only the intensity of the downpour of leaking water astonishes the miners: "However, the cage got past the obstacle. But now it was going down through a stormy deluge [*une pluie d'orage*] so violent that the workmen couldn't help listening anxiously to the sound of the water crashing down." (*eG*, 462)[653] As with the debacles of the human torrent of rebelling strikers rolling down the road that Négrel and his company heard announce itself, it is again sound that speaks of the brewing of heavy weather. It does not take long for Pierron, the worker in charge of loading the tubs at the bottom of the shaft, to make a worrying observation:

> Since the shift had gone down Pierron had been very worried to see how the deluge [*déluge*] pouring down the shaft had increased. While he was loading tubs with two other men, he looked up; his face was drenched with great drops of water, and his ears drummed with the roaring of the tempest above him. But he trembled even more when he looked downwards and noticed that the 'bog', the ten-metre-deep sump, was filling up: the water was already spurting up from underneath and spilling over the iron plates on the floor, proving that the pump wasn't powerful enough to soak up the leaks. He heard it straining, coughing, and spluttering with the effort. (*eG*, 464)[654]

The balance of forces, of 'weathers' (technological vs. natural), is shifted; this is what Pierron observes. The pump that has, as we have seen, constantly been described as the pit's respiration, breathing day and night, signalling the seemingly unshakable, uncanny techno-organic nature of the pits, is suddenly not "powerful enough". Its "coughing [...] and spluttering with the effort" indicates the deathly danger of the situation: the pit is seriously sick, so to speak, and

---

[653] "Pourtant, la cage avait franchi l'obstacle. Elle descendait maintenant sous une pluie d'orage, si violente, que les ouvriers écoutaient avec inquiétude ce ruissellement." (*G*, III 1535)
[654] "Depuis la descente, Pierron, très inquiet, voyait augmenter le déluge qui tombait du puits. Tout en embarquant les berlines avec deux autres, il levait la tête, la face trempée des grosses gouttes, les oreilles bourdonnantes du ronflement de la tempête, là-haut. Mais il trembla surtout, quand il s'aperçut que, sous lui, le puisard, le bougnou profond de dix mètres, s'emplissait : déjà, l'eau jaillissait du plancher, débordait sur les dalles de fonte ; et c'était une preuve que la pompe ne suffisait plus à épuiser les fuites. Il l'entendait s'essouffler, avec un hoquet de fatigue." (*G*, III 1537)

Pierron as well as his superior Dansaert, to whom he reports the fatal fact that "the water was rising" (eG, 465),[655] both know that there is nothing one can do about it.

With his little act of sabotage, by weakening a structure that had already been on the brink of collapsing, Souvarine has initiated a classical climate catastrophe: heavy weather, a "tempest", a stormy rain, a "deluge pouring down", that threatens to drown a world. The situation even worsens from minute to minute, "everything was falling apart up above, and pieces of timber rained murderously down, as if a river had burst its banks" (eG, 466).[656] Soon "the waters of the Torrent, that underground sea with its uncharted tempests and shipwrecks, spilled forth as if a sluice had been opened" (eG, 469).[657] Nothing can stop the "rapid rise of the flood [*l'inondation*]" (eG, 466),[658] that quickly fills up major parts of the pit, and only spares few high galleries where the trapped colliers, if lucky enough, find a place to save themselves from drowning. All they can do is wait to be rescued, or die.

Like Étienne, Souvarine has liberated forces of weather whose dynamism and violence by far surpass the human capacity of control and guidance and that inevitably and directly lead to catastrophe. His act of sabotage has been prefigured by the tragic course of events, by the debacles set free by Étienne's political ambitions. However, whereas these debacles occurred accidentally, as horrible and unintended, as the tragic outcome of Étienne's intervention indicating its complete failure, it is the necessity of debacle that Souvarine affirms with his iteration of events. He purposely repeats and brings to an ultimate end what the natural, weathery forces of the crowd had begun, but had not proved powerful enough to complete: the end of a world. Souvarine, in contrast to Étienne, has understood that change cannot be brought about by rational, political leadership and control; he knows that the Second Empire's climate can only be 'toppled' by itself, it is this self-annihilation that he tries to facilitate. The ally he chooses has, like the mass of miners, all the while been entangled in the conflict about the development of the Second Empire's climate. It is, however, even more powerful ('the Torrent' with a capital 'T') than any torrent of human beings that can, as we have seen, quite easily be stopped by firing bullets at them.

---

[655] "Eh bien, l'eau montait, que pouvait-il y faire ?" (G, III 1537)
[656] "[…] tout crevait là-haut, c'était un fleuve débordé, une pluie meurtrière de charpentes." (G, III 1538)
[657] "[…] les eaux du Torrent, de cette mer souterraine aux tempêtes et aux naufrages ignorés, s'épanchaient en un dégorgement d'écluse." (G, III 1541)
[658] "[…] la hausse rapide de l'inondation […]." (G, III 1539)

The 'local' 'climate catastrophe', the gigantic "terrestrial hurricane" (eG, 475)[659] that Souvarine precipitates indeed reaches its goal, it annihilates the meteorotopos, the coal pit called 'Le Voreux':

> And suddenly, just as the engineers were cautiously advancing, a final convulsion racked the ground and put them to flight. Underground detonations rang out, like a monstrous artillery barrage raking the abyss. On the surface the last buildings toppled over and collapsed. First a sort of whirlwind swept away the remains of the screening shed and the landing-stage. Next the boiler-house burst and disappeared. Then it was the turn of the square tower, where the drainage pump gave a death-rattle and fell flat on its face, like a man mown down by a bullet. And then there was a terrifying scene; they watched as the engine was wrenched from its base, fighting for its life as its limbs were splayed, it straightened out its crank rod like a giant knee, as if attempting to rise to its feet; but then it was crushed and smothered to death. Only the great thirty-metre-high chimney remained standing, battered like a ship's mast in a hurricane. It looked as if it was about to crumble to pieces and disappear in a cloud of dust, when it suddenly plunged straight downwards, swallowed up by the earth, melting like a giant candle; and nothing was left showing above ground level, not even the tip of the lightning conductor. It was finished. The evil beast crouching in its underground cave was sated with human flesh and its harsh wheezing had at last died away. The whole of Le Voreux had now fallen down into the abyss. (eG, 475)[660]

Zola uses several semantic fields to narrate the end of 'Le Voreux'. The most dominant renders the scene as a scene of death: the "evil beast" lies in its final throes, it is shaken by a "final convulsion", desperately and vainly "fighting for its life". This dimension very much resembles the 'death' of the locomotive called La Lison in *La Bête humaine* and takes up the 'machine-as-organism'-imagery pervading the whole cycle. There are, however, also allusions to other semantic

---

[659] "[...] des tempêtes de la terre [...]." (G, III 1546)
[660] "Et, brusquement, comme les ingénieurs s'avançaient avec prudence, une suprême convulsion du sol les mit en fuite. Des détonations souterraines éclataient, toute une artillerie monstrueuse canonnant le gouffre. A la surface, les dernières constructions se culbutaient, s'écrasaient. D'abord, une sorte de tourbillon emporta les débris du criblage et de la salle de recette. Le bâtiment des chaudières creva ensuite, disparut. Puis, ce fut la tourelle carrée où râlait la pompe d'épuisement, qui tomba sur la face, ainsi qu'un homme fauché par un boulet. Et l'on vit alors une effrayante chose, on vit la machine, disloquée sur son massif, les membres écartelés, lutter contre la mort : elle marcha, elle détendit sa bielle, son genou de géante, comme pour se lever ; mais elle expirait, broyée, engloutie. Seule, la haute cheminée de trente mètres restait debout, secouée, pareille à un mât dans l'ouragan. On croyait qu'elle allait s'émietter et voler en poudre, lorsque, tout d'un coup, elle s'enfonça d'un bloc, bue par la terre, fondue ainsi qu'un cierge colossal ; et rien ne dépassait, pas même la pointe du paratonnerre. C'était fini, la bête mauvaise, accroupie dans ce creux, gorgée de chair humaine, ne soufflait plus de son haleine grosse et longue. Tout entier, le Voreux venait de couler à l'abîme." (G, III 1546–1547)

fields that fulfil a specific function. The association of the field of military (the underground detonations sounding "like a monstrous artillery barrage") and the comparison of the falling pump to "a man mown down by a bullet" link the debacle of 'Le Voreux' to two other debacles: to the preceding one of the rebelling mass of strikers shot down by a tempest of bullets and to the future debacle of Sedan, to the hail of shells experienced by the French soldiers. The 'death' of 'Le Voreux' stands in between these two other debacles: on the one hand, it answers the killing of the miners that had been shot by soldiers defending the pit against the rebellion, and translates the conflict about a place to the catastrophic level of annihilating this place. On the other hand, the 'local' end of a world, of the meteorotopos 'Le Voreux', foreshadows the military debacle, the end of the world of the Second Empire. The catastrophe triggered by Souvarine thus functions as a sort of hinge that links the logics and dynamics of the local conflict to the notions and the inevitability of 'local' and 'global' catastrophe. There can be no doubt that a world perishes and mythically sinks into the abyss, as there can be no doubt that this catastrophe, literally, is a climate catastrophe, an event of deluge and heavy weather.

The debacle that takes place at the stock exchange might be less obviously and less literally a climate catastrophe. It provides us, however, with a prime example for understanding the fact that the climate of the age inevitably brews the fatal weather that will, in the end, destroy the very world that had brought it about. The stock exchange is a classical, textbook example of a meteorotopos. It follows the same thermodynamic logic that also drives Octave Mouret's department store: excessive heating serves to 'make profitable weather' – the aim is to "excite [*allumaient*] passers-by and cause millions to rain down" (*eM*, 160).[661] The stock exchange, like the department store, resembles a steam engine, whose "vibration and rumbling, like an engine getting up steam, gr[ows] ever louder, making the whole of the Bourse shake like the flickering of a flame" (*eM*, 22–23).[662] In order to intensify and maximise "the shower of gold he was scattering down on Paris" (*eM*, 271)[663] Saccard "operate[s] in feverish leaps and bounds, applying the methods of intensive farming to the financial terrain, heating and

---

[661] "[...] la noire ignorance du troupeau, prêt à croire tous les contes, tellement fermé aux opérations compliquées de la Bourse, que les raccrochages les plus éhontés allumaient les passants et faisaient pleuvoir les millions." (*Ar*, V 176)

[662] "La trépidation, le grondement de machine sous vapeur, grandissait, agitait la Bourse entière, dans un vacillement de flamme." (*Ar*, V 32)

[663] "Saccard ne vivait plus que dans la fiction exagérée de son triomphe, entouré comme d'une gloire par cette averse d'or qu'il faisait pleuvoir sur Paris, assez fin cependant pour avoir la sensation du sol miné, crevassé, qui menaçait de s'effondrer sous lui." (*Ar*, V 293)

overheating the soil at the risk of burning the harvest" (*eM*, 183).⁶⁶⁴ As with the coal-pit of 'Le Voreux', the extreme exploitation to which Saccard aspires with his bank (aptly named 'L'Universelle') calls for extreme measures and takes enormous risks. Everybody involved in the business knows about the basic truth that "[w]hen you overheat a machine, it sometimes bursts" (*eM*, 312);⁶⁶⁵ nevertheless, hardly anyone can be persuaded to shy away from these risks. The reason for this is as simple as it is paradoxical: extremity lies at the heart of speculation. Zola installs a character, Caroline, to explore and evaluate this 'insight'. In her role of both being somehow complicit in the male protagonist's machinations and holding a certain critical distance to them she is comparable to Denise of *Au Bonheur des Dames*. The vision of a prospering Orient that Saccard sells is based on projects that her brother has developed and attempts to realise, projects that Caroline is proud of. She is drawn as an intelligent and sympathetic character likely to win the readers' identification, so that her reflections on what is going on carry a heavy, authorial weight. She immediately senses the fatal danger of Saccard's proceedings. However, she also understands the fundamental ambivalence of speculations' tendency towards the extreme: on the one hand, risky speculation is necessary for financing the vision of a blooming Orient that she cherishes; on the other hand, the speculation of the 'Universelle' inevitably and directly is rushing towards the "final crash".

> What worried her above all was the terrible pace of it all, the way the Universal was being urged along at such a gallop, like an engine crammed with coal, launched along diabolical rails until the point when everything would shatter and explode in one final crash. She wasn't naïve, nor was she a simpleton, easily fooled; even if she was ignorant about technical banking operations, she well understood the reason for this overdoing of things, this feverish pace, all intended to intoxicate people, and whirl them into the epidemic madness of the dancing millions. Every morning had to produce a rise in the price, people had to be made to believe in ever-greater success, in monumental cash desks, enchanted cash desks, that took in streams of gold and sent back rivers, oceans of gold. (*eM*, 198)⁶⁶⁶

---

664 "Mais Saccard procédait par coups de fièvre, appliquant au terrain financier la méthode de la culture intensive, chauffant, surchauffant le sol, au risque de brûler la récolte [...]." (*Ar*, V 200)
665 "Quand on chauffe trop une machine, il arrive qu'elle éclate." (*Ar*, V 335)
666 "Ce qui surtout l'angoissait, c'était ce terrible train, ce galop continu dont on menait l'Universelle, pareille à une machine, bourrée de charbon, lancée sur des rails diaboliques, jusqu'à ce que tout crevât et sautât, sous un dernier choc. Elle n'était point une naïve, une nigaude que l'on pût tromper ; même ignorante de la technique des opérations de banque, elle comprenait parfaitement les raisons de ce surmenage, de cet enfièvrement, destiné à griser la foule, à l'entraîner dans cette épidémique folie de la danse des millions. Chaque matin devait apporter sa hausse, il fallait faire croire toujours à plus de succès, à des guichets monumentaux, des

With a brutal consistency unequalled by any other novel of the cycle *L'Argent* tells the double story of an enormous capitalistic success, of "the monstrous hurricane of millions" (*eM*, 370)[667] that Saccard manages to liberate and accumulate with his bank and of the "diabolical rails" of this success directly leading towards catastrophe. Everybody, the readers included, knows that a fatal crash is only a question of time. One waits for it, is surprised how astonishingly well and how incredibly long the principle of heating and overheating works – even Saccard's opponent, the almighty and invincible, cold and calculating banker Gundermann acknowledges this 'achievement'.

However, finally, the day of reckoning arrives. It seems to be announced by the "appalling" weather outside:

> Next day, the weather was appalling. It had rained all night, a fine icy rain was swamping the city, now transformed by the thaw into a cesspit of yellow, liquid mud. By half-past twelve, the Bourse was already clamouring under this downpour. The crowd sheltering under the peristyle, and in the hall, was enormous; and the hall, with all the umbrellas dripping on to the floor, soon found itself turned into a vast puddle of muddy water. The walls exuded black filth, and from the glass roof there came only a dim and reddish light, of desperate melancholy. (*eM*, 300–301)[668]

The weather obviously corresponds to the appalling events that will take place in the Bourse that day. It does however not merely evoke the black Friday with the adequate, gloomy atmosphere, but has important things to tell about the logic of catastrophe. With regard to the dismal weather outside it does not come as a surprise that Moser, who is chronically sick and chronically pessimistic about the development of the market, "arrived looking pale after a liverish attack which had kept him awake all the previous night" (*eM*, 301). That day, however, his remark that "everybody [...] looked jaundiced and sickly" (*eM*, 301),[669] for

---

guichets enchantés qui absorbaient des rivières, pour rendre des fleuves, des océans d'or. Son pauvre frère, si crédule, séduit, emporté, allait-elle donc le trahir, l'abandonner à ce flot qui menaçait, un jour, de les noyer tous ? Elle était désespérée de son inaction et de son impuissance." (*Ar*, V 216)

667 "[...] le monstrueux ouragan de millions [...]." (*Ar*, V 397)

668 "Le lendemain, le temps fut exécrable. Il avait plu toute la nuit, une petite pluie glaciale noyait la ville, changée par le dégel en un cloaque de boue, jaune et liquide. La Bourse, dès midi et demi, clamait dans ce ruissellement. Réfugiée sous le péristyle et dans la salle, la foule était énorme ; et la salle, bientôt, avec les parapluies mouillés qui s'égouttaient, se trouva changée en une immense flaque d'eau bourbeuse. La crasse noire des murs suintait, il ne tombait du toit vitré qu'un jour bas et roussâtre, d'une désespérée mélancolie." (*Ar*, V 323)

669 "Il était une heure moins dix, et Moser qui arrivait, blême d'une crise de foie, dont la morsure l'avait empêché de fermer l'œil, la nuit précédente, fit remarquer à Pillerault que tout le monde, ce jour-là, était jaune et avait l'air malade." (*Ar*, V 324)

once, has a ring of truth about it. The atmosphere inside the Bourse is somehow, noticeably changed:

> The truth was, however, that in the general anxiety, the whole room remained gloomy, under the reddish light, and this was especially noticeable in the subdued rumble of the voices. No longer was it the tumultuous roar of the days when prices were rising, that agitation, that din of an all-conquering tide, overflowing on all sides. There was no more running, no more shouting – people sidled along and spoke quietly, as if in a house where someone lay ill. (eM, 301–302)[670]

Again it is noises, the noises of the weather, that forebode the looming debacle: this time it is not the rumbling or thundering of a brewing storm but the treacherous quiet before the storm. As we learn, this absence of the "tumultuous roar" of the "din of an all-conquering tide, overflowing" already has to be read as a worrying abnormality of the stock exchange's 'weather'. The 'actual' disaster that sets in few minutes later only continues this abnormality – the great catastrophe comes as a heavy weather that hits the world and brings with it fatal damage:

> Then, during the last half-hour, it was a disaster [la débâcle], the rout steadily worsening, and carrying people away in a gallop of confusion. After extreme confidence and blind infatuation came the reaction of fear, all now rushing to sell, if there was still time. A hail of orders [grêle d'ordres] to sell beat upon the trading-floor, all one could see was order-slips raining down; and these huge blocks of shares, scattered pell-mell like this, accelerated the fall, made it a real collapse. The prices, going down and down, fell to one thousand five hundred, to one thousand two hundred, to nine hundred. There were no more buyers, nothing was left, the ground was strewn with corpses. [...] By a singular effect of the wind of disaster [vent de désastre] blowing through the room, all agitation had come to a stop and the noise had died down, as in the stupor of a great catastrophe. [...] And the rain went on stubbornly streaming down the windows, which now let in only a sort of sickly twilight; the hall, under the dripping umbrellas and trampling of feet, had become a cesspit, like the muddy floor of an ill-kept stable, littered with all sorts of torn papers; while the trading-floor displayed the bright, multi-coloured slips, the green, the red, the blue, thrown away in handfuls, in such quantities that day that the vast basin was overflowing. (eM, 305–306)[671]

---

[670] "La vérité était que, dans l'anxiété générale, la salle restait morne, sous le jour roussâtre, et cela se sentait surtout au grondement affaibli des voix. Ce n'était plus l'éclat tumultueux des grands jours de hausse, l'agitation, le vacarme d'une marée, débordant de toutes parts en conquérante. On ne courait plus, on ne criait plus, on se glissait, on parlait bas, comme dans la maison d'un malade." (Ar, V 324–325)

[671] "Alors, pendant la dernière demi-heure, ce fut la débâcle, la déroute s'aggravant et emportant la foule en un galop désordonné. Après l'extrême confiance, l'engouement aveugle, arrivait la réaction de la peur, tous se ruant pour vendre, s'il en était temps encore. Une grêle d'ordres de vente s'abattit sur la corbeille, on ne voyait plus que des fiches pleuvoir ; et ce paquets

In fact, the "great catastrophe" at the Bourse is 'less literally' a natural or climate catastrophe than the flooding of 'Le Voreux' in *Germinal*. One could say that the weather here only serves as a metaphorical means of illustrating a debacle that is in itself much too abstract to be related in a novel. However, the novel's employment of weather imagery is too consistent and dominant to dismiss it as merely illustrative. In the way he had proceeded with the dynamic of the political masses that was discussed in the previous section, Zola uses here the dynamics of the weather to conceptualise the dynamic of the financial market. It is obviously no coincidence that Saccard's bank "cause[s] millions to rain down" only to perish in a "hail of orders", to be drowned in the downpour of "order-slips raining down" "in such quantities that day that the vast basin was overflowing". As in the military debacle of Sedan, "the wind had [...] changed": "the monstrous hurricane of millions" that Saccard manages to unleash and that makes him the star of the Second Empire's financial scene, turns into "the wind of disaster", ruining not only him and his bank but also, and most importantly, the vast, anonymous mass of people that has invested in the 'Universelle'. There can be no doubt that the overflowing has been provoked by the very same meteorotopical measures that had made millions rain into Saccard's coffers. He had himself more or less wilfully conjured up the power of the weather that had now turned against him and his enterprise, hitting 'L'Universelle' with full force and annihilating it, sweeping it from the market. The thermodynamic connection between Saccard's intensive heating/overheating and the heavy weather (no matter whether profitable, like the "hurricane of millions", the "streams of gold and [...] oceans of gold", or catastrophic, like the "wind of disaster") constitutes the backbone of Zola's novel about the financial market of the Second Empire.

In the end, this "great catastrophe", this debacle (Zola again alludes to the Second Empire's epochal military *Débâcle*, not only by using this very word, but also by the fact that the bank's "ground was strewn with corpses") has, like the catastrophe of 'Le Voreux', annihilated a world. The meteorotopos 'Bourse' has

---

énormes de titres, jetés ainsi sans prudence, accéléraient la baisse, un véritable effondrement. Les cours, de chute en chute, tombèrent à 1 500, à 1 200, à 900. Il n'y avait plus d'acheteurs, la plaine était rase, jonchée de cadavres. [...] Par un singulier effet du vent de désastre qui traversait la salle, l'agitation s'y était figée, le vacarme s'y mourait, comme dans la stupeur d'une grande catastrophe. [...] Et la pluie ruisselait toujours sur le vitrage, qui ne laissait plus filtrer qu'un crépuscule louche ; la salle était devenue un cloaque, sous l'égouttement des parapluies et le piétinement de la foule, un sol fangeux d'écurie mal tenue, où traînaient toutes sortes de papiers déchirés ; tandis que, dans la corbeille, éclatait le bariolage des fiches, les vertes, les rouges, les bleues, jetées à pleines mains, si abondantes ce jour-là, que le vaste bassin débordait." (*Ar*, V 329)

ceased to be one. Despite its hothouse structure, with its "glass roof" and its windows that the rain, all the time, "went on stubbornly streaming down", there is no difference any more between the horrible weather outside, the thaw having transformed the city "into a cesspit of yellow, liquid mud" and the state of things, the "order-slips raining down" inside the hall. The "trampling of feet" has scrambled the filth and water carried in from outside and the overflowing 'metaphorical' mud of "all sorts of torn papers" into an indistinguishable mixture; the hall itself, like all of Paris outside, "had become a cesspit". It is surely no coincidence that the breakdown, the self-annihilation of a meteorotopos, formerly famous for its (over)heated, its glowing, its hypertrophical atmosphere, seems to share its catastrophic, its devastating state with the whole city surrounding it: it cannot be a good omen that the city of Paris mirrors the "cesspit" of the crashed stock exchange, that it seems to share the fate of a place associated with "an ill-kept stable".

It therefore does not come as a surprise that "the supreme debacle", the Franco-Prussian war of 1870/71, finally 'globally' strikes the Empire and does not spare its core, the city of Paris. In the little summaries of the novels that Zola has his mouthpiece Docteur Pascal present to his niece and future lover Clotilde in the final novel of the cycle, this "supreme debacle" is called "the dreadful and fatal storm [*tempête*] which, from the frontier of Sedan, sweeping away the Empire, threatened to blow away the homeland" (*DP*, V 1014; my transl.).⁶⁷² Zola's 'war novel' titled *La Débâcle* itself confirms the weather 'imagery' of its summary: the military defeat of the French troops is indeed, from the first to the last page, narrated as one gigantic climate catastrophe.

> But now their France was being invaded, the storm was about to break on their own territory, in their own backyards, over their own fields, like one of those dreaded hurricanes which lay waste to whole regions with their hail and thunder in a matter of a couple of hours! (*eD*, 38)⁶⁷³

Even before the French soldiers have encountered a single Prussian soldier, they sense "the new wind of youth and strength blowing in from Germany" (*eD*, 61);⁶⁷⁴ "they could feel the enemy approaching from every side, just as one

---

672 "Jean, le plus humble, le plus ferme soldat de la suprême débâcle, roulé dans l'effroyable et fatale tempête qui, de la frontière à Sedan, en balayant l'Empire, menaçait d'emporter la patrie, toujours sage, avisé, solide en son espoir [...]." (*DP*, V 1014)

673 "Et la France était envahie, et c'était chez eux, autour de leur maison, dans leurs champs, que la tempête crevait, comme un de ces terribles ouragans de grêle et de foudre qui anéantissent une province en deux heures !" (*D*, V 431)

674 "[...] le vent nouveau de jeunesse et de force qui soufflait d'Allemagne [...]." (*D*, V 454)

can sense a storm gathering, before it appears over the horizon." (*eD*, 116)[675] Soon the sound of the cannon comes to metonymically represent the approaching debacle: it booms "like the distant, gathering roar of a storm" (*eD*, 124),[676] it seems "to be approaching from west to east like a relentless rumbling of thunder" (*eD*, 124),[677] before, for the moment, "progressing further and further eastwards, like a hurricane full of hail and disaster, moving on and away" (*eD*, 125).[678]

When the armies finally clash, the heavy weather that had announced itself and that had been anxiously expected by the French soldiers breaks out with full violence. It is not only that "the bullets whistled like desert winds" (*eD*, 185);[679] especially the "terrible artillery duel" (*eD*, 204)[680] unleashes a violent storm whose immense physical force and impact suspends the question of its being a mere 'metaphor': "There was only the thunder, that hurricane of destruction, rumbling across the solitude." (*eD*, 204)[681] "The shells and bullets were hailing down, it was like a hurricane!" (*eD*, 223)[682] "[T]he missiles were raining [*pleuvaient*] down" (*eD*, 232),[683] "the hail of missiles had grown thicker" (*eD*, 250)[684] – this is the way that Zola narrates the scenes of the war, no matter whether they are experienced by the fighting soldiers or by civilians searching their way through the battlefields. Again and again, with every military encounter whose story the novel tells, it, almost stereotypically, comes back to the same description of the war's characteristic heavy weather: the "iron hailstorm" keeps raging and "growing fiercer" (*eD*, 255),[685] the "[m]issiles" keep "raining" (*eD*, 260; transl. altered).[686]

---

[675] "Dans le malaise de cette étape, on sentait de partout l'ennemi approcher, de même qu'on sent monter l'orage, avant qu'il se montre au-dessus de l'horizon." (*D*, V 508)
[676] "[...] le canon tonnait toujours, tout un fracas d'orage éloigné et grandissant [...]." (*D*, V 517)
[677] "Le canon ne cessait pas, semblait avancer de l'ouest à l'est, dans un roulement ininterrompu de foudre." (*D*, V 517)
[678] "[...] le canon [...] allait de plus en plus vers l'est, tel qu'un ouragan de grêle et de désastre, qui marche et s'éloigne." (*D*, V 518)
[679] "Les balles sifflaient comme un vent d'équinoxe [...]." (*D*, V 580)
[680] "[...] le formidable duel d'artillerie [...]." (*D*, V 599)
[681] "Il n'y avait que ce tonnerre, que cet ouragan de destruction, roulant au travers de cette solitude." (*D*, V 599)
[682] "« [...] Une grêle, un ouragan de balles et d'obus ! [...] »" (*D*, V 618)
[683] "[...] les projectiles pleuvaient [...]." (*D*, V 628)
[684] "[...] la grêle des projectiles augmentait [...]." (*D*, V 645)
[685] "[...] la grêle de fer augmentait encore [...]." (*D*, V 649)
[686] "Les projectiles pleuvaient avec la même précision." (*D*, V 654)

> Up there, it was as if a roaring hurricane had been unleashed, shells came sailing over in such huge numbers from Saint-Menges, Fleigneux, and Givonne that it was like a violent rainstorm, the onslaught seeming to make steam rise from the ground. (eD, 254)[687]

> [T]he bullets were whistling past so thick and fast, and such a deluge of shells swept across the empty fields, with no tree in sight, that panic immediately broke out among the men, sending them rushing down the slopes, rolling them headlong like wisps of straw surprised by a storm. (eD, 251–252)[688]

When Zola narrates the tragic story of a character called Weiss, who desperately and, in the end, solitarily, defends his house against the superior power of the Prussians besieging it, he takes up a topos that we have already encountered in Goethe's *Werther*: the topos of the (human-built) house or hovel that fights against the natural forces raging against it from the outside. In contrast to the hovel to which Werther had retreated, it is, however, not "snow and hailstones raging against the windowpane" (84; transl. altered) but "a shower of bullets raking the walls that it sounded like a storm of hailstones" (eD, 238):[689]

> Time and time again, it looked as if it would topple and collapse beneath the storm of metal raining down on it: and yet, battered by volleys of gunfire, surrounded by haze and smoke, still it stood firm, holed and mutilated perhaps, but spitting bullets from every fissure nonetheless. (eD, 240)[690]

In the end, the house falls and Weiss is executed by the Prussian soldiers before the eyes of his wife, who has risked crossing the battlefield, all on her own, to look for her husband. The heavy weather of war thus does not merely paint the picture of a sublime spectacle; it does not merely orchestrate the novel with "the deafening clamour of the storm" (eD, 266).[691] The "dreadful and fatal storm" indeed "sweep[s] away the Empire", in all its literal brutality; it mows down the French army "like wisps of straw surprised by a storm".

---

[687] "C'était, là-haut, un véritable ouragan déchaîné, les projectiles arrivaient en si grand nombre de Saint-Menges, de Fleigneux et de Givonne, que la terre semblait en fumer comme sous une grosse pluie d'orage." (*D*, V 648)

[688] "[M]ais les balles sifflaient si drues, une telle trombe d'obus balayait les champs vides, sans un arbre, que la panique tout de suite se déclara, remportant les hommes le long des pentes, les roulant ainsi que des pailles surprises par un orage." (*D*, V 646)

[689] "[...] une telle pluie de balles fouetta la façade qu'on aurait dit un ouragan de grêle [...]." (*D*, V 633–634)

[690] "En effet, le siège de la petite maison continuait, s'éternisait. Vingt fois elle avait paru devoir emportée dans la tempête de fer dont elle était abattue ; et sous les rafales, au milieu de la fumée, elle se montrait de nouveau debout, trouée, déchiquetée, crachant quand même des balles par chacune de ses fentes." (*D*, V 635)

[691] "[...] clameur de tempête [...]." (*D*, V 661)

Zola illustrates the inconceivable brutality of these weather events with a scene that his two protagonists, Jean and Maurice, themselves exposed to the inferno of the Prussian artillery, watch from their position on the battlefield: the African Chasseurs, a regiment that Zola describes as the bravest of the army and of which Prosper, a friend of Jean and Maurice, forms a part, ride a desperate attack on the overpowering Prussians and are massacred by "a hailstorm" of bullets and shells:

> Before long they were rushing headlong, hell for leather, at an infernal gallop, letting out ferocious yells which the crackling bullets accompanied like a hailstorm, rattling down upon everything metal, mess-tins, water bottles, the copper trim on their uniforms and on the harnesses. Through the hail came the hurricane blast of wind and thunder that set the ground trembling, leaving a smell of scorched wool and sweating beasts rising up to the sunlight. (eD, 266)[692]

"[S]ome men [are] thrown to the ground as if blown off by a gust of wind" (eD, 266),[693] others, like Prosper, fight obstinately before suffering the same fate. When Maurice and Jean, who had himself hardly survived the encounter, having been injured and saved by his friend and comrade, return to the battlefield some days later to find and recover Prosper's corpse, the scenes they are faced with are apocalyptic: the heavy weather of war has reshaped the whole landscape, it is difficult to orient oneself despite the fact that Maurice knows the area extremely well. And, most appallingly, the ground is literally "strewn with corpses". All the images of war, of massacre, of deadly violence that had been used by the previous novels, used to narrate the end of a day of 'battle' at the 'Le Bonheur des Dames', Nana's machinations or the tragic events at the Bourse, are here realised, in their 'literal' sense, by this great, by this "supreme debacle". The 'local' debacles prefigure the 'global' debacle – and they nevertheless possess a metonymic relationship to it. They form part of the same 'whole', they follow the same, weathery logic and dynamic: Zola tells the story of a 'fractal' constellation, where the small scale prefigures the pattern of the larger.

This forewarning link that connects the particular, the local 'event' with the larger historical development, that translates the 'metaphorical' into the 'literal', is most prominently and most explicitly represented with regard to the final, the catastrophic destruction of Paris, its "appalling holocaust" (eD, 509).[694] Several

---

[692] "Bientôt ce fut une course diabolique, un train d'enfer, ce furieux galop, ces hurlements féroces, que le crépitement des balles accompagnait d'un bruit de grêle, en tapant sur tout le métal, les gamelles, les bidons, le cuivre des uniformes et des harnais. Dans cette grêle, passait l'ouragan de vent et de foudre dont le sol tremblait, laissant au soleil une odeur de laine brûlée et de fauves en sueur." (D, V 660)
[693] "[…] des hommes étaient jetés à terre, comme par un coup de vent […]." (D, V 661)
[694] "[…] l'abominable holocauste […]." (D, V 907)

novels of the cycle prefigure the catastrophic vision of Paris burning at climactic points of the plot. They embed the imagery of fire in their tale of an atmosphere of growing heat; they install it as the horrible 'final destination' towards which the 'whole' historical development is moving. Zola's description of the party taking place at the Muffats, which was already analysed in the section on the processes of global heating, constitutes a prime example of this technique of prefiguring 'imagery'. Zola employs the party's decorative use of open fire, its "Venetian lanterns" illuminating the garden, to paint a flaming vision of the end of this world of luxury and excess that presents a forewarning of the "supreme debacle", of the entire city of Paris burning:

> In the garden, the Venetian lanterns looked like the glowing embers of a fire [*lueur de braise*] which lit up the shadowy figures of the men and women strolling off to take a breath of air in the remoter oaths, with a gleam as if from some distant conflagration [*reflet d'incendie*]. And these quaking walls and this red haze [*nuée rouge*] were like a final holocaust [*flambée dernière*] consuming the honour of the whole of this ancient house [...], where a vast accumulation of wealth was suddenly about to go up in flames [*allumées*] and collapse in ruins [...]. (eN, 364)[695]

It is already at the end of *Nana*, when the mass of people gathering in the streets voice their enthusiasm for the war that had just been declared, that this 'fiery' vision is taken up again in a first step towards its 'literalisation':

> But the mob now coming along shouting was carrying torches; from the Madeleine onwards there was a red gleam [*lueur rouge*], like a burning fuse glowing its way through the crowd [*coupait la cohue d'une traînée de feu*] and spreading out over them in a broad sheet of flame [*comme une nappe d'incendie*]. (eN, 418)[696]

The fire is, so to speak, slowly but steadily approximating its future material cause and reality. From the abstract role in an apocalyptic vision of an ancient family it has now become associated with the enthusiasm for war. The dooming fiery fate of the city can already be predicted, it has become thinkable and

---

[695] "Dans le jardin, une lueur de braise, tombée des lanternes vénitiennes, éclairait d'un lointain reflet d'incendie les ombres noires des promeneurs, cherchant un peu d'air au fond des allées. Et ce tressaillement des murs, cette nuée rouge, étaient comme la flambée dernière, où craquait l'antique honneur brûlant aux quatre coins du logis. [...] Ici, sur l'écroulement de ces richesses, entassées et allumées d'un coup, la valse sonnait le glas d'une vieille race [...]." (N, II 1429–1430)

[696] "Mais la bande qui arrivait en vociférant avait des torches ; une lueur rouge venait de la Madeleine, coupait la cohue d'une traînée de feu, s'étalait au loin sur les têtes comme une nappe d'incendie." (N, II 1479)

imaginable: "'[...] And now war's been declared and the Prussians are going to come and set fire to everything ... [...]'" (eN, 421).[697]

The fatal warming of the Muffats, "culminat[ing] in this peak of glittering revelry [*éclat de fête*]" that Zola stylises as the "final holocaust consuming the honour of the whole of this ancient house", and the Second Empire's political ambitions, the enthusiasm for war whose fiery spectacle of torches prefigure the conflagration of Paris, are intimately intertwined. In *L'Argent* we encounter a 'political festivity', constituting a hinge between the Paris of "glittering revelry" and the Paris characterised by political hubris: Saccard's financial triumph at the Bourse is made to coincide with Napoleon III's celebrating himself "as master of Europe" (eM, 182).[698] The Empire seems "at its apogee" (eM, 182):[699] "Paris, the centre of the world, set all her avenues and monuments ablaze with light [*flambait*] on the morrow of Sadowa" (eM, 182).[700] The "festivities at the Tuileries and rejoicing in the streets" (eM, 182)[701] celebrate as if there had been a "great victory" (eM, 182).[702] They do not hear the "protests [in the Chamber of Deputies], some prophets of doom [...] confusedly predicting a terrible future: Prussia made stronger by all that France had tolerated, Austria defeated, and Italy ungrateful" (eM, 182).[703] For the readers, the "blazing Paris [*Paris en flammes*]" (eM, 182),[704] like Saccard's triumph that is the product of overheating the market, portends no good.

The most frighteningly explicit prefiguring vision of Paris in flames is depicted in *Une page d'amour*. It is one of the five famous 'tableaux de Paris', the cityscape of Paris looked upon from the protagonist's, Hélène's, window, situated high above the urban trouble. Her married neighbour, doctor and friend Henri has just confessed his love to her, she has fled back to her flat, and is contemplating the city, tinged by the setting sun:

---

[697] "« [...] Et voilà la guerre déclarée, les Prussiens vont venir, ils brûleront tout... [...] »" (*N*, II 1481)
[698] "[...] maître de l'Europe [...]." (*Ar*, V 199)
[699] "Ce premier triomphe de Saccard sembla être comme une floraison de l'empire à son apogée." (*Ar*, V 199)
[700] "Paris, centre du monde, flambait par toutes ses avenues et tous ses monuments, au lendemain de Sadowa [...]." (*Ar*, V 199)
[701] "[...] des fêtes aux Tuileries, des réjouissances dans les rues, célébraient Napoléon III maître de l'Europe [...]." (*Ar*, V 199)
[702] "[...] ainsi que pour une grande victoire [...]." (*Ar*, V 199)
[703] "A la Chambre, des voix avaient bien protesté, des prophètes de malheur annonçaient confusément le terrible avenir, la Prusse grandie de tout ce que la France avait toléré, l'Autriche battue, l'Italie ingrate." (*Ar*, V 199)
[704] "[...] Paris en flammes [...]." (*Ar*, V 200)

> Right and left alike the edifices were all aflame [*les monuments flambaient*]. The glass roof of the Palais de l'Industrie appeared like a bed of glowing embers amidst the Champs-Elysees groves. [...] [N]earer in, the pavilions of the new Louvre and the Tuileries, were crowned by a blaze, which lent them the aspect of sacrificial pyres [*bûchers gigantesques*]. The dome of the Invalides was on fire, with such brilliancy that you instinctively feared lest it should suddenly topple down and scatter burning flakes over the neighbourhood. Beyond the irregular towers of Saint-Sulpice, the Pantheon stood out against the sky in dull splendour, like some royal palace of conflagration reduced to embers [*pareil à un royal palais de l'incendie qui se consumerait en braise*]. Then, as the sun declined, the pyre-like edifices gradually set the whole of Paris on fire. Flashes sped over the housetops, while black smoke lingered in the valleys. Every frontage turned towards the Trocadéro seemed to be red-hot, the glass of the windows glittering and emitting a shower of sparks, which darted upwards as though some invisible bellows were ever urging the huge conflagration into greater activity. Sheaves of flame were also ever rising afresh from the adjacent districts, where the streets opened, now dark and now all ablaze. Even far over the plain, from a ruddy ember-like glow suffusing the destroyed faubourgs, occasional flashes of flame shot up as from some fire struggling again into life. Ere long a furnace seemed raging, all Paris was burning. (*PA*, II 908–909; my transl.)[705]

In contrast to the previous visions of a "blazing Paris" the scenery that Hélène watches is not triggered by open fire. It is a pure 'weather spectacle', it is produced solely and completely by the interplay of the setting sun, the physics of the light-absorbing atmosphere and the reflections of light produced by the surfaces of the urban architecture. Initially, Zola planned this vision to depict Paris on a "day of public festivity" (Zola 2006, 124; my transl.)[706] – in other words, he had the scenario in mind that he later described in the passage we quoted from *L'Argent*. He obviously abandoned this plan and assimilated

---

[705] "A droite, à gauche, les monuments flambaient. Les verrières du palais de l'Industrie, au milieu des futaies des Champs-Élysées, étalaient un lit de tisons ardents ; [...] plus près les pavillons du nouveau Louvre et des Tuileries, se couronnaient de flammes, dressant à chaque carrefour des bûchers gigantesques. Le dôme des Invalides était en feu, si étincelant, qu'on pouvait craindre à chaque minute de le voir s'effondrer, en couvrant le quartier des flammèches de sa charpente. Au-delà des tours inégales de Saint-Sulpice, le Panthéon se détachait sur le ciel avec un éclat sourd, pareil à un royal palais de l'incendie qui se consumerait en braise. Alors, Paris entier, à mesure que le soleil baissait, s'alluma aux bûchers des monuments. Des lueurs couraient sur les crêtes des toitures, pendant que, dans les vallées, des fumées noires dormaient. Toutes les façades tournées vers le Trocadéro rougissaient, en jetant le pétillement de leurs vitres, une pluie d'étincelles qui montaient de la ville, comme si quelque soufflet eût sans cesse activé cette forge colossale. Des gerbes toujours renaissantes s'échappaient des quartiers voisins, où les rues se creusaient, sombres et cuites. Même, dans les lointains de la plaine, du fond d'une cendre rousse qui ensevelissait les faubourgs détruits et encore chauds, luisaient des fusées perdues, sorties de quelque foyer subitement ravivé. Bientôt ce fut une fournaise. Paris brûla." (*PA*, II 908–909)

[706] Cf. *Ébauche*, "un jour de fête publique" (Zola 2006, 124).

the tableau into the strict composition of the novel. Each of the five parts of the novel ends with a section that centres on a tableau describing Paris, more or less the same vision, varied by weather and 'circumstances': "A morning of clear sunshine, entirely blond", "An afternoon of mi-carême, red and gold, with some clouds", "Paris at night", "Paris grey and muddy from the rain. Upset [*Navré*]", "Winter of a dry freeze, with some threads of snow. Clear weather. No greenery. The Seine bears sediment [*charriant*]" (Zola 2006, 30–32; my transl.).[707] These tableaux, these visions, which Zola wanted to be understood as a sort of antique chorus summing up and commenting on the preceding events,[708] purposely eschew the depiction of anything worth telling, of any historical or political background; they are 'pure' impressionistic tableaux that uncannily correspond to the development of the protagonist's passion. Paris "all aflame" comments on Hélène's reaction to Henri's profession of love, the same way that "Paris grey and muddy from rain" comments on the debacle of Hélène's falling for Henri and her daughter Jeanne's suffering, left alone at the open window, that decisively accelerates her death; "Winter of a dry freeze. [...] No greenery" corresponds to the time after Jeanne's death, to Hélène's new, supposedly passionless life with M. Rambaud.

Its extraordinarily rigid composition seems to detach *Une page d'amour* (Zola's examination of the phenomenon of 'passion') from the cycle's political and societal focus. Like *La Joie de Vivre* it seems to be an odd one out with regard to Zola's project of presenting a critical account of the *Second Empire*. However, as we will soon see, the contrary is true; it is these two novels that provide us with the decisive key for understanding the way that Zola positions himself and his project in relation to the historical development that he reconstructs. In fact, the 'weather spectacle' of Paris "all aflame", which corresponds to Hélène's having fallen in love with Henri, is not at all detached from the cycle's study of the Second Empire's characteristic climate and its tendency towards catastrophe. On the contrary, it tells the very same story that Zola had once planned to tell and that he decided to postpone to *L'Argent*: The city Hélène sees "all aflame" is the very city that Saccard experiences "blazing" "on a day of public festivity", the very same city whose enthusiasm for the war against Prussia makes glow "in a broad sheet of flame". These are all characterisations of the heating climate of the Second Empire (adding to all the furnaces of the

---

[707] Cf. the "plan général du roman", "Une matinée de clair soleil, toute blonde", "Une après-midi de Mi-carême, rouge et or, avec quelques nuage*", "Paris la nuit", "Paris gris et boueux, de la pluie. Navré", "L'hiver par un froid sec, avec quelques [lam] filets de neige. Temps clair. Pas de verdure La Seine charriant." (Zola 2006, 30–32)
[708] Cf. *Ébauche* (Zola 2006, 114–136).

meteorotopoi!) that already portend the fiery catastrophe they inevitably lead to. *Une page d'amour* merely opens up a different view of this general development: focussing on the individual fate of Hélène and her daughter, the novel enacts the Second Empire's historical fate in a sort of chamber play: Hélène gradually 'warms' to Henri, she is set in flames by her passion only to fall in a final, tragic debacle. The tableaux uncannily link the individual fate of Hélène and Jeanne to the historical fate of the Second Empire: Hélène's passion corresponds to the excessive and fatal passions of the city (she may even be said to be infected by these passions): Jeanne watches Paris 'perish' in the deluge of a violent storm "whose violence seemed to announce the end of the city" (*PA*, II 1032; my transl.),[709] showering down "such a torrent that the city was submerged" (*PA*, II 1032; my transl.),[710] while Hélène gives herself to Henri. Jeanne, more or less revengefully (and reacting to the weather), catches a cold that will lead to her death.

Paris does not serve as mere scenery, or a space for reflection in this chamber play. When her daughter joins Hélène watching the fiery sunset at the window in the flat, the mysterious city appears to them to be somehow complicit in what is taking place and what will, fatally, take place in the future:

> Both mother and daughter now sat mutely gazing on Paris all aflame. It seemed to them even more mysterious than ever, as it lay there illumined by blood-red clouds, like some city of an old-world tale expiating its lusts under a rain of fire. (*PA*, II 911; my transl.)[711]

This rain of fire will become reality when the Prussian army eventually besieges Paris. We get two extensive descriptions of the horrible sight of Paris in flames: one from on high, looking down on the city, a perspective similar to the tableaux of Paris 'painted' from Hélène's window; and one from the middle of things, where the focalisers are experiencing the fire rather than watching it from safe distance. It is certainly no coincidence that the first view we get of the burning city, the one from the top, is introduced by a Prussian soldier: "'Paris is burning... Look! [...]'" (*eD*, 489)[712] he tells a young woman, to whom

---

[709] "[...] des rues s'abîmaient, coulant à fond et surnageant, dans des secousses dont la violence semblait annoncer la fin de la cité." (*PA*, II 1032)
[710] "Au fond, sur Notre-Dame, le nuage se partagea, versa un tel torrent, que la Cité fut submergée [...]." (*PA*, II 1032)
[711] "Alors, toutes deux, la mère et la fille, demeurèrent muettes, en face de Paris incendié. Il leur restait plus inconnu encore, ainsi éclairé par les nuées saignantes, pareil à quelque ville des légendes expiant sa passion sous une pluie de feu." (*PA*, II 911)
[712] "« Paris brûle... Tenez ! [...] »" (*D*, V 886)

he happens to be distantly related. Henriette is on her way into the city, searching her brother Maurice. To the soldier, the plan of entering a perishing city must look insane. It is his comments that accompany their viewing the city:

> 'It's all over... Look, there's another district going up, that other fire further to the left... You can quite clearly see that huge line spreading like a river of flames.'
>
> They both fell quiet and a terrified silence reigned. He was right, sudden surges [*crues subites*] of flame were rising incessantly, overflowing [*débordaient*] into the sky like fire streaming from a furnace. With every minute the endless sea of flames spread further in an incandescent swell [*une houle incandescente*], sending up billows of smoke and piling an enormous, thick cloud of dark copper over the city; and there must have been a slight breeze behind it, for it was slowly crossing the black night, blocking out the heavenly vault with its wicked shower of ashes and soot. (*eD*, 490)[713]

Strikingly, the city does not 'merely' burn; it is, at the same time, inundated. The insistency with which this astonishing combination of a 'fiery deluge' appears makes it forceful: "river of flames", "sudden surges of flame", "rising", "overflowing", "fire streaming", "endless sea of flames", "incandescent swell", "shower of ashes and soot". Henriette, the focaliser of this description, is shocked by "the immensity of the catastrophe" (*eD*, 490).[714] She obviously does not care for the imagery of deluge dominating 'her' description, but is deeply affected by the fact that the whole city and her brother are threatened by the flames: "The thought of the fire devouring human lives, the sight of the city in flames on the horizon, casting that infernal glow of cities damned and destroyed, made her cry out in spite of herself." (*eD*, 490)[715] Her association of mythical punishment resonates with the image evoked at the sight of the blazing city in the sunset of *Une page d'amour*, with the vision of "some city of an old-world tale expiating its lusts under a rain of fire". Otto's, the Prussian soldier's reading of the situation confirms this mythical interpretation. Despite the emotionally delicate atmosphere he cannot refrain from voicing his opinion on the catastrophe they are witnessing: "'Ah! It was inevitable,'" he tells Henriette,

---

[713] "« C'est la fin de tout... Un autre quartier s'allume, cet autre foyer, là-bas, plus à gauche... Vous voyez bien cette grande raie qui s'étale, ainsi qu'un fleuve de braise. »

Tous deux se turent, un silence épouvanté régna. En effet, des crues subites de flammes montaient sans cesse, débordaient dans le ciel, en ruissellement de fournaise. A chaque minute, la mer de feu élargissait sa ligne d'infini, une houle incandescente d'où s'exhalaient maintenant des fumées qui amassaient, au-dessus de la ville, une immense nuée de cuivre sombre ; et un léger vent devait la pousser, elle s'en allait lentement à travers la nuit noire, barrant la voûte de son averse scélérate de cendre et de suie." (*D*, V 887–888)

[714] "[...] l'immensité de la catastrophe [...]." (*D*, V 887)

[715] "La pensée du feu dévorant des vies humaines, la vue de la ville embrasée à l'horizon, jetant la lueur d'enfer des capitales maudites et foudroyées, lui arrachaient des cris involontaires." (*D*, V 887)

"'It needed doing.'" (eD, 490)[716] For him there is no doubt that the Prussian army has accomplished a mission of historical, almost providential dimension:

> In any case, his gesture had been enough, he'd expressed his racial hatred, his conviction that he was in France as the dispenser of justice, sent by the God of armies to chastise a perverse nation. Paris was burning as a punishment for centuries of sin, for the long list of its crimes and debauchery. Yet again the Germans would save the world, sweeping away the last specks of Latin dirt and corruption. (eD, 490)[717]

It is, however, very likely that Otto's reading of the situation is indeed shaped by "racial hatred": the narrator seems to believe in the rumours that it was not the Prussians, but rather the Communards who had caused the "turn[ing] [of] the streets and squares into torrents and oceans of flame" (eD, 478)[718] (note again the imagery of a 'fiery deluge'). The personal catastrophe of Jean, who fatally injures his friend Maurice, re-enacts on the level of individuals the historical debacle of the perishing Second Empire as a debacle of civil war rather than as the Germans "sweeping away the last specks" of Latinity. However, the idea that Otto suggests is important. It contributes an essential cue for situating the collapse of the Second Empire in the tradition of imagining historical developments. It confirms Barbara Vinken's claim that Zola aligns himself in the constellations of *translatio imperii* that "have remained decisive in the postrevolutionary nineteenth century" (Vinken 2015b, 159). The Germans "[y]et again" saving the world clearly alludes to the collapse of the Roman Empire and identifies the "Latin dirt and corruption" of late antiquity with the 19th century French Second Empire. As Barbara Vinken writes, unlike Victor Hugo Zola does not regard history completed by the Napoleonic Empire or the Second Empire under Napoleon III; the completion he aspires to is an Anti-Rome that follows the "Latin dirt and corruption" of the Second Empire. Thus in fact, the Prussian soldier Otto articulates the framework of Zola's historical vision. The one deviation is accounted for by Otto's "racial hatred": he overestimates the role of "the Germans". For Zola the collapse of the Second Empire is brought about by the "Latin dirt and corruption" itself. Here a Lucanian

---

716 "« Ah ! c'était certain, ajouta-t-il à voix plus basse. De la grande besogne ! »" (D, V 887)
717 "Et, d'ailleurs, son geste avait suffi, il avait dit sa haine de race, sa conviction d'être en France le justicier, envoyé par le Dieu des armées pour châtier un peuple pervers. Paris brûlait en punition de ses siècles de vie mauvaise, du long amas de ses crimes et de ses débauches. De nouveau, les Germains sauveraient le monde, balayeraient les dernières poussières de la corruption latine." (D, V 887)
718 "Aussi s'enfiévrait-il [Maurice] davantage aux récits qui couraient : les quartiers minés, les catacombes bourrées de poudre, tous les monuments prêts à sauter, des fils électriques réunissant les fourneaux pour qu'une seule étincelle les allumât tous d'un coup, des provisions considérables de matières inflammables, surtout du pétrole, de quoi changer les rues et les places en torrents, en mers de flammes." (D, V 875–876)

perspective comes into play, a perspective whose importance Barbara Vinken has worked out for Gustave Flaubert (Vinken 2015b, 160–161). The Second Empire carries the core of its destruction in itself, it perishes in a necessary and foreseeable process. It is at this point, as we shall see, that the 'imagery' of heavy weather and of inundation comes in.

When Jean and the wounded Maurice fight their way through the burning city, their impressions register from close by what Henriette and Otto had viewed from the distance: "the spectacle of Babylon in flames" (eD, 491).[719] "[T]hey are surrounded by fire "setting the skyline ablaze, flames standing out against more flames in a bloody, endless sea" (eD, 496);[720] a "shower of burning brands rained down on them" (eD, 494)[721] while they struggle along in a little boat on the Seine, which seems to have been transformed to "a river of fire" (eD, 496):[722]

> The light grew so bright that the water was lit up as if by the midday sun, beating straight down, casting no shadows. [...] The bridges stood out particularly strongly, dazzling white, so clear that you could have counted every stone; and it was as if slender footbridges were running intact from one blaze to another, above the fiery, glowing water. At times, sudden creaking could be heard above the constant, rumbling clamour. Flurries of soot came down and foul smells blew over on the wind. And what was so terrifying was that Paris, those other districts far away, beyond the swathe of the Seine through the city, no longer existed. To right and left, the violence of fire was blinding, leaving a black abyss behind it. All that could now be seen was an immense darkness, a void, as if the whole of Paris had been caught and devoured in the fire, and had already vanished into an eternal night. The sky, too, was dead, for the flames reached up so high they extinguished the stars. (eD, 496–497)[723]

The scene is one of apocalypse, with a clear message: "Paris [...] no longer existed." Paris, "the whole of Paris" is "devoured in the fire", and vanishes "into

---

[719] "[...] le spectacle de la Babylone en flammes." (D, V 888)
[720] "Et c'était enfin, derrière, d'autres incendies encore, les sept maisons de la rue du Bac, les vingt-deux maisons de la rue de Lille, embrasant l'horizon, détachant les flammes sur d'autres flammes, en une mer sanglante et sans fin." (D, V 893)
[721] "Une pluie de tisons tombait sur eux, la chaleur était si intense, que le poil de leur face grillait." (D, V 891)
[722] "[...] un fleuve de braise [...]." (D, V 893)
[723] "La clarté devenait telle, que la rivière était éclairée comme par le soleil de midi, tombant d'aplomb, sans une ombre. [...] Surtout, les ponts apparaissaient, d'une blancheur éclatante, si nets, qu'on en aurait compté les pierres ; et l'on aurait dit, d'un incendie à l'autre, de minces passerelles intactes, au-dessus de cette eau braisillante. Par moments, au milieu de la clameur grondante et continue, de brusques craquements se faisaient entendre. Des rafales de suie tombaient, le vent apportait des odeurs empestées. Et l'épouvantement, c'était que Paris, les autres quartiers lointains, là-bas, au fond de la trouée de la Seine, n'existaient plus. A droite, à gauche, la violence des incendies éblouissait, creusait au-delà un abîme noir. On ne voyait plus qu'une énorme ténébreuse, un néant, comme si Paris tout entier, gagné par le feu, fût dévoré, eût déjà disparu dans une éternelle nuit. Et le ciel aussi était mort, les flammes montaient si haut, qu'elles éteignaient les étoiles." (D, V 893–894)

an eternal night". This is the last, the symbolical, the all-encompassing and ultimate catastrophe; the 'global' catastrophe that re-enacts and completes all the 'local' catastrophes, all the apocalyptic scenarios that had pervaded the cycle: the 'apocalypses' of *La Curée* (Kamm 1975, 243, Nelson 1977, 12), of *Une page d'amour* (Nelson 1973, 18), of *Au Bonheur des Dames* (Warning 2005, 159, Vinken 1995, 254), of *Germinal* (Walker 1959, 449, Guedj 1968, 137), of *La Bête humaine* (Jennings 1980, 402), and all the other apocalyptic catastrophes that critics have not given that label, but which clearly also belong to this series (like Coupeau's brutal death, which on the level of one single human body enacts the apocalyptic scenario of overheating and inundation). Zola leaves no doubt that Paris vanishes in "a void" as the coal-pit of 'Le Voreux' had been "swallowed up by the earth". The event is not only of historical, but even of cosmic dimension: "The sky, too, was dead, for the flames reached up so high they extinguished the stars." Zola does not merely tell the story of a city destroyed by (civil) war; it is a world that perishes. As Philipp Walker writes, Zola reconstructs "his age as a major turning point, a time of stupendous change, a veritable apocalypse" (1986, 4). It is this global, this cosmic dimension that make the events that Zola narrates compatible with the figure of *translatio imperii* implied by Otto's interpretation of the catastrophe of Paris burning.

However, Otto's reaction, distorted by racial hatred, does not remain the only interpretation of the debacle with which the novel provides us. As there are two visions on the Paris conflagration, one from the distance, one from the middle of things, there are also two readings. Maurice, whom Jean tries to bring to a safe place after severely injuring him, babbles away in his "delirium of fever":

> Maurice, buoyed up by the delirium of fever, gave a mad laugh.
>
> 'What a beautiful party at the Conseil d'État and the Tuileries... They've lit up the façades, the chandeliers are sparkling, the women are dancing... Oh! Dance, then, dance, in your smouldering petticoats, with your chignons aflame...'
>
> With his good arm he mimed the galas of Sodom and Gomorrah, with the music and flowers and perverted pleasures, the palaces bursting with so much debauchery, lighting up the naked abominations with such a wealth of candles that they'd set fire to themselves. (*eD*, 496–497)[724]

---

[724] "Maurice, que le délire de la fièvre soulevait, eut un rire de fou.

« Une belle fête au Conseil d'État et aux Tuileries... On a illuminé les façades, les lustres étincellent, les femmes dansent... Ah ! dansez donc, dans vos cotillons qui fument, avec vos chignons qui flamboient... »

De son bras valide, il évoquait les galas de Gomorrhe et de Sodome, les musiques, les fleurs, les jouissances monstrueuses, les palais crevant de telles débauches, éclairant l'abomination des nudités d'un tel luxe de bougies, qu'ils s'étaient incendiés eux-mêmes." (*D*, V 894)

Maurice is raving – and (yet) speaks the truth (Serres 1975, 323); he, indeed, "most probably serves as Zola's mouthpiece at this juncture" (Hemmings 1969, 33). He confirms the mythico-historical framework that Otto and others had brought up: here "Sodom and Gomorrah" represent the perversity, the "centuries of sin, [...] the long list of its crimes and debauchery" and the notion of mythical "punishment". The collapse of the Second Empire follows a clear logic of *translatio imperii*, identifying the Second Empire with the decadent Rome, with "Latin dirt and corruption", which, in turn, is identified with the mythical notions of Babylon or, more generally, with 'oriental excess' (cf. Vinken 2015a). When Paris burns, it is therefore Rome that perishes "[y]et again", and, it is, at the same time, "the spectacle of Babylon in flames".

Maurice's interpretation differs, however, from Otto's in one essential aspect: the catastrophic punishment is not brought to the Second Empire from without, by some "dispenser of justice, sent by the God of armies". Like Antoine Macquart "they'd set fire to themselves": it is the candles of the Second Empire's excessive festivities, of "perverted pleasures" and "debauchery" that cause the catastrophe.

Thus on the one hand, Zola rewrites a mythical scenario. As Philipp Walker has shown, Zola's descriptions of catastrophe and heavy weather are pervaded with allusions to "Classical and Biblical myths of the flood" (1971, 214), resorting to the "two principal metaphorical themes, the Underworld and the Deluge" (1959, 449): the "vast, cosmic upheaval" that Zola relates is "reminiscent of the Great Flood of Genesis or of the earthquakes and fiery, watery disasters that recur in early Greek mythology in the wars between the Titans and the early reign of Zeus" (1959, 449). Philip Walker even reads the characteristic "analogy between social upheaval and a catastrophic storm" that we have worked out for *Germinal* as "banal" "universal archetypes of myth" artfully adapted by Zola and turned into "intensely poetic and expressive symbols of his revolutionary modern thought" (1959, 449). There can be no doubt that the *Rougon-Macquart* have sprung from a "mythopoeic mind" (Walker 1971, 215) and that, in a syncretistic fashion, Latin mythology, Arab tales and also, importantly, the Old Testament provide the necessary background for this modern 'history' (Joly 1977, 79). However, Zola does not become "the mythopoet of the modernization process" (Walker 1971, 219) by merely mingling his stories with some wellknown elements of mythical catastrophe; I think that Phillip Walker has come up with a very adequate label, calling the cycle "the product of the peculiarly modern tension between the modern scientific mind and the primordial mythopoeic mind" (1959, 448).

Myth stakes out the scope and the coordinates, the framework of the historical development that Zola narrates with his *Rougon-Macquart*. The collapse of the Second Empire translates mythic and mythico-historic predecessors into the

19th century. It is prefigured by Babylon, by Sodom and Gomorrah, by Rome. "'It was inevitable,'" like the fate of its historical ancestors. However, it was "inevitable" in a different way. It is here that the mythical and the "modern scientific mind" meet – and part ways: Zola's Second Empire does not perish 'for mythical reasons'. 'Fate' does not watch over the empires and intervene like the punishing God of the Old Testament whenever necessary. Despite Otto's attempt to fashion himself and his Prussian comrades as this third, superior authority, Zola's universe does not know any palpable or intelligible "dispenser of justice, sent by the God of armies". The collapse of the Second Empire "was inevitable" for purely 'immanent' reasons. It is laws and regularities of this world, of this modern world of the 19th century (historical, material, cultural, social, 'natural') that account for the necessity of the catastrophe. Thus "human history is [...] incorporated into natural history" (Walker 1982, 261–262), not only in the sense of a mythical worldview, but also regarded from the perspective of modern sciences – sciences concerned with the 'milieu': biology, physiology, sociology.

In other words: on the one hand, there is myth, providing the framework and weight for the historical developments that Zola sets out to narrate; on the other hand, there is 19th century 'science', giving an account of why things happen and have to happen the way they do, filling the gap of the absent transcendent "dispenser of justice". Zola both *re*writes, he iterates ancient and Biblical myth, *and* writes a decidedly modern history of the Second Empire, at the same time. In fact, his characteristic 'natural history' that suspends the difference of nature/culture and accepts 'natural', non-human agents that are somehow 'unleashed' by human activity but develop their own, uncontrollable power, is even in some respects ahead of his own time. It may even be true that the 'scientific' side of Zola's 'natural' history becomes readable as 'scientific' (and not merely as mythic) only in retrospect. It may be true that this (speculative?) dimension of his project can only be taken seriously and be appreciated from our contemporary perspective, in times informed about the fact of mankind-induced climate change, conscious of the 'anthropocene', in times for which the uncontrollable interactions crossing the nature/culture divide have become a fact dominating our view of the world.

The role of the weather/climate in Zola's universe bridges the mythical and the 'modern scientific' dimension: it builds up the productive, "the peculiarly modern tension between the modern scientific mind and the primordial mythopoeic mind" that characterises the *Rougon-Macquart*. It connects the historical development that the cycle narrates, the development of the modern world, to the great mythical or mythico-historical cataclysms, and makes it part of the series of typologies/figurations or *translationes*. As we have seen in many of the previous sections, the weather and its (thermo)dynamics are also a characteristic subject of observation and an epistemological paradigm of the 19th century. As Maurice's reading of burning Paris, of the ultimate catastrophe shows, Zola uses the heavy, catastrophic weather to create an intricate structure of *double figuration*: on the one hand, the 'fiery deluge' destroying Paris and the Second Empire connects this end of a city to historical/mythical predecessors, especially of the Old Testament (the Deluge, the destruction of Sodom and Gomorrah or the fall of Babylon) – and via the *translatio imperii* also to the fall of Rome and the promised 'new Jerusalem' (cf. Warning 2005, 159). On the other hand, the 'fiery deluge' also links this final, ultimate catastrophe to the pre-figurations that had been part of the Second Empire's universe itself; 'internal', 'immanent' pre-figurations that, as we have seen, kept surfacing during the development that the *Rougon-Macquart* narrate; 'local' catastrophes, foreshadowing signals and events that Zola uses to exhibit the logic and dynamic, the 'quasi-natural', the historical force that inevitably drives the Second Empire towards its fatal collapse. The *Rougon-Macquart* thus do not merely re-enact a mythico-historical pattern, they fill and they supplement this pattern with its very own, decidedly modern logic, dynamic and necessity, with a decidedly modern historicity.

Maurice in his fever delirium depicts this second, internal web of figurations. The "galas of Sodom and Gomorrah, with the music and flowers and perverted pleasures, the palaces bursting with so much debauchery" are well known to the readers of the cycle; they have been the object of novels like *La Curée, Nana* or *L'Argent*. In fact, Maurice here hands out the hermeneutic keys for the reading of the cycle that we have been undertaking all this while: the 'metaphorical' fire, the "wealth of candles", the "Venetian lights" of *Nana*, cause 'real' fire. It finally sets Paris ablaze in the end. The ultimate catastrophe turns the 'metaphorical' fire (Paris 'ablaze' in the setting sun, Paris 'burning' of the war enthusiasts' torches) into 'real' fire; it literalises what had been foreshadowed in a metaphorical fashion.

However, the 'typological' connection between the pre-figuring novels and the final catastrophe proves to be more complex. (1) It not only works as a literalisation that turns metaphor into reality, but also makes use of an important metonymic dimension. It continues, to the most extreme extent, the movement of growth and proliferation that we have already observed as typical with regard to the meteorotopoi. The heart of most meteorotopoi (and that is also to say the heart of the process of modernisation), the furnace, that produces the heat for driving the steam engine, has grown to encompass the whole city:

> And above the huge city of Paris, the fire's glow had swelled larger still, the sea of flames appeared to have gained the distant shadows of the horizon, the sky was like the roof of some gigantic oven, heated white-hot. (eD, 510)[725]

Paris "white-hot", turned into one "gigantic oven" marks the endpoint, the extreme point of the process of 'global' heating that the cycle diagnosed as the characteristic trait of the Second Empire. The point of transition from 'metaphorical' to 'metonymic' or to 'real' is impossible to determine; it is however important to note that the movement that Zola traces is no abstract rhetorical operation: it does not merely turn metaphorical into real, but also, and dominantly, contains a line of metonymic continuity that accounts for the story of a historical development. The insistent theme of a fatal proliferation of heat metonymically supplements the cycle's progress towards literalising a metaphor.

(2) The ultimate catastrophe of Paris burning is itself far from purely 'literal'. As the short passage we just quoted again underlines, the fire is consistently conceptualised as an inundation, as a deluge of a "swell[ing]" "sea of flames". It is surely not unintentional that Jean and Maurice make their way through the burning city by boat – as if the city had been washed away by a flood. The elemental combination of a 'fiery deluge' is too paradoxical a combination to carry not the weight of meaning. It takes up and continues the imagery of overflowing, of *débordement*, that pervades the cycle from its first to its last pages. In fact, it is this familiar imagery that makes the ultimate catastrophe readable as another weather/climate catastrophe, as the last, the ultimate item in the series of weather catastrophes handed to us in Zola's cycle. The 'Débâcle' thus brings together all the decisive threads that we have discovered in the previous sections, especially the thermodynamic link between a process of (over)heating and violent weather that threatens to destroy its own place and technology of production. The 'imagery' of deluge, of inundation and overflowing that Zola employs for narrating the perishing of Paris and of the Second Empire in the fires of (civil) war thus connects the ultimate, 'global', historical catastrophe to all the 'local' catastrophes. As we have seen, the 'weathery' logic at play in the local as well as in the global catastrophe is described in great detail in the novels dedicated to the respective milieus – the strike and destruction of the mine in *Germinal*, the collapse of the 'Universelle' in *L'Argent*, the personal catastrophe of Hélène in *Une page d'amour*, only to name some of them. These 'local' catastrophes thus do not merely prophetically foreshadow the great, the

---

[725] "Et, sur Paris immense, le reflet de braise avait encore grandi, la mer de flammes semblait gagner les lointains ténébreux de l'horizon, le ciel était comme la voûte d'un four géant, chauffé au rouge clair." (*D*, V 907)

ultimate catastrophe to come; they are part of the same material formation, they follow the same rules and dynamics and thus provide the readers with explanations for the claim that the 'Débâcle' was "inevitable". The 'Débâcle' is not merely the mythical punishment imposed upon a modern Gomorrah by an abstract instance of justice; it is the "inevitable" result of the Second Empire's 'climate'. It marks the extreme point of a heating gone out of control, when the fires of the furnaces spread all over the city. Paris is flooded by all the torrents that it has unleashed and that have soon started to follow their own, uncontrollable, natural way down the slopes – streams and torrents of people, of goods, of money, of passions. The imagery of overflowing, of *débordement*, linking the burning Paris (and that is to say the collapse of the Second Empire) to the torrents of shoppers in *Au Bonheur des Dames*, to the torrents of orders to sell of *L'Argent*, to the torrents of waters flooding the coal-pit of *Germinal*, to the torrents of fugitives in *La Débâcle*, is the prime example for "the coherence of Zola's novels" that, according to Brian Nelson, "rests on their dense metaphorical structures" (Nelson 1977, 11). It is this coherence of imagery that turns the descriptions of the meteorotopoi and of the 'local' catastrophes into detailed explanations for the 'global' catastrophe.

There can be no doubt that Zola conceptualises his 'Débâcle' as an apocalyptical "great catastrophe". The world of the Second Empire perishes, clearing the way for something new, something better to come. The *Rougon-Macquart* have indeed to be read as a very nuanced interpretation and rewriting of the concept of καταστροφή: once the "wind ha[s] [...] changed" [στρέφειν: to turn] the movement 'downwards' [κατά], towards the final breakdown, towards the end of a world, is "inevitable". As we have seen, Zola even re-actualises the religious connotations of the concept that, according to Judith Kasper, had lost their semantic dominance, almost falling into oblivion, in its 18th century's use (cf. Kasper 2014). Even if the *Rougon-Macquart* do not know an abstract instance of justice, the catastrophe destroying the Second Empire has to do with punishment, it is associated with the Old Testament and its destructive natural forces hitting the cesspools of vice. Moreover, as we will soon see, the destruction of the catastrophe that strikes the world of the Second Empire, in the end aims at a "renewal", like the Biblical and "great mythical themes" (Walker 1971, 216): the world waits for salvation and a saviour. Almost all the dimensions that Judith Kasper assembles in her summary of the concept of catastrophe (cf. Kasper 2014) seem to be at stake in Zola's account of the Second Empire's breakdown. Nevertheless, he seems to have decided to keep a certain distance from this concept of catastrophe. Despite the obvious dependence on its semantic net and traditions, he rarely uses the term *catastrophe*, preferring another, less tradition-laden one: *débâcle*.

This very conscious choice somehow resists the cycle's strong tendency to merge fully into a neo-mythical rewriting of ancient and biblical stories of catastrophic punishment and renewal. It does not omit this dimension either. In fact, the *Rougon-Macquart* tell a mythical story, this is their frame and their scope, this is clearly the line of tradition that they follow. However, there is more, and there is something decidedly 'modern' or contemporary in the cycle that Zola highlights by insisting on the term *débâcle*. He adds a further dimension to the mythical and religious, to the 'traditional' dimensions of catastrophe that are undoubtedly present as well.

The *Petit Robert* lists two meanings for the noun *débâcle*: "In a frozen river, Bursting of the ice covering of which the pieces are carried away by the current" (*PetRob*, débâcle, *n*. 1.; my transl.)[726] and "Sudden flight (of an army) [...] Sudden collapse" (*PetRob*, débâcle, *n*. 2.; my transl.),[727] mentioning Zola's novel and the notion of a financial crash as examples for this meaning. Semantically speaking, *débâcle* is based on the noun *bâcle*, meaning "A wooden or iron bolt with which one locks a door or a window from the interior" (*PetRob*, bâcle, *n*.; my transl.),[728] so that the verb *débâcler* originally signifies "To open (a door, a window) by unlocking the bolt" (*PetRob*, débâcler, *v. tr.* 1.; my transl.).[729] It is only later that the verb takes on the meaning that has survived and that has passed on its semantic core to the noun *débâcle*: "Speaking of a river, Thawing suddenly, the ice breaking up before being carried away by the current" (*PetRob*, débâcler, *v. intr.* 2.; my transl.).[730] In other words, the noun *débâcle* that Zola, very consciously and prominently, has introduced to 'label' the collapse of the Second Empire contributes to and forms part of the 'weathery' 'imagery' that I have claimed is central for the cycle as a whole. *Débâcle* with its notion of sudden thawing, of sudden movement carrying away the debris, the wreckage in the current of a river is closely related to the notion of *débordement*, of overflowing, that pervades the cycle.

---

[726] "Dans un cours d'eau gelé, Rupture de la couche de glace dont les morceaux sont emportés par le courant. [Cf.] dégel ; régional bouscueil." (*PetRob*, débâcle, *n*. 1.)

[727] "Fuite soudaine (d'une armée). Le front percé, ce fut la débâcle. [Cf.] débandade, déroute. Retraite qui s'achève en débâcle. « La Débâcle », roman de Zola (sur la défaite française de 1870). Effondrement soudain. C'est la débâcle pour son entreprise. [Cf.] faillite, ruine. La débâcle d'une fortune. Débâcle financière. [Cf.] krach." (*PetRob*, débâcle, *n*. 2.)

[728] "Barre de bois ou de fer avec laquelle on ferme de l'intérieur une porte, une fenêtre." (*PetRob*, bâcle, *n*.)

[729] "Vieux Ouvrir (une porte, une fenêtre) en enlevant la bâcle*." (*PetRob*, débâcler, *v. tr.* 1.)

[730] "En parlant d'une rivière, Dégeler brusquement, la glace se fractionnant avant d'être emportée par le courant. [Cf.] débâcle." (*PetRob*, débâcler, *v. intr.* 2.)

> It is less the fall [*la chute*] than the waterfall [*la chute d'eau*], less the disaster than the spreading of the multiple by an opening. The bolts are unlocked, the doors open themselves. The definition gapes. This is the torrent. And the crowd rushes. At the stock exchange, on strike, in the *Bonheur*. The mass flows. (Serres 1975, 178; my transl.)[731]

Zola even once, with a witty wink, 'literalises' the *débâcle*, when he 'orchestrates' the collapse of the 'Universelle' with "appalling" weather, with a "thaw" "swamping the city" (*eM*, 300). As we will see in the next section, the gesture of opening the window to violent weather, hoping for its cleansing or purifying, its cathartic effect defines the writing posture that has brought about *The Rougon-Macquart*.

Zola's use of the 'label' *débâcle* for describing the catastrophe of a perishing world thus balances and supplements the mythical dimensions that delineate the framework for his natural and social history of the Second Empire. It shifts the focus to the natural proceedings of a weather-phenomenon, governed by its very own, traceable but complicated logic. As a consequence of this emphasis on the immanence of natural forces rather than on transcendent instances of punishment and justice, one might be tempted to look for a contemporary 'scientific' concept of catastrophe, or at least one developed by the older natural philosophy that Zola might have recurred to. Georges Cuvier with his theory of catastrophism is one candidate that some critics have proposed in this context (Walker 1982, 257, Haavik 2000, 4). However, for Cuvier the catastrophe attacks the world unexpectedly, as a sudden, unforeseeable event interrupting a period of stability. As we have seen, Zola's *débâcle* does not occur in the world of the Second Empire unexpectedly and it does not come from 'without'. On the contrary, it is brought about by the very period that it destroys in the end. It results from a 'stable instability' that follows an immanent, but traceable dynamic and development. It is not a question of contingency, but of necessity: it has to be called "inevitable", because it is a result of certain developments rather than a case of bad luck. With its characteristic process of (over)heating and unleashing weathery forces, the Second Empire (in a quasi-Lucanian fashion) carries its own, necessary collapse within itself; it pays for its huge success by its necessary, huge fall. There is no contemporary 'scientific' theory of catastrophism available for Zola. It would take more than half a decade before René Thom would come up with a mathematical formulation of a theory of catastrophe that could possibly be complex enough to capture Zola's thinking of *débâcle*: both aim at immanently

---

[731] "Et ça finit par la débâcle, qui est moins la chute que la chute d'eau, moins le désastre que le multiple répandu par une ouverture. Les barres sautent, les portes s'ouvrent. La définition bée. C'est le torrent. Et la foule se rue. A la bourse à la grève, au Bonheur. La masse coule." (Serres 1975, 178)

integrating the catastrophe into the 'normal', regular way of the world, they envisage a theory that suspends the binary difference of chaos and order.[732] Even thermodynamics (whose importance for Zola's cycle has been explained by Michel Serres in his *Feux et signaux de brume* (1975)) ceases to be of use with regard to understanding the *débâcle*: the ultimate catastrophe that destroys the Second Empire is not "what one called thermal death [*mort thermique*]" (Serres 1975, 63; my transl.);[733] the Second Empire does not die a "cold death" (Serres 1975, 63; my transl.)[734] that would be characterised by the absence of thermodynamic free energy. It 'makes itself perish' and thereby provides the grounds for a movement of 'renewal'. It is this logic that Zola attempts to capture, a logic that has nothing to do with energy or entropy.

Zola's conceptualisation of the *débâcle* as a 'scientific' phenomenon (balancing and supplementing his mythical framework) thus may be called 'speculative' (or 'literary'?). In his typical, syncretistic way of thinking he combines different, diverse 'scientific' concepts of various fields in order to approach the phenomenon he wishes to 'represent'. In order to understand Zola's notion of *débâcle* there is no alternative to a close reading of his literary descriptions of the 'global' as well as the 'local' *débâcles*, and to reconstructing the fields that he combines into his very idiosyncratic idea of historical development. We have so far explored the different layers of catastrophe (the mythical, Biblical, and the mythico-historical layers that Zola adopts), as well as the theme of the weather inherent in the term *débâcle* itself. There is however a third semantic field that surfaces insistently in the descriptions of the catastrophes and that I have neglected until now: the field of sickness.

Correspondences of the societal *débâcle* with the notion of sickness manifest themselves explicitly on the level of plot and narration: in (at least) three prominent cases Zola makes the catastrophic events that haunt the city of Paris or the Empire as a whole coincide with the narration of the tragic, deadly disease (or injury) of a protagonist. In *Une page d'amour*, it is the little Jeanne, whose fragile health and untimely death correspond to the events taking place outside the flat; in *Nana* the protagonist dies of smallpox under horrible circumstances while the war-enthusiasts flood the streets of Paris; in *La Débâcle* Maurice's slow, feverish death, after having been injured by his friend Jean, corresponds

---

[732] I am grateful to Jörg Dünne for sharing his thoughts on 19th century 'scientific' theories of catastrophe and for pointing me to René Thom.

[733] "Ce qu'on appelait autrefois l'équilibre y est atteint au bout d'un certain temps, celui au cours duquel l'entropie va croissant ; alors, rien ne se passe, et rien ne peut plus arriver. On nommait cet état mort thermique." (Serres 1975, 63)

[734] "La mort froide." (Serres 1975, 87)

to the perishing of the burning city outside. In each of these cases Zola closely interweaves the two narrative threads so that the one uncannily comments on the other. Moreover, Jeanne, Nana and Maurice are all protagonists who are 'typical' for the Second Empire; they perish with and *as* the Empire.

This most obvious presence on the level of plot and narration only points to the less visible but all the more insistent presence of the field of sickness on the level of imagery. There is hardly any climate catastrophe related by the cycle that is not connected to this field. In *Germinal*, as we have seen, "the pump" was "straining, coughing and spluttering with the effort" (*eG*, 464), before "a final convulsion racked the ground"; "the drainage pump gave a death-rattle" and the whole pit "was crushed and smothered to death" (*eG*, 475). The violent storm that Jeanne watches inundate Paris in *Une page d'amour* in a way foreshadows her own death that results from catching a cold at the open window, having herself become drenched by the rain that submerges the city: "Then the vast city, as though overwhelmed and lifeless after some awful convulsion, seemed but an expanse of stony ruins under the invisible heavens." (*PA*, II 1032–1033; my transl.)[735] In *L'Argent*, on the day of the crash, "everybody [...] looked jaundiced and sickly", "people sidled along and spoke quietly, as if in a house where someone lay ill" (*eM*, 301–302). For the experienced brokers who can read the symptoms, the graveness of the situation is quite clear:

> The trading-floor was as nervous as the hall; the brokers, ever since the last settlement, had been feeling the ground shaking beneath their feet, amid symptoms of such gravity as to alarm even them with all their experience. Already there had been some partial collapses, the market, exhausted and overburdened, was showing cracks on all sides. Was this then going to be one of those great cataclysms of the sort that happens every ten or fifteen years, one of those crises that hit speculation when it reaches the point of acute fever, when it decimates the Bourse, and sweeps through like a wind of death? (*eM*, 303)[736]

When all is over, when the 'Universelle' has collapsed and the heating process of speculation has come to an end, the narrator takes up this medical vocabulary to explicate the link between the disaster and a "fatal periodic epidemic":

---

[735] "Alors, l'immense cité, comme détruite et morte à la suite d'une suprême convulsion, étendit son champ de pierres renversées, sous l'effacement du ciel." (*PA*, II 1032–1033)
[736] "La corbeille était tout aussi anxieuse que la salle, les agents sentaient bien, depuis la dernière liquidation, le sol trembler sous eux, au milieu de symptômes si graves, que leur expérience s'en alarmait. Déjà des écroulements partiels s'étaient produits, le marché exténué, trop chargé, se lézardait de toutes parts. Allait-ce donc être un de ces grands cataclysmes, comme il en survient un tous les dix à quinze ans, une de ces crises mortelles du jeu à l'état de fièvre aigue, qui décime la Bourse, la balaye d'un vent de mort ?" (*Ar*, V 326)

> And the Bourse stood out, grey and bleak in the gloom of the crash, which for the last month had left it deserted, open to the four winds, like a marketplace cleared by famine. It was the fatal periodic epidemic that ravages the markets, sweeping through, every ten to fifteen years, the 'black Fridays' as they are called, that strew the ground with wreckage. It takes years for confidence to be restored, and for the great banking houses to be rebuilt, rebuilt until the day when the passion for gambling gradually reawakens, blazes up, and sets the whole process in motion again, bringing a new crisis [*nouvelle crise*], and sending everything crashing into a new disaster. (*eM*, 336)[737]

Certainly, this crash is not just any crash; it foreshadows and precipitates "the imminent end of a world" that "a sort of muffled creaking" from the "far-off parts of the city" (*eM*, 336)[738] announces, as Zola emphasises in the very next sentence. However, this "end of a world", the 'global' catastrophe, will be conceptualised in the same way as the 'local' catastrophes, again resorting to the notions of "epidemic" and "crisis":

> For wasn't this the final, fatal act, the madness in the blood which had germinated on the fields of defeat of Sedan and Metz, the epidemic destruction born of the siege of Paris, the supreme crisis [*la crise suprême*] of a nation in mortal danger, amid all the killing and ruination? (*eD*, 505; transl. altered)[739]

The *débâcles* are not only climate catastrophes – they are also climate crises. *Crises*, understood in its oldest, in its medical, its 'Hippocratic' sense, as: "Pathol. The point in the progress of a disease when an important development or change takes place which is decisive of recovery or death; the turning-point of a disease for better or worse" (*OED*, crisis, *n.* 1.). The notion of crisis that Zola adds to his syncretistic conceptualisation of *débâcle* is of huge consequence. It introduces a decisive deviation from 'classical' or 'traditional' ways of thinking about a catastrophe or apocalypse. When "the wind had [...] changed" signs are not pointing to complete destruction, to a falling into chaos preceding the advent

---

[737] "Et la Bourse, grise et morne, se détachait, dans la mélancolie de la catastrophe, qui, depuis un mois, la laissait déserte, ouverte aux quatre vents du ciel, pareille à une halle qu'une disette a vidée. C'était l'épidémie fatale, périodique, dont les ravages balayent le marché tous les dix à quinze ans, les vendredis noirs, ainsi qu'on les nomme, semant le sol de décombres. Il faut des années pour que la confiance renaisse, pour que les grandes maisons de banque se reconstruisent, jusqu'au jour où, la passion du jeu ravivé peu à peu, flambant et recommençant, l'aventure, amène une nouvelle crise, effondre tout, dans un nouveau désastre." (*Ar*, V 361)

[738] "Mais, cette fois, derrière cette fumée rousse de l'horizon, dans les lointains troubles de la ville, il y avait comme un grande craquement sourd, la fin prochaine d'un monde." (*Ar*, V 361)

[739] "N'était-ce pas, en effet, l'acte dernier et fatal, la folie du sang, qui avait germé sur les champs de défaite de Sedan et de Metz, l'épidémie de destruction née du siège de Paris, la crise suprême d'une nation en danger de mort, au milieu des tueries et des écroulements ?" (*D*, V 903)

of a new world from without. In contrast to the notion of κατα-στροφή, the turn of the medical crisis does not merely lead 'downwards', towards destruction, towards "killing and ruination", but also always implies a solution of the situation: either the re-turn to health, or to an end in death. In fact, crisis in the medical sense does not lead towards chaos, not even in the tragic case of a lethal outcome. It does not mark a turning point linking cosmos and chaos, but rather pertains to a different dimension: the dimension of imbalance and balance, of intemperance and temperance.[740] Crisis thus can be read as the climactic point where the imbalance, the intemperance is turned against itself, as the "point of acute fever" that re-establishes a new state of balance, purifying and cleaning the sick 'body' of its superabundant humours. In the extreme case of fatality it re-establishes balance by dissolving the intemperate 'body'. The "wind of death" that sweeps through the Bourse thus has not only to be read as the means of heavenly punishment that destroys a world of debauchery and vice but also always as a force of recovery that provides for future health. This holds true for the "periodic fatal epidemic" that re-establishes the balance of the financial market as well as for the "supreme crisis" of war, for the French "nation in mortal danger": "'No, no, don't curse the war...'", Zola makes his mouthpiece Maurice explain to the bystanders on his deathbed, "'The war's good, it's doing its work... [...] Maybe this bloodletting's [*cette saignée*] something which needed to happen. War's life, and life can't exist without death.'" (eD, 505)[741] The Second Empire perishes – however, the "nation in mortal danger" survives. The crisis is supreme; the "wind of death" atrociously claims many victims, which is inevitable and necessary, as Maurice explains with regard to his own fate:

> 'Just remember what you told me, the day after Sedan, when you claimed that it wasn't always a bad thing, to get a good slap... And you said, too, that when something somewhere started to rot, like a gangrenous limb, then it was better to see it laying on the ground, lopped off with an axe, than let it kill you, like cholera... I've often thought about what you said, since I've been on my own, shut up in this insane, wretched Paris... So there we are! I'm the rotten limb you've lopped off...' (eD, 509)[742]

---

740 Cf. chapter I, 6 and 68.
741 "« Non, non, ne maudis pas la guerre... Elle est bonne, elle fait son œuvre... [...] C'est peut-être nécessaire, cette saignée. La guerre, c'est la vie qui ne peut pas être sans la mort. »" (D, V 903)
742 "« Rappelle-toi donc ce que tu m'as dit, le lendemain de Sedan, quand tu prétendais que ce n'était pas mauvais, parfois, de recevoir une bonne gifle... Et tu ajoutais que, lorsqu'on avait de la pourriture quelque part, un membre gâté, ça valait mieux de le voir par terre, abattu d'un coup de hache, que d'en crever comme d'un choléra... J'ai songé souvent à cette parole, depuis que je me suis trouvé seul, enfermé dans ce Paris de démence et de misère... Eh bien ! c'est moi qui suis le membre gâté que tu as abattu... »" (D, V 906–907)

Like Jeanne and like Nana, Maurice dies a symbolic death, a death symbolic for the "bloodletting" that is to cure the French nation. His story of being killed by his own comrade thus stands emblematically for the fate of France, which is shattered and, according to Zola, also cured by (civil) war:

> The bloodbath, though, was necessary, and it had to be French blood, this appalling holocaust, this living sacrifice amid the purifying fire. As of now, the calvary had been climbed right to the top, to the most terrifying of agonies, the crucified nation was expiating its sins and was about to be reborn. (eD, 509)[743]

This passage is a good example of Zola's 'syncretistic' 'method' of writing: having introduced the notion of purification in its medical sense by speaking of crisis and fever, Zola now charges this notion with mythical weight by associating it with pagan sacrifice, with the "holocaust". In a further step the "terrifying agonies" of this "living sacrifice" are identified with the Christian Passion narrative. Zola thereby short-circuits the process of crises and recovery with the cleansing from sin and the idea of resurrection. However, as the formulation of being "reborn" (which, in this context, with reference to Christ's suffering on the cross, somehow does not suit the semantic register of the history of salvation) already indicates, the single elements that Zola combines in his syncretistic vision of *débâcle* are each of different, and of limited scopes. Although, for example, "John's Revelations serve as an intertextual grounding" (Mossman 1985, 30) to which Zola comes back with great constancy whenever the fatality of catastrophe and the apocalyptic end of a world needs to be underlined, Christian salvation history does not provide the one, dominant model of historicity that Zola uses for his *Rougon-Macquart*. Zola employs the notion of apocalypse to conceptualise the necessity of a deep historical rupture; an old world perishes as a result of its 'sins', and calls for the advent (or rather the 'growth') of something new. He is, however, not concerned with the important Augustinian difference of *civitas caelestis* and *civitas terrena*. History in the *Rougon-Macquart* (this might change with the later *Quatre Évangiles*) does not follow a transcendent plan, it does not lead to a pre-defined, perfect world. Zola's vision is all about this world. Although pervaded by Christian iconography and Biblical allusions, it can be said to be completely secular and to be fundamentally open with regard to its future. In other words, Zola's thinking about *débâcle* cannot be reduced to any abstract model (i.e. a specific 'scientific' concept of catastrophe, or the theological model of salvation history) available in the discourses of the time. Instead of adopting a single model, Zola fabricates his own concept of *débâcle* by combining different, often conflicting, elements. It is the tension that

---

[743] "Mais le bain de sang était nécessaire, et de sang français, l'abominable holocauste, le sacrifice vivant, au milieu du feu purificateur. Désormais, le calvaire était monté jusqu'à la plus terrifiante des agonies, la nation crucifiée expiait ses fautes et allait renaître." (D, V 907)

the combination of disparate elements (e.g. salvation history and vitalistic immanence) produces that accounts for the specificity and the complexity of Zola's concept.

With regard to the question of the 'rebirth' of the nation and the 'advent' of a new world, the *Rougon-Macquart* give us quite explicit answers. As with the catastrophes, Zola uses the structure of internal, 'local' pre-figuration so that he can narrate this 'rebirth', this post-apocalyptic scenario several times. *Germinal*, *La Terre*, *L'Argent* and *La Débâcle* all end on the same note, so to speak: a (little) world has perished (the coal-pit is destroyed and has vanished into the ground, the farm burned to the walls, the 'Universelle' collapsed, Paris is burning), the protagonist walks by the ruins and is expected to be deeply moved. Instead, a mysterious natural force makes itself felt:

> The sun appeared majestically on the horizon, the whole countryside was experiencing a joyous awakening. A wave of gold light flowed from east to west across the vast plain. This life-giving warmth spread wider and wider, vibrating with youthfulness, throbbing with all the sighs of the earth, with birdsong, and with all the murmurs of the rivers and forests. It was good to be alive, the old world wanted to live for another springtime. (*eG*, 520)[744]

These are Étienne's impressions, when he walks past the over-ground facilities of the coal-pits a last time, on his way to a new, unknown life. His description of idyllic springtime nature can hardly be told apart from Madame Caroline's experiences at the end of *L'Argent*. 'L'Universelle', the bank that she had founded together with Saccard and her brother, has collapsed and drawn a considerable number of victims into the abyss. To make things worse, on a visit and hoping for news concerning Saccard's son Victor whom she had attempted to set back on the track of humanity and morality, Madame Caroline just happens to witness the death of the miserable Busch and hear of Victor's return to the criminal life on the streets. Saddened by these two events, she leaves the building.

> Outside, on the pavement of the Rue Vivienne, Madame Caroline was surprised at the softness of the air. It was five o'clock, the sun was setting in a sky of tender purity, turning to gold the signs far off, hanging high above the Boulevard. This April, so delightful in its new youthfulness, was like a caress for her whole physical being, right down to her heart. (*eM*, 368)[745]

---

[744] "Le soleil paraissait à l'horizon glorieux, c'était un réveil d'allégresse, dans la campagne entière. Un flot d'or roulait de l'orient à l'occident, sur la plaine immense. Cette chaleur de vie gagnait, s'étendait, en un frisson de jeunesse, où vibraient les soupirs de la terre, le chant des oiseaux, tous les murmures des eaux et des bois. Il faisait bon vivre, le vieux monde voulait vivre un printemps encore." (*G*, III 1588)

[745] "Dehors, sur le trottoir de la rue Vivienne, Mme Caroline fut surprise de la douceur de l'air. Il était cinq heures, le soleil se couchait dans un ciel d'une pureté tendre, dorant au loin les enseignes hautes du boulevard. Cet avril, si charmant d'une nouvelle jeunesse, était comme un caresse à tout son être physique, jusqu'au cœur." (*Ar*, V 395)

Étienne and Caroline are both affected by good weather. The "softness of the air", the "warmth spread[ing] wider and wider" irresistibly trigger a "youthfulness": it is not a new world that arrives from without, that is established on the ruins of the old, but "the old world" that "want[s] to live for another springtime", a "new youthfulness" that is obviously introduced by a seasonal logic. It is no coincidence that it is April, in both scenes, the time of the year when good spring weather awakens nature to life, no matter whether the urban life in Paris or the landscape above the coal-pits:

> High in the sky the April sun now shone down in its full glory, warming the bountiful earth and breathing life into her fertile bosom, as the buds burst into verdant leaf, and the fields quivered under the pressure of the rising grass. All around [Étienne] seeds were swelling and shoots were growing, cracking the surface of the plain, driven upwards by their need for warmth and light. The sap flowed upwards and spilled over [*débordement de sève*] in soft whispers; the sound of germinating seed rose and swelled to form a kiss. Again, and again, and ever more clearly, as if they too were rising towards the sunlight, his comrades kept tapping away. Beneath the blazing rays of the sun, in that morning of new growth, the countryside rang with song, as its belly swelled with a black and avenging army of men, germinating slowly in its furrows, growing upwards in readiness for harvests to come, until one day soon their ripening would burst open the earth itself. (eG, 524)[746]

The forces that drive this "new youthfulness" are not new, they are not unknown: it is the "need for warmth and light" that is satisfied – the same need that the Second Empire (over-)satisfied with the help of technology, of hothouses and artificial heating. The intention is obvious: the vocabulary of "swelling", of proliferating nature, with its overflowing saps, driven by the "blazing rays of the sun" takes up vocabulary that also featured prominently in Zola's descriptions of the Second Empire's decadent hothouse proliferations. Étienne and Caroline are not experiencing a new, a different world; it is the same world, working according to the very same mechanisms and the same needs: warmth and light produces growth, this is its simple formula. Not a new world, but a new chance, this is what the post-apocalyptic "new youthfulness" is all about.

---

[746] "Maintenant, en plein ciel, le soleil d'avril rayonnait dans sa gloire, échauffant la terre qui enfantait. Du flanc nourricier jaillissait la vie, les bourgeons crevaient en feuilles vertes, les champs tressaillaient de la poussée des herbes. De toutes parts, des grains se gonflaient, s'allongeaient, gerçaient la plaine, travaillées d'un besoin de chaleur et de lumière. Un débordement de sève coulait avec des voix chuchotantes, le bruit des germes s'épandait en un grand baiser. Encore, encore, de plus en plus distinctement, comme s'ils se fussent rapprochés du sol, les camarades tapaient. Aux rayons enflammés de l'astre, par cette matinée de jeunesse, c'était de cette rumeur que la campagne était grosse. Des hommes poussaient, une armée noire, vengeresse, qui germait lentement dans les sillons, grandissant pour les récoltes du siècle futur, et dont la germination allait faire bientôt éclater la terre." (*G*, III 1591)

By giving his novel on the striking colliers the title *"Germinal"* Zola prominently subjects the social upraising (and that is to say the discourse of revolution) to a seasonal logic. As Sandy Petrey (1969, 60) and others have remarked, the title alludes to the name of the seventh month of the French Republican Calendar, the month of germination, the first month of the spring quarter, which indeed contains and represents the April period of awaking nature. It may however be misleading to claim that the title "embodies the coincidence of man's liberation with that of nature" (Schor 1971, 19); the seasons do not really coincide with the events of the strike (Best 1990, 495), this is, I would surmise, not what the novel is about. Instead, I would suggest reading Zola's associating the social movement of the colliers with germinating nature as a rather provocative comment against a certain messianic idea of history that Zola attributes to movements of socialist revolution: in the course of the novel he developed the idea of a naïve "religious fervour" that the striking colliers harbour, "the fever of hope that the early Christians nourished, waiting for the coming reign of justice" (*eG*, 284; transl. altered).[747] Associating the "black and avenging army of men" with the "swelling" nature of springtime disavows the messianic idea of a "coming reign of justice" without negating the hope for change, transformation and renewal. Zola argues against the model of salvation that fabricates an ideal world, a "reign of justice". He argues against a world radically separated from the old world, a new world set as a *telos* towards which history has to be brought to move, or which just 'arrives' once the old world is destroyed. In the *Rougon-Macquart* (and it is again important to underline that this might change for the late Zola of the *Quatre Évangiles*), Zola does not found his hope for the possibility of a better world on his own ideas of an alternative world to be established once the Second Empire has perished. His tendencies are not utopic. His vision of historicity consciously refrains from positing and investing in a *telos* for the future. Instead, I would maintain, he invests in a radically immanent, vitalistic concept of permanent renewal – and that is to say in a radical openness of the future. Speaking of a 'liberation of nature' makes no sense, because nature does not know a "reign of justice". However, nature exhibits a striking capacity for renewal, for rejuvenation: it follows a seasonal rhythm of decay and transforming re-growth. This abandonment of a linear, messianic concept of history is not to be misunderstood as the adoption of a naïve and fatalistic circular concept of history. Lewis Kamm has summarised the long discussion on the concept of time and history (linear or cyclical?) underlying the *Rougon-Macquart*

---

[747] "Ils ne sentaient plus le froid, ces ardentes paroles les avaient chauffés aux entrailles. Une exaltation religieuse les soulevait de terre, la fièvre d'espoir des premiers chrétiens de l'Église, attendant le règne prochain de la justice." (*G*, III 1380)

that has been going on for decades in Zola criticism (cf. 1992). I think it rather misleading to discuss the question of Zola's concept of history on the abstract level of these two models and their compatibility; all the more so since the notions of 'circular time' or of 'eternal return' are in themselves far from being simple and unequivocal. In the manner of a *bricoleur* Zola crafts his own, very nuanced concept of history, which I am convinced has to be explored in all its different aspects. Zola's apocalyptic *and* vitalistic concept invests in a seasonal logic of (autumn) crisis and (spring) renewal, however, without implying that it is the same that returns again and again.[748] On the contrary, Caroline and Étienne are obviously moving towards a future they know hardly anything about – there is, for them, no reason to be happy or joyful at all:

> And now, as she continued her walk, the wave of joy mounted [*le flot de la joie montait*] within her as if from a bubbling spring, impossible to stop or smother, however hard she tried. She had understood, but unwillingly. No, no, the awful catastrophes were too recent, she could not be gay, could not abandon herself to this uplifting surge of endless life [*ce jaillissement d'éternelle vie qui la soulevait*]. She strove to maintain her grieving, she called herself back to despair, with so many cruel memories! Was she forgetting that she had been complicit? And she recited facts to herself, this fact, that one, and that other, that she should have spent the rest of her life weeping over. But in between her fingers clenched over her heart, that bubbling up of sap gathered strength, and the spring of life overflowed [*la source de vie débordait*], pushing away all obstacles, tossing all debris aside, to flow freely, clear and triumphant in the sunlight.
>
> From that moment Madame Caroline gave in and simply abandoned herself to the irresistible force of continual rejuvenation. (*eM*, 369)[749]

The joyfulness takes hold of Caroline against her will; she cannot help this feeling, it happens to her and she is absolutely powerless against it. The new,

---

[748] Zola's concept of time/history thus can be said to resemble Gilles Deleuze's reading of the Nietzschean 'eternal return' (cf. Deleuze 1962, 1965, 1968).

[749] "Et, maintenant, en elle, tandis qu'elle reprenait sa marche, le flot de la joie montait, comme d'une source bouillonnante, qu'elle aurait tenté vainement d'arrêter, de boucher avec ses deux mains. Elle avait compris, elle ne voulait pas. Non, non ! les affreuses catastrophes étaient trop récentes, elle ne pouvait être gaie, s'abandonner à ce jaillissement d'éternelle vie qui la soulevait. Et elle s'efforçait de garder son deuil, elle se rappelait au désespoir par tant de souvenirs cruels. Quoi ? elle aurait ri encore après l'écroulement de tout, une si effrayante somme de misères ! Oubliait-elle qu'elle était complice ? et elle citait les faits, celui-ci, celui-là, cet autre, qu'elle aurait dû mettre tout son reste d'existence à pleurer. Mais, entre ses doigts serrés sur son cœur, le bouillonnement de sève devenait plus impétueux, la source de vie débordait, écartait les obstacles pour couler librement, en rejetant les épaves aux deux bords, claire et triomphante sous le soleil.

Dès ce moment, vaincue, Mme Caroline dut s'abandonner à la force irrésistible du continuel rajeunissement." (*Ar*, V 396)

unexpected youthfulness she experiences obviously does not accompany the introduction of a new agency of the rational subject that has regained control. On the contrary, Caroline is still relentlessly exposed to the milieu surrounding her, it is this milieu that infects her with "joy" and "life", as count Muffat had been affected by the ruinous warmth radiating from Nana. Strikingly, it is the very same 'weathery' imagery, the same "mount[ing]" "wave[s]", "bubbling spring[s]", "uplifting surge", even "overflow[ing] [*débordait*]" that seize Caroline and trigger her new youthfulness. The fact that the vernal awakening, the overflowing "spring of life" is described as "pushing away all obstacles, tossing all debris aside, to flow freely" even alludes to the notion of *débâcle*, now conceived not as a force of destruction, but of new life. It is the same 'old' world, with the same 'old' forces that brings about rejuvenation. Like Renée in the hothouse, and like the colliers at the end of *Germinal*, Caroline is transformed into a plant whose "sap" rises under the influence of the warming "sunlight". Zola remains faithful to his Tainean "scientific conception": "The character has become the product of the air and the soil, like a plant" (Zola 1893b, 233)[750] – not only with regard to the ruinous influences of the Second Empire's milieu, but also as *the* source of rejuvenating forces!

Against the background of the internal structure of figuration it does not come as a surprise that at the end of *La Débâcle* Jean, looking at the ruins of Paris after the great catastrophe, having just lost his comrade Maurice, almost stereotypically (re-)experiences what Caroline and Étienne had experienced before: "It was then that Jean felt an extraordinary sensation. As the day slowly faded above the flaming city, it seemed to him that a new dawn [*aurore*] was already breaking." (*eD*, 514)[751] This "new dawn", this aurora very precisely mirrors the "wave of gold light", the "gold[en] [...] signs" of the "morning of new growth" that Étienne's and Caroline's new youthfulness has pre-figured. Although separated by hundreds of pages, Zola comes back to the very same images of weather, vegetal life and eternally rejuvenating nature, so that it is imperative to take this complex net of 'imagery' seriously:

> He himself left behind a heart torn in two, with Maurice, Henriette, and his happy future life swept away in the storm. And yet, beyond the still-roaring blaze, life was springing up again, indestructible, far away in the wide, still, supremely clear sky. This was the sure rejuvenation of eternal nature, of eternal humanity, the renewal of life promised to the

---

750 "Le personnage y est devenu un produit de l'air et du sol, comme la plante ; c'est la conception scientifique." (*RE, OC*, IX 425)
751 "Alors, Jean eut une sensation extraordinaire. Il lui sembla, dans cette lente tombée du jour, au-dessus de cette cité en flammes, qu'une aurore déjà se levait." (*D*, V 911)

man who hopes and toils, the tree which sends out a new, strong shoot after the rotten branch, whose poisonous sap has been turning the leaves yellow, has been cut off. (eD, 514)[752]

Although the image of the "man who hopes and toils" already foreshadows a certain normative ideal of a 'just' future that Zola will spell out in his later *Quatre Évangiles*, in the *Rougon-Macquart* he invests in a different, less normative logic of 'critical transformation': his vitalistic affirmation of the "rejuvenation of eternal nature" trusts in forces that cannot be classified according to normative, ethical standards. The "still-roaring blaze", the "storm" that had "swept away" Jean's "happy future life", is an expression of the same "rejuvenation of eternal nature" that also "sends out a new, strong shoot after the rotten branch". The "wide, still, supremely clear sky" is not to be had without the violent "storm" and its devastating consequences. The image of the "rotten branch, whose poisonous sap has been turning the leaves yellow" and that therefore has to be "cut off" may thus be in a certain way misleading, because it nurtures the illusion that the "storm" is controlled by some instance of justice, that it merely concerns the 'sick', morally debased parts and establishes a new, healthy and strong society. This is certainly the proto-fascist idea that Zola harbours in the back of his mind and that he will bring to paper later in his life. However, the dimension of the image that is crucial for the *Rougon-Macquart* concerns the idea of continuity and of radical immanence: the tree, obviously referring to the famous family tree of the Rougon-Macquarts, stays one and the same; the 'new', the 'better', future world has to develop from this tree; the saviour is not sent to the earth from the heavens, but has to be grown from the sullied roots of his degenerate ancestors. There cannot be any guarantee that this would be successful. The little baby with which the cycle ends, and on whose shoulders all the hopes for a better future press heavily, is born of a relation very close to being incestuous (Docteur Pascal being his lover's uncle). Nevertheless, it is exactly this hope, facing a radically open future, affirming this very openness, that the cycle propagates. It is a belief in the "sure rejuvenation of eternal nature", although this rejuvenation is not at all 'guided' by a "reign of justice", but fuelled by blind vital forces void of morality.

---

[752] "Lui-même y laissait son cœur déchiré, Maurice, Henriette, son heureuse vie de demain emportée dans l'orage. Et pourtant, par-delà la fournaise, hurlante encore, la vivace espérance renaissait, au fond du grand ciel calme, d'une limpidité souveraine. C'était le rajeunissement certain de l'éternelle nature, de l'éternelle humanité, le renouveau promis à qui espère et travaille, l'arbre qui jette une nouvelle tige puissante, quand on en a coupé la branche pourrie, dont la sève empoisonnée jaunissant les feuilles." (*D*, V 911–912)

Zola conceptualises the "sure rejuvenation of eternal nature" as the motor of history that drives the process of *translatio imperii*. However, the *débâcle* does not bring about a *tabula rasa* on which a fresh start that builds a new, just world from scratch can be made; the vitalistic concept at the heart of Zola's understanding of history and historic development entails that imbalance, excess and atrocious crisis do not only occur once, only to be overcome for good, but that they are the very forces of history; crises and excess are important aspects of the world that cannot and that should not be contested. At the end of *La Débâcle* the manifest notion that the end of the Second Empire is somehow 'just' and 'deserved' superimposes the ambivalent, the cruel and amoral 'way of the vitalistic world'. However, Maurice at one point voices the fundamental amorality (in the sense of having nothing to do with morals) of life and history: "'The war's good, it's doing its work... [...] Maybe this bloodletting's [*cette saignée*] something which needed to happen. War's life, and life can't exist without death.'" (eD, 505)[753] War is here not only affirmed because it has toppled the corrupt Second Empire. "War's life": war is not opposed to life, it does not threaten life – it is an inherent part of life. Life is war, life is not innocent, it is itself a struggle.

In *L'Argent* Zola spells out this complicated but inherent complicity of destruction and rejuvenation, of life and death, at great length. Caroline, as we have already seen, a sympathetic, ethically sincere and reflective person, is included in the novel as an instance that critically questions the dubious wheelings and dealings of the banker Saccard. She is well aware that what Saccard does is against the law and that it will probably harm or even ruin many of his clients. Nevertheless, she somehow admires him, she even falls in love with him. More than that, she cannot but admire him even after the catastrophe, when all is lost. As much as the novel is a description of the financial market and the speculation of the Second Empire it is a search for the reasons for this attraction between Caroline and Saccard.

The controversial conversations between Saccard and Caroline that Zola stages always treat two things at once: money and life. As a consequence, Caroline and Saccard always also speak about themselves as living beings, because they are both characterised in a similar way as loving life. Saccard's argument is presented quite early in the novel: "'[...] Speculation is the very spur of life itself, the everlasting desire to struggle and go on living... [...]'"

---

753 "« Non, non, ne maudis pas la guerre... Elle est bonne, elle fait son œuvre... [...] C'est peut-être nécessaire, cette saignée. La guerre, c'est la vie qui ne peut pas être sans la mort. »" (*D*, V 903)

(*eM*, 121),⁷⁵⁴ he tells Caroline, "'[...] It's excess that produces what is necessary, isn't it?'" (*eM*, 121)⁷⁵⁵ And also very early, yet without foreseeing the disastrous consequences, Caroline agrees that "'[...] it's all part of nature's plan... You're right, life isn't clean.'" (*eM*, 121).⁷⁵⁶ The money that Saccard cheats out of the pockets of the Parisian crowd and that he fabricates by all kinds of financial tricks, flows, at least in parts, into her brother's projects in the Orient, so that Caroline in a way experiences the amoral cycle of life:

> That excess of passion, and that base expenditure and wasting of life, were all necessary for the very continuation of life. If her brother was rejoicing and singing of victory far away, where construction work was under way and buildings were springing from the ground, it was because in Paris money was pouring down, rotting everything in the madness of speculation. Money, poisonous, destructive money, became the ferment of all social vegetation, providing the necessary compost for the accomplishment of the great works that would bring nations together and create peace on the earth. [...] From money, which did so much evil, everything good was being born. (*eM*, 206)⁷⁵⁷

At this early point, before the catastrophe of the crash has happened, the moral quandary of a vitalistic perspective of social processes already emerges: it is not only that money always produces both, "evil" and "good", so that by affirming money one 'also' has to accept its negative side-effects; worse still, *by* doing evil it does good. The aberration, the excess of money serves as "the ferment of all social vegetation, providing the necessary compost" for all that is good. As indicated by the imagery, Zola here again resorts to the "scientific conception" of a plant's being "the product of the air and the soil"; the metaphor is thus not just any metaphor, but is of particular importance. The surprising formula of "excess that produces what is necessary" describes the conception of life and history that Zola develops in the *Rougon-Macquart* as an answer to messianic concepts of a coming "reign of justice". As Bernd Blaschke has noted, the argument of 'necessary excess' leads the critique of the Second Empire's

---

754 "« Mais la spéculation, c'est l'appât même de la vie, c'est l'éternel désir qui force à lutter et à vivre... [...]. »" (*Ar*, V 135)

755 "« [...] C'est l'excès qui amène le nécessaire, n'est-ce pas ? »" (*Ar*, V 135)

756 "« [...] cela est dans le plan de la nature... Vous avez raison, la vie n'est pas propre. »" (*Ar*, V 136)

757 "Il faut cet excès de la passion, toute cette vie bassement dépensée et perdue, à la continuation même de la vie. Si, là–bas, son frère s'égayait, chantait victoire, au milieu des chantiers qui s'organisaient, des constructions qui sortaient du sol, c'était qu'à Paris l'argent pleuvait, pourrissait tout, dans la rage du jeu. L'argent, empoisonneur et destructeur, devenait le ferment de toute végétation sociale, servait de terreau nécessaire aux grands travaux dont l'exécution rapprocherait les peuples et pacifierait la terre. [...] Tout le bien naissait de lui, qui faisait tout le mal." (*Ar*, V 224–225)

excesses that Zola programmatically formulates in the preface to the first novel to a paradoxical sublation (2005, 49): instead of taking a moralistic point of view, Zola promotes a vitalistic argument that, in the end, even affirms excess and aberration as the driving forces of life's transformations. Instead of condemning the Second Empire's aberrations and contrasting the old reign with a new, future, morally superior reign, Zola makes excess the motor of history and development. History conceived in this way is not a history of linear progress, but of continual crises and rejuvenation. The ambivalence that is so characteristic for Zola's descriptions of the Second Empire's hypertrophic proliferations speaks for this vitalistic standpoint: the enormous forces of life that are, also, carriers of their own death, fascinate Zola and evoke his disgust, at the same time. Despite their ambivalence they have to be affirmed, because it is these deathly carriers of the *débâcle* that will turn the perishing world into "necessary compost" for a rejuvenated future world and will – possibly! – make the rejuvenated world blossom again.

Zola uses the catastrophe of the crash to work out the inevitable ambivalence of this vitalistic force of nature. The crash also brings along a personal crisis for Caroline, who not only feels with the victims of the bankruptcy of the 'Universelle', but also is forced to witness the suicide of a broker and her brother's being sent to prison. Her belief in and love for Saccard is deeply shattered, she is shocked by all the suffering that the mad speculation has caused. However, things change when she gives in to an irrational, unconscious longing to visit Saccard in prison. Despite the failure of the 'Universelle', despite everything apparently having gone wrong, the same old conversation about speculation and life starts again, and, as if nothing had happened, Caroline cannot help admiring the person who has just ruined a part of her life:

> And in spite of herself, even in her alarm, she could feel a certain admiration rising within her. Suddenly, in this bleak and bare cell under lock and key, and cut off from every living soul, she had just had the sensation of an overflowing force [*la sensation d'une force débordante*], an effulgence of life: the eternal illusion of hope, the stubborn refusal of the man who will not die. She sought within herself her anger, her abhorrence of the sins committed, and found they were no longer there. (*eM*, 361)[758]

Caroline's reaction is narrated by using the very same notions of a "rising" and "overflowing" force of life that, as we have seen, reoccurs somewhat later in

---

[758] "Et, malgré elle, de son effroi, une admiration montait. Brusquement, dans cette cellule misérable et nue, verrouillée, séparée des vivants, elle venait d'avoir la sensation d'une force débordante, d'un resplendissement de vie : l'éternelle illusion de l'espoir, l'entêtement de l'homme qui ne veut pas mourir. Elle cherchait en elle la colère, l'exécration des faute commises, et elle ne les trouvait déjà plus." (*Ar*, V 387)

the description of her surprising rejuvenating experience triggered by the springtime weather. Strikingly, the imagery of overflowing that features so prominently in the catastrophic events of crash and *débâcle* is here used in a positive, life-affirming fashion. Saccard embodies the fundamental ambivalence of the force of "an effulgence of life": "As for Saccard, with his heedless, dynamic force [*cette force inconsciente et agissante*], she felt his power once more, as if he were one of those violent, but no doubt necessary, elements of nature." (*eM*, 361)[759] The ambivalence of these "violent, but no doubt necessary, elements of nature" becomes tangible, because Saccard obviously represents both, the violent weather of the *débâcle*, the "hurricane of millions" *and* the rejuvenating sunshine of springtime "sunlight".

Caroline is not deluded by her irrational admiration for this man whom she is suddenly facing again. As the narrator emphasises, she has "retained her hatred of evil-doing, and her pity for suffering" (*eM*, 361).[760] However, no matter whether it proves to be destructive or rejuvenating, the "overflowing force" that she feels affects her (like Étienne and Maurice) on a level different from the moral or the rational: "her normally lofty rationality [has been] devastated by the experience" (*eM*, 361; transl. altered).[761] This unconscious and nevertheless effective force defies the level of rationality, without being merely accidental: on the contrary, it lies at the heart of nature and life; although violent, uncontrollable and 'inhuman', it is "no doubt necessary".

In the end, Caroline has "no illusions left[;] life was decidedly unjust and squalid, like Nature itself" (*eM*, 369).[762] Nevertheless, and this is the important point, she cannot but wholeheartedly affirm this amoral, unjust nature – and its weathery forces. Admiring, and in spite of everything, somehow still loving Saccard inevitably accompanies affirming these ambivalent, "violent, but no doubt necessary, elements of nature", the weathery source of *débâcle* and of rejuvenating sunshine: "It was a triumph of love that this Saccard, this bandit of the financial streets, should be loved so absolutely by this adorable woman, because she saw him as brave and dynamic, creating a world, creating life." (*eM*, 209)[763] In other words, she, despite the catastrophe and all the suffering

---

[759] "Lui [Saccard], cette force inconsciente et agissante, elle le subissait de nouveau, comme une des violences de la nature, sans doute nécessaires." (*Ar*, V 388)
[760] "[Caroline] n'en gardait que sa haine du mal et sa pitié pour la douleur." (*Ar*, V 388)
[761] "[…] sa haute raison dévastée par l'expérience […]." (*Ar*, V 388)
[762] "Certes, aucune illusion ne lui restait, la vie était décidément injuste et ignoble, comme la nature." (*Ar*, V 397)
[763] "C'était l'amour triomphant, ce Saccard, ce bandit du trottoir financier, aimé si absolument par cette adorable femme, parce qu'elle le voyait, actif et brave, créer un monde, faire de la vie." (*Ar*, V 228)

that the 'Universelle' has caused, comes to the final conclusion that Saccard "was right: money was always the manure in which the humanity of tomorrow was growing; money, the compost necessary for the great works that made life easier." (*eM*, 371)[764] More than that, she even sees the controversial argument of the "necessary compost" confirmed, this "ferment of all social vegetation" atrociously produced by the "monstrous hurricane of millions that had run its devastating path through her life": "from [the] ruins [produced by the crash], still warm, she could already sense the growth of a great blossoming opening out in the sun." (*eM*, 370)[765]

It is not a carefully weighed consideration of arguments that leads Caroline to come to this conclusion, but a deeply rooted, intuitive attitude towards life that she and Saccard share. Saccard very early notices this similarity between them when Caroline tells him of her extraordinary talent for coping with crises: "'Oh, you,' he cried, 'you're just made for catastrophes, you really embody the love of life!'" (*eM*, 62)[766] Zola makes Caroline voice an intuition concerning this talent that, behind the heroine's back, is also instructive of the cycle's structure, its technique of emblematic pre-figuration:

> I've often thought that my case is, in microcosm, the case of all humanity, living in the midst of terrible wretchedness, yes, but always cheered by the youthfulness of the next generation. After each one of these crises that knock me down there comes a sort of new youth, a springtime, whose promises of new life revive me and lift up my heart. All of that is so true that after some great sorrow, if I go out into the street in the sun, I immediately begin once more to love, to hope, and be happy. (*eM*, 62)[767]

As we know, some hundred pages later, when the 'Universelle' has crashed and all is lost, Caroline will impressively act according to this talent, she will "go out into the street in the sun", and indeed "begin once more to love, to hope, and be happy". Ever more so, Jean, representative of the French nation after the *débâcle* of 1870, will do the very same thing – and thereby underline

---

[764] "Il avait raison : l'argent, jusqu'à ce jour, était le fumier dans lequel poussait l'humanité de demain ; l'argent, empoisonneur et destructeur, devenait le ferment de toute végétation sociale, le terreau nécessaire aux grands travaux qui facilitaient l'existence." (*Ar*, V 398)

[765] "[...] de ces ruines chaudes encore, elle sentait déjà germer, s'épanouir au soleil toute une floraison." (*Ar*, V 397)

[766] "« Oh ! toi, déclara-t-il, tu es faite pour les catastrophes, tu es l'amour de la vie ! »" (*Ar*, V 74)

[767] "« J'ai pensé souvent que mon cas est, en petit, celui de l'humanité, qui vit, certes, dans une misère affreuse, mais que ragaillardit la jeunesse de chaque génération. A la suite de chacune des crises qui m'abattent, c'est comme une jeunesse nouvelle, un printemps dont les promesses de sève me réchauffent et me relèvent le cœur. Cela est tellement vrai, que, après une grosse peine, si je sors dans la rue, au soleil, tout de suite je me remets à aimer, à espérer, à être heureuse. [...] »" (*Ar*, V 74)

that Caroline's case, indeed, for Zola, represents "the case of all humanity". Caroline's and Saccard's talent, their attitude towards life, is far from banal or ordinary. It does not consist in affirming life's blossoming or a bright, a better future: "she still had hope, but of what? She still had no idea, just the inevitable unknown, that lies at the end of life, at the end of humanity" (eM, 208). It affirms life itself ("just being alive had to be enough, and life would always bring healing for the wounds that it caused" (eM, 208)[768]), it affirms life's forces, that are both violent and rejuvenating.

In other words, the notion of *life* that pervades the *Rougon-Macquart*'s story of *débâcle* and rejuvenation is in itself bare of a 'substantial', of a normative content. Life is a notion of driving forces, beyond morality and rationality, it is the motor that accounts for *the fact that* something is happening in the world: "a perpetual becoming, a constant transformation in this spreading effort, this transmitted power, this trembling that breathes life into matter and that is life itself." (*DP*, V 947; my transl.)[769]

'Life' is the answer to the fundamental question that Zola raises with his huge cycle of novels: "Why and how a new being?" (*DP*, V 944; my transl.)[770] How is transformation possible in a closed world, in a modern world of immanence? With regard to his critical view on the Second Empire this question, despite its rather abstract, ontological quality, is at the core a deeply political one. How are things to change (for the better)? When positing 'life' as a possible answer, the question shifts to a different formulation: "What were the laws of life, this torrent [*torrent*] of beings that made up the world?" (*DP*, V 944–945; my transl.)[771] The question already contains its answer: Zola models his notion of 'life' as a driving force behind all movement in the world on the notion of weather. Life *is* essentially weather: It is not only the "torrent of beings", but also the "stream [*flot*] [...] sweeping away all the wrong connections" (*DP*, V 960; my transl.),[772] a "terrible and vast river, all rolling towards a human sea, that swells

---

[768] "Voilà donc qu'une de ses grandes crises était encore passée, elle espérait de nouveau, quoi ? elle n'en savait toujours rien, l'éternel inconnu qui était au bout de la vie, au bout de l'humanité. Vivre, cela devait suffire, pour que la vie lui apportât sans cesse la guérison des blessures que la vie lui faisait." (*Ar*, V 226)

[769] "Il y avait donc là un perpétuel devenir, une transformation constante dans cet effort communiqué, cette puissance transmise, cet ébranlement qui souffle la vie à la matière et qui est toute la vie." (*DP*, V 947)

[770] "Pourquoi et comment un être nouveau ?" (*DP*, V 944)

[771] "Quelles étaient les lois de la vie, ce torrent d'êtres qui faisaient le monde ?" (*DP*, V 944–945)

[772] "« [...] Une morte d'amour, et comme Albine et Serge s'étaient aimés dans le grand jardin tentateur, au sein de la nature complice ! et quel flot de vie emportant tous les faux liens, et quel triomphe de la vie ! »" (*DP*, V 960)

incessantly for an unknown future" (*DP*, V 1062–1063; my transl.)[773] and the "warming" rejuvenation of "the April sun":

> The life, the life which flows in a torrent, which continues and recommences, towards unknown completion! the life in which we bathe, the life of infinite and contrary flows, always moving and immense, like a limitless sea. (*DP*, V 1219; my transl.)[774]

Climate catastrophes, climate crises, rejuvenation and a radically open future are all connected by the notion of weather. What I have attempted to reconstruct by compiling the protagonists' explicit, reflecting commentaries is taking place all the time on the level of imagery and narratological composition: the world of the *Rougon-Macquart* is essentially a world of weather that can be understood in its totality as a particular climate.

The weather thus does not merely serve as a medium of punishment, bringing justice to a world of debauchery. Neither is it used as a 'tool' to criticise a world; the dominant role of the weather should not be misread as a sign for the fact that this world is out of joint. In the *Rougon-Macquart*, as emblematically personified by Saccard, the weather is both, violent force of catastrophic *débâcle* and force of vernal rejuvenation, and the medical notion of crisis works as the conceptual hinge that holds these two opposing movements together: the *débâcle* thus provides the purification, the purging of superfluous humours, a cathartic moment necessary for the possibility of a rejuvenated future. Zola here employs the same 'physiological' notion of crisis that had already supported Shakespeare's understanding of theatre in *The Tempest* and that is deeply rooted in a view of the world in which the weather is of fundamental importance. This notion, atavistic in the late 19th century, assigns an indispensable, a regulating role to the forces of the weather, a role inconceivable for Goethe and his contemporaries. Whereas in the 18th century the weather had been regarded as a disturbing event, a force of negativity, of imbalance that challenged the 'regular', the 'stable' way and order of the world, it is now conceptualised (again!) as providing for its very regularity and balance, for its purging and rebuilding. A decisive shift separates Zola from Goethe's *Werther*: it is no longer the human *ratio* that carries the hope for 'stability' and balance, but a notion of 'life'. In

---

[773] "« [...] Connais la vie, aime-la, vis-la telle qu'elle doit être vécue. » Mais quel effroyable et vaste fleuve, roulant tout à une mer humaine, qu'il grossit sans cesse pour l'avenir inconnu !" (*DP*, V 1062–1063)

[774] "La vie, la vie qui coule en torrent, qui continue et recommence, vers l'achèvement ignoré ! la vie où nous baignons, la vie aux courants infinis et contraires, toujours mouvante et immense, comme une mer sans bornes !" (*DP*, V 1219)

contrast to the 'stability' of a rational order of the world, the stability that 'life' produces is not substantial and unchanging, it is not inherent in the concrete rational order that organises the world, but is a stability of process: it is not an eternal, rational order that this stability affirms, but the unending process of (re-)ordering, of 'tempering intemperances'. However, viewed more closely, the contrast between Goethe's *Werther* and Zola's *Rougon-Macquart* is not as fundamental as it might seem at first glance: Goethe senses the repressed forces of the weather, he senses that they not only threaten the enlightened world, but also form a necessary part of the dialectical process that creates this world. Zola simply follows Goethe's 'weathery' suspicion and adds one decisive 'turn of the screw': he not only recognises the weather as an important and long-neglected factor of the modern world with which enlightened society has to cope, but affirms it as the 'actual' fundamental force behind life and history as such. The weather becomes the ambivalent ontological basis of the world, a basis that precedes questions of rationality or morality. He thus strategically shifts the line of conflict from the dialectical frontline of rational order versus weathery disturbance to a continual process of weather confronting weather. In this way a self-regulating, creative as well as destructive 'source' or 'torrent' of 'life' forms itself – and a notion of historicity is born.

This shift can not merely be reduced to a strategic decision that separates Zola from Goethe. As we have seen in the preceding sections, the world of the 19th century that Zola sets out to depict and analyse with his *Rougon-Macquart* is a world that has discovered and integrated the forces of the weather as driving forces of 'progress' and 'wealth'. The notion of forces that the human *ratio* has learned to unleash and exploit without being able to exert control over them (thereby subjecting human life, and *ratio* itself to these forces) has replaced the paradigm of an enlightened world that is ordered by human *ratio* itself, by tradition, morality and 'good judgment'. What Zola finds himself confronted with is a 'weathery' world of the Second Empire, a world that he detests, although this world (especially its enormous transformative, modern forces and aesthetics) also fascinates him. Despite his vitriolic critique, he does not reject the specifically weathery character of this world. He does not nostalgically long for the old world of tradition and morality, but, on the contrary, he affirms these very forces of the weather as the bringer of transformation and change.

Affirming 'life' (the basic message of the *Rougon-Macquart*) is therefore not grounded on any rational, theological or other 'abstract', normative basis. There is no 'external' reason for this affirmation, it is the one value, the one "joy" that the cycle posits as a value, as a "joy" in itself: "Ah, the joy of being alive, is there really any other joy than this? Life, just as it is, however abominable it may be, with all its power and its eternal hope!" (*eM*, 370)[775] Affirming life, "however abominable it may be", means affirming the weather and its forces, however violent and abominable they may be: this is, I think, the important message that the *Rougon-Macquart* communicate as a whole.

Zola dedicates one complete novel to this very theme of the 'joy of living'. *La Joie de vivre* is embodied by – the sea! The novel contrasts two attitudes towards the "eternal rhythm of the ocean" (*JV*, III 849; my transl.):[776] Lazare's "resentment [*rancune*] against the sea" (*JV*, III 1016; my transl.)[777] and Pauline's fascination with the sea, her affirmation of its "eternal rocking/balancing [*l'éternel balancement*]" (*JV*, III 847; my transl.).[778] When Pauline, orphaned as a little girl of ten years, arrives one evening at the house of her relatives at the seaside of Bonneville, carried there "by a storm wind" (*JV*, III 968; my transl.),[779] she instinctively "searches the sea":

> [S]he was tormented by the desire of knowing up to where this water was going to rise; and she heard only that the noise was growing, a loud voice, monstrous, whose threat continued to increase every minute, in the middle of the cries of the wind and of the whipping of the rain. Not one glow of light, not even the paleness of foam, on the chaos of the shadows; nothing but the galloping of the waves, whipped by the storm, in the depths of this nothingness. (*JV*, III 820; my transl.)[780]

Even when Pauline learns that the water of the sea "that had appeared so beautiful to her [...] throws itself on the world" (*JV*, III 828; my transl.)[781] and draws a part of the little village into the depths each year, her fascination and affirmation does not cease. Lazare, on the contrary, a nervous, neurotic character, one day decides to stop this atrocious natural spectacle: "The hope of defeating the sea thrilled him feverishly." (*JV*, III 903; my transl.)[782] His plan is to master

---

[775] "Ah ! la joie d'être, est-ce qu'au fond il en existe une autre ? La vie telle qu'elle est, dans sa force si abominable qu'elle soit, avec son éternel espoir !" (*Ar*, V 397)
[776] "Une paix morte retomba sur la petite maison de Bonneville, les jours uniformes se déroulèrent, ramenant les habitudes quotidiennes, en face du rythme éternel de l'océan." (*JV*, III 849)
[777] "[...] sa rancune seule contre la mer le soutenait [...]." (*JV*, III 1016)
[778] "La mer, cependant, battait deux fois par jour Bonneville de l'éternel balancement de sa houle, et Pauline grandissait dans le spectacle de l'immense horizon." (*JV*, III 847)
[779] "[...] lorsqu'elle [Pauline] était arrivée avec elle [sa tante Chanteau] à Bonneville, un soir, par un vent de tempête [...]." (*JV*, III 968)
[780] "[Pauline] cherchait la mer, elle était tourmentée du désir de savoir jusqu'où cette eau allait monter ; et elle n'entendait que la clameur grandir, une voix haute, monstrueuse, dont la menace continue s'enflait à chaque minute, au milieu des hurlements du vent et du cinglement des averses. Plus une lueur, pas même une pâleur d'écume, sur le chaos des ombres ; rien que le galop des vagues, fouetté par la tempête, au fond de ce néant." (*JV*, III 820)
[781] "Cette eau qui lui avait paru si belle et qui se jetait sur le monde." (*JV*, III 828)
[782] "L'espoir de vaincre la mer l'enfiévrait." (*JV*, III 903)

the sea, to build barricades that would protect the village against it: "Since this day, the whole house dreamt only of humiliating the sea, of chaining it at the foot of the terrace with the obedience of a beaten dog." (*JV*, III 903; my transl.)[783] What he does not notice is that his desperate attempt at protecting culture against the forces of nature is but an expression of his neurotic, chronically pessimistic character. His pathologic fear of death engenders a distinct "disgust of life" (*JV*, III 888; my transl.).[784] In his nightly panic attacks a "cold breeze [*souffle froid*] chill[s] his flesh" (*JV*, III 1000; my transl.),[785] he is one of the typical "returned Werthers" that the doctor Cazenove (another of Zola's mouthpieces) speaks of:

> At the very first attempt you want to discover every truth in the sciences, whereas we can barely decipher them, when, maybe, the inquiry will go on forever. Then you begin to say that there is nothing in them, and you try to fall back upon your old faith, which will have nothing more to do with you, and so you drop into pessimism. Yes! pessimism is the disease of the end of the century. You are a set of returned Werthers! (*JV*, III 993; my transl.)[786]

As we have seen in the previous chapter, Werther does indeed know and think about the great disasters of "floods that wash away your villages" (70). He famously discovers that "[t]here is no moment that does not consume you and those near and dear to you, no moment when you are not a destroyer, must be one; the most innocent stroll costs the lives of thousands and thousands of tiny creatures; one footstep shatters the laboriously erected structures of the ant and pounds a tiny world into a miserable grave." (70; transl. altered)[787]

---

[783] "Depuis ce jour, toute la maison ne rêvait plus que d'humilier la mer, de l'enchaîner au pied de la terrasse dans une obéissance de chien battu." (*JV*, III 903)

[784] "[...] dégoût de la vie [...]." (*JV*, III 888)

[785] "Mais, aussitôt, les battements de son cœur emportaient ses serments, et le souffle froid glaçait sa chair, et il tendait les mains en poussant son cri : « Mon Dieu ! mon Dieu ! »" (*JV*, III 1000)

[786] "« [...] Vous voudriez trouver dans les sciences, d'un coup et en bloc, toutes les vérités, lorsque nous les déchiffrons à peine, lorsqu'elles ne seront sans doute jamais qu'une éternelle enquête. Alors, vous les niez, vous vous rejetez dans la foi qui ne veut plus de vous, et vous tombez au pessimisme... Oui, c'est la maladie de la fin du siècle, vous êtes des Werther retournés. »" (*JV*, III 993)

[787] "Kannst du sagen: Das ist! da alles vorübergeht, da alles mit der Wetterschnelle vorüber rollt, so selten die ganze Kraft seines Daseyns ausdauert, ach in den Strom fortgerissen, untergetaucht und an Felsen zerschmettert wird. Da ist kein Augenblik, der nicht dich verzehrte und die Deinigen um dich her, kein Augenblik, da du nicht ein Zerstöhrer bist, seyn mußt. Der harmloseste Spaziergang kostet tausend tausend armen Würmgen das Leben, es zerrüttet ein Fustritt die mühseligen Gebäude der Ameisen, und stampft eine kleine Welt in ein schmähliches

Lazare cannot bear this inherently ambivalent world and life. He is indeed 'a Werther'; 'a Werther', however, bereft of the capacity of transforming this ambivalence into artistic expression. His attitude towards life is clearly marked as pathologic, he is a prime example for the yellow leaves that the crisis will cut off. He cannot follow his doctor's imperative advice: "'But live, isn't life itself sufficient? Happiness consists of action.'" (*JV*, III 994; my transl.)[788] Lazare cannot answer the doctor's rhetorical question the way it has to be answered – by saying 'Yes!', by affirming life, despite its inherent ambivalences. Pauline, on the other hand, "listen[s] with a smile on her face" (*JV*, III 994; my transl.)[789] to the doctor's words. Like Caroline, like Saccard, she instinctively loves life, she is capable of living this joy, despite all the calamities she has had to suffer, having lost her parents, having lost her lover Lazare to her 'rival' Louise, having lost all her money. In contrast to the "cold breeze" haunting Lazare, Pauline seems to "heat the house with a beam of sunlight" (*JV*, III 997; my transl.).[790] Although surrounded by her uncle who is suffering horribly from the gout, by Lazare and Veronique both deeply depressive, especially after the death of Madame Chanteau, she does not "despair of life, judging the world to be altogether good or altogether bad" (*JV*, III 1068; my transl.).[791] Like Saccard, Pauline is capable of affirming life in all its inherent ambivalence. Saccard voices an affirmation of what had driven Werther to suicide. He acknowledges the fact that "life can't exist without death", that "[t]here is no moment that does not consume you and those near and dear to you, no moment when you are not a destroyer, must be one": "'As if life bothered about such matters!'", Saccard says to Caroline, "'With every step we take, we destroy thousands of existences.'" (*eM*, 357)[792] Pauline's affirmation of the sea corresponds to Saccard's attitude towards life, highlighting that this 'love of life' is not merely a cynical way of looking at the world, but the only way to deal with life as it is, to foster

---

Grab. Ha! nicht die große seltene Noth der Welt, diese Fluthen, die eure Dörfer wegspülen, diese Erdbeben, die eure Städte verschlingen, rühren mich. Mir untergräbt das Herz die verzehrende Kraft, die im All der Natur verborgen liegt, die nichts gebildet hat, das nicht seinen Nachbar, nicht sich selbst zerstörte. Und so taumele ich beängstet! Himmel und Erde und all die webenden Kräfte um mich her! Ich sehe nichts, als ein ewig verschlingendes, ewig wiederkäuendes Ungeheuer." (106–108)

[788] "« Mais vivez, est-ce que vivre ne suffit pas ? La joie est dans l'action. »" (*JV*, III 994)
[789] "Et brusquement [le docteur] s'adressa à Pauline, qui écoutait en souriant." (*JV*, III 994)
[790] "Chaque jour vécu était une victoire, sa nièce lui semblait chauffer la maison d'un coup de bon soleil, aux rayons duquel [Chanteau] ne pouvait mourir." (*JV*, III 997)
[791] "Elle avait raison de ne pas désespérer de la vie, en jugeant le monde tout bon ou tout mauvais." (*JV*, III 1068)
[792] "« Est-ce que la vie s'inquiète de ça ! Chaque pas que l'on fait écrase des milliers d'existences. »" (*Ar*, V 383)

hope and keep some joy instead of despairing: the sea both brings violent destruction and "a delicious freshness, a breeze of life [...] with its mounting tide" (*JV*, III 1106; my transl.).[793]

The one is not to be had without the other. Fleeing "to Oceania, to one of those islands where life is so sweet", where "[t]here is no winter, the sky is always blue, and life is passed beneath the sun and the stars" (*JV*, III 1069–1070; my transl.)[794] is but an idle dream comparable to Gonzalo's utopia in *The Tempest*. Above all, it expresses Lazare's incapacity to cope with the complexity of 'real' life. It is no coincidence that the dining-room of the family's house at the seaside is decorated with a "view of Vesuvius and the four lithographs of the Seasons" (*JV*, III 1062; my transl.):[795] (the product of) catastrophe and the seasonal logic of wintry death and vernal rejuvenation, these are the inescapable principles that characterise the way of the narrated world.

With *La Joie de vivre* Zola thus writes a novel that presents us with an emblematic example of how to deal with this 'weathery' world full of suffering. Pauline, who as a character is much less ambivalent than Saccard, is presented as a sort of modern Hiob. She strikingly defies the 'test', because her talent for loving life affirms the very rhythm of suffering and hope, the "'eternal rocking/balancing [*l'éternel balancement*]'" of life and sea. In fact, her attitude towards the weather does not differ widely from the attitude of those that knew how to profit from the Second Empire's heating climate: Saccard, Octave Mouret, Nana, Étienne, none of them try to fight the forces of the weather, but affirm them and attempt to channel the natural energies in order to use them for their own, mostly questionable!, gain. Of course, Pauline's relation to the weather, to the sea and its ambivalent forces does not concern individual profit. The point that Zola makes with this novel is more general: it concerns the relation towards this weathery world as such. However, as Michel Serres has noted, the strategy that Zola propagates with the help of the exemplary character Pauline resembles the strategy that Octave Mouret employs for directing his enterprise: "It is [...] all about acclimatising the catastrophe. Of integrating the *débâcle* in a cycle." (Serres 1975, 267; my transl.) Affirming the weather bets on its "continual inconstancy": "Nothing seemed changed under the sky, the sea was still there, infinite, ceaselessly repeating the same horizons, in its continual inconstancy."

---

[793] "On avait ouvert légèrement la fenêtre, pour chasser l'odeur du sang ; et une fraîcheur délicieuse, un souffle de vie montait avec la marée haute." (*JV*, III 1106)

[794] "« Oui, nous enfuir bien loin, en Océanie par exemple, dans une de ces îles où la vie est si douce. [...] On vit là-bas comme dans un paradis. Jamais d'hiver, un ciel éternellement bleu, une existence au soleil et aux étoiles... [...] »" (*JV*, III 1069–1070)

[795] "[...] la Vue du Vésuve et les quatre lithographies des Saisons [...]." (*JV*, III 1062)

(*JV*, III 1063; my transl.)⁷⁹⁶ It bets on the fact that this continual inconstancy produces new chances, that it does not stop engendering new life, that catastrophe and death always prove to be fertile. In other words, the sea [*la mer*] is conceived of as the primordial mother [*la mère*]: "Why should they have felt anxious? They did not even resist, the sea seemed to lull and fill them with pleasant languor with the eternal monotony of its voice." (*JV*, III 1063; my transl.)⁷⁹⁷ At the end of the novel, Pauline will herself "dandle [*elle berçait toujours*] the child in her arms, with her laughter of bravery" (*JV*, III 1130; my transl.),⁷⁹⁸ the child of Lazare and Louise whom she has taken on the duty of raising. Zola will rewrite this very scene to close the whole cycle with the same image of a child that embodies the hope of a radically open future. (It is important to add that heredity, in both cases, does not favour the fate of the babies, one is born as a child of two parents suffering from the "disease of end of the century", the other springs from a quasi-incestuous encounter with both parents passing on the legacy of the *Rougon-Macquart*). The framing that Zola constructs for his cycle of novels tames the forces of the weather into the balance of "constant inconstancy". It is not coincidentally exemplified by a heroine: this framing is specifically 'female', not only because it takes the rhythm of menstruation and the notion of fertility as its model (cf. Serres 1975, 267), but also, as we will elaborate in the next section, because it conflicts with 'male' notions of control and mastery. The notion of *la mer/mère* supplements the success of the phallic profiteers like Saccard or Mouret; they all rely on the rejuvenation and the energy set free by the power of the *mer/mère* that compels the natural forces into the constant inconstancy of the circle. It is *la mer/mère* that brings about 'fertile' "eternal recommencement" (*JV*, III 1126; my transl.),⁷⁹⁹ and turns dirty love⁸⁰⁰ into a new chance for life, a chance, that is unforeseeable in an open future.

Resisting the mighty circle of nature, and that is to say the forces of the weather, is in vain. Zola stages two attempts, one undertaken by the neurotic, neo-Werther Lazare, the other by one of Zola's archenemies, the Catholic Church. Lazare's 'literal' attempt to tame the sea fails miserably and triggers an unexpected reaction by the fishermen who have just lost their houses to the roaring waves:

---

796 "Rien non plus ne semblait changé sous le ciel, la mer était toujours là, infinie, répétant sans cesse les mêmes horizons, dans sa continuelle inconstance." (*JV*, III 1063)
797 "Pourquoi se seraient-ils inquiétés ? ils ne résistaient même pas, la mer semblait les bercer et les alanguir de l'éternelle monotonie de sa voix." (*JV*, III 1063)
798 "Et elle berçait toujours l'enfant, avec son rire de vaillance [...]." (*JV*, III 1130)
799 "Ah ! quel éternel recommencement, dans ces misères quotidiennes !" (*JV*, III 1126)
800 "L'amour est-il moins souillé, lui qui crée la vie ?" (*Ar*, V 398)

> In less than twenty minutes, indeed, everything had disappeared, the stockades were broken down, the timbers were smashed into matchwood. And [the fishermen] roared with [the waves], and gesticulated and danced like savages, whipped up by the intoxication of the wind and the water, giving in to the horror of the massacre. (*JV*, III 1112; my transl.)[801]

The fishermen have not gone mad; as paradoxical as it might seem, they instinctively celebrate and worship life and its forces, the primordial power of nature weighing much heavier, being rooted much deeper than rational, economic considerations about losing property. In fact, their attitude towards the "horror of the massacre" very much resembles Zola's attitude towards the world of the Second Empire: He as well indulges in the horror of the massacre that many of his novels narrate, his descriptions of perversion and catastrophe unmistakably testify to his fascination with and affirmation of the death-bringing forces of life and the life-bringing forces of death that cause the final *débâcle*. The *Rougon-Macquart*, I maintain, are, as a whole, similarly "whipped up by the intoxication of the wind and the water", they celebrate the constant inconstancy of the weather for the same reason as the fishermen: the weather is life itself.

With *La Faute de l'abbé Mouret* Zola stages one monumental conflict: life against the Catholic Church, which, for Zola, represents the negation of life. L'abbé, having fallen sick, is 'rescued' from his parish by Doctor Pascal and brought to the *locus amoenus* called the Paradou, *the* paradigmatic place of pure, paradisiac life. By taking advantage of the seasonal logic of crisis, he finds his way back to life with the regeneration of nature from winter to spring and falls in love with his 'nurse' Albine. They re-enact the obviously inescapable progression to the Fall. Suddenly, the abbé decides to return to his old 'life', to the Church. Here the Church's negation of life manifests itself most obviously, especially when Albine visits the abbé in order to convince him to come back to the Paradou, claiming that by preferring the Church he has chosen death instead of life. "'You were right'", the abbé tells her, "'[…] this is a place of death, death is what I want, death that delivers and saves us from all corruption… Do you hear? I deny life, I refuse it, I spit on it. […]'" (*eSAM*, 242)[802] He thinks the Church supreme, it towers over Albine's garden of life:

---

[801] "En moins de vingt minutes, en effet, tout avait disparu, les palissades éventrées, les épis brisés, réduits en miettes. Et ils hurlaient avec elle, ils gesticulaient et dansaient comme des sauvages, soulevés par l'ivresse du vent et de l'eau, cédant à l'horreur de ce massacre." (*JV*, III 1112)

[802] "« Tu avais raison, c'est la mort qui est ici, c'est la mort que je veux, la mort qui délivre, qui sauve de toutes les pourritures… Entends-tu ! je nie la vie, je la refuse, je crache sur elle. […] »" (*FaM*, I 1473)

> It is bigger than your garden, this valley, and the whole earth. It's a powerful fortress that nothing will overthrow. In vain will it be assailed by winds and sun, by forests and seas, and by every living thing; it will remain standing, not even shaken. [...] the church, no matter how ruined, will never be carried away in that overflowing of life [*débordement de la vie*]! It is impregnable death... (*eSAM*, 242–243)[803]

Sometime later this scenario of the "overflowing of life" attacking the "powerful fortress" of the church indeed takes place, in a vision that haunts the abbé. 'Nature' (from the red dust and the rocks, to plants and all sorts of animals) unites into a multitude, into a "tempest of life whose breath was like a furnace" (*eSAM*, 256),[804] "beating against the ruined church like living waves" (*eSAM*, 256):[805]

> The village, the animals, this whole tide of overflowing life for an instant swallowed up the church under a frenzy of bodies that made the rafters give way. [...] This was a victorious uprising, Revolutionary Nature was putting barricades with overthrown altars, demolishing the church wich for centuries had overshadowed it. [...] One last blast of hurricane that had fallen upon the church blew away the dust, the shattered pulpit and confessional [...]. The tree of life had just burst the heavens. And it was now higher than the stars. (*eSAM*, 256–258)[806]

It is not the "powerful fortress" of "impregnable death", but the "tree of life" that wins this epic battle. However, instead of being devastated by this outcome, having backed the wrong horse, "Abbé Mouret applauded furiously, like a damned soul, at this vision" (*eSAM*, 258).[807] Like the fishermen, like Zola, he cannot resist being infected by this "storm of life". With this vision Zola not only expresses his stance towards the Catholic Church as a representative of death but also stages another *débâcle*: a mythical debacle of life winning over the Church, over non-fertile death, a *débâcle* that other, local *débâcles* refer to:

---

[803] "Elle est plus grande que ton jardin, que la vallée, que toute la terre. C'est une forteresse redoutable que rien ne renversera. Les vents, et le soleil, et les forêts, et les mers, tout ce qui vit, aura beau lui livrer assaut, elle restera debout, sans même être ébranlée. [...] l'église, si ruinée qu'elle soit, ne sera jamais emportée dans ce débordement de la vie ! Elle est la mort inexpugnable..." (*FaM*, I 1473–1474)
[804] "[...] tempête de vie à l'haleine de fournaise [...]." (*FaM*, I 1488)
[805] "[...] battant l'église en ruine, comme des vagues vivantes [...]." (*FaM*, I 1488)
[806] "Le village, les bêtes, toute cette marée de vie qui débordait, engloutit un instant l'église sous une rage de corps faisant ployer les poutres. [...] C'était l'émeute victorieuse, la nature révolutionnaire dressant des barricades avec des autels renversés, démolissant l'église qui lui jetait trop d'ombre depuis des siècles. [...] Un dernier souffle de l'ouragan, qui s'était rué sur l'église, en balaya la poussière, la chaire et le confessionnal en poudre [...]. L'arbre de vie venait de crever le ciel. Et il dépassait les étoiles." (*FaM*, I 1488–1490)
[807] "L'abbé Mouret applaudit furieusement, comme un damné à cette vision." (*FaM*, I 1490)

for example, when at the end of *La Terre* the farm La Borderie burns to the ground and the ashes are swept away by the wind.

In the world of the *Rougon-Macquart* there is no alternative to affirming these forces of life that are always also forces of the weather. They are inescapable, and it is them, their "continual inconstancy", their "eternal recommencement", their "'eternal rocking/balancing [*l'éternel balancement*]" that "keep the world going". Despite the suffering that this weathery world produces, its "continual inconstancy" always also carries a promise for the future. To be sure, there is no certainty of future prosperity and happiness; on the contrary, it is exactly the openness of the future, the mere fact of the world simply keeping on going that promises transformation and change, that promises rejuvenation:

> And then there was pain and blood and tears, all the things that cause suffering and revolt, the killing of Françoise, the killing of Fouan, the wicked triumphant, and the stinking, bloodthirsty peasants, vermin who disgrace and exploit the earth. But what do we know? Just as the frost that sears the crops, the hail that cuts them to pieces, the thunderstorms that batter them may all be necessary, perhaps blood and tears are needed to keep the world going. Does our unhappiness count for anything in the great system of the stars and the sun? (*eE*, 499)[808]

In this formulation, referring to morality and attempting to 'qualify' human misery, Zola's affirmation of the world characterised by amoral forces of the weather must look rather 'esoteric' and 'mythic'. However, I am convinced that the affirmation of "continual inconstancy", of debacle being preceded by prosperity, joys by sorrows and vice versa, is based on an intuition that is familiar to all of us, an intuition that springs from the observation of the weather:

> For eight days it had been Hélène's diversion to gaze on that mighty expanse of Paris, and she never wearied of doing so. It was as unfathomable and varying as the ocean, fair in the morning, ruddy with fire at night, borrowing all the joys and sorrows of the skies reflected in its depths. A flash of sunshine came, and it would roll in waves of gold; a cloud would darken it and raise a tempest. It always renewed itself [*Toujours, il se renouvelait*]. A complete calm would fall, and everything would assume an orange hue; gusts of wind would sweep by from time to time, and turn everything livid; in keen, bright weather there would be a shimmer of light on every housetop; whilst when showers fell, blurring both heaven and earth, all would be plunged in the debacle of chaos [*débâcle*

---

[808] "Il y avait aussi la douleur, le sang, les larmes, tout ce qu'on souffre et tout ce qui révolte. Françoise tuée, Fouan tué, les coquins triomphants, la vermine sanguinaire et puante des villages déshonorant et rongeant la terre. Seulement, est-ce qu'on sait ? De même que la gelée qui brûle les moissons, la grêle qui les hache, la foudre qui les verse, sont nécessaires peut-être, il est possible qu'il faille du sang et des larmes pour que le monde marche. Qu'est-ce que notre malheur pèse, dans la grande mécanique des étoiles et du soleil ?" (*T*, IV 811)

d'un chaos]. At her window Hélène experienced all the hopes and sorrows that pertain to the open sea. As the keen wind blew in her face she imagined it wafted a saline fragrance; even the ceaseless noise of the city seemed to her like that of a surging tide beating against a rocky cliff. (*PA*, II 846–847; my transl.)[809]

Toujours, il se renouvelait – "It always renewed itself" – this is the intuition on which the *Rougon-Macquart* are built. A thoroughly weathery intuition. The same holds true for the perspective that Hélène's gaze on the city takes: it focuses on the epitome of social or cultural accomplishments, a city, *the* city of the 19th century, but views it as a weather spectacle. It very deliberately and very consistently leaves all moral or evaluative standpoints aside; viewing a city, it does not even talk about humans or humanity. Paris is a reflection of the skies, it is as "unfathomable and varying as the ocean", an "open sea", making the "ceaseless noise" "of a surging tide beating against a rocky cliff". As such, as weather, "[i]t always renewed itself" – not as the achievement of rational or social or moral human beings. It is no coincidence that Hélène's experience at her window approximates Pauline's attitude towards the sea in *La Joie de vivre*: this is the attitude the *Rougon-Macquart* take towards the world they narrate – an observation of a weather phenomenon, of a climate, in which all the trust is placed in the fact that "[i]t always renewed itself".

7 Mastery – the end of modern aesthetics

With the last novel of the cycle called *Le Docteur Pascal*, Zola looks back on all the previous volumes and reflects on the status and the speech act of his narrative project as a whole. Pascal is presented as a figure that projects Zola's role as a 'researcher' of the natural and social history of the Rougon-Macquart family into the diegetic world. Pascal is not a writer, but a doctor, he thus does not produce novels, but keeps dossiers on all of his relatives. He collects and categorises

---

[809] "Hélène, depuis huit jours, avait cette distraction du grand Paris élargi devant elle. Jamais elle ne s'en lassait. Il était insondable et changeant comme un océan, candide le matin et incendié le soir, prenant les joies et les tristesses des cieux qu'il reflétait. Un coup de soleil lui faisait rouler des flots d'or, un nuage l'assombrissait et soulevait en lui des tempêtes. Toujours, il se renouvelait : c'étaient des calmes plats, couleur orange, des coups de vent qui d'une heure à l'autre plombaient l'étendue, des temps vifs et clairs allumant une lueur à la crête de chaque toiture, des averses noyant le ciel et la terre, effaçant l'horizon dans la débâcle d'un chaos. Hélène goûtait là toutes les mélancolies et tous les espoirs du large ; elle croyait même en recevoir au visage le souffle fort, la senteur amère ; et il n'était pas jusqu'au grondement continu de la ville qui ne lui apportait l'illusion que la marée montante, battant contre les rochers d'une falaise." (*PA*, II 846–847)

every piece of information that he gets on his family in order to analyse the influences of heredity and milieu. A large wardrobe contains his precious 'archive', a life's work consisting of thousands of papers. However, his scientific project does not prove to be very popular; especially his mother despises the papers testifying to the corruption of the family she is so proud of. She threatens to burn them once she gets hold of them so that Pascal is always alert to protect the papers from her immediate and mediate access – she has managed to draw the all-too Catholic housekeeper and also Clotilde, Pascal's niece, whom he has taken into his house as a sort of a foster child, on her side. Zola uses the struggle over the wardrobe and its contested contents to make his meta-poetic reflections culminate in a nightly scene between Docteur Pascal and his niece Clotilde:

> One sultry night toward the end of September, Pascal found himself unable to sleep. He opened one of the windows of his room; the sky was dark, some storm must be passing in the distance, for there was a continuous rumbling of thunder. (*DP*, V 1002; my transl.)[810]

Suddenly he remembers that he has left the key to the wardrobe in a piece of clothing so that Clotilde theoretically had the chance to get possession of it. His suspicions prove to be well-founded. When he goes to look for the key he catches his foster child red-handed, emptying the wardrobe. Clotilde, as well, had opened a window:

> Through caution, she had not brought a candle. She had contented herself with opening one of the window shutters, and the continual lightning flashes of the storm which was passing southward in the dark sky, sufficed her, bathing everything in a livid phosphorescence. (*DP*, V 1002–1003; my transl.)[811]

Pascal attacks and bodily subjects her, he even injures her in their short fight so that Clotilde bleeds from a little wound. Having finally surrendered, Clotilde enters into a new kind of relationship with Pascal, a relationship that paves the way for their future love. Despite its future idyllic and ideal aura, their love is brutally founded on bodily subjection and an initial violent, bleeding 'penetration' – it is deeply patriarchal. Their new intimacy finds an expression in Pascal's introducing Clotilde to the 'forbidden' contents of the wardrobe, to the corrupted history of their family. Absorbed in the life-stories of their relatives

---

[810] "Par une nuit lourde de la fin de septembre, Pascal ne put dormir. Il ouvrit l'une des fenêtres de sa chambre, le ciel était noir, quelque orage devait passer au loin, car l'on entendait un continuel roulement de foudre." (*DP*, V 1002)

[811] "Par prudence, elle n'avait pas apporté de bougie, elle s'était contentée de rabattre les volets d'une fenêtre; et l'orage qui passait en face, au midi, dans le ciel ténébreux, les continuels éclairs lui suffisaient, baignant les objets d'une phosphorescence livide." (*DP*, V 1002–1003)

(that is to say in a summary of all the nineteen previous novels of the cycle) the two do not even notice that the thunderstorm outside has reached their house:

> At this moment the edge of the storm which lighted up the sky caught La Souleiade slantingly, and burst over the house in a deluge of rain. But they did not even close the window. They heard neither the peals of thunder nor the ceaseless beating of the rain upon the roof. (*DP*, V 1008; my transl.)[812]

What so captures their attention, the dossiers (i.e. The *Rougon-Macquart*), is itself a weathery spectacle:

> [Pascal] was out of breath, exhausted by his swift course through all this humanity, while, without voice, without movement, the young girl, stunned by this overflowing torrent of life, waited still, incapable of thought or judgment. The storm still beat furiously upon the dark fields with the endless rumbling of its diluvian rain. (*DP*, V 1014–1015; my transl.)[813]

The "overflowing torrent of life" that breaks from Docteur Pascal's research corresponds to the thunderstorm outside. There are two 'storms', one inside the room, raging from the dossiers, one outside. When Pascal and Clotilde have finally completed their course through the life-stories of their relatives, that is to say when the "overflowing torrent of life" ceases, the corresponding storm outside comes to an end as well:

> He stopped, and there was silence for a time. The rain had ceased, the storm was passing away, the thunderclaps sounded more and more distant, while from the refreshed fields, still dark, there came in through the open window a delicious odour of moist earth. (*DP*, V 1021–1022; my transl.)[814]

The scene seems to be plagiarised from the famous ball-scene of Goethe's *Werther*, where, when Lotte and Werther look out of the window after the storm, "[t]hunder rumbled in the distance, a splendid rain was falling on the land, and

---

[812] "A ce moment, un coin de l'orage qui incendiait l'horizon prit en écharpe la Souleiade, creva sur la maison en une pluie diluvienne. Mais ils ne fermèrent même pas la fenêtre. Ils n'entendaient ni les éclats de la foudre, ni le roulement continu de ce déluge battant la toiture." (*DP*, V 1008)

[813] "[Pascal] était hors d'haleine, épuisé d'un tel souffle démesuré, à travers cette humanité vivante ; tandis que, sans voix, sans geste, la jeune fille, dans l'étourdissement de ce torrent de vie débordé, attendait toujours, incapable d'une réflexion et d'un jugement. L'orage continuait à battre la campagne noire du roulement sans fin de sa pluie diluvienne." (*DP*, V 1014–1015)

[814] "Il se tut enfin, il y eut un silence. La pluie avait cessé, l'orage s'en allait, on n'entendait que des coups de foudre, de plus en plus lointains ; tandis que, de la campagne, noire encore, rafraîchie, montait par la fenêtre ouverte une délicieuse odeur de terre mouillée." (*DP*, V 1021–1022)

the most refreshing scent rose up to [them] in the fullness of a rush of warm air." (43) There is, however, one decisive difference between these two scenes: Pascal and Clotilde have not come up with "the clever idea" of retreating to "a room with shutters and curtains" (42) to escape the storm whilst it was raging. On the contrary, both Pascal and Clotilde open the scene by opening windows and shutters, although a storm is brewing, and "they did not even close the window" when the violence of the storm hits their house. Thus from the beginning to the end of this scene the difference of interior and exterior space is suspended – the interior and the exterior 'storm' rage together. Clotilde is exposed to both of these storms and this is what the scene is all about, what Pascal wants her to be. The exposure to the weather that results from opening both the windows and the wardrobe promises to be a kind of cure, which seems to have worked in the end: "Nothing bad had come to her from it. She felt herself beaten by a sharp sea wind, the storm wind which strengthens and expands the lungs." (*DP*, V 1022; my transl.)[815] Her 'rejuvenation' mirrors the state of the nature outside that has also been 'purified' by the crisis of the thunderstorm:

> Day was breaking, a dawn of exquisite purity, far off in the vast, clear sky, washed by the storm. Not a cloud now stained the pale azure tinged with rose colour. All the cheerful sounds of awakening life in the rain-drenched fields came in through the window [...]. (*DP*, V 1024; my transl.)[816]

The scene is obviously a metapoetic representation. We find, hardly disguised, the *Rougon-Macquart* and their author projected into the diegetic world. Beyond this, the 'author' even reads and explains his work to a disciple and thus also stages a scene of exemplary reception. The whole scenario provides Zola with the opportunity to talk about the *Rougon-Macquart* as a whole, to characterise its speech act and its relation to the world surrounding it. Above all, the scenario is steeped in weather: the storm is raging through the open windows, and the dossiers themselves 'are' a weathery spectacle. "There is everything", Pascal tells Clotilde about his 'oeuvre', "the good and the bad, the vulgar and the sublime, flowers, mud, blood, laughter, the torrent of life itself, bearing humanity endlessly on!" (*DP*, V 1016; my transl.)[817] The *Rougon-Macquart* not

---

[815] "Rien de mauvais ne lui en était venu, elle s'était sentie fouettée par un âpre vent marin, le vent des tempêtes, dont on sort la poitrine élargie et saine." (*DP*, V 1022)

[816] "Le jour naissait, une aube d'une pureté délicieuse, au fond du grand ciel clair, lavé par l'orage. Aucun nuage n'en tachait plus le pâle azur, teinté de rose. Tout le gai réveil de la campagne mouillée entrait par la fenêtre [...]." (*DP*, V 1024)

[817] "« [...] Il y a de tout, de l'excellent et du pire, du vulgaire et du sublime, les fleurs, la boue, les sanglots, les rires, le torrent même de la vie charriant sans fin l'humanité ! »" (*DP*, V 1016)

Mastery – the end of modern aesthetics — **535**

only depict a "torrent of life", they not only describe a universe governed by the weather (which confirms the impressions of our readings), the cycle is also itself understood and felt as a weather phenomenon: "a sharp sea wind, the storm wind" experienced by the exemplary reader Clotilde. All this approximates the narrative situation to the Ossian-scene in the *Werther*, where Werther also reads a work by himself, his translation of some passages of 'the Ossian', to an audience consisting of one, beloved female. There as well, the piece read out aloud depicts a world of weather, and, at the same time, it sets free 'weathery forces', it functions *as* a weather event. However, there is one decisive difference between these two meta-poetic scenes: whereas Werther's Ossian transports the weather into the cosy interior space of Lotte's parlour (literature serves as a medium), into an interior space that hermetically wards off the heavy weather outside, the relation of the literary storm and the diegetic world contrasts that of Zola. As his scene so explicitly exhibits by opening the windows to the storm raging outside, the 'literary' storm does not replace, mediate or transport the outer storm – it assists it instead. The two storms are blowing together and Clotilde is exposed to both of them. Literature no longer serves to integrate the weather into a weather-free, enlightened world that is modelled on the notion of human control over interior spaces. Zola's world of the late 19th century is a world of the weather, and the speech-act of the *Rougon-Macquart* affirms the forces of the weather. It merely adds another "sharp sea wind" to the mix, in the hope of "strengthen[ing] and expand[ing]" the readers' "lungs", of bringing about the same 'purging' effect as the thunderstorm that washes the sky. In other words, with his dossiers (i.e. the *Rougon-Macquart*) Pascal has, like his 'successful' but despised relatives, inadvertently fabricated a weather-machine. Nevertheless, he believes himself in control of his weather-machine, he seems to be very sure that its weather contributes to future health. It is here that Pascal's and Zola's projects touch on a paradoxical but decisive point that is crucial for their self-understanding. We have reached the omphalos of the *Rougon-Macquart*: (1) Either the world of the *Rougon-Macquart*, this "torrent of life", regulates itself; weather balances out weather, the world follows the continual inconstancy of the ocean, of the seasons and of the weathery change of the weather – and then Pascal is but a figure of this weathery world, who observes and affirms its logic and power, who facilitates it as far as his position allows him to do, but who inevitably stays exposed to it. His promise of future health and of a better world would however not be assured by this position and would need to be qualified: the torrent of life does not and cannot guarantee a stable 'better world'. It only promises change, for the better and for the worse; it promises rejuvenation, but also brings along the reverse movement of an inescapable tendency towards death. (2) Or, alternatively, an external position, outside the "torrent of life" is available, a position of control, a position from where the weathery world could be overcome; this is not the position of an observer, but of a creator, or at least a cunning manipulator, who uses the weathery forces to construct a non-weathery future. This utopic future will not be subjected to the ambivalent forces of the weather, but follow new, better, 'human' rules. Ultimately, the omphalic question of the cycle concerns the position from where the *Rougon-Macquart* speak: from a superior vantage point in the heavens above the weather, or from somewhere amongst the clouds.

The metapoetic scene we have been reading poses this question of position: Does Docteur Pascal belong to the family of the Rougon-Macquart, does he himself form part of the "torrent of life", or does he stand apart, above or beyond the muddy torrent?

Before passing this question on to Pascal, Clotilde first of all answers it for her own position. She clearly is part of this "muddy torrent [that] had rolled on before her for nearly three hours, and she had heard the most dreadful revelations, the harsh and terrible truth about her people, her people who were so dear to her, whom it was her duty to love" (*DP*, V 1022; my transl.).[818] However, despite the horror of the torrent, she very quickly notices that the torrent is not merely an assemblage of evil: "Was there then only mud in this overflowing stream, whose sluices he had opened? How much gold had passed, mingled with the grass and the flowers on its borders?" (*DP*, V 1022–1023; my transl.)[819] The torrent of life that rages from the wardrobe is deeply ambivalent, and it is in the notion of life itself that this ambivalence is inherent: "Besides, was it not life? There is no absolute evil." (*DP*, V 1023; my transl.)[820] Clotilde's understanding of the "torrent of life" thus mirrors Denise's (*Au Bonheur des Dames*) and Catherine's (*L'Argent*) attitude towards life that is obviously stained with violence and brutality, with death and suffering. In the end, they all come to affirm it in its ambivalence: "In spite of everything, it was a cry of health, of hope in the future." (*DP*, V 1022; my transl.)[821] Affirming this "torrent of life" means affirming its ambivalence, drawing hope from its continual cycle of rejuvenation and death. Pascal's position seems to be different:

---

[818] "Le torrent fangeux avait roulé devant elle, pendant près de trois heures, et c'était la pire des révélations, la brusque et terrible vérité sur les siens, les êtres chers, ceux qu'elle devait aimer :" (*DP*, V 1022)

[819] "Puis, n'y avait-il donc que de la boue dans ce fleuve débordé, dont il lâchait les écluses ? Que d'or passait, mêlé aux herbes et aux fleurs des berges !" (*DP*, V 1022–1023)

[820] "D'ailleurs, n'était-ce pas la vie ? Il n'y a pas de mal absolu." (*DP*, V 1023)

[821] "Malgré tout, c'était un cri de santé, d'espoir en l'avenir." (*DP*, V 1022)

"Well," she resumed, "and you, master?" [...] "I stand apart. [...] Not to be of them, my God! not to be of them! It is a breath of pure air; it is what gives me the courage to have them all here, to put them, in all their nakedness, in their envelopes, and still to find the courage to live!" (*DP*, V 1021; my transl.)[822]

There can be no doubt that this position "apart", as the paradigmatic position of the writer, has an inescapable appeal for Zola. Besides Docteur Pascal, he has placed two doubles of himself in the world of the *Rougon–Macquart*, writers that both hold this position: the tenant of the second floor in *Pot-Bouille* and Sandoz of *L'Œuvre* "live apart, not only of the narrative universe where one encounters them, but also of its laws, and particularly of the ultimate naturalist law, the law that presupposes the ineluctable disaggregation of the living" (Gantrel 2001, 87–88; my transl.). Martine Gantrel finds them 'not natural' and 'without history', so that they are factually excluded from the *Histoire naturelle et sociale* that Zola is writing (2001, 92). According to Martine Gantrel, an ontological difference runs through the narrative universe that reproduces the one that exists between the author and his oeuvre, the subject and the object, the act of writing and the narrated world (2001, 93). Jean Borie observes a similar phenomenon: The passages of *Pot-Bouille* and *L'Œuvre* dedicated to the figures of writers are easily told apart from the rest, they are not really integrated into the texture of the novels. He thinks the authorial intention, the projection of his desire obvious: the depicted writers embody 'success' in life, a good marriage, a family, honest prosperity. However, Borie also regards it as "evident that this success is in truth but an interruption, a blockage of life; these good marriages do not realise desire, they rather bracket it; the innocent prosperity demands absolute isolation" (1970, 23; my transl.). "[W]e do not get to know much of them", Borie adds, "but we can conclude that [the honest writer of *Pot-Bouille*] has to hermetically shut his doors and windows in order to survive in this cesspit" (1970, 23; my transl.). Pascal imagines he "stand[s] apart", like the nameless writer of *Pot-Bouille* – his (more or less unconscious) behaviour in this metapoetic scene that we are still reading, however, contradicts this self-understanding: instead of hermetically shutting his doors and windows, Pascal opens the scene by opening a window. This gesture explicitly and insistently dominates the whole scene: instead of enjoying the "breath of pure air" that his position apart allows him, Pascal is exposed to the same thunderous air that rages through the window opened by

---

[822] "« Eh ! bien reprit-elle, et toi, maître ? » « [...] C'est que je suis à part... [...] N'en être pas, n'en être pas, mon Dieu ! C'est une bouffée d'air pur, c'est ce qui me donne le courage de les avoir tous là, de les mettre à nu dans ces dossiers, et de trouver encoure le courage de vivre ! »" (*DP*, V 1021)

Clotilde. Nevertheless, despite the heavy storm "they did not even close the window". Moreover, it is Pascal who "had opened" the "sluices" of "this overflowing stream" breaking from his wardrobe. Instead of being sealed off from the *Rougon Macquart*'s contagious weather, he stands in the very middle of it, conjuring up, channelling and assisting its violent streams and torrents. This behaviour of one of the intradiegetic mouthpieces of the author confirms Bernd Blaschke's claim that instead of a writer apart, who is condemned to "absolute isolation" and does not quite form part of the narrative universe and its weathery laws, Zola, alias Docteur Pascal, is a soul-mate of Octave Mouret (2005, 44). More than he wants it to do, his job of writing, of dealing with the "torrent of life" resembles the management of torrents that defines Octave's business of the department store.

Despite the dominance of this gesture, the scene remains ambivalent with regard to Pascal's position. The impulse to open the windows and not to shut them as well as their both being exposed to the weather relates Pascal and Clotilde; nevertheless, the scene also emblematically distances the two. It is in this scene that Pascal once and for all establishes the patriarchal hierarchy of the elderly male dominating over the younger female. Zola even resorts to a sort of quasi-ritualistic bodily struggle to make that point; he relates a classical hierarchic encounter that ends by the stronger one's forcing the weaker one to make a submissive gesture. Clotilde is pushed into the passive role, the role of the disciple, whereas Pascal gains authority and control by acting as the teacher, by assuming the active, the strong role of the male. The authority and control *produced* by the patriarchal gender struggle supplements the actual control that Pascal exercises in his work, the control over the Second Empire's and his family's 'weather' that he dreams of. This control is far from obvious; it is heavily contested. However, distancing himself from Clotilde enables Pascal to emphasise his supposed position apart: Clotilde belongs to the ambivalent "torrent of life", he thinks himself beyond it and able to assume an attitude of control and authority that forecloses the actual quandaries of his position.

The novel as a whole addresses the conflict between the two positions: (1) the affirmation of the ambivalent life that one cannot help being subjected to, that defies human control – this is the position explained by Clotilde in the metapoetic scene, a position of immanence; (2) the project of controlling, of mastering, of subjecting life, of intervening and making a better future, a position of transcendence. Pascal oscillates between the two. As we have seen, he, indeed, thinks he occupies a superior position, and he thinks he has made a discovery that promises to make human intervention possible:

And at the thought of this discovery of the alchemy of the twentieth century, an immense hope opened up before him; he believed he had discovered the universal panacea, the elixir of life, which was to combat human debility, the one real cause of every ill; a veritable scientific Fountain of Youth, which, in giving vigour, health, and will would create an altogether new and superior humanity. (*DP*, V 949; my transl.)[823]

Like the nameless tenant of the second floor of *Pot-Bouille* Pascal works on the project of creating "an altogether new and superior humanity" behind the closed doors of his room, hermetically sealed off from the world around him, not wanting to be disturbed, not letting anyone near his little laboratory. He fosters the biopolitical dream of new, strong, healthy and of thus elevated human beings. This dream had already emerged through the surface of some of the preceding novels and is latently present in all of them. In the course of the last novel of the cycle Pascal however also comes to doubt this intervention:

> "[…] To correct nature, to interfere, in order to modify it and thwart it in its purpose, is this a laudable task? To cure the individual, to retard his death, for his personal pleasure, to prolong his existence, doubtless to the injury of the species, is not this to defeat the aims of nature? And have we the right to desire a stronger, a healthier humanity, modelled on our idea of health and strength? What have we to do in the matter? Why should we interfere in this work of life, neither the means nor the end of which are known to us? Perhaps everything is as it ought to be. Perhaps we risk killing love, genius, life itself. Remember, I make the confession to you alone; but doubt has taken possession of me, I tremble at the thought of my twentieth century alchemy. I have come to believe that it is greater and wiser to allow evolution to take its course." (*DP*, V 1084; my transl.)[824]

With this doubt Pascal adopts the position of Clotilde, Denise and Caroline, and affirms nature and life in all their ambivalence, as forces greater than the human "idea of health and strength". "[A]llow[ing] evolution to take its course" also

---

[823] "Et, devant cette trouvaille de l'alchimie du vingtième siècle, un immense espoir s'ouvrait, il croyait avoir découvert la panacée universelle, la liqueur de vie destinée à combattre la débilité humaine, seule cause réelle de tous les maux, une véritable et scientifique fontaine de Jouvence, qui, en donnant de la force, de la santé et de la volonté, referait une humanité toute neuve et supérieure." (*DP*, V 949)

[824] "« […] Corriger la nature, intervenir, la modifier et la contrarier dans son but, est-ce une besogne louable ? Guérir, retarder la mort de l'être pour son agrément personnel, le prolonger pour le dommage de l'espèce sans doute, n'est-ce pas défaire ce que veut faire la nature ? Et rêver une humanité plus saine, plus forte, modelée sur notre idée de la santé et de la force, en avons-nous le droit ? Qu'allons nous faire là, de quoi allons-nous nous mêler dans ce labeur de la vie, dont les moyens et le but nous sont inconnus ? Peut-être tout est-il bien. Peut-être risquons-nous de tuer l'amour, le génie, la vie elle-même… Tu entends, je le confesse à toi seule, le doute m'a pris, je tremble à la pensée de mon alchimie du vingtième siècle, je finis par croire qu'il est plus grand et plus sain de laisser l'évolution s'accomplir. »" (*DP*, V 1084)

entails subjecting oneself to the "torrent of life" and giving up the superior position of control, the position apart, that Pascal so much aspires to occupy. Regarded from this point of view, even the fundamental "desire to cure everything" that not only drives Pascal's life but also pervades the whole project of Zola's *Rougon-Macquart* loses its innocence:

> "[…] Do you not comprehend that to desire to cure everything, to regenerate everything is a false ambition inspired by our egotism, a revolt against life, which we declare to be bad, because we judge it from the point of view of self-interest? […]" (*DP*, V 1085; my transl.)[825]

Despite these arguments that Pascal presents to Clotilde with conviction, he remains divided; he oscillates between the authorial position apart and the sceptical affirmation of life 'from within the torrent'. On his deathbed he again feels the attraction of reaching "human perfection":

> Yes, yes, to begin life over again and to know how to live it, to dig the earth, to study man, to love woman, to attain to human perfection, the future city of universal happiness, through the harmonious working of the entire being, what a beautiful legacy for a philosophical physician to leave behind him would this be! (*DP*, V 1159; my transl.)[826]

Only moments later "humility" wins the upper hand and condemns the vision of creating a better future and the superiority of a solitary position:

> On the contrary, a feeling of humility took possession of him; the idea that all revolt against natural laws is bad, that wisdom does not consist in holding one's self apart, but in resigning one's self to be only a member of the whole great body. Why, then, was he so unwilling to belong to his family that it filled him with triumph, that his heart beat with joy, when he believed himself different from them, without any community with them? Nothing could be less philosophical. Only monsters grew apart. (*DP*, V 1164; my transl.)[827]

I have quoted from these reflections on control and the possibility of human intervention at great length because I assume that Pascal's oscillation characterises very well the ambivalent speech act of the *Rougon-Macquart*. The contradictory impulses that Pascal exhibits and that he elaborates on are impulses that

---

[825] "« […] Ne comprends-tu pas que vouloir tout guérir, tout régénérer, c'est une ambition fausse de notre égoïsme, une révolte contre la vie, que nous déclarons mauvaise, parce que nous la jugeons au point de vue de notre intérêt ? […] »" (*DP*, V 1085)

[826] "Oui, oui ! recommencer la vie et savoir la vivre, bêcher la terre, étudier le monde, aimer la femme, arriver à la perfection humaine, à la cité future de l'universel bonheur, par le juste emploi de l'être entier, quel beau testament laisserait là un médecin philosophe !" (*DP*, V 1159)

[827] "Au contraire, une humilité le prenait, la certitude que toute révolte contre les lois naturelles est mauvaise. Pourquoi donc, autrefois, triomphait-il, exultant d'allégresse, à l'idée de n'être pas de sa famille, de se sentir différent, sans communauté aucune ? Rien n'était moins philosophique. Les monstres seuls poussaient à l'écart." (*DP*, V 1164)

are also pertinent with regard to Zola's project of writing a social and natural history of the Second Empire: On the one hand, the whole project is conceived from a clear ideological point of view. It is critical of the Second Empire and fosters quite a clear-cut idea of a better future that is not described, but that nevertheless shapes Zola's attitude towards the narrated world. On the other hand, Zola's meticulous descriptions of this despised world develops a relation to it and invests it with psychic energy in a way that subverts the distanced, critical and controlled point of view from where the project started. As Rainer Warning observes, denunciation of this world of the Second Empire stands beside secret fascination (2005, 159). In other words, what happens to Zola is what Pierluigi Pellini sees as a common danger for naturalist writers: imitating an often degraded reality risks being contaminated by it and losing the superiority of the positivist scholar (2003, 22). In the case of Zola this does not occur as a mere accident. Zola is well aware of what he is fascinated by when describing the decadent world of the Second Empire: He has discovered enormous, proliferating but ambivalent forces of life. His attraction is coded vitalistically, as Stöber writes (2005, 34), and this fetishism of life (Baguley 1974, 146) affirms the weathery character of the world Zola analyses. We have already seen that life is conceptualised as a "torrent". Moreover, Zola is not only "at once frightened and attracted by the 'red vision of Revolution'" (Gerhardi 1974, 155) conceived of as a violent weather phenomenon, but by "environmental forces" (Bordeau 1998–1999, 104) in general. The continual inconstancy of the weather and its irresistible forces to which we are all subjected serve as the paradigm for thinking and affirming the ambivalent notion of life as a notion that surpasses the individual. The fascination with these forces shifts the strategic orientation of the whole. The project no longer aims at describing the horrors of an old world of the weather and at dreaming of a new weather-free, humane future, but instead attempts to frame, to master and exploit these forces:

> The problem posed by the general *débandade*, the collective madness, of an age is how to control, confine and direct human energies, and how to define the values which must inform the attempt to organize and channel human vitality. (Nelson 1977, 30)

It is not only the "human" energies, as Brian Nelson claims, but also and foremost the non-human, the environmental forces (unleashed by technology, by the masses or by the 'natural' weather) that this vision of mastery attempts to channel and exploit.

Zola's *Docteur Pascal* can be read as a commentary on this vision of mastery. With its very first lines it introduces its readers to a setting that successfully and exemplarily handles excessive environmental forces:

> In the heat of the glowing July afternoon, the room, with blinds carefully closed, was full of a great calm. From the three windows, through the cracks of the old wooden shutters, came only a few scattered sunbeams which, in the midst of the obscurity, made a soft brightness that bathed the surrounding objects in a diffused and tender light. It was cool here in comparison with the overpowering heat that was felt outside, under the fierce rays of the sun that blazed upon the front of the house. (*DP*, V 917; my transl.)[828]

At first glance this setting resembles the unnamed writer's flat in *Pot-Bouille*: The blinds are "carefully closed", creating an interior space that resists the hot weather, that cultivates a pleasant coolness despite the "overpowering heat" and the "fierce rays of the sun" prevailing outside. However, the room is not hermetically sealed. A carefully weighed dose of summer, "a few scattered sunbeams", are admitted into the interior and create a pleasant atmosphere. The room is not entirely governed by "obscurity" but "bathed" in "a soft brightness", "in a soft and tender light". The 'use' of this natural source of lighting indicates that Pascal's house, metonymically standing for Pascal's position towards the world, is not conceptualised as a place that aspires to independence from the weathery world surrounding it. It is rather a place that attempts to exploit these forces in a controlled way. This becomes even more obvious during the cold winter season:

> January was very cold. But the sky remained wonderfully clear, a brilliant sun shone in the limpid blue; and at La Souleiade, the windows of the study facing south formed a sort of hothouse, preserving there a delightfully mild temperature. They did not even light a fire, for the room was always filled with a flood of sunshine, in which the flies that had survived the winter flew about lazily. The only sound to be heard was the buzzing of their wings. It was a close and drowsy warmth, like a breath of spring that had lingered in the old house baked by the heat of summer. (*DP*, V 1036; my transl.)[829]

---

[828] "Dans la chaleur de l'ardente après-midi de juillet, la salle, aux volets soigneusement clos, était pleine d'un grand calme. Il ne venait, des trois fenêtres, que de minces flèches de lumière, par les fentes des vieilles boiseries ; et c'était, au milieu de l'ombre, une clarté très douce, baignant les objets d'une lueur diffuse et tendre. Il faisait là relativement frais, dans l'écrasement torride qu'on sentait au-dehors, sous le coup de soleil qui incendiait la façade." (*DP*, V 917)

[829] "Janvier fut très froid. Mais le ciel restait d'une pureté admirable, un éternel soleil luisait dans le bleu limpide ; et à la Souleiade, les fenêtres de la salle, tournées au midi, formaient serre, entretenaient là une douceur de température délicieuse. On ne faisait pas même de feu, le soleil ne quittait pas la pièce, une nappe d'or pâle, où des mouches, épargnées par l'hiver, volaient lentement. Il n'y avait aucun autre bruit que le frémissement de leurs ailes. C'était une tiédeur dormante et close, comme un coin de printemps conservé dans la vieille maison." (*DP*, V 1036)

Here Pascal is surely at the peak of his craft of mastering the weather. He demonstrates that the hothouse, the paradigmatic weather-machine of the Second Empire, does not have to be (mis)used for excess and perversion, but can be applied as a technology to realise an ancient dream of mankind: to produce the idyllic setting of eternal spring. In this world created and controlled by man, the flies, the most temporal and 'vain' of all species, survive the winter. No heating or air-conditioning has to be installed in order to brave the seasons and preserve a "delightfully mild temperature" in the house: on the contrary, this 'brave new, paradisiac world' is produced by managing and channelling the forces of the weather – it is these forces of the weather that drive the new 'weather-free' world. When the heat of the sun is excessive, it is shut out; when the winter air threatens with deadly cold, the 'sluices' are opened and the warm "flood of sunshine" fills the room. Against the background of control and management of the weather the metapoetic scene analysed above can also be read as conforming to this paradigm: Pascal's exposing Clotilde to the torrent of the dossiers and to the thunderstorm raging in through the open window would then be understood as a cure. Under the medical supervision of the sluice keeper Docteur Pascal, Clotilde received a special treatment consisting of "a sharp sea wind, the storm wind which strengthen[ed] and expand[ed] the lungs." However, the uncanny correspondence of 'outer' and 'inner' weather, of the thunderstorm and the torrent of life breaking from the dossiers, somehow resists the scenario of control. The thunderstorm that has triggered the whole scene defies Pascal's authority; the opening of the windows and shutters happens more or less by chance, at least not in a calculated way. Most importantly, the washing of the sky brought about by the thunderstorm is embedded in a cyclical logic of continual inconstancy that contradicts Pascal's vision of the Souleiade's 'eternal spring': The clear sky will again become clouded, there will be new thunderstorms, new grey days will follow, and so on.

It is this weathery logic that one day indeed afflicts the Souleiade and shatters Pascal's dream of creating for himself and Clotilde a paradise on earth. "[T]he weather unfortunately changed", in a metaphorical as well as a literal sense. The happy times between Pascal and his lover Clotilde come to an abrupt end when the person administering Pascal's fortune suffers bankruptcy and escapes with his clients' money. Since Pascal usually does not even charge his patients and has spent most of the money he earned as a doctor in the last decades on presents for Clotilde, the couple is suddenly left penniless. The heavy weather of the season uncannily corresponds to the hard times the couple is experiencing:

> It was the beginning of September, and the weather unfortunately changed; terrible storms ravaged the entire country; a part of the garden wall was blown down, and as Pascal was unable to rebuild it, the yawning breach remained. (*DP*, V 1130; my transl.)[830]

As the "yawning breach" produced by the "terrible storms" indicates, the weather proves to be more powerful than the human attempts at taming it. Pascal is no longer in control of all the 'sluices', his paradisiac 'fortress' called the Souleiade has suffered 'leakage'. The weather threatens to enter and disturb the "breath of spring" and the "delightfully mild temperature" that Pascal had been so proud of producing. In fact, metaphorically speaking, the "breath of spring" has long given way to the scarcity of winter. The little ménage hardly finds the means to nourish themselves so that Pascal feels forced to make a momentous decision that he actually wanted to avoid by all means: He gives in to his mother's suggestion to send Clotilde to her brother Maxime, who is suffering from paralysis and is in need of care. Pascal knows well that this decision means the end to their love relationship before it has brought about what he is dreaming of: a child.

Pascal's decision triggers a terrible emotional crisis inside the Souleiade that worsens with every hour that Clotilde's departure draws nearer. This crisis is again accompanied by corresponding weather, by a "terrible wind, which threatened to blow down the house" (*DP*, V 1148; my transl.):[831]

> For the past three days the mistral had been blowing. But on this evening its fury was redoubled, and Martine declared, in accordance with the popular belief, that it would last for three days longer. The winds at the end of September, in the valley of the Viorne, are terrible. So that the servant took care to go into every room in the house to assure herself that the shutters were securely fastened. When the mistral blew it caught La Souleiade slantingly, above the roofs of the houses of Plassans, on the little plateau on which the house was built. And now it raged and beat against the house, shaking it from garret to cellar, day and night, without a moment's cessation. The tiles were blown off, the fastenings of the windows were torn away, while the wind, entering the crevices, moaned and sobbed wildly through the house; and the doors, if they were left open for a moment, through forgetfulness, slammed to with a noise like the report of a cannon. They might have fancied they were sustaining a siege, so great were the noise and the discomfort. (*DP*, V 1147; my transl.)[832]

---

[830] "On entrait en septembre, et le temps, malheureusement, se gâtait : il y eut des orages terribles qui ravagèrent la contrée, un mur de la Souleiade fut renversé, qu'on ne put remettre debout, tout un écroulement dont la brèche resta béante." (*DP*, V 1130)

[831] "Et ils entendaient alors le vent, le vent terrible, qui menaçait d'éventrer la maison." (*DP*, V 1148)

[832] "Depuis trois jours déjà, le mistral soufflait. Mais, le soir, il redoubla, avec une violence nouvelle ; et Martine annonça qu'il durerait au moins trois jours encore, suivant la croyance populaire. Les vents de la fin septembre, au travers de la vallée de la Viorne, sont terribles.

Clotilde's departure marks the novel's second crisis: The first had been related in the metapoetic scene where Pascal converted Clotilde by exposing her to the dossiers' "torrent of life". Both crises find an expression in the heavy weather beating against the Souleiade. However, the difference of dealing with the forces of the weather could not be more explicit: Whereas the first crisis was triggered by opening the windows and the wardrobe, the second sets out with Martine's carefully fastening the shutters. The difference in intensity undermines the impression of Pascal's authority over the weather. The thunderstorm raging through the open windows had seemed to assist his cure of exposing Clotilde to "a sharp sea wind, the storm wind". The thunderstorm corresponding to the dossiers' torrent of life had created the impression that Pascal's 'medical' intervention had the blessing of a 'higher authority'. The mistral mirroring the turn of fortune that shattered Pascal's private life qualifies his position towards nature and the weather: Like everybody else, Pascal is subjected to higher forces, his management of the weather's forces is limited. This time, the old house's crevices through which the altered weather enters do not create a pleasant atmosphere as in the novel's first scene; instead, they exhibit the futility of attempting to hermetically seal oneself off from the weather. Despite Martine's precautions, the wind has conquered the Souleiade, it "moan[s] and sob[s] wildly through the house", like a haunting spirit it even challenges Pascal's control over windows and doors:

> The trunks were almost packed when Pascal went to open one of the shutters that the wind had blown to, but so fierce a gust swept in through the half open window that Clotilde had to go to his assistance. Leaning with all their weight, they were able at last to turn the catch. The articles of clothing in the room were blown about, and they gathered up in fragments a little hand mirror which had fallen from a chair. Was this a sign of approaching death, as the women of the faubourg said? (*DP*, V 1149; my transl.)[833]

Aussi eut-elle le soin de monter dans toutes les chambres, pour s'assurer que les volets étaient solidement clos. Quand le mistral soufflait, il prenait la Souleiade en écharpe, par-dessus les toitures de Plassans, sur le petit plateau où elle était bâtie. Et c'était une rage, une trombe furieuse, continue, qui flagellait la maison, l'ébranlait des caves aux greniers, pendant des jours, pendant des nuits, sans un arrêt. Les tuiles volaient, les ferrures des fenêtres étaient arrachées ; tandis que, par les fentes, à l'intérieur, le vent pénétrait, en un ronflement éperdu de plainte, et que les portes, au moindre oubli, se refermaient avec des retentissements de canon. On aurait dit tout un siège à soutenir, au milieu du vacarme et de l'angoisse." (*DP*, V 1147)

833 "Les malles allaient être faites, lorsqu'il voulut rouvrir un volet, que le vent venait de rabattre ; mais, par la fenêtre entrebâillée, ce fut un tel engouffrement, qu'elle dut accourir à son secours. Ils pesèrent de tout leur poids, ils purent enfin tourner l'espagnolette. Dans la chambre, les derniers chiffons s'étaient débandés, et ils ramassèrent, en morceaux, un petit miroir à main, tombé d'une chaise. Était-ce donc un signe de mort prochaine, comme le disaient les femmes du faubourg ?" (*DP*, V 1149)

The readers of *Docteur Pascal* know that death is indeed approaching: Pascal will soon die of a heart disease. The fact that a violent gust of wind conveys this message is highly significant. Pascal's and Clotilde's joint effort of fighting against the weather proves to be vain. It however indicates that Pascal does not occupy the position apart, that position of which he had been so convinced and from which he drew all his "courage to live". His position towards the violent mistral is not any different from Clotilde's. On the contrary, exercising his old imagined mastery over the sluices, trying to adjust a shutter which requires opening a window, Pascal needs his niece and lover to come to his aid. Nevertheless, they cannot prevent the wind from delivering its devastating message. In the face of the mistral and in the face of the financial catastrophe destroying their bliss Pascal is as powerless as Clotilde. The weather-machine has run out of control, the project of controlling and exploiting the forces of the weather in order to create a better, weather-free world of eternal spring has failed. In their despair Pascal and Clotilde can only repeat King Lear's gesture of conjuring up the storm, bidding "the wind blow the earth into the sea, | Or swell the curled water 'bove the main, | That things might change, or cease; [...]" (3.1.1–7):

> How many times during this last day did they not go over to the window, attracted by the storm, wishing that it would sweep away the world. [...] Why could not the mistral take them all up together and carry them off to some unknown land, where they might be happy? (*DP*, V 1148–1149; my transl.)[834]

However, not even the violent mistral proves powerful enough to prevent Clotilde's departure. When he finally watches the train leave the station, standing next to his triumphant mother, Pascal suddenly suffers a Wertherian fit:

> Suddenly Pascal became aware that he was standing alone upon the platform, while the train was disappearing around a bend of the tracks. Then, without listening to his mother, he ran furiously up the slope, sprang up the stone steps like a young man, and found himself in three minutes on the terrace of La Souleiade. The mistral was raging there – a fierce squall which bent the secular cypresses like straws. In the colourless sky the sun seemed weary of the violence of the wind, which for six days had been sweeping over its face. And like the wind-blown trees Pascal stood firm, his garments flapping like banners, his beard and hair blown about and lashed by the storm. His breath caught by the wind,

---

[834] "Que de fois, dans cette dernière journée, ils allèrent jusqu'à la fenêtre, attirés par la tempête, souhaitant qu'elle emportât le monde ! [...] Pourquoi le mistral ne les prenait-il pas ensemble, les jetant là-bas, au pays inconnu, où l'on est heureux ?" (*DP*, V 1148–1149)

his hands pressed upon his heart to quiet its throbbing, he saw the train flying in the distance across the bare plain, a little train which the mistral seemed to sweep before it like a dry branch. (*DP*, V 1154–1155; my transl.)[835]

Unlike his niece Clotilde, Pascal will not be cured by exposing himself to the mistral; "the storm wind" does not "strengthen[ ] and expand[ ] [his] lungs". The second crisis represented by the raging mistral does not restore health; it brings death. The weather, literal and metaphorical, to which he is exposed affects him: "His breath [is] caught by the wind", he presses "his hands [...] upon his heart to quiet its throbbing". He does not care, because, obviously, his actions are not following the paradigm of mastery, of health and control anymore. Like Werther on the day before his suicide, he delivers himself to the forces of the weather. Like Werther's adventurous nightly walk through the "whirling" "mix of rain and snow" (140) Pascal's furious run through the mistral is a premonition of his death.

The whole crisis contributes to Pascal's unexpected demise. It strains his heart that, as Pascal learns, is already weakened due to a hereditary illness. When Pascal and his friend Dr Ramond diagnose the illness, there is official confirmation of a fact that Pascal's relation to the weather had indicated all the while: he does not stand apart.

> His first thought was that he, too, would have to pay for his heredity, that sclerosis was the species of degeneration which was to be his share of the physiological misery, the inevitable inheritance bequeathed him by his terrible ancestry. (*DP*, V 1164; my transl.)[836]

In the metapoetic constellation of the novel, with Pascal representing the position from where the *Rougon-Macquart* are written, this insight is indicative. Pascal is seized and swept away by the "torrent of life" that he had set out to

---

[835] "Brusquement, Pascal s'aperçut qu'il était seul sur le quai, pendant que, là-bas, le train avait disparu, à un code de la ligne. Alors, il n'écouta pas sa mère, il prit sa course, un galop furieux de jeune homme, monta la pente, enjamba les gradins de pierres sèches, se trouva en trois minutes sur la terrasse de la Souleiade. Le mistral y faisait rage, une rafale géante qui pliait les cyprès centenaires comme des pailles. Dans le ciel décoloré, le soleil paraissait las de tout ce vent dont la violence, depuis six jours, lui passait sur la face. Et, pareil aux arbres échevelés, Pascal tenait bon, avec ses vêtements qui avaient des claquements de drapeaux, avec sa barbe et ses cheveux emportés, fouettés de tempête. L'haleine coupée, les deux mains sur son cœur pour en contenir les battements, il regardait aux loin fuir le train, à travers la plaine rase, un train tout petit que le mistral semblait balayer, ainsi qu'un rameau de feuilles sèches." (*DP*, V 1154–1155)

[836] "Sa première pensée venait d'être que lui aussi, à sont tour, payait son hérédité, que la sclérose, cette sorte de dégénérescence, était sa part de misère physiologique, le legs inévitable de sa terrible ascendance." (*DP*, V 1164)

analyse in order to tame it, to gain mastery over it. The project of channelling the forces of the weather and turning them against themselves has failed. Like his relatives Saccard and Octave Mouret, Pascal has unleashed powerful natural forces and has condensed them into one wardrobe full of paper. In the end, this mighty weather-machine outlives the framing and controlling authority that had been supervising it. In the fictional world, Pascal's mother burns the papers soon after Pascal's death and thereby 'averts the danger' issuing from the dossiers' 'torrent of life'. The novels of the *Rougon-Macquart*, however, survive. They depict a world of weather meticulously described by an observer who thinks himself apart, who believes he breathes "pure air" amidst the stormy turbulences he brings to paper. This observer, who draws his "courage to live" from his conviction not to be part of what he describes, secretly delights in seeing the forbidden, in catching nature, life and woman red-handed (Vinken 1996, 218). Nature, life and woman: these are excessive forces that defy male rational control, forces, as I have tried to show, that the cycle conceptualises as the forces of the weather. The tantalising fascination (Vinken 1997, 615) of the male fetishist gaze turns into an existential threat when the (Kantian) sublime constellation collapses; when the observer notices that he is not looking down on the weather spectacle of an inundated valley from the safe distance of a nearby mountain pinnacle but finds himself swept away by the very torrent of life in whose devastating destruction he delighted shortly before.

The weather wins over the authorial control represented by Pascal – and yet Zola finds a way to rescue his vision of male control, of authority over nature and weather. Shortly before Pascal dies, he receives the information that Clotilde has born him a son. The last thing Pascal does in his life is to complete the family tree that had been the centrepiece of his research. He notes down his own death, and the birth of his child named Charles. The coexistence of these two events is crucial. Pascal's vision of a position apart, of a re-establishment of human, rational, male control lives on. It is passed on to his child, it is shifted into the future. Despite his fascination with the weather's continual inconstancy, Zola ultimately does not share Caroline's or Clotilde's (female!) affirmation of the ambivalence of life. As Barbara Vinken has noted, motherliness serves Zola as the classical remedy against threatening femininity (1997, 597). The narrative project represented by Pascal's dossiers has failed to restore the authorial position of manliness, of human control. On the contrary, it has exhibited the inescapability as well as the attraction of a modern world governed by the forces of the weather. Instead of serving as an analysis of the status quo conducted by a neutral and objective observer, instead of providing the foundation for the creation of a future better world, it has revealed the unavailability of the imagined position of authority and control. Against the obvious ideological intention of their author, the *Rougon-Macquart* have become what they set out to frame and control. They are a cycle of novels on the irresistible power of the weather, they *are* themselves a "torrent of life" that their author has unleashed and condensed without proving able to exert control:

> Nature has entered into our works with so impetuous a bound that it has filled them, sometimes swamping the human element, submerging and carrying away characters in the midst of a downfall of rocks and great trees. This was inevitable [*fatal*]. We must leave time to weigh the new formula and to arrive at its exact expression. (Zola 1893b, 233)[837]

Instead of restoring manliness, the *Rougon-Macquart* raise a monument to the weathery threat, to the loss of rational, human control that dominates the modern world (cf. Vinken 1996, 223). Against this background, the fact that Pascal's dossiers, i.e. the fictional twin of the cycle of novels, are burnt at the end gains interesting significance. At first glance Pascal's mother simply celebrates a late triumph over her son; finally she reaches her goal of destroying the dossiers that she despises so much. However, especially the uncanny re-use of the wardrobe attracts attention:

> It yawned open, vast, seemingly bottomless, and on the large bare shelves there was nothing but the baby linen, the little waists, the little caps, the little socks, all the fine clothing, the down of the bird still in the nest. Where so many thoughts had been stored up, where a man's unremitting labour for thirty years had accumulated in an overflowing heap of papers [*débordement de paperasses*], there was now only a baby's clothing, only the first garments which would protect it for an hour, as it were, and which very soon it could no longer use. The vastness of the antique press seemed brightened and all refreshed by them. (*DP*, V 1214; my transl.)[838]

The "overflowing heap of papers" is replaced by the hopeful innocence of infant attire; this image seems to transport the strategy that the last novel of the cycle pursues in order to exorcise the fascination of the weather and re-establish the lost control and manliness (Vinken 1997, 603; 615). Unknowingly Pascal's

---

[837] "La nature est entrée dans nos œuvres d'un élan si impétueux, qu'elle les a emplies, noyant parfois l'humanité, submergeant et emportant les personnages, au milieu d'une débâcle de roches et de grands arbres. C'était fatal. Il faut laisser le temps à la formule nouvelle de se pondérer et d'arriver à son expression exacte." (*RE, OC* IX 425–426)

[838] "Elle semblait sans fond, immense, béante ; et, sur les planches nues et vastes, il n'y avait plus que les langes délicats, les petites brassières, les petits bonnets, les petits chaussons, les tas de couches, toute cette lingerie fine, cette plume légère d'oiseau encore au nid. Où tant d'idées avaient dormi en tas, où s'était accumulé pendant trente années l'obstiné labeur d'un homme, dans un débordement de paperasses, il ne restait que le lin d'un petit être, à peine des vêtements, les premiers linges qui le protégeaient pour une heure, et dont il ne pourrait bientôt plus se servir. L'immensité de l'antique armoire en paraissait égayée et toute rafraîchie." (*DP*, V 1214)

mother might have performed an autodafé that is of central importance for the restitution of the ideological goal that sustains the *Rougon-Macquart*. The strategy of taming the weather's "overflowing" powers by naturalistically describing it has failed; the weather proves to be contagious, describing its forces merely reproduces its powers, as the notion of the "overflowing heap of papers" strikingly shows. Burning this literary weather to ashes (again, it is the diegetic pendant of the *Rougon-Macquart* that is burnt) and instead investing all the hopes for a better future in a little, male (!) baby is a strong gesture. However, some critics have welcomed this turn: according to Chantal Jennings, a first decisive step is made to turn the *Rougon-Macquart*'s reign of nature that Rita Schober (1979, 70) complains about into a reign of man. Men were about to re-establish the upper hand over nature (Bertrand-Jennings 1980–1981, 103), *Le Docteur Pascal* served as a transition between the '*série noire*' of the *Rougon-Macquart* and the '*série rose*' of the Quatre Évangiles (Bertrand-Jennings 1980–1981, 104) and led towards the triumph of man over nature (Jennings 1980, 406). This "reconquête", as Chantal Jennings calls it (1980, 405), this recovery of authority and control, is inseparably linked to a particular relation to the weather. It is no coincidence that the "most triumphant" "victory of man over the world" (Jennings 1980, 408) takes place when in *Travail* man even captivates and domesticates the sun, making himself the uncontested master of light, heat and force (Jennings 1980, 409; my transl.).[839] With this "posthumous revenge for the

---

[839] Cf. "Et, chez [Jordan], c'était donc un culte du divin soleil, le père de notre monde, le créateur et le régulateur [...]. Il était l'éternelle source de vie, parce qu'il était la source de lumière, de chaleur et de mouvement. [...] Et dès lors, pourquoi donc le soleil ne continuerait-il pas, n'achèverait-il-pas son œuvre ? [...] S'il disparaissait chaque soir, s'il pâlissait l'hiver, il fallait lui demander de nous laisser une large part de sa flamme, afin de pouvoir attendre son retour de chaque matin et de patienter sans souffrir pendant les saisons froides. Ainsi, le problème se posait d'une façon à la fois simple et formidable, il s'agissait de s'adresser directement au soleil, de capter la chaleur solaire et de la transformer, à l'aide d'appareils spéciaux, en électricité, dont il faudrait ensuite conserver des provisions énormes, dans des réservoirs imperméables. [...] Et cette force électrique, ravie au soleil créateur, domestiquée par l'homme, serait enfin sa servante docile et toujours prête, le soulageant dans son effort, l'aidant à faire du travail la gaieté, la santé, la juste répartition des richesses, la loi et le culte même de la vie." (*Tr*, *OC* XIX 334)
"« Le jour doit venir où l'électricité sera à tout le monde, comme l'eau des fleuves, comme le vent du ciel. Il faudra non seulement la donner, mais la prodiguer, laisser les hommes en disposer à leur guise, ainsi que de l'air qu'ils respirent. Elle circulera dans les villes telle que le sang même de la vie sociale. Dans chaque maison, il y aura de simples robinets à tourner, pour qu'on ait à profusion la force, la chaleur, la lumière, aussi aisément qu'on a aujourd'hui l'eau de source. Et, la nuit, dans le ciel noir, elle allumera un autre soleil, qui éteindra les étoiles. Et elle supprimera l'hiver, elle fera naître l'éternel été, en réchauffant le vieux monde, en montant fondre la neige, jusque dans les nuages... C'est pourquoi je ne suis pas très fier de ce que j'ai fait, un bien petit résultat, à côté de ce qu'il reste à conquérir. »" (*Tr*, *OC* XIX 261)

'last men' of the *Rougon-Macquart*" (1980, 409; my transl.) Chantal Jennings not only perceptively ascertains a deeply paternalistic, patriarchal and authoritarian ideology (cf. Nelson 1982, 79–80); as Michel Serres has shown, the burning of the "overflowing heap of papers", the leaving behind of the weather of the 19th century world and hoping for a new, weather-free world to come display proto-fascist traces:

> It is against this terrible world that the fascist twentieth century will build its weapons: with its energies and against their work. In the complete silence of new theory, in the repetition of what was said before, before the emergence of this cloudy front [*ce front nuageux*]. (1975, 189; my transl.)[840]

"With *Le Docteur Pascal*, Zola starts to become aesthetically unreadable", writes Rainer Warning (1998, 733). The moment when the "overflowing heap of papers" is burnt and happily replaced by baby clothes makes the difference: Zola has decided for ideology and against aesthetics. It is a decision against the weather, against abandoning oneself to its ambivalent forces – and in favour of a mastery and control that appear to be rather incompatible with artistic production.

---

840 "C'est contre ce monde terrible que le vingtième siècle fasciste va construire ses armes : au moyen de ses énergies et contre leur travail. Dans le silence complet de théorie nouvelle, dans la répétition de ce qui se disait avant, avant l'apparition de ce front nuageux." (Serres 1975, 189)

Conclusion

An archaeology of literature's affinity to the weather tells the story of literature's self-reflection and its repeated creative reinvention as a medium under transforming epistemic and social circumstances. It gives an account of the role and the functioning of 'the literary' and presents them as products of strategic negotiations with the non-literary surroundings.

The three exemplary constellations that I have reconstructed unfold three different actualisations of 'abjuring all roofs':

(1) In Shakespeare's *Tempest* Lear's paradigmatic gesture takes on a metatheatrical meaning: 'abjuring all roofs' characterises the theatrical situation, the 'weathery state of exception', that suspends the worldly hierarchies and, for two or three hours, liberates its participants from the necessities and sorrows of practical life. It is "the enmity o'th'air" against which the audience, like Lear, has "To wage": the intense crisis of theatrical weather raging from the stage (and back!), affects the viewers – and, like Lear, they will probably not be "ague-proof". *The Tempest* reveals how Shakespeare's early modern theatre reflects upon itself as 'theatrical weather'. It 'stages' a theory of the medium theatre that conceptualises the way it works by resorting to the paradigmatic role of the weather in the early modern worldview. For Shakespeare and his contemporaries, the weather represented the ubiquitous processes of correspondences and interactions taking place between the 'components' of the world: between the humours of the human microcosm and the macrocosmic elements. The dominant humoral knowledge of the time constituted an elaborate understanding of the susceptibility of the humoral microcosm to the elemental macrocosm, for which the dynamic processes of the weather served as a decisive conceptual model. Furthermore, the weather played an important role in the Christian tradition: it was regarded as a symbolic medium that communicated God's wrath or benevolence. The theatrical medium that Shakespeare posits as analogous to the weather is thus not only meaningful and needs deciphering; above all, it is responsible for a bodily experience: as *The Tempest* indicates, a theatre performance is a weather event that troubles the viewers' humours and reminds us of the fact that the Aristotelian catharsis is, very literally, to be understood as a purging.

(2) As with Lear and with Shakespeare's *Tempest*, Werther's gesture of 'abjuring all roofs', his urge to go out and, finally, to leave the world, turns out to be a 'literary gesture'. A gesture, however, that demands a medium that, in contrast to *Lear* and the early modern era, has no analogical 'prefiguration' in the enlightened world. On the contrary, Werther embodies the enlightenment's constitutive 'uneasiness' with the weather. In the 18th century's worldview, the

weather has lost its paradigmatic epistemic role. The 'new' regime of knowledge is moulded on the model of an interior space and its controlled stability that the sovereign, rational human being has built for himself. Against this background it is not astonishing that the weather, when experienced collectively, is experienced from 'interior spaces', as in the famous ballroom-scene; it unexpectedly breaks into a world where it does not belong. It disturbs a world that has to find measures to protect itself from the weathery threat and to tame the weather's forces. In fact, the weather turns out to be the constitutive 'outside' of the enlightenment's stable and rational interior; it is by driving out or repressing the weather and related 'unruly' forces that the world centred around the rational human being gains its stability. The tragic story of Werther's 'abjuring all roofs', which is to say of finding no liveable place in enlightened society, is dedicated to these weathery forces that Werther paradigmatically represents. It not only analyses their liminal, but constitutive role for modern subjectivity and its environ-ment; it thereby also creates a space for the weathery forces 'inside' the enlightened 'weather-free' world. The birth of an autonomous medium of literature is inherently linked to the epistemic shift that is marked by the deep rupture between the early modern and the enlightened view and knowledge of the world. The medium of literature serves as a refuge for all that had once been at the epistemic centre ('the fluid', dynamism, interaction, affection, the dominance of becoming and decay as characteristics of the elemental world) and does not find recognition under the 'new' regime of knowledge that operates with the paradigms of 'the solid' and of universal ratio. As Goethe's novel demonstrates, the literary medium successfully transports the weathery forces into the enlightened interior: for example when Werther and Lotte think of the same Klopstock ode, or when Werther reads his translation of Ossian to Lotte. Both times the literary weather is answered by a corresponding 'bodily weather': by tears. The old, and in the enlightened world atavistic knowledge of humoral and elemental correspondences still accounts for the efficacy of the literary medium. However, the medial framing of the 'weather's state of exception' and of the constitution of a critical weathery community has changed significantly.

(3) Unlike Shakespeare's *Tempest* or Goethe's *Werther*, Zola's *Rougon-Macquart* do not produce their literary "horrible pleasure" with a sweeping gesture: Zola can claim a 'scientific method' of naturalistic description and nevertheless write novels that spread "a horror mixed with fascination" (Couillard 1978, 404). This is due to another epistemic and cultural rupture that separates Zola's world of the late 19th from Goethe's of the 18th century: the 'abjuring of all roofs' is no longer a provocative literary gesture, or the decision of a suicidal loaner: it has become the paradigmatic characteristic of the societal realities that Zola sees himself faced with, realities which apparently could not differ more from the

weather-free world of the enlightenment. According to the logic of the literary medium's 'responsibility' for phenomena of the weather and weathery forces, its 'jurisdiction' has broadened dramatically: from marginal phenomena that the 18th century's dominant knowledges did not account for, to no less than the whole of 19th century society. In Zola's monumental literary panorama the Second Empire is captured as a characteristic, warming climate that is produced by and at the same time determines the weathery processes of its various milieus. The paradigmatic locations of the 19th century that Zola portrays, the banking house, the department store, the coal-pit, the bar, the covered markets, the theatre, all turn out to be 'meteorotopoi': locations where (violent) weather is consciously produced mainly by heating and by facilitating circulation in order to create a hypertrophic atmosphere. The enormous forces of the weather that the Second Empire's businessmen unleash (streams of clients, floods of material and goods, rains of millions) account for their success: the more excessive the weather, the more effective their enterprises. Abjuring all roofs does therefore no longer imply turning away from practical life, as it had been with Lear (and Werther), but, on the contrary, emulates and affirms life's very logic; it is associated with gain in property and power.

Zola demonstrates that these locations' local 'climates' transcend the boundaries of the meteorotopoi: they are part of and contribute to the 'global' climate of the Second Empire. It is this climate that determines the catastrophic course of this era's history. Its final debacle is a climate catastrophe that goes back to the heating that had also been responsible for progress and modernisation. The wind has changed, it does not rain millions but shells and fire, the violent and uncontrollable weather does not convey wealth and passion but destruction. In contrast to the epistemic and social surroundings of Shakespeare and Goethe, crisis does not have to be brought to the world of the late 19th century by literature and its (mediated) weather – it is already inherent in it. According to the narratological self-understanding of Zola's writing, the narrator merely observes and analyses a world that follows its own logic – and it is this logic of weathery excess that necessarily leads to the catastrophic (and, potentially, purging and healing) crisis.

The 'weathery state of exception' that Shakespeare's practice of early modern theatre establishes could be called *local*. Here the gesture of 'abjuring all roofs' actually produces a setting that realises a 'genuine' *'outdoor experience'*. This concerns the relation of *appropriation* that early modern theatre, according to Shakespeare's metatheatrical reflections in *The Tempest*, maintains to the dominant worldview and knowledge of the time. Theatre emulates an everyday situation: being exposed to the weather and its effects on the body. It creates a limited situation at a clearly marked-off place: a performance at a theatre. This setting might differ from its surroundings in intensity; it is a hyper-weathery space. However, theatre functions according to the same principles that also govern the rest of the natural world. It is the hegemonic humoral knowledge of the susceptibility of the microcosmic, 'inner weather of the humours' to the 'outer weather of the raging elements' that accounts for theatre's mediated effect, for its purgative catharsis. As a consequence, exposing oneself to the theatrical weather and 'enjoying' its effect does not require any specific cultural technique: the medium theatre works by *tempering*, by exerting forces on the body and its humours.

By contrast, Goethe's *Werther* establishes a *boxed* 'weathery state of exception'. It does not lean on the dominant knowledge of its time in order to account for the way that the literary medium functions. On the contrary, it appropriates the constitutive exclusions of the contemporary hegemonic regime of knowledge: its relation to the epistemic system of its time is one of *supplementation*. In other words, it introduces the weather into the enlightenment's paradigmatic 'interior space'. In the world of the 18th century it has become impossible to experience the 'weathery state of exception' by merely going out of doors. The birth of a medium, of the autonomous medium of literature is needed to make it part of the world: it comes 'boxed', delivered to one's home, to be savoured on the couch in the drawing room, as Lotte and Werther demonstrate with regard to the fashionable *Ossian*. It has become an *'indoor experience'*, which, however demands a cultural technique of 'unboxing' in order to set free the literary weather and its effects: it is no longer an 'immediate' bodily experience, but one mediated by reading. This mediation makes it possible that the boxed weather and its forces that are unleashed by reading work in a fundamentally different way than their weather-free, enlightened surroundings.

The literary medium thus fulfils a clear role in the epistemic and cultural system of the 18th century: it serves as a window that opens the enlightenment's view onto phenomena and forces against which it has built its house of human ratio, control and 'autonomy', a view beyond the defining limitations and boundaries. However, this function is in itself deeply ambivalent: On the one hand, the literary medium thus contributes to the universality of the enlightenment's regime of 'interiority' and its taming of the weather and the weathery forces. On the other hand, the literary weather also shakes the foundations of the 18th century's house of knowledge and self-perception: it not only weakens the house's protective walls against which the weather is raging from without and creates potential spots of intrusion (not without reason the ball-society withdraws to a room that has shutters and curtains); above all it indicates that the human autonomy within this interior space is an illusion; that it is fabricated by excluding the weathery forces which defy the control of human ratio; that in fact even within the house, at its very core, the weathery forces lie repressed – and that it is them (passion, madness, drives) that fill the house with life. Goethe's novel gives an elaborate account of the fact that despite its universal claims, *"the ego is not"* – and cannot be – *"master in its own house"* (Freud 1955, 143). It is no coincidence that the literature of the 18th and early 19th century played an important role for Sigmund Freud's psychoanalytical discoveries, as it is no coincidence that this insight could not become 'official' knowledge until the late 19th century, when another rupture marks the emergence of new epistemic conditions.

Émile Zola's *Rougon-Macquart* relate these new epistemic, social and cultural circumstances. There is one astonishing shift that affects the role and function of the literary medium at the heart: The weather's state of exception has become *permanent* and *general* in the Second Empire (cf. Agamben 2005), it is the paradigm of social reality, of progress and modernity. The relation of literature to the epistemic system shifts from supplementation (focussing on the excluded, the liminal) to *participation*. Shakespeare and Goethe had been concerned with establishing a particular, a literary practice in the socio-cultural assemblage of their time; an effective practice that takes on its very own role, that differentiates itself from other practices and therefore could claim to produce a 'weathery state of exception', no matter whether, like the early modern cultural practice of theatre, limited and set off by the theatrical situation, or by the creation of an autonomous literary medium that has to be read. The socio-historical developments of the 19th century appear to have reversed this process: with the world's taking over the 'weathery state of exception' that could not find a place in the 18th century's enlightened society and demanded the creation of a supplementary medium, this medium, literature, has lost the singularity of its 'subject'. What had once been its particular 'situation', the weathery state of exception, has become generalised and governs the majority of the 19th century's social processes. The supplementary 'box' of the medium literature that had included the excluded (i.e. the weather and its forces) in the enlightened world loses its function and dissolves. Literature, with its affinity to the weather, finds itself in the middle of a world that is now understood to function in a 'weathery' way. Literature thus suddenly participates in, and can be said to contribute to, the dominant knowledge of 'modern' society.

Against this background the question of genre becomes significant. *The Tempest*, as an early modern drama, *Werther*, as a more or less monologic epistolary novel, and *The Rougon-Macquart*, as a naturalistic cycle of novels, could in this regard hardly differ more. And, indeed, genre did not play a role in the compilation of my corpus – which could, as a consequence, be criticised for its arbitrary generic diversity. However, in retrospect, this corpus has shed new light on the emergence of historically formative literary genres, which seems to be correlated to the role of the weather in the respective epistemic settings. The public literary practice of theatre connects to the epistemic 'availability' of the weather's paradigm as a bodily experience; the 'intimate' epistolary novel appears to be made for boxing something (weathery) that works differently than its surroundings; the transparent, 'scientific' description of naturalism only manages to produce "horrible pleasure" and thus could establish itself as a serious, aesthetic practice because it finds the 'weathery state of exception' in the world that it sets out to analyse. The birth of formative literary genres has apparently to do with literature's affinity to the weather that actualised itself differently under transforming epistemic, cultural and social circumstances.

The epistemic framework of Shakespeare's world follows the paradigm of *outdoor processes* (tempering); the enlightened system of the world in which Goethe's *Werther* is embedded is moulded on the model of the *interior space* (ratio's own house). Zola's modern world of the Second Empire is structured by a third epistemic paradigm: by the *suspension of inside and outside*. It is important not to misunderstand the sequence of the three select constellations as a dialectical progress, as a process of sublation: It is a mere product of my study's archaeological layout; I cannot and do not intend to tell a unifying story of development, but contrastingly portray three distinct paradigms that are separated by ruptures. Each of the three paradigms unfolds its very own logic and way of establishing epistemic consistency. The early modern knowledge of *analogies* and *correspondences* does not know an *a priori* foundation of stability or universality. There is only 'outdoor processes', and the correspondences and analogies it posits remain part of this outdoor setting, which is devoid of a stable point of reference. It is by endlessly referring from one analogy to the next, by an infinite process of producing correspondences, that a fragile consistency is established (cf. Foucault 1966, 45). The emergence of an *a priori* foundation of knowledge that makes notions like *a priori* stability or universality possible separates the early modern constellation from its enlightened and 19th century successors. Whereas the enlightened order of the world operated with *limitations*, and produced stability by excluding instability (which in turn creates the need and chance for supplementation), the late 19th century operates with the *universality of communication*. The window is no longer a dialectic threshold between inside and outside, no longer a place of negotiation of inclusion and exclusion and a potentially supplementary place for universalising this dialectic by including the excluded (i.e. universalising the interior space) – it turns into the paradigm for communication, for a universal medium, which suspends the limitations of inside and outside and makes communication across apparently 'absolute' boundaries (the animate – the inanimate; the social – the natural) conceivable. The emergence of the concept of *milieu* in the nascent sciences of the 19th century (physiology, sociology) accounts for the new paradigm: instead of categorising or characterising specific 'objects', it focuses on *interaction* and attempts to find a universal (chemical, physical, literary) 'vocabulary' for it. The atavistic knowledge of the weather as a paradigm for becoming and decay, for influence that crosses all boundaries, and for establishing correspondences serves as an important provisory auxiliary structure for thinking of and conceptualising milieu. This is why Zola can claim a pioneering role for literature in the epistemic project of milieu and universal communication: in its long history of 'abjuring all roofs' and exploring a proximity with the weather, literature has gained a veritable expertise in the weathery processes that are now said to shape the 19th century's society. It has 'cultivated' this 'atavistic' knowledge in its autonomous medium against the enlightenment's paradigm of the 'solid'; in a way it is its very own 'subject' (the weathery state of exception) that has become generalised. The universal medium of milieu, the idea of epistemic consistency produced by *universal communication* exhibits close similarities to and therefore 'favours' the medium of literature.

The development of dedifferentiation (and 'de-mediation'), of dissolving the differentiating and mediating 'box' of the formerly autonomous literary medium, shifts the role of 'literature' in a double and ambivalent way: (1) On the one hand, literature comes to share its 'object of study' with the nascent disciplines of the social and 'human' sciences. It is no coincidence that the *Rougon-Macquart*'s subtitle claims the cycle to be 'social and natural history', *Histoire sociale et naturelle*. The literary is thus invested with the 'serious' function of producing knowledge that surpasses the realm of literature and speaks truth about 'the world'. It *participates* in the epistemic processes. This is accompanied by a shift of paradigms with regard to the functioning and the role of the literary. In Shakespeare's theatre and Goethe's novel the mediating forces of the medium literature had been directed 'vertically' to produce an effect on the viewer or the reader, an effect that surpasses the medium's boundaries. In Zola's *Rougon-Macquart* the medium's mediating forces are primarily working horizontally; they refer back to the level of diegesis and account for the (privileged!) literary approach to the world. The paradigm of the literary medium has therefore shifted from being one of *tempering* and *reading* (both concerned with effects on the 'recipient') to *description* (aiming at the phenomena of the narrated world). The mediating quality of the weather now primarily holds the fictional world together, makes the different milieus communicate and thereby accounts for the universal reach of description and its epistemic relevance. Literature's primary 'effect' is not tears any more – it is knowledge.

(2) On the other hand, as the famous metapoetic scene of Docteur Pascal and Clotilde in the last novel of the cycle exhibits, Zola also regards his literary project as a weathery state of exception, as "a sharp sea wind, the storm wind which strengthens and expands the lungs" (DP, V 1022; my transl.), which is supposed to have a purging, cathartic effect on its readers. Literature is however confronted with a difficult position of enunciation: it has lost the idiosyncratic, differentiating character of its attitude "That things might change or cease". All the world is producing heavy weather, Octave Mouret in his department store as well as the mining company in the coal pit. Are the *Rougon-Macquart* just another meteorotopos, contributing to the warming climate of the late 19th century? Literature's formerly 'critical' position is in danger of being in mere complicity with the world. The 'weathery state of exception' has passed over onto the world; literature's affinity to the weather has in this constellation enhanced its recognition as an epistemic practice – its critical dimension of intervention, of "That things might change or cease", of conjuring up a crisis, has however also been relegated to the world. Can the literary merely analyse, affirm and trust in the world's rejuvenating forces – or is it in need of taking a new standpoint outside the 'weathery' trouble of modern society?

Émile Zola's *Rougon-Macquart* exhibits both these two conflicting tendencies: in large parts it plays out its inclination towards the weather and uses it for a meticulous analysis of the Second Empire. It thereby not only generates knowledge, but also (re)produces and affirms the Second Empire's 'weathery state of exception' and its "horrible pleasure". It, however, also shows traces of a countermovement, of searching for a 'position of resistance' apart. This movement implies a departure from literature's affinity to the weather. The position 'apart' is no longer the 'weathery one' as it had been with Lear and Werther – on the contrary, it is the one unaffected by the weather, the one of control and mastery which allows the reintroduction of order into the weathery chaos of the modern world. Not coincidentally this position apart evokes proto-fascist associations of a better world envisioned by a leader, of a return to 'natural' order, to sane and healthy humankind and of an extinction of everything that has degenerated.

I think that Émile Zola and the conflict that pervades his oeuvre exposes a more general 'problem' that has emerged with the epistemic and social shift I attempted to outline: the generalisation of 'literature's' 'weathery state of exception' appears to provoke a countermovement, an affinity to the 'weather-free', to control and authority. It would be an interesting project to examine literature's affinity to fascist positions and its 'tendency to ideology' that can be observed towards the end of the 19th and the beginning of the 20th century against this background. Paradoxically, it appears to be the approximation of life and art, of society and art, the development of de-mediation and de-differentiation (or of deterritorialisation, as Gilles Deleuze and Félix Guattari would call it (cf. 1972)) that accounts for the uneasy strategic position of literature and the tendency of some writers to abandon the 'critical alliance' with the weather.

These are the results of my archaeological study of literature's affinity to the weather. It reconstructs *how* this affinity actualised itself in different constellations and indicates epistemic shifts as well as literary developments. An archaeology does however not provide us with answers to a question that has certainly been present from the first page of this book: *why* this affinity? What is 'behind' the affinity of literature and weather, and what accounts for its consistency throughout the centuries? In the end, this is *one of many ways* of raising the notorious question of 'the literary'. As there does not appear to be a viable systematic approach to these questions, they can only be tentatively touched upon in the concluding margins and in a merely speculative mood. It is the general and naïve observations of 'similarities' between the three 'texts' that guide and inspire the following thoughts.

'Abjuring the roofs' means affirming the 'weathery *medium*'. The literary medium is characterised by its density and opacity. It is the location for manifold formations and dynamics, for becoming and decay, for movements of all sorts. However, despite producing 'critical' effects, it 'rests in itself'. It does not acquire the transparency of a means that moves towards a non-literary goal. It moves 'in itself' and produces mediated effects.

Literature's 'weathery medium' does not primarily communicate intentions or ideas; it does not draw the alternative plan of a better, a 'weather-free' world. Strikingly, utopic ideas of paradisiac, weather-free places feature in all three constellations that we have read: Gonzalo's plantation in *The Tempest*, Werther's idylls in Goethe's novel, the miners' reign of justice, Lazare's Oceania and Renée's America in the *Rougon-Macquart*. They are all depicted as unliveable illusions, which refer us back to the 'actual', the weathery world. One could say even more generally that representation or the referential function, as Roman Jakobson (cf. 1960) would put it, is not dominant in literature's 'weathery medium' – the literary role of the weather is the best example for this. As an object of representation or description, the weather is indeed rather banal and unspectacular: it is not any different from all the other objects, processes or conditions of the (fictional) world that can become the subject of more or less elaborate literary descriptions. One could write a history of literature's representation of smoking or traffic – on the level of motif and techniques of representation, the weather does not enjoy any privilege. However, in contrast to other subjects, motifs or themes, the weather indicates and exhibits the limits of the notion of representation: it cannot be captured by being described. It does not belong to the order of the representable. On the contrary, representation misses what is characteristic about the weather and what distinguishes it from other 'phenomena': the weather *is* not merely an object that can be observed and described, it *does* something, of itself, without any graspable intention 'behind' it. It has 'serious' effects, it is responsible for life and death, but cannot be reduced to a functional or instrumental logic. This accounts for its characteristic density and opacity: the question of *why* it rains cannot simply and ultimately be answered by referring to the plants' need of water or the benevolent god's care for the thirsty world; the reality of droughts and famines asks for new explanations – and opens up an unending and inescapable process of interpretation. The atmospheric processes somewhat enjoy an 'independent existence', they are the prototype of a differential system that is regulated by universal interaction, loops of self-references and limitless interferences; however, despite this paradigmatic role of self-reference, despite its density and opacity and its apparent 'closure', it is not indifferent to its surroundings. It pervades the world (in fact it is hard to say where the influence of the weather 'ends') and exerts observable, perceptible, palpable effects.

In other words, the weather is a sort of paradigmatic arche-medium. It exhibits similarities to other media, especially to the system of language, and foregrounds characteristics of mediality, particularly its productive, own internal dynamics, that linguistics, as a result of its focus on the instrumentality of language, would find out about only very late in its history. In a way it is the weather's everyday phenomena, its auto-referential processes and their mediated effects, that resemble and indicate literature's own specific attitude towards language and towards the world. This may perhaps account for the fact that using the weather as a literary means to create a specific atmosphere supposedly reveals 'bad authors': reducing the complex medium of the weather to a transparent, manipulative means appears to imply the same sacrilege with regard to the literary medium. I do not think that there is another potential object of description for which the same assertion could be made.

This concerns literature's position of enunciation and its relation to 'the world'. In theory, literary authors exert an absolute and omnipotent authority over their fictional universes. The attitude or gesture of 'abjuring all roofs' implies however a paradoxical 'self-restriction': it is not the attitude of a demiurge, of a creator who is in power of all that is and happens, including the weather, but one of exposing oneself to an existing world. The texts of my corpus do not construct better worlds and they do not merely transparently 'represent' the circumstances of their time either. In a complicated gesture that Aristotle has called *mimesis* they conjure up settings that are oriented towards a specific, contemporary experience of 'life'; in order to be effective, they have to 'abjure the roofs' and deliberately expose themselves to the ambivalences of the world in which they are embedded. The "horrible pleasure" that *Lear*, *The Tempest*, *Werther* and the *Rougon-Macquart* produce are in the end always the horrible pleasures of a historical experience of life itself – and as Lear's gesture so vividly demonstrates, abjuring all roofs is a precondition for this literary relation to the world. In the end, literature is an affirmation of the 'elemental' world; 'abjuring the roofs' has something very 'secular' and anti-escapist to it. It does not construct the ideal, but affirms the ambivalence of a specific given. The weather appears to be the paradigm for this paradoxical literary self-restriction, this exposing oneself to pre-existing 'circumstances' that creates the texts' embeddedness, their effective *mimesis*.

Literature as a weathery medium does not merely represent or depict a world, it makes itself the plaything (Barthes 1975, 34) of this world. It devotes and abandons itself to the characteristics of the 'given': to language as well as to the concrete realities and circumstances, the historical 'semantics' (cf. Luhmann 1980) of life. They form literature's material, 'the stuff that literature is made on', and, at the same time, they are literature's subject, what literature is talking about. Roman Jakobson has called this auto-referential trait the dominance of language's poetical function (cf. 1960). It accounts for the density of the medium described above, for its resting in itself. Literature's mode of 'observation' is special: it 'abjures all roofs' and all safe (scientific) standpoints, all meta-language and 'neutral' conceptual apparatus and experiences the world's 'storm' by exposing itself to it, by conjuring it up, by indulging in and appropriating its materiality, by mapping and making use of its effects. It is built from what it talks about.

As we have seen with *King Lear*, this is not merely a passive gesture: it creates a 'weathery state of exception' that pushes and tests the limits of the given. On the one hand, this is a technique of analysis that reveals the organising structures of a historical world, as *King Lear* and *The Tempest* shed light on authority, *Werther* explores the double concentric structure of modern subjectivity and the *Rougon-Macquart* the weathery nature of late 19th century society. On the other hand, the three examples aim at more than analysis and representation: they give an account of the resistances against the current organising structures, their historicity, their limitations and their vanity. Pushing the limits of the given always also implies focussing on and affirming the excess, the overflowing of the existing epistemic and social frameworks' boundaries. It is no coincidence that Lear "[b]ids the wind blow the earth into the sea, | Or swell the curled water 'bove the main," (*Lr.* 3.1.1–6), that Werther evokes "the torrent of genius [*Strom des Genies*]" which "gush[es] out so rarely, so rarely come[s] rushing in on a spring tide" (30–31) and that Zola puts all his trust in the Second Empire's ubiquitous *débordement* that is to lead to rejuvenation and renewal. Literature *as a weathery medium* does not promote a particular, ascertained, 'true' ideology – it affirms the fundamental 'unorderliness' of the world's existing hegemonic orders. It emphasises and supports the weathery character of development and decay, the emergence and transformations of structuring principles that shape the historical realities of life: "That things might change, or cease".

In the end, all these dimensions of 'abjuring the roofs', and that is to say, of affirming the 'weathery medium' of literature, refer to one central trait: to abjuring mastery. Lear and also Prospero, Werther and Docteur Pascal, they experience their illusion of absolute control; at particular, climactic moments of their stories, we experience them powerless in the face of the weather that they had conjured up. All three are poetological figures that leave their fictional worlds dead, or weak – they all have to step back in favour of the medium that defied their authority, whose "slave" they prove to be, "poor, [and] infirm" (*Lr.* 3.2.19–20). This is not a sign of failure, but the condition of literature's "horrible pleasure", of its characteristic relation to the world and its mediated, critical effect on it. The countercheck might reveal the scope and consequences of this weathery abjuration of mastery: when an author forces absolute control over his literary text, when a text becomes a transparent (political, etc.) message or a particular worldview, literature not only loses its aesthetic appeal, it also forfeits its 'mimetic' relation to the world and turns to ideology or propaganda, to an abstract, lifeless and artless expression.

Does literature's affinity to the weather have a bearing on literary criticism? With my study I attempted to answer this question in the positive. It was an experiment to read the texts as what they presented themselves to be: as weathery media. 'Abjuring all roofs' also describes an attitude of the reader or scholar: the rather unacademic stance of exposing oneself to the 'texts' weather', of renouncing mastery and control: of refraining from bringing conceptual, historical or biographical frameworks to the texts, but of indulging in them, of drifting along with their currents, of being receptive for the minor details that happen to affect oneself while being exposed to them. To be sure, this can at times be a tiring and exhaustive thing to do: one goes astray too often, one travels in repetitive loops rather than telling a well-composed, linear story, one is always in danger of losing oneself in the overflow of detail. Above all, the reader's longing for guidance, for mastery and 'service' is not adequately satisfied. However, "*Drifting* [...] like a cork on the waves" (Barthes 1975, 18) not only establishes an 'intimate' relation to the text (and to the world!), it not only enables an exploration of the main currents of our corpus and being washed ashore of interesting co-texts, but allows participation in a central dimension of literary texts that remains concealed by more 'scientific' approaches with their huge array of tools and technology and their 'ascertained', manifest knowledge: the texts' "horrible pleasure". Their weathery excess, their *débordement* cannot be described or captured in any way. It is what the texts *do* and what the reader 'suffers' (and delights in). As we have learnt from Lear, this "horrible pleasure" is not merely about subjective emotions – it represents the literary practices' *critical* dimension: the affirmation of the fact "That things might change or cease". What about literary criticism's *critical* (some would say 'political') dimension? Is it not about cultivating this affirmation of weathery openness, of de-naturalising hegemonic orders that the weathery medium of literature exhibits? If academic criticism is not to foreclose the critical attitude of its subject and to confine itself to the accumulation of positivistic knowledge 'about' literary texts, there does not appear to be an alternative to joining the 'weathery alliance': this implies abjuring the roofs of a particular epistemic system and its safe ground – the literary texts' weather cannot be calmly observed and analysed from 'in-a-doors' without depriving it of its characteristic, mediated effects.

As Michel Foucault has demonstrated, an archaeological study does not end with the "triumphant, heroic, muscular" (Barthes 1975, 18) gesture of having extended the safe soil of the island of knowledge, of having wrought another piece of land from the broad and stormy ocean, from the true seat of illusion. On the contrary, it concludes with affirming the weathery change of things: any 'safe soil', any arrangement of truth and social order, will "disappear as [it] appeared", "like a face drawn in sand at the edge of the sea". It will be made to crumble by "some event of which we can at the moment do no more than sense the possibility – without knowing either what its form will be or what it promises" (Foucault 1970, 387).

It is precisely at this point that the reconstruction of literature's affinity to the weather and the critical impetus of my study meet: the galloping production of 'scientific' and 'academic' knowledge reproduces the rigid, professional con- and uniformity of the 'office' – the resistances of the weather appear to have been forgotten. This holds true even for literary studies, whose subject might be called the most 'weathery' apart from meteorology's. The future is not open by itself: the rigid roofing, the vaulted domes that we are building every day in order to protect our human, rational mastery from any disturbing influences cement the status quo in a more than questionable and hubris-laden way. Joining Shakespeare's, Goethe's, Zola's and Foucault's 'weathery alliance' I hope to have at least created awareness to the poets' slits "on to the open and windy chaos". It is a challenge to produce knowledge and explore life and the world without erecting too many protective structures that attempt to hold their ground against the creativity of 'the weathery forces', without "patch[ing] the umbrella with [criticism's] painted patch of the simulacrum". Weathery literature is not only a fascinating and uneasy object of study – it is an inspiring example for a humble but critical attitude towards the world. A world that if we do not stifle und ultimately destroy it under our water-proof gear of technology and rationality will always be weathery, will always be a space of creativity and becoming: *Toujours il se renouvelait*.

Nietzsche sensed this: sometimes it is all about having the courage of forgetting one's umbrella.

Works Cited

Oxford English Dictionary. Oxford: Oxford Univ. Press. http://www.oed.com (accessed 30.09.2015).
Acot, Pascal. 2003. *Histoire du climat, Pour l'histoire*. Paris: Perrin.
Adelung, Johann Christoph, D. W. Soltau, and Franx Xaver Schönberger. 1811. *Grammatisch-kritisches Wörterbuch der Hochdeutschen Mundart mit beständiger Vergleichung der übrigen Mundarten, besonders aber der Oberdeutschen*. 4 vols. Wien: Bauer.
Agamben, Giorgio. 2005. *State of Exception*. Translated by Kevin Attell. Chicago: Univ. of Chicago Press.
Albanese, Denise. 1996. *New Science, New World*. Durham, NC: Duke Univ. Press.
Alcorn, Clayton R. 1969. "The Child and His Milieu in *The Rougon-Macquart*." *Yale French Studies* no. 42:105–14.
Althusser, Louis. 1971. "Ideology and Ideological State Apparatus." In *Lenin and Philosophy and Other Essays*, 85–126. London: NLB.
Anderegg, Johannes. 1997. "Werther und Ossian." In *Stile, Stilprägungen, Stilgeschichte. Über Epochen-, Gattungs- und Autorenstile – sprachliche Analysen und didaktische Aspekte*, edited by Ulla Fix and Hans Wellmann, 121–133. Heidelberg: Winter.
Anderson, Katharine. 2005. *Predicting the Weather. Victorians and the Science of Meteorology*. Chicago: Univ. of Chicago Press.
Aurnhammer, Achim. 1995. "Maler Werther. Zur Bedeutung der bildenden Kunst in Goethes Roman." *Literaturwissenschaftliches Jahrbuch im Auftrage der Görres-Gesellschaft* no. 36:83–104.
Back, Guy. 1971. "Dramatic Convention in the First Scene of *The Tempest*." *Essays in Criticism* no. 21:74–85.
Baguley, David. 1974. "Du naturalisme au mythe. L'alchimie du docteur Pascal." *Les Cahiers Naturalistes* no. 48:141–163.
Barker, Francis, and Peter Hulme. 2002. "Nymphs and Reapers Heavily Vanish. The Discursive Con-Texts of *The Tempest*." In *Alternative Shakespeares*, edited by John Drakakis, 195–209. London: Routledge.
Barthes, Roland. 1975. *The Pleasure of the Text*. Translated by Richard Miller. New York: Hill and Wang.
Bartholomaeus. 1582. *Batman Vppon Bartholome. His Booke De Proprietatibus Rerum, Newly Corrected, Enlarged and Amended*. London: Imprinted by Thomas East.
Behringer, Wolfgang. 2007. *Kulturgeschichte des Klimas. Von der Eiszeit bis zur globalen Erwärmung*. München: Beck.
Beizer, Janet. 1989. "The Body in Question. Anatomy, Textuality, and Fetishism in Zola." *L'Esprit Créateur* no. 29 (1):50–60.
Belgrand, Anne. 1987. "Le jeu des oppositions dans *La Curée*." In *La Curée de Zola ou 'la vie à outrance'*, edited by David Baguley, 23–41. Paris: SEDES.
Belton, Ellen R. 1985. "'When No Man Was His Own'. Magic and Self-Discovery in *The Tempest*." *University of Toronto Quarterly* no. 55 (2):127–140.
Bender, John B. 2001. "The Day of *The Tempest*." In *The Tempest. Critical Essays*, edited by Patrick M. Murphy, 200–222. New York: Routledge.
Benjamin, Walter. 1983. *Das Passagen-Werk*. 2 vols, *Edition Suhrkamp*. Frankfurt am Main: Suhrkamp.
Benjamin, Walter. 1999. *The Arcades Project*. Translated by Howard Eiland and Kevin McLaughlin. Cambridge, MA: Harvard Univ. Press.

Bennett, Benjamin. 1980. "Goethe's *Werther*. Double Perspective and the Game of Life." *German Quarterly* no. 53 (1):64–81.
Berger, Harry, Jr. 1969. "Miraculous Harp. A Reading of Shakespeare's *Tempest*." *Shakespeare Studies* no. 5:253–283.
Berger, Karol. 1977. "Prospero's Art." *Shakespeare Studies* no. 10:211–39.
Berthier, Philippe. 1987. "Hôtel Saccard. État des lieux." In *La Curée de Zola ou 'la vie à outrance'*, edited by David Baguley, 107–118. Paris: SEDES.
Bertrand-Jennings, Chantal. 1980–1981. "Zola ou l'envers de la science. De *La Faute de l'abbé Mouret*." *Nineteenth Century French Studies* no. 9 (1–2):93–107.
Best, Janice. 1989. "Espace de la perversion et perversion de l'espace." *Cahiers Naturalistes* no. 63:109–115.
Best, Janice. 1990. "Dégradation et génération du récit. Entropie et chronotopes littéraires." *Poétique* no. 84:483–498.
Bevington, David. 1998. "*The Tempest* and the Jacobean Court Masque." In *The Politics of the Stuart Court Masque*, edited by David Bevington, Peter Holbrook and Leah S. Marcus, 218–243. Cambridge: Cambridge Univ. Press.
Bishop, Tom. 1996. *Shakespeare and the Theatre of Wonder*. Cambridge: Cambridge Univ. Press.
Blaschke, Bernd. 2005. "Literarische Anthropologie im Zeitalter des Hochkapitalismus. Zolas Antinomien des notwendigen Exzesses." *Grenzgänge* no. 12 (23):38–52.
Blumenberg, Hans. 1997. *Shipwreck with Spectator. Paradigm of a Metaphor for Existence*. Translated by Steven Rendall, *Studies in Contemporary German Social Thought*. Cambridge, MA: MIT Press.
Boia, Lucian. 2005. *The Weather in the Imagination*. London: Reaktion Books.
Bordeau, Catherine. 1998–1999. "The Power of the Feminine Milieu in Zola's *Nana*." *Nineteenth-Century French Studies* no. 27 (1–2):96–107.
Borie, Jean. 1970. *Zola et les mythes*. Paris: Éd. du Seuil.
Bradbrook, M. C. 2001. "Romance, Farewell! *The Tempest*." In *The Tempest. Critical Essays*, edited by Patrick M. Murphy, 190–199. New York: Routledge.
Brailow, David G. 1981. "Prospero's 'Old Brain'. The Old Man as Metaphor in *The Tempest*." *Shakespeare Studies* no. 14:285–303.
Brandstetter, Gabriele. 1997. "Tanz und Literatur. Anstöße zu kulturwissenschaftlicher Forschung." *Die Neue Gesellschaft/Frankfurter Hefte* no. 11:1011–1014.
Braswell, Suzanne F. 2013. "Mallarmé, Huysmans, and the Poetics of Hothouse Blooms." *French Forum* no. 38 (1–2):69–87.
Breight, Curt. 1990. "'Treason Doth Never Prosper'. *The Tempest* and the Discourse of Treason." *Shakespeare Quarterly* no. 41 (1):1–28.
Brokaw, Katherine Steele. 2008. "Ariel's Liberty." *Shakespeare Bulletin* no. 26 (1):23–42.
Brook, Peter. 1957. "An Open Letter to Shakespeare, or As I don't Like It." *The Sunday Times*, 1 September.
Brown, Robert H. 1991. *Nature's Hidden Terror. Violent Nature Imagery in Eighteenth-Century Germany*. Columbia, SC: Camden House.
Bruster, Douglas. 2001. "Local Tempest. Shakespeare and the Work of the Early Modern Playhouse." In *The Tempest. Critical Essays*, edited by Patrick M. Murphy, 257–275. New York: Routledge.
Bulger, Thomas. 1994. "The Utopic Structure of *The Tempest*." *Utopian Studies* no. 5 (1):38–47.
Butcher, Samuel Henry, and Aristoteles. 1955. *Aristotle's Theory of Poetry and Fine Art. With a Critical Text and Translation of the Poetics*. 4. ed. New York: Dover.

Buuren, Maarten van. 1987. "*La Curée*, roman du feu." In *La Curée de Zola ou 'la vie à outrance'*, edited by David Baguley, 155–160. Paris: SEDES.

Calvin, Jean. 1578. *A Commentarie of Iohn Caluine, Vpon the First Booke of Moses Called Genesis*. Translated by Thomas Tymme. London: Imprinted by Henry Middleton for Iohn Harison and George Bishop.

Camarani, Ana Luiza Silva. 1990. "Les passions chez Zola." *Revista de Letras* no. 30:183–91.

Campbell, Heather. 1993. "Bringing Forth Wonders. Temporal and Divine Power in *The Tempest*." In *The Witness of Times. Manifestations of Ideology in Seventeenth Century England*, edited by Katherine Z. Keller and Gerald J. Schiffhorst, 69–89. Pittsburgh, PA: Duquesne Univ. Press.

Campmas, Aude. 2003. "Les Fleurs de serres. Entre science et littérature à la fin du dix-neuvième siècle." In *Visions/Revisions. Essays on Nineteenth-Century French Culture*, edited by Nigel Harkness, Paul Rowe, Tim Unwin and Jennifer Yee, 49–61. Oxford: Peter Lang.

Capitanio, Sarah. 1987. "Les mécanismes métaphoriques dans *La Curée*." *Les Cahiers Naturalistes* no. 61:181–193.

Carles, Patricia. 1989. "*L'Assommoir*, une déstructuration impressionniste de l'espace descriptif." *Les Cahiers Naturalistes* no. 63:117–126.

Carnot, Sadi. 1878 [1824]. *Réflexions sur la puissance motrice du feu et sur les machines propres à développer cette puissance*. Paris: Gauthier-Villars.

Carnot, Sadi. 1897. *Reflections on the Motive Power of Heat and on Machines Fitted to Develop That Power*. Translated by Robert Henry Thurston. 2. ed. New York: J. Wiley & sons.

Chakrabarty, Dipesh. 2009. "The Climate of History. Four Theses." *Critical Inquiry* no. 35 (2):197–222.

Chalhoub, Samia. 1993. "L'enfant à travers les déterminismes du milieu dans *Les Rougon-Macquart*." *French Review* no. 66 (4):595–606.

Chevrel, Yves. 1985. "De *Germinal* aux *Tisserands*." *Revue d'histoire littéraire de la France* no. 85 (3):447–463.

Cortés, Martín. 1630. *The Art of Navigation*. Translated by Richard Eden. London: Printed by B. A[lsop]. and T. Fawcet. [sic] for J. Tap.

Couillard, Marie. 1978. "'La fille-fleur' dans *Les Contes à Ninon* et *Les Rougon-Macquart*." *Revue de l'Université d'Ottawa/University of Ottawa Quarterly* no. 48 (4):398–406.

Counter, Andrew J. 2014. "Zola's Reproductive Politics." *French Studies* no. 68 (2):193–208.

Crooke, Helkiah. 1615. *Mikrokosmographia*. London: Printed by William Iaggard.

Cryle, Peter. 2004. "Love and Epistemology in French Fiction of the Fin-de-Siècle. In Search of the Pathological Unknown." *Dix-Neuf* no. 3:55–74.

Davidson, Clifford. 1976. "The Masque within *The Tempest*." *Notre Dame English Journal* no. 10:12–17.

De Gooyer, Alan. 2001. "'Their Senses I'll Restore'. Montaigne and *The Tempest* Reconsidered." In *The Tempest. Critical Essays*, edited by Patrick M. Murphy, 509–531. New York: Routledge.

Deleuze, Gilles. 1962. *Nietzsche et la philosophie*. Paris: Presses universitaires de France.

Deleuze, Gilles. 1965. *Nietzsche, sa vie, son œuvre. Avec un exposé de sa philosophie*. Paris: Presses universitaires de France.

Deleuze, Gilles. 1968. *Différence et répétition*. Paris: Presses universitaires de France.

Deleuze, Gilles. 1969. "Zola et la fêlure." In *Logique du sens*, 373–386. Paris: Éd. de Minuit.

Deleuze, Gilles, and Félix Guattari. 1972. *L'Anti-Œdipe, Capitalisme et schizophrénie*. Paris: Éd. de Minuit.

Deleuze, Gilles, and Félix Guattari. 1980. *Mille plateaux, Capitalisme et schizophrénie*. Paris: Éd. de Minuit.
Deleuze, Gilles, and Félix Guattari. 1991. *Qu'est-ce que la philosophie?, Collection "Critique"*. Paris: Éd. de Minuit.
Delius, Friedrich Christian. 1971. *Der Held und sein Wetter. Ein Kunstmittel und sein ideologischer Gebrauch im Roman des bürgerlichen Realismus*. München: Hanser.
Delius, Friedrich Christian, and Klaus Vogel. 2008. "Der Direktor des DHMD Klaus Vogel und der Schriftsteller Friedrich Christian Delius reden über des Wetter." In *2°. Das Wetter, der Mensch und sein Klima*, edited by Petra Lutz and Thomas Macho, 76–80. Göttingen: Wallstein.
Demaray, John G. 1998. *Shakespeare and the Spectacles of Strangeness. The Tempest and the Transformation of Renaissance Theatrical Forms, Medieval and Renaissance Literary Studies (MRLS)*. Pittsburgh, PA: Duquesne Univ. Press.
Derrida, Jacques. 1967. *De la grammatologie, Collection critique*. Paris: Éd. de Minuit.
Derrida, Jacques. 1972. *La dissémination, Tel quel*. Paris: Éd. du Seuil.
Derrida, Jacques. 1979. *Spurs. Nietzsche's styles/Éperons. Les styles de Nietzsche*. Translated by Stefano Agosti. Chicago: Univ. of Chicago Press.
Derrida, Jacques. 1991. *Donner le temps 1. La fausse monnaie, Collection La philosophie en effet*. Paris: Galilée.
Derrida, Jacques. 2006. *Specters of Marx. The State of the Debt, the Work of Mourning and the New International*. Translated by Peggy Kamuf, *Routledge Classics*. New York: Routledge.
Dessen, Alan C. 1980. "Elizabethan Audiences and the Open Stage. Recovering Lost Conventions." *Yearbook of English Studies* no. 10:1–20.
Donaldson-Evans, Mary. 1992. "The Morbidity of Milieu. *L'Assommoir* and the Discourse of Hygiene." In *Literary Generations. A Festschrift in Honor of Edward D. Sullivan by His Friends, Colleagues, and Former Students*, edited by Alain Toumayan, 150–162. Lexington, KY: French Forum Monographs.
Donat, Sebastian. 2003. "Metrum und Semantik bei Roman Jakobson." In *Roman Jakobsons Gedichtanalysen. Eine Herausforderung an die Philologien*, edited by Hendrik Birus, Sebastian Donat and Burkhard Meyer-Sickendiek, 252–276. Göttingen: Wallstein.
Döring, Tobias. 2013. "Learning to Charm. On the Virtue of Words and the Forgetting of Language in *The Tempest*." In *Critical and Cultural Transformations: Shakespeare's The Tempest – 1611 to the Present*, edited by Tobias Döring and Virginia Mason Vaughan, 99–114. Tübingen: Narr.
Du Bartas, Guillaume de. 1578. *La Sepmaine, ou Création du monde*. Paris: Feurier.
Dumiche, Béatrice. 1995. "Lottes Mutterbindung. Ihre Mitschuld an Werthers Selbstmord." *Orbis Litterarum* no. 50 (5):278–288.
Dumiche, Béatrice. 2000. "Die Vorgängigkeit des Textes. Zur Funktion der Literaturzitate in den *Leiden des jungen Werther*." In *Lectures françaises et allemandes du XVIIIe siècle. Deutsch-französische Interpretationen des 18. Jahrhunderts*, edited by Beatrice Dumiche, Richard Baum and Jean-Louis Haquette, 123–147. Bonn: Romanistischer Verlag Jakob Hillen.
Duncan, Bruce. 1982. "'Emilia Galotti lag auf dem Pult aufgeschlagen'. Werther as (Mis-)Reader." *Goethe Yearbook* no. 1:42–50.
Dunn, E. Catherine. 1952. "The Storm in *King Lear*." *Shakespeare Quarterly* no. 3 (4):329–33.
Ebner, Dean. 1965. "*The Tempest*. Rebellion and the Ideal State." *Shakespeare Quarterly* no. 16 (2):161–173.

Eckermann, Johann Peter, Johann Wolfgang von Goethe, and Frédéric Jacob Soret. 1850. *Conversations of Goethe with Eckermann and Soret*. Translated by John Oxenford. 2 vols. London: Smith.

Edmunds, Kathryn. 1996. "'der Gesang soll deinen Namen erhalten'. Ossian, Werther, and Texts of/for Mourning." *Goethe Yearbook* no. 8:45–65.

Egan, Gabriel. 2006. *Green Shakespeare. From Ecopolitics to Ecocriticism, Accents on Shakespeare*. Abingdon: Routledge.

Egan, Robert. 1972. "This Rough Magic. Perspectives of Art and Morality in *The Tempest*." *Shakespeare Quarterly* no. 23 (2):171–182.

El Kettani, Soundouss. 2010. "Splendeurs et misères de l'architecture des *Rougon-Macquart*." *Nineteenth-Century French Studies* no. 38 (3–4):211–227.

Evans, John X. 1981. "Utopia on Prospero's Island." *Moreana* no. 69:81–83.

Fechner, Jörg-Ulrich. 1998. "Nachwort." In *Sturm und Drang. Ein Schauspiel*, edited by Jörg-Ulrich Fechner, 149–171. Stuttgart: Reclam.

Fine, Gary Alan. 2007. *Authors of the Storm. Meteorologists and the Culture of Prediction*. Chicago: Univ. of Chicago Press.

Fitz, L. T. 1975. "The Vocabulary of the Environment in *The Tempest*." *Shakespeare Quarterly* no. 26 (1):42–47.

Flagstad, Karen. 1986. "'Making This Place Paradise'. Prospero and the Problem of Caliban in *The Tempest*." *Shakespeare Studies* no. 18:205–233.

Flammarion, Camille. 1888. *L'atmosphère. Météorologie populaire*. Paris: Librairie Hachette.

Fleming, James Rodger. 1998. *Historical Perspectives on Climate Change*. New York: Oxford Univ. Press.

Fleming, James Rodger. 2010. *Fixing the Sky. The Checkered History of Weather and Climate Control, Columbia Studies in International and Global History*. New York: Columbia Univ. Press.

Foucault, Michel. 1963. *Naissance de la clinique. Une archéologie du regard médical*. Paris: Presses universitaires de France.

Foucault, Michel. 1966. *Les mots et les choses. Une archéologie des sciences humaines, Bibliothèque des sciences humaines*. Paris: Gallimard.

Foucault, Michel. 1969. *L'archéologie du savoir*. Paris: Gallimard.

Foucault, Michel. 1970. *The Order of Things. An Archaeology of the Human Sciences*. Translated by R.D. Laing. New York: Pantheon.

Foucault, Michel. 1972. *Histoire de la folie à l'âge classique*. Paris: Gallimard.

Foucault, Michel. 1975. *Surveiller et punir. Naissance de la prison, Bibliothèque des histoires*. Paris: Gallimard.

Foucault, Michel. 1984. *L'usage des plaisirs, Histoire de la sexualité 2*. Paris: Gallimard.

Foucault, Michel. 2001 [1967]. "Des espaces autres." In *Dits et écrits. II. 1976–1988*, edited by Daniel Defert and François Ewald, 1571–1581. Paris: Gallimard.

Foucault, Michel. 2001 [1965]. "La pensée du dehors." In *Dits et écrits. I. 1954–1975*, edited by Daniel Defert and François Ewald, 546–567. Paris: Gallimard.

Fowler, Elizabeth. 2000. "The Ship Adrift." In *The Tempest and Its Travels*, edited by Peter Hulme, William H. Sherman and Robin Kirkpatrick, 37–40. Philadelphia, PA: Univ. of Pennsylvania Press.

Fox-Good, Jacquelyn. 1996. "Other Voices. The Sweet, Dangerous Airs of Shakespeare's Tempest." *Shakespeare Studies* no. 24:241–274.

Freud, Sigmund. 1955. "A Difficulty in the Path of Psycho-Analysis." In *The Standard Edition of the Complete Psychological Works of Sigmund Freud, Volume XVII (1917–1919): An Infantile Neurosis and Other Works*, edited by James Stratchey, 137–144. London: The Hogarth Press and the Institute of Psychoanalysis.
Freud, Sigmund. 1964. "Analysis Terminable and Interminable." In *The Standard Edition of the Complete Psychological Works of Sigmund Freud, Volume XXIII (1937–1939): Moses and Monotheism, An Outline of Psycho-Analysis and Other Works*, edited by James Stratchey, 209–254. London: The Hogarth Press and the Institute of Psychoanalysis.
Freud, Sigmund. 1970 [1919]. "Das Unheimliche." In *Psychologische Schriften*, 241–274. Frankfurt am Main: S. Fischer.
Friedrich, Hans-Edwin. 2000. "Autonomie der Liebe – Autonomie des Romans. Zur Funktion von Liebe im Roman der 1770er Jahre. Goethes *Werther* und Millers *Siegwart*." In *Nach der Sozialgeschichte. Konzepte für eine Literaturwissenschaft zwischen Historischer Anthropologie, Kulturgeschichte und Medientheorie* edited by Martin Huber and Gerhard Lauer, 209–220. Tübingen: Niemeyer.
Friedrich, Lars. 2010. "Werthers Resignation." *Poetica* no. 42 (3–4):243–275.
Frye, Northrop. 1965. *A Natural Perspective. The Development of Shakespearean Comedy and Romance, Bampton Lectures in America*. New York: Columbia Univ. Press.
Fulke, William. 1563. *A Goodly Gallerye*. London: Printed by William Griffith.
Furst, Lilian R. 1990. "The 'Imprisoning Self'. Goethe's *Werther* and Rousseau's *Solitary Walker*." In *European Romanticism. Literary Cross-Currents, Modes, and Models*, edited by Gerhart Hoffmeister, 145–161. Detroit, MI: Wayne State Univ. Press.
Gamper, Michael. 2005. "Normalisierung/Denormalisierung, experimentell. Literarische Bevölkerungsregulierung bei Zola." In *Literarische Experimentalkulturen. Poetologien des Experiments im 19. Jahrhundert*, edited by Marcus Krause and Nicolas Pethes, 149–168. Würzburg: Königshausen & Neumann.
Gamper, Michael. 2014. "Rätsel der Atmosphäre. Umrisse einer 'literarischen Meteorologie'." *Zeitschrift für Germanistik* no. 24 (2):229–243.
Gantrel, Martine. 2001. "Zola et ses doubles. Les instances d'auto-représentation dans *Pot-Bouille* et *L'Œuvre*." *Les Cahiers Naturalistes* no. 47 (75):87–98.
Garber, Marjorie B. 1974. *Dream in Shakespeare. From Metaphor to Metamorphosis*. New Haven, CT: Yale Univ. Press.
Garber, Marjorie B. 2004. *Shakespeare After All*. New York: Pantheon Books.
Genette, Gérard. 1972. *Figures III*. Paris: Éd. du Seuil.
Gerhardi, Gerhard. 1974. "*Germinal*. Mass Action and Psychology of the Individual." *Studi di letteratura francese* no. 3:142–156.
Gervinus, Georg Gottfried. 1844. *Handbuch der Geschichte der poetischen National-Literatur der Deutschen*. 3. ed. Leipzig: Engelmann.
Geßner, Salomon. 1973. *Idyllen, Universal-Bibliothek*. Stuttgart: Reclam.
Gilbert, Otto. 1907. *Die meteorologischen Theorien des griechischen Altertums*. Leipzig: Teubner.
Gille, Klaus F. 1998. "Die Leiden und Freuden des jungen Werthers." In *Zwischen Kulturrevolution und Nationalliteratur gesammelte Aufsätze zu Goethe und seiner Zeit*, 11–28. Berlin: Trafo-Verl.
Gillies, John. 1986. "Shakespeare's Virginian Masque." *ELH* no. 53 (4):673–707.
Gilman, Ernest B. 1980. "'All Eyes'. Prospero's Inverted Masque." *Renaissance Quarterly* no. 33 (2):214–230.

Goethe, Johann Wolfgang von. 1848. *The Auto-Biography of Goethe. Truth and Poetry From My Own Life*. Translated by John Oxenford. London: Bohn.

Goethe, Johann Wolfgang von. 1905a. *Briefe 25. April – 31. October 1820*. Vol. IV 33, *Goethes Werke. Weimarer Ausgabe*. Weimar: Böhlau.

Goethe, Johann Wolfgang von. 1905b. *Briefe November 1820 – Juni 1821*. Vol. IV 34, *Goethes Werke. Weimarer Ausgabe*. Weimar: Böhlau.

Goethe, Johann Wolfgang von. 1906a. *Briefe April 1823 – December 1823*. Vol. IV 37, *Goethes Werke. Weimarer Ausgabe*. Weimar: Böhlau.

Goethe, Johann Wolfgang von. 1906b. *Briefe Januar 1824 – October 1824*. Vol. IV 38, *Goethes Werke. Weimarer Ausgabe*. Weimar: Böhlau.

Goethe, Johann Wolfgang von. 1906c. *Briefe Juli 1821 – März 1822*. Vol. IV 35, *Goethes Werke. Weimarer Ausgabe*. Weimar: Böhlau.

Goethe, Johann Wolfgang von. 1907. *Briefe April 1822 – März 1823*. Vol. IV 36, *Goethes Werke. Weimarer Ausgabe*. Weimar: Böhlau.

Goethe, Johann Wolfgang von. 1986. *Gespräche mit Eckermann*. Edited by Heinz Schlaffer. Vol. 19, *Sämtliche Werke. Münchner Ausgabe*. München: Hanser.

Goethe, Johann Wolfgang von. 1987. *Gedichte 1756–1799*. Edited by Karl Eibl. Vol. 1, *Sämtliche Werke, Briefe, Tagebücher und Gespräche. Frankfurter Ausgabe*. Frankfurt am Main: Dt. Klassiker-Verl.

Goethe, Johann Wolfgang von. 1996. *Romane und Novellen*. Edited by Erich Trunz. 14. ed. Vol. 6, *Goethes Werke. Hamburger Ausgabe in 14 Bänden*. München: Beck.

Goethe, Johann Wolfgang von. 1997. *Von Frankfurt nach Weimar. Briefe, Tagebücher und Gespräche vom 23. Mai 1764 – 30. Oktober 1775*. Edited by Wilhelm Große. Vol. 28, *Sämtliche Werke, Briefe, Tagebücher und Gespräche. Frankfurter Ausgabe*. Frankfurt am Main: Dt. Klassiker-Verl.

Goethe, Johann Wolfgang von. 1998. *Ästhetische Schriften 1771–1805*. Edited by Friedmar Apel. Vol. 18, *Sämtliche Werke, Briefe, Tagebücher und Gespräche. Frankfurter Ausgabe*. Frankfurt am Main: Dt. Klassiker-Verl.

Goethe, Johann Wolfgang von. 2006. *Die Leiden des jungen Werthers. Die Wahlverwandtschaften. Kleine Prosa. Epen*. Edited by Waltraud Wiethölter and Christoph Brecht. Vol. 8, *Sämtliche Werke, Briefe, Tagebücher und Gespräche. Frankfurter Ausgabe*. Frankfurt am Main: Dt. Klassiker-Verl.

Goethe, Johann Wolfgang von. 2007. *Aus meinem Leben. Dichtung und Wahrheit*. Edited by Klaus-Detlef Müller. Vol. 14, *Sämtliche Werke, Briefe, Tagebücher und Gespräche. Frankfurter Ausgabe*. Frankfurt am Main: Dt. Klassiker-Verl.

Goethe, Johann Wolfgang von. 2012. *The Sufferings of Young Werther*. Translated by Stanley Corngold. New York: Norton.

Golinski, Jan. 2007. *British Weather and the Climate of Enlightenment*. Chicago: The Univ. of Chicago Press.

Got, Olivier. 2002. *Les jardins de Zola. Psychanalyse et paysage mythique dans Les Rougon-Macquart*. Paris: L'Harmattan.

Graham, Ilse. 1974. "Goethes eigener Werther. Eines Künstlers Wahrheit über seine Dichtung." *Jahrbuch der Deutschen Schillergesellschaft* no. 18:268–303.

Grant, Patrick. 1976. "The Magic of Charity. A Background to Prospero." *Review of English Studies* no. 27 (105):1–16.

Greenblatt, Stephen. 1988. *Shakespearean Negotiations. The Circulation of Social Energy in Renaissance England*. Berkeley: Univ. of California Press.

Grimm, Jacob, and Wilhelm Grimm. 1838–1971. *Deutsches Wörterbuch von Jacob Grimm und Wilhelm Grimm*. Trier: Univ. of Trier. http://urts55.uni-trier.de:8080/Projekte/DWB (accessed 30.09.2015).
Grimm, Reinhold. 1999. "The Last Words of Christ in the Devil's Mouth. A Note on Goethe's Biblical Intertextuality." *Etudes Germano-Africaines* no. 17:59–64.
Guedj, Aimé. 1968. "Les révolutionnaires de Zola." *Les Cahiers Naturalistes* no. 36:123–137.
Gumbrecht, Hans Ulrich. 1978. *Zola im historischen Kontext. Für eine neue Lektüre des Rougon-Macquart-Zyklus*. München: Fink.
Gurr, Andrew. 2010. "The Move Indoors." In *Shakespeare in Stages*, edited by Christine Dymkowski and Christie Carson, 7–21. Cambridge: Cambridge Univ. Press.
Haavik, Kristof Haakon. 2000. *In Mortal Combat. The Conflict of Life and Death in Zola's Rougon-Macquart*. Birmingham, AL: Summa Publications.
Hall, Grace R. W. 1999. *The Tempest as Mystery Play. Uncovering Religious Sources of Shakespeare's Most Spiritual Work*. Jefferson, NC: McFarland.
Hamilton, Donna B. 1990. *Virgil and The Tempest. The Politics of Imitation*. Columbus, OH: Ohio State Univ. Press.
Harris, Claudia W. 2001. "*The Tempest* as Political Allegory." In *The Tempest. Critical Essays*, edited by Patrick M. Murphy, 561–586. New York: Routledge.
Hartmann, Johann Friedrich. 1759. *Abhandlung von der Verwandtschaft und Aehnlichkeit der electrischen Kraft mit den erschrecklichen Luft-Erscheinungen. Mit Kupfern*. Hannover.
Hegel, Georg Wilhelm Friedrich. 1977 [1807]. *Phenomenology of Spirit*. Translated by Arnold V. Miller. Oxford: Oxford Univ. Press.
Hegel, Georg Wilhelm Friedrich. 1986 [1807]. *Phänomenologie des Geistes, Werke*. Frankfurt am Main: Suhrkamp.
Hegel, Georg Wilhelm Friedrich. 2005 [1807]. *Hegel's Preface to the Phenomenology of Spirit*. Translated by Yirmiahu Yovel. Princeton, NJ: Princeton Univ. Press.
Hemmings, F. W. J. 1969. "Fire in Zola's Fiction. Variations on an Elemental Theme." *Yale French Studies* no. 42:26–37.
Heninger, Simeon K. 1960. *A Handbook of Renaissance Meteorology. With Particular Reference to Elizabethan and Jacobean Literature*. Durham, NC: Duke Univ. Press.
Herder, Johann Gottfried von. 1985 [1773]. "Extract from a Correspondence on Ossian and the Songs of Ancient Peoples." In *German Aesthetic and Literary Criticism. Winckelmann, Lessing, Hamann, Herder, Schiller, Goethe*, edited by Hugh B. Nisbet, 151–176. Cambridge: Cambridge Univ. Press.
Herder, Johann Gottfried von. 1773a. "Auszug aus einem Briefwechsel über Ossian und die Lieder alter Völker." In *Von Deutscher Art und Kunst. Einige fliegende Blätter*, 3–70. Hamburg: Bode.
Herder, Johann Gottfried von. 1773b. "Shakespear." In *Von Deutscher Art und Kunst. Einige fliegende Blätter*, 73–118. Hamburg: Bode.
Herder, Johann Gottfried von. 1773c. *Von Deutscher Art und Kunst. Einige fliegende Blätter*. Hamburg: Bode.
Herder, Johann Gottfried von. 1997 [1769]. *Journal meiner Reise im Jahr 1769. Pädagogische Schriften*. Edited by Rainer Wisbert and Martin Bollacher, *Werke*. Frankfurt am Main: Dt. Klassiker-Verl.
Herder, Johann Gottfried von. 2006. *Selected writings on aesthetics*. Translated by Gregory Moore. Princeton, NJ: Princeton Univ. Press.

Hess, Remi. 1998. "Goethe et la valse." In *Sociopoétique de la danse*, edited by Alain Montadon, 149–166. Paris: Anthropos.
Heywood, Thomas. 1964. *The Dramatic Works*. 6 vols. Vol. 2. New York: Russell & Russell.
Hill, Thomas. 1574. *A Contemplation of Mysteries*. London: By Henry Denham.
Hillman, Richard. 1985. "*The Tempest* as Romance and Anti-Romance." *University of Toronto Quarterly* no. 55 (2):141–160.
Hodgkins, Christopher. 2010. "Prospero's Apocalypse." In *Word and Rite. The Bible and Ceremony in Selected Shakespearean Works*, edited by Beatrice Batson and Jill Peleaz Baumgaertner, 153–167. Newcastle upon Tyne: Cambridge Scholars.
Höfele, Andreas. 2006. "Raising Tempests. Religion, Science, and the Magic of Theatre." In *Magic, Science, Technology, and Literature*, edited by Jarmila Mildorf, Hans Ulrich Seeber and Martin Windisch, 25–38. Berlin: Lit.
Hohendahl, Peter U. 1972. "Empfindsamkeit und gesellschaftliches Bewusstsein. Zur Soziologie des empfindsamen Romans am Beispiel von *La vie de Marianne, Clarissa, Fräulein von Sternheim*, und *Werther*." *Jahrbuch der Deutschen Schillergesellschaft* no. 16:176–207.
Holland, Peter. 1995. "The Shapeliness of *The Tempest*." *Essays in Criticism* no. 45 (3):208–229.
Holm, Bent. 1999. "Shakespeare's Ambiguous Magic in *The Tempest*." In *The Renaissance Theatre. Texts, Performance, Design, I. English and Italian Theatre*, edited by Christopher Cairns, 1–11. Aldershot: Ashgate.
Homan, Sidney R. 1973. "*The Tempest* and Shakespeare's Last Plays. The Aesthetic Dimensions." *Shakespeare Quarterly* no. 24 (1):69–76.
Hulme, Peter. 1981. "Hurricanes in the Caribbees. The Constitution of the Discourse of English Colonialism." In *1642. Literature and Power in the Seventeenth Century*, edited by Francis Barker, Jay Bernstein, John Coombes, Peter Hulme, Jennifer Stone and Jon Stratton, 55–83. Essex: University of Essex.
Ide, Richard S. 1991. "*Macbeth* and *The Tempest*. The Dark Side of Prospero's Magic." In *Praise Disjoined. Changing Patterns of Salvation in 17th-Century English Literature*, edited by William P. Shaw, 103–118. New York: Peter Lang.
Jackson, David. 2004. "'Die Leiden der jungen Lotte'. Ironised Patriarchal Perspectives in Goethe's *Die Leiden des jungen Werther*." In *Bejahende Erkenntnis*, edited by Kevin F. Hilliard, Ray Ockenden and Nigel F Palmer, 29–45. Tübingen: Niemeyer.
Jakobson, Roman. 1960. "Closing Statement. Linguistics and Poetics." In *Style in Language*, edited by Thomas A. Sebeok, 350–377. New York: Wiley.
James, David Gwilym. 1967. *The Dream of Prospero*. Oxford: Clarendon Press.
Janković, Vladimir. 2000. *Reading the Skies. A Cultural History of English Weather, 1650–1820*. Manchester: Manchester Univ. Press.
Janković, Vladimir. 2010. *Confronting the Climate. British Airs and the Making of Environmental Medicine, Palgrave Studies in the History of Science and Technology*. New York: Palgrave Macmillan.
Jennings, Chantal. 1973. "La symbolique de l'espace dans *Nana*." *MLN* no. 88 (4):764–774.
Jennings, Chantal Bertrand. 1980. "Le Troisième Règne. Zola et la révolution copernicienne en littérature." *Revue d'histoire littéraire de la France* no. 30:396–410.
Joly, Bernhard. 1977. "Le chaud et le froid dans *La Curée*." *Les Cahiers Naturalistes* no. 51:56–79.
Kaczmarek, Anna. 2011. "Le huis clos zolien. La conception et la signification de l'espace dans le cycle des *Rougon-Macquart* d'Émile Zola." *Études romanes de Brno* (1):27–38.
Kaiser, Elke. 1990. *Wissen und Erzählen bei Zola. Wirklichkeitsmodellierung in den Rougon-Macquart, Romanica Monacensia*. Tübingen: Narr.

Kamm, Lewis. 1974. "People and Things in Zola's *Rougon-Macquart*. Reification Re-humanized." *Philological Quarterly* no. 53 (1):100–109.
Kamm, Lewis. 1975. "The Structural and Functional Manifestation of Space in Zola's *Rougon-Macquart*." *Nineteenth-Century French Studies* no. 3:224–36.
Kamm, Lewis. 1992. "Émile Zola. Time, History, and Myth Reviewed." *Nineteenth-Century French Studies* no. 20 (3–4):384–396.
Kant, Immanuel. 1968 [1787]. *Kritik der reinen Vernunft 2. Auflage 1787*, Akademieausgabe. Berlin: de Gruyter.
Kant, Immanuel. 1968 [1790]. *Kritik der praktischen Vernunft. Kritik der Urtheilskraft*, Akademieausgabe. Berlin: de Gruyter.
Kant, Immanuel. 1998 [1787]. *Critique of Pure Reason*. Translated by Paul Guyer and Allen W. Wood, *The Cambridge Edition of the Works of Immanuel Kant*. Cambridge: Cambridge Univ. Press.
Kant, Immanuel. 2000 [1790]. *Critique of the Power of Judgment*. Translated by Paul Guyer and Eric Matthews, *The Cambridge Edition of the Works of Immanuel Kant*. Cambridge: Cambridge Univ. Press.
Kasper, Judith. 2014. "Für eine Philologie der Kata/strophe." In *Unfälle der Sprache. Literarische und philologische Erkundungen der Katastrophe*, edited by Ottmar Ette and Judith Kasper, 7–20. Wien: Turia + Kant.
Kernan, Alvin B. 1982. "Shakespeare's Stage Audiences. The Playwright's Reflections and Control of Audience Response." In *Shakespeare's Craft. Eight Lectures*, edited by Philip H. Highfill, Jr., 138–155. Carbondale, IL: Southern Illinois Univ. Press.
Kirkpatrick, Robin. 2000. "The Italy of *The Tempest*." In *The Tempest and Its Travels*, edited by Peter Hulme, William H. Sherman and Robin Kirkpatrick, 78–96. Philadelphia, PA: Univ. of Pennsylvania Press.
Kittler, Friedrich A. 1994. "Autorschaft und Liebe." In *Goethes Werther. Kritik und Forschung*, edited by Hans Peter Herrmann, 295–316. Darmstadt: Wissenschaftliche Buchgesellschaft.
Klein, Sonja. 2011. "Goethes *Ossian*-Übersetzung oder Werthers Aufbruch in die deutsche Moderne." In *"Das Fremde im Eigensten". Die Funktion von Übersetzungen im Prozess der deutschen Nationenbildung*, edited by Bernd Kortländer and Sikander Singh, 59–75. Tübingen: Narr.
Klopstock, Friedrich Gottlieb. 1771. *Oden*. Hamburg: Bey Johann Joachim Christoph Bode.
Klopstock, Friedrich Gottlieb. 2010. *Oden*. Edited by Horst Gronemeyer and Klaus Hurlebusch. Vol. 1, *Hamburger Klopstock-Ausgabe*. Berlin: de Gruyter.
Knopp, Sherron. 2004. "Poetry as Conjuring Act. *The Franklin's Tale* and *The Tempest*." *Chaucer Review* no. 38 (4):337–354.
Knowles, James. 1999. "Insubstantial Pageants. *The Tempest* and Masquing Culture." In *Shakespeare's Late Plays. New Readings*, edited by Jennifer Richards and James Knowles, 108–125. Edinburgh: Edinburgh Univ. Press.
Koelb, Clayton. 2008. *The Revivifying Word. Literature, Philosophy, and the Theory of Life in Europe's Romantic Age*. Rochester, NY: Camden House.
Koschorke, Albrecht. 2003. *Körperströme und Schriftverkehr Mediologie des 18. Jahrhunderts*. 2. ed. München: Fink.
Kott, Jan. 1965. *Shakespeare Our Contemporary*. London: Methuen.
Kristeva, Julia. 1974. *La révolution du langage poétique. L'avant-garde à la fin du XIXe siècle: Lautréamont et Mallarmé, Tel quel*. Paris: Éd. du Seuil.

Kurz, Gerhard. 1982. "Werther als Künstler." In *Invaliden des Apoll. Motive und Mythen des Dichterleids*, edited by Herbert Anton, 95–112. München: Fink.

La Primaudaye, Pierre de. 1594. *The Second Part of the French Academie*. Translated by Thomas Bowes. London: Printed by George Bishop.

La Primaudaye, Pierre de. 1601. *The Third Volume of the French Academie*. Translated by R. Dolman. London: Printed by George Bishop.

La Roche, Sophie von. 2011 [1771]. *Geschichte des Fräuleins von Sternheim von einer Freundin derselben aus Original-Papieren und andern zuverlässigen Quellen gezogen*, Reclams Universal-Bibliothek. Stuttgart: Reclam.

Langley, T. R. 1991. "Shakespeare. Dream and Tempest." *The Cambridge Quarterly* no. 20 (2):118–137.

Latour, Bruno. 1993. *Politiques de la nature*. Paris: La Découverte.

Laville, Béatrice. 2012. "Foule et peuple dans les derniers romans zoliens." *Les Cahiers Naturalistes* no. 86:75–86.

Lawrence, David Herbert. 2005. "Chaos in Poetry." In *Introductions and Reviews*, 109–116. Cambridge: Cambridge Univ. Press.

Le Roy Ladurie, Emmanuel. 2004–2009. *Histoire humaine et comparée du climat*. 3 vols. Paris: Fayard.

Leduc-Adine, Jean-Pierre. 1987. "Architecture et écriture dans *La Curée*." In *La Curée de Zola ou 'la vie à outrance'*, edited by David Baguley, 129–139. Paris: SEDES.

Lee, Meredith. 1990. "'Klopstock!'. Werther, Lotte and the Reception of Klopstock's Odes." In *The Age of Goethe Today. Critical Reexamination and Literary Reflection*, edited by Gertrud Bauer Pickar and Sabine Cramer, 1–11. München: Fink.

LeGouis, Catherine. 1993. "Optics and Rhetoric. Images of Light in Zola." *Romanic Review* no. 84 (4):423–36.

Linden, Eugene. 2006. *The Winds of Change. Climate, Weather, and the Destruction of Civilizations*. New York: Simon & Schuster.

Lindenbaum, Peter. 1984. "Prospero's Anger." *Massachusetts Review* no. 25 (1):161–171.

Lipmann, Stephen. 1976. "'Metatheater' and the Criticism of the Comedia." *MLN* no. 91 (2):231–246.

Lüdemann, Susanne. 1994. *Mythos und Selbstdarstellung. Zur Poetik der Psychoanalyse*, Rombach Wissenschaft Reihe Litterae. Freiburg im Breisgau: Rombach.

Luhmann, Niklas. 1980. *Gesellschaftsstruktur und Semantik. Studien zur Wissenssoziologie der modernen Gesellschaft*. Frankfurt am Main: Suhrkamp.

Luhmann, Niklas. 1987. *Soziale Systeme. Grundriß einer allgemeinen Theorie*. Frankfurt am Main: Suhrkamp.

Luhmann, Niklas. 1997. *Die Kunst der Gesellschaft*, Suhrkamp-Taschenbuch Wissenschaft. Frankfurt am Main: Suhrkamp.

Luhmann, Niklas. 2012. *Liebe als Passion zur Codierung von Intimität*. 12th ed, Suhrkamp-Taschenbuch Wissenschaft. Frankfurt am Main: Suhrkamp.

Lumbroso, Olivier. 2012. "'Système des masses et grands ensembles'. Poétique des foules dans *Les Rougon-Macquart*." *Les Cahiers Naturalistes* no. 86:9–26.

Lyne, Raphael. 2004. "Shakespeare, Plautus, and the Discovery of New Comic Space." In *Shakespeare and the Classics*, edited by Charles Martindale and A. B. Taylor, 122–138. Cambridge: Cambridge Univ. Press.

Magnusson, A. Lynne. 1986. "Interruption in *The Tempest*." *Shakespeare Quarterly* no. 37 (1):52–65.

Maione, Michael. 1980. "Critique architecturale dans *Les Rougon-Macquart.*" *Nineteenth-Century French Studies* no. 9:108–116.
Martens, Lorna. 1985. *The Diary Novel*. Cambridge: Cambridge Univ. Press.
McGovern, D. S. 1983. "'Tempus' in *The Tempest.*" *English* no. 32 (144):201–214.
McNamara, Kevin R. 1987. "Golden Worlds at Court. *The Tempest* and Its Masque." *Shakespeare Studies* no. 19:183–202.
Mebane, John S. 1979. "Renaissance Magic and the Return of the Golden Age. Utopianism and Religious Enthusiasm in *The Alchemist.*" *Renaissance Drama* no. 10:117–216.
Mebane, John S. 1988. "Metadrama and the Visionary Imagination in *Dr. Faustus* and *The Tempest.*" *South Atlantic Review* no. 53 (2):22–45.
Mendelssohn, Moses. 1780 [1755]. "Briefe über die Empfindungen." In *Philosophische Schriften*, 1–196. Carlsruhe: Christian Gottlieb Schmieder.
Mendelssohn, Moses. 1997 [1755]. "On Sentiments." In *Philosophical Writings*, 7–95. Cambridge: Cambridge Univ. Press.
Miko, Stephen J. 1982. "Tempest." *ELH* no. 49 (1):1–17.
Molnar, Geza von. 1984. "*Wilhelm Meister's Apprenticeship* as an Alternative to Werther's Fate." In *Goethe Proceedings. Essays Commemorating the Goethe Sesquicentennial at the University Of California*, edited by Clifford A. Bernd, Timothy J. Lulofs, H. Gunther Nerjes, Fritz R. Sammern-Frankenegg and Peter Schaffer, 77–91. Columbia, SC: Camden House.
Montaigne, Michel de. 1603. *The Essayes or Morall, Politike and Millitarie Discourses of Lo: Michaell De Montaigne*. Translated by John Florio. London: Printed by Val. Sims for Edward Blount.
Mossman, Carol A. 1985. "Etchings in the Earth. Speech and Writing in *Germinal.*" *L'Esprit Créateur* no. 25 (4):30–41.
Mowat, Barbara A. 2000. "'Knowing I Loved My Books'. Reading *The Tempest* Intertextually." In *The Tempest and Its Travels*, edited by Peter Hulme, William H. Sherman and Robin Kirkpatrick, 27–36. Philadelphia, PA: Univ. of Pennsylvania Press.
Müller, Peter. 1969. *Zeitkritik und Utopie in Goethes Werther, Germanistische Studien*. Berlin: Rütten & Loening.
Munday, Anthony. 1580. *A Second and Third Blast of Retrait from Plaies and Theaters*. London: Imprinted by H. Denham.
Neill, Michael. 1983. "Remembrance and Revenge. Hamlet, Macbeth and *The Tempest.*" In *Jonson and Shakespeare*, edited by Ian Donaldson, 35–56. Atlantic Highlands, NJ: Humanities.
Nelson, Brian. 1973. "Zola and the Ambiguities of Passion. *Une page d'amour.*" *Essays in French Literature* no. 10:1–22.
Nelson, Brian. 1977. "Speculation and Dissipation. A Reading of Zola's *La Curée.*" *Essays in French Literature* no. 14:1–33.
Nelson, Brian. 1978. "Zola's Metaphoric Language. A Paragraph from *La Curée.*" *Modern Languages* no. 59:61–64.
Nelson, Brian. 1982. "Zola and the Ideology of Messianism." *Orbis Litterarum* no. 37 (1):70–82.
Neppi, Enzo. 2010. "Désir et nature dans *Werther* et *Ultime lettere di Jacopo Ortis.*" In *Ferments d'ailleurs. Transferts culturels entre Lumières et romantismes*, edited by Denis Bonnecase and Francois Genton, 313–338. Grenoble, France: ELLUG.
Neumann, Gerhard. 2000. "Goethes *Werther*. Die Geburt des modernen europäischen Romans." In *Spuren, Signaturen, Spiegelungen. Zur Goethe-Rezeption in Europa*, edited by Bernhard Beutler and Anke Bosse, 515–537. Köln: Böhlau.
Nevo, Ruth. 1999. "Subtleties of the Isle. *The Tempest.*" In *The Tempest. Contemporary Critical Essays*, edited by R. S. White, 75–96. New York: St. Martin's.

Nicolai, Friedrich. 1775. *Freuden des jungen Werthers, Leiden und Freuden Werthers des Mannes Voran und zuletzt ein Gespräch*. Berlin: Nicolai.
Nietzsche, Friedrich. 1988a. *Jenseits von Gut und Böse. Zur Genealogie der Moral*. Edited by Giorgio Colli and Mazzino Montinari. 2. ed, *Kritische Studienausgabe*. Berlin: de Gruyter.
Nietzsche, Friedrich. 1988b. *Nachgelassene Fragmente 1882–1884*. Edited by Giorgio Colli and Mazzino Montinari. 2. ed, *Kritische Studienausgabe*. Berlin: de Gruyter.
Niggl, Günter. 2000. "Ossian in Goethes *Werther*." In *Jenseits der Grenzen. Die Auseinandersetzung mit der Fremde in der deutschsprachigen Kultur*, edited by Margaret Stone and Gundula Sharman, 45–60. Oxford: Peter Lang.
Noiray, Jacques. 1981. *Le romancier et le machine. L'image de la machine dans le roman français (1850–1900)*. 2 vols. Vol. 1. Paris: Corti.
Norbrook, David. 1992. "'What Cares these Roarers for the Name of King?'. Language and Utopia in *The Tempest*." In *The Politics of Tragicomedy. Shakespeare and After*, edited by Gordon McMullan and Jonathan Hope, 21–54. London: Routledge.
Orgel, Stephen. 1971. "The Poetics of Spectacle." *New Literary History* no. 2 (3):367–89.
Ortiz, Joseph. 2011. *Broken Harmony. Shakespeare and the Politics of Music*. Ithaca, NY: Cornell Univ. Press.
Oseman, Arlene. 2003. "Going Round in Circles with Johnson and Shakespeare." *Shakespeare in Southern Africa* no. 15:71–82.
Ovid. 1567. *The. xv. Bookes of P. Ouidius Naso, Entytuled Metamorphosis*. Translated by Arthur Golding. London: By Willyam Seres.
Pabst, Stephan. 2009. "Werthers Ossian. Zur Aporetik des Authentischen." In *Leib/Seele – Geist/Buchstabe. Dualismus in der Ästhetik und den Künsten um 1800 und 1900*, edited by Markus Dauss and Ralf Haekel, 121–145. Würzburg: Königshausen & Neumann.
Pabst, Stephan. 2010. "Das Bild der Idylle. Goethes Kritik an Salomon Gessners Idyllen und ihre Spuren im Werther-Roman." *Goethe-Jahrbuch* no. 127:13–24.
Parkhurst-Ferguson, Priscilla. 1993. "Mobilité et modernité. Le Paris de *La Curée*." *Les Cahiers Naturalistes* no. 67:73–81.
Paster, Gail Kern. 2004. *Humoring the Body. Emotions and the Shakespearean Stage*. Chicago: Univ. of Chicago Press.
Pellini, Pierluigi. 2003. "Archéologie d'une 'maison de verre'. Sur Zola et la folie." *Compar(a)ison* no. 2:5–41.
Peterson, Douglas L. 1973. *Time, Tide, and Tempest. A Study of Shakespeare's Romances*. San Marino, CA: The Huntington Lib.
Petrey, D. Sandy. 1969. "The Revolutionary Setting of *Germinal*." *French Review* no. 43 (1):54–63.
Pieters, Jürgen. 2000. "The Wonders of Imagination. *The Tempest* and Its Spectators." *European Journal of English Studies* no. 4 (2):141–154.
Popelard, Mickael. 2009. "Spectacular Science. A Comparison of Shakespeare's *The Tempest*, Marlowe's *Doctor Faustus* and Bacon's *New Atlantis*." In *The Spectacular In and Around Shakespeare*, edited by Pascale Drouet, 17–40. Newcastle upon Tyne: Cambridge Scholars.
Porter, David. 1993. "His Master's Voice. The Politics of Narragenitive Desire in *The Tempest*." *Comitatus* no. 24:33–44.
Powers, Elizabeth. 1999. "The Artist's Escape from the Idyll. The Relation of Werther to Sesenheim." *Goethe Yearbook* no. 9:47–76.
Pütz, Peter. 1983. "Werthers Leiden an der Literatur." In *Goethe's Narrative Fiction. The Irvine Goethe Symposium*, edited by William J. Lillyman, 55–68. Berlin: de Gruyter.
Rancière, Jacques. 2000. *Le partage du sensible. Esthétique et politique*. Paris: La Fabrique.

Rea, John D. 1919. "A Source for the Storm in *The Tempest*." *Modern Philology* no. 17 (5):279–286.
Reed, Arden. 1983. *Romantic Weather. The Climates of Coleridge and Baudelaire*. Hanover, NH: Univ. Press of New England.
Reid, Robert Lanier. 2007. "Sacerdotal Vestiges in *The Tempest*." *Comparative Drama* no. 41 (4):493–513.
Reinhardt, Olaf. 2003. "Werthers Lektüre." *AUMLA* no. 99–100:55–63.
Renner, Karl Nikolaus. 1985. "'...laß das Büchlein deinen Freund seyn'. Goethes Roman *Die Leiden des jungen Werthers* und die Diätetik der Aufklärung." In *Zur Sozialgeschichte der deutschen Literatur von der Aufklärung bis zur Jahrhundertwende*, edited by Günter Häntzschel, John Ormrod and Karl N. Renner, 1–20. Tübingen: Niemeyer.
Rennie, Nicholas. 1996. "Benjamin and Zola. Narrative, the Individual, and Crowds in an Age of Mass Production." *Comparative Literature Studies* no. 33 (4):396–413.
Riskin, Jessica. 2002. *Science in the Age of Sensibility. The Sentimental Empiricists of the French Enlightenment*. Chicago: Univ. of Chicago Press.
Roach, Joseph R. 1985. *The Player's Passion. Studies in the Science of Acting*. Newark, DE: Univ. of Delaware Press.
Robert, Paul, and Alain Rey. 2015. *Le Petit Robert de la langue française 2016*. Paris: Le Robert.
Rochecouste, Gabrielle Maryse. 1987. "Isotopie catamorphe. Un paragraphe de *La Curée*." In *La Curée de Zola ou 'la vie à outrance'*, edited by David Baguley, 43–51. Paris: SEDES.
Rochecouste, Gabrielle Maryse. 1988. *The Role of Parallel Catamorphic Systems in the Structure of Zola's Rougon-Macquart, Romanistische Texte & Studien*. Hildesheim: Olms.
Ruprecht, Lucia. 2011. "Werthers Walzer. Tanz als kulturelle Codierung von Liebe and Intimität." *Goethe-Jahrbuch* no. 128:44–59.
Ryan, Kiernan. 2003. "Shakespearean Comedy and Romance. The Utopian Imagination." In *Shakespeare's Romances. Contemporary Critical Essays*, edited by Alison Thorne, 27–52. Basingstoke: Palgrave Macmillan.
Saine, Thomas Peter. 1981. "The Portrayal of Lotte in the Two Versions of Goethe's *Werther*." *Journal of English and Germanic Philology* no. 53 (1):54–77.
Saint-Gérand, Jacques-Philippe. 1986. "La serre dans *La Curée* de Zola." *L'Information grammaticale* no. 31:27–33.
Sanchez, Melissa E. 2008. "Seduction and Service in *The Tempest*." *Studies in Philology* no. 105 (1):50–82.
Sauder, Gerhard. 2010. "*Werther*: empfindsam?" In *Neue Einblicke in Goethes Erzählwerk. Genese und Entwicklung einer literarischen und kulturellen Identität. Zu Ehren von Gonthier-Louis Fink*, edited by Gonthier-Louis Fink, Raymond Heitz and Christine Maillard, 27–44. Heidelberg: Winter.
Scherpe, Klaus. 1970. *Werther und Wertherwirkung. Zum Syndrom bürgerlicher Gesellschaftsordnung im 18. Jahrhundert*. Bad Homburg: Gehlen.
Schiller, Friedrich von. 1992. *Gedichte*. Edited by Georg Kurscheidt. Vol. 1, *Werke und Briefe*. Frankfurt am Main: Dt. Klassiker-Verl.
Schlaffer, Heinz. 1978. "Exoterik und Esoterik in Goethes Romanen." *Goethe-Jahrbuch* no. 95:212–26.
Schmidt, Erich. 1875. *Richardson, Rousseau und Goethe. Ein Beitrag zur Geschichte des Romans im 18. Jahrhundert*. Jena: Frommann.
Schober, Rita. 1979. "Le *Docteur Pascal* ou le sens de la vie." *Les Cahiers Naturalistes* no. 53:53–74.

Schor, Naomi. 1969. "Zola. From Window to Window." *Yale French Studies* no. 42:38–51.
Schor, Naomi. 1971. "Zola and *la nouvelle critique*." *L'Esprit Créateur* no. 11 (4):11–20.
Schor, Naomi. 1976. "Le sourire du Sphinx. Zola et l'énigme de la féminité." *Romantisme* no. 13–14:183–195.
Schor, Naomi. 1978. *Zola's Crowds*. Baltimore, MD: The Johns Hopkins Univ. Press.
Schor, Naomi. 1982. "Individu et foule chez Zola. Structures de médiation." *Les Cahiers Naturalistes* no. 56:26–33.
Seiden, Melvin. 1970. "Utopianism in *The Tempest*." *Modern Language Quarterly* no. 31:3–21.
Semon, Kenneth J. 1974. "Fantasy and Wonder in Shakespeare's Last Plays." *Shakespeare Quarterly* no. 25 (1):89–102.
Serres, Michel. 1975. *Feux et signaux de brume. Zola, Figures*. Paris: Grasset.
Serres, Michel. 1977a. *La distribution, Hermès*. Paris: Éd. de Minuit.
Serres, Michel. 1977b. *La naissance de la physique dans le texte de Lucrèce. Fleuves et turbulences*. Paris: Éd. de Minuit.
Serres, Michel. 2000. *The Birth of Physics*. Manchester: Clinamen Press.
Shakespeare, William. 1967. *Measure For Measure*. Edited by J. W. Lever, *The Arden Shakespeare*. London: Arden Shakespeare.
Shakespeare, William. 1979. *A Midsummer Night's Dream*. Edited by Harold Brooks, *The Arden Shakespeare*. London: Arden Shakespeare.
Shakespeare, William. 1995. *King Henry V*. Edited by T. W. Craik, *The Arden Shakespeare*. London: Arden Shakespeare.
Shakespeare, William. 1997. *King Lear*. Edited by R. A. Foakes, *The Arden Shakespeare*. London: Arden Shakespeare.
Shakespeare, William. 1998. *Love's Labour's Lost*. Edited by H. R. Woudhuysen, *The Arden Shakespeare*. London: Arden Shakespeare.
Shakespeare, William. 2002. *King Richard II*. Edited by Charles R. Forker, *The Arden Shakespeare*. London: Arden Shakespeare.
Shakespeare, William. 2006a. *As You Like It*. Edited by Juliet Dusinberre, *The Arden Shakespeare*. London: Arden Shakespeare.
Shakespeare, William. 2006b. *The Merchant Of Venice*. Edited by John Drakakis, *The Arden Shakespeare*. London: Arden Shakespeare.
Shakespeare, William. 2008. *Twelfth Night*. Edited by Keir Elam, *The Arden Shakespeare*. London: Arden Shakespeare.
Shakespeare, William. 2010a. *Shakespeare's Sonnets*. Edited by Katherine Duncan-Jones, *The Arden Shakespeare*. London: Arden Shakespeare.
Shakespeare, William. 2010b. *The Taming of The Shrew*. Edited by Barbara Hodgdon, *The Arden Shakespeare*. London: Arden Shakespeare.
Shakespeare, William. 2011. *The Tempest*. Edited by Virginia Mason Vaughan and Alden T. Vaughan, *The Arden Shakespeare*. London: Arden Shakespeare.
Shakespeare, William. 2012. *Romeo and Juliet*. Edited by René Weis, *The Arden Shakespeare*. London: Arden Shakespeare.
Shakespeare, William. 2013. *Coriolanus*. Edited by Peter Holland, *The Arden Shakespeare*. London: Arden Shakespeare.
Shakespeare, William. 2015. *Macbeth*. Edited by Sandra Clark and Pamela Mason, *The Arden Shakespeare*. London: Arden Shakespeare.
Sidney, Philip. 1595. *An Apologie for Poetrie*. London: Printed for Henry Olney.

Simonds, Peggy Muñoz. 1997. "'My Charms Crack Not'. The Alchemical Structure of *The Tempest*." *Comparative Drama* no. 31 (4):538–570.
Skilleås, Ole Martin. 1991. "Anachronistic Themes and Literary Value. *The Tempest*." *British Journal of Aesthetics* no. 31 (2):122–133.
Slover, George. 1978. "Magic, Mystery, and Make-Believe. An Analogical Reading of *The Tempest*." *Shakespeare Studies* no. 11:175–206.
Smith, Irwin. 1970. "Ariel and the Masque in *The Tempest*." *Shakespeare Quarterly* no. 21 (3):213–222.
Sokol, B. J. 2003. *A Brave New World of Knowledge. Shakespeare's The Tempest and Early Modern Epistemology*. Madison, NJ: Fairleigh Dickinson Univ. Press.
Sousa, Geraldo U. de. 2001. "Alien Habitats in *The Tempest*." In *The Tempest. Critical Essays*, edited by Patrick M. Murphy, 438–61. New York: Routledge.
Stehr, Nico, and Hans von Storch. 1999. *Klima, Wetter, Mensch, Beck'sche Reihe*. München: Beck.
Stern, Tiffany. 2015. "Time for Shakespeare. Hourglasses, Sundials, Clocks, and Early Modern Theatre." *Journal of the British Academy* no. 3:1–33.
Stevens, William Kenneth. 1999. *The Change in the Weather. People, Weather, and the Science of Climate*. New York: Delacorte Press.
Stöber, Thomas. 2005. "Die Ökonomie der 'dépense'. Vitalistisches und ökonomisches Wissen im 19. Jahrhundert (Balzac, Zola, Bataille)." *Grenzgänge* no. 12 (23):22–37.
Stockhammer, Robert. 1991. *Leseerzählungen. Alternativen zum hermeneutischen Verfahren, M-&-P-Schriftenreihe für Wissenschaft und Forschung*. Stuttgart: M & P.
Strauss, Sarah, and Benjamin S. Orlove. 2003. *Weather, Climate, Culture*. Oxford: Berg.
Strier, Richard. 1999. "'I Am Power'. Normal and Magical Politics in *The Tempest*." In *Writing and Political Engagement in Seventeenth-Century England*, edited by Derek Hirst and Richard Strier, 10–30. Cambridge: Cambridge Univ. Press.
Sutton, John. 2007. "Spongy Brains and Material Memories." In *Environment and Embodiment in Early Modern England*, edited by Mary Wilson and Garrett A. Sullivan, 14–34. Basingstoke: Palgrave Macmillan.
Sylvester, Josuah. 1605. *Bartas. His Deuine Vveekes and Workes* London: Printed by Humfrey Lownes.
Taine, Hippolyte. 1863. *Histoire de la littérature anglaise*. 4 vols. Vol. 1. Paris: Hachette.
Taine, Hippolyte. 1920 [1863]. *The History of English Literature*. Translated by Henry van Laun. 4 vols. Vol. 1. London: Chatto and Windus.
Taub, Liba Chaia. 2003. *Ancient Meteorology, Sciences of Antiquity*. London: Routledge.
Thomas, Thomas. 1587. *Dictionarium linguae Latinae et Anglicanae*. London: Printed by Richard Boyle.
Thüsen, Joachim von der. 1994. "Das begrenzte Leben. Über das Idyllische in Goethes *Werther*." *Deutsche Vierteljahrsschrift für Literaturwissenschaft und Geistesgeschichte* no. 68 (3):462–489.
Tonard, Jean-François. 1994. *Thématique et symbolique de l'espace clos dans le cycle des Rougon-Macquart d'Émile Zola*. Frankfurt am Main: Peter Lang.
Tonning, Judith E. 2004. "'Like This Insubstantial Pageant, Faded'. Eschatology and Theatricality in *The Tempest*." *Literature & Theology* no. 18 (4):371–382.
Trüstedt, Katrin. 2011. *Die Komödie der Tragödie. Shakespeares Sturm am Umschlagplatz von Mythos und Moderne, Rache und Recht, Tragik und Spiel*. Konstanz: Konstanz Univ. Press.

Ungelenk, Johannes. 2014. *Sexes of Winds and Packs. Rethinking Feminism with Deleuze and Guattari, Substanz*. Hamburg: Marta Press.
Vaget, Hans. 1983. "Goethe the Novelist. On the Coherence of His Fiction." In *Goethe's Narrative Fiction. The Irvine Goethe Symposium*, edited by William J. Lillyman, 1–20. Berlin: de Gruyter.
Vasak, Anouchka. 2007. *Météorologies. Discours sur le ciel et le climat, des lumières au romantisme, Les dix-huitièmes siecles*. Paris: Champion.
Vaughan, Virginia Mason, and Alden T. Vaughan. 2011. "Introduction." In *The Tempest*, edited by Virginia Mason Vaughan and Alden T. Vaughan, 1–160. London: Arden Shakespeare.
Vedder, Ulrike. 2013. "Eine enzyklopädische Literatur der Dinge. Emile Zolas Warenhausroman *Au Bonheur des Dames*." *Arcadia* no. 48:354–367.
Ventarola, Barbara. 2010. "Der Experimentalroman zwischen Wissenschaft und Romanexperiment. Überlegungen zu einer Neubewertung des Naturalismus Zolas." *Poetica* no. 42 (3–4):277–324.
Vibert, Patrice. 2007. "Vers une pensée de l'événement. Flaubert et Zola." *Revue Flaubert* no. 7.
Vinken, Barbara. 1995. "Temples of Delight. Consuming Consumption in Emile Zola's *Au Bonheur des Dames*." In *Spectacles of Realism. Gender, Body, Culture*, edited by Margaret Cohen and Christopher Prendergast, 247–267. Minneapolis, MN: Univ. of Minnesota Press.
Vinken, Barbara. 1996. "Zola – Alles sehen, alles wissen, alles heilen. Der Fetischismus im Naturalismus." In *Historische Anthropologie und Literatur. Romanistische Beiträge zu einem neuen Paradigma der Literaturwissenschaft*, edited by Rudolf Behrens and Roland Galle, 215–226. Würzburg: Königshausen & Neumann.
Vinken, Barbara. 1997. "Pygmalion à rebours. Fetischismus in Zolas *L'Œuvre*." In *Pygmalion. Die Geschichte des Mythos in der abendländischen Kultur*, edited by Mathias Mayer and Gerhard Neumann, 593–621. Freiburg: Rombach.
Vinken, Barbara. 2015a. "Götzendienst (Émile Zola)." In *Rom rückwärts. Europäische Übertragungsschicksale von Lucan bis Lacan*, edited by Judith Kasper and Cornelia Wild, 61–65. Paderborn: Fink.
Vinken, Barbara. 2015b. *Flaubert Postsecular. Modernity Crossed Out*. Translated by Aarnoud Rommens and Susan L. Solomon, *Cultural Memory in the Present*. Stanford, CA: Stanford Univ. Press.
Walch, Günter. 1996. "'What's Past Is Prologue'. Metatheatrical Memory and Transculturalism in *The Tempest*." In *Travel and Drama in Shakespeare's Time*, edited by Jean-Pierre Maquerlot and Michèle Willems, 223–238. Cambridge: Cambridge Univ. Press.
Walker, Philip. 1959. "Prophetic Myths in Zola." *PMLA* no. 74 (4):444–452.
Walker, Philip. 1971. "Zola, Myth, and the Birth of the Modern World." *Symposium* no. 25 (2):204–220.
Walker, Philip. 1982. "*Germinal* and Zola's Youthful 'New Faith' Based on Geology." *Symposium* no. 36 (3):257–272.
Walker, Philip. 1986. "Zola. Poet of an Age of World Destruction and Renewal." In *Critical Essays on Émile Zola*, edited by David Baguley, 172–185. Boston, MA: Hall.
Walter, James. 1983. "From Tempest to Epilogue. Augustine's Allegory in Shakespeare's Drama." *PMLA* no. 98 (1):60–76.
Waniek, Erdmann. 1982. "*Werther* lesen und Werther als Leser." *Goethe Yearbook* no. 1:51–92.
Ward, David. 1987. "'Now I Will Believe That There Are Unicorns'. *The Tempest* and Its Theatre." *English* no. 36 (155):95–110.

Warning, Rainer. 1998. "Zola's *Rougon-Macquart*. Compensatory Images of a 'Wild Ontology'." *MLN* no. 113 (4):705–733.
Warning, Rainer. 2005. "Der Chronotopos Paris bei Zola." In *Städte der Literatur*, edited by Roland Galle and Johannes Klingen-Protti, 145–160. Heidelberg: Winter.
Warning, Rainer. 2009. *Heterotopien als Räume ästhetischer Erfahrung*. München: Fink.
Wehrs, Donald R. 2011. "Placing Human Constants within Literary History. Generic Revision and Affective Sociality in *The Winter's Tale* and *The Tempest*." *Poetics Today* no. 32 (3):521–591.
Welch, Edward. 2003. "Zola, Jourdain and the Architectonics of Modernity." In *Visions/Revisions. Essays on Nineteenth-Century French Culture*, edited by Nigel Harkness, Paul Rowe, Tim Unwin and Jennifer Yee, 37–47. Oxford: Peter Lang.
Wellbery, David E. 1994. "Morphisms of the Phantasmatic Body. Goethe's *The Sorrows of Young Werther*." In *Body & Text in the Eighteenth Century*, edited by Veronica Kelly and Dorothea von Mucke, 181–208. Stanford, CA: Stanford Univ. Press.
Wells, Stanley. 1994. "Problems of Stagecraft in *The Tempest*." *New Theatre Quarterly* no. 10 (40):348–357.
Whittingham, William. 1560. *The Bible and Holy Scriptures Conteyned in the Olde and Newe Testament*. Edited by Anthony Gilby and Thomas Sampson. Geneva: Printed by Rouland Hall.
Wiegler, Hans. 1905. *Geschichte und Kritik der Theorie des Milieus bei Emile Zola*. Rostock: Schade.
Williams, George W. 1951. "The Poetry of the Storm in *King Lear*." *Shakespeare Quarterly* no. 2 (1):57–71.
Witmore, Michael. 2001. *Culture of Accidents. Unexpected Knowledges in Early Modern England*. Stanford, CA: Stanford Univ. Press.
Wood, Robert. 1769. *An Essay on the Original Genius of Homer*. London.
Woollen, Geoff. 1985. "Zola's Thermodynamic Vitalism." *Romance Studies* no. 4 (1):48–62.
Wright, Neil H. 1977. "Reality and Illusion as a Philosophical Pattern in *The Tempest*." *Shakespeare Studies* no. 10:241–270.
Young, Edward. 1759. *Conjectures on Original Composition in a Letter to the Author of Sir Charles Grandison*. 2. ed. London: Printed for A. Millar; and R. and J. Dodsley.
Zedler, Johann Heinrich. 1732-1754. *Grosses vollständiges Universal-Lexicon aller Wissenschafften und Künste*. 64, 4 suppl. vols. Halle, Leipzig: Zedler.
Zimbardo, Rose Abdelnour. 1963. "Form and Disorder in *The Tempest*." *Shakespeare Quarterly* no. 14 (1):49–56.
Zimmermann, Rolf Christian. 1968. *Das Weltbild des jungen Goethe. Studien zur hermetischen Tradition des deutschen 18. Jahrhunderts*. 2 vols. München: Fink.
Zola, Émile. 1893a. "The Experimental Novel." In *The Experimental Novel and Other Essays*, 1–56. New York: Cassell Publishing.
Zola, Émile. 1893b. "The Novel." In *The Experimental Novel and Other Essays*, 209–290. New York: Cassell Publishing.
Zola, Émile. 1898. *Doctor Pascal*. Translated by Mary J. Serrano. New York: Macmillan.
Zola, Émile. 1901. *The Joy of Life*. Translated by Ernest Alfred Vizetelly. London: Chatto & Windus.
Zola, Émile. 1905. *A Love Episode*. Translated by C. C. Starkweather, *Comédie d'amour* series. Paris: Société des beaux arts.

Zola, Émile. 1960–1967. *Les Rougon-Macquart. Histoire naturelle et sociale d'une famille sous le Second Empire*. Edited by Armand Lanoux and Henri Mitterand. 5 vols, *Bibliothèque de la Pléiade*. Paris: Gallimard.

Zola, Émile. 2000. *La Débâcle*. Translated by Elinor Dorday, *Oxford World's Classics*. Oxford: Oxford Univ. Press.

Zola, Émile. 2002–2010. *Œuvres complètes*. Edited by Henri Mitterand and Françoise Juhel. 21 vols. Paris: Nouveau monde.

Zola, Émile. 2006. *La fabrique des Rougon-Macquart. Édition des dossiers préparatoires*. Edited by Colette Becker and Véronique Lavielle. 7 vols. Vol. 3, *Textes de littérature moderne et contemporaine*. Paris: H. Champion.

Zola, Émile. 2008a. *Germinal*. Translated by Peter Collier, *Oxford World's Classics*. Oxford: Oxford Univ. Press.

Zola, Émile. 2008b. *The Kill*. Translated by Brian Nelson, *Oxford World's Classics*. Oxford: Oxford Univ. Press.

Zola, Émile. 2008c. *The Ladies' Paradise*. Translated by Brian Nelson, *Oxford World's Classics*. Oxford: Oxford Univ. Press.

Zola, Émile. 2008d. *Thérèse Raquin*. Translated by Andrew Rothwell, *Oxford World's Classics*. Oxford: Oxford Univ. Press.

Zola, Émile. 2009a. *The Belly of Paris*. Translated by Brian Nelson, *Oxford World's Classics*. Oxford: Oxford Univ. Press.

Zola, Émile. 2009b. *L'Assommoir*. Translated by Margaret Mauldon, *Oxford World's Classics*. Oxford: Oxford Univ. Press.

Zola, Émile. 2009c. *La Bête Humaine*. Translated by Roger Pearson, *Oxford World's Classics*. Oxford: Oxford Univ. Press.

Zola, Émile. 2009d. *Nana*. Translated by Douglas Parmée, *Oxford World's Classics*. Oxford: Oxford Univ. Press.

Zola, Émile. 2009e. *Pot Luck*. Translated by Brian Nelson, *Oxford World's Classics*. Oxford: Oxford Univ. Press.

Zola, Émile. 2012. *The Fortune of the Rougons*. Translated by Brian Nelson, *Oxford World's Classics*. Oxford: Oxford Univ. Press.

Zola, Émile. 2014. *Money*. Translated by Valerie Minogue, *Oxford World's Classics*. Oxford: Oxford Univ. Press.

Zola, Émile. 2016. *Earth*. Translated by Brian Nelson and Julie Rose, *Oxford World's Classics*. Oxford: Oxford Univ. Press.

Index

Acot, Pascal 10
Agamben, Giorgio 556
Albanese, Denise 69
Alcorn, Clayton R. 326
Althusser, Louis 27
Anderegg, Johannes 302
Anderson, Katharine 10
Aristotle 260
– Meteorology 51
– Poetics 34, 45–47, 552, 561
Augustinus 508
Aurnhammer, Achim 180, 241

Back, Guy 27, 29
Baguley, David 541
Bakhtin, Mikhail Mikhailowich 362, 389
Barker, Francis 24, 124
Barthes, Roland 562–564
Bartholomaeus 54, 98, 138
Baudelaire, Charles 447
Behringer, Wolfgang 10
Beizer, Janet 335, 442
Belgrand, Anne 350
Belton, Ellen R. 60
Bender, John B. 117
Benjamin, Walter 443, 447, 449
Bennett, Benjamin 192, 224
Berger, Harry 38, 78, 108, 118, 140, 145–146
Berger, Karol 21, 44, 130, 144
Berthier, Philippe 362–363, 386, 388, 430, 442
Bertrand-Jennings, Chantal 550
Best, Janice 362, 389, 511
Bevington, David 118–119, 121–123
Bishop, Tom 71
Blaschke, Bernd 328, 516, 538
Blumenberg, Hans 25
Boia, Lucian 10
Bordeau, Catherine 346, 541
Borie, Jean 537
Bradbrook, M. C. 106, 122
Brailow, David G. 105–107
Brandstetter, Gabriele 188, 193, 208

Braswell, Suzanne F. 426, 442
Breight, Curt 102
Brockes, Barthold Heinrich 280
Brokaw, Katherine Steele 21, 49–50
Brook, Peter 18
Brown, Robert H. 151, 193, 208–209, 211, 214, 244
Bruster, Douglas 35, 87, 146
Bulger, Thomas 38, 105–106, 120
Buuren, Maarten van 442, 446

Calvin, Jean 96, 98, 105
Camarani, Ana Luiza Silva 349–350, 355
Campbell, Heather 30, 60, 62, 70
Campmas, Aude 433, 441
Capitanio, Sarah 380, 434
Carles, Patricia 390
Carnot, Sadi 419
Chakrabarty, Dipesh 12, 446
Chalhoub, Samia 349
Chateaubriand, François-René de 335, 339, 341
Chevrel, Yves 447
Cortés, Martín 55, 98
Couillard, Marie 428, 441, 446, 553
Counter, Andrew J. 346
Crooke, Helkiah 26
Cryle, Peter 346
Cuvier, Georges 503

Davidson, Clifford 117, 120–121
De Gooyer, Alan 26
Deleuze, Gilles 16
– Différence et Répétition 235, 512
– L'Anti-Œdipe 418, 560
– Mille plateaux 351, 427
– Nietzsche et la philosophie 512
– Nietzsche, sa vie, son œuvre 512
– Qu'est-ce que la philosophie 265
– Zola et la fêlure 375
Delius, Friedrich Christian 9–10, 182, 318
Demaray, John G. 108

Derrida, Jacques
- De la grammatologie 264
- Donner le temps 292
- Éperons 565
- La dissémination 262
- Spectres de Marx 252
Dessen, Alan C. 89
Donaldson-Evans, Mary 367, 391, 396
Donat, Sebastian 211
Döring, Tobias 116
Du Bartas, Guillaume de Saluste 100–103
Dumiche, Béatrice 192, 296–298
Duncan, Bruce 238, 302
Dunn, E. Catherine 9

Ebner, Dean 94, 107
Eckermann, Johann Peter 315
Edmunds, Kathryn 296–297, 309
Egan, Gabriel 90, 124, 145
El Kettani, Soundouss 363, 438
Evans, John X. 103

Fechner, Jörg-Ulrich 276
Fine, Gary Alan 10
Fitz, L. T. 88, 117
Flagstad, Karen 47, 88–89, 103, 119
Flammarion, Camille 258–260, 262–263, 266, 272, 285
Flaubert, Gustave 495
Fleming, James Rodger 10
Foucault, Michel 11, 16
- Des espaces autres 15, 68, 389
- Histoire de la folie à l'âge classique 270
- Les mots et les choses 12–15, 22–23, 267, 557, 564
- L'archéologie du savoir 12, 14, 22, 360
- L'usage des plaisirs 254, 343
- Naissance de la clinique 270
- Surveiller et punir 179, 215, 270
Fowler, Elizabeth 25, 29
Fox-Good, Jacquelyn 77
Freud, Sigmund 16, 127, 153–154, 202, 215, 252, 287, 309, 556
Friedrich, Hans-Edwin 231
Friedrich, Lars 188
Frye, Northrop 21

Fulke, William 50, 52, 55–56, 59
Furst, Lilian R. 168, 247, 283

Gamper, Michael 11, 346, 449
Gantrel, Martine 537
Garber, Marjorie 45, 63
Genette, Gérard 18, 296
Gerhardi, Gerhard 448, 541
Gervinus, Georg Gottfried 277–278
Geßner, Salomon 241, 245, 247–248
Gilbert, Otto 138
Gille, Klaus F. 231
Gillies, John 20, 47–48, 57, 87–89, 91, 109–110, 112, 117
Gilman, Ernest B. 21, 108, 119, 124
Girard, René 448–449
Goethe, Johann Wolfgang von 317, 342–345, 444, 521–522, 553–554, 556, 564
- Briefe 175–179, 201, 203
- Dichtung und Wahrheit 240, 256–257, 313–314
- Ephemerides 172
- Gedichte 202
- Gespräche mit Eckermann 315
- Kritiken 247, 316
- Meteorologie 173
- Von Deutscher Baukunst 256, 444
- Werther 1, 6–8, 14, 147–317, 319, 329–330, 335, 338–339, 341–343, 414, 486, 521–522, 524–525, 527, 533, 535, 546–547, 552–560, 562–563
- Zwo wichtige bisher unerörterte biblische Fragen, beantwortet von einem Landgeistlichen in Schwaben 246
Goldsmith, Oliver 240, 245–246
Golinski, Jan 10, 174
Got, Olivier 429–430
Graham, Ilse 246
Grant, Patrick 118
Greenblatt, Stephen 124
Grill, Oliver 169
Grimm, Reinhold 290
Guattari, Félix 265, 351, 418, 560
Guedj, Aimé 496
Gumbrecht, Hans Ulrich 326, 330, 350, 359–360, 395, 430
Gurr, Andrew 41

Haavik, Kristof Haakon 503
Hall, Grace R. W. 26–27, 33, 69
Hamilton, Donna B. 67
Harris, Claudia W. 60
Hartmann, Johann Friedrich 172–173
Hegel, Georg Wilhelm Friedrich 16, 284, 286
Heidegger, Martin 286
Hemmings, F. W. J. 363, 497
Heninger, Simeon K. 22
Herder, Johann Gottfried von 16, 147–148, 174, 255, 276–277
– Auszug aus einem Briefwechsel über Ossian und die Lieder alter Völker 256, 316
– Journal meiner Reise im Jahr 1769 174
– Shakespear 256, 281, 410, 424
– Von Deutscher Art und Kunst 256, 444
Hess, Remi 209
Heywood, Thomas 41, 128, 133
Hill, Thomas 52
Hillman, Richard 60
Hippocrates 4, 134–135, 355, 387, 506
Hodgkins, Christopher 30–31, 70
Höfele, Andreas 9, 31, 38, 45, 67, 70, 98
Hohendahl, Peter U. 152, 241, 243
Holland, Peter 27, 40–41, 62, 70, 119, 146
Holm, Bent 117
Homan, Sidney R. 65, 70
Homer 180–181, 233, 235–236, 238–239, 241, 245–246, 255, 309
Horace 25
Hulme, Peter 19, 24, 124

Ide, Richard S. 62, 103

Jackson, David 290
Jakobson, Roman 560, 562
James, David Gwilym 5–6
Janković, Vladimir 10, 174
Jennings, Chantal 330, 389, 428, 447, 496, 550–551
Jerusalem, Karl Wilhelm 207
Joly, Bernhard 362–363, 386–388, 497
Jones, Inigo 91
Jonson, Ben 74, 91

Kaczmarek, Anna 389
Kaiser, Elke 329, 350, 362, 378, 388, 431, 443
Kamm, Lewis 325–326, 330, 351, 389, 496, 511–512
Kant, Immanuel 16, 286
– Kritik der reinen Vernunft 267–274, 276, 279, 283–284, 287, 564
– Kritik der Urteilskraft 281–282, 451, 548
Kasper, Judith 501
Kaufmann, Christoph 276–277, 311, 313
Kernan, Alvin B. 74
Kirkpatrick, Robin 37
Kittler, Friedrich A. 168, 224, 230
Klein, Sonja 309–310
Klinger, Friedrich Maximilian 276–277
Klopstock, Friedrich Gottlieb 216–221, 223–232, 276, 280, 289, 302, 308, 553
Knopp, Sherron 145
Knowles, James 120, 124
Koelb, Clayton 217, 219, 225, 245–246, 297, 302–303
Koschorke, Albrecht 197–201, 203–205, 209, 213, 289
Kott, Jan 19, 41–42, 44, 72, 107, 122–123
Kristeva, Julia 16, 232
Kurz, Gerhard 149

La Primaudaye, Pierre de 37, 52, 98, 131–132, 136–138, 140
La Roche, Sophie von 188
Lacan, Jacques 232
Langley, T. R. 71
Latour, Bruno 12, 446
Lavater, Johann Caspar 276–277
Laville, Béatrice 448
Lawrence, David Herbert 254–255, 257–258, 262–266, 285
Le Roy Ladurie, Emmanuel 10
Leduc-Adine, Jean-Pierre 362–363, 434, 441–444
Lee, Meredith 217, 219, 225
LeGouis, Catherine 442
Linden, Eugene 10

Lindenbaum, Peter 67, 108
Lipmann, Stephen 131
Lucan 494, 503
Lüdemann, Susanne 154
Luhmann, Niklas
– Die Kunst der Gesellschaft 297
– Gesellschaftsstruktur und Semantik 562
– Liebe als Passion 188, 199, 203, 228, 231
– Soziale Systeme 204, 310
Lumbroso, Olivier 447–448
Lyne, Raphael 41, 62

Magnusson, A. Lynne 70, 74, 127
Maione, Michael 442
Martens, Lorna 149
Marx, Karl 447, 464
McGovern, D. S. 18, 20, 73
McNamara, Kevin R. 42, 74, 76, 91, 113, 119–120, 123, 130, 144
Mebane, John S. 27, 61–62, 106
Mendelssohn, Moses 287–289
Miko, Stephen J. 65, 74
Molnar, Geza von 290
Montaigne, Michel de 95–97, 104–106, 118
Mossman, Carol A. 508
Mowat, Barbara A. 25
Müller, Peter 238
Munday, Anthony 58

Neill, Michael 29
Nelson, Brian 320, 325–329, 362, 380, 386, 388, 395–396, 419, 433, 450, 452, 473, 496, 501, 541, 551

Neppi, Enzo 6, 197, 221, 266
Neumann, Gerhard 186, 195–196, 204, 214, 216–217, 220, 227, 229, 290
Nevo, Ruth 44, 54, 109, 131
Nicolai, Friedrich 206
Nietzsche, Friedrich 14, 389, 512, 565
Niggl, Günter 309
Noiray, Jacques 382, 419, 440, 442
Norbrook, David 42

Orgel, Stephen 121
Orlove, Benjamin S. 10
Ortiz, Joseph 77

Oseman, Arlene 60
Ossian 300–311, 315–316, 535, 553, 555
Ovid 99, 104–105, 108, 112, 297

Pabst, Stephan 152, 228, 240, 248, 264
Parkhurst-Ferguson, Priscilla 378, 388
Paster, Gail Kern 52–53
Pellini, Pierluigi 418, 442, 541
Peterson, Douglas L. 21, 26, 73
Petrey, D. Sandy 511
Pieters, Jürgen 25, 69
Plato 95, 250–251, 263
Popelard, Mickael 49, 65
Porter, David 37, 144
Posselt, Johann Friedrich 177
Powers, Elizabeth 152
Pütz, Peter 165, 219, 239, 296, 302

Rancière, Jacques 258
Rea, John D. 31
Reed, Arden 10, 178
Reid, Robert Lanier 77
Reinhardt, Olaf 231–232
Renner, Karl Nikolaus 151
Rennie, Nicholas 447–449
Richardson, Samuel 335
Riskin, Jessica 10
Roach, Joseph R. 53–54, 84
Rochecouste, Gabrielle Maryse 325, 419, 430, 449
Rousseau, Jean-Jacques 277, 339, 341
Ruprecht, Lucia 193, 196, 204–209
Ryan, Kiernan 37

Saine, Thomas Peter 192
Saint-Gérand, Jacques-Philippe 442
Salzmann, Johann Daniel 201, 203
Sanchez, Melissa 108
Sauder, Gerhard 168
Scherpe, Klaus 241, 315–316
Schiller, Friedrich von 73, 105, 211
Schlaffer, Heinz 168, 221, 238
Schmidt, Erich 303, 309
Schober, Rita 424–425, 550
Schor, Naomi 349, 386, 442, 448–449, 511
Schrön, Heinrich Ludwig Friedrich 176
Seiden, Melvin 94

Semon, Kenneth J. 74
Serres, Michel 12, 16, 178, 271
– Feux et signaux de brume 381, 384, 387, 419, 497, 503–504, 526–527, 551
– La distribution 178, 271–272, 274
– La naissance de la physique dans le texte de Lucrèce 271, 279, 285
Shakespeare, William 162, 164, 173–174, 187, 196–197, 256, 274, 276, 281, 289, 317, 342, 367, 410, 424, 552, 554, 556–558, 564
– A Midsummer Night's Dream 114, 129
– As You Like It 131
– Coriolanus 115
– Henry V 89
– King Lear 1–5, 9, 114, 201, 546, 552, 554, 559, 562–564
– Macbeth 94
– Romeo and Juliet 71, 115
– Sonnets 115
– The Merchant of Venice 114
– The Taming of the Shrew 115
– The Tempest 1, 5–6, 9, 14, 17–146, 156, 164, 187, 258, 367–368, 521, 526, 552–554, 556, 560, 562–563
Sidney, Philip 89
Simonds, Peggy Muñoz 134
Skilleås, Ole Martin 68
Slover, George 62, 64–65, 90–91
Smith, Irwin 119
Sokol, B. J. 70–72
Sousa, Geraldo U. de 88
Spinoza, Baruch de 427
Stehr, Nico 10
Stern, Tiffany 71
Sterne, Laurence 296
Stevens, William Kenneth 10
Stöber, Thomas 386, 541
Stockhammer, Robert 238–239, 298
Storch, Hans von 10
Strauss, Sarah 10
Strier, Richard 95, 102
Sulzer, Johann Georg 316
Sutton, John 53
Sylvester, Josuah 59, 100, 102–103, 131, 135–136, 261

Taine, Hippolyte 349–350, 352–356, 359–360, 380, 428, 513
Taub, Liba Chaia 10
Thom, René 503
Thüsen, Joachim von der 149, 157
Tonard, Jean-François 363–364, 375, 389, 442
Tonning, Judith E. 126, 146
Trüstedt, Katrin 46

Ungelenk, Johannes 427

Vaget, Hans 296
Vasak, Anouchka 10–11
Vaughan, Virginia Mason and Alden T. 18, 143
Vedder, Ulrike 423, 443
Ventarola, Barbara 356
Vibert, Patrice 350, 447, 449
Vinken, Barbara 391, 417–418, 448, 494–497, 548–549
Vogel, Klaus 10

Walch, Günter 140
Walker, Philip 351, 362, 380, 404, 442, 449, 496–498, 501, 503
Walter, James 18–19, 132
Waniek, Erdmann 165, 168, 171, 231, 241, 245, 299, 302
Ward, David 72
Warning, Rainer 362–363, 380, 388–389, 433, 444, 446, 473, 496, 499, 541, 551
Wehrs, Donald R. 45, 60, 106, 109
Welch, Edward 413, 438
Wellbery, David E. 149, 190, 196–197, 202, 205, 234, 247
Wells, Stanley 26, 35
Wiegler, Hans 349–350, 355
Wiethölter, Waltraud 221–222
Williams, George W. 9
Witmore, Michael 38, 56, 61
Wood, Robert 180
Woollen, Geoff 346, 350
Wright, Neil H. 25, 60

Young, Edward 180

Zimbardo, Rose Abdelnour 60, 64, 77–78
Zimmermann, Rolf Christian 185, 246, 296
Zola, Émile 1, 7, 14, 551, 553–554, 556–559, 562, 564
- Au Bonheur des Dames 319, 322, 331, 335, 351, 358, 360, 376–380, 382, 388, 403, 411–423, 425, 427, 433, 436, 438, 440–441, 446–447, 453, 479–480, 487, 496, 501, 526–527, 536, 538–539, 554, 559
- Ébauche 490–491
- Germinal 358, 383–385, 387, 402–410, 423, 433, 437–438, 446, 449, 455–465, 472, 474–478, 483, 496–497, 500–501, 505, 509–511, 513, 518, 526, 554, 559–560
- La Bête humaine 317, 331, 358, 382, 404, 437, 478, 496
- La Curée 8, 331, 335, 357, 361–364, 366, 376–378, 380–381, 386–388, 425–426, 428–437, 441, 443–444, 496, 499, 513, 526, 560
- La Débâcle 324–325, 352, 358, 467–472, 474, 479, 483–487, 492–496, 500–501, 504, 506–509, 513–515, 518–519, 554
- La Faute de l'abbé Mouret 383, 386, 428, 430–431, 437, 528–529
- La Fortune des Rougon 328, 335, 360, 402, 450–454, 458, 462, 472
- La Joie de vivre 331, 358, 403, 491, 523–529, 531, 560
- La Terre 317, 324, 335, 385, 509, 530
- Le Docteur Pascal 386–387, 438, 484, 520–521, 531–534, 536–537, 539–542, 544–551, 559, 563
- Le Rêve 335, 383, 387
- Le roman expérimental 326, 339, 342, 344–349, 356–357, 359, 442, 513, 549
- Le Ventre de Paris 331, 335, 357, 390, 395, 398, 402, 427, 439–441, 444, 446, 554
- Les Quatre Évangiles 329, 448, 473, 508, 511, 514, 550
- Les romanciers naturalistes 443
- Lettre à Valabrègue 442
- L'Argent 317, 331, 335, 358, 378, 382, 403, 437–439, 443, 447, 474, 479–484, 487, 489, 491, 499–501, 503, 505–506, 509–510, 512–513, 515–521, 523, 525–527, 536, 539, 548, 554
- L'Assommoir 317, 358, 367, 381–383, 386, 390–394, 396–401, 405, 427, 438–439, 446, 496, 554
- L'Œuvre 537
- Nana 335–342, 345, 352, 357, 360, 363–375, 377, 379–380, 382–383, 385–387, 400, 402–403, 412, 427, 436–437, 446–447, 465–467, 471, 487–489, 499, 504, 508, 513, 526, 554
- Notes préparatoires 442
- Pot-Bouille 332–334, 341–342, 345, 351, 360, 371, 383, 386, 395, 438, 537, 539, 542
- Thérèse Raquin 339, 355–356
- Travail 550
- Une page d'amour 8, 317–318, 320–322, 331, 339, 341–342, 345, 351, 356–357, 360, 383, 386, 390, 437, 489–493, 496, 499–500, 504–505, 508, 531

www.ingramcontent.com/pod-product-compliance
Lightning Source LLC
Chambersburg PA
CBHW020602300426
44113CB00007B/474